SELECTED WRITINGS
ON THE CONSTITUTION

Books By Raoul Berger

CONGRESS V. THE SUPREME COURT, 1969

IMPEACHMENT: THE CONSTITUTIONAL PROBLEMS, 1973

EXECUTIVE PRIVILEGE: A CONSTITUTIONAL MYTH, 1974

GOVERNMENT BY JUDICIARY: THE TRANSFORMATION OF THE FOURTEENTH
  AMENDMENT, 1977

DEATH PENALTIES: THE SUPREME COURT'S OBSTACLE COURSE, 1982

SELECTED WRITINGS ON THE CONSTITUTION, 1987

FEDERALISM: THE FOUNDERS' DESIGN, 1987

SELECTED WRITINGS ON THE CONSTITUTION

by
RAOUL BERGER

Foreword by
Philip B. Kurland

JAMES RIVER PRESS
CUMBERLAND, VIRGINIA

1987

Printed in the United States of America under the direction of James McClellan, and in cooperation with the Center for Judicial Studies, a non-profit, educational organization established in 1983 to promote a better understanding of public policy issues through the study of the Constitution.

Published by James River Press,
Cumberland, Virginia 23040
(804) 492-4949

Library of Congress Cataloging-in-Publication Data

Berger, Raoul, 1901–
    Selected writings on the Constitution.

    Includes index.
    1. United States—Constitutional law.   I. Title.
KF4550.B38   1987   342.73'02   86-27632
                         347.3022

ISBN 0-940973-00-6

CHANNING '86

ACKNOWLEDGEMENTS

A special note of appreciation is extended for permission to reprint the following:

1. "A Fiddler Turned Lawyer," Harvard Law School Bulletin (October 1962), 8–10, 16–17. Copyright© by Harvard Law School Association.
2. "Constructive Contempt: A Post Mortem," 9 University of Chicago Law Review 602–642 (1942). Copyright© by University of Chicago Law Review.
3. "The President, Congress, and the Courts," 83 Yale Law Journal 1111–1155 (1974). Copyright© by Yale Law Journal Co. and Fred B. Rothman & Co.
4. "The Incarnation of Executive Privilege," 22 UCLA Law Review 4-29 (1974). Copyright© by The Regents of the University of California.
5. "Congressional Subpoenas to Executive Officials," 75 Columbia Law Review 865–895 (1975). Copyright© by Directors for the Columbia Law Review Association Inc.
6. "Standing to Sue in Public Actions: Is It a Constitutional Requirement?" 78 Yale Law Journal 816–840 (1969). Copyright© by Yale Law Journal Co. and Fred B. Rothman & Co.
7. " 'Law of the Land' Reconsidered," 74 Northwestern Law Review 1–30 (1979). Copyright© by Northwestern University School of Law.
8. "The Fourteenth Amendment: Light from the Fifteenth," 74 Northwestern Law Review 311–371 (1979). Copyright© by Northwestern University School of Law.
9. "The Ninth Amendment," 66 Cornell Law Review 1–26 (1980). Copyright© by Cornell University and Fred B. Rothman & Co.
10. "Residence Requirements for Welfare and Voting: A Post Mortem," 42 Ohio State Law Journal 853–877 (1981). Copyright© by Ohio State Law Journal.
11. "Insulation of Judicial Usurpation: A Comment on Lawrence Sager's Court-Stripping Polemic," 44 Ohio State Law Journal 611–647 (1983). Copyright© by Ohio State Law Journal.
12. "The Activist Legacy of the New Deal Court," 59 Washington Law Review 751–793 (1984). Copyright© by Washington Law Review Association.
13. "The Constitution and the Rule of Law," 1 Western New England Law Review 261–275 (1978). Copyright© by Western New England Law Review.

CONTENTS

Foreword

Raoul Berger is the dean of scholars of the American Constitution. This is not to say that he is the dean of American constitutional law professors. That title probably still belongs to Professor Paul A. Freund. Nor is Berger the dean of the revisionists of the American Constitution. That laurel today belongs to Mr. Justice William J. Brennan. Berger does not profess constitutional law in the sense of stating or explaining or justifying the law of the Constitution as garnered from the four hundred and sixty-odd volumes of the United States Reports with their annual amendments. He does afford critical commentary, as an academic should, from the all but unique perspective of the scholar of history. He cannot himself rewrite the Constitution for he is not certificated to do so by the Secretary of State of the United States, as a Supreme Court Justice must be. His cogent published arguments, however, do afford those who profess and those who make the Constitution an opportunity to test their handiwork against the intent of the Founders, even if, alas, most modern constitutional law professors and jurists don't seem to care much what the writers of the fundamental document had in mind when they wrote it.

Berger's touchstone has been the text of the Constitution in the light of the history of its origins. It is this stance that has made him anathema to so many of our sitting professors of constitutional law and political science and to judges who are desirous to remake the Constitution in their own image, to reflect their personal tastes rather than to treat it as a document with any fixed meaning. It should be noted that, if Berger is regarded as an iconoclast, he enjoys the role. So, too, he revels in the controversies to which his writings give rise. Although he is several years on the shady side of eighty, he is as vigorous, acute, alert, and, yes, pugnacious as when he first began his legal career, abandoning a career as a virtuoso violinist to do so. Wherever you focus on his career, you will be impressed by the fact that "extraordinary" is the word for Raoul.

To say that Berger believes that the Constitution's words, in the context of their origins, contains the meaning of its provisions which ought to control judgment is not to assert that a dictionary can suffice to supply the answers. "Strict construction" in that sense is merely a shibboleth, a thoughtless oversimplification by political soothsayers of a complex and, at times, an arcane process. As Judge Learned Hand once put it (Learned Hand, *The Spirit of Liberty* 216 (2d ed. 1953).):

> There are indeed political philosophers who insist that a judge must inevitably choose between the dictionary and tabula rasa; but there is a plain distinction between "interpretation" and "legislation," as well as a clear boundary in practice. . . . as soon as a society becomes conscious of self-direction it begins to apply in some measure a "literacy" canon—to borrow from Matthew Arnold—: that is, it begins to read the text, not sub specie aeternitatis; but with the recollection that in origin it served to compose some existing conflict of interest, and that this should serve to interpret it.

Anyone who reads Berger's writings will quickly learn that he was often in disagreement with Felix Frankfurter. And yet, I venture to think that Berger is not in basic disagreement with the well-known dictum of the Justice in *United States v. Monia*, 317 U.S. 424, 431–34 (1943):

> The notion that because the words of a statute are plain, its meaning is also plain, is merely pernicious oversimplification. It is a wooden English doctrine of rather recent vintage, to which lip service has on

i

occasion been given here, but which since the days of Marshall this Court has rejected, especially in practice. A statute, like other living organisms, derives significance and sustenance from its environment, from which it cannot be severed, without being mutilated. Especially is this true where the statute . . . is part of a legislative process having a history and purpose. The meaning of such a statute cannot be gained by confining inquiry within its four corners. Only the historic purpose of which such legislation is an incomplete fragment—that to which it gave rise as well as that which gave rise to it—can yield its true meaning. . . .

The requirement to find in history the guide to the meaning of the words of our Constitution, however, does not mean—and certainly not to Berger—a license to pick and choose historical fragments to sustain a predisposition. Unfortunately, too much of the "history" offered by the Supreme Court and by modern constitutional commentaries is what Professor Alfred Kelly once called "the 'law-office' variety." Kelly took as examples the awesome and awful opinions in *The Dred Scott Case*, 19 How, 393 (1856), and *The Income Tax Cases (Pollock* v. *Farmers' Loan & Trust Co.)*, 157 U.S. 429 (1895); 158 U.S. 601 (1895), of which he wrote (Kelley, *Clio and the Court*, 1963 Supreme Court Review 119, 126):

> In both cases . . . the "history" that Justices of the majority invoked as a precedent breaking device was . . . very bad history indeed. Each of the historical essays in question was partisan; each used evidence wrenched from its contemporary historical context; and each carefully selected those materials designed to prove the thesis at hand, suppressing all data that might impeach the desired historical conclusion.

Unfortunately, the "historical" style of *Dred Scott* and *Pollock* can be found again and again in the United States Reports and many of these cases are brought under the careful scrutiny of Berger in one or more of his books or articles. For, if *Dred Scott* and *Pollock* rested on flawed history, so, too, for examples, did the equally famous *Adamson* v. *California*, 332 U.S. 46 (1947), *Brown* v. *Board of Education*, 347 U.S. 483 (1954), *Baker* v. *Carr*, 369 U.S. 186 (1962), *Griswold* v. *Connecticut*, 381 U.S. 479 (1965), and *New York Times* v. *Sullivan*, 376 U.S. 254 (1964). Each of these, and many more, are treated with the none-too-tender mercies of Berger's acerbic pen. But it is not so much his style of writing as his array of evidence that is so telling.

Perhaps bad judicial history has one merit. It is an acknowledgement, however insincere, that the Court feels obligated to read and to understand the Constitution in the light of the purpose and intent of the Framers. Indeed, Berger's five books, like the articles contained in this collection, are essentially devoted to correcting the "law office" history that has served the Court and its claque in diverting the Constitution from its stated purposes.

When I say that there are five Berger books, I am depending on the shelves of my own library and the expectation that had there been more I should have acquired it or them. I look forward to more, for Berger is still producing like a Picasso. The first of the five books to which I refer is *Congress vs. The Supreme Court* (1965), the contents which may seem a little strange to those "conservatives" who have lately taken Berger to their bosom. In it he evokes history in support of the power of judicial review, particularly against the attacks based on historical arguments of my one-time colleague Professor William Winslow Crosskey (*Politics and the Constitution* (1953), and the rational but unhistorical critique of Learned Hand's *Bill of Rights* (1958). Having recently examined the documentary history of the origins of the Constitution, I have no doubt whatsoever that Berger is absolutely sound about the expectation of the writers of the Constitution that the Supreme Court would exercise judicial review. I was not equally convinced about an inference he drew from the materials he cites that the Founders put it beyond the power of Congress to inhibit judicial review as an "exception" to the appellate jurisdiction of the Court. (Art. III, § 2, ¶ 2.) But he has, in a further demonstration of his commitment to his scholarship, recanted this position. (*Death Penalties*, p. 161, n.31.) It takes a big man publicly to acknowledge error. There are, indeed, several places in Berger's work where I am prepared to do battle over his inferences, although

I have long since learned better than to challenge him on his evidence. (He is equally clear that government cannot evade judicial review on grounds of "sovereign immunity"; I am equally unclear about it.)

That some readers will look askance at such "liberal" views because they don't like them would give little pause to Berger. He doesn't write to please any particular ideologues. Here, as always, he is in the grip of his research and not in the power of any dogma: his conclusions follow from his investigations and not the other way around. And lest judicial activists and deconstructionists take too much heart from the conclusions in this book, they ought carefully to note the important distinction he draws—again on the basis of history—between the legitimacy of the judicial power he defends and the legitimate scope of that power. Thus, he wrote in his concluding chapter (pp. 338–39):

> Unlike Jefferson and Madison, who were "strict constructionists," Marshall was a "loose constructionist," well aware, as he said in *McCulloch* itself, that the Constitution was "to be adapted to various crises of human affairs," yet taking a narrowing view of the "scope of the Court's power to negative legislative and executive choices." Were such views responsive to those of the Founders?
>
> Although confidence in the legislature had been badly eroded by legislative excesses in the 1776–1787 period, not even the most ardent advocate of judicial review suggested that legislative policymaking be supplanted by judicial review. No one, so far as I could find, looked to the courts for "leadership" in resolving problems that the Congress had failed to solve. As the Fathers conceived it, the judicial role was to "negative" or set aside unauthorized action rather than to initiate policy. They looked to the courts to "check" legislative excesses, to "restrain" Congress within its Constitutional "limits," to prevent the "abuse" of power, to guard against the "usurpations" of power withheld. . . .

And his coda is typical of the scholarship in all of his writings (p. 346):

> To those who would turn away from history and maintain that the choices are for us to make, I would suggest that the most generous interpretation of the Constitutional text must still rely on history to buttress the legitimacy of judicial review, and that it would be arbitrary to invoke history for the establishment of the power and to repudiate it when the scope of the power comes into question.

Raoul Berger's 1973 and 1974 books were blockbusters; they probably reached a larger audience than most non-popular historical essays not created as a student text. The first was entitled *Impeachment* and the second, *Executive Privilege*. These had been subjects on which he had been at work over the course of several years. (I remember him discoursing on the subject of executive privilege to Senator Ervin's Senate Judiciary Subcommittee on Separation of Powers, which I was serving as counsel, long before the Watergate scandal broke.) By the time of their publication, the Watergate crisis had completely enveloped the nation and executive privilege and impeachment were central to the resolution of the most pressing public issues. Even the news media in all their pompous ignorance took note of Berger's learning. Whether they did so with more than their usual superficial understanding, I shall leave to others to say.

Berger's initial interest in impeachment was with the question of removability of federal judges from office and whether the Constitution confined judicial removal to the process of impeachment. The book, however, carefully delineates the history, both before and after the framing of the Constitution, of parliamentary powers of retrospective treason, of the meaning of "high crimes and misdemeanors," and of the meaning of "good behavior." He also reviews, with his usual attention to detail, the impeachment trials of Justice Samuel Chase and President Andrew Johnson. Is it impolitic—surely it is impolite—for me to use these pages where I am but a guest at his invitation, to say that while I find his evidence impeccable, I am not persuaded that all his inferences are compelled by that evidence? I depend on his unfailing courtesy even to those who disagree with him. And the chances are that my insights into his evidence are shallower than his. But I am unable to accept that history proves that other means of removal of judges than by impeachment were contemplated by the Founders nor am I convinced that they expected a Senate impeachment trial to be subject to judicial review. We are in agreement, of course, "that history furnishes a plain answer to at least one question that has long cluttered the analysis: the test of an impeachable offense in England was not an indictable, common law crime." (p. 287)

If I cannot agree with all of Berger's conclusions, however, I cannot deny being enlightened by his scholarship. There are times when his scholarship leads ineluctably to an answer. There are other times, however, when the total honesty and fullness of his presentation of history allows a different construction from the one he reached. And I think this usually occurs at times when I think that the founding Fathers were amending our English inheritance while he believes they were affirming it.

His *Executive Privilege* clearly demonstrates that there was not a shred of evidence for the existence of a constitutionally based privilege of the executive to conceal either from Congress or the judiciary information in the executive's possession relevant to the performance of the duties of the other branches. Whether Congress or the judiciary could create such privileges, as they have created other privileges of confidential communications or secrecy or privacy, is a very different question from whether the Constitution mandates such a privilege. It is not surprising, however, that, when the Supreme Court did create such an executive privilege, it purported to derive it from the notion of separation of powers immanent in the Constitution. The Court's *ipse dixit* in *United States* v. *Nixon*, 418 U.S. 683 (1974), purported to rest on constitutional authority which Berger's book demonstrates not to exist. Of course, the sanction given to the concept of executive privilege was dictum, since the Court insisted on the obligation of the President to respond to the judicial subpoena in the case at bar. But with the prolix opinions that are the rule today, little distinction is made between dictum and holding. And with the political nature of the high court, it is frequently the case that dicta have more significance than any holding.

The canvas on which Berger's *Government by Judiciary* (1977) is limned is far more vast than that of his other efforts. It is largely concerned with the meaning of the Fourteenth Amendment's three principal clauses—Privileges and Immunities, Due Process, and Equal Protection—which are at the heart of contemporary Supreme Court constitutional adjudication. The important proofs offered, which can hardly be adumbrated here, show that, contrary to the Court's insistence, these clauses, read in their historical context, do indeed have specific meanings and are not merely *tabula rasa* on which the Justices are licensed to wreak what they will. In Learned Hand's words, already quoted, "there is a plain distinction between "interpretation" and "legislation." It is not, however, a distinction recognized by today's Court or most of today's legal commentators. The result has been a major shift in power from the legislative and executive branches—the democratic ones—to the judiciary. The judiciary has taken over a major part of the policy making function that was assigned by the Founders elsewhere and debarred by them to the courts.

The elasticity of the Due Process and Equal Protection Clauses—Privileges and Immunities remains essentially an unglossed provision still to be exploited—if carried to new limits by the Burger and Warren Courts, is not a notion of their creation. Thus, Professor Felix Frankfurter, as he then was, wrote in 1924 (Kurland, ed., *Felix Frankfurter on the Supreme Court* 163 (1970):

> . . . these broad "guarantees" in favor of the individual are expressed in words so undefined, either by their intrinsic meaning, or by history, or by tradition that they leave the individual Justice free, if indeed they do not actually compel him, to fill in the vacuum with his own controlling notions of economic, social, and industrial facts with reference to which they are invoked. These judicial judgments are thus bound to be determined by the experience, the environment, the fears, the imagination of the different justices.

As a factual description of what took place in the Supreme Court when this was written and what takes place there now, the validity of Frankfurter's statement cannot be denied. As a normative proposition it couldn't be more in error.

Berger in this volume affords what is, to me, conclusive proof that Frankfurter was wrong: all three constitutional phrases do have "intrinsic meaning" and if they didn't, there is adequate historical evidence to reveal specific, limited meanings for each of them, meanings consistent with the structure of the Constitution. That the Fourteenth Amendment, as promulgated, for example, had nothing to say on the subject of the elective franchise is pellucid. That it provides no basis whatsoever for the abortion decisions cannot reasonably be argued.

Again, however, I do not go all the way with Berger. I agree that the authors of the Fourteenth Amendment did not think that they had mandated integrated schools. But I think that Berger affords adequate evidence that they did think that the Equal Protection Clause forbade government classification by race. Indeed, I think that was what the "equal protection of the laws" said and was intended to say. It was the black who was the intended beneficiary of that provision and, probably, he was the only intended beneficiary. Whether a "separate but equal" formula could satisfy the ban on racial classification, I doubt. But then we never had a factual basis on which to test the adequacy of such a standard. The *Brown* case hypothesized the equality of black and white schools against the facts of record, in order to reach out for the brave new world of judicial government, of which, in Alex Bickel's words, *"Brown v. Board of Education* was the beginning."

Whatever the judgment of judicial usurpation in the school cases, however, it remains clear from the evidence that the Fourteenth Amendment did not intend to give to the Justices the power to decide cases according to "the experience, the environment, the fears, the imagination" of each of them. And yet that is exactly what has occurred. That we now have far more "government by judiciary" than the Constitution warrants can hardly by gainsaid even by the most stalwart supporters of judicial activism, although to them, the Constitution is an irrelevancy, at best a symbol, at worst, a relic of a bygone era, an era of limited government and responsible representative democracy, long since dissipated.

Perhaps it bears iteration that Berger's lesson damns such judicial activism whether practiced by "liberal" or "conservative," whether that of Warren and Brennan, or of Burger and Rhenquist. Those who exult in what they see as a recent judicial shift to the right ought not to confuse it with a return to the Constitution.

Of the death penalty cases in the Supreme Court, it may well be said that the wish was father to the absence of thought. The issue is such an emotional one that rational discourse becomes difficult and I must sympathize with those who have what Hans Jonas called "The Imperative for Responsibility" in deciding cases involving capital punishment. What does not draw my sympathy is a patently deliberate distortion of history to justify results that can be sustained only on emotional rather than rational grounds. Indeed, I am one of those who find it abhorrent for the state deliberately to take the life of a human being, however much a monster he may be and however much pain he may have inflicted on his victims.

Would that somehow I could find somewhere in the Constitution a mandate to support Holmes's dictum that the solution to our most difficult problems is for us "to grow more civilized." But I can't. And neither could the Court in the death penalty cases: *Furman v. Georgia,* 408 U.S. 238 (1972): *McGautha v. California,* 402 U.S. 183 (1971), and their progeny. What is to be found in the Constitution on the subject of crime and punishment is the subject of Berger's latest—I am sure it is not his last—book, *Death Penalties* (1982).

Death Penalties is broader in its coverage than its title would suggest although there clearly is an emphasis on the Eighth Amendment and the death penalty cases in which the Court butchered history once more but even then could not reach the results it would have liked. Berger's historical proofs are unassailable in terms of their historical accuracy, again providing the Court with a lesson in historical meaning. But Berger uses some of the pages of this volume for reprises of some of his earlier compositions on the Fourteenth Amendment and the Equal Protection Clause, the incorporation theory, judicial review, the compulsions of the common law in the interpretation of the Constitution, and Congressional powers over Supreme Court jurisdiction. And some space is devoted to refutation and confutation of some of his critics, who challenged his conclusions, not because his history was wrong but because his history did not support desirable ends, *i.e.*, ends they desired. Like his other works, this one too reflects a deep scholarship with a masterful command of language and an ardent plea for intellectual honesty, a rare commodity both in the groves of academe and in the halls of justice.

I have encapsulated the essence of Berger's five books, as I read them, to afford a background against which the essays in this volume may be considered. I could attempt to do the same with the articles offered to you herein. But surely that would be an act of supererogation since these efforts are necessarily at hand. Who needs a commentator to tell an audience of what it will hear when Rudolph Serkin plays a Beethoven sonata for them? So, too, here. Berger's efforts speak for themselves and speak eloquently. Suffice it to say then that you are about to learn how scholarly history can add to your understanding of the meaning of our Constitution.

In October, 1962, Raoul Berger published an autobiographical sketch in the Harvard Law School Record. It was entitled "A Fiddler Turned Lawyer." In it he expressed his credo, "Far down the road lay the hidden lesson that music making is more than a succession of beautiful sounds, more than a medium for mere personal expression, that the prime task of the artist is to search for and lay bare the meaning that is imprisoned in the little black dots which weave their way across the music staves." When he changed professions, he adhered to his belief. For the constitutional scholar, too, interpretation is "more than a medium for personal expression . . . the prime task . . . is to search for and lay bare the meaning that is imprisoned" in the words of the Constitution. Berger reads the Constitution as he reads a Beethoven score, not to "improve" the text but to express it. The success of his efforts are to be found in the pages of the volumes to which I have alluded and the book to which this paean is meant to serve as an introduction. Bravo, maestro!!

Philip B. Kurland
The University of Chicago

CHAPTER I

A Fiddler Turned Lawyer

"Is it not strange that sheeps' guts should hale souls out of men's bodies?" Shakespeare, Much Ado About Nothing, II, iii, 61.

There have been notable shifts from law to music, among others Schumann and the great conductor-pianist, Hans von Bülow. Few musicians, however, have deserted to the law. One who has a true calling to music vibrates to sound much as did Van Gogh to color and light; for him music is more than a vocation, it is an addiction. The law does not invite so ardent a response. It is not, said Mr. Justice Holmes, "the place for the artist or poet" but for the "thinker," though he thought the "Circe of poetry" a "pale phantom" in comparison with the law. Undeniably the unfolding of a great insight has its own solemn splendor. Few, however, can ascend to Holmes' Olympian heights.

For me music never became a "pale phantom." To the contrary, though I have relished forensic clashes and have not infrequently felt the rewarding sense of discovery, nothing has equalled the keen delight of having a great violin come alive under my hands. There is an almost sensual thrill in drawing a glowing flow of sound; and on rare occasion there is the supreme joy of realizing a divine utterance of Bach or Mozart or Beethoven in all its glory. What then, I have often been asked, prompted me to abandon my first love, the violin, for the law. Let me begin with my efforts to become an artist.

From my earliest childhood I was "transported and transpierced," to borrow Montaigne's phrase, by music, whether made by an organ-grinder or band, let alone some early Caruso, Melba or Kreisler record. Well do I recall my first glimpse of the magic concert world, perched high in the top-most gallery of Chicago's Orchestra Hall, when the young Mischa Elman was to play. To a generation jaded by too ready access to fine performances on records and radio, it is impossible to convey the rapture with which I first heard the strains of Elman's Strad. The sound that floated up from the far-off stage was poignant, infinitely moving. For days it haunted my dreams. I was already sawing away on a raucous "factory" fiddle from which emerged sounds that doubtless not a little resembled those which embittered the neighbors of Clarence Day. Far down the road lay hidden the lesson that music making is more than a succession of beautiful sounds, more than a medium for mere personal expression, that the prime task of the artist is to search for and lay bare the meaning that is imprisoned in the little black dots which weave their way across the music staves.

But first came the struggle to escape from the slavery imposed by intractable muscles. That is not a struggle peculiar to the fiddler or pianist; it is common to the player of tennis or billiards. Van Gogh cried out that the pencil dominated his fingers. Whoever seeks to bend muscles to his will comes up against the same seemingly insurmountable wall. The striving for mastery in any medium is like the quest for an ever receding mirage; it is a struggle that the aspiring fiddler wages in the solitude of a cell, and only those persist who are obsessed by a drive for self-expression and to whom the violin alone is adequate to the task.

For me there was in addition the example of a great master, Franz Kneisel. Of his Quartet, James Huneker said, "I would not barter memories of their music making for a wilderness of virtuosi."

Kneisel was a block of a man, impassive and inarticulate, but who could wield a bow with a grace, a flirtatious elegance that a ballerina might envy. His was not the vibrant personality of a Frankfurter, yet he cast an undeniable spell over his pupils. His power derived from the depth of his insight, his immense wisdom in matters technical through which insight alone can be translated into sound and, above all, his complete dedication to the task of teaching. Holmes has said that "If a man is great, he makes others believe in greatness." In Kneisel, worship of the masters burned so high that only a clod could fail to catch fire. He had in addition the surpassing attribute which has ever remained for me the criterion of great teaching—he opened up horizons which but for him we might never have perceived.

My studies extended over a six-year period, broken by a sojourn in Berlin with Carl Flesch, a then renowned virtuoso. It was not an easy school. Kneisel was a severe, even harsh, taskmaster in the old Prussian tradition, impaling the slightest fault or mannerism on a barbed witticism, or blowing it up with uncanny caricature so that even the hapless victim could not resist laughing at himself. That fault would not be soon forgotten. Every lesson involved a search for meaning and essence and the means of making them intelligible by inflection and nuance. Measured by the endlessly lush tone that is the current rage, Kneisel's subtle style would today seem pallid. But this is to prefer the obvious charms of a Betty Grable to the luminous reading of a Julie Harris.

It was with chilling shock that I plunged from this cloistered, ideal world into the struggle for a livelihood. Virtuosity had been lifted by Heifetz to dizzying heights, and the market was flooded with foreign artists who had poured into the United States in the wake of World War I. I make no plea for chauvinism in music; insistence on "Buy American" would have barred artists like Kreisler, Heifetz and Horowitz, who have incalculably enriched our musical life. But not every foreign label is a warranty of sterling artistry. The continuing tragedy of the young artist in America is that he must hit the mark reserved for the five or six who have caught the public fancy or fall to the level of an artisan—there is no in-between. In the law one need not be a Holmes or Cardozo to find an engrossing and rewarding niche. But thirty years ago it was virtually impossible for a young American to make a livelihood as a concert artist, and so it remains today. For one Van Cliburn who rocketed to fame through an enterprising entry into a Moscow competition there are a dozen equally fine pianists who eke out a living teaching other pianists who will likewise have no place to go.

There was nothing for it but the orchestra. Few endeavors are as generally hated by practitioners as membership in a symphony orchestra, the chief reason being that the conductor of a major symphony orchestra exercises tyrannical powers that are scarcely to be duplicated in any other segment of American life. The tongue-lashings that a graduate of the Moscow, Paris, or Leipzig conservatories meekly endured in my time would not for a moment have been stomached by a bricklayer or plumber. Much may be forgiven a Toscanini whose musical goal could compel the enthusiasm of the most hardened orchestra man. But the American orchestral scene has witnessed a procession of conductors whose sole claim to fame is that the orchestral trustees in their wisdom appointed them, so that not without reason do orchestra men wryly reply to the question, "How does one become a conductor?"—"First you get a symphony orchestra."

Nowhere is Acton's axiom that "absolute power corrupts absolutely" better illustrated. Not alone is the conductor accountable only to trustees who are unqualified to criticize his work, his position insulates him from criticism by the men under his command who better than another can perceive his weaknesses[1]; the local music critics for the most part are not worth listening to and local artists cannot afford to offend the reigning deity; the visiting artists will scarcely criticize their host. On

---

[1] Richard Strauss, a great conductor as well as composer, said in 1922: "Down there in the orchestra . . . there are argus-eyed observers . . . who groan if you wave your baton furiously in their faces conducting *Tristan* 'alla breves' in four [when they should be conducted in two]." Reprinted in Kolodin, *The Composer as Listener*, 219 (1958).

all sides he is intoxicated by undiscriminating praise and the heady sense of power. Old Max Hess, that prince of hornists, hit it off superbly: "Conductors, Bah!" he said. "They go like this," with a sweeping gesture as if to hurl a thunderbolt, "the horns go 'Poom'—and they think they are Napoleon."[2]

The strutting and posturing of such pseudo-Napoleons, as they tore a passion to tatters, grew wearisome. Let me recite a recent example. A famous pianist was playing the meditative slow movement of the Schumann Concerto with a well-known orchestra. In the middle section there occurs a song for cello, all tenderness and innocence, about which cluster gentle pianistic arabesques set against so transparent an orchestration that the cello song soars. No conductorial midwifery is required. But our conductor had tarried too long outside the spotlight; turning to the cellos—and to the box holders and occupants of the side balcony—he donned a mask of swooning ecstasy and in a fine frenzy implored the cellos to give their all. Plainly such gratuitous dumb show is meant for the groundlings who listen with their eyes, not their ears.

Orchestra playing suffers from still other infirmities. In the orchestra, only one idea, that of the conductor, can prevail; hence, the orchestra offers no room to the player for the self-expression which is the greatest reward of the artist. Then, too, not all musical works wear well. Before long, for example, the bulk of Wagner appeared a vast sea of tremolo on which forlornly floated a few endlessly-repeated harmonies and banal tunes, the Tchaikowsky Pathétique Symphony, sheer bathos, the modern music which we were premiering, dust and ashes. Some music endured— Haydn, Mozart, Beethoven and Brahms remain eternally fresh and radiant. But it was not enough to rid me of the feeling that I was merely a cog in a machine, engaged in barren drudgery that was numbing to the soul. This was not what I had slaved for and by my mid-twenties I had a sense of hopeless frustration; and though I did not know where to go, like a trapped bear I knew that I had to be on my way.

So I began by entering college while I remained in the orchestra to pay my way. The ensuing four years were hectic, but spiced with the joy of stumbling upon great souls and encountering "ideas that have changed the world." These four college years persuaded me that I had not ossified beyond hope of redemption and hardened my resolve to break away. Upon graduation I resigned from the orchestra and left my string quartet and solo activities. Friends and colleagues regarded this as no less fool-hardy than was Columbus' venture into the unknown. My bridges were burned.

But why the law, why a field so totally removed from what aptitude I had shown? An ill-advised sortie into the dissecting room of a medical school too hastily persuaded me that medicine required a hardier soul than mine. Over-exposure to the task of straightening out the crippled bow-arms of those whom nature had not designed for fiddling turned me against teaching. In my naïveté, business spelled selling, in an era when selling had become synonymous with Babbittry. So I blindly elected the law.

It was my good fortune to begin the study of law at a time of intellectual ferment, when generally accepted conventions were under searching attack. A vigorous group of so-called "realists" had called for a re-evaluation of the law in terms of what courts did rather than what they said in rationalizing their acts; they insisted that judges play a creative "rule-making" role, that courts are not slot machines in which the mere insertion of a properly framed question suffices to produce a "pre-existing" answer. Holmes and others had earlier noted that judges in fact engage in interstitial legislation, and Sir Henry Maine had pointed to the use of "double language"—rationalizations after the fact—to make such legislation palatable. The "realists" focused a spotlight on such facts, insisting that to improve the judicial process it is first essential to understand how it actually

[2]Debussy said of Alfred Cortot, better known to us as a pianist, when conducting a martial passage, that he "advances on the orchestra and aims a threatening baton, like a banderillero when he wants to irritate the bull. The members of the orchestra are as cool as Icelanders: they have been there before." *Ibid.* at 106.

functions and to discard all pretenses as to its nature. The smoke of battle has long since cleared, but when I entered law school the "realist" controversy filled the air. The Dean of my law school, Leon Green, had by virtue of his own publications become a leader of the "Realist" group, hence we had a sense of immediate participation in a vital contemporary movement.

Of Kneisel I spoke with admiration; for Green I must add a note of abiding affection. To him I owe a lasting enthusiasm for the law. He taught us torts. Across the centuries trooped a procession of forgotten men from whose woes legal principles had been distilled; and he unceasingly prodded us to assay the adequacy of the judicial solutions. Daily we re-experienced the perplexity of the judges who were confronted with the proliferation of a rule under the pressure of unforeseen circumstances. Green was a master of Socratic dialogue. Discussion leapt across the room; the air crackled with debate; one solution after another was tried and found wanting. Constantly we were admonished to cut beneath the formula in which decision had been clothed and to dig out the factors on which decision turned. Think things, not words, Holmes has said, and nothing is harder for the lawyer,[3] who insensibly yields to the magic of words sanctified by example and constant repetition. Up to this time I had relied on my fingers to translate my thoughts into sound; now I had to find tongue, to wrestle ideas into words, to state them quickly and precisely. To my great joy, there was a corner of my mind that responded eagerly to the new demands. I had a feeling of high adventure; instead of bogging down in the tedium of learning a new jargon and the elements of a new technique. I found that my study had unexpected zest. Delighted with the give and take of the classroom, before long I was convinced that in blindly choosing law I had chosen better than I knew.

Holmes has said truly that in no other profession "does one plunge so deep in the stream of life—so share its passions, its battles, its despairs, its triumphs, both as witness and actor."

No lawyer worth his salt fails speedily to perceive that law is an instrument for the reconciliation of social conflicts, that lawyers play a pervasive role in shaping human institutions, and that on every level the law affords room for the play of the mind and for shaping the raw materials of life into the stuff that ultimately becomes the law. On the lowest level, each day brings its own legal knot to unravel, each calls for initiative. Even the cub is frequently called upon to frame and recommend a tentative solution, and one of my earliest rewards in the practice was to find that a carefully thought-out analysis was treated with respectful consideration by my betters. This was a world far removed from cut and dried orchestral routine, a world in which no tyrannical conductor rode roughshod over his men. And from time to time there was the zest of a great issue. One such case that fell to me is worth recounting.

It was in 1941, when we were belatedly arming and drafting our boys into training camps to meet the Nazi threat. A group of Jehovah's Witnesses, ranging from 18 to 21 years, had come into a little West Virginia town to proselytize as is their wont. They had been warned during an earlier visit not to return, and now a group of local citizens, borrowing from Mussolini, forcibly fed each of them about 12 ounces of castor oil, tied them along a rope and marched them for several hours through the town while the deputy-sheriff and chief of police stood by. Because of the failure of these officers to protect the victims, the Department of Justice, with which I was then associated, determined to prosecute them for "a denial of equal protection" in violation of the Fourteenth Amendment. At that time is was not clear that such "inaction" was in violation of the Amendment, and the local district attorney, aware of the community hostility to Jehovah's Witnesses, predicted that no grand jury would indict and no petty jury convict. Part of his prophecy was speedily confirmed by the grand jury, which refused to return an indictment and transformed the proceeding into an inquisition as to why the victims would not salute the flag nor serve their country in a crisis.

[3]Holmes too could be seduced by words. See Berger, " 'Disregarding the Corporate Entity' For Stockholders' Benefit," *55 Col. L. Rev.* 808, 809 (1955).

We then determined to file an "information," which dispenses with a grand jury indictment in certain cases. The trial jury was a cross section of local farmers and farm hands, mechanics and small tradesmen. The police authorities were defended by a former president of the State Bar Association—defendants had "done nothing"; a host of witnesses garbed in the uniform of the American Legion marched through the witness box to testify as to the defendants' good reputation; in short, every consideration of local pride and prejudice tugged against us. We hammered away at the folly of drafting sons and brothers to protect us against Hitler's totalitarianism if its hideous features were to find refuge at home; we rang the changes on the danger to cherished rights if fellow Americans could be lynched solely because they professed an unpopular religion while officers stood by. But we feared that our homespun jurors might find these mere abstractions and would decline to send respected local officers to jail for merely "witnessing" an "over-boisterous prank." Never have I been prouder of being an American than when that small-town jury, grasping the real issues, rose above its prejudices and brought in a verdict of guilty against the officers who had failed to protect the unwelcome visitors.[4] In this they underscored a valuable lesson given to me by Mr. Justice Brandeis when he urged me to get some trial practice. His experience as a jury lawyer, he said, was one of the most important parts of his education because it taught him that if the lawyer could frame an issue in terms that the average man could grasp, sturdy common sense would lead him to the right solution. As a result, Brandeis' faith in democracy never wavered.

Much has been said about the drama of the courtroom. It is a drama played before very few spectators and those few generally unaware of the issues or stakes. But there is tension nonetheless, for in every court appearance the chips are down. We may put to one side the criminal cases involving a death penalty or imprisonment where the extreme gravity of the issue is immediately apparent. A civil suit too may be of great moment; it may involve a man's entire fortune or the future of his business or his reputation in the community. By comparison, the task of the artist is relatively simple—to please or delight an audience which has come hoping to be pleased. He plays what he has played countless times before, and if he falls short of the exactions of his own artistic conscience there are few to remark it; if his critiques are lukewarm today he will be enthusiastically acclaimed tommorrow. There is no adversary to punch holes in his performance, no unsympathetic judge to trip him up with searching questions. In contrast, the trial or hearing for all its decorum is a struggle, the lines of which sway this way and that as the struggle proceeds. Often, after fighting an uphill case, I have emerged, whether victorious or defeated, feeling like a boxer who has left a portion of his hide in the ring.

But the lawyer has some pleasures that are withheld from the artist. For one thing he is more likely to be judged by his peers. Those who publish musical criticisms seldom have any real qualification for the post and many an artist has writhed under stupid or utterly unjust criticism at their hands. Although lawyers frequently and justly criticize a system of judicial appointment that is wedded to politics, the fact remains, at least in the federal courts with which I am familiar, that a goodly percentage of the trial judges are schooled and competent men, that in the appellate courts are to be found some judges of exceptional attainments and that in the Supreme Court there have always been some justices of extraordinary talent. Consequently, somewhere down the line a lawyer will be heard by his peers and more often by his betters. Another compensating pleasure is that the lawyer's work is less ephemeral than that of the violinist; however splendid yesterday's concert, it is gone without a trace. Phonograph records which to some extent perpetuate a fine performance, though in the case of the violin they still fall far short of the reality, are for the few. The lawyer's work can leave more enduring impress. True, the magisterial tone of a decision seldom affords an inkling of indebtedness to an advocate's analysis, but the advocate has the quiet satisfaction of knowing that the results were shaped by his hands. Like the architect, he

[4]See *Catlette v. United States,* 132 F.2d 902 (4th Cir. 1943).

may look back along a trail of landmarks that blaze the path he has traversed. If he engages in scholarly researches, he knows the joy of breaking a path that his fellow lawyers will find occasion to use with appreciation of his toil. Not the least of the lawyer's advantages vis-à-vis the fiddler is his freedom from slavery to his fingers. Muscular coordination plays no role in giving effect to hard-won understanding. In sad contrast, as the violinist's experience slowly distills into wisdom his fingers become ever more reluctant servants. Now and then one sees pianists like Backhaus, who retain their powers even into the seventies, and the cellist Casals remains a miracle in his eighties, though it is idle to compare his present performances with those of thirty years ago. But I have never heard a 70-year-old violinist worth listening to, and with the exception of Heifetz and Kreisler, most violinists have gone into a marked decline in their middle fifties. Lawyers are in their prime after 50, and some, e.g., Holmes and Brandeis, have done their finest work when they were past 70. It is not merely that the lawyer may continue to be self-sufficient into his old age but that it is a joy to make the insights which come with experience effective.

There have been times when I regretted that the fanatical zeal which I poured into music was not from the beginning channeled into the acquisition of the intellectual resources that are indispensable to creativity in the higher reaches of the law. But, as I said at the outset, music is an addiction, and I cannot but rejoice that it wrapped its tendrils around my heart, for it has been and remains an undiminished source of joy and wonder. And now let me venture on a proselytizing word.

To most of my brethren at the bar this treasure house remains locked. Now and then one meets a Chief Justice Stone, whose exposure to heroic singing in the Metropolitan at the turn of the century made him a fervent and discriminating devotee of music. In contrast, though Mr. Justice Holmes plumbed virtually all the riches of the mind, not once does he refer to a great composer or mention a concert of the then peerless Boston Symphony Orchestra. This incuriosity about music, I found, is generally characteristic of the cultivated American, in contrast to his opposite English, not to say German or Austrian, number.[5]

Artur Schnabel, the noted pianist, acutely remarked that music constitutes modern Europe's distinctive contribution to Western culture. The Greeks gave us philosophy—including some startling speculations about the nature of matter—poetry, drama, comedy, mathematics, sculpture and architecture. Music alone was left to the future. And in Western culture, I suggest, we encounter no figure of Shakespeare's stature until we come to Bach, Mozart and Beethoven, and, I would add, Brahms.

Entry into this magic world is open to all. The great fraternity of music lovers includes many who do not play or who have had no musical training. Only the tone deaf are excluded. All it needs is listening, listening attentively to great music greatly played. I stress great playing because mediocre performance blocks appreciation no less than a muddy windshield hinders vision. Recall how De Quincey irradiates the knocking at the gate in Macbeth if you would faintly conceive of what Vladimir Horowitz brings to a Chopin mazurka. For those who have yet to enter into this world, there awaits such high adventure as Keats recorded "On First Looking into Chapman's Homer." The lover of letters who has trembled before the mystery of great utterance will find in music communication as searching and profound; he will find intimacy with Beethoven and Brahms as enriching as familiarity with Shakespeare.

---

[5]Hector Berlioz noted in 1862 that "Many highly intellectual people who think they love it [music] have little idea of the emotion it is able to raise." Reprinted in Kolodin, *The Composer as Listener,* 123 (1958).

RAOUL BERGER, a Washington lawyer, began his professional life as a violinist. The music critic of the *Cincinnati Commercial Tribune* in 1929 wrote that a performance by him "stamped him as an artist whose masterly technique is exceeded only by his ambition . . . played a prodigious program . . . equally spectacular was Paganini's caprice in A minor . . ." At this time he was attending the University of Cincinnati, where he received his A.B. in 1932. He had studied violin in New York and in Berlin; he made a number of concert tours and appeared as soloist with the Cleveland Symphony; he served as second concertmaster of the Cincinnati Symphony Orchestra and as first violinist in the Cincinnati String Quartet. After college he went to law school at Northwestern University, which awarded him the J.D. degree in 1935. There followed two years of private practice in Chicago, and then he spent a year at Harvard Law School, receiving the LL.M. degree in 1938. As a government attorney in Washington he served from 1938 to 1940 with the Securities and Exchange Commission on appellate matters; from 1940 to 1942, as a special assistant to the Attorney General; during 1942 to 1946 he was successively assistant general counsel, associate general counsel and general counsel to the Alien Property Custodian. A contributor to various law reviews, he belongs to the American Law Institute and to the American Bar Association. He served last year as chairman of the Association's Administrative Law Section and also as chairman of the Special Committee on Courts of Special Jurisdiction.

CHAPTER II

Constructive Contempt: A Post-Mortem

The expansion of the Fourteenth Amendment in contravention of historic conceptions has become so commonplace[1] that it is doubtless naive to confess astonishment at the latest extension of due process. One hundred and fifty years after the adoption of the Bill of Rights we learn in *Bridges v. California*[2] that the long-recognized summary power of courts over contemptuous publications was curtailed by the First Amendment and later by the Fourteenth. It is remarkable certainly that Mr. Justice Black, who not long ago amazed the profession by urging that corporations are historically outside the protection now afforded them by due process,[3] should be the instrument of this extension. And it is little less remarkable to find Mr. Justice Frankfurter dissenting,[4] in the light of his biting repudiation of the power in 1924.[5] His opinion now posits that the summary power over contemptuous publications, brushed aside as historically "dubious" by Mr. Justice Black,[6] is in fact "deeply rooted" in the common law,[7] and further, that the "power to punish for contempt is not a censorship in advance but a punishment for past conduct and, as such, like prosecution for a criminal libel, is not offensive either to the First or to the Fourteenth Amendments. . . ."[8] It is this position which is to be elaborated in this article.

If it is true, however, that the Fourteenth Amendment does not cut across the contempt power, then it seems to follow that a summary commitment for contemptuous publications, absent other considerations of due process, affords no grounds for reversal by the Supreme Court.[9] But Mr. Justice Frankfurter does not press his logic so far, since he agrees with the majority that two of the contempt judgments in companion cases must be reversed, thereby concurring in the view that the Fourteenth Amendment limits the power.[10] His real difference with the majority appears to arise out of the majority's application of the "clear and present danger" formula to the remaining two cases.[11] Bridges, a labor leader, had virtually threatened to call a strike if a then pending decision was enforced.[12] In a companion case, the *Los Angeles Times* had editorially advised the

---

[1]Cohen, Constitutional and Natural Rights in 1789 and Since, 1 Nat'l Lawyer's Guild Q. 92, 93 (1938); Corwin, Twilight of the Supreme Court 78, 79, 91 (1934). For additional citations see Read, The Constitution Reconsidered 231 n. 26 (1938).

[2]314 U.S. 252 (1941).

[3]Connecticut Gen'l Life Ins. Co. v. Johnson, 303 U.S. 77, 85–90 (1937). We are startled because a Justice cries out "like the child in the story that the king is after all naked," that the Court has woven "imaginary garments for the nakedness of corporate power." Lerner, Ideas Are Weapons 264 (1939).

[4]Stone, C.J., and Roberts and Byrnes, J.J., concurred in the dissent.

[5]Frankfurter and Landis, Power of Congress over Procedure in Criminal Contempts in "Inferior" Federal Courts—A Study in Separation of Powers, 37 Harv. L. Rev. 1010 (1924); cf. page 10–11 infra; Radin, Freedom of Speech and Contempt of Court, 36 Ill. L. Rev. 599, 608 (1942).

[6]Bridges v. California, 314 U.S. 252, 264 (1941).

[7]Ibid., at 284.

[8]Ibid., at 290.

[9]Cf. Patterson v. Colorado, 205 U.S. 454, 462, 463 (1907); Bridges v. California, 314 U.S. 252, 284 (1941).

[10]Ibid., at 297–98; cf. ibid., at 274–75.

[11]Ibid., at 295–303.

[12]Ibid., at 276 n. 20.

judge that he would "make a serious mistake" to grant probation rather than a severe sentence to certain labor "gorillas."[13] The refusal of the majority to find a "clear and present danger" to, or even a "reasonable tendency" to obstruct, impartial arbitrament in these circumstances practically puts it beyond the power of courts to deal with utterances which have hitherto been deemed to constitute an obstruction to the administration of justice.

This was the rock upon which the Supreme Court split, for the minority felt that "trial by newspaper" imperils the fundamental right to an impartial trial.[14] But the reality of this peril was questioned when Mr. Justice Holmes, dissenting in a case that involved threats of a streetcar riders' strike published to deter the judge from entering an order invalidating a fare ordinance, declared that "a judge of the United States is expected to be a man of ordinary firmness of character, and I find it impossible to believe that such a judge could have found in anything that was printed even a tendency to prevent his performing his sworn duty."[15] The realistic analysis of Mr. Justice Black follows this sensible tradition[16] and places free speech beyond the mercies of an offended judge. It requires no extensive reading of contempt cases to awaken distrust of the role played by the personal feeling of the judge.[17] And it cannot be gainsaid that there has been recurring resentment at the use of the contempt power to curb criticism of the bench. Since frequent legislative efforts to curb the power have been rendered abortive by judicial construction,[18] the *Bridges* decision

[13]Ibid., at 272 n. 17.

[14]Ibid., at 283–84. The English practice, cited by the minority, ibid., at 294, goes far beyond the bounds of actual threats addressed to a court. It embraces pre-trial discussion which may influence potential jurors, publications which may discourage parties or witnesses from coming forward, and, in short, extends to all instances which threaten to obstruct the course of impartial justice. See Goodhart, Newspapers and Contempt of Court in English Law, 48 Harv. L. Rev. 885, 888–90, 895 (1935); Sullivan, Contempts by Publication 48 et seq. (2d ed. 1940). As will appear, there is no logical or historical warrant for curtailing such contempts while singling out "intimidation" of the court for favored treatment.

[15]Toledo Newspaper Co. v. United States, 247 U.S. 402, 424 (1918). Mr. Justice Holmes pointed out that the alleged contempt there involved consisted of printed statements approving "a widespread public intent to board the cars and refuse to pay more than three cents [the new fare promulgated by city ordinance] even if the judge condemned the ordinance. . . ." This was of course incitement to disobey a possible court order, and the call for impeachment of the judge was no less "obstructive."

[16]"With an eye on the realities of the situation, we cannot assume that Judge Schmidt was unaware of the possibility of a strike as a consequence of his decision. If he was not intimidated by the facts themselves, we do not believe that the most explicit statement of them could have sidetracked the course of justice." Bridges v. California, 314 U.S. 252, 278 (1941). The "editorial . . . did no more than threaten future adverse criticism which was reasonably to be expected anyway [in view of the Times' well-known policy on labor controversies] in the event of a lenient disposition of the pending case." Ibid., at 273. The masterly espousal of the majority position on this issue by Radin, op. cit. supra note 5, renders further comment superfluous. Here it need only be pointed out that if, as the minority insists, the criterion is to be the threat to impartial decision, Bridges v. California, 314 U.S. 252, 303–4 (1941), why did it sanction an editorial expressing "exulting approval of the verdict" before sentence was imposed in a companion case? Ibid., at 297. For "friendly backing is obviously more likely than hostile aspersion to influence a judge. It is easier to close a mind than to open one. To fortify a judge in his prepossession tends to close his mind and so impede his proper discharge of judicial functions." Nelles and King, Contempt by Publication in the United States, 28 Col. L. Rev. 401, 547 n. 92 (1928); cf. State v. New Mexican Printing Co., 25 N.M. 102, 111–14, 177 Pac. 751, 755 (1918). An acute analysis of the whole question of "trial by publication" in relation to summary procedure is found in Nelles and King, op. cit. supra, at 548 et seq.

[17]The offended judge did not sit in the Bridges case, but that is the exception rather than the rule. The cases are discussed in Nelles and King, op. cit. supra note 16, at 545–47. See Ex parte Nelson, 251 Mo. 63, 157 S.W. 794 (1913) (trial judge had made up his mind and written his opinion before the contempt hearing); United States ex rel. Guaranty Trust Co. v. Gehr, 116 Fed. 520 (C.C. W.Va. 1902); note 229 infra.

[18]Toledo Newspaper Co. v. United States, 247 U.S. 402 (1918); State v. Morrill, 16 Ark. 384 (1855); Bridges v. Superior Court, 14 Cal. (2d) 464, 94 P. (2d) 983 (1939). The cases are collected in Nelles and King, op. cit. supra note 16, at 554–62. The thorny path to amendment is ordinarily cited by those who know that it is generally insuperable.

supplies an eminently practical, if Draconian, solution, unexpectedly cutting down jury trial for contemptuous publications as well.[19]

But, it is the thesis of this article, the evidence that the First Amendment was not designed to curtail the established summary power appears to be so conclusive that the larger question emerges: can the liberals, after steadily criticizing the tendency of the pre-"reconstructed"[20] court to read laissez-faire into the Constitution,[21] afford to sanctify by their own example an interpretive approach which for a generation was employed to block social legislation and may once again be turned against themselves?

That approach, it is trite to remark, purported to give effect to inexorable constitutional mandates, while in fact the prejudices of the justices had become the Procrustean test of overdue social adjustment.[22] Let it be admitted that at the outset the identification by conservative justices of individualistic preferences with constitutional dogma probably reflected the prevailing climate of opinion.[23] But the present Court is too sophisticated to make an analogous identification. Notwithstanding, the liberal justices employ a discredited technique in the *Bridges* case in order to read *their* predilections into the Constitution. To peel the historical veneer from this process we must trace the growth of the contempt power and examine the guarantee of free speech and press against a setting contemporary with its adoption. An adequate description of the present status of the contempt power necessitates discussion of *Nye v. United States*,[24] wherein the Supreme Court recently held that the Act of 1831 limited the exercise of summary power by federal courts over all out-of-court contempts. Thus fell *Toledo Newspaper Co. v. United States*;[25] and the startling echoes of that fall yield only to the reverberations of the *Bridges* case.

COMMON LAW ORIGINS

After reviewing modern studies concerned with published contempts, a recent dissenter concluded that "the courts have built a structure of judicial reasoning upon the sands of precedents which do not exist."[26] This view reflects the historical approach taken in 1924 by Frankfurter and Landis;[27] it rests ultimately on the exhaustive labors of Sir John Charles Fox;[28] and apparently it is now the view of the Supreme Court.[29] The Frankfurter and Landis article furnishes a convenient summary of the animadversions upon the origins of the power strewn throughout the pages of Fox's numerous studies. Roughly, that article states that except for contempts by officers of the court, or in the actual view of the court, trial by jury was had down to the eighteenth century, and

---

[19]The Bridges case does not rest on the *procedural* deprival of due process but upon the infringement of free speech. Curiously enough, Mr. Justice Frankfurter directs attention to the statutes permitting indictment for such contempts but does not advert to the effect of the decision on jury trial. The majority opinion also fails to note the point. Bridges v. California, 314 U.S. 252, 305 (1941); cf. Radin, op. cit. supra note 5, at 609.

[20]See Mr. Justice Frankfurter's concurring opinion in Graves v. New York ex rel. O'Keefe, 306 U.S. 466, 487 (1939).

[21]The classic criticisms are those of Mr. Justice Holmes, dissenting in Lochner v. New York, 198 U.S. 45, 74–76 (1905), and in Baldwin v. Missouri, 281 U.S. 586, 595–96 (1930).

[22]Hamilton and Braden were, it appears, unduly optimistic in stating that recent changes strike at "a dualism between word and deed, by which the Court could act and yet deny the consequences of its own decision. It makes it impossible any longer for the majority of the bench to pretend not to do that in which they were busily engaged." Hamilton and Braden, The Special Competence of the Supreme Court, 50 Yale L.J. 1319, 1329–30 (1941).

[23]Note 258 infra.

[24]313 U.S. 33 (1941).

[25]247 U.S. 402 (1918).

[26]Edmonds, J., dissenting in Bridges v. Superior Court, 14 Cal. (2d) 464, 495, 94 P. (2d) 983, 999 (1939).

[27]Frankfurter and Landis, op. cit. supra note 5; see page 602 supra.

[28]His works are hereinafter cited.

[29]Bridges v. California, 314 U.S. 252, 264 (1941).

that the Star Chamber asserted a summary power over contempts until it was abolished in 1641. To continue in the words of the article:

> But the atmosphere of corrupt and arbitrary practices which it had generated partly survived. Gradually there appear traces of infection in the King's Bench which succeeded to the jurisdiction of the Star Chamber. The odious commitments by the Restoration Parliament . . . reinforced the practice of arbitrary procedure. . . . This infusion of Star Chamber methods on the common law side appears most vigorously in the undelivered judgment of Wilmot, J., in Rex v. Almon. . . . It has bedevilled the law of contempt both in England and in this country ever since. . . . Wilmot's history is fiction. . . .[30]

Thus one gains the impression that this branch of the contempt power is of illegitimate origin, and that, as regards the law courts, it sprang full-armed from the brain of Mr. Justice, later Chief Justice, Wilmot in 1765. Fox, it is to be noted, sought chiefly to demonstrate that Wilmot's sweeping dictum, basing the summary power over contemptuous publications on *immemorial usage,*[31] was unfounded.[32] In this he was unquestionably successful. The very cases collected by Fox, however, disclose that the power was completely established in the early eighteenth century.[33] So much Mr. Justice Frankfurter now postulates in the *Bridges* case.[34] It is the thesis of this section that the power did not spring into being in an eighteenth century void, but that it began long before to develop logically from the comprehensive summary jurisdiction of medieval courts. Not that the argument need for present purposes go so far. Given an established and familiar eighteenth century power at the adoption of the Constitution, the case for the devolution of the power upon the federal courts stands no worse at least than that of familiar equity doctrines of no less recent origin.[35] But it cannot be amiss in considering the constitutional issue raised by the *Bridges* case to dispel the bias that must arise from the current impression that the power is a product of gross usurpation. This task is the more essential because the dissent of Mr. Justice Frankfurter is likely to perpetuate an historical error with respect to the origins of the power, and as he has since remarked, "legal history still has its claims."[36]

The summary power extended from earliest times to disobedience of judicial writs or orders,[37] to all contempts by judicial officers, i.e., jurors, attorneys, and the like,[38] and to contempts

---

[30]Frankfurter and Landis, op. cit. supra note 5, at 1045–47 (the quotation is telescoped). Radin, op. cit. supra note 5, at 609, commenting on the Bridges case, said "It was not assumed, until the posthumously published [1802] judgment in Almon's case, that it [contemptuous publications] could be dealt with summarily. . . ."

[31]Rex v. Almon, Wilm. 243, 254 (K.B. 1765).

[32]"It remains to be determined by an appeal to history whether or not the doctrine is supported by immemorial usage. If it should prove that contempts out of court committed by strangers were before the seventeenth century punished by the common law courts [as distinguished from Chancery], only upon conviction after trial in the ordinary course of law, it follows that the present practice in such cases, though established by a long line of decisions, is based on a misapprehension." Fox, The History of Contempt of Court 43 (1929); see ibid., at 3, 4, 15, 24, 26, 33, 49, 98, 112.

[33]Page 612 infra.

[34]Bridges v. California, 314 U.S. 252, 284–85 (1941).

[35]3 Bl. Comm. *53; 1 Holdsworth, History of English Law 454, 465 (3d ed. 1922); see In re Hallett's Estate, 13 Ch.D. 696, 710 (C.A. 1879).

[36]Federal Power Com'n v. Natural Gas Pipeline Co., 62 S.Ct. 736, 754 (1942). Mr. Justice Frankfurter in the Bridges case rejected that portion of summary jurisdiction known as "scandalizing the court," i.e., bringing it into disrepute, as an "abuse" whereby "some English judges extended their authority," saying that "such foolishness has long since been disavowed in England and has never found lodgment here." Bridges v. California, 314 U.S. 252, 287 (1941).

[37]3 Holdsworth, op. cit. supra note 35, at 391; Fox, op. cit. supra note 32, at 18. Such contempts may appear irrelevant because "civil" rather than "criminal." But Sayles justly remarks that "so sharp a distinction is difficult to uphold in the thirteenth and fourteenth century." 3 Select Cases in the Court of Kings Bench (Edw. I), 58 Seld. Soc. lxxvii (1939).

[38]Fox, op. cit. supra note 32, at 156, 157; Fox, The Summary Process to Punish Contempt, 25 Law Q. Rev. 238, 244 (1909); Fox, The Nature of Contempt of Court, 37 Law Q. Rev. 191, 192 (1921).

committed in the actual view of the court.[39] Contempts committed by strangers out of court, or in the presence but not in the actual view of the court, were tried by jury. Parties were "more strictly amenable than strangers" to the summary jurisdiction.[40] Many, perhaps most, cases of contempts in the actual view of the court were tried by jury.[41] And there are cases in which attorneys were proceeded against by information for misconduct.[42] But there was summary power, and it embraced disobedience to orders, misconduct of officers, and misconduct in the actual view of the court. Except, therefore, for out-of-court contempts by strangers, and possibly by parties, not involving disobedience to process or orders, the summary power of medieval courts was almost modern in scope.

An early example of the summary trial *procedure* is found in the commitment of an attorney upon interrogation in 1310;[43] and in the middle of the fourteenth century "it was probably common custom to examine an officer charged with malpractice. . . ."[44] This was the practice of examination upon interrogatories which derived from the ecclesiastical courts and prevailed in the King's Council.[45] It represents a drastic innovation. Gone are the particularized common law pleadings designed to set out the charge precisely, gone the right to trial by jury. Instead the defendant is summoned to answer a complaint by the plaintiff, and, on appearance, to "answer on oath, and sentence by sentence," the bill of the plaintiff.[46] The justices of both benches were, in the reign of Henry V, assisting in cases pending before the King's Council and thereby becoming familiar with the process of examination.[47] To this may be added the influence exerted by a long line of statutes, from 1402 onwards, extending the summary trial by examination, among other things, to four specific instances of out-of-court contempts by strangers.[48]

The extension of summary procedure to other out-of-court contempts by strangers may be traced from the summary power over their out-of-court disobedience of orders.

At the close of the fourteenth century Chancery was entertaining petitions to punish for contempt not only those who disobeyed, but also those who trampled on or were otherwise disrespectful of its orders.[49] In the middle of the sixteenth century, Chancery began summarily to

---

[39]Fox, op. cit. supra note 32, at ix, 50–52, 116. Sayles accepts the summary punishment of disobedience to process and of court officers, Sayles, op. cit. supra note 37, at lxxvii, lxxix, but questions whether the cases of contempt in the view of the court represent summary *punishment* rather than commitment to await punishment, ibid., at lxxx, lxxxi. Sayles does not explain why flagrant in-court contempts should be remitted to jury trail while often innocuous out-of-court disobedience to court orders would be punished summarily. Fox's citations are persuasive, and his position has been adopted by Holdsworth, op. cit. supra note 35, at 392. This difference of opinion does not affect the present thesis, because the power over contemptuous publications derives from disobedience to court orders, conceded by Sayles to be a branch of the summary jurisdiction.

[40]Fox, op. cit. supra note 32, at 116; cf. Plucknett, Review of Fox, The History of Contempt of Court, 41 Harv. L. Rev. 270 (1928).

[41]Fox, The King v. Almon, 24 Law Q. Rev. 266, 267 (1908); note to Davis's Case, 2 Dyer *188b, 73 Eng. Rep. R. 415, 416.

[42]Fox, op. cit. supra note 32, at 158.

[43]Ibid., at 159, 161, 162; Broke v. Taylard, Y.B. 4 Edw. I, 22 Seld. Soc. 194 (1907).

[44]Fox, op. cit. supra note 32, at 73–74.

[45]Ibid., at 70, 73; Maitland, Equity 5 (1929). Note that summary procedure comprises both examination and attachment, which was initially process to secure appearance in court and did not connote trial by examination. Fox, op. cit. supra note 32, at 56–57.

[46]Maitland, Equity 5 (1929).

[47]Fox, op. cit. supra note 32, at 73; Fox, The Summary Process to Punish Contempt, 25 Law Q. Rev. 354, 356 (1909).

[48]Fox, op. cit. supra note 32, at 77–82. Fox's argument that the explicit statutory authorization in these four instances rules out the existence of a general summary power as to strangers runs afoul of the fact that many statutes dealing with misconduct of officers were only declaratory if by Fox's own testimony disciplinary jurisdiction over court officers was exercised from earliest times.

[49]Select Cases in Chancery, 10 Seld. Soc. 26, 60, 78 (1896).

punish both parties and strangers who resisted the service[50] or who spoke contemptuously of the court on service of process,[51] i.e., of an *order* to appear. In this it followed the example of the Star Chamber, which had since 1495 exercised jurisdiction over resistance to and slander of the process of other courts.[52] It is a mistake to impeach the example of the Star Chamber[53] on the ground of tyrannical excesses at a much later period, for the Star Chamber was a respected and important court as late as the reign of Charles I.[54] If anything, the instances just recited show that Chancery had anticipated the Star Chamber by punishing disrespect of its orders in the fourteenth century. To be sure, Chapter 39 of the Statute of Westminster II had in 1285 provided for jury trial in cases of resistance to a sheriff in execution of process,[55] and Fox lists cases subsequent to the statute in which resistance to execution of process, and contemptuous reference thereto—plainly an extension of statutory authority, which was later taken up in the summary procedure—were tried by jury.[56] We are not, without more, justified in construing the statute as a limitation upon the summary power over disobedience to orders, of which resistance to process was merely a branch.[57] And a striking departure is found in the dreaded writ of subpoena, first met in 1363, which cut through the interminable delays that hamstrung common law process,[58] apparently by means of summary enforcement rather than the recited pecuniary penalty.[59] Even if punishment for contempt of judicial orders, tested by the Statute of Westminster II, represented an arrogation of judicial power, it was nevertheless an established practice by the end of the sixteenth century, and had found formal expression in Lord Bacon's Order No. 77 in 1619.[60]

In short, given the ancient jurisdiction to proceed summarily for disobedience of judicial writs and orders, the extension of the contempt power could and did proceed by easy steps. Fox's sketch of the development in terms of disobedience of mesne process is no less applicable to disobedience of all orders. There was the

> 1st step, disobedience to the writ; 2d, abuse of the process server; 3d, assaulting him; 4th, abusing the writ; 5th, abusing the Court or Judge by whose authority the writ issued; 6th, reducing the abusive words into writing and publishing them; and so the offender arrives at a libel on the Court. The first five

[50]Rove v. West, Cary 38, 21 Eng. Rep. R. 21 (1558); Dastoines v. Apprice, Cary 92, 21 Eng. Rep. R. 49 (1579). The following cases are found in Monro, Acta Cancellariae (1847): St. Johns College v. Pinder (1557) (examination upon interrogatories), at 334; Inhabitants of Lynde v. Byron (1563), at 345; Clement v. Champion (1564), at 352; Churchhouse v. Sherwyn (1566), at 361; Wheteley v. Fenner (1568), at 374; Bowyer v. Samwayes (1572), at 394; see ibid., at 411, 414, 501, 504, 542, 546, 549, 571, 651, 753.

[51]Allen v. Martin (1600), Monro, Acta Cancellariae 753 (1847); cf. Lingen v. Prince (1582), ibid., at 516.

[52]Fox, op. cit. supra note 32, at 109; Idele v. Abbotts, 1 Select Cases in the Star Chamber, 16 Seld. Soc. 50 (1902). Fox cites the summary punishment of "an attempt to discredit justice and jury" in a murder case during the reign of Philip and Mary. Fox, op. cit. supra note 41, at 273; Fox, op. cit. supra note 32, at 84, 116; compare the case of the seizure and detention of the duly elected "bailly" by certain persons displeased with his election "in contempt of your highness and your lawes." 1 Select Cases in the Star Chamber, 16 Seld. Soc. 230–31 (1902).

[53]Fox, op. cit. supra note 32, at 88; Frankfurter and Landis, op. cit. supra note 5, at 1045.

[54]See the comment of Judge Frank in NLRB v. Air Associates, Inc., 121 F. (2d) 586, 589 n. 4 (C.C.A. 2d 1941), and the authorities there cited; Scofield, Court of Star Chamber 45 (1900); Crompton, Star Chamber Cases x (1881); Turner, Star Chamber, Encyc. Brit. 331 (14th ed. 1936); Palgrave, The Original Authority of the King's Council 109–10 (1834); Carr, Concerning English Administrative Law 126 (1941).

[55]Fox, op. cit. supra note 32, at 11–12.

[56]Ibid., at 229–30.

[57]Jury trial in cases of resistance to execution of a writ was not a novelty. See the cases decided in 1254 and 1276, cited in Fox, op. cit. supra note 32, at 226. Perhaps the statute was merely intended to warn the "great men" who alone are mentioned as "resisters" and to embolden the courts to deal with them.

[58]1 Holdsworth, op. cit. supra note 35, at 485 n. 9; 3 ibid., at 623–27.

[59]Palgrave, op. cit. supra note 54, at 131; 1 Spence, Equitable Jurisdiction 369–70 (1846) (authority in the reign of Edw. IV cited); 1 Campbell, Lives of the Lord Chancellors 259 (5th ed. 1868); cf. 1 Holdsworth, op. cit. supra note 35, at 406 n. 6.

[60]Sanders, Chan. Ord. 119 (1845).

steps, ending with abuse of the Judge, were punishable by summary procedure in the Court of Chancery under Lord Bacon's rule, and in the King's Bench after the abolition of the Star Chamber; the sixth, libelling the Court or Judge, was not so dealt with either in the Court of Chancery or at common law, where the contempt was denied, until the eighteenth century.[61]

As we have seen, Chancery had reached the fourth step, abuse of the writ, by the end of the fourteenth century when it was entertaining petitions to punish for contempt those who had trampled on its orders. And by the end of the sixteenth century it was summarily punishing those who abused the court during the service of process (fifth stage). From this it was but a step to commitment for any spoken contempt. There is reason to believe that the step had in fact been taken by the time of Lord Bacon's rule. That rule stated: "In case of contempts granted upon force or ill words upon serving of process, *or upon words of scandall of the Court,* proved by affidavit, the party is forthwith to stand committed."[62] Fox suggests that the phrase "words of scandall of the Court" must "be taken to mean only in connexion with the service of process."[63] But that situation was plainly covered by the phrase "ill words upon service of process," and Lord Bacon was the last man to add purely tautologous matter.

Parliament itself had set the example as early as 1529, when William Thranwis was committed for a contempt in words against the House.[64] An unbroken line of summary commitments for "contumelious words against the House," stretching from 1558 to the case of Sir Francis Burdett in 1810, is recorded in the Journal of Parliament.[65] The practice of commitment for out-of-court contempts had found judicial approval in *Ferrers' Case* in 1543.[66] These cases, and a commitment for libel of the House by one Hall in 1580, are cited by Lord Ellenborough for the proposition that the "House were in the habit of committing for contempt."[67] The power was likewise recognized by Chief Justice Holt,[68] Lord Eldon,[69] and Lord Erskine, who declared that the "House of Commons . . . must, like every other tribunal, have the power to protect itself from obstruction and insult. . . ."[70] So long continued and familiar a practice necessarily influenced the courts; and Fox is plainly mistaken in suggesting that the courts were reflecting the practice of the House in the later Stuart period,[71] for judicial approval reaches back to 1543.

Such is the setting against which the development of the power in the law courts is to be viewed. In 1615, Chief Justice Coke clearly thought he had the power of punishing summarily a person who had treated the process of King's Bench with contempt.[72] An attempt had been made in 1594

---

[61]Fox, op. cit. supra note 32, at 109–10.

[62]Sanders, Chan. Ord. 119 (1845) (italics added); cf. Lingen v. Prince (1582), reported in Monro, Acta Cancellariae 516 (1847), involving a commitment for contemptuous words spoken against the court, though it does not appear where or in what connection the words were spoken. Compare the commitment of counsel for out-of-court criticism of the Lord Chancellor in Brokas v. Savage (1588), ibid., at 581. See the curious Chancery case in 1396 in which John Belgrave was charged with placing in a church, in which an ecclesiastical hearing was to take place, a bill terming the hearing officer an unrighteous judge to the detriment of the execution of the laws. Select Cases in Chancery, 10 Seld. Soc. 106 (1896).

[63]Fox, op. cit. supra note 32, at 109.

[64]Unreported, but cited by Lord Ellenborough in Burdett v. Abbott, 14 East 1, 142, 104 Eng. Rep. R. 501, 555 (K.B. 1811).

[65]The cases are listed in ibid., at 23–26.

[66]Bridgman 625, 124 Eng. Rep. R. 282 (1631).

[67]Note 64 supra.

[68]Regina v. Paty, 2 Ld. Raym. 1105, 1115, 92 Eng. Rep. R. 232, 238 (K.B. 1705).

[69]Burdett v. Abbott, 5 Dow 165, 200, 3 Eng. Rep. R. 1289, 1301 (H.L. 1817).

[70]Ibid., at 201 and 1302; see the Earl of Shaftesbury's Case, 1 Mod. 144, 158, 86 Eng. Rep. R. 792, 800 (K.B. 1677); Murray's Case, 1 Wils. (K.B.) 299, 95 Eng. Rep. R. 629 (1751); Brass Crosby's Case, 3 Wils. (K.B.) 188, 95 Eng. Rep. R. 1005 (1771).

[71]Fox, op. cit. supra note 41, at 275–76.

[72]Bruistone v. Baker, 1 Rol. 315, 81 Eng. Rep. R. 511 (K.B. 1615); 3 Holdsworth, op. cit. supra note 35, at 394 n. 2. Fox stated that this case indicated that a practice of examination upon oath had been "established in Coke's time in some cases." Fox, The Summary Process to Punish Contempt, 25 Law Q. Rev. 238, 250 (1909).

in the Queen's Bench to combine the processes of attachment and examination with respect to a contempt by a stranger out of court.[73] The order then entered apparently came to naught, but there is evidence of examination upon attachment in 1631.[74] Fox remarked that there "is no doubt that summary committal for contempts out of court, except in case of libel on the court . . . was practiced by the common law courts in the middle of the seventeenth century."[75] To discredit the practice by attributing it to the example of a decadent Star Chamber and an arbitrary Restoration Parliament is to ignore the play of forces emanating from the long-familiar parliamentary practice, the well-settled practice of an honored Star Chamber, and, by 1600, the established Chancery practice with respect to slander on the service of process.

The eighteenth century saw the summary power in spate, sweeping on in case after case to encompass contempts by publication. On the King's Bench side were:[76] *Rex v. Barber,*[77] *Rex v. Wilkin,*[78] *Rex v. Colbatch,*[79] *Rex v. Middleton,*[80] *Rex v. Wiatt,*[81] *Rex v. Lawley,*[82] *Anonymous Case,*[83] *Rex v. Carroll,*[84] *Rex v. Almon,*[85] and *Steare's Case.*[86] On the Chancery side were:[87] *Poole*

[73]Fox, op.cit. supra note 32, at 86.

[74]Ibid., at 87, 89. Plucknett stated that the King's Bench, by the end of the sixteenth century, enjoyed considerable powers of summarily trying the more usual contempts. Plucknett, op. cit. supra note 40, at 271.

[75]Fox, op. cit. supra note 72, at 366. Style's Practical Register (1657) under "Attachment": "Generally an attachment doth lie for any contempt done against the court."

[76]Some of the cases are listed in Reports of the Select Committee of the House of Commons appointed to consider Sir Francis Burdett's case, at appendix E, 8 How. St. Tr. 14, 49 (1810), and are discussed in Fox, op. cit. supra note 32, at 25, 112–14, 16, 28, 30, 35, 107. Compare the comment of Lord Kenyon on a commitment for libel by the House of Lords: "This claim of right to punish . . . for such an offense is not peculiar to the House of Lords; it is frequently exercised by this and other courts of record, and that not merely for contempts committed in the presence of the court." Flower's Case, 8 Term R. 314, 323–24 (1799).

[77]1 Stra. 444, 93 Eng. Rep. R. 624 (1721).

[78]Unreported (1722).

[79]Unreported (1723).

[80]Fortes. 201, 92 Eng. Rep. R. 818 (1723).

[81]8 Mod. 123, 88 Eng. Rep. R. 96 (1723). Fox wrote: "The reports in the Middleton and Wiatt cases mistakenly read as if the libel were against a Doctor of Divinity, but it is clear that attachment would not have been granted in the case of a libel on a private individual. The libel in fact contained expressions reflecting on the Court, and the case is so indexed in the Table to 8 Modern and in Viner's Abridgement (vol. xv, p. 90, pl. 3)." Fox, op. cit. supra note 32, at 113.

[82]Unreported (1731).

[83]2 Barn. (K.B.) 43, 94 Eng. Rep. R. 345 (1731).

[84]1 Wils. 75 (1744).

[85]The draft of Chief Justice Wilmot's opinion in Rex. v. Almon has been brushed aside as posthumous. Fletcher, J., dissenting in Taafe v. Downs (1813), quoted in Fox, op. cit. supra note 41, at 187; Frankfurter and Landis, op. cit. supra note 5, at 1046. The copy of his opinion, published in 1802, shows by his endorsement that his brother judges would have agreed in granting the attachment, and more important, it has been explicitly endorsed by the English courts. For citations see Fox, op. cit. supra note 32, at 30. Compare the posthumous opinion of Taney, C.J., in Gordon v. United States, 117 U.S. 697 (1864); Frankfurter and Katz, Cases on Federal Jurisdiction 13 (1931). It was natural that Chief Justice Wilmot, casting about for precedents in a case involving a libel on King's Beach in 1765, should inquire why the printing of scandalous attacks on a judge should go unpunished when attachments were being granted for abusing the process of the Court. Rex v. Almon, Wilm. 243, 256–57 (K.B. 1765).

For parallel independent reasoning see Commonwealth v. Dandridge, 2 Va. Cas. 408, 420 (1823). To this query Fox replied that obstruction of a process server directly interferes with the course of justice whereas a libel on a court is an indirect contempt. Fox, op. cit. supra note 32, at 110. But the distinction between spoken contempts on service of process (which alone are involved) and a libel on the court is unreal. For, as was noted in the Dandridge case, op. cit. supra, at 428, "the process is just as effectual for its end and purpose though spoken of contemptuously, as if received in silence or treated with professed respect." Certainly a slanderous reflection on process can scarcely have a more immediate obstructive effect than a widely published attack on the integrity of the court, particularly when similar cases are pending.

[86]Unreported (1768).

[87]The cases are discussed in Fox, op. cit. supra note 32, at 21–22, 115, 101, 102; see Ex parte Jones, 13 Ves. 237, 33 Eng. Rep. R. 283 (1806).

v. Sacheverel,[88] *In re Dodd,*[89] *Raike's Case,*[90] *Roach v. Garvan,*[91] and *Cann v. Cann.*[92] "Standing by themselves," said Fox, these cases "point to modern innovation rather than to immemorial usage. . . ."[93] This is a just refutation of Chief Justice Wilmot's rash claim. But it goes no further. The towering structure of equity itself would fall were its foundation sought in immemorial usage.[94] And these cases do not stand alone; they are the product of an evolution typical of the common law.[95] If the foregoing analysis is valid, the contempt power over publications was established at the adoption of the Constitution.[96]

THE CONSTITUTION AND THE CONTEMPT POWER

The "sweeping constitutional mandate against any law 'abridging the freedom of speech or of the press' " not alone curtails the summary power of state courts, holds the *Bridges* case, but, the Supreme Court plainly intimates, it limits the power of federal courts, including the Supreme Court itself.[97] The majority, consequently, looks to the First Amendment both for light as to the scope of the Fourteenth and as a direct limitation upon the summary power of federal courts. "Congress shall make no law . . . abridging the freedom of speech or of the press," declares the First Amendment. On its face this prohibition applies only to laws enacted by Congress. Whatever

[88]1 P. Wms. 675, 24 Eng. Rep. R. 565 (1720).

[89]Sanders, Chan. Ord. 538, 542 (1736).

[90]Unreported (1740).

[91]2 Atkyns 469, 26 Eng. Rep. R. 683 (1742).

[92]2 Ves. Sr. 520 (1754). The Cann and Pool cases involve publications of matter relating to the case, rather than criticisms of the court. Of the two groups of cases listed above, the Barber, Wilkin, Colbatch, Middleton, Lawley, Anonymous, Dodd, Raike, Almon, and Steare cases involved libels on the court; and Lord Hardwicke by dictum in the Garvan case mentioned "scandalizing the court" as one of the contempt categories. See note 96 infra; Regina v. Skipworth, 12 Cox C.C. 371 (Q.B. 1873); Regina v. Gray, [1900] 2 Q.B. 36 (non-pending case). Rex v. Editor, 44 T.L.R. 301 (K.B. 1928); Goodhart, op. cit. supra note 14, at 898–904. The foregoing historical materials plainly disclose that "scandalizing the court" is traceable in a direct and logical line from one of the earliest branches of the contempt power, and that it is an accepted doctrine in England today.

The doctrine found acceptance in this country from the beginning; see Respublica v. Oswald, 1 Dall. (Pa.) *319 (1788), and the concession by the learned Storrs in the Peck impeachment proceedings, note 162 infra. See also State v. Morrill, 16 Ark. 384 (1855); Ex parte Barry, 85 Cal. 603, 25 Pac. 256 (1890); Cooper v. People ex rel. Wyatt, 13 Colo. 337, 22 Pac. 790 (1889); In re Hayes, 72 Fla. 558, 73 So. 362 (1916); In re Fite, 11 Ga. App. 665, 76 S.E. 397 (1912); Ray v. State, 186 Ind. 396, 114 N.E. 866 (1917); In re Chadwick, 109 Mich. 588, 67 N.W. 1071 (1896); State v. Shepherd, 177 Mo. 205, 76 S.W. 79 (1903); Territory v. Murray, 7 Mont. 251 (1887); In re Moore, 63 N.C. 389 (1869); State v. Hildreth, 82 Vt. 382, 74 Atl. 71 (1909); Burdett v. Commonwealth, 103 Va. 838, 48 S.E. 878 (1904); State v. Frew & Hart, 24 W.Va. 416 (1884); Nelles and King, op. cit. supra note 16, at 537. Mr. Justice Holmes has summed up this learning in the statement that courts which find "that publications impugning their own reasoning or motives will interfere with their administration of the law" may act summarily. Patterson v. Colorado, 205 U.S. 454, 462–63 (1907). But cf. Mr. Justice Frankfurter's dissent in Bridges v. California, 314 U.S. 252, 287 (1942); note 36 supra.

[93]Fox, op. cit. supra note 32, at 111, 112 (italics added).

[94]See note 35 supra.

[95]As in the case of agreements in restraint of trade, the common law has at times "reversed its old doctrine." Pollock, Principles of Contract 391–92 (10th ed. 1936).

[96]The testimony of contemporary writers is found in 5 Viner, Abridgement 442–53 (5th ed. 1792); 3 ibid., at 236–37 (5th ed. 1791); 2 Hawkins, Pleas of the Crown c. 22 § 36 (6th ed. 1788), citing Rex. v. Barber, 1 Stra. 444 (K.B. 1721); 4 Bl. Comm. *282–85; 2 Comyn's Digest 38–42 (2d ed. 1785). Nor must the importance of Bateman v. Conway, 1 Bro. Parl. Cas. 519 (H.L. 1753) be overlooked in appraising the status of strangers. In that case the House of Lords approved the attachment of a stranger for an out-of-court non-publication contempt. For similar cases see Lea's Case, Gouldsb. 33 (K.B. 1586); Partridge v. Partridge, Toth. 40–41, 21 Eng. Rep. R. 117 (Ch. 1639); Harvey v. Harvey, 2 Cas. in Ch. 82, 22 Eng. Rep. R. 857 (1681); Butler's Case, 2 Salk. 596, 91 Eng. Rep. R. 504 (K.B. 1696); Garibaldo v. Cagnoni, 6 Mod. 90, 87 Eng. Rep. R. 848 (K.B. 1704); Yalden's Case, 1 P. Wms. 697, 24 Eng. Rep. R. 576 (Ch. 1721); Williams v. Lyons, 8 Mod. 189, 88 Eng. Rep. R. 138 (K.B. 1723).

[97]Bridges v. California, 314 U.S. 252, 260 (1941).

be the scope of that limitation, how can a restriction aimed squarely at the legislative power be construed as a limitation upon a familiar co-existing judicial power?[98] The appeal to history by Mr. Justice Black furnishes no adequate answer.

Historically, it is generally agreed that the guarantee of free press was largely designed to bar the Federal Government from licensing or censoring the press.[99] English licensing had by the lapse of a statute expired in 1694, though it maintained itself in the colonies until 1719.[100] Toward the end of the eighteenth century, the dormancy of the licensing power had become identified with a common law right of free press which first found legal formulation at the hands of Blackstone.[101] The "liberty of the press," said Blackstone, whose influence with the colonists is well-known,[102] "consists in laying no previous restraints upon publications and not in freedom from censure for criminal matter when published."[103] It seems improbable that the framers of the Amendment intended to soar far beyond common law confines.[104] For this we have early judicial testimony, as well as that of the great commentators Story and Kent, and more recently, of Mr. Justice Holmes.[105] But why, it has been asked, should the colonists have troubled to push through a constitutional amendment "just to settle an issue that had been dead for decades?"[106] The answer is best given in the words of St. George Tucker, a native annotator of Blackstone, who gave the common law a "strangely republican twist."[107] Referring to the lapse of licensing which established the freedom of the press in England, Tucker wrote:

> But although this negative establishment may satisfy the subjects of England, the people of America have not thought proper to suffer the freedom of speech, and of the press to rest upon such an uncertain foundation, as the will and pleasure of the government. Accordingly . . . the first congress . . . proposed an amendment . . . "that congress shall make no law abridging the freedom of speech, or of the press."[108]

[98]Compare the parallel provision that "No State shall . . . pass any . . . Law impairing the Obligation of Contracts" which time and again has been held inapplicable to impairment by judicial decision. Tidal Oil Co. v. Flanagan, 263 U.S. 444 (1924), and cases cited therein; Stockholders of the Peoples Banking Co. v. Sterling, 300 U.S. 175 (1937); Constitutionality of Judicial Decisions in Their Substantive Law Aspect under the Due Process Clause, 28 Col. L Rev. 619, 627 (1928). "Insofar as the semantics of the eighteenth and early nineteenth centuries are concerned, the word 'laws' did not include decisions but was limited to legislative enactments." Teton, The Story of Swift v. Tyson, 35 Ill. L Rev. 519, 537 (1941), and materials there cited.

[99]2 Story, Commentaries on the Constitution 597–98 (2d ed. 1851); 1 Kent, Commentaries 627 (7th ed. 1851); Pound, Equitable Relief Against Defamation and Injuries to Personality, 29 Harv. L. Rev. 640, 651 (1916); cf. Patterson v. Colorado, 205 U.S. 454 (1907) (per Mr. Justice Holmes); Near v. Minnesota, 283 U.S. 697, 713 (1931) (per Mr. Chief Justice Hughes); see pages 19–20 infra.

[100]2 Story, op. cit. supra note 99, at 599; Vance, Freedom of Speech and of the Press, 2 Minn. L. Rev. 239, 247 (1918).

[101]Pound, op. cit. supra note 99, at 650; Corwin, Freedom of Speech and Press under the First Amendment: A Résumé, 30 Yale L.J. 48, 49 (1920).

[102]Ibid., at 49; Pound, op. cit. supra note 99, at 650; cf. Frankfurter and Landis, op. cit. supra note 5, at 1046 n. 128.

[103]4 Bl. Comm. *151.

[104]Corwin, op. cit. supra note 101, at 49; Pound, op. cit. supra note 99, at 651. All "that the earlier sages of the Revolution had in view," according to Kent, was to erect "barriers against any previous restraints upon publication." 1 Kent, Commentaries 627 (7th ed. 1851); see Robertson v. Baldwin, 165 U.S. 215, 281 (1897).

[105]Respublica v. Oswald, 1 Dall. (Pa.) *319 (1788); note 99 supra. For a qualification by Mr. Justice Holmes, see note 171 infra.

[106]Chafee, Freedom of Speech in War Time, 32 Harv. L. Rev. 932, 945 (1919).

[107]Hamilton and Adair, The Power to Govern 201–2 (1937). Tucker was professor of law at William and Mary, and a judge of the General Court of Virginia. It is at least singular that so "republican" a glossator, one thoroughly alive to the difference between English and American limitations on free press, should have been completely oblivious of the "menace" to free press implicit in Blackstone's sweeping formulation of the summary power over publications.

[108]1 Bl. Comm. pt. 2, app. at 13 (Tucker ed. 1803).

This was likewise the explanation offered by Story.[109] And, it is submitted, this is all that Madison meant when he declared that "the freedom of the press and rights of conscience, those choicest privileges of the people, are unguarded in the British Constitution."[110]

Admittedly, the Blackstonian interpretation was from early times criticized on the ground that subsequent punishment under repressive laws might as effectively stifle harmless publication as previous restraints. In the words of Madison: "It would seem a mockery to say that no laws should be passed preventing publications from being made, but that *laws might be passed* for punishing them in case they should be made."[111] This feeling found powerful expression in the English movement led by Fox and Erskine to reform repressive libel laws, culminating in Fox's Libel Act of 1792.[112] But it is of great significance that these leaders, though indubitably familiar with the summary power over contemptuous publications, should have ignored the "threat" to free speech inherent in the power and confined themselves exclusively to reforming libel trials by jury. Lord Erskine, in fact, later approved the contempt power over publications.[113] Chief Justice Hughes summarized the matter in *Near v. Minnesota,* a decision that went far to extend protection to the press:

> But it is recognized that punishment for the abuse of the liberty accorded to the press is essential to the protection of the public, and that the common law rules that subject the libeler to responsibility for the public offense, as well as for the private injury, are not abolished by the protection extended in our constitutions. . . . The law of criminal libel rests upon that secure foundation. There is also the conceded

[109] 2 Story, op. cit. supra note 99, at 399.

[110] 1 Annals Cong. 434 (1789), quoted in Bridges v. California, 314 U.S. 252, 264 (1941).

[111] 6 Writings of James Madison 386 (Hunt ed. 1906) (italics added). These remarks, parenthetically, occur in the same discussion of free speech from which Mr. Justice Black culled the quotation that the "common law cannot be admitted as the universal expositor of American terms. . . ." Bridges v. California, 314 U.S. 252, 265 n. 10 (1941); see Near v. Minnesota, 283 U.S. 697, 714–15 (1931). As Chafee puts it: "A death penalty for writing about socialism would be as effective suppression as a censorship." Chafee, op. cit. supra note 106, at 940.

[112] Chafee, op. cit. supra note 106, at 939, 945.

[113] Burdett v. Abbott, 5 Dow 165, 200, 3 Eng. Rep. R. 1289, 1302 (H.L. 1817). See also his statement in the text at note 70 supra. A word against the temptation to equate contemptuous publications with seditious libels. According to Stephen, the eighteenth century defined seditious libel as "written censure upon public men for their conduct as such, or upon the laws, or upon the institutions of the country." 2 Stephen, The History of the Criminal Law of England 348 (1883). This language, to be sure, is broad enough to include publications which "scandalize" the courts. But Blackstone does not make the identification. Instead, he treats them in separate categories, explaining that libels, "especially of a magistrate," may lead to breach of the peace by inciting "to revenge, and perhaps to bloodshed." 4 Bl. Comm. *150. Punishment for contemptuous publications, on the other hand, proceeds from the need for law enforcement, since "laws, without a competent authority to secure their administration from disobedience and contempt, would be vain and nugatory." Ibid., at *282. And summary punishment of contemptuous publications has a line of descent quite distinct from that of the crime of libel. Pages ii–ix supra. Moreover, despite the frequent trials for seditious libel, the leading contempt cases do not cite them as analogies, nor do the leading seditious libel cases invoke the contempt cases.

Indeed, Erskine, who had been preeminent for the defense in the leading seditious libel cases, plainly excepted contempts from the broad protection of free press. Thus, in the argument on behalf of Thomas Paine, he said that if one "calumniates living magistrates . . . he is then a criminal upon every principle of rational policy, as well as upon the immemorial precedents of English justice. . . ." Paine's Case, 22 How. St. Tr. 358, 415 (K.B. 1792); ibid., at 424. Again, referring to the need to preserve the "impartial administration of justice," Erksine said that the "circulation of any paper" that tends to prejudice a "British tribunal" is "highly criminal," a quite inclusive formula guarding "freedom of trial." Ibid., at 417. Finally, emphasis upon incitement to disaffection, to violent alteration of established institutions, runs through the libel cases; see Dean of St. Asaph's Case, 21 How. St. Tr. 847, 898, 906, 1011 (K.B. 1784). It is therefore understandable that, as fear of revolution diminished, English prosecutions for seditious libel practically ceased, 2 Stephen, op. cit. supra, at 373, whereas English courts continue to punish contemptuous publications because they obstruct the administration of justice. See note 92 supra.

authority of courts to punish for contempt when publications directly tend to prevent the proper discharge of judicial functions.[114]

The general statements by Madison, cited by the majority, to the effect that "the state of the press . . . under the common law, cannot . . . be the standard of its freedom in the United States,"[115] do not impair the position that the contempt power was untouched by the guarantee of free press. As their immediate context shows, these statements were merely intended to emphasize, in the course of the controversy that raged about the Alien and Sedition Laws, that Americans, in contrast to the English, were protected against subsequent punishment under *laws* as well as prior executive licensing. Madison's statement immediately preceding the last quotation makes this emphatically clear: "In the United States the great and essential rights of the people are secured against legislative as well as against executive ambition. . . . This security of freedom of the press requires that it should be exempt not only from previous restraints by the Executive, as in Great Britain, but from legislative restraint also; and this exemption, to be effectual, must be an exemption not only from the previous inspection of licensors, but from the subsequent penalty of laws."[116]

We turn to contemporary constructions that are more directly in point. It will be recalled that there was an established summary power over contemptuous publications at the adoption of the Constitution. In 1789 Congress conferred upon the federal courts the power to punish for contempts,[117] a grant which the Supreme Court before long held was merely declaratory of the inherent judicial power.[118] Acting under a Constitution that set up courts of "law and equity" after the English pattern, and prompted by the statutory technical term, *contempts,* the courts properly turned to the common law for light as to the scope of their powers.[119] That the courts would in consequence emerge with summary punishment for contemptuous publications could not have been unforeseen by Congress. Just one year before the Act of 1789, *Respublica v. Oswald*[120]—a

---

[114]Near v. Minnesota, 283 U.S. 697, 715 (1931). Cf. Frohwerk v. United States, 249 U.S. 204 (1919); Schenck v. United States, 249 U.S. 47 (1919); Gitlow v. New York, 268 U.S. 652 (1925). Compare the many early constitutional provisions proclaiming the responsibility of those who enjoyed a free press for its "abuse." Cf. the Pennsylvania Constitution of 1790, 2 Poore, Constitutions and Charters 1554 (2d ed. 1878).

[115]Bridges v. California, 314 U.S. 252, 264 (1941); 6 Madison, op. cit. supra note 111, at 387.

[116]6 Madison, op. cit. supra note 111, at 387. Mr. Justice Black quotes Schofield's statement that "one of the objects of the Revolution was to get rid of the English common law on liberty of speech and of the press." Freedom of the Press in the United States, 9 Pub. Am. Sociol. Soc. 67, 76 (1914); Bridges v. California, 314 U.S. 252, 264 (1941). But Schofield cites no authority for the proposition that the contempt power was curbed.

[117]Judiciary Act of 1789, § 17, 1 Stat. 83 (1789).

[118]United States v. Hudson & Goodwin, 7 Cranch (U.S.) *32, *34 (1812); Anderson v. Dunn, 6 Wheat. (U.S.) *204, *227 (1821).

[119]Cf. the statement of Harlan, J., in Savin, Petitioner: "The act of 1789 did not define what were contempts. . . . Under that statute the question whether particular acts constitute a contempt . . . was left to be determined according to such established rules and principles of the common law as were applicable to our situation." Savin, Petitioner, 131 U.S. 267, 275–76 (1889).

[120]1 Dall. (Pa.) *319 (1788), discussed in Nelles and King, op. cit. supra note 16, at 410, 412. Echoes of the case even reached Jefferson in Paris. He then wrote the details of the case to Shippen, saying that it was "likely to make a noise." 7 Writings of Thomas Jefferson 152 (mem. ed. 1903). If to this the acceptance of the power by such contemporary writers as Blackstone, Hawkins, Comyn, and Viner, note 96 supra, and the contemporaneous use of the power by Congress in 1795 and 1800 is added, the fact that the framers could not have heard of Rex v. Almon prior to its publication in 1802 becomes irrelevant; cf. Radin, op. cit. supra note 5, at 614. A hasty search of colonial materials suggests that the power was not a nineteenth century exotic; it was employed in Massachusetts in 1721, 1 Parrington, Main Currents in American Thought 128 (1927), and in Delaware, between 1678 and 1681. Records of the Court of Newcastle in Delaware 496–97, 514–18 (1904). The Records report another case wherein the sheriff "indytes" a man and his wife for slandering the court. Ibid., at 226. Since no mention is made of jury trial, a strange omission in the light of the almost invariable emphasis upon jury participation where a jury was employed, ibid., at 307, 358, 410, 436, 443, 458, 469, the case seems to represent summary procedure. Compare the binding over of one Henry Salter to answer for his slander of the court before the Governor of New York. Ibid., at 287.

case that excited widespread public interest—was tried in Philadelphia under the very nose of Congress. Oswald, arrested for publishing a libel upon one Browne, published an article stating that he could not expect a fair trial because of the prejudice of the bench, and because Browne was merely a tool of Dr. Rush, a brother of a member of the Pennsylvania court. This was plainly an attempt to "create a public sentiment which would deter a jury from a just finding of his guilt in the libel case. . . ."[121] and Oswald was attached for contempt. The case is especially significant because the protection of the state free press clause was expressly invoked[122] and unequivocally denied—some three years before the adoption of the federal Bill of Rights. Chief Justice McKean of the Supreme Court of Pennsylvania, a signer of the Declaration of Independence[123] and an "ardent advocate of the Constitution,"[124] declared:

> What then is the meaning of the bill of rights, and constitution of Pennsylvania, when they declare, "That the freedom of the press shall not be restrained," and "that the printing presses shall be free to every person who undertakes to examine the proceedings of the legislature, or any part of the government?" . . . Will it be said, that the constitutional right to examine the proceedings of government, extends to warrant an anticipation of . . . the judgments of the court? . . . The futility of any attempt to establish a construction of this sort, must be obvious to every intelligent mind.[125]

In 1801 the doctrine of the *Oswald* case received the approval of the Pennsylvania federal circuit court in *United States v. Duane,*[126] and it was reaffirmed by the Pennsylvania Supreme Court in *Respublica v. Passmore.*[127] Shortly thereafter Kent employed the summary power in still another publication case, *People v. Freer.*[128] State and federal courts have ever since uniformly declared that the contempt power falls without the ambit of the free speech and press clauses of state constitutions.[129]

Congress had in fact set a precedent for the early federal cases. In 1800, the Senate, following the English practice earlier noted, attached Duane, the same editor that was subsequently the subject of the contempt proceeding in *United States v. Duane,*[130] for a libel on the Senate. The

[121]Nelles and King, op. cit. supra note 16, at 411.

[122]Respublica v. Oswald, 1 Dall. (Pa.) *319, *321 (1788).

[123]Nelles and King, op. cit. supra note 16, at 409 n. 45. Lord Mansfield wrote McKean that the Pennsylvania reports, sent to him by McKean, "do credit to the court . . . they show readiness in practice, liberality in principle, strong reason and legal learning." 1 Dall. (Pa.) *vii (1788).

[124]1 Beveridge, Life of John Marshall 332 (1916).

[125]1 Dall. (Pa.) *319, *325 (1788); see Commonwealth v. Brown (1789), decided by the same court. The case is not officially reported but is set out in full in Hamilton, Trial of Justice Shippen 365, 425 (1805).

[126]Fed. Cas. No. 14,997 (C.C. Pa. 1801), at 922. Referring to Oswald's case, the court said: "The present governor of Pennsylvania was then chief justice. He is well versed in the general principles of the law as well as the usages and customs of the United States, and cannot be supposed to have favored constructions unfriendly to true liberty, or unwarranted by the genuine sense of the constitution." See the elaborate examination of the Oswald case by counsel in Hollingsworth v. Duane, Fed. Cas. No. 6,616, at 362 (C.C. Pa. 1801); Fry's Case, cited by counsel in the Peck case; Stansbury, Trial of James H. Peck 352 (1833); Nelles and King, op. cit. supra note 16, at 428 n. 142, 422 n. 116.

[127]3 Yeates (Pa.) 438, 441, 442 (1802).

[128]1 Caines (N.Y.) *518 (1804); cf. Yates v. Lansing, 9 Johns. (N.Y.) 396, 417 (1811): "This power extends . . . to consequential, indirect and constructive contempts, which obstruct the process, degrade the authority, or contaminate the purity of the court."

[129]State v. Morrill, 16 Ark. 384, 402, 404 (1855); In re Cheeseman, 49 N.J.L. 115, 141, 6 Atl. 513, 516 (1886); Cooper v. People ex rel. Wyatt, 13 Colo. 373, 376 (1889); State ex rel. Haskell v. Faulds, 17 Mont. 140, 145, 42 Pac. 285, 286 (1895); State v. Tugwell & Baker, 19 Wash. 238, 253, 52 Pac. 1056, 1061 (1898); State v. Shepherd, 177 Mo. 205, 244, 76 S.W. 79 (1903); Burdett v. Commonwealth, 103 Va. 838, 847, 48 S.E. 878 (1904); McDougall v. Sheridan, 23 Idaho 191, 193, 218, 128 Pac. 954, 955, 963 (1913); In re Haynes, 72 Fla. 558, 73 So. 362 (1916); Dale v. State, 198 Ind. 110, 124, 150 N.E. 781, 786 (1926); In re Stolen, 193 Wis. 602, 216 N.W. 127 (1927); State v. Lovell, 117 Neb. 710, 718, 222 N.W. 625, 628 (1929); In re Shuler, 210 Cal. 377, 404, 292 Pac. 481, 493 (1930); cf. Tenney's case, 23 N.H. 162 (1851); see Watson v. Williams, 36 Miss. 331 (1858). Contra: Ex parte Hickey, 12 Miss. 751, 782 (1844).

[130]See note 126 supra.

freedom of the press was urged,[131] but the Senate voted for Duane's attachment, following the view of Senator Tracy who declared that the contempt power of the Senate was no less requisite than freedom of the press.[132] Previously the House, in 1795, had attached Randall for contempt on two charges—bribery of its members, and a slander on the House in that Randall had alleged that some thirty or forty members were already parties to the bribery scheme.[133] It is highly significant that Madison, the advocate of protection for the press against subsequent punishment under *laws,* should have participated actively in these proceedings without protesting against the exercise by the House of the summary power to curb free speech.[134] The vote of 78 to 17 for attachment[135] in a period of "party dissention and political animosity"[136] is assuredly the most eloquent testimony of contemporaries, many of whom had joined in submitting the Bill of Rights, that the guarantes of free press were not intended to deprive federal tribunals of the power to repel "disrespect and insult."[137]

The early cases are dismissed without mention by Mr. Justice Black as "attempts to expand" the contempt power which "evoked popular reactions that bespeak a feeling of jealous solicitude for freedom of the press."[138] These reactions were episodes in the turbulent struggle for political supremacy between the Federalists and Republicans. Thus Oswald was the editor of a newspaper given to intemperate anti-Federalist abuse, and it is possible to regard his attachment for what was a flagrant and apparently un-political contempt as a covert Federalist gag.[139] After sentence, Oswald's cause was adopted by members of the Pennsylvania legislature, but a resolution to label the attachment an unconstitutional exercise of judicial power was defeated by a considerable majority,[140] which one again can attempt to explain in terms of Federalist bias.[141] What are we to think, however, of the abandonment by Albert Gallatin, a leading Republican, of an attempt to modify the contempt power in the state constitutional convention of 1790 on the ground that it was "involved in difficulties" and it was "most prudent to leave the matter where it stood?"[142] It is the impeachment proceedings against the members of the Pennsylvania Supreme Court in 1805, arising out of the *Passmore* case, and the attempted impeachment of Federal Judge Peck in 1831, that are chiefly relied on to demonstrate the early belief that summary proceedings were incompatible with the guarantee of free press.[143] Of these in turn.

---

[131]10 Annals Cong. 75, 85 (1800).

[132]Ibid., at 87, 111, 113.

[133]5 Annals Cong. 168 (1795). The references to the slander charge are in ibid., at 175, 177, 214, 215. Counsel for Randall asked: "Are the House to lock up the mouths of the people?" Ibid., at 215.

[134]At one point Madison expressed himself in "favor of allowing counsel" to defendant. Ibid., at 181. At another, he pointed out that the elaborate argument was premature since Randall might "Save all this trouble" by confessing his guilt. Ibid., at 187.

[135]5 Annals Cong. 220 (1795).

[136]This point was made in the subsequent attachment proceeding of Anderson. 31 Annals Cong. 642 (1818).

[137]5 Annals Cong. 189, 193 (1795).

[138]Bridges v. California, 314 U.S. 252, 266 (1941).

[139]Nelles and King, op.cit. supra note 16, at 410.

[140]Respublica v. Oswald, 1 Dall. (Pa.) *319, 329–29g (1788).

[141]The adoption of the Constitution during this very period is susceptible of an explanation in similar terms. And it is worth noting that Oswald "kept up the bombardment of the Constitution and its advocates" after ratification took place in Pennsylvania; cf. 1 Beveridge, Life of John Marshall 334–38 (1916). Madison commented that the "minority . . . of Pennsylvania has been extremely intemperate. . . ." Ibid., at 338.

[142]Hamilton recites the conversation of Jared Ingersoll, counsel for the justices, a former attorney general of Pennsylvania and a member of the Federal Constitutional Convention, with Peter Duponceau, a noted Pennsylvania lawyer who "never evinced any interest in politics," and a letter from Duponceau to Ingersoll, which sets out the Gallatin incident. Hamilton, op. cit. supra note 125, at 454, 467. Dictionary Am. Biography (1935).

[143]Nelles and King, op. cit. supra note 16, at 414, 553; Bridges v. California, 314 U.S. 252, 264–66 (1941).

Passmore sued Bayard and Petit on a policy of insurance and secured a favorable referee's report. The defendants then filed exceptions, whereupon Passmore published a charge that they were "basely" keeping him from his money. He was attached by the Supreme Court of Pennsylvania, where a hearing on the exceptions was pending, and was held in contempt.[144] By this time, be it recalled, contemptuous publications had been punished by the Pennsylvania state and federal courts, and by the Senate and House in the *Duane* and *Randall* cases. Consequently there were American as well as common law precedents. Nevertheless the *Passmore* case was now taken up with a great fanfare in the legislature. Although Hugh H. Breckinridge, the sole Republican member of the Pennsylvania Supreme Court, had not participated in the *Passmore* proceedings, he endorsed the action of his associates and begged to be impeached with them.[145] The "fustian character of the whole proceeding" receives its due from Nelles, an unrelenting critic of the contempt power:

> A majority of the Republican majority, both in Pennsylvania and in Congress, were, however, at this period bloodthirsty for Federalist judicial scalps. . . . Until 1805, when the impeachment of Justice Chase of the Supreme Court failed by two votes, Federalist judicial tenure was precarious. It was touch and go whether impeachment would not become an established procedure for taking the judges of a defeated party out of politics.[146]

Touch and go it assuredly was in the *Passmore* proceedings, for the State Senate voted 13 to 11 for impeachment,[147] failing by just two votes to attain the majority of two-thirds necessary for impeachment. Even in this jaundiced proceeding, the eminent advocate for the legislature, Caesar Rodney,[148] conceded that the guarantee of free press did not limit summary punishment of a publication in a pending case,[149] and indeed the proceeding turned on the specious argument that the case was no longer pending.[150] The "maddened Republicans" stormed the polls to secure a convention for the purpose of amending the Constitution, but lost.[151] When they came to power some years later, they limited the contempt power by *statute*.[152]

We come now to the case most frequently cited for the "abuse" of the contempt power, the "flagrant case of Judge Peck."[153] It is one of the ironies of history that Judge Peck should be singled out as a horrible example, and that he should have waited one hundred years for vindication at the hands of one who strenuously opposed the summary power. The vindication of Judge Peck is a monument to the lofty scholarship of the late Professor Nelles, who alone summoned the patience to disentangle the facts from the morass of Spanish land grant law and Missouri politics out of which the case arose.[154] Luke Lawless, a crony of Senator Benton of Missouri, and his successor as legal representative of many speculative land claimants, lost a case involving one such claim before Judge Peck, and thereupon published a criticism, artfully temperate in tone, yet as "unfair

[144]Bayard and Petit v. Passmore, 3 Yeates (Pa.) *438 et seq., *442 et seq. (1802); Nelles and King, op. cit. supra note 16, at 413.

[145]3 McMaster, History of the People of the United States 159 (1892).

[146]Nelles and King, op. cit. supra note 16, at 414.

[147]Hamilton, op. cit. supra note 125, at 491.

[148]Rodney had been one of the Managers for the House of Representatives in the impeachment proceedings of both Federal Judge Pickering and Supreme Court Justice Chase in 1804, and became Jefferson's Attorney General in 1807. Dictionary Am. Biography (1934).

[149]Hamilton, op. cit. supra note 125, at 357.

[150]This argument was specious because Passmore's own former counsel had advised Passmore that the case was pending and had subsequently declined to represent him in the proceedings. Ibid., at 146, 150, 152–53; cf. ibid., at 8, 20, 49.

[151]3 McMaster, op. cit. supra note 145, at 160; Nelles and King, op. cit. supra note 16, at 414.

[152]The statute is quoted in Bridges v. California, 314 U.S. 252, 266 n. 11 (1941).

[153]Ibid., at 287; Thomas, Problems of Contempt of Court 25–27 (1934); Boyd v. Glucklich, 116 Fed. 129, 136 (C.C.A. 8th 1902).

[154]Nelles and King, op. cit. supra note 16, at 423–30.

as can be imagined,"[155] of Judge Peck's opinion. The case was on appeal at the time of the publication, and it raised the identical issues of numerous cases then pending before Judge Peck. To quote Nelles, "it could have no end except to subject the court to contumely and promote sympathy with the land claimants, making fair juries unobtainable in their cases. . . ."[156] This was obstructing the fair course of justice with a vengeance. Assuming a recognized contempt power, Judge Peck, "exasperated by propaganda in aid of fraud,"[157] had rich justification for its exercise. The Congress to which Lawless turned for aid had not been untouched by the "Spanish" land squabbles, and it numbered few more potent statesmen than Senator Benton, himself an advocate of the speculative interests.[158] Judge Peck narrowly escaped impeachment. We may give thanks that he did, for his impeachment would have been a lasting reproach to American justice. The precedents, and certainly the dicta,[159] might well have led a sound lawyer to believe that the summary power extended to non-pending cases. If he erred, to borrow his own words, Peck erred "in company with judicial characters with whom any judge might be proud to associate."[160] This argument was emphasized throughout by his great counsel, William Wirt,[161] and a study of the proceedings convinces one that it is unanswerable. Men are not put away for what is at worst a mistake of judgment.

But even the heat of advocacy did not lead the Managers for the House into sweeping denial of the existence of summary power over all contemptuous publications. On the contrary, the Managers, with the exception of Buchanan, repeatedly recognized the common law power over publications in pending cases. Their criticism was reserved for Peck's use of the power in a non-pending case,[162] and their generalizations about free press are to be viewed in this frame. Nor did these strictures purport to explain *how* the free press guarantee had limited the contempt power. To be sure, popular repudiation of the Alien and Sedition Laws was used to point the moral—that Judge Peck sought to exercise by implication a power denied to Congress.[163] But the First Amendment expressly denies the power to Congress, not to the courts. Assuming that the Peck proceedings have a wider significance than is here indicated, can an advocate's interpretation, forty years after the adoption of the amendment, be dignified as a contemporary construction? Surely the contemporary judicial and congressional interpretations of the First Amendment earlier noted more

[155]Ibid., at 428.
[156]Ibid.
[157]Ibid., at 525.
[158]Ibid., at 425, 426, 429.
[159]Rex v. Barber, 1 Stra. 444 (K.B. 1721), and Rex v. Lawley (1731) (unreported), were instances of libels on the court in non-pending cases. The dicta of Lord Hardwicke in Roach v. Garvan, 2 Atkyns 469 (Ch. 1742), and of Wilmot, J., in Rex v. Almon, Wilm. 243 (K.B. 1765), page 15 supra, pointed the same way. By this time, it may be added, Rex v. Almon had been expressly approved in Rex v. Clement, 4 B. & Ald. 218, 233 (K.B. 1821), and Rex v. Davison, 4 B. & Ald. 329, 337 (K.B. 1821).
[160]Stansbury, op. cit. supra note 126, at 45.
[161]Ibid., at 486–97.
[162]Ibid., at 88, 298, 299, 312, 314, 315, 372, 376, 380, 381, 382, 395, 400. Early in the argument McDuffie tacitly, ibid., at 88, and Spencer, ibid., at 298, and Wickliffe explicitly, ibid., at 314, 315, recognized the summary power over publications in pending cases. Meredith, opening for Peck, sought to narrow the issue by stating this concession, but Buchanan rejected the proposition and insisted that there was no power in pending cases as well. Ibid., at 385. Associate counsel, heeding the dictates of courtesy, of course could not flatly repudiate Buchanan. But Storrs, who followed Meredith, stated the issue in terms of a "libel on the court, not relating to any cause or matter pending. . . ." Ibid., at 372. He repeatedly indicated his acceptance of prevailing case law with respect to pending cases, ibid., at 376, 380, 381, 382, 395, 400, saying for example, "We do not deny here that one class of contempt is scandalizing the court. But we say that these scandals must relate to matters pending in judicature before the judges." Ibid., at 382. These expressions have been explained away as illustrative of the advocates' skill. Nelles and King, op. cit. supra note 16, at 526. If we are merely dealing with an exhibition of advocacy, the proceedings have no place as legislative history.
[163]Stansbury, op. cit. supra note 126, at 90, 447.

accurately reflect the intention of the framers than do the views of the zealous prosecutors in the *Peck* case forty years after the event.[164]

If the summary power was not limited by the First Amendment, it was not limited by the Fourteenth. Mr. Justice Black recognizes that the Court, under the Fourteenth Amendment, has applied to the states "the same standards of freedom of expression as, under the First Amendment, are applicable to the federal government."[165] Finally, the issue whether the guarantee of free press curtails the summary power was submitted to the Supreme Court in *Patterson v. Colorado*[166] and was there decided in the negative in an opinion by Mr. Justice Holmes. The statement by Mr. Justice Black that the *Patterson* case "cannot be taken as a decision squarely in point" relies on Mr. Justice Holmes' remark that: "We leave undecided the question whether there is to be found in the Fourteenth Amendment a prohibition similar to that in the First."[167] But Mr. Justice Holmes found it unnecessary to decide that question because, assuming that the prohibition was found in the Fourteenth Amendment, he held that it did not limit the contempt power.

The *Patterson* case grew out of a publication reflecting on the Supreme Court of Colorado, for which the publisher was summarily held in contempt. A motion to quash, based upon the Fourteenth Amendment, was overruled below; Colorado urged in the United States Supreme Court that there was no jurisdiction to review, in the absence of a federal question, since the guarantee of free press did not extend to a publication that obstructed the administration of justice.[168] On the issue thus presented, Mr. Justice Holmes declared:

> We leave undecided the question whether there is to be found in the Fourteenth Amendment a prohibition similar to that in the First. But even if we were to assume that freedom of speech and freedom of the press were protected from abridgment on the part not only of the United States but also of the States, still we should be far from the conclusion that the plaintiff in error would have us reach. In the first place, the main purpose of such constitutional provisions is "to prevent all such *previous restraints* upon publications as had been practiced by other governments," and they do not prevent the subsequent punishment of such as may be deemed contrary to the public welfare . . . Respublica v. Oswald. . . . In the next place, the rule applied to criminal libels, applies yet more clearly to contempts. A publication likely to reach the eyes of a jury, declaring a witness in a pending cause a perjurer, would be none the less a contempt that it was true. It would tend to obstruct the administration of justice. . . . What is true with reference to a jury is true also with reference to a court. . . . Judges generally, perhaps,

---

[164]Apart from the cases, it is significant that the brilliant Edward Livingston, who leveled a penetrating attack against the contempt power early in the nineteenth century, a criticism that was of great influence, and was in fact argued to the Senate in the Peck case, should have completely ignored the free speech clauses in considering the problem. Stansbury, op. cit. supra note 126, at 441–44, 474; Nelles and King, op. cit. supra note 16, at 418–21, 527; 1 Livingston, Works on Criminal Jurisprudence 258 et seq. (1873). Mr. Justice Curtis, a former member of the Supreme Court, after quoting the Act of 1831, note 178 infra, which was enacted after the Peck proceedings, stated that "the common-law authority of the courts, as it has been exercised in England and in this country, and as it was exercised by Judge Peck . . . extended much wider than this." Curtis, Jurisdiction of the United States Courts 181–82 (1880).

[165]Bridges v. California, 314 U.S. 252, 268 (1941). Compare the statement in Mobile & Ohio R. Co. v. Tennessee, 153 U.S. 486, 506 (1894): "[The Fourteenth Amendment] conferred no new and additional rights, but only extended the protection of the Federal Constitution over rights of life, liberty, and property that previously existed under all state constitutions." Compare the state cases cited in note 129 supra. The expansion of due process to embrace freedom of speech and press dates back only to Gitlow v. New York, 268 U.S. 652 (1925). In 1922 the Court had stated that "neither the Fourteenth Amendment nor any other provision of the Constitution of the United States imposes upon the States any restrictions about 'freedom of speech.'. . ." Prudential Ins. Co. v. Cheek, 259 U.S. 530, 543 (1922). Freedom of speech is traditionally not comprehended by the term "liberty." Warren, The New "Liberty" under the Fourteenth Amendment, 39 Harv. L. Rev. 431 (1926); Shattuck, The True Meaning of the Term "Liberty" in those Clauses in the Federal and State Constitutions which Protect "Life, Liberty, and Property," 4 Harv. L. Rev. 365 (1891).

[166]205 U.S. 454 (1907).

[167]Bridges v. California, 314 U.S. 252, 267–68 (1941).

[168]Patterson v. Colorado, 205 U.S. 454, 457–58 (1907).

are less apprehensive that publications impugning their own reasoning or motives will interfere with their administration of the law. But if a court regards, as it may, a publication concerning a matter of law pending before it, as tending toward such an interference, it may punish it as in the instances put . . . the propriety and necessity of preventing interference with the course of justice by premature statement, argument or intimidation can hardly be denied. . . . We have scrutinized the case, but cannot say that it shows an infraction of rights under the Constitution of the United States. . . .[169]

Any doubt as to the scope of the decision is removed by the dissent of Mr. Justice Harlan, who flatly declared that "the action of the court below was in violation of the rights of free speech and a free press as guaranteed by the Constitution."[170] That the decision denied the existence of immunity from summary punishment by virtue of the "free press" guarantee has hitherto been unquestioned.[171] And, as the foregoing historical résumé attempts to demonstrate, the *Patterson* case more closely approximates the late eighteenth century view of the relation between summary power and the First Amendment[172] than does the present day reading of Madison's generalizations by Mr. Justice Black.[173]

His argument that the First Amendment plainly prohibits religious test oaths or restrictions upon assembly—practices then prevalent in England—and that the right of free press was consequently similarly enlarged beyond the then existing English right,[174] leaves open the scope of the enlargement. If Madison's views faithfully mirror contemporary opinion, the right was extended beyond freedom from prior executive restraints to limit subsequent legislative restraints. But it is even plainer that contemporary construction rejected the view that the guarantee curtailed the summary power over contemptuous publications. It may well be that there is no logical basis for a differentiation between subsequent legislative and judicial restraints. But this is to substitute twentieth century logic for the "environment in which the First Amendment was ratified,"[175] upon which Mr. Justice Black purports to rely. Certainly Madison, whose equivocal utterances the majority invoke to recreate that environment, would have been the first to repudiate the substitution of present-day logic for "the sense in which the Constitution was accepted and ratified by the Nation." For, continued Madison, "In that sense alone it is the legitimate Constitution. And if that be not the guide in expounding it, there can be no security for a consistent and stable government, more than for a faithful exercise of its powers."[176]

[169]Ibid., at 462–63.

[170]Ibid., at 465.

[171]This case has been cited by Mr. Justice Holmes in Gitlow v. New York, 268 U.S. 652, 666 (1925), and by Mr. Chief Justice Hughes in Near v. Minnesota, 283 U.S. 697, 715 (1931). Mr. Justice Holmes' qualification in Schenck v. United States, 249 U.S. 47, 51 (1919), that the prohibition of an abridgment of free speech is not confined to previous restraints, indicates his attitude towards restraints under repressive laws rather than a departure from his view that the Fourteenth Amendment left the summary power untouched. Counsel for Bridges himself has declared in a more dispassionate atmosphere that "Mr. Justice Holmes for the majority, in dismissing the writ of error, indicated that in any event the constitutional provision did not prevent punishment of publications after they were made." Fraenkel, One Hundred and Fifty Years of the Bill of Rights, 23 Minn. L. Rev. 719, 759 n. 206 (1939). See Vance, op. cit. supra note 100, at 253. Contra: Schofield, op. cit. supra note 116, at 107.

[172]Note Mr. Justice Holmes' citation of Respublica v. Oswald, 1 Dall. (Pa.) *319 (1788), in the Patterson case.

[173]"It is the importation of meaning, opinion, and intellectual procedure from the alien world of here and now which makes evidence inconclusive, muddles understanding, and shunts inquiry to false leads." Hamilton and Adair, op. cit. supra note 107, at 104.

[174]Bridges v. California, 314 U.S. 252, 265 (1941).

[175]Ibid., at 264.

[176]9 Madison, op. cit. supra note 111, at 191, 372.

THE FEDERAL ACT OF 1831

Twenty-three years ago the city of Toledo was engaged in a controversy with the local traction company about a franchise that was shortly to expire. The city passed an ordinance establishing a three-cent fare, to take effect upon expiration of the franchise. The traction company then sought injunctive relief, and the local newspaper, espousing a popular cause, commented unfavorably upon this turn of affairs, and continued thereafter to publish comments and cartoons which were doubtless unflattering to the court. The federal district court held the publishers in contempt; this judgment was affirmed by the Supreme Court in *Toledo Newspaper Co. v. United States.*[177] The case hinged on the Act of 1831,[178] which had followed on the heels of Judge Peck's acquittal. Prior to the *Toledo* case, it had long been believed that the act had deprived the inferior courts of summary power over contemptuous publications.[179] When, therefore, Mr. Chief Justice White declared in 1918 that the Act of 1831 left the summary jurisdiction untouched, the decision appeared to its critics to nullify the express will of the American people.[180] Unruffled by this criticism, the Supreme Court continued in subsequent decisions to adhere to the doctrine of the *Toledo* case.[181] The sanction thus given to the example set by state courts during the second half of the nineteenth century in rendering largely nugatory state statutes patterned after the Act of 1831[182] gave the law a deceptive air of immutability.[183] The *Toledo* case was overruled at the last term of court in *Nye v. United States.*[184]

The unsuspecting medium of history was an illiterate old man who had brought a wrongful-death action in a federal district court. He had been plied with liquor by a relative of the defendant and induced to abandon the suit. Thereupon the district court, located about one hundred miles from the scene of these events, held the relative in contempt for obstructing the administration of justice. The jurisdiction of the district court to proceed summarily if the contempt was in fact criminal was not challenged by the petitioner in the Supreme Court. But the Government, sensing that the specter of contempt by publication lurked behind these drab facts, conceded that the summary power had been curtailed by the Act of 1831, and urged merely that the act was not intended to limit jurisdiction over out-of-court contempts which, as in the case of Nye, actually obstructed the administration of justice.[185] The majority of the Court, speaking by Mr. Justice Douglas, found the contemnor's conduct "highly reprehensible,"[186] but held that the district court could not proceed summarily because the summary power, since the Act of 1831, extends to *no* out-of-court contempt which is not "so near" the presence of the court "as to be disrupting to

---

[177]247 U.S. 402 (1918).

[178]4 Stat. 487 (1856). The present form of this statute is found in 18 U.S.C.A. § 241 (1927); 28 U.S.C.A. § 385 (1928).

[179]See notes 209, 220, 221 infra.

[180]Nelles and King, op. cit. supra note 16, at 533, 541, 543; cf. Frankfurter and Landis, op. cit. supra note 5, at 1037, 1058.

[181]Craig v. Hecht, 263 U.S. 255 (1923); Cooke v. United States, 267 U.S. 517 (1925); Sinclair v. United States, 279 U.S. 749 (1929).

[182]Nelles and King, op. cit. supra note 16, at 533, 537, and cases cited therein.

[183]Thus Nelles and King dolefully remarked that "it might be vain to hope that a long stream of adjudication would reverse its course and flow back up-hill on news that its source was a poisoned spring." Nelles and King, op. cit. supra note 16, at 401.

[184]313 U.S. 33 (1941).

[185]Brief for the United States 36, 39, (No. 558, Oct. 1940).

[186]Nye v. United States, 313 U.S. 33, 52 (1941).

quiet and order."[187] The minority, in an opinion by Mr. Justice Stone, concurred in by Mr. Chief Justice Hughes and Mr. Justice Roberts, agreed that the Act of 1831 curtailed the contempt power,[188] thus joining in the erasure of Mr. Chief Justice White's amazing dictum that the act had "imposed no limitations not already existing,"[189] but denied that the limitation extended to such out-of-court behavior as was present in the *Nye* case.

The *Nye* decision was rested almost exclusively on the history of the *Peck* case and the structure of the statute. The *Peck* case, however, turned on considerations of free speech not present in the *Nye* case; it is therefore proposed to ascertain the bearing of the Peck proceedings on both publication and non-publication cases, to discuss contemporaneous construction of the Act of 1831, and to consider factors of policy that may influence decision.

Although the general references to free press by the Peck prosecutors shed little light on the intention of the framers of the First Amendment forty years earlier, they are obviously relevant to the statute enacted immediately upon Peck's acquittal. Throughout the hearings the Managers hammered home the need for enforcing judicial responsibility by means of unfettered criticism.[190] As Wickliffe, one of the Managers for the House, put it:

> We have been laboring under a most fatal delusion upon the subject of our constitutional rights and guarantees, if we are to be told by this high tribunal, that there is one department of our Government, the Judiciary, exempt from free, open and public investigation; one department which can shield itself from responsibility to public opinion by this impenetrable armor, the power to punish for contempts.[191]

To countenance such judicial insulation would, in the words of Buchanan, result in the erection of "one of the most formidable engines of oppression that was ever set up in a free state."[192] And, as if to give effect to these sentiments forthwith, Congress immediately after the acquittal declared in the Act of 1831 that the contempt power:

> Shall not be construed to extend to any cases except the misbehavior of any person or persons in the presence of said courts, *or so near thereto* as to obstruct the administration of justice, the misbehavior

---

[187]In dissenting, Mr. Justice Stone stated that the majority opinion "implicitly holds that no contempt is summarily punishable unless it is either in the presence of the court or is some kind of physical interference with or disturbance of its good order. . . ." Ibid., at 54. This seems a fair statement of the majority's position.

Among the issues presented was whether a criminal or civil contempt was involved. The rule to show cause had issued on the motion of counsel for the plaintiff in a civil suit; the Government was first joined on appeal by the clerk of the circuit court of appeals, and participated actively for the first time in the Supreme Court. Applying familiar criteria, the Supreme Court decided that the contempt was criminal. Application of such criteria in the lower courts has proven most unsatisfactory, and the Circuit Court of Appeals for the Second Circuit finally revolted at scanning records with the "object of catching at straws, which lead us first one way and then another, and in the end force us to guess about a matter which could so easily be set right at the beginning." In re Guzzardi, 74 F. (2d) 671, 673 (C.C.A. 2d 1935). Where a court of such distinction must guess, a respondent may understandably first learn on appeal that he was tried below on a criminal charge.

The potential severity and stigma of a criminal sentence require that a defendant be apprised at the outset that he is facing criminal charges. He can then invoke the presumption of innocence, require proof beyond a reasonable doubt, refuse to testify without risking unfavorable comment, and invoke certain defenses, among them a more favorable statute of limitations, and the like. Cf. Civil and Criminal Contempt of Court, 46 Yale L. J. 326 (1936). Under the rule advanced by Judge Learned Hand in McCann v. New York Stock Exchange, 80 F. (2d) 211 (C.C.A. 2d 1935), a criminal contempt is either prosecuted by the district attorney or by another attorney directed by the court to prosecute criminally under a written order served on respondent. The fairness of this procedure needs no emphasis. And it will be speedily established when a failure to follow it is attended by reversal on appeal.

[188]Nye v. United States, 313 U.S. 33, 53 (1941).

[189]Frankfurter and Landis, op. cit. supra note 5, at 1029–30; cf. Ex parte Wall, 107 U.S. 265, 302 (1882).

[190]Stansbury, op. cit. supra note 126, at 92, 297, 426.

[191]Ibid., at 314.

[192]Ibid., at 437.

of any of the officers of the said courts in their official transactions, and the disobedience or resistance by any officer of the said courts, party, juror, witness, or any person or persons, to any lawful writ, process, order, rule, decree, or command of the said courts.[193]

Were the remarks about free speech the sole background of the act, it should properly be construed to deprive the lower federal courts of summary power over all out-of-court criticism of the judiciary. But the Managers time and again conceded the existence of the power over contemptuous publications in *pending* cases.[194] It is equally plain that the Managers had no thought of striking down summary control over other out-of-court contempts. True, Spencer, Buchanan, and Storrs referred during the proceedings to contempts committed in the face of the court or its immediate precincts by tumultuous conduct and the like.[195] But these references were illustrative rather than restrictive. In closing the case Buchanan had posed the issue in terms of an absence of power "to punish in a summary manner, as contempts, *publications* reflecting on the court. . . ."[196] And though Storrs put the example of the assault upon a judge who was entering the courthouse, he went on to say: "It was as much a contempt and a direct obstruction to the administration of justice as to have kept a juror or witness away by force. . . ."[197] Storrs had earlier stated in discussing a paragraph of Blackstone that:

> In a note to this very paragraph Chitty has put the case, by way of illustration, of attempting to influence a jury. . . . So, said Mr. Storrs, he might add . . . offering to bribe a judge; writing him a threatening letter relating to a cause; assaulting a judge on his way to the courthouse . . . libelling the parties in the cause in reference to the merits. . . . All these contempts show that gross want of respect to courts of justice and their proceedings, without which their legal authority and moral weight would both be lost and the courts of justice made a mere mockery.[198]

In a similar vein, Wickliffe enumerated, among other contempts, "attempts to bribe the witnesses or jurors in a cause, all attempts to prevent an attorney or officer of the court from the discharge of his duty as such. . . ."[199]

These statements, conjoined with the concessions as to publications in pending cases, make indisputable an intention to conserve the familiar summary jurisdiction except for publications in non-pending cases. All this may, of course, be dismissed as the prosecutors' astute attempt so to narrow the issue as to avoid making the impeachment turn on the need for a radical overhauling of the entire contempt power. It is precisely this possibility—that we are confronted with *advocacy,* with the heated partisanship revealed by resort to impeachment for what was at worst an error of judgment—that suggests it is a mistake to regard the proceedings as evidence of legislative deliberations, i.e., legislative history. But, if the proceedings are invoked as legislative history, those portions which are presently unpalatable cannot be dismissed as mere evidence of forensic skill. So much for the gleanings of legislative intention from the impeachment proceedings.

The actual legislative proceedings contribute only one important fact. In its original form as introduced by Buchanan, the Act of 1831 contained but one section,[200] the section heretofore considered, limiting the contempt power. Though the bill was enacted in the rush at the end of the session,[201] the Senate yet found time to add a second section punishing by fine and impris-

---

[193]4 Stat. 487 (1856), 28 U.S.C.A. § 385 (1928) (italics added).

[194]See note 162 supra; cf. Bridges v. California, 314 U.S. 252, 287 n. 3 (1941).

[195]Stansbury, op. cit. supra note 126, at 291, 399, 439; cf. Nelles and King, op. cit. supra note 16, at 530.

[196]Stansbury, op. cit. supra note 126, at 434 (italics added).

[197]Ibid., at 399.

[198]Ibid., at 397. Compare Storrs's reaffirmation of his early position that out-of-court bribery was a contempt. Ibid., at 403.

[199]Ibid., at 313.

[200]Nelles and King, op. cit. supra note 16, at 531 n. 27.

[201]Ibid., at 528.

onment after conviction attempts "corruptly, or by threats or force" to influence jurors, witnesses, and officers of the court, or to obstruct the administration of justice.[202] The Senate, Nelles argues, would scarcely have stopped in the rush of a closing session to add a merely cumulative remedy; the more reasonable purpose was to cover matters *not* covered by Section 1, such as corrupt, out-of-court overtures to jurors and the like.[203] This was the construction adopted by Justice Baldwin on circuit shortly after passage of the Act of 1831, and on this construction the *Nye* case to some extent rests.[204]

But the face of Section 2 raises a doubt whether it covers the out-of-court contempts allegedly not embraced by Section 1. For example, unless contemptuous publications, assuming them to be withdrawn from Section 1, constitute an attempt to obstruct justice by "threats," they must be "corrupt" attempts to be comprehended in Section 2. The term "corrupt," however, ordinarily connotes "bribery,"[205] a connotation also suggested by its use in connection with jury-tampering and the like in the first clause of Section 2. A contemptuous publication will not normally be corrupt in this sense, nor, to take a broader definition, will it be "depraved or debased" if it merely expresses honest indignation, although such criticism might be a common law contempt. To this extent, therefore, Section 2 would not cover matters withdrawn from Section 1. Then too, Section 1, responding to the desire of the Managers to curb summary control of criticism while preserving some of the common law contempt power over court officers,[206] patently extends to all out-of-

[202]Ibid., at 531 n. 24. Section 2 provides: "That if any person or persons shall, corruptly, or by threats or force, endeavour to influence, intimidate, or impede any juror, witness, or officer, in any court of the United States, in the discharge of his duty, or shall, corruptly, or by threats or force, obstruct, or impede, or endeavour to obstruct or impede, the due administration of justice therein, every person or persons, so offending, shall be liable to prosecution therefor, by indictment. . . ." 4 Stat. 488 (1856). An amended version of this statute is still in effect. 18 U.S.C.A. § 241 (1927).

[203]Nelles and King, op. cit. supra note 16, at 531. Some confirmation for the position that the two sections are mutually exclusive is perhaps to be found in the commentary of the New York revisers on the scope of the parallel indictment section in the structurally similar New York Act of 1829 which was possibly called to the attention of Congress. Judge Spencer, a manager in the impeachment proceeding, was the father of one of the revisers. Ibid., at 416, 421 n. 110, 527. In discussing that portion of the New York act, the revisers said: "In the fourth part, many of the offenses which are now punished as contempts, and which are omitted in the preceding section, will be included among misdemeanors. It cannot be necessary at this day, to urge any reason for substituting the trial by jury in all possible cases, instead of a trial by an offended tribunal." Nelles and King, op. cit. supra note 16, at 421–22 n. 112. The federal, New York and Pennsylvania acts are set out in parallel columns, ibid., at 528–29. It is curious that Congress employed the ambiguous phrase "misbehaviour . . . so near [the presence of the courts] . . . as to obstruct the administration of justice," if the unequivocal New York phrase "any breach of the peace, noise or other disturbance, directly tending to interrupt its proceedings," was before it.

[204]Ex parte Poulson, Fed. Cas. No. 11,350 (C.C. Pa. 1835); see Nye v. United States 313 U.S. 33, at 49–50 (1941); Coll v. United States, 8 F. (2d) 20, 22 (C.C.A. 1st 1925).

[205]See Black, Law Dictionary (1933); Murray, New English Dictionary (1928). For citations to cases, see 20 C.J.S. 239; Words and Phrases (perm. ed.). If the word "corruptly" is not given some such connotation, *any* attempt to "influence" a juror or "impede" the administration of justice will be penalized; and it follows that the entire adverbial phrase "corruptly, or by threats or force" will be reduced to surplusage, the very result rejected under § 1 in the Nye case, with respect to the phrase "so near thereto." But see Bosselman v. United States, 239 Fed. 82 (C.C.A. 2d 1917).

[206]In his memorial to the House, Judge Peck had called attention to the broad power of a court over its officers. Stansbury, op. cit. supra note 126, at 42. This power rests on almost immemorial usage. See Fox, op. cit. supra note 32, at 249 "officer." One of the earliest cases, that of John de Northampton (1344) involved the summary punishment of an attorney who had written a letter reflecting on the court. 3 Select Cases in the King's Bench (Edw. I), 58 Seld. Soc. lxxxii, cxxxiii–iv (1939), quoted also in Reports of the Select Committee of the House of Commons appointed to consider Sir Francis Burdett's Case, 8 How. St. Tr. 14, 41 (1810). Coke cites the case as a contempt, Co. Third Inst. *174, as does Holdsworth, 3 Holdsworth, op. cit. supra note 35, at 390. But see Fox, op. cit. supra note 32, at 24; Fox, op. cit. supra note 41, at 269. In 1588 Chancery ordered that an attorney be committed for contemptuous speeches against the Lord Chancellor. Brokas v. Savage, reported in Monro, Acta Cancellariae (1847). See also Ex parte Ingles (1740), Sanders, Chan. Ord. 552 (1845) (solicitor committed for libel); Fox, op. cit. supra note 32, at 102. The Managers in the Peck impeachment rejected a curb on an attorney's right to criticize the court, but they explicitly recognized the summary jurisdiction over attorneys acting "in the execution of their offices." Stansbury, op. cit. supra note 126, at 91, 376, 406. The act of 1831 was practically framed in those terms; see Ex parte Wall, 107 U.S. 265, 273 (1882).

court misconduct by such officers since it penalizes their misbehavior "in their *official* transactions."[207] An exclusory construction of Section 2 with reference to this clause of Section 1 would appear strained. This branch of the argument based on the structure of the statute does not therefore appreciably advance the case for limitation of all out-of-court contempts. There remains the argument that "so near thereto," read in juxtaposition to "presence," suggests physical proximity rather than causal relation.[208] It does seem that the phrase should be read in this sense; otherwise it is practically reduced to surplusage, since any obstruction however remote becomes an "obstruction to the administration of justice."

Contemporaneous construction, except for expressions that the summary power over contemptuous publications was curtailed, ends with the above-mentioned decision of Mr. Justice Baldwin.[209] There is little in *Ex parte Robinson*,[210] decided in 1873, to support the assertion that the "Supreme Court unequivocally confirmed" Mr. Justice Baldwin's construction.[211] In the *Robinson* case the district court disbarred an attorney for a disrespectful refusal to answer in open court, and the Supreme Court held the *disbarment* improper. In passing, the Court, describing the Act of 1831 in hasty shorthand, said:

> The power of these courts in the punishments of contempts can only be exercised to insure order and decorum in their presence, to secure faithfulness on the part of their officers in their official transactions, and to enforce obedience to their lawful orders, judgments, and processes.[212]

This obviously incomplete description which makes no mention of contempts "so near" the presence of the court sheds uncertain light on the scope of that phrase.

The question whether the Act of 1831 limited the summary power to tumultuous disturbances and the like was first presented to the Supreme Court in *Savin, Petitioner*.[213] The *Savin* case is cited by both the majority and the minority of the Supreme Court in the *Nye* case for confirmation of opposing positions,[214] which suggests that it is not an unequivocal authority for either. Savin had attempted to bribe a witness in a pending case, the acts occurring in a witness room not seven feet from, and in the hallway immediately adjoining, the courtroom. The Court recognized that there may be misbehavior "in the vicinity of the building in which the court is held, which, on account of its disorderly character, would actually interrupt the court, being in session, in the conduct of its business, and consequently obstruct the administration of justice."[215] But the Court found it unnecessary to decide whether the phrase "so near thereto" was *limited* to such cases,[216] basing its decision on an expanded concept of the presence of the court: "the court, at least when in session, is present in every part of the place set apart for its own use, and for the use of its officers, jurors and witnesses; and misbehavior anywhere in such place is misbehavior in the

---

[207](Italics added.) Cf. Ex parte Bradley, 7 Wall. 364, 374 (1868).

[208]Nye v. United States, 313 U.S. 33, 49 (1941); Nelles and King, op. cit. supra note 16, at 530.

[209]Ex parte Poulson, Fed. Cas. No. 11,350, at 1208 (C.C. Pa. 1835); see the remarks of Justice Baldwin in United States v. Holmes, Fed. Cas. No. 15,383, at 363 (C.C. Pa. 1842). But Justice Baldwin's contemporaries appear to regard the Act of 1831 as a limitation upon libels alone. Thus Buchanan said on the floor of Congress on March 2, 1836: "A few days after the acquittal of this Judge [Peck], the Senate . . . passed a bill . . . under which no Federal Judge will ever again dare to punish a libel as a contempt." 3 Moore, Works of James Buchanan 13 (1908). Chancellor Kent declared that "The act of Congress . . . prohibits all interference by attachment and summary punishment for contempts committed out of the presence of the court, by libels upon the court and the parties. . . ." 1 Kent, Commentaries 300 n. d (3d ed. 1836).

[210]19 Wall. (U.S.) 505 (1873).

[211]Nelles and King, op. cit. supra note 16, at 532 n. 28.

[212]Ex parte Robinson, 19 Wall. (U.S.) 505, 510–11 (1873); see the dissent of Mr. Justice Field in Ex parte Wall, 107 U.S. 265, 302–3 (1882).

[213]131 U.S. 267 (1889).

[214]Nye v. United States, 313 U.S. 13, 52, 55 (1941).

[215]Savin, Petitioner, 131 U.S. 267, 276 (1889).

[216]Ibid., at 278.

presence of the court."[217] Whereupon some of the lower federal courts, apparently unaware that this interpretation of "presence" had been rested on the time-worn notion that judicial precincts were hallowed,[218] reasoned that if quiet bribery on the threshold of the courthouse, i.e., "in the presence" of the court, were a contempt, then it would be equally contemptuous to do the same thing "so near thereto," e.g., "on the street opposite the court building, or four blocks away."[219] Thus resulted the expansion of the phrase "so near thereto,"[220] though there remained courts which took a narrower view.[221] But the remarkable opinion of Mr. Justice Holmes in *Patterson v. Colorado* furnished scant comfort to proponents of the latter view.[222]

Summarizing the foregoing, the Peck proceedings merely disclose a desire to strike down the summary power over contemptuous publications in non-pending cases, and they seem to indicate an intention to conserve the balance of the common law jurisdiction. The proceedings are of dubious weight as legislative history because highly colored by advocacy. The structure of the statute is inconclusive so far as concerns the inference to be drawn from the separate provisions of Sections 1 and 2, but the need for giving meaning to the phrase "so near thereto" suggests a construction limiting all out-of-court contempts. Such a limitation was adopted in the contemporary construction of Mr. Justice Baldwin.[223] As to the other cases, prior to the *Toledo* case, the Supreme Court had recognized that the Act of 1831 effected a curtailment of the contempt power, but it may be fairly stated that the utterances of the Court as to the scope of the curtailment were equivocal. The lower courts, on the other hand, almost unanimously regarded the Act of 1831 as a restriction on the summary power in publication cases, and were about evenly divided as to whether the "so near" phrase was limited to noisy disturbance of orderly proceedings.[224]

---

[217]Ibid., at 277.

[218]There was early common law authority for a construction of "in the presence" extending to the precincts of the court. See Fox, op. cit. supra note 72, at 244. But the Court relied instead on Bacon's statement that "The place of justice is an hallowed place; and therefore not only the bench but the footpace and precincts and purprise thereof ought to be preserved against scandal and corruption." Savin, Petitioner, 131 U.S. 267, 277 (1889).

[219]In re Brule, 71 Fed. 943, 948 (D.C. Nev. 1895); United States v. Huff, 206 Fed. 700, 705 (D.C. Ga. 1913) (letter delivered to judge at home). Compare Mr. Justice Stone's dissent in Nye v. United States, 313 U.S. 33, 56 (1941).

[220]One court actually expanded the "presence of the court" to include a juror's place of business half a mile away from the court. McCaully v. United States, 25 App. D.C. 404, 413 (1905). In addition to the McCaully case, and the Brule and Huff cases cited in note 219 supra, see In re May, 1 Fed. 737, 742 (D.C. Mich. 1880) (summary punishment of juror); United States v. Anonymous, 21 Fed. 761, 771 (C.C. Tenn. 1884) (threatening equity examiner on street); Sharon v. Hill, 24 Fed. 726, 732–33 (C.C. Cal. 1885) (misconduct before equity examiner a contempt, but proceeding by indictment instead); Ex parte McLeod, 120 Fed. 130 (D.C. Ala. 1903) (assault upon federal commissioner on the highway); United States v. Zavelo, 177 Fed. 536 (C.C. Ala. 1910) (service on out-of-state witness); Kirk v. United States, 192 Fed. 273 (C.C.A. 9th 1911) (attempt to corrupt juror). It is to be emphasized that the May, Anonymous, and Kirk cases recognized the delimitation effected by the Act of 1831 with respect to contempt by publication. In re May, 1 Fed. 737, 743 (D.C. Mich. 1880); United States v. Anonymous, 21 Fed. 761, 768 (C.C. Tenn. 1884); Kirk v. United States, 192 Fed. 273, 277 (C.C.A. 9th 1911). Ex parte McLeod lends lip service to this interpretation but finds a specious distinction with respect to publications designed to influence the court in a pending cause. Ex parte McLeod, 120 Fed. 130, 137, (D.C. Ala. 1903).

[221]Cuyler v. Atlantic & North Carolina R. Co., 131 Fed. 95 (C.C.N.C. 1904), squarely held that the Act of 1831 curtailed the summary power in publication cases; see Morse v. Montana Ore-Purchasing Co., 105 Fed. 337, 347 (C.C.Mont. 1900). The Cuyler case, like Ex parte Schulenburg, 25 Fed. 211, 218 (C.C. Mich. 1885), declared that the power extended only to loud noises or disturbances so near as to interrupt orderly proceedings. Cuyler v. Atlantic & North Carolina R. Co., 131 Fed. 95, 98 (C.C. N.C. 1904). For similar constructions see Hillmon v. Mutual Life Ins. Co., 79 Fed. 749 (C.C. Kan. 1897) (intimidation of litigant); Atwell v. United States, 162 Fed. 97 (C.C.A. 4th 1908) (disclosure by juror of grand jury proceedings); Asbestos Shingle, Slate & Sheathing Co. v. Johns-Manville Co., 189 Fed. 611 (C.C. N.Y. 1911) (misstatement in advertisement of effect of decision). For a similar result under a "so near" phrase in state statutes, see Commonwealth v. Deskins, 4 Leigh. (Va.) 685 (1834) (concealment to avoid service), Va. Rev. Code (Supp. 1833) c. 109, § 25; Baldwin v. State, 11 Ohio St. 681 (1860) (substituting false return in court files), 1 Ohio Rev. Stat. (Curwen, 1853) 122.

[222]Patterson v. Colorado, 205 U.S. 454 (1907); pages 24–25 supra; Nelles and King, op. cit. supra note 16, at 539–40.

[223]But see note 209 supra.

[224]See notes 219 and 220 supra.

It is not a little remarkable that the opinion of Mr. Justice Douglas in the *Nye* case should earn praise as an example of "consummate technique in concealing policies beneath artful rhetoric."[225] The considerations that prompted him to eschew a discussion of policy in the face of an equivocal statute are obscure. Surely policy is entitled to greatest weight when interstitial legislation is unavoidable. And it is a tenet of the Realist school, to which Mr. Justice Douglas has made distinguished contributions, that legal problems should be articulated in the social terms they really involve, the better to grapple with them.[226] It is scarcely necessary to remark that no contradiction is involved in accepting the policy factors behind the *Bridges* decision in a statutory context while rejecting them in the constitutional frame. Policy is an almost inescapable guide to the interpretation of an equivocal statute. It is, however, something else to depart from the historic content of constitutional language in order to give effect to personal prejudices, e.g., to employ the historically procedural due process in order to outlaw minimum wage legislation. We turn now to policy considerations.

Blackstone, though taking a broad view of the contempt jurisdiction, uneasily notes that this method of making the defendant answer upon oath to a criminal charge is not agreeable to the genius of the common law.[227] Not alone is it disquieting that a man is by his own admission compelled to convict himself,[228] and that he is tried for a criminal charge without benefit of jury, but also that his prosecutor is at the same time judge and jury in a situation which is frequently charged with personal feeling.[229] And in the publication cases there is the more potent objection that a judiciary placed beyond the realm of criticism may become a "formidable engine of oppression."[230] Apart from the check furnished by public opinion, the judiciary is practically free from all restraints. An awakened public opinion not only restricts the growth of arbitrary power, but also exerts a salutary influence on the judicial lag,[231] as is illustrated by the minimum wage cases.[232] Or it ultimately produces legislation that overleaps judicial reluctance to adapt the law to a changing economic environment—witness the relation of Workmen's Compensation Acts to intolerable "master and servant" cases.[233] But free criticism cannot flourish in the *in terrorem* atmosphere of

---

[225]Hamilton and Braden, op. cit. supra note 22, at 1319, 1363 n. 194.

[226]This was emphasized by Mr. Justice Holmes, copiously quoted in Frank, Law and the Modern Mind 253, 258 (1930); cf. ibid., at 230; see also Holmes, Collected Legal Papers 126, 167 (1920); Nelles, Towards Legal Understanding, 34 Col. L. Rev. 1041, 1073 (1934). Compare Mr. Justice Douglas' opinion in Textile Mills Securities Corp. v. Com'r, 314 U.S. 326 (1941).

[227]4 Bl. Comm. *287–88; see the remarks of Lord Fitzgerald, concurred in by Lord Bramwell, quoted in Fox, op. cit. supra note 32, at 42.

[228]Fox, op. cit. supra note 32, at 70.

[229]Mr. Justice Holmes, dissenting in the Toledo case, said: "when it is considered how contrary it is to our practice and ways of thinking for the same person to be accuser and sole judge in a matter which, if he be sensitive, may involve strong personal feeling, I should expect the power to be limited by the necessities of the case to insure order and decorum in their presence." Toledo Newspaper Co. v. United States, 247 U.S. 402, 423 (1918). Mr. Chief Justice Taft later remarked: "The delicacy there is in the judge's deciding whether an attack upon his own judicial action is mere criticism or real obstruction, and the possibility that impulse may incline his view to personal vindication are manifest." Craig v. Hecht, 263 U.S. 255, 279 (1923). See note 17 supra. A significant recognition of the importance of these factors is found in Cooke v. United States, 267 U.S. 517, 539 (1925). The Supreme Court suggested that if a judge should be personally attacked he might properly call a fellow judge to act for him; see Cornish v. United States, 299 Fed. 283, 285 (C.C.A. 6th 1924); Frankfurter and Landis, op. cit. supra note 5, at 1056; Frankfurter and Greene, The Labor Injunction 190 (1930) (quoting Senator Bacon). It is uncertain whether this is an adequate safeguard, in view of what Nelles and King describe as the tendency of judges to maintain the prestige of their class. Nelles and King, op. cit. supra note 16, at 547.

[230]Stansbury, op. cit. supra note 126, at 437; Nelles and King, op. cit. supra note 16, at 403.

[231]Cf. Stone, The Common Law in the United States, 50 Harv. L. Rev. 4, 12 (1937).

[232]Compare Morehead v. New York ex rel. Tipaldo, 298 U.S. 587 (1936), with West Coast Hotel Co., v. Parrish, 300 U.S. 379 (1937).

[233]Laski, Procedure for Constructive Contempt in England, 41 Harv. L. Rev. 1031, 1032 (1928).

a pervasive contempt power. Men will not freely speak their minds at the risk of offending a judge who may read criticism as an obstruction of justice.[234]

Against such considerations, it was urged in the *Peck* proceedings that a judge could not in pursuit of vindication forsake his duties to dance attendance upon grand and petit juries.[235] Chancellor Kent could not believe that a judge would get a fair hearing from a jury;[236] Goodhart more recently shrank from the spectacle of a judge undergoing cross-examination.[237] Others say that ordinary criminal process is too slow to cure the mischief occasioned by published contempts, or that lacking summary punishment an offender may persevere in his misconduct.[238] Such arguments cannot tip the scales against the potentiality of arbitrary power,[239] and arbitrary power is today not a rhetorical flourish but a matter of life or death. There remains the claim that without summary power against contemptuous publications "no court could possibly exist."[240] This so-called "law of necessity," remarks Judge Thomas, is no law at all, for, if it were, "*no* court could exist without it."[241] No tribunal has been more frequently and harshly criticized than the Supreme Court, yet it has never attempted to stifle criticism by summary punishment.[242] Respect will not be coerced; it must be won. The true measure of necessity is to be found in the power required to insure orderly procedure, to compel attendance and testimony, and to repel clamorous invasion.[243] Even this power, as Edward Livingston acutely remarked, need only go so far as to repel, and not to punish. Temporary confinement would sufficiently control contumacious persons, and punishment could be reserved to an impersonal tribunal.[244] Livingston was a member of the Senate[245] to which Buchanan presented the argument in his very words;[246] it was there rejected. But its logic

---

[234]Ibid., at 1033. It is worth noting that Kent and Buchanan appeared, shortly after the passage of the Act of 1831, to regard it as applicable to all libels on the court. Note 209 supra.

[235]Stansbury, op. cit. supra note 126, at 355, 506.

[236]"If a judge was called a blockhead or a fool, one half of the rude and vulgar jurors of the country might think it a very smart and, possibly, a very true saying. . . . I never would accept judicial office . . . if I was to be left so naked and defenseless. . . ." Nelles and King, op. cit. supra note 16, at 420 n. 107, quoting Kent's letter.

To this the complete answer is found in Stuart v. People, 3 Scam. (Ill.) 395, 405 (1842): "An honest, independent and intelligent court will win its way to public confidence, in spite of newspaper paragraphs, however pointed may be their wit or satire, and its dignity will suffer less by passing them by unnoticed, than by arraigning the perpetrators, trying them in a summary way, and punishing them by the judgment of the offended party." See Laski, op. cit. supra note 233, at 1040.

[237]Goodhart, op. cit. supra note 14, at 903.

[238]Skipworth's and Castro's Case, 9 Q.B. 230, 233 (1873); Respublica v. Oswald, 1 Dall. (Pa.) 319, 326–27 (1788). Can it be seriously doubted that the lodging of an information against an offender will cause him to desist, or if he persist, that arrest and bond will act as a deterrent pending trial?

[239]Nelles and King enumerate other social interests "paramount to the insulation of the administration of justice": 1) judges deal with problems of statesmanship which involve off-the-record factors and which merit thorough discussion; 2) consistent and logical suppression of discussion likely to affect pending cases would mean that some continuing grievances would never be discovered at all; for example, a judicial "dry" bias would escape comment so long as a prohibition law bred new cases; 3) newspaper comment is merely one of myriad outside influences that are always at work, and it may serve as a corrective to less desirable influences. Nelles and King, op. cit. supra note 16, at 550–52.

[240]Respublica v. Oswald, 1 Dall. (Pa.) 319, 326–27 (1788); see Nelles and King, op. cit. supra note 16, at 537.

[241]Thomas, The Law of Constructive Contempt 69 (1904); People ex rel. Att'y Gen'l v. News-Times Pub. Co., 35 Colo. 253, 430, 84 Pac. 912, 968 (1906).

[242] Thomas, op. cit. supra note 241, at 67–69.

[243]Stansbury, op. cit. supra note 126, at 441; Frankfurter and Landis, op. cit. supra note 5, at 1022; Nelles and King, op. cit. supra note 16, at 418–19.

[244]1 Livingston, Complete Works 264 et seq. (1873), quoted in Nelles and King, op. cit. supra note 16, at 419; Stansbury, op. cit. supra note 126, at 441 et seq.; 3 Wharton, Criminal Procedure §§ 1905, 1906 (1846). Judge Spencer for the Managers, and Meredith in behalf of Judge Peck, emphasized that the summary power arises out of the right of self-defense. Stansbury, op. cit. supra note 126, at 296–329.

[245]Stansbury, op. cit. supra note 126, at 474.

[246]Ibid., at 441–44; Nelles and King, op. cit. supra note 16, at 527.

reinforces the social considerations that dictate curtailment of summary power over all contemptuous publications.

In the non-publication cases, the convenience of summary punishment is not opposed by such social pressures as are generated when criticism is inhibited by summary power. And in this field, Livingston's proposal, though logical, would practically confer immunity on petty offenders.[247] But in such non-publication cases as may engender judicial resentment, Livingston's analysis buttresses the considerations which suggest that jury trial is to be preferred to summary procedure. Even within the summary jurisdiction outlined in the *Nye* and *Savin* cases it may on occasion be judicious to exercise the power of judicial self-limitation.[248] For this we have the example of English courts which have frequently resorted to,[249] and possibly prefer, jury trial,[250] be the cases as provoking as that in which a brickbat was thrown at the judge and "narrowly mist."[251] Immediate and severe punishment might in such cases seem called for and yet be suspect as the retaliatory reflex of an offended judge. Our deep-rooted instinct for impersonal trial demands that not even the shadow of personal pique should cloud the face of justice.[252] This ideal must, however, yield when outrageous misconduct that falls within the statutory jurisdiction would otherwise go unpunished.[253] With the exception, therefore, of cases in which summary procedure is expedient because petty offenses will otherwise go unpunished to the detriment of orderly proceedings, the ripe wisdom of Jessel, Master of the Rolls, furnishes a complete guide:

> I have myself had on many occasions to consider this jurisdiction, and I have always thought that necessary though it be, it is necessary only in the sense in which extreme measures are sometimes necessary to preserve men's rights, that is, if no other pertinent remedy can be found. Probably that will be discovered after consideration to be the true measure of the exercise of the jurisdiction.[254]

CONCLUSION

Not long ago Mr. Justice Jackson, then Solicitor General, published an article entitled "Back to the Constitution,"[255] in which he compared the recent emergence of the constitutional text from beneath a laissez faire gloss to the rediscovery of an Old Master after the retouching brushwork of succeeding generations has been removed. Despite the excellence of the rediscovered Constitution, it was yet obliquely intimated that the document was to be refurbished with a more fitting gloss,[256] for in the article was quoted Marshall's famous dictum that the Constitution is "intended to endure

---

[247]"An efficient *in terrorem* power to maintain order and decorum must have teeth. Peccadilloes too trifling to be worth the bother of sending to another court for prosecution should not for that reason be committed with impunity." Nelles, The Summary Power to Punish for Contempt, 31 Col. L. Rev. 964–66 (1931).

[248]Cf. Finkelstein, Judicial Self-Limitation, 37 Harv. L. Rev. 338 (1924); Berger, Exhaustion of Administrative Remedies, 48 Yale L. J. 981, 994 (1939).

[249]Cf. Fox, op. cit. supra note 32, at 241–42.

[250]Cf. Ex parte Grossman, 267 U.S. 87, 116 (1925).

[251]Note to Davis's Case, 2 Dyer 188b, 73 Eng. Rep. R. 415–16 (1631).

[252]See Sharon v. Hill, 24 Fed. 726, 733 (C.C. Cal. 1885); cf. note 229 supra.

[253]Cf. United States v. Pendergast, 39 F.Supp. 189 (Mo. 1941). It is not intended to express an opinion as to whether the misconduct in the Pendergast case took place in the presence of the court; see Sharon v. Hill, 24 Fed. 726, 733 (C.C. Cal. 1885); In re May, 1 Fed. 737, 742–43 (D.C. Mich. 1880); Nelles, The Summary Power to Punish for Contempt, 31 Col. L. Rev. 956, 966 (1931).

[254]In re Clements v. Erlanger, 46 L.J. (Ch.) 375, 383 (1877); cf. Frankfurter and Landis, op. cit. supra note 5, at 1051. This discussion has been confined to such contempts as constitute an obstruction to the administration of justice. But the need for judicial self-limitation is no less present in the field of disobedience of injunctive orders issued in labor controversies. Legislative policy has been indicated by repeated limitation of injunctive interference in labor disputes, and by the provision of the Clayton Act for jury trial in the case of contempts which also constitute criminal offenses. 38 Stat. 738 (1914), 28 U.S.C.A. § 387 (1940); see Frankfurter and Landis, op. cit. supra note 5, at 1038–41, 1053.

[255]25 A.B.A.J. 745 (1939).

[256]Cf. Hamilton and Adair, op. cit. supra note 107, at 104.

for ages to come, and consequently to be adapted to the various crises of human affairs."[257] Perhaps adaptation of the Constitution by the Court to the needs of a rapidly changing society is indeed a law of constitutional survival. And now that the first fine rapture of debunking has passed, we can perceive that in its early stages the extension of substantive due process was on the whole an adaptation to the needs of an expanding industrial society.[258] It was the refusal of the Court over a long period to make the *readaptation* necessitated by our changing economic world, to relax the bonds of a once beneficent individualism, that proved crucial.[259]

The costs of this wilfulness in terms of a generation of sweated labor and unchecked industrial piracy should remind us that a Court which can read a beneficial power into the Constitution today can read out cherished rights tomorrow.[260] Possibly the menace of arbitrary power should lead us with Madison and Taney to prefer a Constitution carrying the meaning and intent it had for the framers.[261] This is not the place to evaluate the divergent theories of Madison and Marshall,[262] though a reappraisal of those theories in the light both of liberal ascendancy on the Court and the sharpened conflict between totalitarianism and constitutional authority is needed. Here it may be assumed that adaptation and survival are inseparable. But adaptation to what? To "the dominant political forces of the country as revealed at the ballot box," says Corwin.[263] Yet an "unadapted" Constitution may be the last refuge of minorities if a national Huey Long comes to power. Such fears must be set aside when the nation seeks to cope with an unprecedented emergency, a "crisis in human affairs."[264] Adaptation may then be imperative, and possibly that is a test of the need for adaptation. But can it be seriously urged that the sporadic exercise of summary power over contemptuous publications provokes such a crisis, particularly when such redoubtable liberals as Mr. Chief Justice Stone and Mr. Justice Frankfurter believe that the *Bridges* decision imperils rather than rescues civil liberties?[265] Even advocates of a flexible Constitution recognize that judicial exercise of the vast power of adaptation can be tolerated only when tempered by self-restraint. It is the melancholy lesson of the *Bridges* case that it is easier to preach self-restraint to the opposition than to practice it oneself.[266]

[257]Jackson, Back to the Constitution, 25 A.B.A.J. 745, 748 (1939).

[258]"Due process was fashioned from the most respectable ideological stuff of the later nineteenth century. The ideas out of which it was shaped were in full accord with the dominant thought of the age. . . . In philosophy it was individualism, in government laissez faire, in economics the natural law of supply and demand, in law the freedom of contract. The system of thought had possessed every other discipline; it had in many a domain reshaped the law to its teachings. . . . An impact that had been irresistible elsewhere should surely have won its way into constitutional law." Hamilton, The Path of Due Process of Law, in Read, The Constitution Reconsidered 167, 189 (1938). Corwin calls the extension of due process "an achievement which the American democracy tolerated, even welcomed, in the name of prosperity." Corwin, op. cit. supra note 1, at 91, 101. See Borchard, The Supreme Court and Private Rights, 47 Yale L. J. 1051, 1054, 1057, 1058 (1938).

[259]Borchard, op. cit. supra note 258, at 1055; Hamilton and Adair, op. cit. supra note 107, at 193.

[260]See McIlwain, Constitutionalism and the Changing World 264, 270 (1939); Hamilton and Braden, op. cit. supra note 22, at 1375.

[261]For the views of Madison, see page 627 supra; for those of Taney, see Scott v. Sandford, 19 How. (U.S.) 393, 426 (1856). Yet in the very same opinion Taney could find substantive due process in the Constitution. Ibid., at 450. See also the Passenger Cases, 7 How. (U.S.) *283, *478 (1849).

[262]See Corwin, op. cit. supra note 1, at 7–15.

[263]Corwin, Court Over Constitution 126 (1938).

[264]The attempt to deal with the staggering effects of the depression is an example, though only a scraping of the barnacles from the Constitution was necessary to loose national powers. Compare Hamilton and Adair, op. cit. supra note 107.

[265]One may differ with the minority's estimate of the perils and yet believe that the existence of such a difference between those who cherish liberal ideals indicates the absence of a crisis.

[266]That lesson is to be found in the dissent of Mr. Justice Frankfurter as well. "We must," he adjures the majority, "be fastidiously careful not to make our private views the measure of constitutional authority." Bridges v. California, 314 U.S. 252, 293 (1941); see ibid., at 279. The learning cited by him with respect to non-curtailment of the contempt power by the First and Fourteenth Amendments, page 8 supra, should lead him to reject any limitation on the power. Instead, he agrees that there is a limitation with respect to the cases in which he finds the threat to impartial trial negligible, note 10 supra, and calls for self-restraint only in the two cases where, parting from the majority, he finds the threat real.

CHAPTER III

The President, Congress, and the Courts

I. SUBPOENAING THE PRESIDENT: JEFFERSON V. MARSHALL IN THE BURR CASE

We do not think that the President is exalted above legal process . . . and if the President possesses information of any nature which might tend to serve the cause of Aaron Burr, a subpoena should issue to him, notwithstanding his elevated station.

Alexander McRae, of counsel for President Jefferson[1]

Chief Justice Marshall's rulings on President Jefferson's claim of right to withhold information in the trial of Aaron Burr have been a source of perennial debate. Eminent writers have drawn demonstrably erroneous deductions from the record. For example, Edward Corwin stated that Jefferson "refuse[d] to respond to Chief Justice Marshall's subpoena,"[2] a statement recently repeated by Circuit Judge George MacKinnon.[3] More recently still, Irwin S. Rhodes, on the basis of "newly discovered" evidence,[4] has charged that Chief Judge John J. Sirica, "by asserting the right of the court to order presidential submission and to review and revise the president's judgment in the exercise of executive privilege," laid claim to "a power that Chief Justice Marshall disavowed." In

---

[1] 1 T. CARPENTER, THE TRIAL OF COLONEL AARON BURR 75 (1807). McRae's co-counsel, William Wirt, who served as Attorney General of the United States for twelve consecutive years, stated that "if the production of this letter would not compromit [sic] the safety of the United States, and it can be proved to be material to Mr. Burr, he has a right to demand it. Nay, in such a case, I will admit his right to summon the President. . . ." Id. at 82. His associate, George Hay, the United States Attorney, stated,

I never had the idea of clothing the President . . . with those attributes of divinity. . . . That high officer is but a man; he is but a citizen; and, if he knows anything in any case, civil or criminal, which might affect the life, liberty or property of his fellow-citizens . . . it is his duty to . . . go before a Court, and declare what he knows. And what would be the process, in case he failed to attend? Why, the common means would be, for the Court to issue an attachment to force him. . . .

Id. at 90–91.

Later Wirt, arguing in Cherokee Nation v. Georgia, 30 U.S. (5 Pet.) 1 (1831), stated: Shall we be asked . . . how this Court will enforce its injunction. . . . I answer, it will be time enough to meet that question when it shall arise. . . . In a land of laws, the presumption is that the decision of the Courts will be respected; and, in case they should not, it is a poor government indeed in which there does not exist power to enforce respect.

What is the value of that government in which the decrees of its Courts can be mocked at and defied with impunity? . . . It is no government at all. . . . [This Court is not] to anticipate that the President will not do his duty.

2 C. WARREN, HISTORY OF THE SUPREME COURT 207–08 (1922). Although this was uttered against a background of veiled presidential threats not to enforce a decree against Georgia, the reasoning extends to a subpoena against the President. Id. at 205.

[2] E. CORWIN, THE PRESIDENT: OFFICE AND POWERS 139 (3d ed. 1948). Compare the statement by Dumas Malone at p. 41 infra.

[3] Nixon v. Sirica, 487 F.2d 700, 748 (D.C. Cir. 1973) (dissenting opinion) ("the President, through his attorney, refused to disclose certain passages").

[4] Rhodes, What Really Happened to the Jefferson Subpoenas, 60 A.B.A.J. 52 (1974). He alleges that the courts relied on the "incomplete record." They "failed to uncover the complete contemporaneous reporting of the case taken in shorthand by Thomas Carpenter . . ." and to consult the archives wherein he located a copy "of the controversial letter of General Wilkinson to President Jefferson. . . ." Id.

following him, Rhodes states, the Court of Appeals, which "limited or opposed the absolute character of presidential privilege departed from the rulings of Chief Justice Marshall. . . ."[5] And he concludes that insofar as the courts "depart from precedent under assertions of perpetuating it, the law as well as history is not well served."[6]

This is a ringing condemnation, and I may be indulged for being equally blunt: The courts were right and Rhodes is wrong. With the "tapes" issue threatening to boil up anew in consequence of President Nixon's refusal to furnish further information to Special Prosecutor Leon Jaworski, and the even more serious limits set by the President on "cooperation" with the impeachment investigation by the House Judiciary Committee,[7] the issue posed by Rhodes is of greatest importance. It is high time that the issue be removed from the realm of opinion, that the Burr record be permitted to speak for itself, and that the several Marshall pronouncements be set out so that one may judge where the truth lies.

As Rhodes remarks, "the proceedings were in four stages: commitment during the grand jury inquiry, trial and acquittal on a charge of treason, trial and acquittal on a charge of misdemeanor, commitment to the United States Circuit Court of Ohio on a misdemeanor charge."[8] The "new" evidence upon which Rhodes relies comes from the fourth stage; and he notices that Marshall

> recognized that if Burr could prove the relevancy of the material withheld and if the proceedings were a prosecution in chief [instead of commitment proceedings], he might discontinue the case.[9]

Apparently Rhodes did not realize that this statement demolished his argument.

In the preliminary first stage proceedings, Burr sought to procure a letter of October 21, 180[6], written by General Wilkinson to Jefferson, by means of a subpoena calling both for Jefferson's attendance and production of the letter,[10] though Burr repeatedly stated that he was content merely to obtain the letter.[11] Alexander McRae, of counsel for Jefferson, "admitted that the President might be summoned to attend,"[12] an admission to which Marshall later adverted,[13] but George Hay, the United States Attorney, disputed issuance of a subpoena duces tecum.[14] Because Marshall fully appreciated the importance of the personal summons, he was not content to rest on the concession of counsel but rendered a written opinion on June 13, 1807, in which he concluded that "any person charged with a crime in the courts of the United States, has a right before, as well as after indictment, to the process of the Court, to compel the attendance of his witnesses."[15]

Turning to the subpoena duces tecum Marshall stated: "In the provisions of the Constitution and of the statute which give to the accused a right to the compulsory process of the Court there is no exception whatever." Likening the President to the Governor of a State, he observed that "it is not known ever to have been doubted, that the Chief Magistrate of a State might be served with

---

[5]*Id.*

[6]*Id.* at 54.

[7]N.Y. Times, Feb. 15, 1974, at 1, col. 8; Wall St. J., Feb. 20, 1974, at 7, col. 2.

[8]Rhodes, *supra* note 4, at 52.

[9]*Id.* at 54. On the preponderant role of "relevancy," *see* note 33 *infra.*

[10]1 T. CARPENTER, *supra* note 1, at 65, 124.

[11]*Id.* at 62, 64, 70; 2 *id.* at 4.

[12]1 *id.* at 77, 84. While Jefferson wrote that personal attendance might hale him to all parts of the vast hinterland, he stated that if Burr should "suppose there are any facts within the knowledge of the Heads of departments or of myself . . . we shall be ready to give him the benefit of it, by way of deposition . . . ," a plea of inconvenience rather than of lack of jurisdiction. 9 JEFFERSON WRITINGS 57 (P. Ford ed. 1898) [hereinafter cited as Ford]. Compare this with Rhodes' statement that Jefferson wrote Hay on June 17 "denying the right to demand his personal attendance. Rhodes, *supra* note 4, at 53. No such representation was ever made to the court. To the contrary, his counsel professed readiness to have him appear. *See* note 1 *supra.*

[13]"We observed that Mr. Hay admitted, that the President might be subpoenaed." 1 T. CARPENTER, *supra* note 1, at 70.

[14]*Id.* at 84, 127.

[15]*Id.* at 127.

a subpoena *ad testificandum.*" He added that "it has never been alledged [*sic*]" that in England "a subpoena might not be directed" to members of the "cabinet council," who, instead of the King, he correctly noted, were the analogue of the American executive.[16] Marshall could "perceive no legal objection to issuing a subpoena *duces tecum,* to any person whatever, provided the case be such as to justify the process."[17] If the papers "may be important in the evidence—if they may be safely read at the trial—would it not be a blot in the page which records the judicial proceedings of this country, that, in a case of such serious import as this, the accused should be denied the use of them?"[18]

Marshall then addressed the argument that "the letter contains matter which ought not to be disclosed;" he said, "There is certainly nothing before the Court, which shews, that the letter in question contains any matter, the disclosure of which, would endanger the public safety. If it does contain any matter which it would be imprudent to disclose, which it is not the wish of the Executive to disclose, such matter, if it be not immediately and essentially applicable to the point, will of course, be suppressed."[19] As further developments indicate, Marshall was not to waver from this view. Should Burr be found guilty, he added, all concerned "should certainly regret that a paper which the accused believed to be essential to his defence . . . had been withheld from him"; and "it would justly tarnish the reputation of the Court which had given its sanction to its being withheld." Sounding a personal note, Marshall went on to say that he would feel "self-reproach" were he to "declare on the information now possessed, that the accused is not entitled to the letter in question, if it should be really important to him."[20]

In sum, Marshall made the touchstone of nondisclosure danger to the public safety, not "confidentiality," as President Nixon urges; and even such matter would be sheltered only if it were not "essentially applicable" to the defense. He regarded a judicial sanction to withhold such "essential" information as a "blot" which would "tarnish the reputation of the Court."

Corwin's statement that Jefferson "refuse[d] to respond to Chief Justice Marshall's subpoena" is also inaccurate. On June 12 Jefferson wrote to Hay that he had delivered the papers to the Attorney General and instructed the War Department to review its files with a view to compliance with the subpoena.[21] In a second letter to Hay on June 17, Jefferson wrote that "the receipt of these papers [by Hay] has, I presume, so far anticipated, and others this day forwarded will have substantially fulfilled the object of a subpoena. . . ."[22] When Jefferson learned that the Attorney General did not have the Wilkinson letter subpoenaed by Burr, he wrote Hay on June 23 that "[N]o researches shall be spared to recover this letter, & if recovered, it shall immediately be sent on to you."[23] Hay advised the court that "[W]hen we receive general Wilkinson's letter, the return will be completed."[24] This is hardly a "refusal" to comply with the subpoena. Apparently the letter "had been put in the hands of the clerk."[25]

---

[16]*Id.* at 127–28. Marshall rejected the reservation in the law of evidence for the King—which was based on the ground that it was "incompatible with his dignity to appear under the process of the court"—because the "principle of the English constitution that the king can do no wrong" was inapplicable to our government whereunder "the President . . . may be impeached and may be removed from office." *Id.*

[17]*Id.* at 129.

[18]*Id.* at 130.

[19]*Id.* at 133.

[20]*Id.* at 134.

[21]Ford, *supra* note 12, at 55–56.

[22]*Id.* at 56.

[23]*Id.* at 61.

[24]1 D. ROBERTSON, TRIAL OF AARON BURR 256 (1808). Like the Carpenter report, the Robertson report is a stenographic record of the trial.

[25]3 T. CARPENTER, *supra* note 1, at 14. Rhodes, *supra* note 4, at 53, states that "a copy of the letter of October 21, which had been lost, [was] submitted."

The treason trial commenced on August 3, and on September 1, Burr was acquitted.[26] On September 2, the misdemeanor proceedings commenced, and on September 3, Burr called for a second letter from Wilkinson to Jefferson, dated November 12, 1806.[27] Hay replied that the letter contained "several strictures upon certain characters in the Western country. . . . Would it not be better, to trust the Court with the selection of such parts, as it might deem necessary to the defence of the accused?" Luther Martin objected to a "secret tribunal," whereupon Hay proposed to "submit those letters to the inspection of either Mr. Randolph, or Mr. Botts, or Mr. Wickham [Burr counsel]; the man so selected, to pledge himself upon honour, not to divulge the confidential contents. If there was any difference of opinion as to what were confidential passages, the Court were to decide."[28] Burr's counsel insisted that Burr too should see the letter and demanded production in "public."[29] This is worlds apart from the Nixon claim of blanket "confidentiality," of a right to withhold from court as well as counsel. Instead, Hay left the final determination to the court.

What were the "strictures" Jefferson's counsel were so zealous to shield? Rhodes, who apparently consulted true copies of the letter in the archives, stated that Wilkinson referred to the "complicity of Governor Claiborne of Louisiana and his secretary, Cowles Meade, in the [Burr] conspiracy. Claiborne was a trusted appointee of Jefferson, who was adamant that the charges against Claiborne and his aide not be made public."[30] Since Wilkinson was to testify against Burr, this attempted suppression is not the most glorious chapter in Jefferson's history. A subpoena issued on September 4 and Hay promptly made a return with a copy of the letter;

> excepting such parts thereof as are, in my opinion, not material for the purposes of justice, for the defence of the accused, or pertinent to the issue. . . . The accuracy of this opinion, I am willing to refer to the judgment of the Court, by submitting the original letter for its inspection.[31]

Earlier, on June 12, Jefferson had devolved on Hay "the exercise of that discretion, which it would be my right and duty to exercise by withholding . . . any parts of the letter, which are not directly material for the purposes of justice."[32] Neither Jefferson nor Hay invoked an absolute claim of right to withhold information from the court. They restricted themselves to matters irrelevant to the cause and Hay was willing to leave the judgment on relevancy to the Court.[33] Burr's counsel, Botts, then moved that the "prosecution should stand, and be continued until that letter shall be in the possession of your Clerk."[34]

---

[26]2 T. CARPENTER, *supra* note 1, at 3; 3 *id.* at 3.

[27]3 *id.* at 9, 20, 21.

[28]*Id.* at 20.

[29]*Id.* Robertson reports that Martin also claimed the right to hear the Wilkinson letter "publicly," 2 D. ROBERTSON, *supra* note 24, at 502, and that Hay said, "I wish the court to look at the letter and say whether it does not contain what ought not to be submitted to public inspection." *Id.* at 509. It "cannot be right," said Hay, that Burr "shall have . . . access to the letter, merely for the purpose of making it public." 3 T. CARPENTER, *supra* note 1, at 25. In his opinion of September 4, Marshall took account of this dispute; he said,

> With respect to the secrecy of these parts which it is stated are improper to give out to the world, the Court will take any order that may be necessary. I do not think that the accused ought to be prohibited from seeing the letter: but . . . I will order that no copy of it be taken for public exhibition; and that no use shall be made of it but what is necessarily attached to the case. . . . [I]f it is necessary to debate it in public, those who take notes may be instructed not to insert any part of the arguments on that subject.

Id. at 38.

[30]Rhodes, *supra* note 4, at 52, 53.

[31]3 T. CARPENTER, *supra* note 1, at 27–28.

[32]1 *id.* at 10 (second series of pagination).

[33]Throughout, "relevancy" was the touchstone. *See* pp. 38, *supra*, text accompanying notes 32–33; *infra* note 37; p. 41, text accompanying note 46, *infra*, p. 42.

[34]3 T. CARPENTER, *supra* note 1, at 30.

On this state of facts Marshall delivered a second opinion on September 4. Rhodes asserts that rather than review "the withheld data *in camera* or otherwise and weighing relevant interests," Marshall "repeatedly sidestepped or ignored suggestions by one or the other of the parties to examine the letter and determine the validity of the president's assertion."[35] Rhodes bases his argument on Marshall's statement, "I never ought to have heard it at all, and which I must treat as though I have never heard. I cannot, therefor, speak from any knowledge I have of the letter."[36] The reason for this statement, which escaped Rhodes, was in Marshall's own words that "it is impossible that either the Court or the attorney [for the President] can know in what manner it is meant to be used: I must, therefore, consider declaration made upon the subject, as though they had not been made."[37] In other words Marshall sought to determine a broad issue of law, divorced from his premature and incomplete knowledge of the facts, which he broadly hinted did not really demand nondisclosure.[38] Marshall emphasized that only the defendant knew what was essential to his case and refused to take from him the right of making that decision.

Marshall phrased the issue in broadest terms: "If then the executive possesses a paper which is really believed by the accused to be material to his defence, ought it to be withheld?"[39]

That the President . . . might be subpoenaed and examined as a witness, and called upon to produce any paper which is in his possession, is not controverted, indeed that has once been decided. . . . I can very readily conceive, that the President might receive a letter which it would be very improper to require for public exhibition, because of the manifest inconvenience of the exposure. There ought, in such a case, to be an extremely strong occasion for its demand[40]. . . . I do think that a privilege does exist with respect to a private letter of the President ['which might relate to public concerns'[41]]

. . . . Now, it is a very serious question, when such letters may be supposed to contain something very material to the defence of any individual, that he should not be able to avail himself of the advantage of it. . . . [P]erhaps the Court ought to consider . . . the reasons which induced the President to refuse the paper as a governing principle to induce them to refuse its exhibition, except as it shall be made to appear absolutely necessary in the defence.[42]

Burr had filed an affidavit that the letter "may be material" to his defense and Marshall held that since "no sufficient reason is adduced, except in the affidavit of the accused . . . the Court must suppose that the paper ought to be produced; and if that is refused, the Court must take the proper means of ordering the continuance of the case until it is produced."[43] He concluded that "I do not

[35]Rhodes, *supra* note 4, at 54. There is, however, no evidence that Burr's counsel at any point suggested that "relevancy" be left to Marshall.

[36]*Id.*

[37]3 T. Carpenter, *supra* note 1, at 37. Marshall subsequently repeated that "it was impossible for him to determine, even if he saw the letter, how much of it was relevant to the present case, because he could not anticipate what ground of defence would be taken by the accused." *Id.* at 279–80.

[38]It is extremely probable that the letter, or the parts of the letter called for

. . . is [*sic*] of infinitely less importance, if it should be looked into, than gentlemen suppose; and that the objections . . . would vanish at its production; because it is probable, that, if it was produced and read, very much of the suspicions now entertained, would be wiped away. . . .

Id. at 35.

[39]*Id.* at 36.

[40]Robertson reports this as follows: "The occasion for demanding it ought, in such a case, to be very strong, and to be fully shown to the court before its production could be insisted on." 2 D. Robertson, *supra* note 24, at 535–36.

[41]3 T. Carpenter, *supra* note 1, at 37.

[42]*Id.* at 36–37. The challenge to the sufficiency of Burr's allegation that the letter "may be material" was thus met by Marshall:

[I]f a paper be in the possession of the opposite party, what statement of its contents or applicancy can be expected from the person who claims its production, he not knowing its contents? . . . It has always been thought sufficient to describe the paper, and identify its general nature and authenticity. . . .

Id. at 35.

[43]*Id.* at 36–37.

think that the accused ought to be prohibited from seeing the letter."[44] Thus, although Marshall attached great weight to presidential representations that a document should be withheld, he reaffirmed what he had earlier held: that the needs of the accused were primary.

For the purpose of weighing presidential claims against those needs, Marshall had said in his September 4 opinion that the President himself, not his delegate, must "judge as to his motives for withholding the letter."[45] To meet this requirement, Hay had sent an express letter to Jefferson at Monticello on September 5, and on September 9 he read into the record a certificate from Jefferson (to which was annexed a copy of the Wilkinson November 12 letter) in which Jefferson recited that he had deleted passages "in no wise material to the purposes of justice, on the charges of treason or misdemeanor. . . . [T]hey are on subjects irrelevant to any issue which can arise out of those charges, and could contribute nothing towards his acquittal or conviction."[46] That is all that the reports of the trial contain on the subject.[47] Nothing appears in Carpenter's report to indicate what was done with the letter; it was not read into the record. Dumas Malone, biographer of Jefferson, concluded that "[t]he document was accepted without comment. Thus there was an assertion and a recognition of a degree of executive privilege";[48] and Judge MacKinnon likewise states that Marshall "accepted" the deletions, that they "were not contested."[49]

Such statements overlook the mechanics of litigation. The letter had been subpoenaed by Burr; thus it would be his counsel who would introduce it in evidence. There is no mention of an offer in evidence of the letter by anyone. Earlier, Luther Martin, answering an objection ("if this evidence [a letter] came, what would be done with it?"), replied, "The answer is obvious; that it must be retained by the court till it is wanted,"[50] at which point it could be called for by counsel for the purpose of introduction in evidence. Throughout, Burr had insisted, and was again to insist, on production of the whole letter, and there is nothing to show that at this stage he had withdrawn his objections to deletions.[51] As Marshall stated at another juncture, "the Court are bound to hear the evidence; if there are any objections made, it will hear them, and decide upon their force."[52] Of an offer of the letter, or of rulings by Marshall there is not a trace.

Malone and Judge MacKinnon would transform Jefferson's compliance with Marshall's requirement of a personal claim of privilege, as a preliminary to Marshall's balancing of that claim against Burr's needs, into Marshall's silent withdrawal of the two careful opinions he had delivered. It is violent presumption that Marshall, without apparent reason, suddenly overruled his opinions sub silentio, that he no longer felt that a denial of a needed document to the accused would be a "blot" on American judicial proceedings, "tarnish the reputation of the Court," and fill Marshall himself with "self-reproach." Views so deeply felt, so often repeated, are not lightly abandoned. Stronger

---

[44]*Id.* at 38.

[45]*Id.* at 37; Rhodes, *supra* note 4, at 53. Robertson reports, "The propriety of withholding it must be decided by himself, not by another for him." 2 D. ROBERTSON, *supra* note 24, at 536.

[46]3 T. CARPENTER, *supra* note 1, at 46.

[47]United States v. Burr, 25 F. Cas. 187, 192–93 (No. 14,694) (C.C. Va. 1807), which purports to draw on the Carpenter and Robertson reports, states that Hay "presented a certificate from the President. . . ." Neither report contains such language. Robertson does not even record the express letter to Hay from Jefferson. 2 D. ROBERTSON, *supra* note 24, at 537.

[48]N.Y. Times, Nov. 26, 1973, at 30, col. 5.

[49]Nixon v. Sirica, 487 F.2d 700, 748 (D.C. Cir. 1973) (dissenting opinion).

[50]1 D. ROBERTSON, *supra* note 24, at 169. Compare Burr's statement on September 3: "A letter has been demanded from the President . . . which has often been promised, but never produced. I wish to know if that letter is in Court, and whether it cannot be put into the hands of the clerk." 3 T. CARPENTER, *supra* note 1, at 14.

[51]*See, e.g.,* 3 T. CARPENTER, *supra* note 1, at 30, *quoting* Botts. Rhodes states that on "September 16, Burr reasserted his demand for the November 12 letter, saying that 'the court ought to make no question how to proceed on it,' undoubtedly referring to his prior motion to continue the case." Rhodes, *supra* note 4, at 54. Marshall had earlier stated that he would follow that course. *See* p. 38 *supra.* Burr continued to demand the entire letter. *See* p. 42 *infra.*

[52]2 T. CARPENTER, *supra* note 1, at 125.

evidence than Jefferson's mere compliance with Marshall's requirement of a personal presidential claim of privilege is needed to prove that Marshall silently jettisoned his two decisions.[53] There is none.

Instead, the gloss which Malone and Judge MacKinnon put upon Hay's production of the letter is further rebutted by subsequent developments in the case: the Rhodes "discovery." On September 15, Burr was found not guilty on the misdemeanor charges.[54] Proceedings for the commitment of Burr for trial in another district where Burr was present when some overt act occurred then began.[55] On September 29, Wilkinson testified that the November 12 letter had been submitted to the grand jury; the presidential mantle of secrecy had been rent. Wickham called for the letter, but Hay stated that Chief Justice Marshall had remarked that "he could not think of requiring from General Wilkinson the exhibition of those parts of the letter which the president was unwilling to disclose."[56] Rhodes quotes this statement[57] but fails to take into account the implications of further developments. When Wickham, urging that the letter had been laid before the grand jury, renewed the demand, Marshall again emphasized relevancy:

[A]fter such a certificate from the president . . . as has been received, I cannot direct the production of those parts of the letter, without a sufficient evidence of their being relevant to the present prosecution.[58]

The implication that if the deleted portions were shown to be "relevant" their production would be "directed" repels the inference that Marshall had earlier "accepted" the deletions.

After further argument Marshall "determined that the correct course, was to leave the accused all the advantages which he might derive from the parts actually produced; and to allow him all the advantages of supposing that the omitted parts related to any particular point. The accused may avail himself as much of them, as if they were actually produced."[59] When Hay objected to Wickham's deduction that defendant's suppositions should be received as evidence in place of Jefferson's deletions, Marshall responded:

It is certainly fair to supply the omitted parts by suppositions. . . . If this were a trial in chief, I should perhaps think myself bound to continue the cause, on account of the withholding the parts of this paper; and I certainly cannot exclude the inferences which gentlemen may draw from the omissions.[60]

This was the last word spoken by Marshall on the subject; it reaffirmed the earlier opinions that the needs of the accused would override presidential reasons for withholding. In this less formal commitment proceeding, Marshall permitted Burr to fill the place of the deleted parts by suppositions that would be given the force of evidence.

As Rhodes summarized:

The chief justice placed considerable emphasis on the president's assertion of irrelevancy of the parts withheld, stating that in order to make further demand for the letter Burr must give "sufficient evidence" of relevancy. He recognized that if Burr could prove the relevancy of the material withheld and if the proceedings were a prosecution in chief, he might discontinue the case, but in the absence of that proof

---

[53]Note Marshall's remark on September 4: "[I]ndeed that has once been decided." *See* p. 40 *supra.* Later he stated in another context, "I have already decided this question." 3 T. CARPENTER, *supra* note 1, at 284.

[54]3 T. CARPENTER, *supra* note 1, at 110.

[55]Rhodes adverts to Marshall's ruling "that to constitute treason by acts of war the principal must be physically present at the place of committing the acts, in this case at Blannerhasset Island, a requirement the testimony could not meet." Rhodes, *supra* note 4, at 54.

[56]3 T. CARPENTER, *supra* note 1, at 254.

[57]Rhodes, *supra* note 4, at 54.

[58]3 T. CARPENTER, *supra* note 1, at 280-81.

[59]*Id.* at 281–82.

[60]*Id.* at 284.

and circumstances he refused further steps than allowing Burr to make the most favorable inference of the omitted part.[61]

That allowance made the letter superfluous. Against this background, Mr. Rhodes' deduction, that "[i]t is eminently clear that President Jefferson['s] . . . claim to an exclusive exercise of executive privilege, unreviewed and unreviewable by the courts, was upheld by Chief Justice Marshall,"[62] boggles the mind.

No more tenable is Rhodes' view that the misdemeanor trial "concluded without a definitive ruling on the president's right to withhold the letter."[63] In his September 4 opinion, a reaffirmation of the principles enunciated in the June 13 opinion, Marshall laid down the rules of law that should guide counsel and firmly indicated that presidential nondisclosure claims must yield to the real needs of the accused. Before applying these rules to the facts, he required a personal claim of privilege by Jefferson. This was not the only time that Marshall delineated the applicable legal principles for the future guidance of counsel. In an opinion rendered on September 14 respecting the admissibility of certain testimony, Marshall laid down the governing rules and added, "Gentlemen well know how to apply these principles. Should any difficulty occur in applying them, the particular cases will be brought before the Court and decided."[64] The fact that Marshall had no occasion at the fourth stage commitment hearing to apply the law to the facts, because Burr could be richly content to substitute his "suppositions" for the deleted letter, does not render the opinions of June 13 and September 4 any less the law of the case.[65]

The heart of Marshall's opinions was therefore justly summarized by the Court of Appeals in the "tapes" case: "The court was to show respect for the President's reason . . . but the ultimate decision remained with the Court."[66] If the courts are the "ultimate interpreters" of the Constitution and can therefore constrain Congress to operate within constitutional bounds,[67] they are no less empowered to measure presidential claims of constitutional power. The "mystique" of the President stops at the courthouse doors.

II. MUST IMPEACHMENT PRECEDE INDICTMENT?

A great debate has been raging about whether the President or Vice President must be impeached before he can be indicted. It turns on the provisions of Article I, § 3 of the Constitution:

Judgment in Cases of Impeachment shall not extend further than to removal from Office, and disqualification . . . but the Party convicted shall nevertheless be liable and subject to Indictment, Trial. . . .[68]

[61]Rhodes, *supra* note 4, at 54.

[62]*Id.*

[63]*Id.* at 53.

[64]3 T. CARPENTER, *supra* note 1, at 103.

[65]*See* p. 40 and note 53 *supra*.

[66]Nixon v. Sirica, 487 F.2d 700, 710 (D.C. Cir. 1973).

[67]*See* Powell v. McCormack, 395 U.S. 486, 521 (1969).

[68]U.S. CONST. art. I, § 3. It is reported that Special Prosecutor Leon Jaworski advised the grand jury not to indict President Nixon: "It was researched at the time and the conclusion was that legal doubt on the question was so substantial that a move to indict a sitting President would touch off a legal battle of gigantic proportions." N.Y. Times, Mar. 12, 1974, at 24, col. 1.

When I first studied Article I, § 3, I was engrossed in the *separation* of the removal on impeachment from the indictment and unwittingly wrote that "[r]emoval would enable the government to replace an unfit person with a proper person, leaving 'punishment' to a later and separate proceeding. . . ." R. BERGER, IMPEACHMENT: THE CONSTITUTIONAL PROBLEMS 79 (1973). At that time the problem whether impeachment *must* precede indictment had never crossed my mind; since then my incautious words have been read to endorse that view. Nixon v. Sirica, 487 F.2d 700, 757 (D.C. Cir. 1973) (MacKinnon, J., dissenting); Brief for Appellant at 20, Nixon v. Sirica, *supra*. I hereby repudiate such endorsement, for study of the problem has convinced me that § 3 has no such requirement.

Let us begin with the words themselves; "nevertheless" is defined as "notwithstanding or in spite of." Consequently § 3 must be understood to mean that an indictment may be filed "in spite of" a prior removal or impeachment. It does violence to language to twist this into a requirement that an impeachment must precede indictment. The implication of "shall nevertheless be liable" to indictment is that the given party is already liable, that the words are merely designed to preserve existing criminal liability rather than to qualify it.[69] It would be unreasonable to attribute to the Framers an intention to insulate officers from criminal liability by mere appointment to office; like all men they are responsible under the law.[70] Thus Solicitor General Robert H. Bork concluded in a brief designed to demonstrate that Vice President Spiro Agnew could be indicted before he was impeached: "[A] civil officer could be both impeached and criminally punished even absent the Article I, Section 3 proviso."[71]

Since Article II, § 4, provides without discrimination for the impeachment of the "President, Vice President and all civil officers," Mr. Bork's statement should be equally applicable to the President. Furthermore, after impeachment and removal the President is returned to the body of the citizenry.[72] No special dispensation is required to allow prosecution of a citizen; nor is there a scrap of evidence that the Framers were minded to clothe an ex-President in any immunity whatsoever. On the contrary, immunity was denied to him as President. It follows that the President is criminally triable while in office, because no special provision is required for trial of an ex-President. An interpretation of the saving clause that makes the President triable only *after* removal from office would therefore reduce the clause to "mere surplusage,"[73] unless we adopt an alternative—that it was designed solely to foreclose the argument of double jeopardy.

Solicitor General Bork justly concluded, as did Justice Story 140 years ago,[74] that the "sole purpose" of the Article I, § 3 "indictment" proviso "is to preclude the argument that the doctrine of double jeopardy saves the offender from the second trial."[75] That danger arose from the English practice, wherein criminal punishment and removal were wedded in one proceeding; hence it was the part of caution to ward off an inference that a prior impeachment would constitute a bar to indictment. With Solicitor General Bork, I would conclude that the "nevertheless . . . subject to indictment" clause was not designed "to establish the sequence of the two processes, but solely to establish [that a prior conviction upon impeachment] does not raise a double jeopardy defense in a criminal trial."[76] So viewed, the "nevertheless" clause seeks to *preserve* the right to a subsequent criminal prosecution, not to prescribe that it must be preceded by impeachment. Justice Miller's statement in *Langford v. United States* that "the ministers personally, like our President, may be

---

[69]*See* discussion of double jeopardy *infra*.

[70]"[N]o officer of the law may set that law at defiance with impunity. All the officers of government, from the highest to the lowest . . . are bound to obey it." United States v. Lee, 106 U.S. 196, 220 (1882). *See* note 84 *infra*.

[71]Memorandum for the United States at 10n.**, Application of Spiro T. Agnew, Civil No. 73-965 (D. Md.) (memorandum filed Oct. 5, 1973, concerning the Vice President's claim of constitutional immunity, prepared by Solicitor General Robert H. Bork) [hereinafter cited as Bork].

[72]As Chief Justice Marshall stated, he "is elected from the mass of the people" and "returns to the mass of the people." 1 D. ROBERTSON, *supra* note 24, at 181.

[73]Cohens v. Virginia, 19 U.S. (6 Wheat.) 264, 394 (1821). Chief Justice Marshall added, "This cannot, therefore, be the true construction of the article."

[74]1 J. STORY, COMMENTARIES ON THE CONSTITUTION OF THE UNITED STATES § 782 (5th ed. 1905).

[75]Bork, *supra* note 71, at 8.

[76]*Id.* at 10. Mr. Bork properly points out that "impeachment and the criminal process serve different ends so that the outcome of one has no legal effect upon the outcome of the other," a conclusion justly rested on James Wilson:

Impeachments . . . come not . . . within the sphere of ordinary jurisprudence. They are founded on different principles; are governed by different maxims, and are directed to different objects; for this reason, the trial and punishment of an offense in the impeachment, is no bar to a trial of the same offense at common [criminal] law.

Bork, *supra* note 71, at 8–9, *citing* 1 J. WILSON, WORKS 324 (R. McCloskey ed. 1967).

impeached; or if the wrong amounts to a crime, they may be indicted"[77] likewise rebuts insistence that indictment must follow after impeachment.

This conclusion is further buttressed by other factors. "The only explicit immunity in the Constitution," said Solicitor General Bork, "is the limited immunity granted Congressmen"[78] in Article I, § 6, which provides:

The Senators and Representatives . . . shall in all cases, except treason, felony or breach of the peace, be privileged from arrest during their attendance at the session of their respective Houses, and in going to and returning from the same.

In the words of Mr. Bork:

Since the Framers knew how to, and did, spell out immunity, the natural inference is that no immunity exists where none is mentioned.[79]

The Supreme Court has employed that principle of construction.[80] Not only is this the "natural inference," but we have the testimony of Charles Pinckney, one of the most active participants in the Constitutional Convention, who, in explaining the Constitution to the South Carolina Ratification Convention, stated that no immunity for the President was intended. Speaking in the Senate in 1800, Pinckney said that "it never was intended to give Congress . . . any but specified [privileges], and those very limited privileges indeed."[81] And addressing himself to certain privileges under discussion, he stated, "No privilege of this kind was intended for your Executive, nor any except which I have mentioned for your Legislature. The Convention . . . well knew that . . . no subject had been more abused than privilege. They therefore determined to set the example, in merely limiting privilege to what was necessary, and no more."[82] James Wilson, considered by Washington "to be one of the strongest men in the Convention,"[83] assured the Pennsylvania Ratification Convention that "not a *single privilege* is annexed to his [the President's] character."[84] Remarks such as these were a response to the pervasive distrust of executive power.[85] Nothing in

Bork, at 11, also cites cases in state courts that reached a similar conclusion under constitutional provisions modeled on Article I, § 3, such as Commonwealth v. Rowe, 112 Ky. 482, 66 S.W. 29 (1902); State v. Jefferson,, 90 N.J.L. 507, 101 A. 569 (Ct. Err. & App. 1917). In addition, Bork, at 16n., points to United States v. Kerner (involving an indictment and conviction of Circuit Judge Otto Kerner prior to impeachment) then pending in the 7th Circuit and since decided in favor of the Department of Justice position that such a judge is a subject of indictment and conviction prior to impeachment and removal. N.Y. Times, Feb. 21, 1974, at 6, col. 1. To this may be added that Justice William Rehnquist, then Assistant Attorney General, Office of Legal Counsel, advised Attorney General John Mitchell that the United States could prosecute Justice Abe Fortas without waiting on impeachment. Keeffe, *Explorations in the Wonderland of Impeachment*, 59 A.B.A.J. 885, 886 (1973).

[77]101 U.S. 341, 343 (1879).

[78]Bork, *supra* note 71, at 4.

[79]*Id.* at 5.

[80]*See, e.g.,* T.I.M.E., Inc. v. United States, 359 U.S. 464, 471 (1959): "We find it impossible to impute to Congress an intention to give such a right to shippers under the Motor Carriers Act when the very sections which established that right in Part I [for railroads] were wholly omitted in the Motor Carriers Act."

[81]10 ANNALS OF CONG. 72 (1800).

[82]*Id.* at 74. In the course of his remarks, Pinckney addressed himself to the questions "why the Constitution should have been so attentive to each branch of Congress . . . and have shown so little to the President . . . in this respect. Why should the individual members of either branch . . . have more privileges than him *[sic]*." *Id.* Thus the withholding of presidential immunity was no oversight; it was intentional. The explanation lies in history cited by the Supreme Court. *See* p. 48. *infra.*

[83]M. FARRAND, THE FRAMING OF THE CONSTITUTION 21 (1913).

[84]2 J. ELLIOT, DEBATES IN THE SEVERAL STATE CONVENTIONS ON THE ADOPTION OF THE FEDERAL CONSTITUTION 480 (1836). In his Lectures of 1791, James Wilson, a Justice of the Supreme Court, rephrased this as follows: "[T]he most powerful magistrates should be amenable to the law. . . . No one should be secure while he violates the constitution and the laws." 1 J. WILSON, *supra* note 76, at 425.

[85]R. BERGER, EXECUTIVE PRIVILEGE: A CONSTITUTIONAL MYTH 49–50, 52–53 (1974). Hamilton was constrained to rebut

the prior English practice, with which the Framers were familiar,[86] suggests a requirement that impeachment had to precede indictment. On several occasions the Parliament preferred to refer the case to the courts; and one of the most learned lawyers in Parliament, Sir John Maynard, said of the charges against Sir Adam Blair: "I would not go before the Lords, when the law is clear, and may be tried by juries."[87] Constitutional history therefore confirms the inference properly drawn from the face of the Constitution that no immunity was given to the President.

By a feat of legerdemain Mr. Bork would read the President out of this history. He recognizes that the impeachment debate "related almost exclusively to the Presidency" and that "the impeachment clause was expanded to cover the Vice President and other civil officers only toward the very end of the Convention."[88] Mr. Bork's view presents the anomaly that the history of the impeachment provision, framed entirely in the context of the President, refers only to the "Vice President and all civil officers," who were virtually unmentioned and were added as a last-minute afterthought. Thus a provision the "sole purpose" of which was to forfend the double jeopardy argument, which was not designed "to establish the sequence" of impeachment or indictment, and which is accompanied by an "immunity" provision limited to Congress (without immunity for felonies) so that "the natural inference is that no immunity exists where none is intended," suddenly is found to establish precisely that "sequence" and to confer exactly that un-"natural" immunity on the President. When we emerge from Bork's elaborate argument that the President must be impeached before he is indicted, it adds up to a claim of immunity from criminal prosecution that was denied him. On what grounds is this analytical somersault justified?

Mr. Bork first states that the Framers' "remarks strongly suggest an understanding that the President, as Chief Executive, would not be subject to the ordinary criminal process. . . . For example . . . Gouverneur Morris observed that the Supreme Court would 'try the President after the trial of the impeachment.' "[89] That this is ill-considered shorthand emerges from the reference to a trial by the Supreme Court, which can only hear an appeal. Bork also cites Hamilton for the assertion that "the Framers' discussion assumed that impeachment would precede criminal trial."[90] Hamilton's participation in the Convention was sporadic and had little, if any, influence.[91] At the close of the Convention he handed Madison a plan in which he proposed that the President be impeached and removed and "be afterwards tried and punished."[92] So far as the records show, it was not considered by the Convention. The Framers were fastidious draftsmen, keenly alive to the weight of every word.[93] They employed neither "after" nor "afterwards";[94] and it is not for us

---

attacks upon grants to the President by those who, "[c]alculating upon the aversion of the people to monarchy," portrayed the President "as the full-grown progeny of that detested parent." THE FEDERALIST No. 68, at 448 (Mod. Lib. ed. 1937) (A. Hamilton).

[86]R. BERGER, supra note 68, at 328 (See pages cited under heading "Founders."). Compare id. at 70, with id. at 89; and see id. at 171 n.217.

[87]Id. at 49.

[88]Bork, supra note 71, at 6–7.

[89]Bork, supra note 71, at 6, citing 2 M. FARRAND, THE RECORDS OF THE FEDERAL CONVENTION OF 1787, at 500 (1911) [hereinafter cited as FARRAND].

[90]Bork, supra note 71, at 17. Another citation by Bork, at 6, is to 2 FARRAND 64–69, 626. Nothing relevant to the impeachment-indictment sequence is contained in those pages.

[91]J. MILLER, ALEXANDER HAMILTON: PORTRAIT IN PARADOX 174–76, 178 (1959).

[92]3 FARRAND, supra note 89, at 617, 625.

[93]Compare their rejection of "high misdemeanor" because it has a "technical meaning too limited" and the substitution of "high crimes and misdemeanors" for "mal-administration." R. BERGER, supra note 68, at 74. As was said by Chief Justice Taney: "[N]o word was unnecessarily used, or needlessly added. . . . Every word appears to have been weighed with the utmost deliberation, and its force and effect to have been fully understood." Holmes v. Jennison, 39 U.S. (14 Pet.) 540, 571 (1840).

[94]Compare Hamilton's suggestion that on impeachment the President be suspended until judgment, 3 FARRAND, supra note 89, at 617, 625, with the rejection of such a motion made by Morris and Rutledge. 2 FARRAND 612. When Hamilton

to supply a word thus omitted, to convert "nevertheless" (in spite of) into "afterward," that is, to transform a nonsequential provision into a prescribed sequence. Nor can the mistaken Morris-Hamilton versions of the provision be read to create the very immunity that the Framers intentionally withheld from the President when they squarely faced the issue. The § 3 proviso must be read together with the immunity provision; if possible both should be given effect.[95] Above all, we "cannot rightly prefer" a meaning "which will defeat rather than effectuate the Constitutional purpose."[96]

If, however, the remarks of Morris and Hamilton are to override this withholding of immunity, they no less demand that the "Vice President and all civil officers" likewise first be impeached and then indicted. Mr. Bork's anticipatory answer was that "[i]t is, of course, significant that such remarks referred only to the President, not to the Vice President and other civil officers."[97] How could it be otherwise when the President was the sole object of discussion? There was no allusion to impeachment of the others until the end when the "Vice President and all civil officers" were casually added to the impeachment provision without discussion.[98] As Bork himself has stated, "[N]one of the general debates addressed or considered the particular nature of the powers [or immunities] of the Vice President or other civil officers."[99] How then could the Framers consider the denial to them of an immunity allegedly granted to the President? The fact is that all the history cited by Mr. Bork to establish the prior indictability of the Vice President had reference to the President alone and establishes *his* prior indictability.

After his bow to history, Mr. Bork turns to the structure of the Constitution, wherein he finds "embedded" reasons for drawing the distinction between the President and the others.[100] No such distinction was, of course, drawn by the Founders; it is the product of presidential counsel 185 years after the event. In a nutshell, Bork rings the changes on "the singular importance of the President."[101] The crucial nature of the President's executive responsibilities, on which Mr. Bork lays such great store, played no role in the impeachment debate. Instead, opponents of impeachment urged that it would invade the President's "independence" and violate the separation of powers,[102] a central principle from which the Framers proceeded. The felt necessity for a curb on presidential transgressions, however, overcame this "independence" argument; despite the "crucial nature" of his powers, the Framers gave Congress power to oust him for various noncriminal offenses.[103] They made no move to interfere with the normal criminal process that applied to every

stated in THE FEDERALIST No. 69, *supra* note 85, at 446, that "[t]he President would be liable [in impeachment] and would afterwards be liable to [criminal] prosecution," he was referring to his own plan rather than a faithful rendition of Article I, § 3.

[95]For the appropriate rule of construction, *see, e.g.,* United States v. Menasche, 348 U.S. 528, 538–39 (1955); *cf.* Fisher v. District of Columbia, 164 F.2d 707, 708–09 (D.C. Cir. 1948).

[96]United States v. Classic, 313 U.S. 299, 316 (1941).

[97]Bork, *supra* note 71, at 6.

[98]R. BERGER, *supra* note 68, at 146–47.

[99]Bork 7.

[100]*Id.*

[101]*Id.* at 18.

[102]Rufus King referred "to the primitive axiom that the three great departments of Govts. should be separate & independent," and asked, "Would this be the case if the Executive should be impeachable?" 2 FARRAND, *supra* note 89, at 66. Charles Pinckney stated that impeachment by the Legislature would give it "a rod over the Executive and by that means effectually destroy his independence." *Id.*

[103]George Mason, expressing the view that prevailed, stated, "No point is of more importance than that the right of impeachment should be continued." *Id.* at 65. Edmund Randolph stated, "The Executive will have great opportunity for abusing his power." *Id.* at 67. *See also* the remarks of James Madison and Elbridge Gerry. *Id.* at 66. The vote was 8 to 2 in favor of retaining the impeachment power. *Id.* at 69. For a discussion of noncriminal offenses, see R. BERGER, *supra* note 68, at 53–93.

person; on the contrary, they withheld from him an immunity from criminal prosecution that, but for felonies, they expressly conferred upon Congress.

"This limited grant of immunity" to Congress, Bork explains, "demonstrates a recognition that, although the functions of the legislature are not lightly to be interfered with, the public interest in the expeditious and even-handed administration of the criminal law outweighs the cost imposed by the incapacity of a single legislator. Such incapacity does not seriously impair the functioning of Congress."[104] A very different conclusion needs to be drawn from the fact that "a limited grant of immunity" was conferred upon members of Congress, whereas none whatever was given to the President: The President was not nearly as "important" in the eyes of the Framers as he is in those of Bork. "There is little doubt," said the Supreme Court, "that the instigation of criminal charges against the critical or disfavored legislators by the executive in a judicial forum ['the judges were often lackeys of the Stuart monarchs'[105]] was the chief fear prompting the long struggle for parliamentary privilege in England."[106] Both the "speech and debate" clause and the "immunity from arrest" clause were "consciously" drawn by the Framers "from this common historical background,"[107] which bespeaks fear of rather than special solicitude for executive power. Moreover, the Founders had observed that the most powerful ministers could be condemned to death without endangering the continuity of government, indeed, in the case of the Earl of Strafford, conducing to the preservation of liberty.[108] It is no answer to point to the invulnerability of the King because first, as Gouverneur Morris pointed out, "[the first Magistrate] is not the King but the Prime-Minister,"[109] and second, as James Iredell emphasized, the President, unlike the King, was made triable.[110]

A kindred speculation is that "[t]he Framers could not have contemplated prosecution of an incumbent President because they vested in him complete power over execution of the laws, which includes, of course, the power to control prosecutions."[111] When President Nixon acted on this premise and discharged Special Prosecutor Archibald Cox, who was engaged, among other things, in investigating whether the President was implicated in the Watergate coverup and other criminal acts, a storm of outrage swept over the White House.[112] It is reasonable to infer that the Framers never intended to permit the President to shield himself from criminal indictment by the control given him over such prosecutions. Next Mr. Bork argues that the presidential pardoning power extends to a pardon for himself, thus rendering criminal conviction ineffectual.[113] Such a pardon after conviction would be an even greater affront to the nation than Nixon's discharge of Cox to impede his own prosecution. The "pardon" provision must be read in harmony with the "immunity" provision; it was not designed to confer an immunity intentionally withheld.[114] Constitutional construction should not depart from common sense;[115] it should not proceed from

---

[104]Bork, *supra* note 71, at 16.

[105]United States v. Johnson, 383 U.S. 169, 181 (1966).

[106]*Id.* at 182. *See also id.* at 178.

[107]K. BRADSHAW & D. PRING, PARLIAMENT AND CONGRESS 95 (1972).

[108]R. BERGER, *supra* note 68, at 30–33, 39.

[109]2 FARRAND, *supra* note 89, at 69.

[110]4 J. ELLIOT, *supra* note 84, at 109.

[111]Bork, *supra* note 71, at 20.

[112]The discharge was held illegal by District Judge Gerhard Gesell. Nader v. Bork, 366 F.Supp. 104 (D.D.C. 1973).

[113]Bork, *supra* note 71, at 20.

[114]In *Ex parte* Grossman, 267 U.S. 87, 121 (1925), the Court said that the pardoning power "is a check entrusted to the executive for special cases. To exercise it to the extent of destroying the deterrent effect of judicial punishment would be to pervert it; but whoever is to make it useful must have full discretion to exercise it. Our Constitution confers this discretion on the highest officer in the nation in confidence that he will not abuse it." An abuse "would suggest a resort to impeachment. . . ."

[115]A respected scholar and judge, Herbert F. Goodrich, stated that "[i]f a legal rule fails to satisfy the untechnical

horribles that the nation would reject and that would have even more greatly affronted the Founders.

Like Solicitor General Bork, Professor Alexander Bickel declares that the Article I, § 3 provision "does not remotely say that impeachment must precede indictment" and like him he considers that the "case of the President . . . is unique." He does not base this on the "original intention" but on the premise that "[i]n the presidency is embodied the continuity and indestructibility of the state."[116] He would thereby import into our system the monarchical notion that the continuity of the state was embodied in the crown: *"L'Etat c'est moi."*[117] But by the eighteenth century, Parliament had prevailed in its struggle with the King; and the downfalls of Charles I and James II had shown that the indestructibility of a King was not synonymous with the "indestructibility of the state." For Blackstone the "sovereign power" meant "the making of the laws"; it had come to rest in Parliament, "this being the place where that absolute despotic power, which must in all governments reside somewhere, is entrusted by the constitution of these kingdoms."[118] Therefore, if we are to look to the history the Founders had before them, the Parliament rather than the King was the repository of sovereignty, the symbol of "continuity." Among the revolutionary changes made by the Founders was to establish that sovereignty resided in the people and that the officers of government were merely their servants and agents.[119] In the words of Gouverneur Morris, "[T]he people are the King."[120] Presidents come and go but the people remain. The consensus of the Founders was that the President's main function was to execute the laws, that as commander in chief he was merely the "first General."[121] Such functionaries are expendable rather than indispensable; thus the view of the President taken by the Framers is incompatible with the proposition that in him the Framers "embodied the continuity and indestructibility of the state." The fact that they made him removable from office alone suggests that a hiatus in his office was not thought to threaten that "indestructibility." This also emerges from Hamilton's statement about the King: There is "no punishment to which he can be subjected without involving the crisis of a national revolution,"[122] implying thereby that removal or indictment of the President could have no calamitous effect.

The nation has also survived a number of presidential deaths and assassinations without impairment of the presidency or the "indestructibility of the state." It is a mistake, I suggest, to identify the "continuity" of the presidency with that of a given President. Whatever befalls a President, the state and the presidency are "indestructible."[123] The fact is that a Vice President is immediately available to assume executive functions without skipping a beat; and if he is unavailable there is

requirements of ordinary common sense the premises behind the rule had better be carefully examined." Gavin v. Hudson & Manhattan Co., 185 F.2d 104, 105–06 (3d Cir. 1950).

[116]Bickel, *The Constitutional Tangle,* THE NEW REPUBLIC, Oct. 6, 1973, at 14, 15.

[117]Gibbon says of Rome that "the obsequious civilians unanimously pronounced that the republic is contained in the person of its chief." 4 E. GIBBON, THE HISTORY OF THE DECLINE AND FALL OF THE ROMAN EMPIRE 509 (Nottingham Soc'y ed. undated). A current illustration is furnished by the statement of Emperor Haile Selassie of Ethiopia on March 11, 1974, albeit with recognition of the winds of change: "[W]hile the monarchy was a durable institution needed to hold Ethiopia together, its once overwhelming political power was not 'eternal' and could be varied according to the requirements and exigencies of the times." N.Y. Times, Mar. 12, 1974, at 13, col. 1.

[118]1 W. BLACKSTONE, COMMENTARIES ON THE LAW OF ENGLAND 49, 160–61 (1765).

[119]R. BERGER, CONGRESS V. THE SUPREME COURT 174–75 (1969). *See also* G. WOOD, THE CREATION OF THE AMERICAN REPUBLIC, 1776–1787, at 362, 377, 382, 530 (1969).

[120]2 FARRAND, *supra* note 89, at 69.

[121]R. BERGER, *supra* note 85, at 51–52, 61–63.

[122]THE FEDERALIST No. 69, *supra note 85,* at 446.

[123]In the words of Arthur Schlesinger, Jr.: "The Presidency, though its wings could be clipped for a time, was an exceedingly tough institution. . . . It had endured many challenges and survived many vicissitudes. It was nonsense to suppose that its fate as an institution was bound up with the fate of the particular man who happened to be President at any given time." A. SCHLESINGER, JR., THE IMPERIAL PRESIDENCY 405 (1973).

a row of statutory successors. William Henry Harrison died and was succeeded by John Tyler, James A. Garfield by Chester A. Arthur, Warren G. Harding by Calvin Coolidge, and Franklin D. Roosevelt by Harry Truman. Upon assassination, Lincoln was succeeded by Andrew Johnson, William McKinley by Theodore Roosevelt, and John F. Kennedy by Lyndon B. Johnson. One may hazard that Tyler was an improvement on Harrison; certainly Theodore Roosevelt was an improvement on McKinley, as was Coolidge on Harding; Truman was at least an adequate substitute for an ailing and sinking Franklin Roosevelt. That is not a bad list to pit against the unfortunate succession of Andrew Johnson to the chair of Abraham Lincoln. A senseless assassination creates a shock for which the nation is utterly unprepared, in contrast to a removal on impeachment or conviction on indictment of a President in whom the nation has lost confidence.

Obviously, Professor Bickel states, "the presidency cannot be conducted from jail, nor can it be effectively carried on while an incumbent is defending himself in a criminal trial."[124] The second proposition is by no means obvious; Andrew Johnson did not personally participate in his impeachment and he continued to perform the duties of his office.[125] A President equally may entrust his defense in a criminal trial to his counsel. If he feels constrained to be present, that is no more disturbing to the performance of his duties than his parallel presence at an impeachment trial; in either case the effect on his functioning is the same. While it is true that the presidency "cannot be conducted from jail," it is unrealistic to postulate that a convicted President could not be released on bail pending appeal. Moreover, the attempt of a convicted President to hang on to his office would present a spectacle that the nation would find intolerable. A storm of public outrage such as would make the "firestorm" after the Cox discharge seem like a sputtering candle could sweep him from office. If the President lacked the sensitivity to resign,[126] an impeachment could speedily follow; the most partisan congressman would hardly summon the hardihood to reject the verdict of the people. The test of the availability of criminal process, I suggest, should not turn on hypotheticals that strain credulity. "[O]f what value," said Macaulay, "is a theory which is true only on a supposition in the highest degree extravagant?"[127]

There is a last practical consideration, which Solicitor General Bork summarized in the context of "civil officers":

> [I]f Article I, Section 3, clause 7, were read to mean that no one not convicted upon impeachment could be tried criminally, the failure of the House to vote an impeachment, or the failure of the impeachment in the Senate, would confer upon the civil officer accused complete and—were the statute of limitations permitted to run—permanent immunity from criminal prosecution however plain his guilt.[128]

That would be no less true of the President. No great stretch of the imagination is required to conceive that partisanship in Congress may defeat an impeachment of the President in the House or conviction by two-thirds of the Senate. Suppose that Special Prosecutor Leon Jaworski were convinced that he had evidence that would establish the President's guilt. Although a partisan one-third of the Senate might differ, can it be reasonable that he should be barred from prosecution because an impeachment fell prey to partisanship?

A mistake against which we must be ever vigilant is to read our own predilections back into the minds of the Framers.[129] One of the most eminent of the Founders, James Iredell, later a Justice of the Supreme Court, cautioned:

[124]*See* Bickel, *supra* note 116, at 15.

[125]The Framers rejected suspension prior to conviction. *See* note 94 *supra.*

[126]Vice President Spiro Agnew resigned after indictment and before trial, explaining in part that the welfare of the nation would thereby be served. N.Y. Times, Oct. 11, 1973, at 35, col. 3.

[127]2 T. Macaulay, Critical and Historical Essays 128 (1980).

[128]Bork, *supra* note 71, at 9–10.

[129]Compare Justice Sutherland on "sovereignty" in United States v. Curtiss-Wright Export Corp., 299 U.S. 304 (1936), *discussed in* Berger, *The Presidential Monopoly of Foreign Relations,* 71 Mich. L. Rev. 1, 26–33 (1972).

We are too apt, in estimating a law passed at a remote period, to combine, in our consideration, all the subsequent events which have had an influence upon it, instead of confining ourselves (which we ought to do) to the existing circumstances at the time of its passing.[130]

These are not merely the yearnings of a legalistic "strict constructionist"; they are a canon of historiography. The task of the historian, Ranke taught, is to establish the facts of history *wie es eigentlich gewesen war*; the search must be for what actually happened and, if we find it, not to substitute for it what should have happened. As in the task of construing any document, the primary function is to ascertain the intention of the draftsmen. When that intention is discovered, what Iredell said becomes of prime importance: "The people have chosen to be governed under such and such principles. They have not chosen to be governed, or promised to submit upon any other."[131]

It is easier, however, to preach such vigilance than to practice it, as I can testify from personal experience in the very context of the distinction here under discussion. Influenced by the difficulty of giving the words "high crimes and misdemeanors" a narrow construction in the case of the President and a broad one for judges, I initially concluded that they must be given a single meaning. But I was led to alter my view upon consideration of the fact that judges were added to the impeachment provision at the last minute with no reference either to judges or to governing standards. From this and other data I reasoned that stricter standards of conduct might be required of a judge, that is, that the range of impeachable offenses might be broader.[132] Whatever the validity of that reasoning, it cannot be invoked for the President, who was the subject of the debates and the constitutional restrictions; a broader application of those restrictions to judges does not warrant a total immunity from criminal prosecution for the President. Sensible, however, of the "difficulties involved in adoption of the view that impeachment of judges requires a less restricted reading of those words [high crimes and misdemeanors] than does that of the President," I suggested that "[p]erhaps a better solution is to take a more hospitable approach to removal of judges *by judges* for infractions of good behavior. . . ,"[133] indicating thereby that I entertained some doubts about my change of position.

The problem of giving two meanings to the same words in the very same context has continued to trouble me, the more so as I examined the difficulties which Mr. Bork's analysis engendered, his attempt to render utterances exclusively directed at the President applicable solely to "the Vice President and all civil officers," who were not mentioned. My thinking has reverted to my initial view, additionally influenced by the statement of the Supreme Court in *Atlantic Cleaners & Dyers v. United States:* "[T]here is a natural presumption that identical words used in different parts of the same act are intended to have the same meaning . . ."[134] Here the presumption is fortified by the fact that the words are used not in different parts of the Constitution but in one place, in the very same context; and Mr. Bork seeks to give them a different meaning with respect to whom they apply. No trace of an intention to give them that dual meaning is to be found in the history of the provision. This is not to say that the presumption is irrebuttable,[135] but that the

---

[130]Ware v. Hylton, 3 U.S. (3 Dall.) 199, 267 (1796). *See* R. BERGER, *supra* note 119, at 22–23.

[131]2 G. McREE, LIFE AND CORRESPONDENCE OF JAMES IREDELL 146 (1857–1858).

[132]R. BERGER, *supra* note 68, at 91–93.

[133]*Id.* at 93.

[134]286 U.S. 427, 433 (1932).

[135]The Court stated,

Where the subject matter [impeachment] to which the words refer is not the same in the several places where they are used, or the conditions are different, or the scope of the legislative power exercised in one case is broader than that exercised in another, the meaning may well vary to meet the purposes of the law, to be arrived at by a consideration of the language in which those purposes are expressed, and of the circumstances under which the language was employed.

Id.

rebuttal cannot rest on factors that were not before the Framers, on an image of the presidency which is a product of our times and which they emphatically did not share.

Such distinctions represent but another attempt to revise the Constitution under the guise of euphemisms, derived from an exalted notion of the presidency which is far removed from the egalitarian sentiments of the Founders.[136] When the subpoena to Jefferson issued, Albert Beveridge, who had scoured the newspapers of the time, comments "For the first time, most Republicans approved of the opinion of John Marshall. In the fanatical politics of the time there was enough honest adherence to the American ideal, that all men are equal in the eyes of the law, to justify the calling of a President, even Thomas Jefferson, before a court of justice."[137] It is we who have surrounded the President with a mystique that has contributed heavily to an "imperial presidency."[138] When we forget that the President is "but a man . . . but a citizen"[139] we are on the road that has unfailingly led to Caesarism. It was because the Founders had learned this lesson from history that presidential powers were enumerated and limited, and that immunity from arrest was altogether withheld.

III. IMPEACHMENT: MR. ST. CLAIR'S "INSTANT HISTORY"

If the House "be found incompetent to one of the greatest [causes] . . . it is impossible that this form of trial should not, in the end, vanish out of the constitution. For we must not deceive ourselves: whatever does not stand with credit cannot stand long. And if the constitution should be deprived . . . of this resource, it is virtually deprived of everything else, that is valuable in it. For this process is the cement which binds the whole together . . . here it is that we provide for that, which is the substantial excellence of our constitution . . . by which. . . . no man in no circumstance, can escape the account, which he owes to the laws of his country."[140]

When a client proclaims that he will "fight like hell" to balk impeachment it may be expected that his lawyer will follow suit. Not surprisingly, therefore, James St. Clair, chief defense counsel for President Nixon, has favored the House Judiciary Committee with a lengthy memorandum that purports to prove by recourse to history that the President may only be impeached for an indictable crime.[141] That standard would virtually nullify impeachment for the nonindictable offenses which were the chief concern of the Founders and which the evidence plainly shows they considered impeachable. Despite its issuance from the august precincts of the White House, the memorandum is but "lawyer's history," a pastiche of selected snippets and half-truths, exhibiting a resolute disregard of adverse facts, and simply designed to serve the best interests of a client rather than faithfully to represent history as it actually was.

Although defense lawyers are notoriously not the best source of constitutional history,[142] such

---

[136]. *See* 1 *supra.* Herbert Butterfield, who has considered the problems of historiography in his penetrating study, *George III and the Historians* (rev. ed. 1969), remarked that "it is often necessary to know a great deal of history before one is equipped for the interpreting of historical documents." *Id.* at 18. This is more essential with respect to a constitution. *See* p. 51 *supra.*

[137]3 A. BEVERIDGE, LIFE OF JOHN MARSHALL 450 (1919).

[138]*See* A. SCHLESINGER, JR., *supra* note 123, at ix.

[139]1 T. CARPENTER, *supra* note 1, at 90.

[140]7 E. BURKE, WORKS 14 (1839) (Burke's opening statement at the trial of Warren Hastings).

[141]J. St. Clair, An Analysis of the Constitutional Standard for Presidential Impeachment, issued in late February, 1974 [hereinafter cited as St. Clair]. The memorandum consists of six pages of summary and a body of 61 pages.

[142]The value of such "history" is illuminated by the citation, St. Clair at 42–43, of the argument of Luther Martin on behalf of Justice Samuel Chase in 1805. Martin, a heavy drinker, appeared in 1810 before Justice Chase on circuit in Baltimore, somewhat more inebriated than usual. Chase complained, "I am surprised that you can so prostitute your talents." Martin replied, "Sir, I never prostituted my talents except when I defended you and Col. Burr;" and turning to the jury he added confidentially, "[A] couple of the greatest rascals in the world." P. CLARKSON & R. JETT, LUTHER MARTIN OF MARYLAND 280 (1970). *In vino veritas.*

pseudo-history cannot be ignored because, as J. R. Wiggins said of a similar submission by the then Deputy Attorney General William P. Rogers on the issue of executive privilege, "Unless historians bestir themselves . . . the lawyers' summary that has placed 170 years of history squarely behind the assertion of unlimited executive power to withhold information threatens to get incorporated into that collection of fixed beliefs and settled opinions that governs the conduct of affairs. History thereafter may become what lawyers mistakenly said it was therefore."[143] "Legal history," said Justice Frankfurter, "still has its claims."[144]

In the present controversial atmosphere it is all too easy to say "a plague on both your houses" and evenhandedly to attribute partisan readings of history to one and all. My study, however, of the meaning of "high crimes and misdemeanors," the central issue of impeachment, was undertaken in 1968–1970, submitted to the *Southern California Law Review* in mid-summer of 1970, and published in 1971,[145] long before Watergate surfaced and before there was any thought that President Nixon might be impeachable. Composed in the quiet of a university, uninfluenced by fees or hopes of preferment, my study may or may not be mistaken, but it can hardly be dismissed as biased, simply because there then was no occasion whatsoever for partisan bias.

A. Indictable Offenses

Let us begin in midstream with the Nixon-St. Clair thesis that impeachment is available only for an indictable crime. Former Attorney General Elliot L. Richardson recently stated, "It seems clear to me as a matter of common sense that impeachable offenses cannot be limited to matters defined in the U.S. Penal Code."[146] Common sense is buttressed by the historical record. Mr. St. Clair, quoting the Supreme Court, recognizes that under federal law there are no crimes except as declared by statute: "The legislative authority of the Union must first make an act a crime, affix a punishment to it. . . ."[147] That is what the Act of 1790 did for treason and bribery;[148] but with the exception of a handful of statutes, such as those that make "high misdemeanors" of privateering against friendly nations,[149] launching military expeditions against them from American soil,[150] practicing law by a federal judge,[151] conspiring or counseling to insurrection or riot,[152] there are

---

[143]Wiggins, *Lawyers as Judges of History,* 75 PROCEEDINGS MASS. HIST. SOCY' 84, 104 (1963).

[144]FPC v. Natural Gas Pipeline Co., 315 U.S. 575, 609 (1942) (concurring opinion).

[145]Berger, *Impeachment for 'High Crimes and Misdemeanors,'* 44 S. CAL. L. REV. 395 (1971).

[146]Harv. L. Record, Mar. 15, 1974, at 9.

[147]St. Clair, *supra* note 141, at 17, *quoting* United States v. Hudson & Goodwin, 11 U.S. (7 Cranch) 32 (1812).

[148]Act of Apr. 30, 1790, ch. 9, §§ 1, 21, 1 Stat. 112, 117.

Professor Jefferson Fordham states that "treason is defined as a crime by the Constitution in the judicial article with the element of sanction left to the Congress." Fordham, Book Review, 47 S. CAL. L. REV. 673, 676 (1974). The Supreme Court held that, to constitute a crime, it is necessary to "affix a punishment to proscribed conduct." United States v. Hudson & Goodwin, 11 U.S. (7 Cranch) 32 (1812). Had Congress elected not to "affix a punishment," treason would not have constituted a "crime"; no one could have been prosecuted for treason. By the Act of 1790, treason was made a crime; it will hardly be maintained that prior thereto treasonable acts were indictable. An unpunishable "crime" is like "a grin without a cat."

Since, as Fordham recognized, "the definition appears to be intended for all purposes, including impeachment," 47 S. CAL. L. REV. at 676, it cannot be *assumed* that impeachment for treason was criminal in nature. The fact that George Mason emphasized that "treason" as defined would not reach "subversion of the Constitution" and suggested "maladministration" which, to say the least, comprehended *some* acts of noncriminal nature, alone argues against such an assumption. *See* 2 FARRAND, *supra* note 89, at 550, *cited in* R. BERGER, *supra* note 68, at 86. The substitution of "high crimes and misdemeanors" for Mason's "maladministration" indicates that the association of "high crimes and misdemeanors" with "treason" was not thought to render "high crimes and misdemeanors" criminal for impeachment purposes.

[149]Act of June 14, 1797, ch. 1, § 1, 1 Stat. 520.

[150]Act of June 5, 1794, ch. 50, § 5, 1 Stat. 384.

[151]28 U.S.C. § 454 (1970).

[152]Act of June 5, 1794, ch. 50, § 1, 1 Stat. 381–82.

no indictable "high misdemeanors." Consequently, the offenses the Founders particularly had in mind would be unimpeachable. Consider "subversion of the Constitution"—usurpation of power, the very offense that prompted the addition of the words "high crimes and misdemeanors." George Mason said in the Federal Convention:

> Treason as defined in the Constitution will not reach many great and dangerous offenses. Hastings is not guilty of Treason. Attempts to subvert the Constitution may not be Treason as above defined. . . . It is the more necessary to extend the power of impeachments.[153]

Under Mr. St. Clair's interpretation the manifest intention of the Framers to reach such subversion would be frustrated by the lack of an indictable crime, for no federal statute has made it a crime. So too, other categories of "high crimes and misdemeanors," under the English practice upon which our impeachment provisions were modeled and which were mentioned by the Founders, such as "abuse of power," "betrayal of trust," and "neglect of duty," would also fall by the wayside. Yet Madison stated that protection against presidential "negligence" was indispensable, that perversion of the office "into a scheme of . . . oppression," that is, "abuse of power," should be impeachable.[154] Madison, C. C. Pinckney, and Gouverneur Morris referred to "betrayal of trust";[155] Edward Rutledge spoke of "abuse of trust," as did Hamilton in *The Federalist.*[156]

Madison, the leading architect of the Constitution, furnished three illustrations of impeachable offenses that have never been made indictable crimes: (1) In the Virginia Ratification Convention he stated that "if the President be connected, in any suspicious manner with any person, and there be grounds to believe that he will shelter him," he may be impeached.[157] (2) In the First Congress—that "almost adjourned session of the Convention"—he said that the President would be impeachable if he "neglects to superintend [his subordinates'] conduct, so as to check their excesses."[158] (3) There too he stated that "the wanton removal of meritorious officers" would be impeachable.[159] To this day all of these categories of "high crimes and misdemeanors" have not been made indictable crimes, reflecting a continuing judgment by Congress, which has the "sole" jurisdiction of impeachment, that indictable crimes are not a prerequisite to impeachment, as four convictions by the Senate for nonindictable offenses confirm.[160]

One hundred and forty years ago Justice Story pointed out that only treason and bribery were made indictable offenses by statute and that insistence on indictable crimes would enable impeachable offenders to escape scot-free and render the impeachment provisions "a complete nullity."[161] The absurdity of Mr. St. Clair's analysis is pointed up by his incongruous juxtaposition of the 1790 treason and bribery statutes. "Any person" could be indicted under the "treason" Act whereas the "bribery" Act was specifically directed against judges who had accepted bribes.[162] Even today it is open to question whether the bribery statute embraces the President.[163] Judicial bribery was not

---

[153] R. BERGER, *supra* note 68, at 86. Chapter 2 of my book incorporates the article cited in note 145 *supra.*

[154] R. BERGER, *supra* note 68, at 89.

[155] *Id.*

[156] THE FEDERALIST No. 65, *supra* note 85, at 423.

[157] R. BERGER, *supra* note 68, at 89.

[158] 1 ANNALS OF CONG. 372–73 (1789) (page running head "History of Congress").

[159] 1 ANNALS OF CONG. 498 (1789) (page running head "History of Congress").

[160] R. BERGER, *supra* note 68, at 57 n.15.

[161] *Id.* at 77. *See* 1 J. STORY, COMMENTARIES ON THE CONSTITUTION OF THE UNITED STATES §§ 796, 798 (5th ed. 1905). An earlier work, W. RAWLE, A VIEW OF THE CONSTITUTION 273 (2d ed. 1829), had come to the same conclusion.

[162] *See* note 148 *supra.*

[163] Members of Congress and officers of the United States were added by the Act of Feb. 26, 1853, ch. 81, § 6, 10 Stat. 171. Today, 18 U.S.C. § 201 (1970) covers "public official[s]," defined as "member[s] of Congress . . . or an officer or employee or person acting for or on behalf of the United States, or any department." Under the prior Act, an "officer of

mentioned in the Convention, but Gouverneur Morris emphasized that the President "may be bribed," and he instanced that "Charles II was bribed by Louis XIV"[164] and that therefore the President ought to be impeachable. Notwithstanding that the President was the only mentioned object of constitutional impeachment for "bribery," he would be unimpeachable on Mr. St. Clair's reasoning because the penal "bribery" statute was confined to judges. Nor can we take seriously Mr. St. Clair's argument that "high crimes and misdemeanors" must involve criminal "offenses of such a serious nature [as] to be akin to treason and bribery."[165] Treason and bribery are rank unequals. Treason is the arch offense—betrayal of the state to the enemy—whereas acceptance of so much as $50 as a bribe for favorable official action suffices to constitute bribery. Who would maintain that acceptance of such a petty bribe is more heinous than presidential usurpation or abuse of power?

It remains to add two Founders' statements that repel the equation of an impeachable offense with an indictable crime. After adverting to impeachment in the North Carolina Ratification Convention, James Iredell stated that "the person convicted is *further liable* to a trial at common law, and may receive such common-law [criminal] punishment as belongs to a description of such offenses, *if it be punishable by that law*."[166] In other words, an offense may be impeachable although it is not criminally punishable. Similar recognition is evidenced by George Nicholas' distinction in the Virginia Ratification Convention between disqualification from office and "further punishment if [the President] has committed such high crimes as are punishable at common law."[167] This clearly implies that some "high crimes" are not thus punishable and nevertheless impeachable. Finally, there is Hamilton's statement in *The Federalist* No. 65 that an impeachment proceeding "can never be tied down by such strict rules . . . as in common [criminal] cases [which] serve to limit the discretion of the courts in favor of personal security,"[168] an analysis which Department of Justice lawyers concede "cuts against the argument that 'high crimes and misdemeanors' should be limited to criminal offenses."[169] We can hardly prefer Mr. St. Clair to Hamilton, Madison, *et al.* as an expounder of the Framers' intention. That Mr. St. Clair can maintain against this background that we should "*uphold the intent of the drafters* of the Constitution that impeachable offenses be limited to criminal violations"[170] only illustrates to what lengths advocacy will go.

B. High Crimes and Misdemeanors

Mr. St. Clair belabors the fact that in England, where removal from office and criminal punishment were united in one and the same proceeding, impeachment was criminal in nature,[171] a fact no one would dispute, albeit the crime, as we shall see, was of a peculiar sort. He totally ignores the impact of a momentous departure from the prior English practice, embodied in Article I, § 3(7), the separation between removal and criminal proceedings:

the United States" was deemed one "appointed by the President . . . or the head of some executive department." United States v. Van Wert, 195 F. 974, 976 (N.D. Iowa 1912); *cf.* United States v. Germaine, 99 U.S. 508, 510 (1878); and under the maxim *noscitur et sociis* the words "employee or person" might similarly exclude the President.

[164]R. BERGER, *supra* note 68, at 89.

[165]St. Clair, *supra* note 141, at 34.

[166]R. BERGER, *supra* note 68, at 75 n.111 (emphasis added).

[167]*Id.* at 79. *See* note 184 *infra* for Hamilton's similar statement.

[168]THE FEDERALIST No. 65, *supra* note 85, at 425–26.

[169]Office of Legal Counsel, Dep't of Justice, Legal Aspects of Impeachment: An Overview, February 1974, at 14 [hereinafter cited as Justice Dep't Memorandum].

[170]St. Clair, *supra* note 141, at 38–39 (emphasis in original).

[171]*Id.* at 7, 10, 12, 13, 20, 26, 38. "To further reinforce the criminal nature of the process," says St. Clair, *id.* at 26–27, "an early draft provided that an impeachment was to be tried before the Supreme Court," as if the Court was to hear no civil cases. By the same reasoning, the subsequent transfer of the trial to the Senate should mark the offense as noncriminal.

Judgment in Cases of Impeachment shall not extend further than to removal . . . and disqualification to hold and enjoy any Office . . . but the Party convicted shall nevertheless be liable . . . to Indictment . . . and Punishment, according to Law.[172]

In other words, if criminal law covered the offense, it would be indictable. Thus removal was to be a prophylactic measure, to remove an unfit man from office; criminal punishment was left to a separate proceeding. As Justice Story stated in 1830, impeachment "is not so much designed to punish an offender as to secure the state against gross official misdemeanors. . . . [I]t simply divests him of his political capacity,"[173] it removes and disqualifies him from office. Thus, in place of the combined English removal and criminal proceedings the Framers divorced the two, with consequences that James Wilson immediately perceived:

> Impeachments . . . come not . . . within the sphere of ordinary [*i.e.,* criminal] jurisprudence. They are founded on different principles; are governed by different maxims, and are directed to different objects; for this reason, the trial and punishment of an offense on impeachment, is no bar to a trial of the same offense at common law.[174]

When Mr. St. Clair emphasizes the criminal nature of impeachment in England, he overlooks that there it was part and parcel of a criminal proceeding. The separation of the two in our Constitution demands a construction of impeachment in noncriminal terms lest it fall afoul of other constitutional provisions.

First there is double jeopardy. Were impeachment criminal in nature, as Mr. St. Clair repeatedly stresses, a conviction or acquittal on impeachment would bar a criminal indictment and a prior conviction or acquittal on indictment would bar an impeachment, for no man can be tried twice for the same offense.[175] Both Wilson and Story were aware of the play of double jeopardy in the constitutional provision.[176] The Framers meant to have both impeachment and indictment available, not to put Congress to a choice between either one or the other. Mr. St. Clair says not a word of the impact on double jeopardy of the separation of removal from indictment, a matter set forth for Mr. St. Clair in my book, *Impeachment: The Constitutional Problems,* which he quotes when it fits his needs.[177] Another example of selective history in this same focus is his citation of the Article III, § 3(3) provision that "trial of all crimes except . . . impeachment shall be by jury" in order to demonstrate that impeachment was limited to "criminal matters."[178] He ignores the fact, which I had also pointed out, that, with this exception before them, the draftsmen of the Sixth Amendment omitted it and extended trial by jury to "all criminal proceedings." Presumably they felt no need to exempt impeachment from the Sixth Amendment because they did not consider it a criminal prosecution. If impeachment be indeed criminal in nature, as Mr. St. Clair maintains, it must be tried by jury, not by the Senate, because "all criminal proceedings" means *all,* particularly after the omission of the prior exception, and second, because the Bill of Rights modifies all prior provisions of the Constitution that are in conflict with it.[179]

Constitutional analysis need not depart from common sense;[180] the fact that the criteria of what were impeachable crimes in England were employed by the Framers to identify causes for removal from office does not serve to make removal criminal, as a familiar example will make clear. Suppose

[172]U.S. Const. art. I, § 3.

[173]R. Berger, *supra* note 68, at 79. *See* note 184 *infra.*

[174]*Id.* at 80.

[175]*Id.* at 80–81.

[176]*Id.;* 1 J. Story, *supra* note 161, § 782, *see* J. Wilson, *supra* note 76.

[177]St. Clair, *supra* note 141, at 3.

[178]*Id.* at 37–38.

[179]R. Berger, *supra* note 68, at 81–82.

[180]*See* note 115 *supra.*

that Jones runs a red light at 80 miles an hour and crashes into Smith, severely injuring Smith and destroying his car. Such reckless driving constitutes a criminal offense, but that does not convert a civil suit to recover damages on those facts into a criminal proceeding. The difference was appreciated by Solicitor General Bork, who pointed out that "just as an individual may be both criminally prosecuted and deported for the same offense . . . a civil officer could be both impeached and criminally punished. . . ."[181] Deportation, the Supreme Court held, "is not punishment for a crime. . . . It is but a method of enforcing the return to his country of an alien who has not complied with the conditions" laid down for his residence,[182] exactly as impeachment is designed solely to remove an unfit officer for the good of the state. That criminal prosecution may also be had on the same grounds does not render either deportation or removal by impeachment criminal. Solicitor General Bork justly concluded that "conviction of impeachment under our Constitution has no criminal consequences," whereas "impeachment in England was designed to accomplish punishment as well as removal."[183] Without criminal penalties such as fine or imprisonment, and limited to removal of an unfit officer, impeachment cannot be criminal in nature.[184]

But, Mr. St. Clair argues, such terms as "convicted" and the like "are all terms limited in context to criminal matters."[185] This terminology was taken into account by me in 1970, and I suggested that the Framers, engaged in an immense task—the drafting of a written Constitution for a new nation in the short space of fourteen weeks—could not at each step undertake "to coin a fresh and different vocabulary." That would have involved an insuperable labor.[186] As the Department of Justice lawyers recognize, quoting Professor John Pomeroy's mid-19th century treatise, "The word is borrowed, the procedure is imitated, and no more; the object and end of the process are far different."[187] To give this borrowed terminology conclusive effect on the issue of criminality is to invite the application of double jeopardy and trial by jury rather than by the Senate, as well as to disregard all of the statements by the Founders that clearly demonstrate their intention to make nonindictable offenses impeachable, an intention that courts normally strive to effectuate. Were these conflicting pulls between terminology and "original intention" and the like to be posed to a court, it would attempt to balance them, not, like Mr. St. Clair's selective history, to avoid the inescapable task of weighing heavily countervailing factors.

More than a little confusion has resulted from the fact that the Constitution employs the words "high crimes and misdemeanors." The starting point is that "high crimes and misdemeanors" and ordinary "crimes and misdemeanors" are altogether different in meaning and origin. "High crimes and misdemeanors," which the historical evidence shows meant "high crimes and *high* misdemeanors," referred to offenses against the state, as the companion words "treason, bribery" indicate. Such offenses were triable by Parliament under the *Lex Parliamentaria* or law of Parliament. When the words were first employed in 1386 there was no such ordinary crime as "misdemeanor"; lesser crimes were then punishable as "trespasses." "Misdemeanors" supplanted "trespasses" early in the 16th century, and, as Fitzjames Stephen pointed out, they were proceedings for wrongs against the individual and were triable in the courts rather than in Parliament.[188] It is safe to say that "high crimes and misdemeanors" were words of art peculiar to parliamentary

---

[181]Bork, *supra* note 71, at 10n.**.

[182]R. BERGER, *supra* note 68, at 81.

[183]Bork, *supra* note 71, at 10n.**.

[184]Hamilton distinguished between "their removal from office" and "*their actual punishment* in cases which would admit of it." THE FEDERALIST No. 70, *supra* note 85, at 461 (emphasis added). He thus recognized, as did Iredell and Nicholas, that *some* impeachable offenses could not be punished criminally. *See* p. 55 *supra*.

[185]St. Clair, *supra* note 141, at 38.

[186]R. BERGER, *supra* note 68, at 85.

[187]Justice Dep't Memorandum, *supra* note 169, Appendix I at 24. *Compare* pp. 56–57 *supra*.

[188]J. STEVENS, THE CRIMINAL LAW OF ENGLAND 60 (1863) *cited in* R. BERGER, *supra* note 68, at 61.

impeachment[189] and had no relation to ordinary "crimes and misdemeanors" that were triable by the courts. "High misdemeanors," it may be added, never entered the criminal law administered by the English courts, nor were ordinary "misdemeanors" a criterion for impeachments.[190]

In the main, Mr. St. Clair accepts this analysis: He states that "high crimes and misdemeanors" "was *the standard phrase*" used in "*parliamentary impeachments*," "a unitary phrase *meaning crimes against the state, as opposed to those against individuals.*"[191] He agrees that the word "high" modifies both "crimes and misdemeanors," and "refers to official conduct, conduct relating to one's function with respect to the State."[192] But he repeatedly skitters from "high misdemeanor" to "misdemeanor"; he cites, for example, Blackstone's distinction between "crimes" and "smaller faults and omissions . . . termed misdemeanors," notwithstanding that Blackstone, as Mr. St. Clair notices, differentiated "high misdemeanors" as "high offenses against the King and government."[193] The Framers well understood that "high misdemeanors" had a "technical meaning too limited";[194] and intellectual honesty demands an end to such verbal play on "misdemeanor," an end to shifts from historical meaning to "its present day context," whereunder "the purpose of inclusion of the *word 'misdemeanor' is to include* lesser *criminal* offenses that are not felonies."[195] For the Framers undeniably borrowed "high misdemeanor" from the law of Parliament; they did not borrow "misdemeanor" from the "criminal" law of the courts. To glide from *their* meaning to the "modern context" and to a view that "misdemeanor" "include[s] lesser *criminal* offenses" is to revise the Constitution, the very thing Mr. St. Clair should most fear, lest it lead to the unbridled discretion not long since attributed to Congress by Vice President Gerald Ford and former Attorney General Kleindienst.[196]

---

[189]Justice Frankfurter stated, "Words of art bring their art with them. They bear the meaning of their habitat . . . whether it be loaded with recondite connotations of feudalism." Frankfurter, *Some Reflections on the Reading of Statutes,* 47 COLUM. L. REV. 527, 537 (1947). For the meaning of "high crimes and misdemeanors," *see* pp. 53–54 *supra.*

[190]R. BERGER, *supra* note 68, at 61–63.

[191]St. Clair, *supra* note 141, at 19 (emphasis in original).

[192]*Id.* at 25, 33. His explanation of "high" is rested on "modern usage," citing to the HOUSE JUDICIARY COMM., 93d CONG., 1st SESS., IMPEACHMENT: SELECTED MATERIALS 622 (Comm. Print 1973). The citation to page 622 is to a reprint of my 1971 article, at which point I was tracing the centuries-long development, culminating in Blackstone!

[193]St. Clair, *supra* note 141, at 21–22, 23. He neglected to notice Blackstone's statement in his discussion of "Misprisons . . . generally denominated *contempts* or *high misdemeanors;* of which 1. The first and principal is the *mal-administration* of such high officers, as are in public trust and employment. This is usually punished by the method of parliamentary impeachment. . . ." 4. W. BLACKSTONE, *supra* note 118, at 121 (emphasis in original). Contempts were punished by the respective tribunals against whom contemptuous conduct was proven, the courts or the Parliament. I recall no case in which Parliament turned to a court for punishment of a contempt against itself.

[194]R. BERGER, *supra* note 68, at 86.

[195]St. Clair, *supra* note 141, at 34 (emphasis in original). It is beside the point to say that "in *common parlance* a misdemeanor is considered a crime by lawyers, judges, defendants, and the general public," *id.* at 33, first, because a "high misdemeanor" is quite different from a "misdemeanor," and second, because the test of such a "technical" common law term is not present "common parlance" but what it meant to the Framers.

The language of the Constitution cannot be interpreted safely except by reference to the common law and British institutions as they were when the instrument was framed and adopted. The statesmen and lawyers of the Convention who submitted it to the ratification of the Conventions of the Thirteen States, were born and brought up in the atmosphere of the common law and thought and spoke in its vocabulary. . . . [T]hey expressed [their conclusions] in terms of the common law, confident that they could be shortly and easily understood.

Ex parte Grossman, 267 U.S. 87, 108 (1925); *cf.* United States v. Barnett, 376 U.S. 681, 688 (1964).

To import "high" by resort to history as a special species of crime and then to argue that the words " 'high crimes and misdemeanors' . . . are so clear and unequivocal in and of themselves" that it is not "necessary to look beyond the words," St. Clair, *supra* note 141, at 32, 38, indicates that the right hand knew not what the left was doing. This maneuver was designed to invoke the "plain meaning" rule, which once shut off extrinsic evidence, but which has been badly battered in the last fifty years. Wirtz v. Bottle Blowers Ass'n, 389 U.S. 463, 468 (1968); United States v. American Trucking Ass'ns, 310 U.S. 534, 543–44 (1940); Boston Sand & Gravel Co. v. United States, 278 U.S. 41, 48 (1928) (Holmes, J.).

[196]*See* R. BERGER, *supra* note 68, at 53; Wash. Star-News, Apr. 11, 1973, at A2, col. 1.

C. Mr. St. Clair's Theories

Mr. St. Clair does not attempt to deal with the constitutional separation between impeachment and indictment, the consequent problems of double jeopardy, trial by jury of "all criminal prosecutions," or the long-standing dichotomy between parliamentary trials of political "high misdemeanors" and court trials of criminal "misdemeanors," but he comes up with some far-fetched theories. He begins with the American "commitment to two central and interrelated ideas. The first is the theory of limited government and the second is the mechanism of separation of powers."[197]

Both President Nixon and Mr. St. Clair disregard the fact that the Framers adopted impeachment as *a breach* in the separation of powers. In the Federal Convention, Rufus King dwelt on the "primitive axiom that the three great departments of Govts. should be separate & independent. . . . Would this be the case if the Executive should be impeachable? . . . [It] would be destructive of his independence and of the principles of the Constitution."[198] Charles Pinckney likewise urged that it would "effectually destroy his independence."[199] But such views were decisively rejected by a vote of 8 to 2, because, as George Mason stressed, "[N]o point is of more importance than that the right of impeachment should be continued." Madison "thought it indispensable that some provision should be made for defending the Community against the incapacity, negligence or perfidy of the chief Magistrate." Impeachment was favored by Edmund Randolph because the "Executive will have great opportunity of abusing his power."[200] It was precisely to effectuate the limits on executive power embodied in the Constitution that impeachment was adopted. As Elias Boudinot, for years President of the Continental Congress, said in the First Congress, impeachment is an "exception to a principle," the separation of powers.[201] Commenting on Hamilton's statement that impeachments were regarded "as a bridle in the hands of the legislative body upon the executive servants. . . ."[202] Department of Justice lawyers state that Hamilton was "justifying the exceptions to the separation of powers found in the American provisions relating to impeachment."[203] The extraordinary spectacle now presented by presidential attempts to define the jurisdiction of the House Judiciary Committee and to limit its access to White House documents based on an invocation of the separation of powers stands history on its head. This invasion of the House's "sole" power to impeach, expressed in the Constitution, is more grotesque when it is compared to Mr. Nixon's strenuous claims of inviolable "confidentiality" of which the Constitution contains not a trace.

Mr. St. Clair muddies the waters when he cites James Iredell's 1786 statement that the North Carolina Constitution was not designed to fashion a legislative "despotism" but to "guard against the abuse of unlimited power."[204] First, in 1788 the Framers accomplished that purpose by a careful grant to Congress of enumerated and limited powers. And second, that Iredell himself believed that impeachment for nonindictable offenses was not identifiable with legislative "despotism" is evident in his reference to "impeachment for concealing important intelligence from

---

[197] St. Clair, *supra* note 141, at 2.

[198] *Id.* 2 FARRAND, *supra* note 89, at 66–67.

[199] Particularly disconcerting is St. Clair's non sequitur that that President "was, while President, unindictable by ordinary criminal process. This, of course, is why some members of the Constitutional Convention, Mr. Pinckney, for example, thought impeachment was wholly unnecessary." St. Clair, *supra* note 141, at 10. Pinckney explained to the Senate in 1800 that congressmen were given specific and very limited privileges (immunity from arrest) and none were given to the President. 10 ANNALS OF CONG. 72, 74 (1800). This ill comports with an attribution to him of presidential unindictability.

[200] 2 FARRAND, *supra* note 89, at 69, 65, 67; R. BERGER, *supra* note 68, at 89.

[201] R. BERGER, *supra* note 68, at 118 n.73.

[202] THE FEDERALIST No. 65, *supra* note 85, at 425.

[203] Justice Dep't Memorandum, *supra* note 169, Appendix 1 at 23.

[204] St. Clair, *supra* note 141 at 4.

the Senate" respecting foreign relations.[205] Mr. St. Clair himself quotes Madison's statement that "the executive magistracy is carefully limited," whereas the "legislative department derives a superiority . . . , its constitutional powers being at once more extensive, and less susceptible of precise limits."[206] "In republican government," said Madison, "the legislative authority necessarily predominates."[207] What we are witnessing is a presidential effort to abort the accountability to Congress that the Founders designed in the impeachment process. This process does not endow Congress with unlimited power, for it must act within the confines of "high crimes and misdemeanors."[208] It is Mr. St. Clair who would confer illimitable power on the President by making him unaccountable in an impeachment proceeding except on terms that the President lays down. As well may a banker under suspicion dictate the terms of investigation to a bank examiner.

One of Mr. St. Clair's mistakes is to postulate two unpalatable alternatives: at one pole indictable crimes, at the other unlimited congressional discretion.[209] But there is a median possibility which in fact was the choice of the Framers: Impeachment would be both limited and noncriminal. In noticing that "high crimes and misdemeanors" had a "technical meaning too limited," the Framers exhibited awareness that the words had a "limited" content defined by the English practice at the adoption of the Constitution. As we have seen, they repeatedly referred to the established categories, namely, subversion of the Constitution, abuse of power, neglect of duty—all nonindictable and *limited* offenses.[210] To be sure, these are broad categories, but no more so than many standards employed by the law, such as restraint of trade, the care of an ordinary prudent man, or due process itself.

The English categories expressed the evils at which the Framers squarely aimed; Mr. St. Clair's attempts to explain them away are a grasping at straws. Consider his argument based on the rejection of "maladministration" as an impeachable offense in favor of "high crimes and misdemeanors" in an effort to show that "impeachment was designed to deal exclusively with indictable criminal conduct." "Thus," he states, the Framers "manifested their intention to narrow the scope of impeachable offenses."[211] Without doubt the phrase "high crimes and misdemeanors" is narrower than "maladministration," which might include minor examples of mismanagement. But rejection of "maladministration" does not spell a "narrowing" of "high crimes and misdemeanors"; we need to look to "high crimes and misdemeanors" itself for the content the phrase had in both parliamentary practice and the eyes of the Framers. Each of the categories recognized by the Founders, such as "abuse of power" and "neglect of duty," was a category at English law of "high crimes and misdemeanors" and each represents a form of maladministration, that is, "improper management of public affairs." Thus "maladministration" within the parameters of "high crimes and misdemeanors" undoubtedly was to be impeachable. For this we have Madison's testimony. Referring to displacement "from office [of] a man whose merits require that he should be continued in it" (wanton discharge), Madison stated that the President "will be impeachable by this House, before the Senate, for such an act of maladministration."[212]

---

[205]R. BERGER, *supra* note 68, at 79.

[206]St. Clair 5

[207]R. BERGER, *supra* note 68, at 100.

[208]*Id.* at 86–90.

[209]St. Clair 14.

[210]R. BERGER, *supra* note 68, at 70, 89.

[211]St. Clair, *supra* note 141, at 30–31, 32. He argues that Gouverneur Morris' argument for retention of Mason's proposed "maladministration" on the ground that "it will not be put in force & can do no harm—an election of every four years will prevent maladministration," 2 FARRAND, *supra* note 89, at 550, "expressed the will of the Convention," St. Clair 31, notwithstanding that the Convention then proceeded to reject Morris' plea for "maladministration" and substituted "high crimes and misdemeanors." Such analysis is sloppy.

[212]1 ANNALS OF CONG. 517 (1789) (page running head "History of Congress").

Equally without merit is Mr. St. Clair's assertion that "[t]he Convention rejected all noncriminal definitions of impeachable offenses. . . . Terms like 'malpractice,' 'neglect of duty' . . . and 'misconduct' were all considered and discarded."[213] In fact, however, "malpractice" and "neglect of duty" were considered and "agreed to" at an early stage;[214] later, when the issue was whether the President should be impeachable, Franklin urged that impeachment was needed when the President's "misconduct should deserve it."[215] This was not put to a vote and it was not "rejected." Instead, the Framers adopted "high crimes and misdemeanors," which *included* "neglect of duty" and serious "misconduct" in office, as the Framers were well aware. Since the generic "high crimes and misdemeanors" embraced those particulars, there was no need to spell them out; an omission to do so cannot therefore be twisted into a "rejection" of the particulars.

Next Mr. St. Clair scoffs at the Framers' comments on impeachable categories because they antedated the Convention's decision on the "nature of the executive branch." Hence there was "no clear concept of who would be impeached."[216] But by July 20, the date of the early remarks, it had been settled, in Madison's words, that "the Executive Magistracy . . . was to be administered by a single man."[217] The later discussions avouched by Mr. St. Clair merely have reference to the several methods of electing the President; they did not alter impeachability of that "single man."[218] By his own admission, the last discussion of the subject on September 8 was Mason's admonition that provision must be made for "great and dangerous offenses," such as the nonindictable subversion of the Constitution, which led directly to the adoption of the phrase "high crimes and misdemeanors."[219] Moreover, when the Founders referred to the earlier categories in the several Ratification Conventions, they clearly demonstrated their satisfaction with the noncriminal content of "high crimes and misdemeanors"; and, as we have seen, Madison listed still other nonindictable offenses in the First Congress.

To illustrate "the opposition of the Framers to the abuse in the English tradition," Mr. St. Clair points to their proscription of bills of attainder, corruption of blood, and narrow definition of treason.[220] These examples demonstrate, however, that the Framers well knew how to reject undesirable practices. The fact that they defined treason narrowly and left "high crimes and misdemeanors" untouched indicates that they were content to follow English practice in "high crimes and misdemeanors,"[221] as their references to the several categories confirm. Mr. St. Clair further argues that the treason and attainder examples "express the deep commitment to due process which permeates the Constitution. This due process would be emasculated if the impeach-

---

[213]St. Clair, *supra* note 141, at 31.

[214]1 FARRAND, *supra* note 89, at 88.

[215]2 *id.* at 65.

[216]St. Clair 27–30.

[217]2 FARRAND 66.

[218]St. Clair 28–29.

[219]*Id.* at 30–31.

[220]*Id.* at 14, 16–17, 40.

[221]A striking example of the Founders' assumption that English law would be applicable unless barred is exhibited by the First Congress' prohibition of resort to "benefit of clergy" as an exemption from capital punishment, an exemption first afforded by the common law to the clergy and then to such of the laity as could read. R. BERGER, *supra* note 68, at 76.

St. Clair also argues that because the "pardon power is explicitly excluded for impeachment convictions" it "can only be understood as a reaction to and rejection of the English political impeachments." The exclusion proves exactly the contrary: The fact that a pardon *can not* save one convicted on impeachment shows an intention to *preserve* impeachments of whatever nature. The exception for pardons derived from English history and practice, when the pardon of the Earl of Danby by Charles II, after his impeachment, blew up a storm. As a result, the Act of Settlement fashioned a partial bar to such pardons; and a remark by George Nicholas in the Virginia Ratification Convention shows that the Founders were aware of this history: "Few ministers will ever run the risk of being impeached, when they know the King cannot protect them by a pardon." R. BERGER, *supra* note 68, at 45, 55 n.7, 101.

ment process were not limited to indictable offenses."[222] Since it is the intention of the Framers that Mr. St. Clair purports to seek, we must view due process as they did. For them due process merely demanded conformity with the procedure required by the law of the land. Hamilton gave, as an example, "due process of law, that is by indictment or presentment of good and lawful men, and trial and conviction in consequence."[223] Charges filed by the House and trial by the Senate under the ascertainable law were all that due process required in the eyes of the Framers.

Still another of Mr. St. Clair's contributions to history is his dismissal of the "impeachments between 1621 and 1715 [which] had as their main purpose the achievement of parliamentary supremacy." Indeed, "some individuals were impeached merely because they . . . were favorites of the King and hence rivals of the Parliament in settling State policy."[224] Shades of the dissolute Duke of Buckingham! His "boundless influence over both James I and Charles I," said Professor Chafee, "was one of the greatest calamities which ever hit the English throne," and he, Macaulay stated, illustrates why "favorites have always been highly odious."[225] Such impeachments, according to Mr. St. Clair, "distorted" the process in order to achieve "parliamentary supremacy," which he labels an "abuse."[226] This is a hair raising description of a process that halted the tide of monarchical absolutism which was sweeping over Europe. Mr. St. Clair's conclusion that this aspect of impeachment was opposed by the Framers as "an abuse in the English tradition"[227] reveals unfamiliarity with the fact that for them that parliamentary struggle was the cradle of liberty.[228] In truth, their expressions of distrust of "favorites," their hatred of Stuart absolutism[229] which had engendered the great English impeachments, their abiding faith in the legislature[230] which led the Framers to give it a "bridle" on the executive, their repeated references to impeachable offenses such as subversion of the Constitution, abuse of power, and even to the giving of "bad advice" by Ministers to the Crown[231] that emerged from this struggle for parliamentary supremacy, demonstrate that the Framers, far from regarding these as "abuses" and "distortions" to be repudiated, adopted them en bloc in order to save the nascent democracy from executive usurpations and excesses. Mr. St. Clair's reading of history underlines anew the wisdom of Pope's injunction—"Drink deep, or taste not the Pierian spring."

D. Selectivity: Other Examples

Let me close with a few additional examples of discriminatory selectivity which a lawyer employs to acquit a client but which hardly comport with the duty of one who professes to give a faithful historical account. After alluding to treason and bribery, Mr. St. Clair states, "Other crimes for which impeachments were brought included the misappropriation of government funds, partici-

---

[222]St. Clair, *supra* note 141, at 17.

[223]4 A. HAMILTON, WORKS 237 (Lodge ed. 1904). The "due process" of the Fifth Amendment, said Charles Curtis, incontrovertibly "meant a procedural due process, which could be easily ascertained from almost any law book." Curtis, *Review and Majority Rule,* in SUPREME COURT & SUPREME LAW 177 (E. Cahn ed. 1954). The shift to "substantive" due process began in the late 19th century. R. MCCLOSKEY, THE AMERICAN SUPREME COURT 128–32 (1960); Hamilton, *The Path of Due Process of Law,* in THE CONSTITUTION RECONSIDERED 167 (C. Read ed. 1938).

[224]St. Clair 12–13, 15.

[225]R. BERGER, *supra* note 68, at 72.

[226]St. Clair, *supra* note 141, at 13, 16.

[227]*Id.* at 16.

[228]"The privileges of the House of Commons, for which the people had fought in the seventeenth century . . . [they] held to be synonymous with their liberty. . . ." J. CLIVE, MACAULAY 124–125 (1973).

[229]R. BERGER, *supra* note 68, at 5 n.9, 99 n.215, 101 n.228.

[230]Justice Brandeis referred to the deep-seated conviction of the English and American people that they "must look to representative assemblies for the protection of their liberties." Myers v. United States, 272 U.S. 52, 294–95 (1926) (dissenting opinion). The constitutional provision for impeachment is one piece of evidence for that view.

[231]R. BERGER, *supra* note 68, at 71–72, 71n.91, 89.

pation in various plots against the government . . . and voicing religious beliefs prohibited by the laws." By the First Amendment, he continues, the Constitution "specifically rejected the English precedents of impeaching individuals for their religious beliefs."[232] From this one might conclude that he had exhausted the roster of impeachable offenses. Where is mention of subversion of the Constitution, abuse of power, betrayal of trust, and neglect of duty, which were impeachable offenses in England, and to which the Founders adverted?

Again, Mr. St. Clair quotes Erskine May for the proposition that "impeachments are reserved for extraordinary crimes and extraordinary offenders,"[233] but he neglects to add May's statement that "[i]mpeachments by the Commons, for high crimes and misdemeanors beyond the reach of the [criminal] law . . . might still be regarded as an ultimate safeguard of public liberty."[234] Throughout, Mr. St. Clair plays a tattoo on the fact that impeachment was a proceeding "for great men and great causes."[235] Would he read out of the Constitution the express provision for impeachment of "all civil officers" who are not "great men"? Is not the President a "great man" by any standard? Then too, "great offenses" for the Founders were the impeachable offenses that they enumerated, for which we cannot now substitute a new version supplied by defense counsel.

Consider finally Mr. St. Clair's selection from Edmund Burke at the trial of Warren Hastings:

> We say, then, not only that he governed arbitrarily, but corruptly . . . that is to say, that he was a giver and receiver of bribes. . . . In short, money is the beginning, the middle, and the end of every kind of act done by Mr. Hastings.[236]

The emphasis on "money" is apt to overshadow that Hastings was charged with governing "arbitrarily," the classic impeachable offense, and that Burke's accusations reached far deeper than "bribery." In his opening statement before the Lords he stated,

> It is by this tribunal that statesmen who *abuse their power* . . . are tried . . . not upon the niceties of a narrow [criminal] jurisprudence, but upon the enlarged and solid principles of morality.[237]

Observe that Burke, the hero of the Founders for his defense of the American revolt, emphasized that "abuse of power" was not to be tried by the narrow principles of criminal law. And he concluded, "I impeach Warren Hastings of high crimes and misdemeanors. I impeach him in the name of the Commons . . . whose *trust* he has betrayed. . . ."[238] To ignore these statements while concentrating attention on "bribery" is to deal in halftruths and to stray from candor.

Enough has been set out to expose Mr. St. Clair's cavalier treatment of history; and though it is tempting to invoke the Latin maxim, so often applied by the courts—false in one thing, false in everything—I prefer rather to forego analysis of the rest of the 61-page St. Clair memorandum in order to spare the reader a needlessly wearisome and tedious journey. Against this background it is sheer effrontery to say, as does Mr. St. Clair,

> [a]ny analysis that broadly construes the power to impeach and convict can be reached only by reading Constitutional authorities selectively, by lifting specific historical precedents out of their precise historical context, by disregarding the plain meaning and accepted definition of technical, legal terms—in short, by placing a subjective gloss on the history of impeachment that results in permitting the Congress to do whatever it deems most politic.[239]

[232]St. Clair, *supra* note 141, at 12.
[233]*Id.* at 9.
[234]T.E. MAY, PARLIAMENTARY PRACTICE 39 (17th ed. 1964).
[235]*See, e.g.,* St. Clair 9.
[236]*Id.* at 14.
[237]7 E. BURKE, *supra* note 140, at 11, 14.
[238]*Id.* at 267.
[239]St. Clair 60.

In conclusion, Mr. St. Clair has resolutely closed his eyes to adverse facts throughout, to the impact of the American separation of removal on impeachment from criminal trial by jury of "all criminal prosecutions" if, as he argues, the removal proceeding must be regarded as criminal in nature. "Historical reconstruction," said a distinguished English historian, Sir Herbert Butterfield, "must at least account for the evidence that is discrepant, and must explain how the rejected testimony came to exist."[240] Judges too require lawyers to meet the arguments of opposing counsel. When Mr. St. Clair neglects to do so and wraps himself in the cloak of pseudo-history, he lays himself open to the suspicion that he is not so much engaged in honest reconstruction of history as in propaganda whose sole purpose is to influence public opinion in favor of a client who is under grave suspicion. An "acquittal so obtained," said Macaulay, "cannot be pleaded in bar of the judgment of history."[241]

---

[240]H. BUTTERFIELD, *supra* note 136, at 225.
[241]T. MACAULAY, *supra* note 127, at 516.

CHAPTER IV

The Incarnation of Executive Privilege

I. INTRODUCTION

From the banner headlines that greeted the Supreme Court's decision ordering President Nixon to turn over to Judge John J. Sirica certain tapes of White House conversations, one might conclude that it represented a startling innovation. It was, however, President Nixon's claim that he was the sole and final arbiter of the limits of his powers that was novel. On his behalf it was argued that, "[i]nherent in that executive power, as part and parcel of the separation of powers, is executive privilege. . . ."[1] The separation of powers doctrine, which "makes one master in his own house precludes him from imposing his control in the house of another who is master there."[2] This doctrine "necessarily includes the right of the holder of the privilege to decide when it is to be exercised."[3] Consequently the central question "so powerfully put by Judge Wilkey in his dissent in Nixon v. Sirica . . . is 'Who Decides?' "[4] The answer, presidential counsel, James St. Clair, urged, required affirmance of "the proposition . . . that it is for the Chief Executive, not for the judicial branch, to decide when the public interest permits disclosure of Presidential discussions."[5]

Had the Court accepted this "proposition," which rests on a claim of implied power—for no mention is made of executive privilege in the Constitution or in its history, it would have opened the door to unchecked executive power, an evil dreaded by the Founders.[6] And it would have undermined judicial review altogether; for by parity of reasoning, Congress, which is given the express power to legislate, might equally maintain that it too is "master in its house," that it alone may determine what legislation it is authorized to enact, that the courts may not intrude into that legislative function. Yet, as the Court noted, acts of Congress are declared unconstitutional[7] notwithstanding that the power to legislate is vested exclusively in Congress. What makes the implied power of the Executive more sacrosanct than the express power of Congress? In furnishing an unequivocal answer to "Who Decides?" the limits of the respective powers conferred by the Constitution, the Court merely reaffirmed a doctrine of long standing, expressed by Chief Justice Marshall in *Marbury v. Madison:* The Court is the ultimate interpreter of the Constitution; and since the Constitution sets up a Government of limited powers, it is the function of the Court to

---

[1]Brief for Respondent at 49, United States v. Nixon, 94 S. Ct. 3090 (1974) [hereinafter cited as Respondent].

[2]*Id.* at 74, *quoting* Humphrey's Ex'r v. United States, 295 U.S. 602, 629–30 (1935).

[3]*Id.* at 73.

[4]Reply Brief for Respondent at 2-3; United States v. Nixon, 94 S. Ct. 3090 (1974) [hereinafter cited as Reply].

[5]*Id.* at 3.

[6]R. BERGER, EXECUTIVE PRIVILEGE: A CONSTITUTIONAL MYTH 49–50, 53, 58, 62 (1974) [hereinafter cited as EXECUTIVE PRIVILEGE].

Believing the surrounding material to be most valuable in understanding the concept of executive privilege, I have cited extensively to my book, *Executive Privilege.* To facilitate reference to the original source, however, citations to such sources will appear parenthetically after citation to EXECUTIVE PRIVILEGE.

[7]United States v. Nixon, 94 S. Ct. at 3105.

decide their parameters.[8] This, the historical evidence shows, was the design of the Founders.[9]

When St. Clair further alleged that his "proposition [was] not seriously challenged for the first 184 years of our constitutional history,"[10] he overlooked Chief Justice Marshall's treatment of the very issue in *United States v. Burr.*[11] There Aaron Burr sought to procure from President Jefferson a letter written to him by General Wilkinson, and Jefferson's counsel, George Hay, offered the letter,

> excepting such parts thereof as are, in my opinion, not material for the purposes of justice, for the defence of the accused, or pertinent to the issue. . . . The accuracy of this opinion, I am willing to refer to the judgment of the Court, by submitting the original letter for its inspection.[12]

When Jefferson, in compliance with Marshall's request that he himself designate the reasons for nondisclosure, submitted the letter with certain deletions, he too explained that the deleted passages were "in no wise material to the purposes of justice . . . . [T]hey are . . . irrelevant to any issue which can arise out of those charges . . ."[13] Thus neither Jefferson nor Hay invoked a blanket right to withhold; they restricted themselves to matter not material or relevant to the issue, as to which the court would have the final say. Above all, Jefferson, whatever his fulminations in private, "in no way publicly challenged [the court's] authority."[14] There was no insistence that the court was deprived of jurisdiction by virtue of the separation of powers, and Marshall made no mention of it. As one of the leaders in the Virginia battle for adoption of the Constitution, he can hardly have been oblivious to an issue of such dimensions. Instead, Marshall proceeded on the theory that the claim of limited nondisclosure was a branch of *evidentiary* privilege, akin to that of lawyer-client, doctor-patient, a creation of the courts.

It does less than justice to the *Burr* case to single out Marshall's statement that "in no case of this kind would a court be required to proceed against the President as against an ordinary individual."[15] Marshall more than once emphasized that a presidential representation that non-disclosure was essential must yield to the needs of the defendant for evidence. Early on Marshall stated that there was no showing that the letter,

> contains any matter, the disclosure of which, would endanger the public safety. If it does contain any matter which it would be imprudent to disclose, which it is not the wish of the Executive to disclose, such matter, if it be not immediately and essentially applicable to the point, will of course, be suppressed.[16]

---

[8]5 U.S. (1 Cranch) 137 (1803). *See also* Powell v. McCormack, 395 U.S. 486 (1969).

[9]*See* R. BERGER, CONGRESS V. THE SUPREME COURT (1969). The Court also gave short shrift to Respondent's argument that this "was an intra-branch dispute between a subordinate and superior officer of the Executive Branch and hence not subject to judicial resolution," Respondent, *supra* note 1, at 7, holding that a suit for production of evidence by one official, resisted by another, exhibits "that concrete adverseness" which presents a justiciable controversy and confers standing. 94 S. Ct. at 3102. For a more extended discussion of these issues, see Berger, *Congressional Inquiry v. Executive Privilege,* 12 UCLA L. REV. 1287, 1335–60 (1965).

[10]Reply, *supra* note 4, at 3.

[11]25 F. Cas. 55 (No. 14693) (C.C.D. Va. 1807). For a detailed discussion see Berger, *The President, Congress and the Courts,* 83 YALE L.J. 1111 (1974) [hereinafter cited as *The President*].

[12]*The President, supra* note 11, at 1116 (3 T. CARPENTER, THE TRIAL OF COLONEL AARON BURR 27–28 (1807) [hereinafter cited as CARPENTER]).

[13]*Id.* at 1118 (3 CARPENTER, *supra* note 12, at 46).

[14]EXECUTIVE PRIVILEGE, *supra* note 6, at 193 (H. RANDALL, LIFE OF JEFFERSON 218 (1858)).

[15]94 S. Ct. 3090, 3108, 3111 (1974). During the Burr trial, the United States Attorney, who spoke for Jefferson on the subpoena issue, stated that the President "is but a man; he is but a citizen," and were he summoned and failed to attend, "the common means would be, for the Court to issue an attachment to force him." *The President, supra* note 11, at 1111 n.1. It was a time, as Albert Beveridge stated, of "honest adherence to the American ideal that all men are equal in the eyes of the law. . . ." EXECUTIVE PRIVILEGE, *supra* note 6, at 365 (3 A. BEVERIDGE, LIFE OF JOHN MARSHALL 450 (1919)).

[16]*The President, supra* note 11, at 1114 (CARPENTER, *supra* note 12, at 133).

Thus Marshall made the touchstone of nondisclosure danger to the public safety, not "confidentiality," and even such matter would not be sheltered if it was "essentially applicable" to the defense. In his written opinion of September 4th, Marshall repeated:

> I can very readily conceive, that the President might receive a letter which it would be very improper to require for public exhibition, because of the manifest inconvenience of the exposure. There ought, in such case, to be an extremely strong occasion for its demand. . . .
>
> . . . .
>
> [P]erhaps the Court ought to consider . . . the reasons which induced the President to refuse the paper as a governing principle to induce them to refuse its exhibition, except as it shall be made to appear absolutely necessary in the defence.[17]

Behind Marshall's courtly bows to Jefferson there was unwavering emphasis on the overriding right of a defendant to evidence—a letter from General Wilkinson to Jefferson—even from the President. The decision in *United States v. Nixon* is not therefore a novel expansion of judicial review; what was new was President Nixon's insistence that he alone could determine the breadth of his powers.

II. THE IMPACT ON EXECUTIVE PRIVILEGE

For the first time in our history the Court has rooted executive privilege in the Constitution and held that the necessity of "confidentiality" for high level communications "is too plain to require further discussion."[18] Arguably the Court made a very narrow opening in this doctrine:

> [W]e cannot conclude that advisers will be moved to temper the candor of their remarks by the infrequent occasions of disclosure because of the possibility that such conversations will be called for in the context of a criminal prosecution.[19]

"Confidentiality," in short, will rarely be invaded because White House participation in another Watergate conspiracy is quite unlikely. On this view, the impact on executive privilege is restricted to the facts of the case. This restriction is reinforced by the Court's caution that it was not concerned with the weight to be given confidentiality,

---

[17]*Id.* at 1117–18 (3 CARPENTER, *supra* note 12, at 36–37).

[18]94 S. Ct. at 3106. These matters are examined in greater detail in text accompanying notes 32–126 *supra*.

Not the least curious aspect of the Court's opinion is the fact that but for a reference to the district court's holding that the judiciary "was the final arbiter of a claim of executive privilege," *id.* at 3098, the Court eschews further employment of the words "executive privilege" and refers instead to "presidential privilege," *id.* at 3106, "privilege for presidential communications," *id.* at 3107.

But there are intimations that these utterances are not confined to presidential communications: (1) the reference to "military, diplomatic or sensitive national security secrets" surely reaches across the entire executive spectrum, *id.* at 3107; (2) the reference to communications between "high government officials and those who advise and assist them," *id.* at 3106; (3) the derivation "from the supremacy of each branch within its own assigned area," *id.*; and (4) the citation to Kaiser Alum. & Chem. Corp. v. United States, 157 F. Supp. 939 (Ct. Cl. 1958), which discussed low level interchanges in terms of executive privilege, *id.* at 3107 n.17. Consequently, I shall employ the familiar term "executive privilege" throughout.

[19]94 S. Ct. at 3109. Criminal conspiracies by White House aides against the public welfare do not emerge panoplied with evidence that proves the crime. If investigation is to be effective, it must commence before proof of misconduct eventuates in prosecution, at a time when the miscreants, with all the leverage of the executive department will insist that investigation represents a vile attack by enemies of the administration. Compare executive resistance to the Teapot Dome investigation, EXECUTIVE PRIVILEGE, *supra* note 6, at 6 n.27 (Frankfurter, *Hands Off the Investigations,* 38 NEW REPUB. 329 (1924)).

in civil litigation, nor with [the balance] between the confidentiality interest and congressional demands for information. . . . We address only the conflict between the President's assertion of a generalized privilege of confidentiality against the constitutional need for relevant evidence in criminal trials.[20]

On the other hand, the Court repeatedly justified its breach in executive privilege by resort to a broad principle:

[T]he ends of criminal justice would be defeated if judgments were to be founded on a partial or speculative presentation of the facts. The very integrity of the judicial system and public confidence in the system depend on full disclosure of all the facts. . . .[21]

It adverted to "the inroads of such a privilege on the fair administration of criminal justice";[22] "the allowance of the privilege . . . would cut deeply into the guarantee of due process of law and gravely impair the basic function of the courts";[23] the privilege "cannot prevail over the fundamental demands of due process of law in the fair administration of criminal justice."[24] Such principles burgeon by analogy. Are the claims of privilege less likely to impair the "fair administration" of justice in a civil suit than in a criminal trial? A litigant in a civil proceeding, particularly against the government, is not less entitled to due process than is a defendant in a criminal prosecution. The progress of civil liberties is marked by a succession of appeals to due process in civil suits. And Marshall drew in the *Burr* case on the analogy to civil litigation.[25]

The functions of Congress as the organ for impeachment and removal of the President would also seem to override executive privilege. For it can hardly be maintained that the public interest in the criminal prosecution of a White House aide outweighs the public interest in the "full disclosure of all the facts" before Congress when it is engaged in the impeachment of a President. Surely those functions far surpass in national importance the administration of criminal justice by a district court in an individual criminal case. Just as in that individual criminal case, the "fair administration of justice" by Congress demands a "full disclosure of all the facts"; here too the privilege for "confidentiality" must yield lest the grand function of Congress be impaired. Mindful that the sole power to impeach is vested in the House, and that the Senate has the sole power to try an impeachment, it seems clear that they alone are empowered to weigh claims of privilege made by the President.[26] It cannot be left to the subject of an investigation to determine its bounds, otherwise accountability would be undermined. Whatever the weight to be given to the separation of powers argument, a matter more closely examined hereafter, it has no place in an impeachment. For the Framers made it clear that impeachment itself was to be a considered breach in the separation of powers."[27] Inquiry is not only a traditional prelude to impeachment, but it is dictated

[20]94 S. Ct. at 3109 n.19.

[21]*Id.* at 3108.

[22]*Id.* at 3109.

[23]*Id.* at 3110.

[24]*Id.*

[25]EXECUTIVE PRIVILEGE, *supra* note 6, at 191 n.156 (United States v. Burr, 25 F. Cas. 187, 191 (No. 14694) (C.C.D. Va. 1807)).

[26]When I advanced the heterodox view that judicial review was available against a Senate verdict that was in excess of its powers, Berger, *Impeachment for "High Crimes and Misdemeanors,"* 44 U. SO. CAL. L. REV. 395, 443–57 (1971), I did not have in mind interlocutory interference with its exclusive right to "try" an impeachment. *See* Endicott Johnson Corp. v. Perkins, 317 U.S. 501, 507 (1943); Myers v. Bethlehem Shipbuilding Corp., 303 U.S. 41, 48 (1938).

[27]In the Federal Convention, Rufus King argued that impeachment would violate the separation of powers and destroy the independence of the President, as did Charles Pinckney. 2 M. FARRAND, THE RECORDS OF THE FEDERAL CONVENTION OF 1787, at 66–67 (1911) [hereinafter cited as FARRAND]. Their view was decisively rejected by a vote of eight to two. As Elias Boudinot, for years President of the Continental Congress, stated in the First Congress, impeachment was an "exception to a principle," *i.e.* to the separation of powers. 1 ANNALS OF CONG. 548 (2d ed. 1834) (print bearing running heads "History of Congress").

by common sense. Who would urge "hang him first, investigate afterwards?"[28]

The general investigatory power of Congress is not less important, for thereby the Teapot Dome scandal and vast areas of the Watergate scandal were explored. Paraphrasing J.S. Mill, Woodrow Wilson said that, " '[t]he informing function of Congress should be preferred even to its legislative function.' "[29] " 'The country,' [he stated], 'must be helpless to learn how it is being served' unless Congress have and 'use every means of acquainting itself with the acts and disposition of the administrative agents of the government.' "[30] The accuracy of this statement has been illustrated by recent events. No more than trial court functions may congressional investigatory functions be permitted to suffer impairment by executive withholding of "confidential" communications. A House committee justly emphasized in 1843 that the public interest served by legislative inquiries rises above that invoked in the administration of justice in particular cases:

> [I]n parliamentary inquiries, where the object is generally to investigate abuses in the administration itself, and where such inquiry would be defeated if the chief of the administration or his subordinates were privileged to withhold the information or papers in their possession . . . the public safety requires that it should be disclosed.[31]

On the reasoning of the Court, this function also may not be "impaired" by claims of "confidentiality." In sum, notwithstanding the Court's caution that it was deciding no more than the case before it—as is eminently appropriate—the principles it enunciated will lend themselves to the decision of other and quite different cases.

III. THE BASIS OF EXECUTIVE PRIVILEGE

The executive privilege controversy has revolved around claims that the President has the absolute, unreviewable right to refuse information to Congress and the courts.[32] So far as the courts are concerned, such claims were routed in the *Nixon* case; and by parity of reasoning they should not stand up against Congress. The case, therefore, can hardly be viewed as a victory for executive privilege.[33] Nevertheless the Court's legitimation of executive privilege in sweeping terms sows the seeds of future problems. The dicta of "presumptive privilege," of the indispensability of "confidentiality," the special warning against *in camera* examination of "military, diplomatic or sensitive national security secrets," will lead district courts to view attempts to obtain information unsympathetically. With surprising casualness the Court found that the privilege for presidential communications "is inextricably rooted in the separation of powers"[34] and that "the importance of this confidentiality is too plain to require further discussion."[35] Against the sleazy background of "White House Horrors"[36] which emerged in the Watergate testimony and which Mr. Nixon cloaked under the garb of "confidentiality" and "executive privilege," these facile assumptions are

---

[28] " 'Would not a Physician be a Madman,' said a member of the House of Commons in 1742 (when it was considering an inquiry into the regime of the fallen Robert Walpole), to 'prescribe to a Patient, without first examining into the State of his Distemper, the Causes from which it arose.' " EXECUTIVE PRIVILEGE, *supra* note 6, at 15 (13 R. CHANDLER, HISTORY AND PROCEEDINGS OF PARLIAMENT FROM 1621 TO THE PRESENT 85 (1743)).

[29] *Id.* at 2–3 (W. WILSON, CONGRESSIONAL GOVERNMENT 297, 303 (1913)).

[30] *Id.* (W. WILSON, CONGRESSIONAL GOVERNMENT 297, 303 (1913)).

[31] *Id.* at 184 (H.R. REP. NO. 271, 27th Cong., 3d Sess. 10 (1843)).

[32] See Attorney General Rogers' claim of "uncontrolled discretion" to withhold. Berger, *Congressional Inquiry v. Executive Privilege,* 12 UCLA L. REV. 1043, 1045 (1965).

[33] Mr. Nixon stated, "I was gratified, therefore, to note that the court reaffirmed both the validity and the importance of the principle of executive privilege. . . . [T]his [case] will prove to be not the precedent that destroyed the principle but the action that preserved it." Washington Post, July 25, 1974, at A16, col. 4. *See also* note 138 *infra.*

[34] 494 S. Ct. at 3107.

[35] *Id.* at 3106.

[36] The quoted words are those of Mr. Nixon's former Attorney General, John Mitchell.

little short of astonishing. They legitimate and anoint presidential claims that are vitiated by historical facts and which have been perverted by the grossest abuses.

My chief criticism of the remarks devoted by the Court to "confidentiality" and "presidential privilege" is that they rise little above *ipse dixits*. The respect enjoyed by the Court derives in no small part from its appeal to reason, its attempts to explain the basis of its decisions. There is no such appeal where there are little more than summary assertions. There is not a hint in the opinion that there may be evidence that may lead to a contrary conclusion, that there is an alternative explanation; no question is raised whether inferences from the historical facts militate against those assertions. Even more than an historian, the Court is called upon to take discrepant evidence into account, to explain why it was given no weight.[37] Nine years ago I set forth my initial studies of executive privilege in the pages of this very Review;[38] since then I have spent three more years in a reexamination and expanded study of the field.[39] In the interim no piece rejecting my findings was to my knowledge published.[40] Consciousness of fallibility haunts every student;[41] but I hope it is not immodest to insist that upon so momentous an issue such findings call for examination until proven untrustworthy or wrong. And in remaining an unrepentant heathen, I am emboldened by the statement of Justice Iredell in *Ware v. Hylton:*

> [H]owever painful it may be, to differ from gentlemen whose superior abilities and learning I readily acknowledge, I am under the indispensable necessity of judging according to the best lights of my own understanding, assisted by all the information I can acquire.[42]

Temerarious though it may be to sally forth in the face of a unanimous Supreme Court decision,[43] I submit, as Senator George Wharton Pepper boldly stated at the bar of the Court, that though we bow to the "law" declared by the Court, "history remains history, in spite of judicial utterances upon the subject."[44] And since the only restraint upon the Court is its own sense of self-restraint,[45] it is of utmost importance that its opinions be subjected to searching scrutiny. For this I have the

---

[37]"Historical reconstruction must at least account for the evidence that is discrepant, and must explain how the rejected testimony came to exist." H. BUTTERFIELD, GEORGE III AND THE HISTORIANS 225 (rev. ed. 1969).

[38]Berger, *Congressional Inquiry v. Executive Privilege,* 12 UCLA L. REV. 1287 (1965).

[39]EXECUTIVE PRIVILEGE, *supra* note 6.

[40]After this Article was submitted, a rancorous review, which jumps off from the proposition that my scholarly reputation is an utterly unfounded product of the media, was published by Professor Ralph Winter, 83 YALE L.J. 1730 (1974). As I shall demonstrate in a forthcoming article, Winter substitutes derision and expletives for analysis; his views run counter to those of more distinguished reviewers: former Justice Arthur J. Goldberg, Christian Science Monitor, May 15, 1974, at 5F, col. 3; Professor Phillip B. Kurland, NEW REPUB., June 15, 1974, at 21; Louis Pollak, Washington Post, June 30, 1974, Book World, at 1; Garry Wills, N.Y. Times, May 5, 1974, Book Review, at 1. *See also* Professors John P. Dawson & Willard Hurst, dust jacket of EXECUTIVE PRIVILEGE, *supra* note 6.

[41]James Iredell's fine statement in the North Carolina Ratification Convention has long been before me: "Nothing is more fallible than human judgment. No gentleman will say that his is not fallible. Mine, I am sure, has often proved so." 4 J. ELLIOT, DEBATES IN THE SEVERAL STATE CONVENTIONS ON THE ADOPTION OF THE FEDERAL CONSTITUTION 14 (2d ed. 1836).

[42]3 U.S. (3 Dall.) 199, 265 (1796).

[43]Compare the eight to one decision in the "flag salute" case with its eight to one repudiation three years later. Minersville School Dist. v. Gobitis, 310 U.S. 586 (1940); West Virginia State Bd. of Educ. v. Barnette, 319 U.S. 624 (1943).

[44]Myers v. United States, 272 U.S. 52, 70 (1926) (argument of Senator Pepper). Recall the Court's erroneous view that the House of Commons was a court, Kilbourn v. Thompson, 103 U.S. 168 (1880). Coke stated in the Commons in 1621 that "we have no power to [judge], we may examine." 3 W. NOTESTEIN, F. RELF & H. SIMPSON, COMMONS DEBATES: 1621 54 (1935). *See* Stockdale v. Hansard, 112 Eng. Rep. 1112, 1196 (Q.B. 1839).

One of the earliest and most acute students of the Constitution, Judge St. George Tucker of the Virginia Supreme Court of Appeals, said of judicial opinions, "where any doubt is entertained of their correctness . . . they ought to receive an early and full discussion; otherwise they will soon acquire the force of *precedents.* These are often more difficult to be shaken than the most cogent arguments, when drawn from reason alone." 1 W. BLACKSTONE, COMMENTARIES ON THE LAW OF ENGLAND (Tucker ed. 1803).

[45]United States v. Butler, 297 U.S. 1, 78–79 (1936) (Stone, J., dissenting).

testimony of a great member of the court. In 1942 I published an article[46] critical of Justice Black's opinion in *Bridges v. California,*[47] and ventured to send it to him. Back came a letter stating that he had read it with "a great deal of interest," took note of our differences, and regarded such criticism of the Court's opinions as "most helpful in efforts ultimately to arrive at right conclusions."

A. Evidentiary Privilege in Court Litigation

Let us begin with the evidentiary privilege which was at issue in the *Nixon* case. It is not a little remarkable that the principle that the privilege is "inextricably rooted in the separation of powers" should completely have escaped the notice of Chief Justice Marshall in the *Burr* case. That was a threshhold question, to which he—a powerful advocate of adoption of the Constitution by Virginia—can scarcely have been oblivious.[48] One will vainly search other cases under evidentiary privilege for any reference to the separation of powers. English cases at or about the time of the adoption of the Constitution—among them one involving an Order of Council in the midst of our Revolutionary War—rejected executive claims to withhold confidential information from litigants in court,[49] an implicit holding that "confidentiality" was not crucial to administration. When the claim was first advanced in 1950 before a federal district court in what was later to be known as *United States v. Reynolds,* Judge Kirkpatrick stated that "the Government claims a new kind of privilege . . . I can find no recognition in the law of such a privilege."[50] On appeal, the Court of Appeals for the Third Circuit, by Judge Albert Maris, refused to recognize the claim that a disclosure "would have a deterrent effect upon the much desired objective of encouraging uninhibited statements," saying that "such a sweeping privilege . . . is contrary to sound public policy."[51] The Supreme Court reversed the case on the ground that the respondent failed to prove the necessity for disclosure of military secrets since alternative sources were available to him. Not a word was said by the Court about "confidentiality." On the other hand, the three dissenting Justices, Black, Frankfurter and Jackson, endorsed the opinion of the court of appeals, thereby approving that court's rejection of the "confidentiality claim," an issue on which the majority was silent.[52]

Thus stood the law when *Kaiser Aluminum & Chemical Corp. v. United States,*[53] the earliest case cited by Chief Justice Burger in the *Nixon* case, came down in 1958.[54] That was a court of claims opinion, per Justice Reed sitting by designation; and in the words of the St. Clair Reply Brief, "the court defined the privilege claimed solely in terms of the law of evidence, with its foundation in custom or statute."[55] Reed himself stated that the assertion of such a privilege, either

---

[46]Berger, *Constructive Contempt: A Post-Mortem,* 9 U. CHI. L. REV. 602 (1942).

[47]314 U.S. 252 (1941).

[48]EXECUTIVE PRIVILEGE, *supra* note 6, at 364.

[49]*Id.* at 215–16 (The Ship Columbus, 1 Collectanea Juridica 88, 92 (1789)).

[50]Brauner v. United States, 10 F.R.D. 468, 472 (E.D. Pa. 1950), *aff'd sub nom.* United States v. Reynolds, 192 F.2d 987 (3d Cir. 1951), *rev'd on other grounds,* 345 U.S. 1 (1952).

[51]United States v. Reynolds, 192 F.2d 987, 994–95 (3d Cir. 1951).

[52]EXECUTIVE PRIVILEGE, *supra* note 6, at 354–55 (United States v. Reynolds, 345 U.S. 1, 12 (1952)). When Wigmore came to sum up, he stated that the scope of the privilege beyond secrets "in the military or international sense is by no means clearly defined; and . . . it has not become a matter of precedent or even of debate in more than a few jurisdictions;" and "ordinarily there are [not] any matters of fact, in the possession of officials, concerning solely the internal affairs of public business, civil or military, which ought to be privileged from disclosure." *Id.* at 232 (8 J. WIGMORE, EVIDENCE IN TRIALS AT COMMON LAW § 2378a, at 788–89 (3d ed. 1940)). Justice Reed, sitting by designation in Kaiser Alum. & Chem. Corp. v. United States, 157 F. Supp. 939, 946 (Ct. Cl. 1958), stated that "the privilege for intradepartmental advice would very rarely have the importance of diplomacy or security. It does not have in this case."

[53]157 F. Supp. 939 (Ct. Cl. 1958).

[54]494 S. Ct. at 3107 n.17.

[55]Reply, *supra* note 4, at 16; *see* Kaiser Alum. & Chem. Corp v. United States, 157 F. Supp. 939, 944 (Ct. Cl. 1958). Justice Reed, however, was more concerned with protection of the reasoning process preliminary to decision than with "confidentiality." *Id.* at 945–46. For the absence of "custom," see EXECUTIVE PRIVILEGE, *supra* note 6, at 353–55.

against Congress or the courts, was a "judicially undecided issue."[56] As in *Reynolds,* the discussion of privilege was sheer dictum, for in both cases the court held that no need for the information had been made out. And like Chief Justice Burger, Reed *assumed* that candid interchange among executive officials was essential to good government.[57] *Kaiser* did not involve *presidential* communications; echoing the 1954 Eisenhower directive it referred to "confidential" communications at every lower level of the executive branch.[58] No roots in the separation of powers can be traced to *Kaiser.*

In addition to cases that followed *Kaiser,* Chief Justice Burger cited *The Federalist No. 64,*[59] which dealt with the treaty power, a power shared with the Senate. John Jay stated that though he appreciated that negotiations with those who preferred to "rely on the secrecy of the president" might arise, he stressed that such secrecy was with respect to "those preparatory and auxiliary measures which are no [*sic*] otherwise important in a national view, than as they tend to facilitate the attainment of the objects of the negociation."[60] By the terms of the Constitution, treaties require the "advice and consent" of the Senate, so that secrecy from the Senate was not rested by Jay on the separation of powers but rather on expedient yielding to hypothetical foreign desires, which by no means adds up to an unlimited claim of privilege. Assuming that Jay may be read to the contrary, the historical evidence indicates that the Founders considered the zone of secrecy exceedingly limited.[61] High as is the authority of *The Federalist,* it is not irrebuttable. Marshall stated that "No tribute can be paid to [its authors] which exceeds their merit; but in applying their opinions to the cases which may arise in the progress of our government, a right to judge of their correctness must be retained. . . ."[62] The interested reader will find extended exposition of the Founders' view that the Senate would participate in treaty-*making* in my chapter on secrecy in foreign relations.[63] It must suffice here to note James Wilson's statement at the Pennsylvania Ratification Convention that he was "not an advocate for secrecy . . . even *in forming* treaties."[64] Speaking to "intercourse with foreign powers," James Iredell stated in the North Carolina Convention that it is the President's "duty to impart to the Senate every material intelligence he receives."[65] In the words of McDougal and Lans, "[t]he testimony of delegates to the Constitutional Convention clearly indicates the intention of the draftsmen that the Senate participate equally with the President in the step-by-step negotiation of treaties."[66] Blind-folded participation was far removed from their design. A far-reaching claim of confidentiality for presidential communications can not therefore be rested on *The Federalist No. 64.*

For the proposition that there is "nothing novel about governmental confidentiality," Chief Justice Burger stated that "[t]he meetings of the Constitutional Convention in 1787 were conducted in complete privacy."[67] Notwithstanding this experience, however, when they came to set down

---

[56]EXECUTIVE PRIVILEGE, *supra* note 6, at 355, (157 F. Supp. at 944 n.7).

[57]157 F. Supp. at 945–46.

[58]"[W]e do not think this record shows the need for examination of the privileged document"; "[t]his should not be ordered without definite showing by plaintiff of facts indicating reasonable cause for requiring such a submission." *Id.* at 947 & 948.

[59]94 S. Ct. at 3107 n.17.

[60]THE FEDERALIST NO. 64, at 435 (Mod. Lib. ed. 1937) (J. Jay).

[61]EXECUTIVE PRIVILEGE, *supra* note 6, at 120–35.

[62]McCulloch v. Maryland, 17 U.S. (4 Wheat.) 316, 433 (1819).

[63]EXECUTIVE PRIVILEGE, *supra* note 6, at 121–40.

[64]*Id.* at 128 (2 J. ELLIOT, DEBATES IN THE SEVERAL STATE CONVENTIONS ON THE ADOPTION OF THE FEDERAL CONSTITUTION 506 (2d ed. 1836) [hereinafter cited as ELLIOT].

[65]*Id.* at 129 (4 ELLIOT, *supra* note 64, at 127).

[66]*Id.* (McDougal & Lans, *Treaties and Congressional-Executive or Presidential Agreements: Interchangeable Instruments of National Policy,* 54 YALE L.J. 181, 539 n.25 (1945)).

[67]94 S. Ct. at 3106 n.15.

the Constitution, the Framers authorized secrecy only by Congress: Article I, § 5(3) requires Congress to keep and publish Journals, except "such Parts as may in their Judgment require Secrecy." Initially six states supported this provision, four states opposed it and one was divided. Wilson, whose state, Pennsylvania, opposed it, said that "The people have a right to know what their Agents are doing or have done, and it should not lie in the option of the Legislature to conceal their proceedings."[68] When George Mason and Elbridge Gerry pressed for publication of "all the proceedings of the House," the "other side" countered that "cases might arise where secrecy might be necessary in both Houses—Measures preparatory to a declaration of war."[69] Such fears also agitated the Ratification Conventions. Patrick Henry stated in Virginia that "the liberties of a people never were . . . secure when the transactions of their rulers may be concealed from them."[70] Mason said: "Under this veil they may conceal anything and everything."[71] To set such fears at rest, John Marshall assured the Virginia Convention that "secrecy is only used when it would be fatal and pernicious to publish the schemes of government."[72] These and similar remarks testify to the apprehension that was engendered by an *express* congressional authorization to keep parts of its Journals secret *from the public,* and they explain restrictive readings to allay such fears. The fact that the Convention deliberated in secret is therefore of no moment, for in the Constitution the Framers provided for limited secrecy by Congress alone, thereby excluding executive secrecy from the public.[73] Executive *secrecy from the Congress* raises altogether different problems.

B. The "Precedents" of Presidential Withholding from Congress

Troubled by the paucity of precedent in the evidentiary privilege cases, Mr. Nixon's counsel, James St. Clair, invoked the "precedents" of presidential withholding from Congress,[74] largely self-serving assertions by a number of Presidents which crumble under scrutiny.[75] Here the Court's statement that presidential privilege is "inextricably rooted in the separation of powers" meets its severest test. Looking to the parliamentary practice at the adoption of the Constitution, the Court in *McGrain v. Daugherty,*[76] held that "the power of inquiry—with enforcing process—was regarded and employed as a necessary and appropriate attribute of the power to legislate—indeed, was treated as inhering in it," and that the grant of legislative power was "intended to include this attribute. . . ."[77] For the scope of this power we turn to its source. A random sampling of parliamentary records stretching from 1621 to 1742 disclosed that the inquiry power had its inception as a prelude to impeachment, and before long covered the entire spectrum of executive conduct: inquiries into corruption, the conduct of war, the basis for legislation, disbursement of appropriations, conduct of foreign relations, and execution of the laws. Legislative oversight of administration was exercised across the board.[78] No member of the executive branch has ever advanced a pre-1787 precedent in English history for an executive refusal to turn over information to the legislature. I found a solitary instance of a refusal by a Solicitor of the Treasury; he was promptly thrown into the Tower.[79] In 1701 Charles Davenant stated that "no one has ever questioned the

---

[68]EXECUTIVE PRIVILEGE, *supra* note 6, at 204 (2 FARRAND, *supra* note 27, at 260).

[69]*Id.* (2 FARRAND, *supra* note 27, at 613).

[70]*Id.* (3 ELLIOT, *supra* note 64, at 170).

[71]*Id.* at 205 (3 ELLIOT, *supra* note 64, at 404).

[72]*Id.* at 205 (3 ELLIOT, *supra* note 64, at 233, 170, 222).

[73]*See* EXECUTIVE PRIVILEGE, *supra* note 6, at 206–07.

[74]Respondent, *supra* note 1, at 54–58.

[75]EXECUTIVE PRIVILEGE, *supra* note 6, at 163–208.

[76]273 U.S. 135 (1927).

[77]*Id.* at 175.

[78]EXECUTIVE PRIVILEGE, *supra* note 6, at 15–31.

[79]*Id.* at 170 (13 R. CHANDLER, HISTORY AND PROCEEDINGS OF PARLIAMENT FROM 1621 TO THE PRESENT 224–25 (1943) [hereinafter cited as CHANDLER]).

legislative authority 'to enquire into, and correct the Errors and Abuses committed' " by those who exercised executive power.[80] That was confirmed 130 years later by the great English constitutional historian, Henry Hallam.[81] In a word, there is no historical basis for the proposition that there was an "inherent" executive power to withhold information from the legislature. The evidence is to the contrary.

To root such an executive withholding power in the separation of powers is to beg the question. The separation of powers does not generate power; it only serves to protect *granted* powers from encroachment. Where is the grant? To this question by Special Prosecutor Leon Jaworski[82] and by Justices Douglas and Thurgood Marshall,[83] Chief Justice Burger responds that "the silence of the Constitution on this score is not dispositive," and invokes the rule " 'that which [is] reasonably appropriate and relevant to the exercise of a granted power' " accompanies the grant.[84] His analysis is undercut by a number of considerations. First, as Justice William Johnson stated in 1821, "the genius and spirit of our institutions are hostile to the exercise of implied powers."[85] True, he did go on to say that express powers draw after them implied powers "vital to their exercise."[86] But this "vital" need may not be assumed, particularly when implied powers are "hostile" to our institutions; they should therefore meet a high and proven standard of necessity. Second, the implied executive power to withhold information curtails legislative inquiry which the Court, looking to parliamentary practice, justly stated was an "attribute" of the legislative power and, as has been noted, was untrammelled. In the words of Chief Justice Marshall,

> [i]t would . . . be expected that an opinion which is to overrule all former precedents, and to establish a principle never before recognized, should be expressed in plain and explicit terms. A mere implication ought not to prostrate a principle which seems to have been so well established.[87]

A Convention which was at pains expressly to authorize the President to ask for written opinions from Executive department heads—a power which, as Justice Jackson said, was "inherent" if any

---

[80]Bestor, *Separation of Powers in the Domain of Foreign Affairs: The Interest of the Constitution Historically Examined,* 5 SETON HALL L. REV. 527, 558–59 (1974).

[81]EXECUTIVE PRIVILEGE, *supra* note 6, at 18 (3 H. HALLAM, CONSTITUTIONAL HISTORY OF ENGLAND 143 (1884)).

[82]94 S. Ct. at 3106 n.16.

[83]Record at 90–91, United States v. Nixon, 94 S. Ct. 3090 (1974).

[84]94 S. Ct. at 3106 n.16, *quoting* Marshall v. Gordon, 243 U.S. 521, 527 (1917). It may be thought that the principle "which exempts judges . . . from liability in a civil action for acts done by them in the exercise of their judicial functions," Bradley v. Fisher, 80 U.S. (13 Wall.) 335, 347 (1872), an immunity not mentioned in the Constitution, furnishes an apt analogy for evocation of a constitutional power by implication. But there the Court stated that this exemption "has been the settled doctrine of the English courts for many centuries, and has never been denied . . . in the courts of this country. It has, as Chancellor Kent observes, 'a deep root in the common law.' " *Id.* The presidential claim of a right to withhold information from Congress is altogether without common law roots; Chief Justice Burger's "implied" power would curtail a legislative power that *is* deeply rooted in the common law. *See* text accompanying note 87 *infra.*

[85]Anderson v. Dunn, 19 U.S. (6 Wheat.) 204, 225 (1821).

[86]*Id.* at 225–26.

[87]EXECUTIVE PRIVILEGE, *supra* note 6, at 51 (United States v. Burr, 25 F. Cas. 55, 165 (No. 14693) (C.C.D. Va. 1807)). This holding was given powerful reaffirmation in Pierson v. Ray, 386 U.S. 547 (1967). After adverting to the decision in Bradley v. Fisher, 80 U.S. (13 Wall.) 335 (1872) which held that the immunity of judges from actions for acts performed in their official capacity was deeply rooted in the common law, the Court stated:

> We do not believe that this settled principle of law was abolished by § 1983, which makes liable "every person" who under color of law deprives another person of his civil rights. . . . The immunity of judges . . . [is] well established and we presume that Congress would have specifically so provided had it wished to abolish the doctrine.

386 U.S. at 554–55.

Thus express words, "every person," were refused comprehensive effect where that would curtail an established common law immunity. How can an "implied" executive power be permitted to curtail an equally well established legislative power to require information from the executive?

power was[88]—was little likely to endow him with an "implied" power to diminish the established investigatory power of the Grand Inquest of the Nation.[89] Presidential excesses were feared, as the impeachment debate alone testifies; and the Founders knew from English experience that legislative oversight was an indispensable check upon such abuses.[90] The need for "confidentiality" is a creature of our times, and it would hardly have weighed in the scales against the Founders' fear of arbitrary executive power and familiarity with the legislative inquisitorial check upon such excesses. Third, the express grant of the privilege to Congress by the "Speech and Debate" clause precludes the inference that it was impliedly given to the President. As Solicitor General Robert Bork stated, the Framers well knew how to confer immunity, and where it was not conferred, it was withheld, as is confirmed by the history of the cognate express immunity from arrest conferred upon members of Congress and consciously withheld from the President.[91] Chief Justice Burger's assumption that the need for "confidentiality" is abundantly plain is far removed from the view of Founders, as expressed by James Wilson:

> The executive power is better to be trusted *when it has no screen* . . . [the President cannot] hide either his negligence or inattention . . . not a *single privilege* is annexed to his character.[92]

It cannot often enough be repeated that the Founders did not view the President with awe but with apprehension.

C. Lack of Historical Basis for Privilege

In addition to the lack of precedent for the assumption that presidential privilege is "inextricably rooted in the separation of powers," there are historical materials that contradict that assumption. Prior to 1787, it will be recalled, no challenge to parliamentary inquiry into executive conduct or to its scope is recorded. Consequently, there is no basis for a conclusion that an executive right to withhold information from the legislature was deemed an "attribute" of the "executive power." That is confirmed by Montesquieu, the oracle of the separation of powers, interminably cited by the Founders. He said, the legislature "has a right, and ought to have the means, of examining in what manner its laws have been executed," in which the English, he stated, enjoy an advantage over some governments where public officers "gave no account of their administration."[93] Not only were the Founders thus alerted by Montesquieu that the inquisitorial function was not barred by the separation of powers, but there is James Wilson's tribute to the House of Commons, the Grand Inquest of the Nation, which has "checked the progress of arbitrary power. . . . The proudest ministers of the proudest monarchs . . . have appeared at the bar of the house to give an account of their conduct. . . ."[94] References to the House as the "Grand Inquest of the Nation" are sprinkled through the records of the several Conventions.[95] In no case was protest made that this power was too broad or had to be curtailed for the protection of the President. From Montesquieu they had

---

[88]EXECUTIVE PRIVILEGE, *supra* note 6, at 56 (Youngstown Sheet & Tube Co. v. Sawyer, 343 U.S. 579, 640–41 (1952) (Jackson, J., concurring)). For Justice Jackson's rejection of "inherent" presidential powers, see EXECUTIVE PRIVILEGE, at 86 (343 U.S. at 646–50).

[89]"Every grant to the President," said Professor Louis Henkin, "was in effect a derogation from Congressional power, eked out slowly, reluctantly. . . ," L. HENKIN, FOREIGN AFFAIRS AND THE CONSTITUTION 23 (1972).

[90]For English inquiry into damaging confidential communications at the highest levels in 1714, see note 108 *infra*. In 1741, William Pitt, summarizing the English experience, stated: "We are called the Grand Inquest of the Nation, and as such it is our duty to inquire into every Step of publick Management, either Abroad or at Home, in order to see that nothing has been done amiss." EXECUTIVE PRIVILEGE, *supra* note 6, at 29 (13 CHANDLER, *supra* note 79, at 172–73).

[91]*The President, supra* note 11, at 1125.

[92]EXECUTIVE PRIVILEGE, *supra* note 6, at 49 (2 ELLIOT, *supra* note 64, at 480 (quoting James Wilson) (emphasis added in original)).

[93]*Id.* at 4 (C. MONTESQUIEU, THE SPIRIT OF THE LAWS 187 (1802)).

[94]*Id.* at 33 (2 J. WILSON, THE WORKS OF JAMES WILSON 731 (1967)).

[95]*Id.* at 35 (2 FARRAND, *supra* note 27, at 154).

again learned that the power was essential, and the lesson was reinforced by a dread of executive excesses so deep-seated as to welcome another check, in Wilson's words, to "the progress of arbitary power." Today we are painfully aware of the ultimate check, the power of impeachment, to which President Nixon had also interposed executive privilege in reliance on the separation of powers, notwithstanding that in the Convention impeachment was regarded as an indispensable *breach* in the separation of powers.[96]

Then too, the Act of July 31, 1789, confirms that the separation of powers was in no wise conceived to curtail the legislative inquiry function. It imposed,

> the duty of the Secretary of the Treasury . . . to . . . give information [to both Houses of Congress] . . . respecting *all matters . . . which shall appertain to his office.*[97]

During the Nixon administration members of the cabinet, indeed of the White House staff, have repeatedly sought refuge in executive privilege. Are we to conclude that this act drafted by Alexander Hamilton, co-author of *The Federalist,* enacted by the First Congress, in which sat about twenty Framers and Ratifiers of the Constitution, and signed by President Washington, who had presided over the Convention, violated the separation of powers?[98] Before legitimizing executive privilege, the Court, I submit, should have explained why these historical facts were immaterial. My analysis, of course, is aimed at those who consider that the Constitution is to be construed in light of the original intention of those who framed and adopted it.[99] That the Court can "make" history in disregard of that "original intention" is known to the bar but not to the general public.

Given the sorry role played by executive secrecy in recent years—secret executive agreements, secret bombing of Cambodia, President Nixon's secret obstruction of the Watergate investigation—and given its proven capacity to hamper the legislative process, the nation is entitled to a better explanation of how executive secrecy is protected by the Constitution.

Some bizarre side-effects of the rooting of executive privilege in the separation of powers deserve to be noted. Consider the Freedom of Information Act.[100] In what had appeared an exuberant flight of fancy, Judge Malcolm Wilkey, speaking with reference to information sought by a member of the *public* under the Act, stated that "the executive may still assert a constitutional privilege on the ground that Congress may not compel by statute disclosure of information which it would not be entitled to receive directly upon request." He reasoned that, "[o]bviously Congress could not surmount constitutional barriers . . . by conferring upon any member of the general public a right which Congress, neither individually nor collectively, possesses."[101] The Court, it will be recalled, fashioned an escape hatch from the separation of powers barrier by reasoning that "the separate powers were not intended to operate with absolute independence," but must be integrated "into a workable government," so as not to "gravely impair the role of the courts."[102] Congress too can protect itself against impairment of its function. But how would executive privilege impair the role of Congress when it seeks to provide for executive information *to the public*? To deprive Congress

[96]*See* note 27 *supra.*

[97]Executive Privilege, *supra* note 6, at 38 (5 U.S.C. § 242 (Supp. V, 1959–63) (originally enacted as Act of July 31, 1789, 1 Stat. 65, 66)) (emphasis added).

[98]*See* Executive Privilege, *supra* note 6, at 46–47 (3 Annals of Cong. 934 (1793)), for Madison's comments.

[99]That was the view of Jefferson and Madison. Executive Privilege, *supra* note 6, at 97 (4 Elliot, *supra* note 64, at 446); 9 J. Madison, Works 191, 372 (Hunt ed. 1900–10). The contrary meaning given to Marshall's reference to a Constitution "to be adapted to the various crises in human affairs" was categorically repudiated by him. Executive Privilege at 960. (McCulloch v. Maryland, 17 U.S. (4 Wheat.) 316, 415 (1819) (G. Gunther, John Marshall's Defense of *McCulloch v. Maryland* 182, 184 (1969)).

[100]5 U.S.C. § 552 (1970).

[101]Executive Privilege, *supra* note 6, at 210 n.5 (Soucie v. David, 448 F.2d 1067, 1082–83 (D.C. Cir. 1971) (Wilkey, J., concurring)).

[102]94 S. Ct. at 3107.

of information needed for its *own* role—legislation, appropriation and the like—is one thing; but it is something else again to insist that legislative provision for information to the public is essential to the congressional role. Is the Freedom of Information Act then unconstitutional? Was the people's long struggle to learn how their government operates in vain?

Similar questions arise from the provisions for discovery against the Government in the discovery rules of the Federal Rules of Civil Procedure.[103] Resort to executive privilege will be found in criminal and civil discovery proceedings, now authorized by statute.[104] Given the fact that Congress may authorize suits against the Executive Branch, that administrators may be brought into court by summons, it would seem that the lesser power to compel them to produce documents logically follows.[105] Or are we to conclude that congressional authorization of such suits violates the separation of powers?

IV. CONFIDENTIALITY

The Court assumed a "valid need for protection of communications between high government officials and those who advise and assist them . . . the importance of this confidentiality is too plain to require further discussion." It posited "the necessity for protection of the public interest in candid, objective, and even blunt or harsh opinions in presidential decision making."[106] Preliminarily, how high is "high"? The "advice" given by the Attorney General to the President cannot be better than the weakest link in the chain of advice *he* receives, and it is the soundness of the Attorney General's advice that the Court would insure. Is an Assistant Attorney General, to whom the Attorney General must turn, entitled to similar immunity for communications from *his* advisers; may his subordinate Section Chiefs equally invoke the privilege? In each case the soundness of a subordinate's advice to his chief supposedly rests on the "uninhibited" nature of such advice.

Few would quarrel with the proposition that as a practical matter the President should be free to consult with his immediate advisers in confidence, and in practice Congress has respected such communications.[107] But because a result is practical it does not follow that it is constitutionally required. Indeed, there is evidence that the Founders did not consider "confidentiality" as a *sine qua non* of the Presidency. There had been a number of impeachments of English ministers who had given "bad advice" to the Crown; in several State Ratification Conventions members referred to the giving of "bad advice" as impeachable,[108] a view that is at war with the assumption that presidential "confidentiality" is anchored in the Constitution.

The real problem is not posed by confidentiality between the President and his immediate advisers, members of his cabinet and the like; it arises from the fact that the claim for executive privilege has sprawled far beyond presidential precincts. The Eisenhower directive of 1954, from

---

[103]FED. R. CIV. P. 26–37. *See generally* Berger & Krash, *Government Immunity From Discovery,* 59 YALE L.J. 1451, 1454–55 (1950).

[104]Berger & Krash, *supra* note 103, at 1456–57; 18 U.S.C. § 3489 (1970).

[105]*Id.* at 1459. In the *Kaiser* case, Justice Reed stated that executive privilege "finds its strongest expression in the government's absolute freedom from suit except as it may consent." 157 F. Supp. at 944.

[106]94 S. Ct. at 3106. Compare with EXECUTIVE PRIVILEGE, *supra* note 6, at 349.

[107]*Hearings on Executive Privilege Before the Subcomm. on Separation of Powers of the Senate Comm. on the Judiciary,* 92d Cong., 1st Sess., at 423 (1971). Compare respect for withholding of "raw and unevaluated evidence" expressed by Chairman Sam J. Ervin, Jr., of that Subcommittee. *Id.* at 440.

[108]R. BERGER, IMPEACHMENT: THE CONSTITUTIONAL PROBLEMS 71, 89 (1973). Among those impeachments, with which the Founders were manifestly familiar, was that of the Earl of Oxford and other high Ministers in 1714. In a preliminary inquiry, Thomas Harley, brother of Oxford, and Matthew Prior, envoys to France, were interrogated as to their instructions by the Ministers to negotiate a secret treaty behind the back of their Dutch allies, a disgraceful incident which, William Pitt said, left an indelible stain on English honor. EXECUTIVE PRIVILEGE, *supra* note 6, at 256. (W. CHURCHILL, MARLBOROUGH: HIS LIFE AND TIME 890 (1968)).

which the doctrine largely derives, ordered that communications and conversations *between employees* of the executive branch must be withheld from Congress so that they may "be completely candid in advising with each other."[109] Therefore, it was not without "precedent" that Attorney General Richard Kleindienst claimed this immunity in April, 1973, for every employee in the executive branch—circa 2,500,000 in all; he went on to assert that the President is empowered to forbid federal employees to testify before Congress under any circumstances and to block congressional demands for *any* documents within the executive branch. The President, Kleindienst claimed, could "forbid federal employees from testifying before Congress under any circumstances—including impeachment."[110] Once the shelter of the separation of powers is available to the President, on what logic may it be denied his agents in the entire executive department? President Eisenhower's directive to federal "employees," he explained, was designed "to maintain the proper separation of powers. . . ."[111] What this shelter for "uninhibited interchange" can mean is illustrated by a remark by Acting Director Saccio of the International Cooperation Administration: "If ICA wanted to apply the 'executive privilege,' GAO [General Accounting Office, the congressional watchdog] would not see one thing because practically every document in our agency has an opinion or piece of advice."[112] Eisenhower's invitation to withholding was speedily cashed in on a broad scale.[113] In measuring the impact of the *Nixon* case, therefore, the scope of the claims hitherto made for executive privilege, its shelter for tier upon tier of little officials and petty communications, needs constantly to be borne in mind.

In the larger framework of the entire federal establishment, for which the Eisenhower and Nixon administrations increasingly claimed "confidential" immunity, Chief Justice Burger's "valid need" is by no means " too plain to require discussion." Despite the English reluctance to overrule a precedent of long standing, they found that an earlier sweeping pronouncement had given "free rein . . . to the tendency to secrecy which is inherent in the public service,"[114] with the foreseeable result that "candid interchange," in the words of Lord Radcliffe, came to be claimed for "everything, however commonplace, that has passed between one civil servant and another."[115] In *Conway v. Rimmer*[116], the House of Lords, to borrow from the eminent English commentator H. W. R. Wade, "shattered" the "candid interchange" argument "without mercy."[117] Justices Black, Frankfurter and Jackson had earlier endorsed the court of appeals' rejection of that argument in the *Reynolds*

---

[109]EXECUTIVE PRIVILEGE, *supra* note 6, at 234 (100 CONG. REC. 6621 (1954)).

[110]*Id.* at 254–55. (Washington Post, Apr. 11, 1973, at A1, col. 3). Commenting on the effect of the Eisenhower directive, Professor Telford Taylor stated in 1955 that congressional committees would "frequently be shut off from access to documents to which they were clearly entitled by tradition, common sense and good governmental practice." EXECUTIVE PRIVILEGE at 235–36 (T. TAYLOR, GRAND INQUEST 133 (1955)).

[111]C. MOLLENHOFF, WASHINGTON COVER-UP 210 (1962) [hereinafter cited as MOLLENHOFF].

[112]EXECUTIVE PRIVILEGE, *supra* note 6, at 236 (Kramer & Marcuse, *Executive Privilege: A Study of the Period 1953–1960*, 29 GEO. WASH. L. REV. 827, 852 (1961) [hereinafter cited as Kramer & Marcuse]). *See* text accompanying note 135 *infra*.

[113]EXECUTIVE PRIVILEGE, *supra* note 6, at 236–39.

[114]*Id.* at 231 (H. WADE, ADMINISTRATIVE LAW 285 (2d ed. 1967) [hereinafter cited as WADE]). An English scholar refers to the "civil servant's occupational love of secrecy," as the "official instinct of hiding as much as possible from the public gaze." EXECUTIVE PRIVILEGE at 367 n.109 (H. WADE, ADMINISTRATIVE LAW 16 (1961)).

The instinct of bureaucracy, as Max Weber pointed out, was "to increase the superiority of the professionally informed by keeping their knowledge and their intentions secret." The concept of the "official secret" was "the specific invention of bureaucracy," and officials defended nothing so "fanatically" as their secrets. A. SCHLESINGER, THE IMPERIAL PRESIDENCY 337 (1973).

[115]EXECUTIVE PRIVILEGE, *supra* note 6, at 231 (Glasgow Corp. v. Central Land Bd., [1956] Scots L.T.R. 41).

[116][1968] 1 All E.R. 874.

[117]EXECUTIVE PRIVILEGE 231 (Wade, *Crown Privilege Controlled at Last*, 84 L.Q. REV. 171, 172 (1968)). But compare this to Chief Justice Burger's statement: "Human experience teaches that those who expect public dissemination of their remarks may well temper candor with a concern for appearances and for their own interests to the detriment of the decision making process." 94 S. Ct. at 3106.

case.[118] So the "valid need" for protection of such communications cannot be regarded as self-evident.

Indeed, Eisenhower's assumption, which anticipated that of the *Nixon* case, that protection of "candid interchange" among subordinates is indispensable to good government is disproved by the fact that our nation flourished and prospered from 1789 to 1954 without the benefit of the Eisenhower curtain, as is attested by innumerable investigations of the executive branch in which we have no record that "confidentiality" was claimed.[119] It is disproved by the fact that Peruvian foreign-aid documents tied into an investigation of corruption and mismanagement, which were withheld by Eisenhower because disclosure allegedly "would gravely impair" administration, were promptly released by President Kennedy without untoward results.[120] It is disproved by the fact that Presidents Kennedy and Johnson drastically curtailed claims of executive privilege[121] and administration was not noticeably hampered. It is again disproved by the fact that in some agencies "anything in the department is open to" the GAO, including evaluation reports, internal staff memoranda and the like.[122] In fact, the former Legal Counsel to the Department of Justice pointed to the "vast outpouring of data, reports, letters . . . which flow from the executive to Congress,"[123] suggesting that withholding is occasioned not to encourage "candid interchange" but to escape embarrassment or conceal what should be made public, a point freshly underscored by President Nixon's confession that the tapes he had withheld (on pleas of executive privilege and the indispensability of "confidentiality" to the very survival of the Presidency) actually were concealed because they would disclose his orders to halt the investigation of the Watergate conspiracy.[124] Against the Court's assumption that "confidentiality" is indispensable to executive governance there is the fact that in carrying out its judicially acknowledged function of ferreting out corruption, inefficiency and waste in the Executive Branch, Congress has been compelled to require "confidential" communications. Without them Congress would have been unable to reveal the complicity of Secretaries Denby and Fall, and Attorney General Daugherty in the Teapot Dome scandal and of Attorney General John Mitchell *et al.* in the Watergate scandal; the list can be multiplied.[125] Against the debatable assumption that fear of disclosure to Congress may inhibit "candid interchange" and impair administration, there is the proven fact that such exchanges have time and again served as the vehicles of corruption and malversation, so that, to borrow from Lord Morris, "a greater measure of prejudice to the public interest would result from their non-production."[126] In an era given to "balancing" opposing policy considerations, such factors need to be taken into account; and we are entitled to be told why they are deemed insubstantial.

---

[118]United States v. Reynolds, 345 U.S. 1, 12 (1952).

[119]Executive Privilege, *supra* note 6, at 44 n. 171.

[120]*Id.* at 239–40. For a similar Pakistan incident, see *id.* at 237. A former Assistant Attorney General stated that the "Pakistan incident shows how embarrassing and damaging it may become to the concept of Executive privilege, if a congressional investigation, originally strongly resisted by an agency, proves to have been justified." *Id.* at 237 (Kramer & Marcuse, *supra* note 112, at 911.) More important, the incident shows that if the executive may censor what Congress may see, it can hamstring a badly needed exposé.

[121]Executive Privilege, *supra* note 6, at 252 n.107 (N.Y. Times, Aug. 20, 1973, at 31, col. 5).

[122]Executive Privilege, *supra* note 6, at 240.

[123]*Id.* at 241 n.44 (N.Y. Times, Mar. 23, 1973, at 35 col. 2).

[124]*See* note 132 *infra.*

[125]It had been vital to learn the nature of advice and recommendations of both high-level and low-level officials on settlements of huge tax cases . . . Caudle [Assistant Attorney General] and White House Aide Matthew Connelly could have claimed that their communications were "confidential executive business." As it was, the Caudle-Connelly communications were actually used as the basis of criminal charges on which Caudle and Connelly were convicted. . . ." Mollenhoff, *supra* note 111, at 50.

[126]Executive Privilege, *supra* note 6, at 243 (Mollenhoff, *supra* note 111, at 50).

V. MILITARY AND NATIONAL SECURITY SECRETS

In what may prove to be one of the costliest of its dicta, the Court raised a statement in *United States v. Reynolds,* itself pure dictum, to the level of dogma:

> It may be possible to satisfy the court, from all the circumstances of the case, that there is a reasonable danger that compulsion of the evidence will expose military matters which, in the interest of national security, should not be divulged. When this is the case, the occasion for the privilege is appropriate, and the court should not jeopardize the security which the privilege is meant to protect by insisting upon an examination of the evidence, even by the judge alone, in chambers.[127]

Earlier in the *Nixon* opinion, the Court had excluded "a claim of need to protect military, diplomatic or sensitive national security secrets" from *in camera* inspection.[128] Current events, one might expect, should have persuaded the Court that a Judge John J. Sirica or Gerhard Gesell is more to be trusted *in camera* with such matters than a John Ehrlichman or his like. Mr. Ehrlichman has been sentenced to prison for a break-in sought to be justified on grounds of "national security"; and the incident may serve to illustrate the difficulties which will confront a district judge in applying the *Reynolds* formula. The break-in to the office of psychiatrist Dr. Lewis Fielding, masterminded by the White House "Plumbers," had for its purpose the procurement of derogatory information respecting Daniel Ellsberg that could be used for political purposes. In what is one of the most fascinating portions of the President's taped conversations, we see him in conference with chief aide H.R. Haldeman and White House counsel John Dean, canvassing possible explanations of the break-in. Slowly it dawns on them that to invoke "national security" would interpose a shield against charges of illegality.[129] Suppose Dr. Fielding filed a suit for the break-in, and that Ehrlichman, one of the President's very closest advisers, represented to the court that further inquiry must be barred because "national security" would be imperilled, relying on vague representations, *e.g.* disclosure of wire-tapping to trace military leaks to Soviet Russia were involved. Given also Chief Justice Burger's quotation from the *C. & S. Air Lines v. Waterman Steamship Corp.* case: "The President . . . has available intelligence services whose reports are not and ought not to be published to the world,"[130] and it would have been a stout judge (before Watergate) that would have dared, in the teeth of such a representation, to jeopardize "national security" by *in camera* inspection. It should be noted that the author of the *Waterman* opinion, Justice Jackson, later stated with respect to bureaucratic claims that disclosure threatens national security: "security is like liberty in that many crimes are committed in its name,"[131] a statement freshly proven by Mr. Nixon's disclosure that he tried to halt the FBI investigation of the Watergate break-in on the ground, among others, that it might reopen the Bay of Pigs incident.[132]

---

[127]94 S. Ct. at 3109, *quoting* United States v. Reynolds, 345 U.S. 1 (1952).

[128]94 S. Ct. at 3107.

[129]On March 21, 1973, Nixon, Haldeman and Dean were discussing how to deal with the break-in:

President: How you keep it out, I don't know. You can't keep it out if Hunt talks. . . .

Dean: You might put it on national security grounds basis.

. . . .

President: National Security. We had to get information for national security grounds.

. . . .

President: With the bombing coming out and everything coming out, the whole thing was national security.

Dean: I think we could get by on that.

THE WHITE HOUSE TRANSCRIPTS 163 (Bantam ed. 1974).

[130]94 S. Ct. at 3109, *quoting* C. & S. Air Lines v. Waterman Steamship Corp., 333 U.S. 103, 111 (1948).

[131]EXECUTIVE PRIVILEGE, *supra* note 6, at 224 (Knauff v. Shaughnessy, 338 U.S. 537, 551 (1951) (Jackson J., dissenting)).

[132]Mr. Nixon has virtually admitted that his representations on May 22, 1973 that the "F.B.I. investigation might lead to the exposure either of unrelated covert activities of the C.I.A. or of sensitive national security matters" and therefore gave

The exception for military secrets and national security needs to be examined in light of bureaucratic infatuation with secrecy.[133] The English experience, an English scholar found, demonstrated that whenever the bureaucracy is "given a blank cheque," it unfailingly yields "to the temptation to overdraw,"[134] as is confirmed by our own experience. The potential scope of the exception may be gathered from the statement of Professor Joseph Bishop, former General Counsel to the Army:

> [T]here is not much information in the files of the State and Defense Departments—of a sort likely to attract congressional interest—which could not with some plausibility be given a security classification, if the executive wished to withhold it on that [or any other] ground.[135]

The *Reynolds* statement that "[j]udicial control over the evidence in a case cannot be abdicated to the caprice of executive officers"[136] is no less true in this than in other areas of executive privilege.

Against the *Reynolds-Nixon* dicta, which rest on pure assumption, I would cite the sober reflections of a long-time high officer of the State Department, Charles W. Yost, former Ambassador to the United Nations. "National security," he stated,

> is a godsend. It enables a government official to justify keeping his actions and intentions secret even when they might lead the nation into war.
>
> Genuine considerations of national security may require secrecy in regard to the character and deployment of certain weapons. In my thirty-five years in foreign affairs, however, I almost never found that the public disclosure of political measures or plans could be truthfully said to jeopardize national security or to be more than temporarily inconvenient.
>
> Once "national security" has come to be accepted as a cloak for the conduct of foreign affairs, [or military, *e.g.* the secret bombing of Cambodia] it is all too likely that public officials will find it irresistibly convenient for cloaking also some of their more far-out domestic activities [*e.g.* the White House "Plumbers"]. In fact, once they slip into the national security psychosis, they easily begin to equate, as we have so often seen, the nation's security with their own political power or their partisan aims.[137]

These are the realities which the Court, in my opinion, should have weighed before it gave fresh currency to the *Reynolds* anti-*in camera* dictum.[138] Finally, when one compares the Nixon aides with Judges Sirica and Gesell, fresh point is given to the 1951 statement of Circuit Judge Albert Maris: There is no "danger to the public interest in submitting the question of privilege to the

instructions to "ensure that investigation not expose these sensitive national security matters" was false. "The June 23 tapes clearly show," he continues, "that at the time I gave those instructions I also discussed the political aspects of the situation, and that I was aware of the advantages . . . [of] limiting possible public exposure of involvement [in the Watergate break-in] by persons connected with the re-election committee." The tapes show not only that he was "aware" but that he gave orders to abort the FBI investigation. N.Y. Times, Aug. 6, 1974, at 1, 15, col. 8. "National security" was an unadulterated sham. Such are the uses of "confidentiality."

[133]*See note 114 supra.*

[134]EXECUTIVE PRIVILEGE, *supra* note 6, at 219 (WADE, *supra* note 114, at 285).

[135]*Id.* at 216 n.39 (Bishop, *The Executive's Right of Privacy: An Unresolved Constitutional Question,* 66 YALE L.J. 477, 487 (1957). *See also* text accompanying note 112 *supra.* A former Pentagon security officer testified that "less than one-half of 1 per cent . . . actually contain information qualifying for the lowest defense classification." *Id.* at 368 n.114, (A. SCHLESINGER, THE IMPERIAL PRESIDENCY 344 (1973)).

[136]345 U.S. 1, 9–10 (1953).

[137]EXECUTIVE PRIVILEGE, *supra* note 6, at 369 (Yost, *Security Cloak Has Way of Deceiving the Deceiver,* Baltimore Sun, Nov. 3, 1973, Opinion Section, at 17.

[138]A former Nixon aide, William Safire, commented,

Future Presidents, with the ghost of Mr. Nixon nodding approvingly over their shoulders, will take the Court's decision to mean that a "need to protect military, diplomatic or sensitive national security secrets" gives the Chief Executive the privilege of withholding anything—anything—from even the in camera inspection of a Federal judge . . . [Mr. Nixon's] winning of national security privilege is a dark victory.

N.Y. Times, July 29, 1974, at 23, col. 5–6.

decision of the courts. The judges . . . are public officers whose responsibility under the Constitution is just as great as that of the heads of the executive departments."[139] The Founders had far greater confidence in the courts than in the executive; and it is passing strange in light of the pronounced current preference for courts over President Nixon and his henchmen that this view is not shared by the Court.

Secrecy in the operations of government is an abomination, as Mr. Nixon has demonstrated anew. In the hands of his administration, "confidentiality" was the vehicle for the cover-up of criminal acts and conspiracies by his aides, an instrument he repeatedly employed for the obstruction of justice. This was not the finest hour for the legitimation of "confidentiality," but rather for searching examination of the evils perpetrated in its name, for limiting it, as Marshall did with respect to the express grant to Congress, to *matters* which it would be "fatal and pernicious" to disclose.[140]

---

[139]EXECUTIVE PRIVILEGE, *supra* note 6, at 219–220 (Reynolds v. United States, 192 F.2d 987, 997 (3d Cir. 1951)).
[140]*See* text accompanying note 72 *supra*.

CHAPTER V

Congressional Subpoenas to Executive Officials

How far a court is warranted in substituting its judgment for that of a congressional committee when asked to enforce its subpoena presents vexing questions that were not considered in *Senate Select Committee v Nixon*.[1] In the "first such case in our history,"[2] the Senate Select Committee on Presidential Campaign Activities (Ervin Committee), created by a resolution of the Senate to investigate improper activities during the 1972 presidential election,[3] brought an action to enforce its subpoena to President Nixon for some of his tape-recorder "confidential" communications with his principal aides. The United States Court of Appeals for the District of Columbia Circuit held that presidential communications are "presumptively privileged";[4] that "the presumption can be overcome only by an appropriate showing of public need"[5] by the suitor; and that the Committee had failed to make the requisite showing.[6] The case is truly unprecedented; and it is not surprising under the unique circumstances that the court did not come to grips with fundamental issues that needed to be examined. It assumed, rather, that it could build on its earlier decision, *Nixon v. Sirica*,[7] respecting enforcement of a grand jury subpoena to the President, a situation that differs markedly from a congressional subpoena to a member of the executive branch. An adequate treatment of the issues involved requires (1) a survey of the historical roots of judicial review of congressional subpoenas, (2) an evaluation of the considerations governing judicial review of congressional subpoenas to private individuals, and (3) of the applicability of such considerations to congressional subpoenas issued to executive officials. The Supreme Court's decision in *United States v. Nixon*,[8] involving the Special Prosecutor's subpoena to the former President, elevated the D.C. Circuit's rule of "presumptive privilege" to a constitutional level.[9] Its impact upon future cases of congressional subpoenas to the executive branch must also be examined in light of the congressional oversight power. Finally, the various methods of enforcing congressional subpoenas to executive officials will be briefly discussed.

I. HISTORY OF JUDICIAL REVIEW OF CONGRESSIONAL SUBPOENAS

For the first ninety years of our history, the courts acknowledged the immunity of congressional investigations from curtailment by judicial intervention. The authority to conduct congressional inquiries and the auxiliary contempt power to compel testimony pursuant to such investigations,

---

[1]498 F.2d 725 (D.C. Cir. 1974).
[2]*Id.* at 733.
[3]S. Res. 60, 93d Cong., 1st Sess. § 1(a) (1973).
[4]498 F.2d at 731.
[5]*Id.* at 730.
[6]*Id.* at 733.
[7]487 F.2d 700 (D.C. Cir. 1973).
[8]418 U.S. 683 (1974).
[9]*Id.* at 708; *see notes* 95-133 and accompanying text *infra*.

it is generally agreed, are rooted in English history. For the scope of Parliament's power, we have the testimony of the Supreme Court in *Watkins v. United States*:[10]

> The rudiments of the power to punish for "contempt of Congress" come to us from the pages of English history. . . . [Both Houses of Parliament] claimed absolute and plenary authority over their privileges. . . . [O]nly Parliament could judge what conduct constituted a breach of privilege.
>
> . . . [This] precluded judicial review of the exercise of the contempt power or the assertion of privilege. Parliament declared that no court had jurisdiction to consider such questions.[11]

But, the Court mistakenly concluded, "[u]nlike the English practice, from the very outset the use of contempt power by the legislature was deemed subject to judicial review."[12] The case cited for this proposition, *Anderson v. Dunn*,[13] however, supports the opposite position, that congressional exercise of the contempt power within its jurisdiction was nonreviewable.

In *Anderson*[14] an action of trespass was brought against the Sergeant-at-Arms of the House of Representatives for assault and battery and false-imprisonment. The plaintiff had been taken into custody by the Sergeant-at-Arms pursuant to a warrant issued by the House and brought before the bar of the House to answer a charge of attempted bribery of a member of the House. He had been found guilty, reprimanded by the Speaker, and then discharged from custody. The issue before the Supreme Court was "whether the House of Representatives can take cognizance of contempts committed against themselves under any circumstances?"[15] The Court found that such power exists in the Congress as a necessary incident to the exercise of its express powers.[16]

There is not the faintest claim by the Court in *Anderson* that it had the power to set a congressional contempt aside. In fact, Justice William Johnson, one of the ablest judges who ever graced the Court, gave every indication to the contrary. He noted the acknowledged power of the House summarily to commit for a contempt in its presence and asked, "why should the house be at liberty to exercise an ungranted, an *unlimited,* and undefined power within their walls, any more than without them?"[17] And in *Kilbourn v. Thompson*[18] Justice Miller, who was no friend of the congressional contempt power, stated that *Anderson* held that

> there is in some cases a power in each House of Congress to punish for contempt: that this power is analogous to that exercised by courts of justice, and that it being the well-established doctrine that when it appears that a prisoner is held under the order of a court of general jurisdiction for a contempt of its authority, no other court will discharge the prisoner or make further inquiry into the case of his commitment.[19]

As the Court in *Kilbourn* noted, *Anderson* "was decided . . . undoubtedly under pressure of the strong rulings of the English courts in favor of the privileges of the two Houses of Parliament."[20]

---

[10]354 U.S. 178 (1975). *See also* Berger, *Constructive Contempt: A Post Mortem,* 9 U. CHI. L. REV. 602, 611 (1942).

[11]354 U.S. at 188.

[12]*Id.* at 192.

[13]19 U.S. (6 Wheat.) 204 (1821).

[14]According to Chief Justice Warren in *Watkins, Anderson* was the "first case [of this sort] to reach this Court. . . ." 354 U.S. at 192 n.20.

[15]19 U.S. at 224–25.

[16]*Id.* at 225–26.

[17]*Id.* at 299 (emphasis supplied).

[18]103 U.S. 168 (1880); *see* text accompanying notes 28–33 *infra.*

[19]103 U.S. at 197, *See* Marshall v. Gordon, 243 U.S. 521, 537 (1971); text accompanying notes 34–38 *infra.*

[20]103 U.S. at 198. Justice Johnson in *Anderson* stressed the appropriateness of drawing from the English practice in construing the Constitution:

> [T]he constitution . . . rests at every point on received opinions and fixed ideas. It is not a new creation, but a combination of existing materials, whose properties and attributes were familiarly understood, and had been determined by reiterated experiments.

The English practice was next referred to by Justice Story in *Ex parte Kearney*,[21] which involved a contempt of a circuit court. There, Justice Story, who had sat with Johnson in *Anderson*, cited the leading British case, *Brass Crosby's Case*,[22] involving a contempt against the House of Commons. Story quoted Justice Blackstone who had lumped together the practices of "the two Houses of Parliament, and the courts of Westminster-Hall."[23] In *Brass Crosby* both Blackstone and Justice Gould concurred with Lord Chief Justice de Grey that "this Court hath no cognizance of contempts or breaches of privilege of the House of Commons: they are the only judges of their own privileges. . . ."[24] Thus, Story drew on the practice which insulated the House of Commons from judicial review in order to justify similar restraint with respect to a court.

The next case was *In re Nugent*[25] in the circuit court for the District of Columbia, where Chief Justice Cranch's opinion for a unanimous court contains a comprehensive review of the English cases, not paralleled in the Supreme Court decisions. On the basis of the English precedents, he held:

> The law as stated by the court in [Brass] Crosby's Case was the law of the land both in this country and in England before our Revolution, and has so continued to the present time.[26]
>
> . . . .
>
> These cases and authorities, we think, show conclusively that the senate . . . has power to punish for contempts of its authority in cases of which it has jurisdiction; that every court, including the senate and house of representatives, is the sole judge of its own contempts; and that in case of the commitment for contempt in such a case, no other court can have a right to inquire directly into the correctness of propriety of the commitment.[27]

Thus stood the law until *Kilbourn v. Thompson*[28] was decided in 1880. The Court there rejected the English practice altogether on the ground that the House of Commons was a court whereas the House of Representatives was not. In fact, however, the Commons enjoyed no part in the process of adjudication, for that was the exclusive prerogative of the House of Lords.[29] Coke stated in 1621 in the Commons that "we have no power to iudg [*sic*]; we may examine," that is, investigate;[30] and in 1667 the Commons "thought the judicial power better lodged with [the Lords] than in the Commons themselves."[31] In *McGrain v. Daugherty*[32] the Court flatly rejected *Kil-*

---

19 U.S. at 230. *See also* Chief Justice Taft's opinion in *Ex parte* Grossman, 267 U.S. 87, 108–09 (1925).

[21]120 U.S. (7 Wheat.) 38 (1822).

[22]3 Wils. 188, 95 E.R. 1005 (1771).

[23]20 U.S. at 41, 43–44, *quoting* Brass Crosby's Case, 3 Wils. 188, 204, 95 E.R. 1005, 1014 (1771).

[24]3 Wils. at 203, 95 E.R. at 1013. In *Brass Crosby's Case* Serjeant Glynn, arguing on the writ of habeas corpus for Brass Crosby, Lord Mayor of London, that the cause of the latter's commitment was insufficient in law to justify his detention, urged the Court to discharge him from the custody of the Lieutenant of the Tower of London. In refusing the writ, Lord Chief Justice de Grey stated:
The House of Commons therefore having an authority to commit, and that commitment being an execution, the question is, what can this Court do? It can do nothing when a person is in execution, by the judgment of a Court having a competent jurisdiction [that is, the House of Commons]; in such a case, this Court is not a Court of Appeal.
Id. at 199, 95 E.R. at 1011.

[25]18 Fed. Cas. 471 (No. 10,375) (C.C.D.C. 1848).

[26]*Id.* at 473.

[27]*Id.* at 481.

[28]103 U.S. 168 (1880).

[29]*See* R. BERGER, IMPEACHMENT: THE CONSTITUTIONAL PROBLEMS 18–20 (1973) [hereinafter cited as BERGER, IMPEACHMENT].

[30]3 W. NOTESTEIN, F. RELF & H. SIMPSON, COMMONS DEBATES: 1621, at 54 (1935).

[31]6 HOWELL'S STATE TRIALS 360. Indeed, the Court in *Kilbourn*, 103 U.S. at 198, quoted from Justice Coleridge in Stockdale v. Hansard, 9 Ad. & E. 1 (1839):
The House is not a court of law at all in the sense in which that term can alone be properly applied here. Neither originally nor by appeal can it decide a matter in litigation between two parties . . . it claims no such power; powers of inquiry and accusation it has, but it decides nothing judicially, except where it is itself a party, in the case of contempts.

[32]273 U.S. 135 (1927).

bourn's historically unsound intimation that "neither house of Congress has power to make inquiries and exact evidence in aid of contemplated legislation."[33]

McGrain had been anticipated by *Marshall v. Gordon,*[34] where Chief Justice White stated that *Anderson*

> explicitly decided that from the power to legislate given by the Constitution to Congress there was to be implied the right of Congress to preserve itself, that is, to deal by way of contempt with direct obstructions to its legislative duties.[35]

This implied power, he stated, "rests solely upon the right of self-preservation to enable the public powers given to be exerted,"[36] that is, "the right to prevent acts which in and of themselves inherently obstruct or prevent the discharge of legislative duty or the refusal to do that which there is an inherent legislative power to compel in order that legislative functions may be performed."[37] Coming from Louisiana, a Civil Law state, White found the argument from principle more congenial than resort to the common law. But it was on that law that the legislative power was modelled; and the authority to issue contempts was an attribute of common law conceptions of legislative authority.[38]

In sum, the courts did not interfere with Parliament's investigations into executive conduct nor its exercise of the contempt power; and for the first ninety years of our history American judges considered—and with good reason—that our American law followed this practice. No intimation is to be found in the records of the several Conventions that the traditional power of inquiry with its accompanying attributes was to be curtailed in any particular.[39]

Judicial review of congressional subpoenas entered the law for the protection of private individuals from investigations in excess of jurisdiction or in violation of constitutional guarantees; and its limits were epitomized by Chief Justice White in *Marshall:*

> unless there be . . . a mere exertion of arbitrary power coming within the reach of constitutional limitations, the exercise of the [investigatory] authority is not subject to judicial interference.[40]

Thus, judicial review was limited to inquiry whether the particular investigation was within the jurisdiction of Congress and whether the demand for information was consistent with Bill of Rights guarantees. Congressional subpoenas to executive officials, however, involve considerations that differ from those present in the private individual subpoena context and call for a greater degree of judicial restraint.

II. SUBPOENAS TO PRIVATE INDIVIDUALS CONTRASTED WITH SUBPOENAS TO OFFICIALS

Spurred by excesses which discredited congressional investigations during the Communist witch-hunting era,[41] and to counter what the Supreme Court characterized as "broad-scale intru-

---

[33]*Id.* at 171. It further explained and distinguished *Kilbourn* on the ground that there "the resolution contained no suggestion of contemplated legislation; that the matter was one in respect to which no valid legislation could be had"; and consequently that the House had exceeded its powers and assumed to exercise clearly judicial power. *Id.*

[34]243 U.S. 521 (1917).

[35]*Id.* at 537.

[36]*Id.* at 541.

[37]*Id.* at 542.

[38]*See* text accompanying note 157 *infra.*

[39]*See* text accompanying notes 163–67 *infra.*

[40]243 U.S. at 545.

[41]*See* W. GOODMAN, THE COMMITTEE (1968).

sion into the lives and affairs of private citizens,"[42] undertaken "without justification in terms of the functions of Congress,"[43] the Court began to pay special attention to its "responsibility . . . to insure that Congress does not unjustifiably encroach upon an individual's right to privacy nor abridge his liberty of speech, press, religion or assembly."[44] The guarantees of the fourth and fifth amendments played an increasingly important role.[45] With respect to congressional demands for the testimony of private individuals, the state of the law was well summarized in *Quinn v. United States:*[46]

> Without the power to investigate—including of course the authority to compel testimony . . . Congress could be seriously handicapped in its efforts to exercise its constitutional function wisely and effectively.
>
> But the power to investigate, broad as it may be, is also subject to recognized limitations. It cannot be used to inquire into private affairs unrelated to a valid legislative purpose. Nor does it extend to an area in which Congress is forbidden to legislate [for example, by the First Amendment]. . . . Still further limitations . . . are found in the specific individual guarantees of the Bill of Rights, such as the Fifth Amendment's privilege against self-incrimination. . . .[47]

But even as the Court set out "limitations" upon the power of inquiry, it carefully set to one side "the powers of Congress to inquire into and publicize corruption, maladministration or inefficiency in the agencies of the Government."[48] There are solid reasons for differentiating broad inquiries into executive conduct from the protection of private individuals, which I shall discuss under two headings: (1) the different nature of the rights involved, and (2) the different responsibilities of Congress and the attendant role of the courts in the two situations.

A. Different Nature of the Rights

The private rights protected by the Constitution are, to my mind, not generally relevant to inquiries into executive conduct. Misconduct in office can hardly be shielded as a private or personal affair.[49] As James Wilson assured the Pennsylvania Ratification Convention, "[t]the executive power is better to be trusted when it has no screen . . . [The President cannot] hide either his negligence or inattention,"[50] much less his affirmative misconduct.

In his brief filed on behalf of the President in *United States v. Nixon,*[51] Mr. James St. Clair based his client's claim of absolute presidential discretion to withhold "confidential" communications on "the right of privacy and the constitutionally protected freedom of expression."[52] Mr. St. Clair's springboard was a remark by Judge Wilkey, dissenting in *Nixon v. Sirica,*[53] that "[t]o breach [the President's] privacy would unquestionably have a 'chilling effect' on those who otherwise would

---

[42]Watkins v. United States, 354 U.S. 178, 195 (1957).

[43]*Id.* at 187.

[44]*Id.* at 198–99. For an earlier allusion to the "right of privacy," *see* Sinclair v. United States, 279 U.S. 263, 292 (1929).

[45]Watkins v. United States, 354 U.S. 178, 188 (1957); Quinn v. United States, 349 U.S. 155, 160–61 (1955).

[46]349 U.S. 155 (1955). *See also* McGrain v. Daugherty, 273 U.S. 135, 175 (1927); Barenblatt v. United States, 360 U.S. 109, 111 (1959).

[47]349 U.S. at 160–61 (citations omitted).

[48]Watkins v. United States, 354 U.S. 178, 200 n.33 (1957).

[49]Even in the case of a private individual who deals with the government, as in Harry Sinclair's negotiation of oil leases on naval reserves, the investigation no longer relates "merely to . . . [his] private or personal affairs"; the matter becomes "of concern to the United States." Sinclair v. United States, 279 U.S. 263, 294 (1929). The question whether a broker bought sugar stocks on behalf of a Senator was not an unreasonable search into the private affairs of the witness." In re Chapman, 166 U.S. 661, 669 (1897).

[50] 2 J. ELLIOT, DEBATES IN THE SEVERAL STATE CONVENTIONS ON THE ADOPTION OF THE FEDERAL CONSTITUTION 480 (1896) [hereinafter cited as ELLIOT].

[51]418 U.S. 683 (1974); *see* notes 95–133 and accompanying text *infra.*

[52]Brief for Respondent and Cross-Petitioner at 69, United States v. Nixon, 418 U.S. 683 (1974).

[53]487 F.2d 700 (D.C. Cir. 1973).

counsel and confide in the President with complete candor and honesty."[54] But as one of the cases cited by Mr. St. Clair, *Griswold v. Connecticut,*[55] observed, the "right of privacy . . . [was] carefully and particularly reserved to the people."[56] And *Griswold* further stated that the fourth and fifth amendments provided "protection against all governmental invasions 'of the sanctity of a man's home and the privacies of life.' "[57] In short, the Bill of Rights was designed to secure protection to the people against the government,[58] not to insulate government officers from accountability or to envelop government files in secrecy.[59] This is made crystal clear by the first amendment on which Mr. St. Clair relied for his "freedom of expression." For example, the companion phrase—"the right of the people . . . to petition the Government for a redress of grievances"—testifies that the first amendment is concerned with "the right of the people peaceably to assemble," not of officers of government against whom protection was thus guaranteed.

This is not to say that government officers may not invoke the fifth amendment rights against self-incrimination and double jeopardy, or the sixth amendment right to trial by jury. The sixth amendment, however, refers to the "accused" in "all criminal prosecutions," and the fifth amendment is cast in terms of "No person" and "any person." In contrast, the fourth amendment speaks of "The right of the people to be secure in their persons, houses . . . against unreasonable seizures." The Founders well knew how to broaden rights secured to "the people" so as to embrace "any person," including officers of the government. They were aware that inquiries by the Grand Inquest of the Nation into executive conduct and files knew no bounds.[60] Where they omitted to speak in terms of "any person," reliance by government officers on the Bill of Rights should be unavailing as a defense to congressional inquiries into their official conduct.

On its face, therefore, the fourth amendment affords no protection to government officers from searches of government files as distinguished from searches of their "houses" for private "papers and effects." And though an officer may avail himself of the privilege against self-incrimination with respect to his private affairs, that privilege is unavailable to him when it is government records that are sought, on the analogy of corporate records which, it is settled, afford no basis to the individual for a claim against self-incrimination.[61]

Similarly, outcries against "fishing expeditions" into executive department files should be discounted as attempts to transplant a slogan which had its source in fourth amendment appeals by private individuals and corporations to the wholly inapposite context of legislative investigation of official conduct. Moreover, the invocation of "no fishing expeditions" resurrects a slogan that was interred in the private rights field by Justice Jackson. He explained in *United States v. Morton*

[54]*Id.* at 767.

[55]381 U.S. 479 (1965).

[56]*Id.* at 485, *quoting* Mapp v. Ohio, 367 U.S. 643, 656 (1961).

[57]381 U.S. at 484–85.

[58]"The 'Bill of Rights' is concerned only with the protection of the individual against the impact of federal or state law." L. HAND, THE BILL OF RIGHTS 31 (1962).

[59]The Court's statement in United States v. Nixon, 418 U.S. 683, 708 (1974), that presidential confidentiality "has all the values to which we accord deference for the privacy of all citizens," should not be read to import a "right of privacy" into executive affairs.

[60]*Compare* the Act of September 2, 1789, which made it "the duty of the Secretary of the Treasury" to "give information to either branch of the legislature . . . respecting *all* matters . . . which shall pertain to his office." 1 Stat 65—66 (emphasis supplied). It was to the honor of the House of Commons, said James Wilson, that they "checked the progress or arbitrary power" by calling on the "proudest ministers of the proudest monarchs . . . to give an account of their conduct." 2 J. WILSON, WORKS 731, (McCloskey ed. 1967). For the great sweep of parliamentary investigations, *see* R. BERGER, EXECUTIVE PRIVILEGE: A CONSTITUTIONAL MYTH 15–31 (1974) [hereinafter cited as BERGER, EXECUTIVE PRIVILEGE].

[61]It is well settled that "[b]ooks and records kept in a representative rather than in a personal capacity cannot be the subject of personal privilege against self-incrimination, even though production of the papers might tend to incriminate [their keeper] personally." United States v. White, 322 U.S. 694, 699 (1944); *see* McPhaul v. United States, 364 U.S. 372, 380 (1960); Curcio v. United States, 354 U.S. 118, 122 (1957); Shapiro v. United States, 335 U.S. 1, 17 (1948).

Salt Co.,[62] after a review of earlier cases, that the courts are confined to the "adjudication of cases," and since they could not go fishing, neither could anyone else. Administrative investigations fell before the colorful and nostalgic slogan "no fishing expeditions."[63] Not a little of this attitude, one may surmise, sprang from early judicial distrust of administrative investigations,[64] for the analogous grand jury practice was much broader. A witness before a grand jury, for example,

> is not entitled to urge objections of incompetency or irrelevancy, such as a party [to a trial] might raise, for this is no concern of his. . . . He is not entitled to set limits to the investigation that the grand jury may conduct. . . . It is a grand inquest, a body with powers of investigation and inquisition, the scope of whose inquiries is not to be limited narrowly by questions of propriety or forecasts of the probable result of the investigation.[65]

In *Morton Salt*, Justice Jackson placed administrative agencies on an equal footing as investigatory bodies with grand juries, stating that an administrative agency, under powers conferred by Congress, "has a power of inquisition . . . analogous to the Grand Jury, . . . [and] can investigate merely on suspicion that the law is being violated, or even just because it wants assurance that it is not."[66]

"Fishing expeditions" are often unavoidable. Consider the bank examiner who calls at a bank and is confronted by row upon row of filing cabinets. Whether there is fraud or embezzlement only appears after examination; and to designate "relevant" documents before such examination would require X-ray eyes.[67] Assistant Attorney General Hansen "admitted that it might be difficult for a subcommittee to make demands for specific documents without having examined the files,"[68] as Professor Bernard Schwartz learned when he was cast in the role of investigator.[69] Chief Justice Marshall asked on the trial of Aaron Burr, "if a paper be in the possession of the opposite party, what statement of its contents or applicancy can be expected from [his opponent] he not knowing of its contents?"[70] Insistence upon a preliminary bill of "relevant" particulars would abort congressional investigation at the threshold.

B. Different Responsibilities of Congress and Attendant Role of the Courts

1. *Congressional Oversight Responsibility over the Executive.* General oversight of the conduct of the Executive Branch was confided to the Legislature, not to the Judiciary. Chief Justice Marshall disclaimed such oversight responsibilities in *Marbury v. Madison:*[71]

> The province of the court is, solely, to decide on the rights of individuals, not to inquire how the executive, or executive officers, perform duties in which they have a discretion.[72]

---

[62]338 U.S. 632 (1950). *See also* United States v. Powell, 379 U.S. 48, 57 (1965).

[63]338 U.S. at 641–42.

[64]As late as 1939, the Court cautioned the lower courts that administrative agencies cannot "rightly be regarded . . . as an alien intruder." United States v. Morgan, 307 U.S. 183, 191 (1939).

[65]Blair v. United States, 250 U.S. 273, 282 (1919). *See also* Oklahoma Press Publishing Co. v. Walling, 327 U.S. 186, 216 (1946).

[66]338 U.S. at 642–43. The Court added:
> Even if one were to regard the request for information in this case as caused by nothing more than official curiosity, nevertheless law-enforcing agencies have a legitimate right to satisfy themselves that corporate behavior is consistent with the law and the public interest.

Id. at 652. *See* 1 K. DAVIS, ADMINISTRATIVE LAW TREATIES 188 (1958) ("The breadth of an investigation is for the investigators to determine").

[67]An administrative investigation cannot be "limited . . . by the forecasts of the probable result of the investigation." Blair v. United States, 250 U.S. 273, 282 (1919).

[68]Kramer & Marcuse, *Executive Privilege—A Study of the Period* 1953–1960, 29 GEO. WASH. L. REV. 827, 890 (1961).

[69]Schwartz, *Executive Privilege and Congressional Investigatory Power*, 47 CALIF. L. REV. 3, 4 (1959).

[70]3 T. CARPENTER, TRIAL OF AARON BURR 35 (1808).

[71]5 U.S. (1 Cranch) 137 (1803).

[72]5 U.S. at 169–70; *see also* text accompanying note 84 *infra*.

Precisely that function—inquiry into the manner in which executive officers have performed their official duties—lies within the province of the legislature.[73] Thus, congressional interrogation of executive officials rests not only on the need for their testimony in aid of general congressional functions, as in the case of private individuals, but also upon its responsibility to oversee the conduct of the executive branch.[74] This additional congressional responsibility, not present in the private individual subpoena cases, calls for a different judicial role.

2. *The Select Committee Roadblock. Senate Select Committee v. Nixon*[75] exhibits a disquieting inroad on the exclusive congressional oversight responsibility. There the Ervin Committee[76] sought enforcement of its subpoena duces tecum directing President Nixon to produce "original electronic tapes" of five conversations between the President and his former Counsel, John W. Dean, III.[77] The Committee asserted that it needed the subpoenaed materials in order to resolve conflicts in testimony it had already taken involving "the extent of malfeasance in the executive branch," and possible direct presidential participation in criminal conduct.[78]

In refusing to enforce the Committee's subpoena, the D.C. Circuit found no occasion to "deny that the Congress may have, quite apart from its legislative responsibilities, a general oversight power,"[79] for it rested its decision on the insufficiency of the Committee's showing that the subpoenaed evidence was "demonstrably critical to the responsible fulfillment of the Committee's functions."[80] Since the House Judiciary Committee had already begun an inquiry into the possibility of presidential impeachment and had possession of copies of the tapes, the court found that as regards the subpoenaed tapes, the "investigative objectives of the two committees substantially overlap. . . . [so that the] Select Committee's immediate oversight need for the subpoenaed tapes is, from a congressional perspective, merely cumulative."[81]

Such a conclusion represents an unwarranted interference with congressional oversight powers. It is a preclusive view that was not shared by President Washington. Although he refused the Jay Treaty papers to the House, after furnishing them to his Senate treaty-partner, he explained that the House had no part in treaty-making so that the papers were not "relative to any purpose under the cognizance of the House."[82] But he emphasized that he had no disposition to "withhold any information . . . which could be required of him as a right"[83]—in other words, where the House

---

[73]*See* text accompanying notes 157–67 *infra*.

[74]Tocqueville noted in 1831 that "In the exercise of the executive power the President . . . is constantly subject to a jealous supervision." 1 A. DE TOCQUEVILLE, DEMOCRACY IN AMERICA 123 (Colonial Press 1899). Holmes "saw it as a basic value in the separation of powers that ultimate surveillance should rest in the legislature." W. HURST, JUSTICE HOLMES ON LEGAL HISTORY 99 (1964). The "celebrated Montesquieu," who is "the oracle who is always consulted and cited on [the separation of powers] subject," THE FEDERALIST No. 47, at 313 (Mod. Lib. ed. 1937) (J. Madison), stated that the legislature "has a right, and ought to have the means, of examining in what manner its laws have been executed," in which the English enjoy an advantage over some governments where public officers "gave no account of their administration." C. MONTESQUIEU, THE SPIRIT OF THE LAWS 187 (Philadelphia ed. 1802). Professors Gellhorn and Byse state that "one of the fundamental concepts of our form of government is that the legislature, as representative of the people, will maintain a degree of supervision over the administration of governmental affairs." W. GELLHORN & C. BYSE, ADMINISTRATIVE LAW: CASES AND COMMENTS 166 (1960). *See also* T. TAYLOR, GRAND INQUEST 7 (1955).

[75]498 F.2d 725 (D.C. Cir. 1974).

[76]*See* note 3 and accompanying text *supra*.

[77]498 F.2d at 726.

[78]*Id.* at 731.

[79]*Id.* at 732, *See* note 74 *supra*.

[80]*Id.* at 731.

[81]*Id.* at 732. The court went on to reject the contention that the subpoenaed tapes were needed for the Select Committee's or Congress' legislative functions, stating that "Congress frequently legislates on the basis of conflicting information provided in its hearings." *Id. See* text accompanying note 86 *infra*.

[82]BERGER, EXECUTIVE PRIVILEGE, *supra* note 60, at 172.

[83]*Id.*

had jurisdiction to inquire. The Senate's possession of the papers, Washington thereby indicated, would not foreclose the right of the House to have them, if this were an area of House responsibility. Senate and House Committees have long carried on their own independent investigations, often into the same subject matter; and each has been the sole judge of what its own functions require. And in *Oceanic Steam Navigation Co. v. Stranahan*[84] the Court rejected the assumption, with respect to the scope of legislative authority,

> that it is within the competency of judicial authority to control legislative action as to subjects over which there is complete legislative authority, on the theory that there was no necessity calling for the exertion of legislative power.[85]

Courts are likewise "incompetent" to inquire into the necessity or usefulness of a particular exercise of Congress's oversight power.

The distinction drawn by the D.C. Circuit between grand jury needs and those of the Select Committee also seems to me to be mistaken and inverted. The court stated:

> There is a clear difference between Congress's legislative tasks and the responsibility of a grand jury. . . . [Unlike] the grand jury's need for the most precise evidence . . . [there is no] comparable need in the legislative process. . . .[86]

The needs of the grand jury and those of an investigating committee of Congress exercising the oversight function are indeed incommensurable. The Grand Inquest of the Nation, looking into executive conduct that affects the nation, historically has played a grander role than the grand inquest of the county engaged in examining individual criminality. In the words of Justice Coleridge,

> the general inquisitors of the realm . . . may inquire into everything which it concerns the public weal for them to know; and they themselves, I think, are entrusted with the determination of what falls within that category.[87]

One needs only to read James Wilson's eulogy of that function to realize that the Founders had no intention of curtailing it.[88]

The D.C. Circuit in *Select Committee* rested its ruling on the "decisional structure"[89] it had earlier established in *Nixon v. Sirica*,[90] that the executive branch enjoyed a "presumptive privilege" of confidentiality rebuttable only by an appropriate showing of "public need" by the party seeking to pierce the veil of secrecy. This is the conceptual framework that the Supreme Court more fully developed in *United States v. Nixon*.[91] It is submitted, however, that this "structure" is of questionable relevance to the situation presented in *Select Committee,* and that the failure of the D.C.

---

[84]214 U.S. 320 (1909).

[85]Professor Archibald Cox agrees:
[T]he legislature's right should prevail in every case in which either the Senate or House of Representatives votes to override the Executive's objections, provided that the information is relevant to a matter which is under inquiry and within the jurisdiction of the body issuing the subpoena, including its constitutional jurisdiction.
Cox, *Executive Privilege,* 122 U. PA. L. REV. 1383, 1434 (1974).

[86]498 F.2d at 732. The court here was referring to Congress' legislative function, but the proper comparison would have been between Congress' informational needs in fulfilling its oversight responsibilities and the needs of a grand jury in unearthing private criminality.

[87]Howard v. Gossett, 10 Q.B. 359, 379–80, 116 E.R. 139, 147 (1845).

[88]*See note 60 supra.*

[89]498 F.2d at 730.

[90]487 F.2d 700 (D.C. Cir. 1974) (en banc) (per curiam).

[91]418 U.S. 683 (1974).

Circuit to distinguish the Ervin Committee's suit to enforce its subpoena from the grand jury context of *Sirica* led it to misapprehend its proper review function in the case of a congressional subpoena.[92] A grand jury is an arm of the court, and it is appropriate for a court to decide what its adjunct requires for the performance of its duties. It does not necessarily follow, however, that the courts may equally control the independent oversight function of Congress, a matter more fully discussed hereafter.

When I urged in 1965 that the controversy between Congress and the President over the claim of executive privilege be submitted to judicial arbitrament as a dispute over constitutional *boundaries*,[93] it was not my thought that courts should supervise the exercise of congressional discretion, but rather, as in the private individual subpoena cases, the courts would limit themselves to ensuring that Congress acted within its jurisdictional limits and invaded no constitutional guarantees.[94] In rejecting the Committee's exercise of discretion, the *Select Committee* court exceeded the proper scope of judicial intervention.

III. *UNITED STATES V. NIXON:* THE CONSTITUTIONALIZATION OF PRESUMPTIVE PRIVILEGE

A. Extraconstitutional Judicial "Blending" between the Separate Powers

In casting its decision in terms of a qualified or "presumptive privilege" against any "judicially compelled intrusion into presidential confidentiality"[95] which "can be overcome only by an appropriate showing of public need,"[96] the *Select Committee* court apparently followed the "evidentiary privilege" path whereunder courts had created the common law privileges of lawyer-client, doctor-patient, and so on.[97] It remained for the Supreme Court in *United States v. Nixon*[98] to lift the President's presumptive privilege to the level of Constitutional dogma,[99] a temptation that Justice Reed had resisted.[100]

The Court held that "a presumptive privilege for confidential communications . . . is fundamental to the operation of government and inextricably rooted in the separation of powers,"[101] that "to the extent this interest relates to the effective discharge of a President's powers, it is constitutionally based,"[102] and that the privilege "derive[s] from the supremacy of each branch within its own

---

[92]The court in *Select Committee* nowhere considers whether different considerations should apply if Congress, rather than the Special Watergate Prosecutor, were seeking information from the President. Rather, it attempts to most "accurately [reflect] the doctrines of *Nixon v. Sirica,* doctrines that, at least by analogy, we think controlling here." 498 F.2d at 729.

[93]Berger, *Executive Privilege and Congressional Inquiry,* 12 U.C.L.A. L. REV. 1044, 1288, 1335–62 (1965).

[94]Although the courts may therefore be called on for "automatic" enforcement of congressional subpoenas, that does not diminish the judicial function. Courts routinely enforce administrative subpoenas, for example. *See also* text accompanying notes 155–56 *infra.*

[95]498 F.2d at 731.

[96]*Id.* at 730.

[97]*See* BERGER, EXECUTIVE PRIVILEGE, *surpa* note 60, at 232, 355. In the words of the reply brief filed on behalf of President Nixon, "the court defined the privilege claimed solely in terms of the law of evidence with its foundation in custom or statute." Brief for the Respondent and Cross-Petitioner at 16, United States v. Nixon, 418 U.S. 683 (1974).

[98]418 U.S. 683 (1974).

[99]The Court, however, expressly avoided any decision on "the balance between the President's generalized interest in confidentiality . . . and congressional demands for information. . . ." *Id.* at 712 n.19.

[100]*See* note 110 and accompanying text *infra.*

[101]418 U.S. at 708. Chief Justice Burger "reported that one Supreme Court Justice had said in a seminar that the presumption of innocence is 'rooted in the Constitution' " and commented, " 'Well, it may be rooted there, but you cannot find it there.' " L. LEVY, AGAINST THE LAW 18 (1974).

[102]418 U.S. at 711.

assigned area of constitutional duties."[103] Elsewhere I have sought to show that the Court's *assumption* that "confidentiality" is "fundamental to the operations of government and inextricably rooted in the separation of powers"[104] is without historical roots.[105] Parliament was no respecter of such confidences, as the Founders were all aware.[106] In this country, administration of government long proceeded without the benefit of such a doctrine,[107] and there is good reason to believe that the Founders did not conceive that the President was shielded from congressional inquiry by the separation of powers.[108] For practical purposes, the privilege was first enunciated in 1954 by President Eisenhower and was claimed for communications between *any* employees of the executive branch, not merely for the President.[109] It was very guardedly picked up by Justice Reed without the help of the separation of powers doctrine.[110] There is no need to restate my critique of the historical argument made in *United States v. Nixon*,[111] here I shall proceed from the Court's premise that executive privilege is rooted somewhere in the Constitution and examine the basis on which the Court held that the privilege must not be permitted to "impair" the judicial administration of justice.

---

[103]*Id.* at 705.

[104]*Id.* at 708.

[105]Berger, Executive Privilege, *supra* note 60, at 11–12, 45–47; Berger, *The Incarnation of Executive Privilege*, 22 U.C.L.A. L. Rev. 4, 19–20 (1974) [hereinafter cited as Berger, *Incarnation*].

[106]That no such principle obtained in the practice of Parliament is exemplified by its inquiry in 1714 as a prelude to the impeachment of the Earl of Oxford and other high ministers. Among the witnesses examined were Thomas Harley, brother of Oxford, and Mathew Prior, envoys to France, who were interrogated as to their instructions by the ministers to negotiate a secret treaty behind the back of their Dutch allies. Berger, Executive Privilege, *supra* note 60, at 23.

"Pernicious advice" to the Crown by its ministers was a repeated cause for impeachment; and Corbin in the Virginia Ratification Convention, Pendleton in South Carolina and Iredell in North Carolina alluded to such "advice" as within the scope of impeachment. *Id.* at 185–86. Given the impeachability of such "advice," inquiry as to whether it was given was an indispensable prerequisite.

[107]See Berger, *Incarnation*, *supra* note 105, at 4, 24–25 (1974); note 74 *supra*.

[108]James Wilson told the Pennsylvania Ratification Convention that "The Executive power is better to be trusted when it has no screen . . . [The President cannot] hide either his negligence or inattention . . . [and] not a single privilege is annexed to his character." 2 Elliot, *supra* note 50, at 480.

When Jefferson first encountered the problem in connection with the St. Clair expedition (1792), he made no mention of the separation of powers but turned to English precedents to learn what were the respective powers of the legislature and executive. Berger, Executive Privilege, *supra* note 60, at 169. Nor did Marshall take account of it in the Burr trial. *See* text accompanying note 70 *supra*. It would be wondrous strange if Marshall, who had vigorously defended the Constitution in Virginia, was obvious to the threshold separation issue. One must conclude that it played no role in his analysis, which proceeded rather on customary evidentiary privilege grounds. Reliance on the evidentiary privilege analogy, rather than any attempt to locate presidential confidentiality in constitutional structure, is apparent in President Tyler's explanation of his partial refusal to turn over requested papers to the House. Enumerating certain categories of information in reliance on the evidentiary privileges recognized in judicial proceedings instituted by private litigants, he said: "these principles are as applicable to evidence sought by a legislature as to that required by a court. . . ." 3 A. Hinds, Precedents of the House of Representatives 182 (1939).

[109]Berger, Executive Privilege, *supra* note 60, at 213–14. Professor Freund agrees that, "the term appears to be of recent origin." Freund, *Foreword: On Presidential Privilege, The Supreme Court, 1973 Term*, 88 Harv. L. Rev. 13, 18 (1974).

[110]Kaiser Aluminum & Chem. Corp. v. United States, 157 F. Supp. 939 (Ct. Cl. 1958); *see* Berger, Executive Privilege, *supra* note 60, at 232, 355.

[111]*See* Berger, *Incarnation*, *supra* note 105. Professor Paul Mishkin comments:
The substantial body of scholarly learning on the subject, which includes careful historical and analytical treatments, is not considered or refuted, but simply ignored. The generalized constitutionally-based privilege seems to emerge full-blown from the head of the court.
Mishkin, *Great Cases and Soft Law, A Comment on United States v. Nixon*, 22 U.C.L.A. L. Rev. 76, 83–84 (1974). *See also* Kurland, *United States v. Nixon: Who Killed Cock Robin*, *id.* at 68, 74.

The Supreme Court held that it could restrict the exercise of the "constitutionally based" privilege in order to satisfy the demands of due process in the context of a "demonstrated, specific need for evidence in a pending criminal trial."[112] The Court reasoned that "the separate powers were not intended to operate with absolute independence,"[113] quoting Justice Jackson's statement in *Youngstown Sheet & Tube Co. v. Sawyer*[114] that the Constitution contemplated that "practice will integrate the dispersed powers into a workable government."[115]

The necessary interdependence of the separate branches, however, does not confer on the Court a "roving commission" to integrate "the dispersed powers" to any greater extent than mandated by the Constitution. It is clear that an invasion by one branch of the exclusive province of another is outside the purview of integration into a "workable government" by practice. The Court in the *Steel Seizure* case recognized this basic proposition,[116] as did Chief Justice Burger, writing for a unanimous Court, in *United States v. Nixon* itself:

> Notwithstanding the deference each branch must accord the others, the "judicial power of the United States" vested in the federal courts by Art. III, § 1 of the Constitution can no more be shared with the Executive Branch than the Chief Executive, for example, can share with the Judiciary the veto power, or the Congress share with the Judiciary the power to override a presidential veto. Any other conclusion would be contrary to the basic concept of separation of powers and the checks and balances that flow from the scheme of a tripartite government.[117]

Indisputably, the separate powers of the distinct governmental departments were never meant to operate with absolute independence. They were indeed "blended." When the proposed blending of powers provoked charges that the Constitution "violat[ed] the sacred maxim of free government"[118]—Montesquieu's separation of powers—Madison showed[119] that Montesquieu's model, the British Constitution, as well as various state Constitutions, exhibited blendings such as executive veto of legislation, executive appointment of judges, and the like.[120] But because some powers were similarly blended in our Constitution, it does not follow that the Supreme Court enjoys a free hand to do additional blending in the interest of a "workable government." On the contrary, the rule as stated by Chief Justice Taft in *Myers v. United States*[121] was one of strict construction of any provision of the Constitution which "blends" the powers of the separate branches:

> From this division on principle, the reasonable construction of the Constitution must be that the branches should be kept separate in all cases in which they were not expressly blended, and the Constitution should be expounded to blend them no more than it affirmatively requires.[122]

[112]418 U.S. 683, 713 (1974).

[113]*Id.* at 707.

[114]343 U.S. 579 (1952).

[115]*Id.* at 635 (Jackson, J., concurring).

[116]Notwithstanding Justice Jackson's statement, the Court enjoined President Truman's seizure of the steel mills on the grounds that "[t]he Founders of this Nation entrusted the lawmaking power to the Congress alone in both good times and bad," *id.* at 589, and that "[t]he Constitution does not subject this law making power of congress to presidential or military supervision or control," *id.* at 588. Justice Jackson pointed out that the seizure did not fall within the "Twilight" zone, where the distribution of powers is uncertain, because Congress "has covered [the issue of the propriety of seizures] by three statutory policies inconsistent with this seizure." *Id.* at 639.

[117]418 U.S. at 704.

[118]THE FEDERALIST No. 47, at 320 (Mod. Lib. ed. 1937).

[119]*Id.* Nos. 47–48.

[120]*Id.* No. 47, at 320, 315.

[121]272 U.S. 52 (1926).

[122]*Id.* at 116. *See also* Chief Justice Waite's statement in *The Sinking-Fund Cases*, 99 U.S. 700 (1879):
One branch of the government cannot encroach on the domain of another without danger. The safety of our institutions depends in no small degree on a strict observance of this salutary rule.
Id. at 718. *Cf.* text accompanying notes 84–85 *supra*.

This had been even more forcefully stated by Madison.[123]

If, therefore, the privilege for confidentiality is in fact "inextricably rooted in the separation of powers," and indeed "derives from the supremacy of each branch" within its own sphere, and is related "to the effective discharge" of executive powers, as Chief Justice Burger posits, then it should be inviolable, and curtailment in the interest of the judicial function would be an encroachment on the executive power. The Court's appeal to "due process" does not, in my judgment, advance the argument. "Due process" was not designed to redistribute the constitutional grants to the separate branches but to secure to each citizen rights under "the law of the land," including the guarantees of the Constitution. And one may ask, with Professors Henkin and Kurland, why the President's "constitutional" privilege must yield to judicial necessities while the lawyer-client and doctor-patient privileges—judicial constructs—remain untouchable.[124]

Not for a moment do I concede that presidential "confidentiality" is rooted in the Constitution; my object is solely to show that the Court's breach in its "inextricably rooted" assumption in order to save judicial administration from impairment raises a grave constitutional question: where is the authority for such judicial "blending?"

The assumption in *United States v. Nixon* that courts should engage in a balancing of competing interests whenever information is sought from the Executive raises still other doubts with respect to congressional demands for information pursuant to its legislative and oversight responsibilities. In the cases of congressional demands for information directed to private citizens, it has been shown that the courts have confined themselves to a refusal to enforce subpoenas or punish for contempt where Congress acted in excess of its jurisdiction or in violation of express constitutional safeguards;[125] the courts do not attempt to weigh the manner in which Congress exercises its discretion in requesting certain information or subpoenaing certain witnesses against other values, provided Congress is acting within the scope of its jurisdiction. A grant of discretion, by definition, leaves the grantee freedom of choice within the jurisdiction. Traditionally, control of discretion lies beyond judicial functions, as Chief Justice Marshall recognized in *Marbury v. Madison*,[126] and as early cases like *Decatur v. Paulding*[127] have underscored. In *Decatur* mandamus was sought to compel the Secretary of the Navy to pay certain sums of money, which, under the circumstances, was a discretionary rather than a ministerial act of the kind regularly subject to judicial compulsion. Chief Justice Taney refused to issue a mandamus:

> The court could not entertain an appeal from the decision of one of the Secretaries, nor revise his judgment in any case where the law authorized him to exercise discretion, or judgment. Nor can it by mandamus, act directly upon the officer, and guide and control his judgment or discretion in the matters commited to his care, in the ordinary discharge of his official duties.
> . . . .

---

[123]In his discussion of "blending" in FEDERALIST No. 48, at 321 (Mod. Lib. ed. 1937), Madison stated:

It is equally evident, that none of [the departments] ought to possess, directly or indirectly, an overruling influence over the others, in the administration of their respective powers. It will not be denied that power is of an encroaching nature, and that it ought to be effectually restrained from passing the limits assigned to it.

And he emphasized the need "to provide some practical security for each, against the invasion of others." *See also* L. HAND, *supra* note 58, at 66; note 129 *infra*.

An argument to the contrary by Professor James M. Landis and then Professor Felix Frankfurter is examined in the Appendix; they use the term "interaction" in place of "blending." Their citations, it will be found, largely involve common law attributes of a given power, that is, long established exceptions to strict separation of powers.

[124]*See* Henkin, *Executive Privilege: Mr. Nixon Loses But the Presidency Prevails*, 22 U.C.L.A. L. REV. 40, 44 (1974); Kurland, *supra* note 111, at 73.

[125]*See* notes 40–47 and accompanying text *supra*.

[126]5 U.S. (1 Cranch) 157, 168–70 (1803); *see* text accompanying note 71 *supra*.

[127]39 U.S. (14 Pet.) 497 (1840); *see also* text accompanying note 84 *supra*.

The interference of the courts with the performance of the ordinary duties of the executive departments of the government, would be productive of nothing but mischief; and we are quite satisfied, that such a power was never intended to be given to them.[128]

Similarly, interference with discretionary legislative authority was no more "intended to be given" to the courts.

Against this it may be argued that it is the task of the Judiciary to demark the constitutional boundaries between the branches and to accommodate or reconcile conflicting claims to power. The distinction between judicial demarcation of constitutional boundaries and interference with executive or legislative choices within those boundaries must constantly be borne in mind.[129] It was because the Court lost sight of that distinction that we have the lamentable line of pre-1937 decisions striking down much socio-economic legislation.[130] When the Court in *United States v. Nixon* held that presidential confidentiality "derived from the supremacy" of the Executive "within its own sphere" and was related "to the effective discharge" of executive powers,[131] it held that the power to withhold information from the sister branches was included in the "executive power." Within those boundaries, it was for the President, on the Court's premises, to make the choices and to determine what the "effective discharge" of the executive powers required. The assumption of power by the Court to make a breach in its newly fashioned presidential privilege, therefore, constitutes an interference with that executive discretion and authority. The Court cannot have it both ways.[132]

Although the Court in *United States v. Nixon* expressly reserved decision on how it would resolve a clash between "the confidentiality interest and Congressional demands for information,"[133] the rooting of the executive interest in "confidentiality" in the separation of powers doctrine is at odds with the traditional legislative oversight function. Chief Justice Burger's assumption that a presidential privilege to withhold information is constitutionally based curtails the historically untrammeled legislative power to inquire into executive conduct, ignoring the fact that congressional oversight was never challenged by the Executive, and that the Founders consciously adopted the English practice under which "confidentiality" was no bar to legislative inquiry. The claims of history are fortified by the resulting formidable difficulties—extraconstitutional "blending" and unprecedented judicial interference with legislative discretion—that flow from *United States v. Nixon* and call for a reexamination of that assumption in the context of congressional inquiry into the executive branch.

B. Executive Privilege and Congressional Demands for Information

1. *Inquiry Incident to Impeachment Proceedings.* Whatever the weight to be given to the presidential privilege which Chief Justice Burger rooted in the separation of powers, claims of

---

[128]39 U.S. at 515–16.

[129][P]ublic functionaries must be left at liberty to exercise the powers which the people by the Constitution . . . have intrusted them. They must have a wide discretion as to the choice of means. . . . If the means are within the reach of the power, no other department can inquire into the policy or convenience of the use of them. If there be excess by overleaping the just boundary of the power, the judiciary may generally afford the proper relief. . . . J. STORY, COMMENTARIES ON THE CONSTITUTION OF THE UNITED STATES § 432 at 330 (1905). In the words of Learned Hand, judicial review "should be confined to occasions when the statute or order was outside the grant of power to the grantee, and should not include a review of how the power has been exercised." L. HAND, *supra* note 123, at 66. It is important, he stressed, "that within its prescribed borders each 'Department' . . . shall be free from interference." *Id.* at 31.

[130]*See, e.g.,* Lochner v. New York, 198 U.S. 45 (1905).

[131]418 U.S. at 705.

[132]*See note* 129 *supra.*

[133]418 U.S. at 712 n.19.

executive privilege have no place in impeachment inquiries because the Framers made clear that impeachment was a studied breach in the doctrine.[134] Hostile as Justice Miller was to congressional inquiry as a prelude to legislation in *Kilbourn v. Thompson*,[135] he unhesitatingly made an exception in the case of impeachment:

> Where the question of . . . impeachment is before either body acting in its appropriate sphere on that subject, we see no reason to doubt the right to compel the attendance of witnesses, and their answer to proper questions, in the same manner and by use of the same means that courts of justice can in like cases.[136]

When this is juxtaposed with his statement that the "general rule [developed in the initial case of *Anderson v. Dunn*[137]] . . . as regards the relation of one court to another" is that "no other court will discharge the prisoner or make further inquiry into the cause of his commitment [for contempt],"[138] it is reasonable to deduce that he ruled out judicial intervention with respect to commitments for contempt in the course of impeachment proceedings.

Justice Miller's position on impeachment reflects the orthodox view that given the "sole" power of the Senate to "try" impeachments, a Senate verdict is unreviewable.[139] When I advanced the heterodox view that judicial review was available for a Senate impeachment verdict that was in excess of its powers,[140] I did not have in mind *interlocutory* interference with its exclusive right to "try" an impeachment.[141]

2. *Inquiry Preliminary to Impeachment Proceedings.* Of inquiry preliminary to impeachment, it may even more truly be said that "[t]he scope of the power of inquiry . . . is as penetrating and far-reaching as the potential power to enact and appropriate. . . ."[142] Instances of inquiry by the House of Commons as a prelude to impeachment can be found as early as 1621.[143] To impeach without inquiry is to risk groundless accusations and rank injustice. Strictly speaking, such inquiries do not enjoy express constitutional authorization; rather they are a necessary attribute of the power to impeach, anchored in long historical practice.[144]

---

[134]In the Federal Convention, Rufus King dwelt on the "primitive axiom that the three great departments of Govts. should be separate & independent: . . . Would this be the case if the Executive should be impeachable? [It] would be destructive of his independence and of the principles of the Constitution." 2 M. FARRAND, THE RECORDS OF THE FEDERAL CONVENTION OF 1787, at 66–67 (1911). Charles Pinckney likewise urged that it would "effectually destroy his independence." *Id.* at 66. Those views were rejected by a vote of 8 to 2. As George Mason stressed, "No point is of more importance than that the right of impeachment should be continued." *Id.* at 65.

Elias Boudinot, for years President of the Continental Congress, said in the First Congress, impeachment is an "exception to a principle." 1 ANN. CONG. 527 (print bearing running-head "History of Congress") (1834).

[135]103 U.S. 168 (1880); *see* notes 28–31 and accompanying text *supra.*

[136]*Id.* at 190.

[137]19 U.S. (6 Wheat.) 204 (1821); *see* notes 14–20 and accompanying text *supra.*

[138]103 U.S. at 197.

[139]BERGER, IMPEACHMENT, *supra* note 29, at 103.

[140]Berger, *Impeachment for "High Crimes and Misdemeanors,"* 44 SO. CAL. L. REV. 395, 443–57 (1971).

[141]*See* notes 150–56 and accompanying text *infra.*

[142]Barenblatt v. United States, 360 U.S. 109, 111 (1959).

[143]*See* BERGER, EXECUTIVE PRIVILEGE, *supra* note 60, at 15–16.

[144]The D.C. Circuit's statement in *Select Committee* that "[t]he investigative authority of the Judiciary Committee with respect to presidential conduct has an express constitutional source," 498 F.2d at 732, may suggest that the authority of the Select Committee is open to question. The express authority of Congress is to impeach and to try; and as Professor Bickel has pointed out, "[i]t doesn't say anything about how you get information." Wall Street Journal, June 5, 1974, at 18, col. 4. Nevertheless, although the fifth amendment, which requires indictment by a grand jury, does not expressly state how it is to obtain the information to support an indictment, the right of a grand jury to subpoena those who may have information is hardly debatable.

Recognition of this "far-reaching" power was expressed by President Polk in 1846. When the House sits as the Grand Inquest of the Nation, he said, it can "penetrate into the most secret recesses of the Executive Departments."[145] This was the original design, as James Wilson noted.[146] President Nixon's insistence that he alone had a right to determine what information the Grand Inquest may have from executive files in an investigation of his own misconduct was without parallel. It undermined the basic supremacy of the Constitution, and constituted a long step toward the very executive unaccountability that the Founders meant to prevent.

Within jurisdictional bounds, the House, no less than the Executive or a mere administrative agency, is entitled to exercise its discretion in determining what evidence it requires to perform its exclusive responsibility to impeach, that is, to accuse government officials of misconduct in office. Although the late Professor Alexander Bickel thought it "plain . . . that there can't be judicial review of the impeachment process," he maintained that a judge may determine that the information sought by subpoena of the House Judiciary Committee is "not relevant to what would properly be an impeachable offense."[147] Questions of "relevance," as we have seen,[148] may not be raised before the cognate grand jury. And given that there can be no review of the "impeachment process," I should have concluded that the greater includes the less, particularly because the House is given the "sole power of impeachment." But dismayed by the "absolute horror" of a result that would enable the House to "turn almost everything into an impeachable offense" merely by so holding a refusal to tender subpoenaed information, Professor Bickel concluded that "there ought to be limits on the impeachment power," and that courts ought to have "some control over the impulse to use the impeachment power in unbridled fashion."[149] But this would substitute a judgment of a court for that of the Senate, which is given the sole, and in Bickel's view unreviewable, power to try an impeachment.[150]

Judicial review at the subpoena stage is *premature* and runs contrary to the settled course of practice. "Investigation will be paralyzed," said Chief Judge Cardozo, "if arguments as to materiality or relevance, however appropriate at the hearing, are to be transferred" to the subpoena enforcement stage.[151] One under investigation may object before the *adjudicatory* tribunal to the admis-

---

[145] 4 J. RICHARDSON, COMPILATION OF THE MESSAGES AND PAPERS OF THE PRESIDENTS, 1789–1897, at 434 (1897). In such cases, said President Polk, "all the archives and papers of the Executive Departments, public or private, would be subject to the inspection and control of a committee of [Congress] and every facility in the power of the Executive be afforded them to enable them to prosecute an investigation." *Id.* at 435.

John Quincy Adams, then a revered ex-President, said in the House of Representatives on June 4, 1842:

[W]hat mockery it would be . . . to say that the House should have the power of impeachment, extending even to the President . . . himself, and yet to say that the House had not the power to obtain the evidence and proofs on which their impeachment is based.

11 CONG. GLOBE 580.

[146] *See* text accompanying note 50 *supra.*

[147] Wall Street Journal, June 5, 1974, at 18, col. 4.

[148] *See* notes 65–66 and accompanying text *supra.*

[149] Wall Street Journal, June 5, 1974, at 18, col. 4.

[150] As Professor Gerald Gunther points out:

Courts could not adjudicate the relevance of the information sought by the subpoenas without taking some position as to the scope of impeachable offenses—an issue ultimately for Congress under its "sole impeachment" power.

Gunther, *Judicial Hegemony and Legislative Autonomy: The Nixon Case and the Impeachment Process,* 22 U.C.L.A. L. REV. 30, 38 (1974).

[151] In Matter of Edge Ho Holding Corp., 256 N.Y. 374, 381–82, 176 N.E. 537, 539 (1931). Cardozo would permit interlocutory judicial interference in very limited circumstances: "Only where the futility of the process to uncover anything legitimate is inevitable or obvious must there be a halt upon the threshhold." *Id.* at 382.

sibility of any particular document.[152] It suffices, the Supreme Court held in *Hannah v. Larche*,[153] with respect to a Federal Trade Commission investigation, that "any person investigated . . . will be accorded all the traditional judicial safeguards at a subsequent adjudicative proceeding."[154] Since the House has the sole power to impeach, it must likewise have the sole power to determine what evidence is required for this purpose. A useful analogy may be drawn from the rationale of the "primary jurisdiction" doctrine. When Congress vested exclusive power to prevent unfair labor practices affecting interstate commerce in the National Labor Relations Board, subject to review by the circuit courts, the Supreme Court held that the district court was without jurisdiction to enjoin hearings before the Board, and that the statute vested the Board with power to determine in the first instance whether the particular controversy fell within the jurisdiction granted.[155] By the same token, the House is entitled "in the first instance" to determine the "coverage" of "high crime and misdemeanors," and whether the subpoenaed information falls within it.[156] Vested by the Constitution itself with the "sole" power to impeach, the House cannot be entitled to less exclusivity than is recognized in the case of an administrative agency. And the Senate may be relied upon to reject an article of impeachment for contemptuous refusal of information to which the House is not entitled, subject, in my view, to judicial review if the article is erroneously sustained by the Senate.

3. *General Investigations.* If the general investigatory or oversight power of Congress does not stand on as high a footing as its power to inquire before impeaching, it is nevertheless anchored solidly enough. As the power to conduct inquiries preliminary to impeachment is a necessary "attribute" of the power to impeach, rooted in long historical practice, the general investigatory power is likewise an implied attribute of the legislative power having similar historical roots. In the aftermath of the Teapot Dome scandal, the Supreme Court held in *McGrain v. Daugherty*[157] that at the time of the adoption of the Constitution "the power of inquiry—with enforcing process—was regarded . . . as a necessary and appropriate attribute of the power to legislate—indeed, . . . as inhering in it."[158] The scope of the "attribute" was justly summarized by William Pitt in 1742:

> We are called the Grand Inquest of the Nation, and as such it is our Duty to inquire into every step of publick Management, either Abroad or at Home, in order to see that nothing has been done amiss.[159]

Parliamentary inquiries stretched across the entire spectrum of executive conduct; nothing was sacred.[160] No member of this country's executive branch, but for Jefferson's mistaken citation to the Walpole hearings in 1741–1742, has ever cited an instance where an English minister chal-

---

[152]*See* Civil Aeronautics Board v. Hermann, 353 U.S. 322 (1957). Similarly, objections to the particular article of impeachment may be taken before the Senate, the adjudicatory tribunal which by no means has seen eye to eye with the House over the years.

[153]363 U.S. 420 (1960).

[154]*Id.* at 446.

[155]Myers v. Bethlehem Shipbuilding Corp., 303 U.S. 41, 48 (1938) (per Brandeis, J.).

[156]*Cf.* Endicott Johnson Corp. v. Perkins, 317 U.S. 501, 507 (1943) (the determination whether subpoenaed information fell within the coverage of the statute "was primarily the duty of the Secretary," not of the enforcing court).

[157]273 U.S. 135 (1927).

[158]*Id.* at 175. It was for this reason that the Court concluded that "the constitutional provisions which commit the legislative function to the two houses are intended to include this attribute." *Id.; see also* Quinn v. United States, 349 U.S. 155, 160–61 (1955).

[159]13 R. CHANDLER, HISTORY & PROCEEDINGS OF THE HOUSE OF COMMONS 172 (1743). After adverting to the investigations of 1691 and 1694 into the Admiralty, Hallam stated, "it is hardly worth while to enumerate later instances of exercising a right which had become indisputable, and, even before it rested on the basis of precedent, could not reasonably be denied to those whom might advise [that is, participate with the King in legislating], remonstrate and impeach." 3 H. HALLAM, CONSTITUTIONAL HISTORY OF ENGLAND 144 (1884).

[160]*See* BERGER, EXECUTIVE PRIVILEGE, *supra* note 60, at 15–31.

lenged the scope of a parliamentary inquiry.[161] On four or five occasions the Founders referred to the Grand Inquest of the Nation (which had come to identify the entire investigatory function) in the several Ratifying Conventions,[162] with never a protest that the powers of the Grand Inquest should be curtailed in the interest of the President. Widespread dread of executive usurpation[163] counselled the broadest inquisitorial power to uncover presidential excesses.[164] Those who provided for impeachment of the President in conscious breach of the separation of powers were hardly likely to shrink from plenary preliminary inquiry. Nor was a Convention that was at pains to authorize the President to ask for written opinions from executive department heads[165] likely to endow him with an implied power to diminish the established investigatory power of the Grand Inquest,[166] which James Wilson exalted because it had "checked the progress of arbitrary power."[167] History in short, demonstrates that Congress was designed to exercise the inquisitorial power exercised by Parliament, that this power was unqualified, that no member of the English executive had claimed to be exempt from this power, and that no member of several Conventions had claimed for the President any exemption from this power of the Grand Inquest of the Nation.

Practical considerations reinforce the teaching of history. Woodrow Wilson stated that "[u]nless Congress have and use every means of acquainting itself with the acts and the dispositions of the administrative agents of the government, the country must be helpless to learn how it is being served."[168] A glaring illustration is furnished by President Nixon's long course of deception about the participation of his closest aides, indeed of Nixon himself, in the conspiracy to conceal the executive involvement in the attempted burglary of the Watergate Hotel. Sweet are the uses of "confidentiality." Our generation has witnessed a steadily mounting tide of executive recalcitrance in supplying information to Congress, ranging from the trivial to matters of gravest import,[169] thereby obstructing important functions of Congress—inquiries into disbursement of appropria-

---

[161]In 1701, Charles Davenant wrote:
[N]o one has ever questioned the legislative authority "to enquire into, and correct the Errors and Abuses committed by those upon whom the Prince has devolved any part of the Executive Power." Accordingly, "if Ministers of State advise an unnecessary War, a dishonorable Peace, or a dangerous Alliance, they are as much accomptable to Parliament, as for any other Neglect or Crime in the administration of affairs."
Bestor, *Separation of Powers in the Domain of Foreign Affairs: The Original Intent of the Constitution Historically Examined,* 5 SETON HALL L. REV. 527, 558–59 (1974). Speaking of the 1689 inquiries, Hallam stated, "No courtier [Minister] has ever since ventured to deny the general right of inquiry." 3 H. HALLAM, *supra* note 159, at 143. My research uncovered no earlier challenge. To the contrary, after Lord Chancellor Francis Bacon had been impeached, he wrote to congratulate "the Treasurer on his advancement" and stated that "he had one rule for all great officers of the Crown: 'Remember, a Parliament will come.'" C. BOWEN, THE LION AND THE THRONE 462 (1957). For similar remarks by Samuel Pepys in 1776, then a navy official, see BERGER, EXECUTIVE PRIVILEGE, *supra* note 60, at 17. For detailed discussion of the Walpole citation, *see id.* at 24–30, 169–71.

[162]For citations, *see* BERGER, EXECUTIVE PRIVILEGE, *supra* note 60, at 35–36; *cf. id.* at 37, 168, 262.

[163]*See, id.* at 49–50, 53, 62.

[164]*See, e.g.,* James Wilson's statement to the Pennsylvania Ratification Convention, *quoted in* note 108, and text accompanying note 50 *supra.*

[165]Justice Jackson viewed this as the quintessential "inherent" executive power. Youngstown Sheet & Tube Co. v. Sawyer, 343 U.S. 579, 640–41 & n.9 (1952) (Jackson, J., concurring).

[166]Chief Justice Marshall stated that it is
to be expected that an opinion which is to overrule all former precedents, and to establish a principle never before recognized, should be expressed in plain and explicit terms. A mere implication ought not to prostrate a principle which seems to have been so well established.
United States v. Burr, 25 Fed. Cas. 55, 165 (No. 14,693) (C.C.Va. 1807). To the same effect, *see* Pierson v. Ray, 386 U.S. 547, 554–55 (1967).

[167]*See* note 60 *supra.*

[168]*Quoted in* United States v. Rumely, 345 U.S. 41, 43 (1953).

[169]BERGER, EXECUTIVE PRIVILEGE, *supra* note 60, at 236–40, 245–49, 254, 257–60, 263. "The central problem today is how to deal wth governmental secrecy and—to be blunt—with governmental deception. A congressional power to inquire, freely exercised, could help to provide the necessary information." Cox, *supra* note 85, at 1434.

tions, conduct of war, of impeachment itself. What the Court said in the frame of a contempt against a private individual is even more applicable to executive withholding:

> A legislative body cannot legislate wisely or effectively in the absence of information respecting the conditions which the legislature is intended to affect or change; and where the legislative body does not itself possess the requisite information—which not infrequently is true—recourse must be had to others who do possess it. . . . [S]ome means of compulsion are essential to obtain what is needed.[170]

Inquiry into executive conduct should not be handcuffed by presidential conditions upon its exercise. The rationale of *United States v. Nixon* extends to this legislative function; here too the "generalized interest in confidentiality" must not be permitted to impair Congress' performance of this vital function.[171]

In sum, what information Congress requires for the performance of its investigatory functions was left in the discretion of Congress. To extend *United States v. Nixon* to make the courts the supervisor of Congress' exercise of that discretion is to assume a power that Chief Justice Marshall disclaimed,[172] and that *Decatur v. Paulding*[173] later held was not given to the courts; it is to engage in unauthorized "blending" of powers. The precedents counsel that the rule of *Nixon v. Sirica* and *United States v. Nixon* should be confined to their facts—judicial supervision of a branch of the courts. Even more than in the private industrial cases, we need to heed the caution of Justice Frankfurter with respect to drawing "constitutional limits upon the investigatory power of Congress": "Experience admonishes to tread warily in this domain."[174]

IV. ENFORCEMENT PROCEDURES FOR CONGRESSIONAL SUBPOENAS[175]

For the moment we may put to one side the exceptional problem posed by a President's refusal to honor a congressional subpoena in the course of an impeachment inquiry. The vast bulk of congressional investigations are not concerned with impeachments nor with the President but rather with calls for information from lesser officials in the course of inquiry into administration of the executive branch.[176] In such cases, there is first the traditional contempt procedure which

---

[170]McGrain v. Daugherty, 273 U.S. 135, 175 (1927); *see also* Quinn v. United States, 349 U.S. 155, 160–61 (1955).

[171]Professor Henkin has made a similar point:

But since the Court also found the privilege conditional, Congress will surely assert its own legislative and investigative needs as public interests which are also greater than the interest in executive confidentiality.

Henkin, *supra* note 124, at 43, Speaking of the Court's dictum that the claim of presidential privilege may enjoy its greatest force when "national security" is served by confidentiality, 418 U.S. at 706, Professor Henkin commented:

An absolute privilege against disclosure in court . . . does not necessarily imply that it is similarly absolute vis-a-vis Congress, which has its constitutional claims to know national secrets at least on a classified basis.

Id. at 45.

The position asserted in the text that the "generalized interest in confidentiality" must fall before congressional demands for information necessary to exercise its oversight function is confirmed in part by President Ford's view in deciding to appear before a Subcommittee of the House Judiciary Committee to answer questions regarding the circumstances surrounding his pardon of Richard Nixon, that executive privilege "is not [an] absolute right," N.Y. Times, Oct. 2, 1974, at 24, col. 4. President Ford thus recognized that the privilege stands no higher against Congress than the courts. In responding to Committee inquiries about communications with White House aides regarding various options that might be taken upon President Nixon's resignation, Mr. Ford demonstrated that "confidentiality" is not really indispensable to the conduct of the presidency. A "confidentiality" that can be turned on or off as presidential convenience dictates belies the justification for the privilege: selective disclosure will inhibit "candid interchange" between members of the executive branch, for subordinates can never be certain when presidential convenience will lead to disclosure.

[172]*See* notes 71–72, 176 and accompanying text *supra*.

[173]39 U.S. (14 Pet.) 497 (1840); *see* notes 127–28 and accompanying text *supra*.

[174]United States v. Rumely, 345 U.S. 41, 46 (1953).

[175]This section is a summary of an earlier discussion in BERGER, EXECUTIVE PRIVILEGE, *supra* note 60, at 309–41.

[176]*Id.* at 234–64.

the Supreme Court has recognized in the case of private individuals.[177] Its applicability to officials was noted by Professor Joseph Bishop: "Congress undoubtedly has power to punish contempts . . . by the simple and forthright process of causing the Sergeant-at-Arms to seize the offender and clap him into the common jail of the District of Columbia or the guardroom of the capitol police."[178] If that seems drastic, it should be regarded merely as a necessary means of opening the door to judicial review. Once the recalcitrant officer is in the custody of Congress, he can challenge its right to the required information by a petition for a writ of habeas corpus.[179] Suppose, however, that the President himself invokes executive privilege—pending legislation would require him to do so for every claim of a subordinate to withhold information from Congress[180]—and suppose that he directs the subordinate not to furnish the information. Indeed, Theodore Roosevelt went so far as to take the subpoenaed records into his own possession and to defy the Senate Judiciary Committee.[181]

Where the records remain in the officer's possession, the President's directive plainly should furnish no shield. In *Kendall v. United States*,[182] for example, the Postmaster General, acting on presidential instructions, had refused to pay monies owed by the United States for the carriage of mails. Congress thereupon passed a law directing payment, and when the Postmaster General again refused to make payment, mandamus was brought to compel it. The Court held that the vesting of executive power in the President did not mean that "every officer in every branch of that department is under the exclusive direction of the President. . . . [I]t would be an alarming doctrine, that Congress cannot impose upon any executive officer any [constitutional] duty. . . ."[183] That a duty to turn over information is a constitutional one may be deduced from the Act of September 2, 1789, which made it the duty of the Secretary of the Treasury to furnish to Congress information "respecting all matters . . . which shall appertain to his office."[184] In 1854 Attorney General Caleb Cushing held that "by legal implication the same" duty is imposed upon all other members of the cabinet.[185] Justice William H. Rehnquist, then Assistant Attorney General, acknowledged that a "member of the executive branch who himself has custody of the documents for which the President is seeking to assert executive privilege might . . . be at least a compellable witness in the sense that he would have to respond to a subpoena,"[186] subject to judicial review.

---

[177]*See* notes 14–20, 40–48 and accompanying text *supra*.

[178]Bishop, *The Executive's Right of Privacy: An Unresolved Constitutional Question*, 66 YALE L.J. 477, 484 (1957). *See also* BERGER, EXECUTIVE PRIVILEGE, *supra* note 60, at 309–13.

[179]*Cf.* Freund, *Foreword: On Presidential Privilege, The Supreme Court, 1973 Term*, 88 HARV. L. REV. 13, 38 (1974). For the unavailability of habeas corpus in the absence of such custody, see BERGER, EXECUTIVE PRIVILEGE, *supra* note 60, at 293 n.323.

[180]H.R. 12462, 93d Cong., 2d Sess. (1974); S. 2432, 93d Cong., 1st Sess. § 342a (1974).

[181]This incident set forth more fully in BERGER, EXECUTIVE PRIVILEGE, *supra* note 40, at 228–30, represents a striking example of executive highhandedness; a supine Committee failed to pursue its right to the information. In *United States v. Nixon*, as Professor Paul Freund stated, President Nixon's action "in formally taking sole custody of the tapes" made "the usual suit against a subordinate . . . impossible, and a confrontation was compelled," thus serving to "solidify the principle of presidential amenability to process." Freund, *Foreword: On Presidential Privilege, The Supreme Court, 1973 Term*, 88 HARV. L. REV. 13, 20 (1974). Professor Cox states: "To recognize presidential power to defeat the legal process merely by substituting the President's person for the person of the customary subordinate would not only exalt form over substance but also confer a king-like prerogative to set aside the laws according to the Executive's will. . . ." Cox, *supra* note 85, at 1389. *See also* Karst & Horowitz, *Presidential Prerogative and Judicial Review*, 22 U.C.L.A. L. REV. 47, 52 (1974).

[182]37 U.S. (12 Pet.) 524 (1838).

[183]*Id.* at 610, 613.

[184]1 Stat. 65–66, presently codified as 31 U.S.C. § 1002 (1970).

[185]6 OP. ATT'Y GEN. 326, 333 (1854). "Congress," Cushing summed up, "may at all times call on them [the cabinet departments] for information or explanation in matters of official duty." *Id.* at 344.

[186]*Hearings Before a Subcomm. on U.S. Government Information Policies and Practices—The Pentagon Papers of the House Comm. on Government Operations*, 92d Cong., 1st Sess. pt. 2, at 385 (1971). *See also id.* at 379.

But just as Congress has been pressing for invocation of executive privilege by the President alone,[187] a contempt citation should similarly have authorization from the given House. As I wrote in 1965:

> Not all demands for information represent a considered congressional judgment. Too often they are pressed by head-line hunting members of Congress, and often the leadership finds itself trapped into a showdown that might have been averted by intervention at an earlier stage.[188]

On the basis of the analysis earlier set forth, the courts should decline to interfere with the legislative demand, provided Congress is acting within its jurisdiction, and reaffirm the legitimacy of wide-ranging congressional inquiry into "corruption, inefficiency or waste."[189] It would not require many such decisions to bring home to executive officials that they must comply with congressional subpoenas.[190]

A second method of enforcement could be by suit brought by the given congressional committee. For this purpose, I suggested in 1965 that a Committee be authorized by statute to institute suit in a district court, and that the statute also confer jurisdiction on a district court to entertain the suit.[191] For want of such a statute, the United States District Court for the District of Columbia dismissed the first suit brought by the Senate Select Committee to obtain information in the course of the Watergate investigation.[192] The mills of Congress grind slowly; on December 18, 1973, the Senate passed a bill which would authorize the Chairman of a Committee, with approval of the given House, to institute suit for enforcement of a subpoena and confer jurisdiction of such suit upon the United States District Court for the District of Columbia.[193] At this juncture, the House has yet to pass the bill. It is to be hoped that the House will remove jurisdictional hurdles to the exercise of its own powers.

A third alternative is resort to the statute which makes it a misdemeanor to be in contempt of Congress.[194] In conflicts between Congress and the executive branch, it is idle to look to the Attorney General to institute a criminal proceeding against an official who has the seal of the President's claim of executive privilege. Consequently, a Special Prosecutor is needed who can handle enforcement of such criminal statutes against members of the executive branch on behalf of Congress. He should be made a permanent officer; before long he would acquire expertise in the executive privilege area and be qualified to counsel the several Committees before enforcement proceedings come to a head.

There remains enforcement of a subpoena to the President in the course of an impeachment— that tremendous power lodged in Congress in deliberate breach of the separation of powers. There is no power conferred upon the courts that equals in importance the congressional power to

---

[187]*See* note 180 and accompanying text *supra.*

[188]Berger, *Executive Privilege and Congressional Inquiry,* 12 U.C.L.A. L. REV. 1044, 1335 (1965).

[189]Watkins v. United States, 354 U.S. 178, 187 (1957). The Court there adverted to the "danger to effective and honest conduct of the Government if the legislature's power to probe corruption in the executive branch were unduly hampered." *Id.* at 194–95. *See also* text accompanying note 48 *supra.*

[190]As Theodore Sorenson, special counsel to President Kennedy, stated: "All Congress has to do is once to hold an executive witness in contempt for improperly invoking executive privilege, and it will be illegally invoked a lot less in the future." Sorenson, *The Case for a Strong Presidency, in* HAS THE PRESIDENT TOO MUCH POWER? 24, 28 (C. Roberts ed. 1974).

[191]Berger, *supra* note 188, at 1334. Recent developments, writes Professor Cox, "probably make it desirable to put the force of [statutory] law behind some congressional subpoenas addressed to the President. . . ." Cox, *supra* note 85, at 1434.

[192]Senate Select Committee v. Nixon, 366 F. Supp. 51 (D.D.C. 1973). For details of later proceedings, *see* 498 F.2d 725, 727 (D.C. Cir. 1974).

[193]S. 2432, 93d Cong., 1st Sess. (1973); 119 CONG. REC. S23191–92 (daily ed. Dec. 18, 1973).

[194]2 U.S.C. § 194 (1970). The statute applies to contempts by "all persons"; no exception is made for government officials. Former Assistant Attorney General Robert Kramer assumed that it applied to them. Kramer & Marcuse, *supra* note 68, at 313 n.46.

impeach and remove the President; and this power equally carries with it the right "to prevent acts which . . . prevent the discharge of legislative duty." And so I would conclude that the House has the constitutional power to hold a President in contempt and a right to bring him before the bar of the House. During the recent crisis, Representative Don Edwards lamented that the House Judiciary Committee cannot force its will upon Mr. Nixon because "he's got the Army, Navy, and Air Force and all we've got is Ken Harding," the Sergeant-at-Arms.[195] Although the Supreme Court likewise cannot call on the armed forces for enforcement of its decrees, it has nevertheless assumed from Chief Justice Marshall onwards that its decrees would be obeyed.[196] That belief was once again vindicated by the capitulation of President Nixon.

The President must "take care that the laws be faithfully executed"; among those laws is the constitutional provision for impeachment of which the House and Senate were given "sole" control. It appears beyond cavil that the law does not permit him to set the bounds of an impeachment inquiry. It was open to the Judiciary Committee to ask the House to summon Mr. Nixon to show cause why he could not be held in comtempt, if only to dramatize, by his intransigent refusal, his contempt for law. Those who shrink from exercising constitutional powers when occasion demands contribute to their decay.[197] We need to recall the statement by President Jefferson's lawyer, George Hay, who, speaking before Chief Justice Marshall on the issue of Aaron Burr's subpoena for a letter from General Wilkinson to Jefferson—a confidential communication—stated that the President

> is but a man; he is but a citizen; and if he knows anything in any case, civil or criminal, which might affect the life, liberty, or property of his fellow citizens . . . it is his duty to . . . go before a Court, and declare what he knows. And what would be the process, in case he failed to attend? Why, the common means would be, for the Court to issue an attachment to force him. . . .[198]

This was not empty rhetoric but a studied response to the egalitarian spirit of the times. It could not be otherwise in a system where no man is above the law, "from the highest to the lowest,"[199] where all officers, the President included, are but the "servants and agents"[200] of the people. Given a duty there must be a means to compel compliance,[201] and Jefferson's lawyers understood and declared that the President, like every other man, could be so constrained.

During the course of the recent impeachment hearings before the House Judiciary Committee, it was suggested from time to time that the Committee ought to request the courts to enforce its subpoena to President Nixon. Historically, a judicial subpoena stood no higher than one from

---

[195]N.Y. Times, May 23, 1974, at 32, col. 3.

[196]When Marshall was told in 1805 that "there was no means of compelling" the United States to pay costs, he replied, "[t]hat would make no difference, because we are to presume they would pay them if bound by law so to do." United States v. Hooe, 7 U.S. (3 Cranch) 73, 90 (1805). "Later he decided against Georgia in spite of the high probability that the order would be disregarded, undeterred by President Jackson's reported assurances that he would not lend his aid to enforcement." BERGER, EXECUTIVE PRIVILEGES, *supra* note 60, at 338. See McPherson v. Blacker, 146 U.S. 1, 24 (1892).

President Truman acquiesced in this view when he complied with the decision of the Court in Youngstown Sheet & Tube Co. v. Sawyer, 343 U.S. 579 (1952); *see* notes 114–16 and accompanying text *supra*. Asked earlier whether he would accept the Court's decision, Truman replied that he had "no ambition to be a dictator." N.Y. Times, May 2, 1952, at 1, col. 5.

[197]Perhaps the Committee concluded that it could not have mustered the votes in the House; a consensus for impeachment was slow in forming.

[198]3 T. CARPENTER, *supra* note 70, at 90–91.

[199]United States v. Lee, 106 U.S. 196, 220 (1882).

[200]James Iredell, 4 ELLIOTT, *supra* note 50, at 9.

[201]Berger, *Judicial Review: Countercriticism in Tranquility,* 69 Nw. U.L. REV. 390 (1974). Professor Philip Kurland justly asks: "why, if it is dubious ["an open question"] that a President may be subject to a contempt citation, was it certain that he was properly subjected to the kind of order that was before the Court for review? If the answer turns on the availability of sanctions, the answers to both questions would seem to be the same." Kurland, *supra* note 111, at 70–71.

Parliament; and until Mr. Nixon bowed to the order of the Supreme Court there was no assurance that he would comply with the judicial subpoena any more than he did with the congressional directive.[202] Even so, there was an advantage in turning to the courts—the gain that would accrue from the high esteem in which the courts are held, and the unfavorable impact on public opinion of a presidential confrontation with both Congress and the courts. On the other hand, possibly the Committee was reluctant to surrender a jot of its paramountcy in conducting an impeachment investigation; and it did have an ultimate sanction—to add an article for contempt of the House by refusal to comply with its subpoena.[203] Presidential infringements on the prerogatives of the House are impeachable.[204]

CONCLUSION

Courts did not interfere with Parliament's investigations or exercise of the contempt power; and for the first 90 years of our history American judges considered—and with good reason—that this also represented American law. No indication is to be found in the records of the several Conventions that the traditional power of inquiry with its accompanying attributes was to be curtailed in any particular. The limits of judicial review may again be set forth in the words of Chief Justice White:

> unless there be . . . a mere exertion of arbitrary power coming within the reach of constitutional limitations, the exercise of the [investigatory] authority is not subject to judicial interference.[205]

The recent confrontation between President Nixon and both Congress and the courts must not distort our vision. Such occasions are likely to be rare indeed; the norm is refusals of information by subordinates of the President. It needs to be understood that the "separation of powers," on which Chief Justice Burger relied to shield "presidential privilege," was invoked by President Eisenhower in 1954 to shelter communications between *all* employees of the federal establishment lest their "candid interchanges" be inhibited.[206] It is against this far-reaching claim that judicial supervision of congressional subpoenas needs to be measured.[207]

APPENDIX

Frankfurter's and Landis' Appeal to "Interaction"

In order to defend the Clayton Act's provision for trial by jury of criminal contempts committed outside the presence of the court, and punished to vindicate the authority of the court rather than to provide relief at the behest of a complainant,[a] against charges that it infringed upon the principle of separation of powers, Professors Frankfurter and Landis argued that the "Court had refused to

---

[202]*See* Mishkin, *supra* note 111, at 86–87; Karst & Horowitz, *supra* note 181, at 53.

[203]It may be thought that such an article required a preliminary decision by the House that the President was in contempt. But that judgment could be made by the House when voting on the contempt article. There would be no deprivation of a hearing because the President could show at the trial by the Senate that his refusal was not contemptuous.

[204]Berger, Impeachment, *supra* note 129, at 70.

[205]Marshall v. Gordon, 243 U.S., 521, 545 (1917).

[206]Berger, Executive Privilege, *supra* note 60, at 234–35. Hence it was that Attorney General Kleindienst told the Senate that the President is empowered to forbid over two-and-a-half million federal employees to testify before Congress under any circumstances and to block congressional demands for any document in the possession of the executive branch. *Id.* at 254–55.

[207]Professor Telford Taylor foresaw that under the Eisenhower doctrine, congressional committees would "frequently be shut off from access to documents to which they are clearly entitled by tradition, common sense and good governmental practice." T. Taylor, Grand Inquest 133 (1955).

[a]Act of October 15, 1914, ch. 323, §§ 21–25, 38 Stat. 730, *repealed by* Act of June 25, 1948, ch. 645, § 21, 62 Stat. 862.

draw abstract, analytical lines of separation and has recognized necessary areas of interaction."[b] When the issue came before the Supreme Court in *Michaelson v. United States ex rel. Chicago, St. Paul, Minneapolis & Omaha Ry. Co.,*[c] it conceded that if the provision were actually an invasion of the province of a court of equity, it would present a "grave constitutional question."[d] The Court held, however, that the proceeding for criminal contempt "is between the public and the defendant, is an independent proceeding at law, and no part of the original cause,"[e] and therefore did not interfere with the settled practice of suits in equity. Justice Holmes had noted in *Gompers v. United States*[f] that in early English law contempts were "punished only by the usual criminal procedure," that is, trial by jury, and still "preferably are tried in that way."[g] The Clayton Act's criminal contempt provision, then, is an example of "interaction" based on common law practice, and not an invasion of the province of the courts.

The "interaction" cases cited by Frankfurter and Landis largely illustrate that "the Supreme Court has consistently sustained congressional discretion when moving in the general legislative field not bound by specific limitations, even though the particular field may border on territory dominantly in control of another department of the government,"[h] and generally, it may be added, when the legislation rested on common law practice. Such a case was *The Laura,*[i] cited by Frankfurter and Landis for the proposition that "the President's power to pardon offenses" does not "preclude Congress from giving the Secretary of the Treasury the authority to remit fines and forfeitures."[j] The Supreme Court upheld the Treasury Secretary's fine remitting authority as resting on a "practice [that] commenced very shortly after the adoption" of the Constitution, probably patterned upon English Acts that "invested certain subordinate officers with authority to remit penalties and forfeitures."[k] And Congress merely delegated routine, burdensome duties to a subordinate of the President, presumably with his concurrence—hardly an invasion or redistribution of executive power. Of the same order is *Brown v. Walker,*[l] cited by Frankfurter and Landis to show that the President's pardoning power "does not invalidate congressional acts of amnesty."[m] The particular Act, the Court said, "belongs to a class of legislation which is not uncommon either in England . . . or in this country."[n] Another Frankfurter-Landis example of "interaction" is the President's "power to pardon punishment for a contempt of court;"[o] but here too "the common law and English history before the American Revolution . . . show that criminal contempts were within the understood scope of the pardoning power. . . ."[p]

Finally, *Cary v. Curtis,*[q] say Frankfurter and Landis, illustrates that "matters have been withdrawn from courts and vested in the executive."[r] The statute there provided that duties paid to the Collector under protest should be covered into the Treasury and refunded when shown "to

---

[b]Frankfurter & Landis, *Power of Congress Over Procedure in Criminal Contempts in "Inferior" Federal Courts—A Study in Separation of Powers,* 37 HARV. L. REV. 1010, 1014 (1924).

[c]266 U.S. 42 (1924).

[d]*Id.* at 64.

[e]*Id.*

[f]233 U.S. 604 (1914).

[g]*Id.* at 610–11.

[h]Frankfurter & Landis, *supra* note a, at 1016.

[i]114 U.S. 411 (1885).

[j]Frankfurter & Landis, *supra* note a, at 1015.

[k]114 U.S. at 414.

[l]161 U.S. 591 (1896).

[m]Frankfurter & Landis, *supra* note a, at 1015.

[n]161 U.S. at 601.

[o]Frankfurter & Landis, *supra* note a, at 1015 n.21.

[p]*Ex parte* Grossman, 267 U.S. 87, 112 (1925).

[q]44 U.S. (3 HOW.) 236 (1845).

[r]Frankfurter & Landis, *supra* note a, at 1014.

the satisfaction of the Secretary of the Treasury" that a refund was due.[s] This provision, the Court held, barred access to the courts; and it sustained the bar on the ground that the judicial power is dependent for its distribution on congressional action.[t] Thus, the "withdrawal" was deemed to have express constitutional sanction. Justice Story dissented on the ground that Congress was not authorized to deny access to the courts for complaints of illegal exercise of power,[u] and that Congress had no such bar in mind.[v] Justice Story's view was speedily confirmed by a second Act which provided that nothing contained in the earlier one shall deprive any person who made payment of the right to maintain an action at law.[w] Thus, *Cary* represents both a mistaken construction of a statute and a constitutional grant of power to Congress to reallocate the judicial power.

---

[s]Act of March 3, 1839, ch. 82, § 2, 5 Stat. 339.
[t]44 U.S. at 240–41, 245.
[u]44 U.S. at 253. *See also* R. BERGER, CONGRESS V. THE SUPREME COURT 285–96 (1969).
[v]44 U.S. at 257.
[w]Act of February 26, 1845, ch. 22, 5 Stat. 727.

CHAPTER VI

Standing to Sue in Public Actions: Is it a Constitutional Requirement?

Confusion twice-confounded reigns in the area of federal jurisdiction described as "standing to sue." That concept, it has been justly observed, is "among the most amorphous in the entire domain of public law," one of "uncertain content,"[1] of such complexity that Justice Frankfurter, a pioneering student of federal jurisdiction, "found himself reduced to a nearly unprecedented degree of inarticulateness" in dealing with one of its many aspects.[2] Not a little of the confusion originated in *Frothingham v. Mellon,*[3] which left uncertain whether "standing" was a constitutional requirement or simply a "rule of self-restraint."[4] A contributing factor was Justice Frankfurter's own attempt to ground the standing doctrine firmly on constitutional compulsions. In endowing the Court with "judicial Power," he stated, Article III "presupposed an historic content for that phrase," and in limiting the sphere of judicial action to "Cases" and "Controversies" the Framers had reference to "the familiar operations of the English judicial system," whereunder "[j]udicial power could come into play only in matters that were the traditional concern of the courts in Westminister and only if they arose in ways that to the expert feel of lawyers constituted 'Cases' or 'Controversies.' "[5] Given a document which employed familiar English terms—*e.g.,* "admiralty," "bankruptcy," "trial by jury"—it is hardly to be doubted that the Framers contemplated resort to English practice for elucidation, and so the Supreme Court has often held.[6] Indeed, on the very issue of "judicial Power" Madison emphasized in the Convention that it ought "to be limited to cases of a Judiciary Nature," implying that past practice would supply the criterion.[7]

---

[1]*Hearings on S. 2097 Before the Subcomm. on Constitutional Rights of the Senate Comm. on the Judiciary,* 89th Cong., 2d Sess. 498 (March 1966) [hereinafter cited as *Hearings*]. "Uncertainty," said John Streater, invoking a maxim in his defense against a commitment by Parliament in 1654, is "the mother of all debate and confusion, than which there is nothing more odious in law." Streater's Case, 5 How. St. Trials 365, 399.

[2]L. JAFFE, JUDICIAL CONTROL OF ADMINISTRATIVE ACTION 461 (1965).

[3]262 U.S. 447 (1923).

[4]Flast v. Cohen, 392 U.S. 83, 92 (1968).

[5]Coleman v. Miller, 307 U.S. 433, 460 (1939) (dissent). This was a "political question" case; Justice Frankfurter went on to lift his view to the level of generalized doctrine in Joint Anti-Fascist Refugee Comm. v. McGrath, 341 U.S. 123, 150–59 (1951) (concurring opinion).

[6]The language of the Constitution cannot be interpreted safely except by reference to the common law and to British institutions as they were when the instrument was framed and adopted. The statesmen and lawyers of the Convention who submitted it to the ratification of the Conventions of the thirteen States, were born and brought up in the atmosphere of the common law and thought and spoke in its vocabulary. They were familiar with other forms of government, recent and ancient, and indicated in their discussions earnest study and consideration of many of them, but when they came to put their conclusions into the form of fundamental law in a compact draft, they expressed them in terms of the common law, confident that they could be shortly and easily understood.

Ex Parte Grossman, 267 U.S. 87, 108–09 (1925). As was said in Glidden Co. v. Zdanok, 370 U.S. 530, 563 (1962), one touchstone of justiciability to which this Court has frequently had reference is whether the action sought to be maintained is of a sort "recognized at the time of the Constitution to be traditionally within the power of courts in the English and American judicial systems."

See also Goebel, *Constitutional History and Constitutional Law,* 38 COLUM. L. REV. 555, 557 (1938).

[7]2 M. FARRAND, RECORDS OF THE FEDERAL CONVENTION OF 1787, at 411 (1911) [hereinafter cited as FARRAND].

It has been too easily assumed, however, that English practice had at its core the necessity of showing injury to a personal interest as a prerequisite to an attack on jurisdictional usurpation.[8] In seeking to clarify *Frothingham* in *Flast v. Cohen*, moreover, the Court, in my opinion, has further confused analysis by extracting from the separation of powers and advisory opinion doctrines "implicit policies embedded in Article III"[9] with which to bolster dubious implications drawn from the "case or controversy" phrase.[10] A first step towards clarification would be to clear the ground of unhistorical notions of constitutional restrictions, to free consideration of the perplexing and wide-ranging issues of policy that cluster about the problem of standing from the constriction of fancied constitutional bonds. I propose to show that the English practice on which Justice Frankfurter relied did not in fact demand injury to a personal interest as a prerequisite to attacks on jurisdictional excesses,[11] and that neither the separation of powers nor advisory opinion doctrines as originally envisaged require insistence on a personal stake as the basic element of standing to make such challenges.

Unlike "case or controversy," which can summon the express terms of Article III, "standing" is not mentioned in the Constitution or the records of the several conventions. It is a judicial construct pure and simple[12] which, in its present sophisticated form, is of relatively recent origin. Professor Jaffe encountered "no case before 1807 in which the standing of the plaintiff is mooted. . . ,"[13] and found that objections to the standing of a private individual to enforce a "public right" were first squarely presented in 1897.[14] *Locus standi* was employed by two English Courts in 1874 and 1879 in not really relevant circumstances,[15] and appears in connection with referral by the House of Commons to a Court of Reference of objections that certain private bills may interfere with private

[8]Joint Anti-Fascist Refugee Comm. v. McGrath, 341 U.S. 123, 151–54 (1951) (Frankfurter, J., concurring). Professor Bickel deduces from the fact that the judicial power "may be exercised only in a case," that courts "may not decide non-cases, which are not adversary situations and in which nothing of immediate consequence to the parties turns on the results." Bickel, *Foreword: The Passive Virtues, The Supreme Court, 1960 Term*, 75 HARV. L. REV. 40, 42 (1961) [hereinafter cited as Bickel].

[9]392 U.S. 83, 96 (1968).

[10]That the matter is by no means academic may be deduced from the fact that Chairman Sam Ervin of the Senate Subcommittee on Constitutional Rights felt constrained in 1966 to call hearings in order to ascertain from divers scholars whether Congress was empowered to confer standing, not dependent upon a personal interest, to attack the constitutionality of legislation that would assist the educational and welfare programs of religious institutions. *Hearings* 5. In those hearings government counsel repeatedly urged that such legislation would raise constitutional doubts. *Id.* 76, 85, 127, 137. Professor P. G. Kauper stated that "absent a showing of injury" to the suitor in some "specific or concrete way," he "would not suppose that Congress has the power to direct the Federal courts to take jurisdiction of such citizen's suits." *Id.* 502. Professor A. S. Miller stated that there is "some doubt of the extent to which Congress can confer 'standing' upon those the Supreme Court has said do not have it." *Id.* 509.

[11]This is not a novel proposition. In a pathbreaking article, Professor Jaffe sought to demonstrate via the history of mandamus that "the public action—an action brought by a private person primarily to vindicate the public interest in the enforcement of public obligations—has long been a feature of our English and American law." Jaffe, *Standing to Secure Judicial Review: Private Actions*, 75 HARV. L. REV. 255, 302 (1961) [hereinafter cited as Jaffe, *Private Actions*], summarizing his companion article, *Standing to Secure Judicial Review: Public Actions*, 74 HARV. L. REV. 1265 (1961) [hereinafter cited as Jaffe, *Public Actions*]. In the latter he noted that *Frothingham* appealed to "a questionable dogma." *Id.* 1266. In *Hearings* 451, he characterized the requirement that a plaintiff have "a special, pecuniary interest" as "unhistorical."

[12]Jaffe, *Private Actions* 256.

[13]Jaffe, *Public Actions* 1270. There is an earlier American case, State v. Corporation of New Brunswick, 1 N.J.L. 393 (1795), in which the argument was made, without employing the word "standing," and was rejected. For discussion see TAN 99 *infra*. See note 38 *infra* for a rejection in a quo warranto case in 1789.

[14]Jaffe, *Public Actions* 1271–72.

[15]James v. The Queen, [1874] 5 Ch. D. 153, 160 (one to whom a statute does not make a grant has no *locus standi* to compel one to him); *In re* Gold Co., [1879] 12 Ch. D. 77, 83.

rights of others.[16] As late as 1955, an English writer examining the availability of the writ of certiorari could say that the subject of *locus standi* had not been "treated in a satisfactory way by any one, judge or jurist."[17] In any case "standing" was neither a term of art nor a familiar doctrine at the time the Constitution was adopted. Although it has been explained as a description of "the constitutional limitation on the jurisdiction of the Court to 'cases' and 'controversies,' "[18] it apparently entered our law via *Frothingham* in 1923.[19]

When we turn to pre-Constitution English law for light on the meaning of "case or controversy," we find that attacks by strangers on action in excess of jurisdiction were a traditional concern of the courts in Westminster. The writ of prohibition supplies perhaps the clearest example. Coke tells us of a complaint by the clergy to the King of undue granting of writs of prohibition by the courts against the exercise of ecclesiastical jurisdiction, which the judges were then called upon to answer. "[A]ll the judges of England, and the barons of the Exchequer, with one unanimous consent," records Coke, made answer in a document known as the *Articulo Cleri*. In their Third Answer the judges stated:

> Prohibitions by law are to be granted at any time to restraine a court to intermeddle with, or execute any thing, which by law they ought not to hold plea of, and they are much mistaken that maintaine the contrary. . . . And the kings courts that may award prohibitions, being informed either by the parties themselves, or by any stranger, that any court temporall or ecclesiasticall doth hold plea of that (whereof they have not jurisdiction) may lawfully prohibit the same, as well after judgement and execution, as before.[20]

No English court, so far as I can discover, has ever rejected the authority of *Articulo Cleri* or denied that a writ of prohibition may be granted at the suit of a stranger. On the contrary, Coke was cited by the 18th century Abridgments[21] and by English courts throughout the 19th century,[22] and his rule remains the law in England today.[23] Thus at the time of the Revolution, the "courts in Westminster" afforded to a stranger a means of attack on jurisdictional excesses without requiring a showing of injury to his personal interest.

[16]Constable, *Principles and Practice Affecting Locus Standi*, 9 Jurid. Rev. 47, 55 (1897): "The principle of *locus standi* is that there is something in the bill which, if passed into law, would injure the parties petitioning" (quoting Mr. Richards). The fact that the words *locus standi* have not found their way into the indices of the English digests itself suggests relative novelty. And to this day in England "there is no serious trouble over standing (*i.e., locus standi*)." Wade, *Anglo-American Administrative Law: More Reflections*, 82 L.Q. Rev. 226, 249 (1966).

[17]Yardley, *Certiorari and the Problem of Locus Standi*, 71 L.Q. Rev. 388, 393 (1955).

[18]Barrows v. Jackson, 346 U.S. 249, 255 (1953); C. Wright, Federal Courts 36 (1963), states that "standing to sue is an element of the federal constitutional concept of 'case or controversy.' " *See also* note 8 *supra*.

[19]Professor Jaffe states that "[t]he first significant controversy . . . concerning standing had reached the Supreme Court in 1911," but that the Court "found it unnecessary to decide the standing question." The "criterion of standing was brought into focus" with Baltimore & Ohio R.R. v. United States, 264 U.S. 258 (1924). Jaffe, *Private Actions* 261–262.

[20]2 E. Coke, Institutes of the Laws of England* 602 (1797) [hereinafter cited as *Inst.*]. "In Roman law it was open to any citizen to bring an *actio popularis* in respect of a public delict or to sue for a prohibitory or restitutory interdict for the protection of *res sacrae* and *res publicae*." S. de Smith, Judicial Review of Administrative Action 423 (2d ed. 1968) [hereinafter cited as De Smith].

[21]4 J. Comyns, Digest, "Prohibition" (E) (1766); 4 M. Bacon, Abridgment, "Prohibition" (C) (3d ed. 1768).

[22]In Wadsworth v. Queen of Spain [1851] 17 Q.B. 171, 214, Lord Campbell stated: "we find it laid down in books of the highest authority that, where the court to which prohibition is to go has no jurisdiction, a prohibition may be granted upon the request of a *stranger*, as well as of the defendant himself. 2 Coke 607; *Com. Dig. Prohibition (E).*" *See also* Mayor of London v. Cox [1867] L.R. 2 E. & I. App. 239, 279 (H.L.); Worthington v. Jeffries [1875] L.R. 10 C.P. 379, 383. *See* note 108 *infra*.

[23]H. Wade, Administrative Law 125–26 (2d ed. 1967) [hereinafter cited as Wade].

Coke was a revered figure in the Colonies, and his record of *Articulo Cleri* was presumably familiar to Colonial lawyers.[24] In addition, his doctrine had been picked up by the Bacon and Viner *Abridgments,* to which they frequently turned, as well as by the respected *Comyns' Digest.*[25] Of course the availability of prohibition did not constitute "common law precedent on standing to attack the constitutionality of a statute,"[26] both because written constitutions were a distinctive product of post-revolutionary America, and because the doctrine of "constitutionality" was a peculiarly American development. But a challenge to action in excess of authority conferred by the Constitution was well within the rationale of the writ of prohibition.

There was also the analogous practice of certiorari. Both the writs of certiorari and prohibition, said Lord Atkin,

> are of great antiquity, forming part of the process by which the King's Courts restrain courts of inferior jurisdiction from exceeding their power. Prohibition restrains the tribunal from proceeding further in excess of jurisdiction; certiorari requires the record or order of the court to be sent up to the King's Bench Division, to have its legality inquired into, and, if necessary, to have the order quashed. It is to be noted that both writs deal with questions of excessive jurisdiction.[27]

Certiorari, stated Chief Justice Holt in 1702, would issue to examine the "proceedings of all jurisdictions erected by Act of Parliament . . . to the end that this court may see that they keep themselves within their jurisdiction; and if they exceed it, to restrain them."[28] That certiorari was available to a stranger may be inferred from a 1724 case which drew a distinction between a party aggrieved and "one who comes merely as a stranger," for purposes of deciding whether issuance of the writ was discretionary or a matter of right.[29] In 1870 an English court examining the writ looked to "the very analogous case of prohibition,"[30] and without an air of fresh-minting law the Court of Appeal flatly stated in 1957 that "the remedy by certiorari . . . extends to any stranger."[31] I know of no English case that has denied this proposition.

Originally, both certiorari and prohibition "dealt almost exclusively with the jurisdiction of what is described in ordinary parlance as a Court of Justice";[32] but very early they were employed with

---

[24]In New York, "Coke was by all odds the writer most used and cited. There are many indications that this was true in other provinces." Goebel, *supra* note 6, at 564 n.25. Jefferson stated that there never was "one of profounder learning in the orthodox doctrines of the British Constitution or what is called British rights" than Coke. E. CORWIN, THE DOCTRINE OF JUDICIAL REVIEW 31 n.45 (1914).

[25]*See* note 21 *supra;* C. VINER, ABRIDGMENT, "Prohibition" (M) 14 (1743). "A lot of American law came out of Bacon's and Viner's Abridgments." Goebel, *Ex Parte Clio,* 54 COLUM. L. REV. 450, 455 (1954). Justice Willes stated in Mayor of London v. Cox [1867] L.R. 2 E. & I. App. 239, 285 (H.L.): "the law is laid down in Comyn's Digest." 2 J. ADAMS, LEGAL PAPERS (Wroth & Zobel eds. 1965) contains frequent citations of the Abridgments by James Otis, Adams, and Blowers. *Id.* 128 n.73, 163, 228, 269, 284, 341, 350, 424, 428, 430.

[26]Jaffe, *Public Actions* 1308.

[27]Rex v. Electricity Commissioners [1924] 1 K.B. 171, 204–05. Lord Atkin stated that he could "see no difference in principle between certiorari and prohibition, except that the latter may be invoked at an earlier stage." *Id.* at 206.

[28]Rex v. Inhabitants in Glamorganshire, 91 Eng. Rep. 1287, 1288 (1702) (certiorari to bring up a levy of moneys to repair Caerdiffe Bridge). If there was a "personal stake" *quaere* whether it amounted to a "cause of action." *See* note 47 *infra.*

[29]Arthur v. Commissioners of Sewers, 88 Eng. Rep. 237 (1725). The case was so read by Justice Blackburn in Regina v. Justices of Surrey, [1870] L.R. 5 Q.B. 466, 472–73.

[30]*Id.* at 472.

[31]Regina v. Thames Magistrates Court, *ex parte* Greenbaum [1957] Local Gov't Rep. 129, 132, 125–36. In England, an applicant for certiorari or prohibition does not have to show that some legal right of his is at stake. If the action is an excess or abuse of power, the court will quash it at the instance of a mere stranger . . . [T]hese remedies are not restricted by the notion of *locus standi.* Every citizen has standing to invite the court to prevent some abuse of power, and in doing so he may claim to be regarded not as a meddlesome busybody but as a public benefactor. WADE 125–26.

[32]Rex v. Electricity Commissioners [1924] 1 K.B. 171, 205.

respect to what we term "administrative" functions. Because the justices of the peace were the local county administrators, charged with supervising road construction and maintenance, licensing alehouses, setting wage-scales for laborers and apprentices and administering the poor-laws, and were at the same time courts of record,[33] review of administrative functions was handily accomplished by means of these self-same writs. As Professor de Smith remarks:

> It was assumed that the writs of certiorari and prohibition by which [the justices] were controlled in their capacity as courts of summary jurisdiction, were equally appropriate devices for superintending the exercise of their multifarious governmental functions. All those functions of the justices which were not purely ministerial were regarded for this purpose as being judicial: no separate category of discretionary "administrative" acts, immune from the reach of certiorari and prohibition, was yet recognized. A no less broad conception of "judicial" functions governed review of orders made by the Commissioners of Sewers, who presided over a court of record which performed administrative duties under judicial forms.[34]

In the course of the meandering development of English administrative law many such functions were transferred from "courts of record" to administrative agencies. In keeping with existing practice Parliament not infrequently provided for review by certiorari—as, for example, in the case of Poor Law administration. And despite the lack of such express provisions in other statutes, from which the courts might have inferred that Parliament intended to exclude certiorari in certain cases, it was concluded instead that "common-law certiorari and prohibition could properly issue to other authorities discharging similar functions."[35] In one such case the court rejected an attempt by the Inclosure Commissioners to question whether prohibition would lie to review an attempted enclosure with the remark that the case was "too clear."[36] Evaluation of a colonial lawyer's

---

[33] DE SMITH 386–87; E. HENDERSON, FOUNDATIONS OF ENGLISH ADMINISTRATIVE LAW 18–25 (1963) [hereinafter cited as HENDERSON].

[34] DE SMITH 387. Review of a non-judicial function of the Commissioners is illustrated by Arthur v. Commissioners of Sewers, 88 Eng. Rep. 237 (1725), in which certiorari brought up an order ousting plaintiff who had been chosen by the Commissioners as their clerk at an earlier meeting. If, as Professor Henderson emphasizes, the Commissioners, like the justices of the peace, were courts of record, HENDERSON 112, 116, the predominant consideration was prevention of jurisdictional excess, as two notable utterances testify. In Commins v. Massam, March 196 (1643), Justice Heath stated:
> notwithstanding that the act leaves the proceedings to the discretion of the Commissioners [of Sewers], nevertheless this discretion is examinable and controllable in this Court. Suppose that the Commissioners do anything without or against their commission, without doubt this is reformable and examinable here.
Quoted in HENDERSON 146. In the *Caerdiffe Bridge Case* (Rex v. Inhabitants in Glamorganshire, 91 Eng. Rep. 1287 (1702)), the justices of the peace had levied money for repair of the bridge, and objection to ceritorari was made that a new statute had reposed the jurisdiction, *i.e.*, the discretion, in the justices. To this Chief Justice Holt replied:
> this Court will examine the proceedings of all jurisdictions erected by Act of Parliament. And if they, under pretense of such Act, proceed to incroach jurisdiction to themselves greater than the Act warrants, this Court will send a certiorari to them . . . to the end that this Court may see, that they keep themselves within their jurisdiction, and if they exceed it, to restrain them.
Id. at 1288.

[35] DE SMITH 388.

[36] Church v. Inclosure Commissioners, 142 Eng. Rep. 956 (1862). Rex v. Electricity Commissioners, [1924] 1 K.B. 171, 209, noted this act of a distinguished bench.
The relevance of the early cases was made explicit in 1924 when *Rex v. Electricity Commissioners* pointed to the *Caerdiffe* holding that "certiorari lies to justices of peace in a county in respect of a statutory duty to fix a rate for the repair of a county bridge." *Id.* 205. Stress in that case upon the "judicial" nature of the reviewable administrative function is to be read against the facts: "the Electricity Commissioners have to decide whether they will constitute a joint authority in a district in accordance with law, and with what powers they will invest that body." In "deciding upon the scheme and in holding the inquiry, they are acting judicially. . . ." *Id.* 206–07. Professor Henderson reminds us that the orders issued by the early courts of record are "very different from the judicial business 'between party and party' which is characteristic of courts of record." HENDERSON 116.
It would have been anomalous indeed had agency excesses been given immunity denied to judicial usurpations, and this at a time when deference to vaunted agency expertise lay far in the future. In applying the *Caerdiffe* ruling to purely

hypothetical appraisal of English practice in curbing action in excess of jurisdiction should not therefore be made to turn on a "court of record" distinction which the English judiciary, so respectful of precedent, found of no moment. Colonial observers would see administrative functions being reviewed without reason to conclude that future transfers from courts of record to administrative agencies would liberate those functions from surveillance.

In addition to prohibition and certiorari there were other writs, which had no "court of record" antecedents. An information in the nature of quo warranto antedates the statute of 9 Anne, which allowed anyone who so desired to make use of the name of the Clerk of the Crown, with the leave of Court, for the purpose of prosecuting usurpers of franchises.[37] The breadth of the statute envisaged suits by a stranger; and at least one case in 1789[38] held that the writ was available to a stranger, as had earlier been held with respect to other prerogative writs. The analogy to prohibition was clearly drawn in 1915, when Lord Reading observed that "a stranger to a suit can obtain prohibition . . . and I see no reason why he should not in a proper case obtain an information of quo warranto."[39]

Professor Jaffe considers mandamus and injunctions as the "most significant prototypes the public action," certiorari of "considerably lesser significance," and prohibition and quo warranto least important of all.[40] As a résumé of the American development this is unexceptionable, but it probably was not intended to describe the course of events in England, where the availability of prohibition and quo warranto as public actions, as Professor Jaffe himself notes, "has been clearer than that of either mandamus or injunction"[41] and where even today certiorari and prohibition remain available to strangers.[42] Since my concern is with the state of English law before 1787, with the question whether that law, as viewed by the Framers, could be understood to permit attacks by strangers upon jurisdictional unsurpations, the early English practice in prohibition, certiorari, and quo warranto, which permitted such attacks, is for me the more significant.

For purposes of such attacks, I suggest, the early English mandamus practice was not highly relevant. Mandamus was largely designed to compel action by one who was under a duty to act, who was *authorized* to act in the premises; it was not a vehicle for the restraint of unauthorized action. As Blackstone put the distinction, mandamus was used to direct persons, corporations or inferior courts "to do some *particular* thing . . . which appertains to their office and duty," while "encroachment of jurisdiction, or calling one *coram non judice,* to answer in a court which has

---

administrative agencies the English courts were true to the common law canon that the scope of a principle is not limited to the facts that fortuitously gave it birth.

[37]9 Anne, c. 20 (1710). *See* Rex v. Trelawney, 97 Eng. Rep. 1010 (1765); J. Shortt, Informations (Criminal and Quo Warranto) Mandamus and Prohibition 112–14 (1888) [hereinafter cited as Shortt].

[38]Rex v. Smith, 100 Eng. Rep. 740 (1790), contains a note on *Rex v. Brown* (1789), which was an information in the nature of quo warranto that councilmen were under disqualification because they had not received the sacrament within twelve months previous to the election as required by statute. Erskine argued that "it does not appear here that the party making the application has any connection with the corporation." Lord Kenyon, however, held: "We are bound to grant this information. The law has said that the magistracy of the country shall be in the hands of those who profess the religion of the Church of England." Justice Ashurst added: "the ground on which this application is made is to enforce a general Act of Parliament, which interests all the corporations in the kingdom; and therefore it is no objection that the party applying is not a member of the corporation."

Cf. Rex v. Mayor of Hartford, 91 Eng. Rep. 325 (1700), where quo warranto issued against the mayor and aldermen of Hartford to show "by what authority they admitted persons to be freemen of the corporation who did not inhabit in the borough. The motion was pretended to be on behalf of the freemen, who by this means were encroached upon." *See* note 47 *infra.*

[39]Rex v. Speyer [1916] L.R. 1 K.B. 595, 613. "Every subject," said Justice Lush, "has an interest in securing that public duties shall be exercised only by those competent to exercise them. . . ." *Id.* at 628.

[40]Jaffe, *Public Actions* 1269.

[41]*Id.*

[42]*See* note 31 *supra.*

no legal cognizance of the cause, is . . . a grievance for which the common law has provided a remedy by the writ of prohibition."[43]

Mandamus, however, did have an important complementary role to play in the enforcement of duties colored with a public interest, duties in which the "personal interest" did not rise to the dignity of a "cause of action." In 1652, mandamus was granted to the parishioners and officers of the parish of Clerkenwell "to make scavengers that are elected to that office to serve the office."[44] In the *Case of the Borough of Bossiny*, mandamus issued to hold an election for mayor;[45] a mandamus commanded in 1733 that an election be held to fill a vacancy on the corporation of Esham;[46] and it had issued in 1698 to compel justices of the peace "to make rates for the relief of the poor."[47] From such cases a colonial lawyer might well have concluded that mandamus was capable of issuance at the suit of a stranger who sought to assert the public interest,[48] especially because the analogy of mandamus to prohibition was early drawn, and because Coke, who had unequivocally stated the availability of prohibition to strangers, also made a massive assertion of mandamus jurisdiction.[49] To King's Bench, he declared in *James Baggs' Case*,

> belongs authority, not only to correct error in judicial proceedings, but other errors and misdemeanors extrajudicial, tending to breach of peace, or oppression of the subjects, or to the raising of faction, controversy, debate or any manner of misgovernment, so that no wrong or injury, either private or public, can be done but what it shall be here reformed or punished by due course of law.[50]

This was not long after *Articulo cleri* had categorically asserted the right of strangers to attack jurisdictional usurpations in prohibition proceedings. Scarcely less encompassing was Lord Mansfield's statement in 1762 that mandamus

> was introduced to prevent disorder from failure of justice and defect of police. Therefore, it ought to be used upon all occasions where the law has established no specific remedy, and where in justice and good government there ought to be one.[51]

The fact that mandamus subsequently "developed along more modest lines"[52] should not obscure the potential effect of these grandiose claims on the minds of the Founders. In weighing whether "case or controversy" was framed restrictively, we should not too hastily assume that the contem-

---

[43] 3 W. BLACKSTONE, COMMENTARIES* 110–11. 3 M. BACON, ABRIDGMENT, "Mandamus" (A) (3d ed. 1768) states that the writ was used "to oblige inferior Courts and Magistrates to do that Justice, which, without such Writ, they are in Duty, and by virtue of their Offices, obliged to do." *Compare* J. COMYNS, DIGEST, "Mandamus" (B) (1766): it "does not lie to prevent a Molestation against Law: As not to molest a Preacher." Regina v. Peach, 91 Eng. Rep. 482 (1705). In denying a writ in such circumstances, Peat's Case, 87 Eng. Rep. 979 (1704), explained that "a *mandamus* is always to do something in execution of law."

[44] Anonymous, 82 Eng. Rep. 765 (1652).

[45] 93 Eng. Rep. 996 (1735).

[46] Anonymous, 94 Eng. Rep. 471 (1733).

[47] Lidleston v. Mayor of Exeter, 90 Eng. Rep. 567 (1697).

Such cases, as well as *Rex v. Mayor of Hartford*, discussed *supra* note 38, and *Rex v. Inhabitants of Glamorganshire*, *supra* note 28, speak against the narrow requirement of Tennessee Electric Power Co. v. TVA, 306 U.S. 118, 140 (1939), that a plaintiff who would complain of invalid action must show injury to "a legal right—one of property, one arising out of contract, one protected against tortious invasion, or one founded on a statute which confers a privilege."

[48] Professor Jaffe points out that "the lists of the cases in the digests strongly suggest that the plaintiff in some of them was without a personal interest." Jaffe, *Public Actions* 1270. Case titles furnish no clues because the King or Queen are "invariably the prosecutors of the writ." T. TAPPING, THE LAW AND PRACTICE OF THE HIGH PREROGATIVE WRIT OF MANDAMUS at viii (1848). *Cf.* note 57 *infra*.

[49] E. HENDERSON 72; Jaffe & Henderson, *Judicial Review and the Rule of Law: Historical Origins*, 72 L.Q. REV. 345, 359 (1956).

[50] 77 Eng. Rep. 1271, 1277–78 (1615).

[51] Rex v. Barker, 97 Eng. Rep. 823, 824–25 (1762).

[52] Jaffe & Henderson, *supra* note 49, at 360.

porary view was ours, but rather should consider that Coke's and Mansfield's sweeping assertions of mandamus jurisdiction reflected English practice in other prerogative writs.[53]

The early English practice in prohibition, certiorari, and quo warranto is not the sole indication of easy access to "public actions"; there were in addition the centuries-old "informers" actions. These went beyond making *available* procedures to control unlawful conduct, and offered financial *inducements* to strangers to prosecute such actions, provided for by a "very large" number of statutes "in which the public at large was encouraged to enforce obedience to statutes by the promise of a share of the penalty imposed for disobedience. . . ."[54] Such informers had "no interest whatever in the controversy other than that given by statute,"[55] and the pecuniary reward thus offered to strangers was little calculated to lead colonial lawyers to read cognate remedies narrowly. There were also the "relator" actions, deriving from the Crown's duty "to see that public bodies kept within their lawful powers."[56] Blackstone cites the quo warranto statute of Queen Anne for a suit "at the relation of any person desiring to prosecute the same, (who is then styled the *relator*). . . ."[57] The relator action flourished in England, where it is brought by the Attorney General "at the relation (*i.e.*, at the instance) of some other person," being a proceeding "against any public authority which is abusing its power."[58] "It is not absolutely necessary," said Lord Hardwicke in 1741, that "relators in an information for a charity, should be the persons principally interested. . . . [A]ny persons, though the most remote in the contemplation of the charity, may be relators in these cases"; and other cases dispensed with "the least particle of interest."[59]

At the adoption of the Constitution, in sum, the English practice in prohibition, certiorari, quo warranto, and informers' and relators' actions encouraged strangers to attack *unauthorized action.* So far as the requirement of standing is "used to describe the constitutional limitation on the jurisdiction of this Court to 'cases' and 'controversies' ";[60] so far as "case" and "controversy" and

[53]De Smith notes that Mansfield seems to have been the first to perceive the close relationship between what are now classed as the "prerogative" writs. DE SMITH 384.

[54]4 W. HOLDSWORTH, A HISTORY OF ENGLISH LAW 356 (2d ed. 1937).

[55]Marvin v. Trout, 199 U.S. 212, 225 (1905): "Statutes providing for actions by a common informer, who himself had no interest whatever in the controversy other than that given by statute, have been in existence hundreds of years in England, and in this country ever since the foundation of our Government." The use of such actions to police official misconduct is noted by Blackstone, who refers to suits for forfeitures by persons who "being in particular offices . . . neglect to take the oaths to the government; which penalty is given to him or them that will sue for the same." 2 W. BLACKSTONE, COMMENTARIES* 437. A New York informer's statute of 1692 to restrain privateers and pirates provides for one-half the recovery of fines against an "officer that shall omitt or neglect his duty herein." SUPREME COURT OF THE JUDICATURE OF THE PROVINCE OF NEW YORK, 1691–1704, 30 n.77, 71 n.74 (1959).

[56]WADE 113.

[57]3 W. BLACKSTONE, COMMENTARIES* 264. He also alludes to informations exhibited in the name of the king, in which, "though the king is the nominal prosecutor, yet it is at the relation of some private person or common informer. . ." 4 *id.** 308. A couple of pre-1788 relator cases are Attorney General v. Parker, 26 Eng. Rep. 1132 (Ch. 1747) (action to set aside election to a curacy); Attorney General v. Middleton, 28 Eng. Rep. 210 (1751) (action concerning charitable trust for a school; dismissed because colored by relator's private motive of revenge).

[58]WADE 113.

[59]Attorney General v. Bucknall, 26 Eng. Rep. 600 (Ch. 1741). *See* Rex v. Mayor of Hartford, 91 Eng. Rep. 325 (1700). *See also* Attorney General v. Vivian, 38 Eng. Rep. 88, 92 (1825): "The character of relator . . . does not seem to require the least particle of private interest in the due administration of that charity." To the same effect see Attorney General v. Logan, [1891] L.R. 2 Q.B. 100, 103. Professor Wade states that

To require public authorities to keep within their powers generally is not normally the business of the ordinary citizen. But it is the business of the Crown, and the Crown will lend its help to any subject who reasonably wants to borrow— or rather to hire—it. . . . [I]t is a beneficial arrangement, since it enables a private citizen to assert his concern as a member of the public that public authorities should not abuse their powers.

WADE 114.

Professor Finer states that the Attorney General "invariably permits the use of his name." H. FINER, ENGLISH LOCAL GOVERNMENT 220 (4th ed. 1950), quoted in Jaffe, *Public Actions* 1274.

[60]Barrows v. Jackson, 346 U.S. 249, 255 (1953); *cf.* C. WRIGHT, FEDERAL COURTS 36 (1963); Bickel 42.

"judicial power" "presuppose an historic content";[61] and so far as the index of that content is the "business of the . . . courts of Westminster when the Constitution was framed,"[62] the argument for a constitutional bar to strangers as complainants against unconstitutional action seems to me without foundation. When the Court stated in *Flast v. Cohen* that

> in terms of Article III limitations on federal court jurisdiction, the question of standing is related only to whether the dispute sought to be adjudicated will be presented in an adversary context and in a form historically viewed as capable of judicial resolution. It is for that reason that the emphasis . . . is on . . . "a personal stake in the outcome" of the controversy,[63]

it misinterpreted English history. For that history discloses that one without a "personal stake," a mere stranger to the action complained of, was allowed to initiate and maintain an "adversary" proceeding in the public interest to challenge a jurisdictional usurpation. Such a proceeding was "historically viewed as capable of judicial resolution." Those who would complain that the evidence of English practice is scanty should remember that the argument to the contrary rests on no evidence at all, but on the mistaken assumption that the practice in such strictly private actions as tort and contract governed "public actions" as well.[64]

Possibly entertaining doubts about Justice Frankfurter's reference to the "practices of the courts of Westminster," *Flast v. Cohen* adverted to the "uncertain historical antecedents of the case and controversy doctrine" and sought to bolster it by arguments derived from the separation of powers and advisory opinion doctrines, emerging with what were termed "implicit policies embodied in Article III."[65] The phrase "cases and controversies" was explained primarily as defining "the role assigned to the judiciary in a tripartite allocation of power to assure that the courts will not intrude into areas committed to the other branches of the government."[66]

---

[61]Coleman v. Miller, 307 U.S. 433, 460 (1939) (Frankfurter, J., concurring).

[62]Joint Anti-Fascist Refugee Comm. v. McGrath, 341 U.S. 123, 150 (1951) (Frankfurter, J., concurring). *See* TAN 5 *supra*.

[63]392 U.S. at 101. "If our constitutional notions of proper judicial business are grounded to a significant degree in history it is next to impossible to conclude—as was attempted in *Frothingham*—that a taxpayer's action does not fulfill the constitutional requisites of case or controversy." Jaffe, *Private Actions* 302.

Justice Harlan was closer to the mark in concluding that non-personal stake public actions are "within the jurisdiction conferred upon the federal courts by Article III." 392 U.S. at 130. *See also id.* at 120.

[64]*See* Tennessee Electric Power Co. v. TVA, 306 U.S. 118, 140 (1939). Even when tempted to disbelieve a witness, courts have said that "Mere disbelief of testimony [not inherently incredible] is not the equivalent of evidence to the contrary." Phillips v. Gookin, 231 Mass. 250, 251, 120 N.E. 691 (1918); Mosson v. Liberty Fast Freight Co., 124 F.2d 448, 450 (2d Cir. 1942); Eckenrode v. Pennsylvania R.R., 164 F.2d 996, 999 n.8 (3d Cir. 1947); Magg v. Miller, 296 F. 973, 979 (D.C. Cir. 1924).

[65]392 U.S. 83, 95–96 (1968).

[66]*Id.* at 95. The Court was careful to separate the issue of "capacity to sue" from the question whether it had Article III jurisdiction of the subject matter.

"[W]hen standing is placed an issue in a case, the question is whether the person whose standing is challenged is a proper party to request an adjudication of a particular issue and not whether the issue itself is justiciable." *Id.* at 99–100.

In Berger, *Executive Privilege v. Congressional Inquiry*, 12 U.C.L.A.L. Rev. 1288, 1342 (1965), I directed attention to the fact that this distinction had been drawn in Tileston v. Ullman, 318 U.S. 44, 46 (1943): "Since the appeal must be dismissed on the ground that appellant has no standing to litigate the constitutional question . . . it is unnecessary to consider whether the record shows the existence of a genuine case or controversy essential to the exercise of the jurisdiction of this court"; and also noticed in Willing v. Chicago Auditorium Ass'n, 277 U.S. 274, 289 (1928), where, although there was "no lack of a substantial interest of the plaintiff in the question" of standing, Justice Brandeis concluded that "still the proceeding is not a case or controversy within the meaning of Article III. . . ."

For a similar differentiation in the field of conflicts between the jurisdiction of a court over the subject matter—the power confided by a state to decide in the premises—and the capacity of a party to sue, see A. Ehrenzweig, Conflict of Laws 35, 71, 72, 120 (1962).

Flast goes on to state that whether "a particular person is a proper party to maintain the action does not, by its own force, raise separation of powers problems related to improper judicial interference with other branches." 392 U.S. at 100.

Overemphasis of the "separation of powers," however, is apt to obscure the no less important system of "checks and balances." Judicial checks on legislative excesses represent a deliberate and considered departure from an abstractly perfect separation of powers, part of what Madison called a necessary "blending" of powers that was required to make the separation work.[67] Litigation that challenges unconstitutional legislation does not constitute an "improper interference" with nor an "intrusion" into the legislative domain. No authority to make laws in excess of granted powers was "committed" to Congress; instead courts were authorized to check Congressional excesses. "Case or controversy," to be sure, seeks to confine the courts to what Madison termed cases of a "judiciary nature" as distinguished from a roving revision of legislation. Legislation is emphatically not for the courts; but after the legislative process is completed the courts may decide in the frame of litigation that a statute is invalid as a legislative usurpation.[68] A legislative usurpation does not change character when it is challenged by a stranger; and judicial restraint thereon remains a "judicial" function, not an "intrusion," though undertaken at the call of one without a personal stake.[69] No hint that judicial restraint of legislative usurpation was to hinge on the suitor's "interest" is to be found in the records of the Constitutional Convention. Having made review available to curb usurpations of power not "committed" to Congress, the Founders could assume that traditional remedies in "cases" of a "judiciary nature" would be available to curb such

Then, after stating that "in deciding the question of standing, it is not relevant that the substantive issues in the litigation might be non-justiciable," *Flast* declares that it is "necessary to look to the substantive issues . . . to determine whether there is a logical nexus between the status asserted and the claim sought to be adjudicated." *Id.* at 101–02. How the irrelevant thus again becomes relevant is too subtle for my comprehension.

[67]Explaining the limitations of the separation of powers doctrine in *Federalist* 47, Madison said that Montesquieu "did not mean that these departments ought to have . . . no *control* over, the acts of each other." In No. 48 he stated that "unless these departments be so far connected and blended as to give to each a constitutional control over the others, the degree of separation which the maxim requires, as essential to a free government, can never in practice be duly maintained." So too, Davie met criticism in the North Carolina convention with the reply that

> Montesquieu, at the same time he laid down this maxim, was writing in praise of the British government. At the very time he recommended this distinction of powers, he passed the highest eulogium on a constitution wherein they were all partially blended.

4 J. ELLIOT, DEBATES IN THE SEVERAL STATE CONVENTIONS ON THE ADOPTION OF THE FEDERAL CONSTITUTION 121 (1881). *See also* Frankfurter & Landis, *Power of Congress Over Procedure in Criminal Contempts in "Inferior" Federal Courts—A Study in Separation of Powers,* 37 HARV. L. REV. 1010 (1924). In short, the separation of powers was tempered by a system of "checks and balances," and the reach of the separation in a given case must be evaluated against the purpose that the given "check" was to serve.

[68]For this reason, Justice Harlan seems to me mistaken in saying that "unrestricted public actions" would "go far toward the final transformation of this Court into the Council of Revision which, despite Madison's support, was rejected by the Constitutional Convention." Flast v. Cohen, 392 U.S. 83, 130 (1968) (dissent). For that Council was to participate in the *enacting* process by way of an Executive veto (in which the judges would take part), as distinguished from judicial review *after* enactment and in the course of litigation. The matter was put in a nutshell by James Wilson, who argued in behalf of judicial participation in the Council that "[i]t will be better to prevent the passage of an improper law, than to declare it void when passed." 2 FARRAND 391. King urged the exclusion of judges because they "ought to be able to expound the law as it should come before them, free from the bias of having participated in its formation." 1 *id.* 98. Charles Pinckney also objected that such participation would "give a previous tincture to their opinions." 2 *id.* 298. *See also* Gerry, 1 *id.* 97. The Council of Revision was rejected, judicial participation and all. That the judicial function was to begin after completion of the legislative process appears again in Wilson's statement to the Pennsylvania convention:

> it is possible that the legislature . . . may transgress the bounds assigned to it, and act may pass, in the usual mode, notwithstanding that transgression; but when it comes to be discussed before the judges—when they consider its principles, and find it incompatible with the superior power of the Constitution,—it is their duty to pronounce it void.

2 J. ELLIOT, *supra* note 67, at 446.

[69]Compare the reasoning of Justice Brett, *infra* note 108. Professor Jaffe also finds it difficult to accept the conclusion "that an issue in every other respect apt for judicial determination should be non-justiciable because there is no possibility of a conventional plaintiff—an issue in short in which every one has a legitimate interest but only as a citizen." Jaffe, *Private Actions* 305.

excesses, particularly in light of their desire to leave all channels open for attacks on congressional self-aggrandizement.[70]

The history of advisory opinions similarly lends small comfort to insistence on a personal stake in protests against unconstitutional action. That history exhibits not so much a shrinking from "improper interference" with Congress as a desire to shield the judicial invalidation of statutes from the "bias" of prior advice to Congress, a consideration that bulked large with the Framers.[71] When Jefferson asked Chief Justice Jay in 1793 whether President Washington might avail himself of the advice of the Justices on questions arising out of the Franco-British war, Jay called attention to the fact that the constitutional authority to call for the opinion of the Cabinet "seems to have been *purposely* as well as expressly limited to the *executive* departments."[72] In addition, Jay remarked that the three departments "being in certain respects checks upon each other, and our being judges of a court in the last resort, are considerations which afford arguments against the propriety of our extra-judicially deciding the questions alluded to. . . ."[73] By this time several Justices had decided in a number of cases on Circuit, in one of which Chief Justice Jay partici-pated,[74] that, as Justice Chase phrased it in 1800, "the supreme court can declare an act of congress to be unconstitutional and therefore, invalid. . . ."[75] Jay's emphasis that the courts were to serve as a check on the other departments indicates that the chief objection to "advisory opinions" was that the Justices were loath to render "extra-judicial" advice on questions that might later come before them for judicial decision. His desire to insulate constitutional decisions from the tug of prior judicial advice suggests no fear of improper intrusion into the congressional sphere; nor would decision of a stranger's suit render probable a biased declaration of unconstitutionality. In view of the fact that under the English practice attacks on jurisdictional excesses had traditionally been welcome, a logical nexus between "advice" and such attacks needs to be demonstrated, not assumed.[76] So, too, Professor Frankfurter's argument against submission to the courts for advice of "legislative proposals rather than deliberate enactments," and his statement that such "advisory opinions are bound to move in an unreal atmosphere"[77] can have little bearing on a suit instituted

---

[70]*See* pp. 120–121 *infra.*

[71]Hamilton explained in *Federalist* 73 that one reason judges were excluded from the executive veto was that "the judges, who are to be the interpreters of the law, might receive an improper bias, from having given a previous opinion in their revisionary capacities. . . ." Hamilton is richly confirmed by the statements of the framers themselves.

Strong opposed judicial participation in the Council of Revision because "[t]he Judges in exercising the function of expositors might be influenced by the part they had taken, in framing the laws." 2 FARRAND 75. To the same effect see Gorham, *id.* 79, Rutledge, *id.* 80 Pinckney, 2 *id.* 298. King urged exclusion of the judges because "they ought to be able to expound the law as it should come before them, free from the bias of having participated in its formation." 1 *id.* 98.

[72]3 H. JOHNSTON, CORRESPONDENCE AND PUBLIC PAPERS OF JOHN JAY 486–89 (1891).

In the convention Charles Pinckney had proposed a provision which would authorize both Congress and the President "to require the opinions of the supreme Judicial Court upon important questions of law. . . ." That provision was referred to the Committee on Detail and was heard of no more. FARRAND 341, 334. Instead there emerged the present Article II, Section 2, clause 1 provision authorizing the President to require the opinions of the Departments.

[73]3 H. JOHNSTON, *supra* note 72, at 486–89.

[74]The Circuit Court cases are reported in a note to Hayburn's Case, 2 U.S. (2 Dall.) 408, 409–14 (1792); that of Jay's Circuit at 409.

[75]Cooper v. Telfair, 4 U.S (4 Dall.) 14, 18 (1800):

It is, indeed, a general opinion, it is expressly admitted by all this bar, and some of the judges have, individually, in the circuits, decided, that the supreme court can declare an act of congress to be unconstitutional, and therefore, invalid; but there is no adjudication of the supreme court itself upon the point. I concur, however, in the general sentiment. . . .

Earlier Justice Iredell had adverted to the judicial power to set aside unconstitutional acts in Ware v. Hylton, 3 U.S. (3 Dall.) 199 (1796), and in Calder v. Bull, 3 U.S. (3 Dall.) 386, 395, 399 (1798).

[76]At least as regards a stranger's attack on unconstitutional action, the *Flast* statement that "the rule against advisory opinions implements the separation of powers prescribed by the Constitution and confines federal courts to the role assigned them by Article III," 392 U.S. at 96, seems to me unilluminating.

[77]Frankfurter, *Advisory Opinions,* in 1 ENCYC. SOC. SCI. 475, 478 (1930).

by the American Civil Liberties Union to test an already enacted measure.[78] An advisory opinion in response to a Congressional solicitation may be undesirable for a variety of reasons of policy, but it cannot be said to constitute an "intrusion" or "improper interference."[79] Its only relevance to the "standing" issue lies in its character as a non-judicial, non-"case or controversy" function; and in that aspect it is irrelevant to the propriety of a stranger's suit which was traditionally adjudicated by the English courts and was therefore comprehended as a "case" of a "judiciary nature."

But, it may be asked, does it follow that American judges, acting under a novel written constitution that set up three co-equal branches, were bound to follow the English practice when strangers attacked unconstitutional actions by Congress or the President? For the American legislature and executive occupied a far more exalted position than the petty officials and inferior courts that the King's Bench had been wont to keep in bounds.

We must remember that the present stature of Congress by no means corresponds to the place it occupied in the minds of the Founders. For them Congress was an object not of awe but of apprehension. They were far more anxious to defend against unconstitutional action by Congress than were English judges to curb unauthorized action by subordinate public bodies. At the several conventions the atmosphere was charged with an almost obsessive concern with Congressional "usurpations," and a drumfire of criticism was directed against feared congressional "tyranny" and "oppression." A few examples must suffice. Gouverneur Morris considered "[l]egislative tyranny the great danger to be apprehended."[80] Without "effective checks" against legislative "encroachments," said Madison, "a revolution . . . would be inevitable."[81] James Wilson warned against the

---

[78] For the founders, "advice" to Congress before enactment was altogether different from adjudication of a suit challenging the constitutionality of an enacted bill. If this seems an uncertain distinction to our subtle-minded generation, it was amply clear to the founders, *See* note 68 *supra.*

[79] Even less can the term "intrusion" be applied to a statute whereby Congress authorizes a stranger to challenge the constitutionality of a law. Judicial entry in response to an invitation cannot constitute an "improper interference." From the beginning, the First Congress recognized that its own constitutional interpretations as a prelude to legislating were necessarily subject to judicial review. Thus, Peter Sylvester said, "If we are wrong, they can correct our error," 1 ANNALS OF CONG. 585 [1789] (1834) (print bearing running page head: *Gales & Seaton's History of Debates in Congress*); John Lawrence: "If the laws shall be in violation of any part of the Constitution, the judges will not hesitate to decide against them," *id.* 505; Fisher Ames: "if we declare improperly the judiciary will revise our decision," *id.* 496; Abraham Baldwin: "if they find this clause to be unconstitutional, they will not hesitate to declare it so," *id.* 582; Elbridge Gerry: "Our exposition, therefore, would be subject to their revisal," *id.* 596.
The possibility that thereby he might be saved from his mistakes, said Congressman Elias Boudinot, gave him added confidence in carrying out his legislative tasks:
The last objection was that by adopting this bill [of which Boudinot was a proponent] we exposed the measure to be considered and defeated by the Judiciary . . . who might adjudge it to be contrary to the Constitution, and therefore void. . . . This, he alleged, gave him no uneasiness. He was so far from controverting this right in the Judiciary, that it was his boast and his confidence. It led him to greater decision on all subjects of a constitutional nature, when he reflected that if, from inattention, want of precision, or any other defect, he should do wrong, that there was a power in the Government which could constitutionally prevent the operation of such a wrong measure from effecting his constituents. He was legislating for a nation, and for thousands unborn; and it was the glory of the Constitution that there was a remedy even for the failures of the supreme Legislature itself. 2 ANNALS, *supra* at 1978–79 [1791]. In his *Lectures on the Law* in 1791, Justice James Wilson, who had been a leading participant in both the federal and Pennsylvania Ratification conventions, and was then also Professor of Law, quoted Boudinot's statement. 1 J. WILSON, WORKS 330–31 (McCloskey ed. 1967).

[80] 2 FARRAND 551, 76.

[81] *Id.* 35. Though Madison and Morris were here concerned with state excesses, Madison also referred to the "strong propensity" of state legislatures "to a variety of pernicious measures" and stressed the need "to controul the Natl. Legislre. so far as it might be infected with a similar propensity." 2 *id.* 110. Mason stated that the national legislature "would so much resemble that of the individual States, that it must be expected frequently to pass unjust and pernicious laws. This restraining power was therefore essentially necessary." *Id.* 78. "All agree," said Nathanial Gorham, "that a check on the Legislature is necessary." *Id.* 79.

danger of "legislative despotism."[82] This from advocates of the Constitution. In the Ratification conventions opponents such as Patrick Henry said, "I trust I shall see Congressional oppression crushed in embryo."[83] In North Carolina, Timothy Bloodworth warned that "[w]ithout the most express restrictions," going beyond those contained in the proposed Constitution, "Congress may trample on your rights."[84] There were others.[85].

To quiet such fears there were repeated assurances that Congress "has no power but what is expressly given it,"[86] that it has "no authority" to make a law "beyond the powers" enumerated,[87] that "[i]f Congress, under pretence of executing one power should in fact usurp another, they will violate the Constitution."[88] The legislature, said Archibald Maclaine in North Carolina, "cannot travel beyond [the Constitution's] bounds";[89] it cannot, Governor Johnston added, "assume any other powers than those expressly given [it], without a palpable violation of the Constitution."[90] A law "not warranted by the Constitution," said James Iredell, a leader of the adoption forces in the same convention, "is barefaced usurpation."[91] Lee assured the Virginia convention that "[w]hen a question arises with respect to the legality of any power, exercised or assumed by Congress" the question will be *Is it enumerated in the Constitution?* . . . It is otherwise arbitrary and unconstitutional."[92] As Iredell said in North Carolina, "the question . . . will always be, whether Congress had exceeded its authority."[93] Any assumption that congressional excesses were regarded more indulgently than were the "usurpations" of the English magistracy simply does violence to the facts. Rather, I would say, the founders raised the English policy of policing jurisdictional excesses to the highest power.

In the process they were not content with assurances that congressional transgressions would be void and would be so declared by the courts,[94] but stressed that all channels of resistance

[82]1 *id.* 261: "May there not be legislative despotism if in the exercise of their power they are unchecked or unrestrained by another branch?"

[83]3 ELLIOT 546; *cf. id.* 396.

[84]4 *id.* 167.

[85]*E.g.,* William Lenoir in North Carolina: "When we consider the great powers of Congress, there is great cause for alarm." *Id.* 203. "Let us," William Lancaster there said, "exclude the possibility of tyranny," *id.* 213; and William Goudy warned, "beware the iron glove of tyranny." *Id.* 10. The ratification debates are replete with remarks to the same effect. *See generally* R. BERGER, CONGRESS V. THE SUPREME COURT (to be published: Harvard University Press, 1969). As Jefferson was later to say:

It is jealousy and not confidence which prescribes limited constitutions to bind down those whom we are obliged to trust with power. Our Constitution has accordingly fixed the limits to which, and no further, our confidence will go. In questions of power, then, let no more be heard of confidence in man, but bind him down from mischief by the chains of the Constitution.

Quoted in C. WARREN, CONGRESS, THE CONSTITUTION AND THE SUPREME COURT 153 (1925).

[86]3 ELLIOT 464 (Randolph).

[87]4 *Id.* 166 (MacLaine). In Massachusetts, Samuel Stillman acknowledged that Congressional powers were "great and extensive" but maintained that they are "defined and limited, and . . . sufficiently checked." 2 *id.* 166.

[88]4 *id.* 179 (Iredell).

[89]*Id.* 63; *see also id.* 140–41.

[90]*Id.* 142.

[91]*Id.* 194.

[92]*Id.* 186.

[93]4 *id.* 179. Earlier Iredell expressed the "utmost satisfaction" with the "jealousy and extreme caution with which gentlemen consider every power to be given to this government." 4 *id.* 95. *See also* p. 834 *infra.*

When Chief Justice Shaw relied on "respect for the legislature" and "well-established principles" to bar a stranger's assault on a state law, Wellington, Petr., 16 Pick. (33 Mass.) 87, 96 (1834), he did not, of course, take account of the relevant history of the Federal Constitution, nor did he mention the relevant English practice in prohibition, certiorari, and the like, but concluded that an unconstitutional Act was merely voidable, not void, and consequently could be challenged only by those persons whose rights were affected.

[94]In *Federalist* 78, Hamilton alluded to the "clear principle" that "every act of delegated authority, contrary to the tenor of the commission, under which it is exercised, is void. No legislative act, therefore, contrary ot the Constitution, can be

remained open. Thus Parsons stated in the Massachusetts convention that "[a]n act of usurpation is not obligatory; it is not law; and any man may be justified in his resistance."[95] In North Carolina Steele said, "[i]f the Congress make laws inconsistent with the Constitution, independent judges will not uphold them, nor will the people obey them. A universal resistance will ensue."[96] Even so fervid a proponent of judicial review as Iredell said that "[t]he people will resist if the government usurp powers not delegated to it."[97] Would proponents of the Constitution have preferred "universal resistance" to a suit by a disinterested representative of the public interest that would resolve the issue peaceably? One who pores over the ratification debates is driven to conclude that the founders must have welcomed *any* traditional mechanism that could aid in keeping Congress within bounds.

Two early, post-1787 state cases indicate how naturally American courts did in fact adapt English practice to the problem of dealing with invalid laws. *Zylstra v. Charleston* arose on a motion for a prohibition to restrain an inferior court from levying a fine (under a city ordinance) that was allegedly "unconstitutional and out of its jurisdiction." The threatened action was held "*void, as being contrary to the constitution of the state,*" and a prohibition issued.[98] In *State v. Corporation of New Brunswick* a citizen moved for certiorari to the mayor to return a by-law of the corporation in order to test its validity. Against the motion it was argued that "[t]he court ought not to award a *certiorari* on the mere prayer of an individual, unless he will previously lay some case before them tending to show that he is or may be affected by the operation of the by-law, and is, therefore entitled to question its validity." The court ignored this argument and issued the writ.[99] Although these cases dealt with minor governmental bodies, the fact remains (1) lack of jurisdiction was matter-of-factly equated with unconstitutionality, and (2) a personal interest was not deemed necessary for an attack upon the validity of a law. Of course this is not conclusive evidence that contemporary judges had generally assimilated English practice to the American condition,[100] but it is better than unsubstantiated twentieth century speculation that would assign our values to the eighteenth century founders.

Flast v. Cohen makes yet another dubious contribution to the alleged constitutional derivation of "standing" in the shape of a distinction between a "challenged enactment [that] exceeds specific constitutional limitations," *e.g.*, express prohibitions, and one that "is generally beyond the powers delegated to Congress."[101] Whatever its desirability on policy grounds, the distinction seems to be without historical warrant. Little stress was placed in the several ratifying conventions on the possibility that Congress might act in defiance of express Constitutional prohibitions; the gnawing

---

valid." If Congress exceeds its powers, said George Nicholas in the Virginia convention, "the judiciary will declare it void." 3 ELLIOT 443. Samuel Adams said in the Massachusetts convention that "any law . . . beyond the power granted by the proposed constitution . . . [will be] adjudged by the courts of law to be void." 2 *id.* 131. Oliver Ellsworth told the Connecticut convention that "a law which the Constitution does not authorize" is void, and the judges "will declare it to be void." *Id.* 196. Similar statements were made by Wilson in Pennsylvania, 2 *id.* 446, and by John Marshall in Virginia, 3 *id.* 553.

[95]2 *id.* 94.

[96]4 *id.* 71.

[97]*Id.* 185. In the First Congress Madison referred to "the general principle, that laws are unconstitutional, which infringe rights of the community." 1 ANNALS, *supra* note 79, at 458 [1789]. Colonists considered that "no obedience is due to arbitrary, unconstitutional edicts," and that "the invasion of the liberties of the people 'constitutes a state of war with the people' who may use 'all the power which God has given to them' to protect themselves." B. BAILYN, THE IDEOLOGICAL ORIGINS OF THE AMERICAN REVOLUTION 142 (1967).

[98]1 Bay 382, 390 (S. C. 1794).

[99]1 N.J.L. 393 (1795). Mark that this argument was cast in terms of what is now called "standing," not in terms of a failure to state a cause of action because of *damnum absque injuria. Cf.* note 47 *supra.*

[100]*But see* Strong's Case, Kirby 345, 351 (Conn. 1785–88), where counsel on both sides cited English law on mandamus and the court laid down that the "statute of Anne should be the rule of the proceeding." Colonial reliance on English authority was the practice. *See* notes 24 & 25 *supra.*

[101]392 U.S. at 102–03. For Justice Fortas, concurring, "This thesis, slender as its basis is, provides a 'nexus' for the action." *Id.* at 115. *Cf.* Justice Douglas, concurring, *id.* at 110.

fear was rather that Congress might usurp powers in excess of those conferred. To cite only a few examples, Wilson assured the Pennsylvania convention that if any congressional act should be "inconsistent with those powers vested by this instrument in Congress, the judges, as a consequence of their independence, and the particular powers of the government being defined, will declare such laws to be null and void."[102] Archibald MacLaine said in the North Carolina convention that "[i]f Congress should make a law beyond the powers and spirit of the Constitution, should we not say to Congress, 'You have no authority to make this law. There are limits beyond which you cannot go. You cannot exceed the power prescribed by the Constitution.' "[103] Policing of such excesses was paramount in the minds of the founders, and it may fairly be concluded that they expected that both jurisdictional usurpations and defiance of prohibitions would equally be set aside. Thus Hamilton coupled the two forms of excess when, in *Federalist* 78, arguing from principles of agency, he derided the notion that those who act under delegation "may do not only what their powers do not authorize, but what they forbid." Similarly Luther Martin, who opposed the Constitution, understood nonetheless that the judicial power extended both to Acts *"contrary to"* and to those *"not warranted* by the Constitution. . . ."[104] With Justice Harlan, I am "quite unable to understand, how, if a taxpayer believes that a given expenditure is unconstitutional . . . his interest in the suit can be said necessarily to vary according to the constitutional provision under which he states his claim."[105]

[102]2 ELLIOT 489.

[103]4 *id.* 161. Governor Johnston reassured North Carolina: "The powers of Congress are all circumscribed, defined, and clearly laid down. So far they may go, but no farther." 4 *id.* 64 *See also id.* 185, 188. In the Massachusetts convention, Samuel Adams said that the courts would adjudge "void" any federal law "extended beyond the power granted by the proposed Constitution." 2 *id.* 131. And John Marshall told the Virginia convention that were Congress to "go beyond the delegated powers," "to make a law not warranted by any of the powers enumerated," the courts would "declare it void." 3 *id.* 553. *See also* p. 833 *supra.*

[104]3 FARRAND 220.

[105]Flast v. Cohen, 392 U.S. 85, 124.
We have seen that the English practice did not require statement of a "cause of action" as a prelude to maintenance of what Professor Jaffe has aptly termed a "public action." *See* note 11 *supra.* As regards such actions, I would therefore dissent from Professor Wechsler's view that the judicial power extends to all cases arising under the Constitution "only when the standing law, decisional or statutory, provides a remedy to vindicate the interest that demands protection. . . ." Weschsler, *Toward Neutral Principles of Constitutional Law,* 73 HARV. L. REV. 1, 6 (1959), assuming that by such "interest" he means a personal stake." My own reading in the records of the several conventions turned up no relevant limitation beyond Madison's proposal to confine Article III to cases of a "judiciary nature." Suits by strangers were of that nature. To make existence of a "remedy" a component of the Article III power raises still other problems. Suppose there is a deprivation of constitutional rights for which no "remedy," statutory or decisional, exists, can it be that such a case "arising under the Constitution" lies outside the "judicial power?" Can it be that an invasion of constitutional rights would be without remedy? If the Constitution provides its own "remedy" in such cases, we are engaged in circular reasoning. Suppose that the Court proceeds to fashion a new remedy—Marshall laid claim in *Marbury v. Madison* to the common law power to fashion a remedy for the protection of every right, 5 U.S. (1 Cranch) 137, 163 (1803)—and suppose that the *existence* of a remedy is an indispensable element of "judicial power"; is not this the creation of bootstrap jurisdiction? Analytically, the Article III "judicial power" is jurisdictional, and to make it depend upon the availability of remedies is to leave the jurisdiction at the mercy of Court or Congress, who can then contract it at will.
Elsewhere I have sought to show that the Article III authorization to make "exceptions" to the Supreme Court's appellate jurisdiction was not designed to permit Congress to deprive the Court of Jurisdiction of constitutional controversies, that a federal court—either an inferior court or the Supreme Court on appeal from a state court—must be open for assertion of a constitutional right, and that Congress's power to withdraw or withhold consent to suit likewise may not be employed to bar access to a federal court for relief from federal invasions of Constitutional rights. R. BERGER, CONGRESS V. THE SUPREME COURT (to be published: Harvard University Press, 1969).
The judicial power, I submit, is best viewed as a constitutional grant of jurisdiction of the subject matter described in Article III, which exists independently of whether a litigant can state a cause of action. A word is in order about the mistaken identification of jurisdiction with failure to state a cause of action, of which the classic example is Tennessee Elec. Power Co. v. TVA, 306 U.S. 118, 140, 147 (1939). In that case eighteen power companies sought to enjoin operation of the Tennessee Valley Authority, asserting that it lacked constitutional power to act in the premises. The Court held that

There remains the question whether allowance of a suit by a stranger who lacks a personal interest to challenge action that is in excess of power granted by the Constitution lies within judicial discretion or is a matter of right. Except for prohibition, issuance of the other prerogative writs—mandamus, certiorari, and quo warranto—seems clearly to have been a matter of judicial discretion.[106] Coke's record of *Articulo Cleri,* however, suggests that the writ of prohibition would issue as a matter of right. Replying in the Tenth Answer to the objection that a plaintiff who sued in the ecclesiastical court should be precluded from obtaining prohibition of his own action, the judges stated:

> None may pursue in the ecclesiastical court for that which the kings court ought to hold plea of, but upon information thereof given to the kings courts, either by the plaintiff, or by any mere stranger, they are to be prohibited, because they deal in that which appertaineth not to their jurisdiction. . . . [P]rohibitions thereupon are not of favour, but of justice to be granted.[107]

In modern terms, such writs would issue as of right. *Articulo Cleri* remained vital in England, where in 1875 its principles were powerfully restated in *Worthington v. Jeffries* by Justice Brett.[108]

---

the plaintiff lacked standing because the "damage consequent on competition, otherwise lawful, is in such circumstances *damnum obsque injuria.* . . ," *id.* 140, the Latin tag generally associated with injuries that do not give rise to a cause of action. *Compare,* note 47 *supra.* Failure to state a cause of action is not normally regarded as jurisdictional; it "calls for a judgment on the merits and not for a dismissal for want of jurisdiction." Bell v. Hood, 327 U.S. 678, 682 (1946). One may have a cause of action and fail, for example, to come within the "diversity" jurisdiction of Article II, or come within that jurisdiction and fail to state a cause of action. Justice Frankfurter justly objected to "confounding the requirements for establishing a substantive cause of action with the requirements of diversity jurisdiction." Smith v. Sperling, 354 U.S. 91, 98 (1957) (dissent); Romero v. International Terminal Co., 358 U.S. 354, 359 (1959). No more should the other branch of the "judicial power"—"case or controversy"—be identified with statement of a cause of action. It needs to be kept firmly in mind that "a court may have jurisdiction of the subject matter of an action though the complaint therein does not state a claim upon which relief can be granted." Weiss v. Los Angeles Broadcasting Co., 163 F.2d 313, 314 (9th Cir. 1947). "Jurisdiction . . . is not defeated . . . by the possibility that the averments might fail to state a cause of action." Bell v. Hood, 327 U.S. 678, 682 (1946).

[106]Certiorari: 1 M. BACON, ABRIDGMENT, "Certiorari" (A) (3d ed. 1768); Rex v. Lewis, 98 Eng. Rep. 288 (1769); Regina v. Justices of Surrey, [1870] L.R.5 Q.B. 466, 472–73.

Quo Warranto: For early statutory requirement of leave of court, see SHORTT 113–14; Rex v. Trelawney, 97 Eng. Rep. 1010 (1765); Rex v. Wardroper, 98 Eng. Rep. 23 (1766).

Mandamus: 3 M. BACON, ABRIDGMENT, "Mandamus" (E) (3d ed. 1768): the Court of King's Bench "are not obliged to [issue mandamus] in all Cases wherein it may seem proper, but herein may exercise a discretionary power, as well in refusing, as granting such Writ. . . ."

[107]2 INST.* 607. Blackstone states that from *Articulo Cleri* "much may be collected concerning the reasons of granting and methods of proceeding upon prohibitions." 3 W. BLACKSTONE, COMMENTARIES* 113. Professor Henderson states that the "theoretical emphasis" of the seventeenth and eighteenth centuries "was on 'jurisdiction,' an elusive concept of the agency's or justices' 'power' to hear the question at all or to take a given action. Questions that had been labelled as 'jurisdictional' could be reviewed as of right." HENDERSON 6.

[108]These authorities show that the ground of decision, in considering whether prohibition is or is not to be granted, is not whether the individual suitor has or has not suffered damage, but is, whether the royal prerogative has been encroached upon by reason of the prescribed order of administration of justice having been disobeyed. If this were not so, it seems difficult to understand why a stranger may interfere at all. . . . If it is the absolute duty of the superior Court to enforce order on being convinced of a breach of it by information given by the defendant in the suit below, why should it be a less absolute duty if it is convinced of the same breach of order by information given by a stranger? Order is no less broken, the prerogative is no less invaded. . . . [T]he real ground of the interference by prohibition is not that the defendant below is individually damaged, but that the cause is drawn in *aliud examen,* that public order in administration of law is broken. And inasmuch as the duty of enforcing such order is imposed on the superior Courts, and the issue of a writ of prohibition is the means given to them by law of enforcing such order, it seems to us that, upon principle and in the absence of enactment, it must be their duty to issue such writ whenever they are clearly convinced by legal evidence, by whomsoever brought before them, that an inferior Court is acting without jurisdiction, or exceeding its jurisdiction. . . .

Justice Brett further remarked that in *Articulo Cleri* "the duty is declared in absolute terms applicable to all cases." L.R. 10 C.P. 379, 382, 383.

Our concern, however, is with how English law appeared to the eyes of a colonial lawyer who did not have the benefit of nineteenth century cases. It is generally acknowledged that at the time of the Revolution and before, there was considerable disagreement as to whether prohibition, even in the case of one who had a personal interest, was a matter of discretion or of right.[109] When regard is had to this division of opinion, noted in Bacon's *Abridgment*,[110] and to the discretionary nature of the other prerogative writs, it is difficult to attribute to colonial lawyers the view that the writ of prohibition had to issue to a stranger as of right. Neither, however, may we attribute to them the view that prohibition could be denied out of hand, for Bacon's *Abridgment* emphasized that "the Superior Courts are at liberty to exercise a legal Discretion herein, but not an arbitrary one, in refusing Prohibitions, where in such like cases they have been granted. . . ."[111]

Finally, there appears to be no impediment to the creation by Congress of an absolute right to prohibition, even when sought by a stranger.[112] It has never been suggested that there are any limits on the creation of the cognate "informers" actions, which create indefeasible causes of action at least until Congress withdraws jurisdiction from the courts.[113] Taking note of the "informers" statutes, and doubtless cognizant of "relators" actions as well, Judge Jerome Frank drew from *FCC v. Sanders Brothers Radio Station*[114] and *Scripps-Howard Radio, Inc. v. FCC*[115] the proposition that "Congress can constitutionally enact a statute conferring on any non-official person

Although the nineteenth century English cases exhibit some differences of opinion, the later and more numerous cases are with Brett. Among the latter is Burder v. Veley, 113 Eng. Rep. 801 (Q.B. 1840), where Denman, C.J., stated: "In whatever stage that fact ['want of jurisdiction'] is made manifest, either by the Crown, or by any one of its subjects, we are bound to interpose," *id.* at 812–13; "the Courts of Westminster Hall have no discretion to award or refuse the writ, but are bound to award it." *Id.* at 810. An influential case contra is Forster v. Forster, 4 B. & S. 187, 199 (Q.B. 1863), in which Cockburn, C. J., distinguished the case of a stranger from that of a party aggrieved, stating that although the Court will listen to a stranger, "[Y]et this is not ex debito justitiae, but a matter upon which the Court may properly exercise its discretion. . . ." Cockburn's statement apparently was approved in Mayor of London v. Cox, [1865] L.R. 2 E. & I. App. 239, 280 (H. L.), where the same point "came indirectly before the House of Lords." So Master of Rolls Jessel concluded in Chambers v. Green, [1875] L.R. 20 Eq. Cases 552, 555, choosing to rely on *Forster* and *Cox* rather than on the subsequent opinions in *Worthington v. Jeffries*. When *Chambers v. Green* was later pressed on Justice Brett, he adhered to *Worthington* in Ellis v. Fleming, [1876] L.R. 1 C.P. Div. 237, 239–40.

In Farquharson v. Morgan, [1894] 1 Q.B. 552, 556, the Court of Appeals followed the Coke rule; Lord Halsbury stated: It has long been settled that, where an objection to the jurisdiction of an inferior Court appears on the face of the proceedings, it is immaterial by what means and by whom the Court is informed of such objection. The Court must protect the prerogative of the Crown and the due course of the administration of justice by prohibiting the inferior Court from proceeding in matters as to which it is apparent that it has no jurisdiction. . . . I find no authority justifying the withholding of a writ of prohibition in such case.

Professor de Smith states that "If a defect of jurisdiction is apparent on the face of the proceeding, the application may be brought . . . by a complete stranger . . . and the court is obliged to allow the application." DE SMITH 427.

[109]Ford v. Welden, 83 Eng. Rep. 50 (1664); Clay v. Snelgrove, 91 Eng. Rep. 1285, 1286 (1701); Parish of Aston v. Castle-Birmidge Chapel, 80 Eng. Rep. 215 (c 1603–1625). See also Mayor of London v. Cox, [1865] L.R. 2 E. & I. App. 239, 278 (H.L.).

[110]4 M. BACON, ABRIDGMENT, "Prohibition" (B) (3d ed. 1768).

[111]*Id.* Of the related quo warranto writ, Lord Mansfield said the Court must "exercise a sound discretion." Rex v. Wardroper, 98 Eng. Rep. 23 (1766). There "is no clear decision that the court can use its discretion arbitrarily" in the field of certiorari, and discretionary denials of certiorari involve cases where evidence "showed ground on which the adjudication attacked would be upheld." Gordon, *Certiorari and the Problem of Locus Standi*, 71 L.Q. REV. 483, 485 (1955).

[112]For the contrary view, see note 10 *supra*.

[113]Blackstone said that "by commencing the suit the informer has made the popular action his own private action, and it is not in the power of the crown, or of any thing but parliament, to release the informer's interest." 2 W. BLACKSTONE, COMMENTARIES* 437. See also Sherr v. Anaconda Wire & Cable Co., 149 F.2d 680, 681 (2d Cir. 1945), which held that Congress may deprive the district court of jurisdiction after the informer has filed his action, leaving him to seek compensation, if any, in the Court of Claims.

[114]309 U.S. 470 (1940).

[115]316 U.S. 4 (1942). For discussion of *Sanders* and *Scripps-Howard*, see Jaffe, *Private Actions* 272–74.

. . . authority to bring a suit to prevent action by an officer in violation of his statutory powers; for then . . . there is an actual controversy. . . . Such persons, so authorized, are so to speak, private Attorney Generals."[116] When this statement appeared in 1943, those who were under the spell of the Court's earlier decisions regarded it as a daring break with tradition, whereas in fact it is solidly rooted in the common law. It is difficult to see how the power of Congress to confer standing by statute can be open to question when its power to create informers' actions is beyond doubt.[117] Since the monetary recovery is only an incentive to, rather than an element of, the action, it cannot be that the payment of a financial inducement to a stranger alone legitimizes his suit. This would too much resemble Charles Lamb's Chinaman who thought it necessary to burn down the house in order to roast the pig.

In sum, the notion that the constitution demands injury to a personal interest as a prerequisite to attacks on allegedly unconstitutional action is historically unfounded. The "matters that were the traditional concern of the courts in Westminster" upon which such an interpretation of the "case or controversy" phrase has been premised were not in fact as limited as Frankfurter and his successors have supposed. Public suits instituted by strangers to curb action in excess of jurisdiction were well established in English law at the time Article III was drafted. Nor were the concerns of the Founders with separation of powers and advisory opinions germane to the issues involved in standing to challenge action either in defiance of or beyond the authority granted by the Constitution. There may well be policy arguments in favor of a "personal interest" limitation on standing, but they cannot rest on historically-derived constitutional compulsions.

---

[116]Associated Industries, Inc. v. Ickes, 134 F.2d 694, 704 (2d Cir. 1943), *vacated as moot,* 320 U.S. 707 (1943).

[117]Justice Harlan, who questions the wisdom of broadening the standing of strangers, states that "[a]ny hazards to the proper allocation of authority among the three branches of the Government would be substantially diminished if public actions had been pertinently authorized by Congress and the President." Flast v. Cohen, 392 U.S. at 116, 131–32 (1968) (dissent). *See also* note 79 *supra.*

CHAPTER VII

"Law of the Land" Reconsidered

The famous thirty-ninth chapter of Magna Carta provides, roughly speaking, that no man shall be deprived of life, liberty, or property unless by the lawful judgment of his peers and (or) by the law of the land: *"nisi per legale judicium parium suorum vel per legem terre."*[1] Almost every one of these words has been the subject of interminable controversy among leading legal historians.[2] Yet, despite the massive literature and Lord Coke's identification of "law of the land" with "due process of law,"[3] considerable uncertainty remains. It has been said that "law of the land" has a meaning broader than and different from due process.[4] What did it mean over the centuries in England; in colonial America? Did it embrace judicial power to set legislation aside on "substantive" grounds? Such questions are the more relevant because each of the pre-1787 state constitutions employed the "law of the land" rather than the "due process" phraseology, and a few early state courts purported to find warrant in the phrase for overruling legislation on substantive grounds, though others rejected such arguments.

In 1926, Dr. Rodney Mott, in a mountainous treatise,[5] which a commentator recently stated "is still the most authoritative work on the historical development of due process,"[6] categorically asserted that due process of law had from the beginning comprehended judicial power to test legislation for reasonableness. Some greeted this study as a monument of learning;[7] others who went behind his voluminous citations dismissed it out of hand.[8] That split of opinion led me to re-examine his study and the relevant sources.

This article seeks to fill a significant gap which exists in the history of substantive due process, of which I became aware while writing the chapters on due process in my recent study of the fourteenth amendment and the exercise of judicial power under its supposed mandate.[9] The materials relied upon to correct this deficiency in the historical perception of due process are

---

[1]W. McKechnie, Magna Carta: A Commentary on the Great Charter of King John 375 (2d ed. 1914).

[2]For citations to various interpretations, see R. Mott, Due Process of Law 32 n.9 (1926). For example, does "vel" translated mean "and," "or," or "and/or." W. McKechnie, *supra* note 1, at 381; *see also* the discussion of *lex terrae* in text accompanying notes 12–26 *infra*. For a summary of the "vel" arguments, see B. Keeney, Judgment by Peers 64–66 (1949).

[3]2 E. Coke, The Second Part of the Institutes of the Laws of England 50 (1628). Coke was followed by Story, 3 J. Story, Commentaries on the Constitution of the United States § 1789 (1833), J. Kent, Commentaries on American Law 620–21 (9th ed. 1858), and others.

[4]*See* Jurow, *Untimely Thoughts: A Reconsideration of the Origins of Due Process of Law,* 19 Am. J. Leg. Hist. 265, 278–79 (1975).

[5]R. Mott, note 2 *supra.*

[6]Jurow, *supra* note 4, at 271.

[7]Brown, Book Review, 25 Mich. L. Rev. 565 (1927); Cushman, Book Review, 12 Cornell L.Q. 423 (1927).

[8]Brown, Book Review, 40 Harv. L. Rev. 800 (1927); Plucknett, Book Review, 27 Colum. L. Rev. 628 (1927); Rottschaefer, Book Review, 11 Minn. L. Rev. 481 (1927).

[9]R. Berger, Government by Judiciary: The Transformation of the Fourteenth Amendment (1977) [hereinafter cited as R. Berger 1977].

developments in early English and colonial history, and the pre-1787 state cases on judicial review, which have never been examined for their due process implications.

ENGLISH MATERIALS

What did the "lex terrae"—the law of the land—mean to the barons at Runnymede? One thing seems tolerably plain: it was not a synonym for the "due process of law" with which Coke four centuries later identified it,[10] borrowing from fourteenth-century statutes which first spelled out that the law of the land required that a defendant be afforded an opportunity to answer by service of proper process in due course.[11] Conflict has swirled about the issue, neatly phrased by Charles McIlwain: "Does *lex terrae* mean the 'law of the land' or is it merely a mode of trial?"[12] William McKechnie, Melville Bigelow, and John Selden concluded, pinning their case to the word "lex," that it merely had reference to a mode of trial, *i.e.,* by "duel, ordeal, or compurgation."[13] McIlwain agrees that in 1215 "lex" was often employed in this sense;[14] but he musters historical materials to show that it was also employed in a wider sense, *i.e.,* a trial in accordance with the "law of the land."[15] He reasons that the chief grievance of the barons was the king's seizure of their persons without first convicting them of some offense in his curia.[16] They were not so much concerned with "abuses of judicial process" as with attacks "without any process whatever."[17] Looking to the associated "lawful judgment of his peers," McIlwain reads it to preclude attacks "except *after a judgment* obtained in the ordinary course, *i.e.,* by a judicium parium."[18] On this McKechnie apparently is in accord; he had earlier observed that the main and "obvious" contention of the barons was that "John was no longer to take the law into his own hands: the deliberate judgment of a competent court of law must precede any punitive measures. . . ."[19]

A judicial judgment posits some antecedent law that governed, the violation of which gave rise to the proceeding. As McIlwain puts it, the judgment of the peers "prescribes the manner of application," the *lex terrae,* "the law to be applied."[20] G.B. Adams likewise concluded that the barons "were demanding that they should not be imprisoned . . . except after a trial in the King's Court 'by a judgment of their peers and by the whole body of law and custom which such judgments are intended to interpret and apply.' "[21] Most of the law of the early period was customary law, deeply embedded customs, and the common law fashioned by the courts was rooted in this

---

[10]"*Nisi per legem terrae*. But by the law of the land: For the true sense and exposition of those words, see the statute of [37 Edw. III, c.8 (1363)], where the words, by the law of the land, are rendered without due process of law. . . ." 2 E. COKE, *supra* note 3, at 50. *See* Jurow, *supra* note 4, at 268, 276.

[11]For a discussion of the fourteenth-century statutes, see Jurow, *supra* note 4, at 266–71. For example, 25 Edw. III, st. 5, c.4 (1352), provided in relevant part that "none shall be taken . . . unless . . . by process made by writ original at the common law; and none shall be put out of his franchise of freehold, unless he be duly brought to answer . . . by 'voie de lei.' "

[12]McIlwain, *Due Process of Law in Magna Carta,* 14 COLUM. L. REV. 27, 44 (1914).

[13]*Id.* at 32–33; W. MCKECHNIE, *supra* note 1, at 379 (quoting M. BIGELOW, HISTORY OF PROCEDURE IN ENGLAND 155 n.3 (1880)).

[14]McIlwain, *supra* note 12, at 45.

[15]*Id.* at 46–47.

[16]*Id.* at 41.

[17]*Id.* at 43.

[18]*Id.* (emphasis added).

[19]W. MCKECHNIE, *supra* note 1, at 381; *see also* 9 W. HOLDSWORTH, HISTORY OF ENGLISH LAW 61 (1922).

[20]McIlwain, *supra* note 12, at 50.

[21]Powicke, *Per Judicum Parium Vel Per Legem Terrae,* in MAGNA CARTA: COMMEMORATION ESSAYS 96 (H. Malden ed. 1971) (quoting G. ADAMS, THE ORIGIN OF THE ENGLISH CONSTITUTION 266 (1912)) [hereinafter cited as MALDEN ESSAYS]. As said by Vinogradoff: "The struggle was waged to secure trial in properly constituted courts of justice in accordance with established law." Vinogradoff, *Magna Carta, c. 39,* in MALDEN ESSAYS, *supra,* at 78, 85.

customary law.[22] While there was as yet no sharp articulation of the Roman maxim "nulla poena sine lege"—"no person shall be punished except in pursuance of a statute which fixes a penalty for criminal behavior"[23]—it is instinct in King John's oath of 1213 that "he would restore the good laws of his ancestors and especially the laws of King Edward,"[24] a promise that was picked up by the barons, in contrast to what the contemporary Annals of Waverly refer to as "his tyrannical will was his only law."[25] Magna Carta, in sum, laid down that the laws bind the king.[26]

From the foregoing it is apparent that the chief, if not the sole, object of the barons was protection against the king's arbitrary will.[27] The then rudimentary Parliament, in which the Commons did not as yet participate,[28] posed no threat to the barons. As the Supreme Court observed in *Hurtado v. California:*[29] "It did not enter into the minds of the barons to provide security against their own body . . . by limiting the power of Parliament. . . ."[30] Nevertheless, Mott locates as early as 1290 the expression "in a clear cut fashion the conception of a fundamental statute by which other statutes might be tested as regards their validity" which he translates as "certain substantive limitations of due process of law upon legislation."[31] Thus he deduces from a statement in the Mirrour of Justices that chapter 39 invalidates the Statute of Merchants provision for imprisonment for debt because "none is to be taken unless it be by warrant founded on a personal action," *i.e.,* imprisonment must be preceded by a judgment.[32] Some early statutes expressly provided that a statute in contravention of a provision of Magna Carta would be void,[33] just as denial by federal statute of jury trial would violate the sixth amendment. That one could be tried for violation of a "substantive" law is not equivalent to a sanction for judicial overthrow of a substantive law because it did not satisfy the "law of the land" in the sense of a substantive due process.

Mott's citation of the *Case of the Ordinance of St. Albans*[34] is rejected by Theodore Plucknett in a scathing review of Mott's English materials.[35] *St. Albans* held that "a municipal ordinance is void against Magna Carta and that the ordinance would be void even if it were part of the municipal charter. . . ."[36] Plucknett acidly comments:

> [I]t has never been disputed that a statute is superior to by-laws and to charters. A labored demonstration that charters have been held void for contravening Magna Carta proves nothing; the same would be true if they contravened any other statute. What is wanted is a case where a statute was held invalid, and it is this that Dr. Mott fails to give us.[37]

[22]C. McILWAIN, THE HIGH COURT OF PARLIAMENT 42–47, 51 (1910).

[23]Hall, *Nulla Poena Sine Lege,* 47 YALE L.J. 165 (1937).

[24]McIlwain, *supra* note 12, at 47.

[25]*Id.* at 49.

[26]G. ADAMS, CONSTITUTIONAL HISTORY OF ENGLAND 138 (rev. ed. 1935).

[27]*Id.* at 128; W. McKECHNIE, *supra* note 1, at 381.

[28]Stephenson, *The Representatives and Taxation,* in EARLY ENGLISH PARLIAMENTS 56, 60 (G. Bodet ed. 1968).

[29]110 U.S. 516 (1884).

[30]*Id.* at 531. "Fundamental laws (and Magna Carta itself) were valued for the protection they afforded against the arbitrary power of kings. There was no suggestion yet that the people's representatives themselves . . . might be tyrannical." J. GOUGH, FUNDAMENTAL LAW IN ENGLISH CONSTITUTIONAL HISTORY 65 (2d ed. 1961) (footnote omitted).

[31]R. MOTT, *supra* note 2, at 44, 43 (footnotes omitted).

[32]*Id.* at 43 n.53.

[33]W. McKECHNIE, *supra* note 1, at 159; McIlwain, *Magna Carta and Common Law,* in MALDEN ESSAYS, *supra* note 21, at 174, 176.

[34]The case is unreported.

[35]Plucknett, note 8 *supra.*

[36]*Id.* at 629 (citing F. DWARRIS, DWARRIS ON STATUTES (1873)).

[37]*Id.* Plucknett makes no mention of Mott's citation of the Mirrour of Justices, which Maitland dismisses as "a leaven of falsehood that was introduced by this fantastic and unscrupulous pamphleteer." F. MAITLAND, A HISTORY OF ENGLISH LAW BEFORE THE TIME OF EDWARD I, 304, 312 (1898), *reprinted in* 3 HISTORIANS AT WORK 301–02 (P. Gay & V. Wexler eds. 1975).

Apparently Mott himself was of two minds, for he remarks that some scholars see in chapter 39 "the general norm of all governmental actions. . . . It can hardly be contended that such a conception of 'due process of law' gained any wide acceptance before the time of the Stuarts. . . . The idea of a residual substantive content of 'due process of law' was at most exceedingly nebulous."[38]

What was thus "exceedingly nebulous" now allegedly became clear at the hands of Lord Coke. In "the early part of the Seventeenth Century," Mott writes,

> it almost seemed as if the courts were establishing the principle of judicial control through the interpretation of Magna Carta. Sir Edward Coke laid the foundations for this development in Calvin's case and the year following he decided Dr. Bonham's Case in which his position was stated more clearly and forcefully.[39]

The *Bonham*[40] statute, Coke held, was against "common right and reason,"[41] by which *Calvin* makes plain he meant the law of nature, not Magna Carta.[42] No mention of Magna Carta in this context is made in either *Bonham* or *Calvin*.[43] Mott also notes William Penn's protest against a denial of due process, "based almost entirely upon the Great Charter as interpreted by Coke," during his 1670 trial in England but observes that "the remedy for *legislative* violations of due process of law was to be found largely in an enlightened public opinion, according to Penn."[44] The state of English law is thus summarized by Hazeltine: "In England the provisions of Magna Carta, including chapter thirty-nine, were originally intended, and have since been regarded, as a limitation upon the executive and judicature, not upon the legislature."[45]

COLONIAL MATERIALS

So it was understood in the colonies, as is evidenced by one of the great Founders, James Iredell, who stated in the North Carolina Ratification Convention, "neither that instrument [Magna Carta], or any other instrument every attempted to abridge the authority of parliament. . . ."[46] And that understanding was buttressed, as will presently appear, by earlier evidence. Although Mott notes that "[f]requently the [colonial] conflicts had centered around the question of the exercise of arbitrary power of these [royal executive] officials,"[47] he goes on to state of due process of law:

> Nevertheless, its ambiguity must not be taken to prove that the colonists did not consider that it limited the legislative bodies as well as the executive or judiciary. The evidence on this matter is clearly all on one side. Practically without exception, strenuous objections were raised whenever the colonists were

[38]R. MOTT, *supra* note 2, at 74, 75.

[39]*Id.* at 49.

[40]77 Eng. Rep. 646 (K.B. 1610).

[41]*Id.* at 652.

[42]77 Eng. Rep. 377 (K.B. 1608).

[43]For discussion of Calvin's Case, 77 Eng. Rep. 377 (K.B. 1608), see R. BERGER, CONGRESS V. THE SUPREME COURT 351–52, 355 (1969) [hereinafter cited as R. BERGER 1969].

[44]R. MOTT, *supra* note 2, at 107 (emphasis added) (footnote omitted).

[45]Hazeltine, *The Influence of Magna Carta on American Constitutional Development,* in MALDEN ESSAYS, *supra* note 21, at 180, 222. The references to due process and law of the land in W. HOLDSWORTH, note 19 *supra,* are to judicial procedure, not to judicial power to overthrow legislation. 2 *id.* at 169 (2d ed. 1914); 9 *id.* at 112 (2d ed. 1938). *See also* B. KEENEY, *supra* note 2, at 55, 66–68; F. THOMPSON, MAGNA CARTA: ITS ROLE IN THE MAKING OF THE ENGLISH CONSTITUTION 1300–1629, at 87–88 (1948).

[46]4 J. ELLIOT, THE DEBATES IN THE SEVERAL STATE CONVENTIONS ON THE ADOPTION OF THE FEDERAL CONSTITUTION 158 (2d ed. 1836).

[47]R. MOTT, *supra* note 2, at 141.

met with a situation involving a legislative violation of due process of law. So overwhelming is the proof of the importance of this protection in this regard that it is difficult to understand how there would have been any serious question regarding it when the courts considered it a half century later.[48]

Mott illustrates a common frailty: we overlook what we do not want to see.

Apart from James Otis's stirring appeal against the writs of assistance in 1761, citing the dicta of Coke in *Bonham's Case,* coupled with the "law of the land" provision of Magna Carta,[49] Mott builds largely on the colonial protests against "taxation without representation," noting, however, that the "colonists were not daunted by the difficulty of tying their principles of taxation to any particular section of Magna Carta," that they appealed "rather to the spirit of the Great Charter than to particular parts of it. . . ."[50] But in 1627 when Parliament protested to Charles I in the Petition of Right against taxation "without the common consent by act of parliament," they appealed not to Magna Carta but directly to statutes of Edward I and Edward III.[51] That example was followed by the New York Assembly in 1683, when it enacted The Charter of Liberties and Privileges declaring that no taxes were to be levied without its consent.[52] Almost a century later Patrick Henry stirringly framed the issue: "no taxation without representation,"[53] thus rejecting the prevailing English view that every man was "virtually represented" in the Parliament.[54] But the colonists denied its power to tax them in the absence of actual representation, and insisted in the First Continental Congress (1765) that "no taxes ever have been, or can be constitutionally imposed on them, except by their respective legislatures."[55] Thus the argument was an expression of incipient revolt against a remote oppressor, a claim to the right of self-government, rather than

[48]*Id.* at 142. Mott acknowledges that "[i]t is more probable that arbitrary procedure on the part of officers not chosen by the colonists formed the root of their demands. . . . For the most part the colonists had little cause to fear the colonial legislatures. . . ." *Id.* at 105. James Wilson, second only to Madison as an architect of the Constitution, noted colonial partiality to the legislature because the assemblies were their own whereas governors were royal appointees. 1 J. WILSON, WORKS 292–93 (R. McCloskey ed. 1967).

[49]R. MOTT, *supra* note 2, at 125–27.

[50]*Id.* at 132, 137. Mott states that the colonists

may very well have had in mind the twelfth section of Magna Carta, although that seems unlikely when we find but one specific reference to that section in this protest literature, while there are many indisputable citations of and quotations from the thirty-ninth section. . . . [I]n so far as they did think of any particular chapters, it is reasonable to presume that one was the due process provision.

Id. at 132 (footnotes omitted).

Section 12 provided: "No scutage nor aid shall be imposed on our kingdom unless by common Counsel of our kingdom. . . ." W. McKECHNIE, *supra* note 1, at 232. "Aid," McKechnie states, "can be regarded as, in any sense, a freewill offering." *Id.* at 234. Scutage was a payment by a tenant "in lieu of actual attendance in the army of his feudal lord." *Id.* at 70, 233. Rejecting the notion that § 12 evidences an "absolute surrender of all powers of arbitrary taxation," McKechnie comments:

The doctrine of the day was that the King in normal times ought "to live of his own," like many other land-owning gentleman. A regular scheme of "taxation" to meet the ordinary expenses of government was undreamt of. It is too much to suppose, then, that our ancestors in 1215 sought to abolish something which, strictly speaking, did not exist. The famous clause treats, not of "taxation" in the abstract, but of the scutages and aids already discussed.

Id. at 239.

[51]3 Car. 1, c.1, at 317–19 (1627). So too, the Bill of Rights flatly declares that "the levying of money for or to the use of the crown by pretence of prerogative without grant of parliament for a longer time or in other manner than the same is or shall be granted is illegal." 1 W. & M. Sess. 2, c.2(4) (1688).

[52]S. MORISON, THE OXFORD HISTORY OF THE AMERICAN PEOPLE 78 (1965). This was disallowed by the crown, as were several other similar colonial statutes, but they testify to a legislative determination.

[53] S. MORISON & H. COMMAGER, GROWTH OF THE AMERICAN REPUBLIC 51 (4th ed. 1950). Henry had been anticipated by James Otis. 1 P. SMITH, JOHN ADAMS 80 (1962).

[54]G. WOOD, CREATION OF THE AMERICAN REPUBLIC 1776–1787, at 173–85 (1969).

[55]S. MORISON & H. COMMAGER, *supra* note 53, at 151–52.

a charge that taxation was a violation of due process vindicable in English courts,[56] the less likely because Parliament was then regarded as "omnipotent."[57] "It was perceived" during the Revolutionary War, Mott remarks, "that there were no real precedents for the colonial difficulties. . . ."[58]

As in England, so in the colonies; protests largely arose out of the struggle with the royal executives the Crown had saddled on them; the colonists were attached to their assemblies which they elected and could control.[59] When they came to draft state constitutions they reflected this attachment and placed the vast bulk of power in the legislature, reduced the governor almost to the status of a "Cypher,"[60] and neither gave "arising under this Constitution" jurisdiction to the courts nor provided a "supremacy clause" whereby to test enactments. Pre-1787 state court attempts to declare statutes unconstitutional were confined to infringements of express provisions of the Constitution or a treaty, and did not proceed on a theory that courts, under the "law of the land," could substitute their views of policy for those of the legislature.[61] Even so, they met with vigorous criticism and opposition.[62]

To retrace our steps, Mott, commenting on a 1692 Massachusetts Act that included "the first use of the phrase 'due process of law' which has been found in American documents,"[63] stated of this and similar New York acts: "In none of these cases, nor indeed in the similar attempts in Massachusetts, is there any evidence that the colonists desired protection from legislative abuses."[64] Some early colonial enactments will illuminate the scene. The Massachusetts Body of Liberties of 1641 provided that "[n]o mans life shall be taken away . . . , no mans goods or estate shall be taken away from him . . . , unlesse it be by vertue or equitie of some expresse law of the Country warranting the same, established by a generall Court [Assembly] and sufficiently published. . . ."[65] Mott remarks: "The wording would indicate that it was intended that there should be no limitation upon the legislative power, and that it merely required that the law be published. . . ."[66] A similar provision is found in a Rhode Island law of 1647: "[N]o person . . . shall be taken or imprisoned . . . but by the lawful judgment of his peers, or by some known law . . . ratified and confirmed by the major part of the General Assembly. . . ."[67] Such provisions indicate that Massachusetts and Rhode Island understood the parallel "law of the land" to mean a law of the province, not some supra-"constitutional" test of a statute.[68] The distinction between such "law" and due process was sharply drawn in a Massachusetts Act of 1692. Section I provided: "That no freeman shall be taken

---

[56]"Simple assertion that taxation without representation violated the Great Charter was very common, for nearly all those engaged in the political debate wished to buttress their cause if possible, by reference to the venerable document." R. Mott, *supra* note 2, at 130–31.

[57]1 W. Blackstone, Commentaries on the Law of England 91 (3d ed. 1769).

[58]R. Mott, *supra* note 2, at 138 (footnote omitted). "There is also little question that the colonists looked upon the 'law of the land' as being the common law of England. . . ." *Id.* at 142. In England, no case had held that Magna Carta applied to legislation.

[59]*See* note 48 *supra*.

[60]2 M. Farrand, The Records of the Federal Convention of 1787, at 35 (1911). *See* R. Berger 1969, *supra* note 42, at 49.

[61]*See* text accompanying notes 90–124 *infra*.

[62]R. Berger 1969, *supra* note 43, at 40, 142.

[63]R. Mott, *supra* note 2, at 97 (footnote omitted). The Act is discussed in text accompanying notes 69–70 *infra*.

[64]R. Mott, *supra* note 2, at 99.

[65]*Quoted in* Hazeltine, *supra* note 45, at 193. Article VII of the 1627 Petition of Right read the Great Charter to require that "no man ought to be adjudged to death but by the laws established in this realm, either by the customs of the same realm, or by acts of parliament." 3 Car. 1, c.1 (1627).

[66]R. Mott, *supra* note 2, at 93–94.

[67]The Earliest Acts & Laws of the Colony of Rhode Island and Providence Plantations 1647–1719, at 12 (J. Cushing ed. 1977).

[68]Prefixed to these laws of Rhode Island "was a reaffirmation of chapter thirty-nine of Magna Carta . . . and a declaration that by law of the land ('lex terrae') was meant the law enacted by the General Assembly of the colony itself—not the law of England. . . ." Hazeltine, *supra* note 45, at 195 (footnote omitted).

or imprisoned or be disseized of his freehold . . . , nor shall be . . . condemned, but by the lawful judgment of his peers or the law of this province."[69] Section 5 declared that "[n]o man . . . shall be put out of his lands, or tenements, nor be taken or imprisoned . . . without being brought to answer by due process of law."[70] Here we have an unmistakable distinction between due process as the means of affording a defendant opportunity to answer in court and the paraphrase of the law of the land as "the law of this province."

A similar provision is contained in the New York Charter of Liberty of 1683:

> That no freeman shall be . . . imprisoned or be disseized of his freehold . . . nor shall be passed upon adjudged or condemned but by the lawful judgment of his peers and by the law of the province. . . . That no man . . . shall be put out of his lands or tenements, nor taken, or imprisoned, nor . . . any ways destroyed without being brought to answer by due course of law.[71]

Mott remarks that "the English wording of section thirty-nine [was] being copied almost verbatim,"[72] a curious "verbatim" indeed. The distinction again drawn between being "brought to answer by due course of law" and the "law of this province" precludes, in my judgment, a reading of "law of the land" as a means of testing legislative policy. The East New Jersey Act of 1698, like those of Massachusetts and New York, provides separately for condemnation "by the laws of this Province" and "being first brought to answer by due course of law."[73]

To round out the picture, consider a Virginia incident that Mott cites as being the "first instance on record in which an exercise of the police power was questioned, as being opposed to the 'law of the land.' "[74] In 1657, the House of Burgesses sent an act regulating lawyers to the governor and council for approval, who answered: "The Governor and council will consent to this proposition so farr as it shall be agreeable to Magna Charta."[75] To this equivocal statement the burgesses replied: "[W]ee have considered Magna Charta and wee cannot discerne any prohibition conteined therein but that these propositions may pass into lawes."[76] It was the burgesses, not the royal governor, who represented the colonial understanding, paralleled as we have seen by that of other colonies.[77]

From such materials and protests against "arbitrary taxation" Mott concludes that

> the colonists looked upon due process of law as a guarantee which had a wide, varied, and indefinite content. . . .

[69] 1692 Mass. Acts § 1, *quoted in* R. MOTT, *supra* note 2, at 97 n.43.

[70] 1692 Mass. Acts § 5, *quoted in* R. MOTT, *supra* note 2, at 97 n.43. For the fourteenth-century statutes which viewed due process as the "method of summoning the person to appear . . . to answer the accusation made against him," see Jurow, *supra* note 4, at 266–70.

[71] 1 Colonial Laws of New York 113 (Albany 1894), *quoted in* R. MOTT, *supra* note 2, at 11 n.35. The New York and Massachusetts statutes were disallowed, *id.* at 101; nevertheless they exhibit the colonial understanding. Mott adds, there is "little evidence to support the view that the provisions were expected to restrict the legislature." R. MOTT, *supra* note 2, at 11 n.35.

[72] R. MOTT, *supra* note 2, at 11 (footnote omitted).

[73] *Id.* at 11 n.39. The Continental Congress of 1774 claimed the "privilege of being tried by their peers of the vicinity, according to the course of that law. . . ." *Id.* at 13 n.42. A similar construction was put upon Magna Carta by Blackstone: "For exile, or transportation, is a punishment unknown to the common law; and, wherever it is now inflicted, it is . . . by the express direction of some modern act of parliament. To this purpose the great charter (p) declares, that no freeman shall be banished, unless by the judgment of his peers, or by the law of the land." 1 W. BLACKSTONE, *supra* note 57, at 137.

[74] R. MOTT, *supra* note 2, at 115.

[75] *Id.* at 114 n.20.

[76] *Id.* at 115 n.20.

[77] *See* note 71 *supra.* Virginia adhered to the colonial confinement of "law of the land" to a known law; in 1753 a "fee" for the issuance of a patent upon crown lands caused a protest which was in part obviously copied from the thirty-ninth chapter of the Great Charter. The Assembly cited the provision "that no Man's . . . Freehold, or goods, be taken away . . . but by established and known Laws. . . ." But the charging of the fee was not by any known law. R. MOTT, *supra* note 2, at 122.

. . . It is but a small step from the view that the procedure in a civil case must be according to the law, to the conception of the law of the land as a limitation upon the impairment of vested rights or the tyrannical exercise of the police power.[78]

From judicial procedure "in a civil case" to the overturn of the legislature's "tyrannical exercise of the police power" is not a "small" but a giant, unbridged step. "In a few cases," says Mott, "the colonial lawyers made this step, but . . . the cases involving such questions were consequently very few,"[79] a confession that there are no judicial precedents, presumably because the colonial confinement of due process to service in "due course" and the assimilation of "law of the land" to "law of the province" blocked the way.

Mott would wrest an inference to the contrary from an utterance of Madison in sponsoring the Bill of Rights in the First Congress:

If they are incorporated into the Constitution independent tribunals of justice will consider themselves in a peculiar manner the guardians of those rights; they will be an impenetrable bulwark against every *assumption* of power in the legislative or executive; they will be naturally led to resist every encroachment upon rights *expressly stipulated* for in the constitution by the declaration of rights.[80]

This was in keeping with the contemplated judicial role, to police the constitutional boundaries so that the legislative and executive would not "overleap their limits," that they would not "assume" powers not granted to them,[81] that the legislature would not "encroach upon rights expressly stipulated for," *e.g.*, that they would not deprive a citizen of the trial by jury secured to him by the sixth amendment.[82] Madison did not mean that *within* those boundaries the courts would control the legislative discretion, for it was he who wrote in *Federalist No. 51* that in a republican form of government, the legislature naturally predominates.[83] In a contemporary letter to Jefferson, he wrote: "My own opinion has always been in favor of a bill of rights, provided it be so framed as *not to imply* power not meant to be included in the enumeration."[84] Now Mott would have it that the judiciary, which Hamilton assured the ratifiers "is next to nothing,"[85] was in fact made a "superlegislature," and this through the medium of the words "due process" which Mott agrees

---

[78]*Id.* at 123.

[79]*Id.*

[80]*Id.* at 155 (quoting 1 ANNALS OF CONG. 439 (1836; print bearing running title "History of Congress")) (emphasis added).

[81]R. BERGER 1969, *supra* note 43, at 16, 13–16.

[82]This plainly appears from Jefferson's letter to F. Hopkinson of March 13, 1789:

What I disapproved from the first moment also was the want of a bill of rights to guard liberty against the legislature as well as executive branches of the government, that is to say to secure freedom in religion, freedom of the press, freedom from monopolies, freedom from unlawful imprisonment, freedom from permanent military, and a trial by jury. . . .

Letter from T. Jefferson to F. Hopkinson (Mar. 13, 1789), *quoted in* R. MOTT, *supra* note 2, at 157 n.60.

[83]THE FEDERALIST No. 51, at 338 (Mod. Lib. ed. 1937). In Ware v. Hylton, 3 U.S. (3 Dall.) 199 (1796), Justice Iredell, one of the Founders, put the matter plainly: "The power of the Legislatures is limited" by the several Constitutions. *Id.* at 266. Beyond those limitations . . . their acts are void, because they are not warranted by the authority given. But *within* them, I think, they are in all cases obligatory . . . because . . . the Legislatures only exercise a discretion expressly confided to them by the constitution. . . . It is a discretion no more controllable (as I conceive) by a Court of Justice, than a judicial determination is by them.

Id. (emphasis added). This is also the view of L. HAND, THE BILL OF RIGHTS 31, 66 (1962); Thayer, *The Origin and Scope of the American Doctrine of Constitutional Law,* 7 HARV. L. REV. 129, 135 (1893). That executive discretion lies beyond judicial control was held in Marbury v. Madison, 5 U.S. (1 Cranch) 137, 169–70 (1803), and in Decatur v. Paulding, 39 U.S. (14 Pet.) 497, 515 (1840).

[84]Letter from J. Madison to T. Jefferson (Oct. 17, 1788), *reprinted in* 1 J. MADISON, WRITINGS 424 (1884) (emphasis added).

[85]THE FEDERALIST No. 78, at 504 note (Mod. Lib. ed. 1937). The words were quoted from Montesquieu, regarded as an oracle by the Founders. Montesquieu also stated: "The national judges are no more than the mouth that pronounces the words of the law, mere passive beings, incapable of moderating either its force or rigour." C. MONTESQUIEU, SPIRIT OF THE LAWS, bk. XI, ch. V, *quoted in* C. MCILWAIN, *supra* note 22, at 323.

were not mentioned in the Convention "a single time,"[86] words that had a familiar historical content relating solely to procedure in the courts, not to legislative acts.

The foregoing history confirms the statement Alexander Hamilton made in the New York Assembly on the eve of the Philadelphia Convention:

> The words "due process" have a precise technical import, and are only applicable to the process and proceedings of the courts of justice; they can never be referred to an act of legislature.[87]

Against this background the oft-cited dictum of Justice Johnson is without historical foundation:

> As to the words from Magna Charta . . . after volumes spoken and written with a view to their exposition, the good sense of mankind has at length settled down to this: that they were intended to secure the individual from the arbitrary exercise of the powers of government, unrestrained by the established principles of private rights and distributive justice.[88]

So far as the English and colonial records go, Anglo-Americans understood Magna Carta to mean only that a man would not be imprisoned or dispossessed but by a judgment after due opportunity to answer and under a standing law. Johnson did not profess to repudiate accepted learning; he merely held that a statute giving a bank summary process by execution against a debtor who consented thereto in writing was constitutional. Like a waiver of trial by jury, consent may be given to summary process. In fact, Justice Johnson recognized the paramountcy of the legislature: "The forms of administering justice, and the duties and *powers* of courts as incident to the exercise of a branch of sovereign power, must ever be subject to legislative will. . . ."[89]

STATE PRECEDENTS BEFORE 1789

Most of the discussion of the pre-1789 state precedents has centered on whether they asserted the power of judicial review; so far as my reading goes, inquiry has not been directed to whether the power extended to overrule legislation as in derogation of some penumbra of "law of the land," *i.e.,* to substitute judicial for legislative policy. The authenticity of some of the cases has been hotly disputed, but for present purposes such authenticity may be assumed.

---

[86]R. MOTT, *supra* note 2, at 145. Mott also states that in the "flood" of post-Convention literature "there has not been found a single mention of due process of law," *id.* at 147, an extraordinary neglect of what Mott considers so important a provision.

[87]4 THE PAPERS OF ALEXANDER HAMILTON 35 (H. Syrett & J. Cooke eds. 1962) [hereinafter cited as HAMILTON PAPERS]. Following Coke, Justice Story wrote that due process means "being brought in to answer . . . by due process of the common law. So that this clause in effect affirms the right of trial according to the process and proceedings of the common law." J. STORY, *supra* note 3, § 1789 (footnotes omitted). Pomeroy's inclusion of the legislature is without historical warrant:

> It is plain that any statute which Congress or legislature may see fit to pass, is not, in the sense in which the words are used in the Constitution, 'due process of law,' or 'the law of the land'. Otherwise this safeguard of private rights would become a mere empty form.

J. POMEROY, INTRODUCTION TO THE CONSTITUTIONAL LAW OF THE UNITED STATES 156 (1880).

[88]Bank of Columbia v. Okely, 17 U.S. (4 Wheat.) 235, 244 (1819). In Davidson v. New Orleans, 96 U.S. 97 (1877), the Court stated that the norm for "law of the land" is to be found in those fundamental principles of liberty and justice which lie at the bases of our civil and political institutions. *Id.* at 102. More surprising is Justice Field's statement in Barbier v. Connolly, 113 U.S. 27 (1885):

> But neither the [fourteenth] amendment . . . nor any other amendment, was designed to interfere with the power of the State, sometimes termed its police power, to prescribe regulations to promote the health . . . education . . . and good order of the people, and to legislate so as to increase the industries of the State, develop its resources, and add to its wealth and prosperity.

Id. at 31.

[89]Bank of Columbia v. Okely, 17 U.S. at 245 (emphasis added).

Josiah Philips: Virginia 1778.[90]—In 1778 the Virginia Assembly passed a bill of attainder against Josiah Philips and a band of outlaws who were terrorizing certain Virginia communities. When he was seized, he was tried by a court in a criminal prosecution rather than being sentenced to death in execution of the bill of attainder. In 1803 St. George Tucker, then a judge of the Virginia court, explained that this was "a decisive proof of the importance of the separation of the powers of government, and of the independence of the judiciary. . . ."[91] In other words, the act of attainder was void so that sentence could not be passed thereunder. But Jefferson, who was a member of the legislative committee that recommended the bill of attainder, later wrote that

> Randolph being Attorney General and apprehending he [Philips] would plead that he was a British subject, taken in arms in support of his lawful sovereign, and as a prisoner of war was entitled to the protection of the law of nations, he thought the safest proceeding would be to indict him as a felon and robber. Against this, I believe, Phillips urged the same plea; but was overruled and found guilty.[92]

Corwin regards Tucker as "a zealous champion of judicial review . . . seeking to create a precedent out of hand."[93] On a more charitable view he was mistaken. For centuries, bills of attainder had been a rubric of Parliament's power;[94] as an attribute of the legislative function, they were included in state grants of legislative power.[95] The fact that a number of state constitutions, though not Virginia's, expressly prohibited bills of attainder indicates that absent the prohibition the power was possessed by the legislature. Such prohibitions were regarded by Hamilton as "exceptions to the legislative authority."[96] A few years before Tucker wrote, the Supreme Court declined in *Cooper v. Telfair*[97] to hold that a Georgia bill of attainder passed in 1782 was "excepted from the legislative jurisdiction, by a necessary implication" where the Georgia constitution did not "expressly interdict" it.[98] Even on Tucker's view, the Court decided an issue of constitutional boundaries, not whether jurisdiction within such boundaries could be displaced by the judiciary.

Holmes v. Walton: New Jersey 1780[99].—A New Jersey Act of 1788 provided for the seizure of enemy goods, subject to trial by a six-man jury; apparently the court held the six-man jury provision void. Article 22 of the 1776 New Jersey Constitution declared that "the inestimable right of trial by jury shall remain confirmed as a part of the law of this Colony. . . ."[100] A twelve-man jury was the invariable practice since "sometime in the 14th century,"[101] Coke and Blackstone regarded a twelve-man jury as of the essence.[102] In the Virginia Ratification Convention, Governor Edmund Randolph said: "There is no suspicion that less than twelve jurors will be thought sufficient."[103] So important was this deemed that seven states had enacted statutes providing that the petit jury must be composed to twelve men.[104] In that light the case merely upset action in derogation of a constitutional requirement.

[90]For a discussion and various citations, see C. HAINES, THE AMERICAN DOCTRINE OF JUDICIAL SUPREMACY 89–95 (1932).

[91]1 TUCKER'S BLACKSTONE, app. 293 (1803).

[92]E. CORWIN, THE DOCTRINE OF JUDICIAL REVIEW 72 (1914).

[93]*Id.* at 71.

[94]Berger, *Bills of Attainder: A Study of Amendment by the Court,* 63 CORNELL L. REV. 355, 374 (1978).

[95]*Id.* at 386.

[96]THE FEDERALIST No. 78, at 505 (Mod. Lib. ed. 1937).

[97]4 U.S. (4 Dall.) 14 (1800).

[98]*Id.* at 18.

[99]C. HAINES, *supra* note 90, at 92–95.

[100]2 B. POORE, THE FEDERAL AND STATE CONSTITUTIONS, COLONIAL CHARTERS 1313 (1878).

[101]Williams v. Florida, 399 U.S. 78, 89 (1970).

[102]3 W. BLACKSTONE, *supra* note 57, at 379; 1 E. COKE, *supra* note 3, at 48a.

[103]3 J. ELLIOT, *supra* note 46, at 467.

[104]New Hampshire Act of Jan. 17, 1777, Acts and Laws of New Hampshire 65 (1780); New York: Act of Apr. 19, 1786, art. XVI, Laws of New York, p. 266 (Greenleaf 1792); North Carolina: Act of Nov. 10, 1779, ch. VI, Laws of North Carolina, p. 388 (Iredell 1791); Pennsylvania Act of Mar. 19, 1785, § 9, Laws of Pennsylvania, pp. 262–65 (Dallas 1793); Rhode

Commonwealth v. Caton: Virginia 1782[105].—Caton was judicially condemned for treason; the lower house of the Virginia legislature passed a pardoning resolution, in which the Senate did not concur. This issue was whether a constitutional provision, "no reprieve or pardon shall be granted, but by resolve of the House of Delegates,[106] conflicted with a statute providing that "the general assembly . . . shall determine" whether a person or persons are the "proper objects of mercy or not."[107] This was an issue whether an express provision of the constitution was violated, not an attempt to control legislative discretion.

Rutgers v. Waddington: New York 1784[108].—Elizabeth Rutgers brought suit against Josiah Waddington, a Loyalist, under the New York Act of 1783, "designed for the relief of those patriots who had fled occupied territory" by giving them an action against persons who had used their property.[109] At issue was whether the statute offended the Peace Treaty of 1783 with England. The court stated that "[t]he supremacy of the legislature need not be called into question; if they think fit positively to enact a law, there is no power to control them."[110] But "when a law is expressed in general words" and some collateral matter arising therefrom "is unreasonable, then the judges are in decency to conclude that the consequences were not forseen by the legislature; and therefore they are at liberty to expound the statute by equity, and only *quoad hoc* to disregard it,"[111] a paraphrase of Blackstone's tenth rule of statutory construction.[112] Here the supremacy of the legislature is acknowledged, but its enactment is construed to avoid an "unforeseen" and "unreasonable" result.

Trevett v. Weeden: Rhode Island 1786[113].—In violation of a Rhode Island statute, John Weeden had refused to accept payment for meat in paper money. The Act provided that such violations were to be tried without a jury; Weeden was indicted; his counsel, James Varnum, maintained that the Act was unconstitutional. Since Rhode Island had no written constitution and operated under its colonial charter which contained no relevant provision, Varnum claimed that trial by jury was a fundamental right confirmed by Magna Carta.[114] It was adjudged that the "[c]omplaint does not come under the Cognizance of the Justices . . . and . . . is hereby dismissed."[115] Two of the five justices orally stated that the court could not take cognizance because the law was unconstitutional.[116] *Trevett* therefore may be read to disclaim jurisdiction to declare a law unconstitutional; in any event the issue of constitutionality turned on a direct violation of a "fundamental" requirement—trial by jury—not the judicial displacement of legislative discretion.

The "Ten Pound Case": New Hampshire 1786[117].—According to Wiliam Crosskey, no friend of judicial review, the New Hampshire court treated an Act providing for the expeditious recovery of

---

Island: Session of Mar. 18, 1776, p. 316; South Carolina: Act of Aug. 20, 1731, Public Laws of South Carolina, p. 125 (Grimke 1790); Virginia: Session of Oct. 20, 1777, ch. XVII, art. XI, Collection of Public Acts 1776–1783 (1785).

[105]C. HAINES, *supra* note 90, at 95–98; the case is reported in 4 Call. 5 (1782). Louis Boudin's charge that this is a "mythical" case, L. BOUDIN, GOVERNMENT BY JUDICIARY 531–35 (1932), has been disproved. 2 D. MAYS, EDMUND PENDLETON 196 (1952).

[106]2 D. MAYS, *supra* note 105, at 195.

[107]*Id.* at 168.

[108]C. HAINES, *supra* note 90, at 98–104.

[109]Act of Mar. 17, 1783, 6th Sess., ch. 31, 1 Laws of New York 62 (Greenleaf 1792); 1 J. GOEBEL, HISTORY OF THE SUPREME COURT OF THE UNITED STATES 132 (1971).

[110]C. HAINES, *supra* note 90, at 99.

[111]*Id.*

[112]J. GOEBEL, *supra* note 109, at 136.

[113]C. HAINES, *supra* note 90, at 105–12.

[114]*Id.* at 105, 112; J. GOEBEL, *supra* note 109, at 139.

[115]J. GOEBEL, *supra* note 109, at 140 (footnote omitted).

[116]*Id.*

small debts without trial by jury as "unconstitutional and therefore not binding upon them."[118] Article 20 of the 1784 New Hampshire Constitution provided that "[i]n all cases concerning property . . . the parties have a right to a trial by jury" except where the usage had been otherwise.[119] The prior practice was to afford trial by jury where more than forty shillings was involved, so that the withdrawal of jury trial for less than ten pounds violated an express constitutional guarantee.

Bayard v. Singleton: North Carolina 1787[120].—An Act confiscating Loyalist property provided that suits against purchasers of the property from the commissioners were to be dismissed on motion. The court declined to dismiss a suit, saying: "[B]y the Constitution every citizen had undoubtedly a right to a decision of his property by trial by jury."[121] So Article 14 of the 1776 North Carolina Constitution expressly provided: "[I]n all controversies at law, respecting property, the ancient mode of trial, by jury . . . ought to remain sacred and inviolable."[122]

"Remonstrance," Case of the Judges: Virginia 1788[123].—The judges of the Court of Appeals of Virginia filed a Remonstrance with the General Assembly in May, 1788, protesting that a statute which imposed new duties on the courts without corresponding compensation constituted an assault upon the independence of the judges in violation of the separation of powers.[124]

Summary.—In sum, none of the pre-1789 "precedents" assert a right to displace legislative discretion, and, of course, they do not appeal to Magna Carta for that purpose; rather the statutes were in direct conflict with constitutional requirements, *e.g.,* trial by jury. In two of the cases, the courts disclaimed jurisdiction to override the legislature; even so the suggestion of unconstitutionality was followed by violent criticism and attempts to remove the offending judges, a consequence that makes meaningful the veteran Judge Pendleton's statement that he regarded the power to nullify legislation as a "deep, important and I will add, a tremendous question, the decision of which might involve consequences to which gentlemen may not have extended their ideas."[125] It was the legislature that was the darling of the colonists; of the three branches, Hamilton assured the Founders, the judiciary was "less than nothing."[126] Such sentiments counsel, given the background of judicial review limited to policing constitutional boundaries, against a reading of "the law of the land" to embrace judicial displacement of legislative discretion within those boundaries.

STATE PRECEDENTS AFTER 1789

In evaluating the post-1789 precedents, it is to be borne in mind that toward the turn of the century courts began to see themselves as instruments of social change in the common law areas of torts and contracts that had long been confided to them. "Instrumentalism" was not the pre-1789 fashion; social change was brought about through legislation. "Fear of judicial discretion had long been part of colonial political rhetoric,"[127] nowhere better exemplified than in the utterance

[117]*See* 2 W. Crosskey, Politics and the Constitution in the History of the United States 969-71 (1953).

[118]*Id.* at 969.

[119]2 B. Poore, *supra* note 100, at 1282.

[120]1 N.C. (Mart. 42) (1787), *quoted in* C. Haines, *supra* note 90, at 112–20.

[121]C. Haines, *supra* note 90, at 112, 114 (quoting Bayard v. Singleton, 1 N.C. (Mart.) 42, 47 (1787)).

[122]2 B. Poore, *supra* note 100, at 1410.

[123]J. Goebel, *supra* note 109, at 129; C. Haines, *supra* note 90, at 150–52. The case is appended to Kamper v. Hawkins, 3 Va. (1 Va. Cas.) 22, 98, 100–02 (1793).

[124]J. Goebel, *supra* note 109, at 129.

[125]Commonwealth v. Caton, 4 Call. 5, 7 (1782).

[126]The Federalist No. 78, at 504 (Mod. Lib. ed. 1937).

[127]Horwitz, *The Emergence of an Instrumental Conception of American Law, 1780–1820,* in 5 Perspectives in American History 287, 303 (1971).

of Chief Justice Hutchinson of Massachusetts in 1767: "[T]he *Judge* should never be the *Legislator:* Because then the Will of the Judge would be the Law: and this tends to a State of Slavery."[128] These were the norms, the presuppositions of those who created the several judiciaries, and they may fairly be said to demark the boundaries of the judicial function.

Ham v. M'Claws: South Carolina 1789[129].—A resident of British Honduras brought negro slaves into South Carolina upon being informed that actual settlers were not barred from doing so, as an existing act provided at the time of setting sail. They arrived a few days after a new act, of which they could not have known, provided for forfeiture of any slave brought into the state. The court held that

> statutes passed against the plain and obvious principles of common right, and common reason [Coke's *Bonham* dictum], are absolutely null and void, as *far as they are calculated to operate against these principles.* . . . We are, therefore, bound to give such a construction to this . . . act . . . as will be consistent with justice, and the dictates of natural reason, though contrary to the strict letter of the law; and this construction is, that the legislature never had it in their contemplation to make forfeiture of the negroes in question. . . .[130]

This was not a holding that the statute was void because in derogation of the "law of the land," but an attempt by construction to mitigate the hardship that the statute imposed in an unforeseen and patently unjust situation.

Bowman v. Middleton: South Carolina 1792[131].—In 1677 Nicholls obtained a grant of 510 acres; Cattell obtained an adjoining grant in 1701 that included 146 acres of the Nicholls tract. An act of 1712 confirmed Cattell's title, including the 146 Nicholls acres. The court held that "it was against common right, as well as against *Magna Carta,* to take away the freehold of one man and vest it in another. . . ."[132] Magna Carta, as we have seen, had no application to acts of the legislature.

Kamper v. Hawkins: Virginia 1793[133].—The Virginia constitution required that judges be appointed by joint ballot of both houses and be commissioned by the governor. A statute which appointed judges, but not in this manner, was held unconstitutional, a violation of an express constitutional provision.[134]

---

[128]*Id.* at 292 (emphasis in original).

[129]1 S.C.L. (1 Bay) 93 (1789).

[130]*Id.* at 98 (emphasis in original). After the Revolution of 1688, wrote Haines, "English courts gradually restricted the *[Bonham]* principle to acts which were impossible to be performed and acts wherein absurd consequences might arise." C. HAINES, *supra* note 90, at 98 (footnote omitted). McIlwain observes that after the Restoration, "[t]he temptation to use the courts for social or political objects was . . . greatly lessened by the frequency and regularity of the sessions of Parliament. If a grievance was felt, if a change was wanted . . . , the result could easily be brought about by a statute. . . ." C. McILWAIN, *supra* note 22, at 354 (quoting 2 A. LOWELL, THE GOVERNMENT OF ENGLAND 476 (1912)).

It is worth recalling that the colonists invoked Coke's *Bonham* dictum because it was congenial to the forces that were mounting an attack on parliamentary supremacy. But does it follow that the Founders therefore meant to make their own darling assemblies subject to judicial control under the "law of nature," for so Coke himself regarded his appeal to "common . . . reason"? R. BERGER 1969, *supra* note 43, at 351–52. In resorting to written constitutions—positive law—that "would determine explicit . . . allocations of power and its corresponding limits," R. BERGER 1977, *supra* note 9, at 252, the Founders embraced positivism rather than the law of nature. They had no thought of handing over lawmaking to the branch which Hamilton assured the Ratifiers "is next to nothing." THE FEDERALIST No. 78, at 504 (Mod. Lib. ed. 1937).

[131]1 S.C.L. (1 Bay) 252 (1792).

[132]*Id.* at 254 (emphasis in original).

[133]3 Va. (1 Va. Cas.) 20 (1793).

[134]Judge St. George Tucker quoted Vattel: the legislators "ought to consider the fundamental laws as sacred, if the nation has not *in express terms given them power to change them.* . . ." *Id.* at 75 (emphasis added). Of the courts he stated, their duty is "declaring what the law is, and not making a new law." *Id.* at 96.

Zylstra v. Charleston: South Carolina 1796[135].—Zylstra was tried under a city bylaw by a court of wardens and fined one hundred pounds for keeping a tallow-candler's shop within the city. The act of 1784 gave the court of wardens jurisdiction of "causes as far as 20 [pounds] without the intervention of a jury." Hence Judge Burke held the bylaw void because "jury trial . . . is . . . guaranteed to us expressly by our constitution," in which view Judge Waties joined.[136]

Vanhorne's Lessee v. Dorrance: Federal 1795[137].—*Vanhorne* is of particular interest because Justice Paterson, a prominent delegate to the Convention, sat on the trial of the case. It arose under the Pennsylvania, not the federal, constitution; a Pennsylvania statute "confirmed" title to certain disputed lands. In his charge to the jury, Paterson stated that "[t]he preservation of property then is a primary object of the social compact, and, by the late [1776] Constitution of Pennsylvania, was made a fundamental law."[138] Consequently the legislature "had no authority to make an act divesting one citizen of his freehold, and vesting it in another, without a just compensation."[139] He likewise held that just compensation could be fixed only by a jury.[140] It required no invocation of supraconstitutional power, or the Magna Carta—which was unmentioned—for there were express governing constitutional provisions. Article 8 of the Declaration of Rights provided that "no part of a man's property can be justly taken from him, or applied to public uses, without his consent."[141] And Article II declared that "in controversies respecting property, . . . the parties have a right to trial by jury. . . ."[142]

Trustees of the University of North Carolina v. Foy: North Carolina 1805[143].—An act repealed grants of property earlier made to the university, and ordered that it revert to the state. To the argument that the "law of the land" does not impose any restriction on the legislature, the court replied that the provision was designed to apply to some branch, that it was not applicable to the executive because of his limited powers; nor to the judiciary, for they are "only to expound and enforce the law and have no discretionary powers";[144] consequently it was designed to apply only to the legislature, and to require that a deprivation of property must be by judicial trial.[145] Obviously this stands the history earlier detailed on its head: the "law of the land" was aimed at the executive and required that individual property could only be taken under existing law after trial; it had no application to the legislature.

Holden v. James: Massachusetts 1814[146].—The legislature had suspended the statute of limitations so as to permit a named individual to bring suit against an administrator after the statute of limitations had run. Article 20 of the Massachusetts Declaration of Rights declared that "the power of suspending the laws . . . ought never to be exercised but by the legislature . . . in such particular cases only as the legislature shall expressly provide for."[147] Nevertheless the court held: "It is manifestly contrary to the first principles of civil liberty and natural justice, and to the spirit

[135]1 S.C.L. (1 Bay) 382 (1796).

[136]*Id.* at 388, 394. Compare this with Mott's rendering of *Zylstra:* "due process of law . . . certainly did not permit the legislature to allow summary convictions." R. MOTT, *supra* note 2, at 197.

[137]2 U.S. (2 Dall.) 304 (1795).

[138]*Id.* at 310.

[139]*Id.*

[140]*Id.* at 310, 313.

[141]2 B. POORE, *supra* note 100, at 1541.

[142]*Id.* at 1542.

[143]5 N.C. (1 Mur.) 53, 58 (1805).

[144]*Id.* at 79, 88.

[145]*Id.* at 78–79, 87–88.

[146]11 Mass. 396 (1814).

[147]*Id.* at 403, 404.

of our constitution and laws, that any one citizen should enjoy privileges and advantages which are denied to all others under like circumstances. . . ."[148] Although the reasoning appeals to our sense of justice, it overrides the discretion expressly conferred on the legislature to provide for "particular cases." The appeal to "natural justice" was an appeal to natural law, which Dean Pound characterized as "purely personal and arbitrary,"[149] and which permitted the judges to override the Constitution. When it was later argued before Chief Justice Shaw that enforcement of the Fugitive Slave Act offended against natural rights, he held that "an appeal to natural rights . . . was not pertinent! It was to be decided by the Constitution . . . and by the Law of Congress. . . . These were to be obeyed, however disagreeable to our natural sympathies or views of duty."[150] And before long natural law was ostensibly repudiated by the New York court in *Wynehamer v. People.*[151]

 Gardner v. Village of Newburgh: New York 1816[152].—*Gardner,* one of the earliest and the most frequently cited precedents for substantive due process, carries the authority of Chancellor Kent. An act authorized a village to supply water; the village diverted a stream without compensating one riparian owner. The case could have been decided on the narrow ground that the particular taking without compensation was not within the contemplation of the draftsmen; this was in fact the third ground that Chancellor Kent advanced:

> [T]he legislature never intended . . . to . . . interfere with this great and sacred principle of private right. This is evident from the care which this act bestows on the rights of the owners of the spring, and of the lands through which the conduits are to pass. . . . [I]n these cases due provision is made for its protection, or for just compensation. There is no reason why the rights of the plaintiff should not have the same protection as the rights of his neighbors; and the necessity of a provision for his case could not have occurred, or it, doubtless, would have been inserted.[153]

Consequently, Kent held that it was "contrary to the intention of this statute" to deprive him of the right without compensation,[154] an appeal to Blackstone's tenth rule of construction, for which he could have cited *Rutgers v. Waddington*[155] and *Ham v. M'Claws.*[156]

 Bent, however, on riveting the doctrine of vested rights on the New York Constitution, he opened by holding that the right to the stream is property "of which no man can be disseised 'but by lawful judgment of his peers, or by due process of law.' " This is an "ancient and fundamental maxim . . . which the legislature has incorporated into an act. . . ."[157] But in explaining this very act to the Assembly in 1787, Hamilton had declared that "[t]he words 'due process' . . . are only applicable to the process and proceedings of the courts of justice; they can never be referred to an act of legislature."[158] Kent's application of "due process" to the statute gave it a meaning flatly in contradiction to its historical meaning and the understanding of the Assembly who incorporated it in the 1787 statute.

---

[148]*Id.* at 403, 405.

[149]Pound, *Common Law and Legislation,* 21 HARV. L. REV. 383, 393 (1908).

[150]Account in The Liberator, Nov. 4, 1842, at 3, *quoted in* R. COVER, JUSTICE ACCUSED: ANTI-SLAVERY AND THE JUDICIAL PROCESS 169 (1975). In The Antelope, 23 U.S. (10 Wheat.) 66 (1825), Chief Justice Marshall declared in a slave trade case: "[T]his court must not yield to feelings which might seduce it from the path of duty, and must obey the mandate of the law." *Id.* at 114.

[151]13 N.Y. 378, 430, 453, 390, 391, 476 (1856). In Hanson v. Vernon, 27 Iowa 28 (1869), Chief Justice Dillon discarded the time-worn argument that acts could be declared void because they violated notions of natural equity or justice. *Id.* at 41.

[152]2 Johns. Ch. 162 (N.Y. 1816).

[153]*Id.* at 168.

[154]*Id.*

[155]*See* text accompanying notes 108–12 *supra.*

[156]*See* text accompanying notes 129–30 *supra.*

[157]2 Johns. Ch. at 166 (citing Act of Jan. 26, 1787, 1 Laws of New York 1778–1787 (Greenleaf 1792)).

[158]HAMILTON PAPERS, *supra* note 87, at 35. *See* text accompanying note 87 *supra.*

Next, Kent engrafted a requirement of just compensation on the New York Constitution, from which it was absent, first leaning on Blackstone.[159] Blackstone, however, does not root just compensation in Magna Carta or in any other governing statute but in the beneficent *practice* of the legislature. The legislature interposes "[n]ot by absolutely stripping the subject of his property in an arbitrary manner; but by giving him a full indemnification and equivalent for the inquiry thereby sustained."[160] But Blackstone also wrote that "if the parliament will positively enact a thing to be done which is unreasonable, I know of no power that can control it."[161] Kent then avers that " 'just indemnity' has been deemed of such importance, that is has frequently been made the subject of an express and fundamental article of right," citing the Pennsylvania, Delaware, and Ohio constitutions.[162] These, however, indicate that an express provision was deemed necessary to curtail the legislative power.[163]

What Kent regards as "of higher authority, and [as] absolutely decisive of the sense of the people of this country, it is made a part of the constitution of the United States, 'that private property shall not be taken for public use, without just compensation.' "[164] It will be recalled that Kent first found just compensation to be a requirement of due process. The framers of the fifth amendment, however, expressly provided against the deprivation of property without due process and then added a separate provision for just compensation, testimony that they did not consider it to be covered by due process. Elsewhere I have shown that the Founders were fastidious draftsmen who rejected surplusage even to make assurance doubly sure.[165] Consequently, the lesson of the fifth amendment is that just compensation was deemed to require an express provision. Of course, I am not an advocate of takings without just compensation but rather an opponent of judicial revision of a Constitution to conform it to a judge's sense of justice.[166] For me, Madison, chief architect of the Constitution, furnishes the guide: "Had the power of making treaties, for example, been omitted, however necessary it might have been, the defect could only have been lamented, or supplied by an amendment of the Constitution."[167]

Kent was preeminently not a disinterested judge divorced from political passions. His "political convictions were fierce"; he became known as one who "tended to erect barriers to the broadening of economic or political power," so much so that the New York legislature invoked the mandatory retirement statute when he reached age sixty.[168] That his transparent manipulation of legal doctrine

---

[159] 2 Johns. Ch. at 167.

[160] 1 W. BLACKSTONE, *supra* note 57, at 139.

[161] *Id.* at 91.

[162] 2 Johns. Ch. at 167.

[163] *See* text accompanying note 98 *supra*. It may be thought that I employ a double standard, citing seven state constitutional provisions for jury trial to confirm its centrality and rejecting similar evidence with respect to just compensation. Trial by jury, however, has an unbroken centuries-old tradition: no privilege was more precious to the Founders, so that the seven express state provisions may be regarded as declaratory or confirmatory. No such traditions exist for just compensation.

[164] 2 Johns. Ch. at 167.

[165] *See* Berger, *supra* note 94, at 363–64.

[166] *See* note 150 and accompanying text *supra*. For Kent's "sense of justice," see note 168 *infra*.

[167] 2 ANNALS OF CONG. 1800–01 (Feb. 2, 1791). Kent, on the other hand, was addicted to lawmaking. For example, in Dash v. Van Kleeck, 7 Johns. Ch. 502 (N.Y. 1811), he held:

An *ex post facto* law, in the strict technical sense of the term is usually understood to apply to criminal cases, and this is its meaning when used in the Constitution of the United States; yet laws impairing previously acquired civil rights are equally within the reason of that prohibition, and equally to be condemned.

Id. at 505. The Framers gave the clause what they considered was its common law meaning; they debated and rejected the extension of the terms to retroactive civil statutes, making an exception for impairment of contracts. *See* Berger, *supra* note 94, at 365–67. *See also* Satterlee v. Matthewson, 27 U.S. (2 Pet.) 380, 413 (1829); Calder v. Bull, 3 U.S. (3 Dall.) 386, 391–93, 397 (1798) (wherein Justice Chase quoted three state constitutions restricting ex post facto to criminal cases).

[168] G. WHITE, THE AMERICAN JUDICIAL TRADITION 32 (1976). Consider Kent's appeal to the New York Constitutional Convention of 1821 to reject universal suffrage:

to enshrine vested rights in response to his own socioeconomic prejudices has any credence is a reproach to a democracy that has steadily moved in the opposite direction.

Mayo v. Wilson: New Hampshire 1817[169].—A case more responsive to history is *Mayo v. Wilson,* decided one year later. A statute authorized selectmen to arrest persons suspected of traveling unnecessarily on Sunday. An arrested defendant invoked the "law of the land" provision, arguing that there can be no arrest without a warrant. The court held that "an arrest if authorized by the statute or common law, though without writ or warrant in deed, has always been considered in England as warranted *per legem terrae....* We think that the 15th article in our Bill of Rights [analog of the Magna Carta 39th] ... was not intended to abridge the power of the legislature...."[170] Statutes "made in pursuance of the constitution" are the "law of the land."[171]

Against this Judge Waties argued in *Lindsay v. Commissioners*[172] that "[i]f the *lex terrae* meant any law which the legislature might pass, then the legislature would be authorized by the constitution to destroy the right."[173] Historically, however, that lay within the power of Parliament, as Blackstone emphasized. And Justice Iredell, one of the most cogent advocates of judicial review prior to adoption of the Constitution, maintained that given a "Constitution, which imposed no limits on the legislative power ... whatever the legislative power chose to enact, would be lawfully enacted."[174] One may, like Justice Chase, look to supraconstitutional power, to natural law,[175] but warrant to thwart the legislative will cannot be traced to the *lex terrae* phrase.

In sum, several of the post-1789 state cases represent a rising tide of judicial assertiveness, laying claim to a right to mold the Constitution to conform to the judge's sense of justice, going so far, as in *Holden v. James,*[176] to substitute that sense for the express constitutional terms, or, as in *Trustees of the University of North Carolina v. Foy,*[177] erroneously reading the *lex terrae* as not

That extreme democratic principle ... has been regarded with terror, by the wise men of every age....

. . . .

... The tendency of universal suffrage, is to jeopardize the rights of property, and the principles of liberty. ... [T]here is a tendency in the poor to covet a share in the plunder of the rich ...; in the indolent and profligate, to cast the whole burthens of society upon the industrious and the virtuous....

See H. COMMAGER, DOCUMENTS OF AMERICAN HISTORY 232, 233 (7th ed. 1962). His opponents carried the day. *Id.*

[169] 1 N.H. 53 (1817).

[170] *Id.* at 57.

[171] *Id.* at 57, 58. In the same year the court held in Dartmouth College v. Woodward, 1 N.H. 111, 129–30 (1817), that "[i]t is evident, from all the commentaries upon [Magna Carta] by *English* writers, that it was intended to limit the powers of the crown, and not of parliament," and that "all statutes, not repugnant to any other clauses in the constitution, seem always to have been considered as 'the law of the land'...." *Id.* (emphasis in original). The decision was reversed in Dartmouth College v. Woodward, 17 U.S. (4 Wheat.) 518 (1819), not on "due process" or "law of the land" grounds but on "impairment of contract."

"Story was the only one of the justices of the Supreme Court to consider this point: 'Each trustee has a vested right, and legal interest in his office, and it cannot be devested but by due course of law.' " R. MOTT, *supra* note 2, at 203 n.42 (quoting 17 U.S. (4 Wheat.) at 705 (Story, J.)). Mott arrives at the singular conclusion that the "Supreme Court ... in so far as an opinion was expressed on this subject [by Story alone], adopted his viewpoint, and if anything, carried his definition a step further, distinctly linking up the principles of vested rights with due process of law." *Id.* at 203 (footnotes omitted).

Yet Story later held in Watson v. Mercer, 33 U.S. (8 Pet.) 88 (1834), that the federal courts had "no right to pronounce an act of the state legislature void, as contrary to the Constitution of the United States, from the mere fact that it devests antecedent vested rights of property." *Id.* at 110.

[172] 1 S.C.L. (2 Bay) 38 (1796).

[173] *Id.* at 59. The court was evenly divided; Justices Grimke and Bay argued that an act authorizing the appropriation of land for highways was part of the *lex terrae* and "declaratory of the well known and established laws of the kingdom." *Id.* at 57.

[174] Calder v. Bull, 3 U.S. (3 Dall.) 386, 398 (1798).

[175] *Id.* at 388. *But see* R. BERGER 1969, *supra* note 43, at 252–53.

[176] 11 Mass. 396 (1814). *See* text accompanying notes 146–51 *supra.*

[177] 5 N.C. (1 Mur.) 53 (1805). *See* text accompanying notes 143–45 *supra.*

applicable to the executive and judiciary but only to the legislature, a reading unmistakably contradicted by history. Such decisions must rest on the force of their reasoning;[178] so tested, they are a poor foundation for judicial power to take over policymaking. And they are counterbalanced by *Mayo v. Wilson*[179] and *Kamper v. Hawkins*.[180] The Virginia court that decided *Kamper* was probably the best qualified court in the land at that time. In *Kamper,* one of the most powerful early decisions to lay claim to the power of judicial review, the Virginia judges were at pains to disclaim policymaking. So Judge St. George Tucker, a vigorous proponent of judicial review and noted commentator on the Constitution, declared that the judicial duty is "declaring what the law is, and not making a new law."[181] Judge Henry more fully stated:

> The judiciary, from the nature of the office . . . could never be designed to determine upon the equity, necessity, or usefulness of a law; that would amount to an express interfering with the legislative branch. . . . [N]ot being chosen immediately by the people, nor being accountable to them . . . they do not, and ought not, to represent the people in framing or repealing any law.[182]

That view had been forcibly expressed by the Framers in rejecting a move for the participation of the Justices in policymaking. Elbridge Gerry, one of the most vigorous proponents of judicial review, declared: "It was quite foreign from the nature of ye office to make them judges of the policy of public measures. . . ."[183] "It was making Statesmen of the Judges. . . ."[184] Nathaniel Gorham observed that judges "are not to be presumed to possess any peculiar knowledge of the mere policy of public measures."[185] Immured in cloistered cells, remote from the political struggles that shape public policy, the Justices are peculiarly unfitted to shape it.

MOTT'S INFERENCES

So massive a study as that of Mott deserves better than curt dismissal; hence I shall examine a number of his findings in detail so that the reader may judge for himself whether they are worthy of credence. His treatment of the Northwest Ordinance of 1787 offers a good starting point. Article 2 provided in the context of criminal procedures that "[t]he inhabitants . . . shall always be entitled to . . . judicial proceedings according to the course of the common law. . . . No man shall be deprived of his liberty or property, but by the judgment of his peers or the law of the land. . . ."[186] Mott comments:

> Because of its close textual connection with certain other procedural protections for persons accused of crime, one might be led to think that it was considered merely as a procedural protection. Likewise, the fact that trial by jury and the well known "proceedings according to the course of the common law" are especially provided for, might seem to imply that it was neither of these protections which the framers of the article had in mind. Neither of these assumptions, however, seems to be warranted. In the first place, the framers of the bills and drafters of legislation in the formative years . . . were by no means so punctilious in the observance of the subtleties of statutory construction as one might wish. To say, therefore, that no two parts of a document were expected to cover the same ground, is to

---

[178]Judicial authority, Chief Justice Taney declared, should "depend altogether on the force of the reasoning by which it is supported." The Passenger Cases, 48 U.S. (7 How.) 283, 470 (1849) (Taney, C.J., dissenting).

[179]1 N.H. 53 (1817).

[180]3 Va. (1 Va. Cas.) 20 (1793).

[181]*Id.* at 96.

[182]*Id.* at 47. Justice Tyler stated: "[O]ur constitution was made . . . for ages to come, subject only to such alterations as the people may please to make." *Id.* at 65.

[183]1 M. FARRAND, *supra* note 60, at 97–98.

[184]2 *id.* at 75.

[185]2 *id.* at 73. *See* R. BERGER 1977, *supra* note 9, at 300.

[186]H. COMMAGER, *supra* note 168, at 130.

attribute to the legislators of this period a wisdom which, unfortunately, they did not possess. In the second place, there seems to have been a universal tendency in this period to put ambiguous, general, and abstract clauses in protections of this sort for good measure. Although the protection of trial by jury appeared in the Federal Constitution as adopted a few months later, one of the chief objections to the document was that it contained no general reservation of rights to the people. In the third place, there is evidence that some of the citizens of the confederation considered a jury trial as part of the protection of the law of the land.[187]

To begin with the third point, the special provision for jury trial showed that the draftsmen, as distinguished from "some citizens," separated jury trial from "law of the land."

In charging the framers of that period with lack of punctiliousness in matters of drafting Mott discloses he read the records of the Constitutional Convention on the run. The Framers, who sat coterminously with the draftsmen of the Ordinance, were in fact fastidious draftsmen. James Wilson adverted in the Pennsylvania Ratification Convention to "the care that the Convention took in selecting their language."[188] Two examples must suffice. When the impeachment clause came to the floor of the Convention, it referred only to "Treason and bribery." George Mason said: "Treason as defined in the Constitution will not reach many great and dangerous offences. . . . Attempts to subvert the Constitution may not be Treason as above defined. . . ."[189] Mason therefore moved to add "or maladministration"; but Madison objected that "[s]o vague a term will be equivalent to a tenure during pleasure of the Senate."[190] Thereupon Mason proposed "other high crimes & misdemeanors"[191] which, like "due process," had a familiar "technical, limited" meaning.[192] Consider also Madison's question "whether it was not going too far to extend the jurisdiction of the Court generally to cases arising Under the Constitution, & whether it ought not to be limited to cases of a Judiciary Nature."[193] His suggestion was rejected, "it being generally supposed that the jurisdiction given was constructively limited to cases of a Judiciary nature," that is, to "cases and controversies."[194] Thus the Framers exhibited a sure grasp of words that exactly expressed their aims and a distaste for unnecessary verbiage.

In the "flood" of post-Convention literature, Mott states, "there has not been found a single mention of due process of law."[195] Mott explains that the most common criticisms were "[o]mission of statements guaranteeing freedom of religion, liberty of the press, and trial by jury. . . ."[196] "In spite of the rather nebulous concept which the anti-federalists had of the contents of the [proposed] Bill of Rights," he observes, "there is abundant evidence to show that it was expected that those articles should apply to the legislature as well as to the other organs of government. It was a favorite contention that the power of Congress over both the *states* and the individuals was much too

---

[187]R. MOTT, *supra* note 2, at 143–44 (footnotes omitted).

[188]2 J. ELLIOT, *supra* note 46, at 452. Later, Chief Justice Taney observed: "Every word appears to have been weighed with the utmost deliberations, and its force and effect to have been fully understood." Holmes v. Jennison, 39 U.S. (14 Pet.) 540, 571 (1840).

[189]2 M. FARRAND, *supra* note 60, at 550.

[190]*Id.*

[191]*Id.*

[192]*See* R. BERGER, IMPEACHMENT: THE CONSTITUTIONAL PROBLEMS 86–87, 106–07 (1973).

[193]2 M. FARRAND, *supra* note 60, at 430.

[194]*Id.* Compare also Mott's denial to the draftsmen of the capacity to perceive "that no two parts of a document were expected to cover the same ground," with an interchange between Luther Martin and Gouverneur Morris. Martin moved to amend U.S. CONST. art. IV, § 3, cl. 2, which provided that "[n]othing in the Constitution shall be so construed as to prejudice any claims of the United States, or of any particular State" by adding, "[b]ut all such claims may be examined into & decided upon by the Supreme Court of the U—States." Morris replied: "[T]his is unnecessary, as all suits to which the U.S.—are parties are already to be decided by the Supreme Court." 2 M. FARRAND, *supra* note 60, at 466.

[195]R. MOTT, *supra* note 2, at 147.

[196]*Id.* at 147 n.18; *see* note 82 *supra*.

great."[197] The Bill of Rights, however, was not made applicable to the states, so that Mott's "evidence" merely reflects objections to the unduly broad grants to Congress. Moreover, to rely on "Agrippa's" remark, deemed "especially in point" by Mott, that "[a]ny system therefore which appoints a legislature, without any reservation of the rights of individuals, surrenders all power in every branch of legislation to the government,"[198] for proof that "due process" was designed to confer judicial authority to control legislative policymaking is to engage in circular reasoning. No one stated in the First Congress that the due process clause would serve to restrict the broad grants to Congress, a strange omission given the conventional view that the work applied only to judicial proceedings. In what Mott finds "the only instance of a direct reference to the thirty-ninth article of Magna Carta" by the antifederalists, there was "a long section protecting the rights of those accused of crime," concluding "that, no man be deprived of his liberty, except by the law of the land, or the judgment of his peers,"[199] the classic *procedural* formula. No pre-1787 precedent, we have seen, struck down legislation on substantive policy grounds; the cases proceeded for violations of express constitutional provisions, such as trial by jury. Moreover, some of those who urged that a Bill of Rights was unnecessary, Mott tells us, "declared that even if enacted, it would not limit the legislature. . . ."[200]

Another bit of evidence proffered by Mott is George Mason's insistence that "without a Bill of Rights the people would not be protected in their common-law privileges which would certainly indicate that he feared legislative as well as judicial and executive tyranny."[201] Without doubt the Bill of Rights was designed to protect the *enumerated* rights from Congress, as the first amendment makes clear; legislative violations of other express guarantees, *e.g.*, trial by jury, were likewise precluded. But there was no "common law privilege" to have legislation set aside because the judiciary entertained different views of policy. Mason's attempt to have judges included in the Council of Revision for the veto of legislation on policy grounds was rejected, for the reason among others that the delegates to the Convention put their trust in the legislature rather than in the judges, who were deemed to have no special competence for the determination of policy. How Mott deduced from such materials that "the Fifth Amendment was expected to limit arbitrary abuses of the power of government from whatever source abuse might come. . . ."[202] is indeed mystifying.[203]

Mott also invoked the Committee Report to the New York Convention of 1777, that would prohibit "the disfranchisement of persons 'unless by the act of the legislature of this State.' "[204] Livingston offered a substitute article which was adopted: " 'No member of this State shall be disfranchised, or deprived of any of the rights or privileges secured to the subjects of this State by this Constitution, unless by law of the land, or the judgment of his peers.' "[205] Mott construes this "law of the land" to mean something more than a "legislative enactment."[206] As far back as 1683, New York, like some of the other colonies, had associated the "judgment of his peers" with "the law of the province." The Committee Report had recognized the legislative power of disfranchisement; Livingston picked it up and expanded the rights to be protected. Before this is read as Mott's

---

[197]R. MOTT, *supra* note 2, at 148 (emphasis added) (footnote omitted).

[198]*Id.* at 149 n.20.

[199]*Id.* at 149 & n.24.

[200]*Id.* at 150 (footnote omitted).

[201]*Id.* at 146–47 (footnote omitted).

[202]*Id.* at 159.

[203]Of the same order is his paraphrase of Sir John Fortescue's statement that the king can make no "change in laws of the realm without the consent of the subject" as "no one should lose either his life or property without a regular trial before the courts according to the law of the land. . . ." *Id.* at 41 & n.48.

[204]*Id.* at 169 n.11.

[205]*Id.* at 169–70 n.11 (quoting 1 C. LINCOLN, CONSTITUTIONAL HISTORY OF NEW YORK 522 (1906)).

[206]*Id.* at 170.

substantive "law of the land" it needs to be shown that Livingston's substitute was designed to deny the legislative power to disfranchise which the Committee had recommended, and to depart from the "law of the province" pattern that had obtained.

The "essence of an adequate constitutional guarantee," Mott recognized, is that "it already has been given a reasonably clear cut meaning by the courts."[207] Yet he argued that

> [t]his view that due process of law was considered as a general phrase designed to prevent general arbitrary action on the part of the government is strengthened when we consider that even though it had been frequently used in the colonies and in England, no settled meaning was yet attached to it.[208]

One need only recall Hamilton's summation in 1787, that the words "due process of law" applied only to proceedings in the courts, never to acts of the legislature, to perceive that Mott has not properly evaluated the evidence. His view is further vitiated by his concession that

> [n]ot every statesman, and certainly not all the people, understood the broad character of this protection (it would have evoked considerably more discussion if they had understood it); but it is reasonable to suppose that *some* of those who were law-trained and understood the nature of the common law *had a glimpse* at least of the importance of such a basis for future judicial adjudication.[209]

That is a sorry basis for a revolutionary departure from the well-settled meaning that due process had from 1352 to 1787. No revolutionary departure found expression in the First Congress which inserted the words in the fifth amendment. Nevertheless, Mott declared that the evidence that the colonists considered that due process of law "limited the legislative bodies as well as the executive or judiciary" is

> clearly all on one side. Practically without exception, strenuous objections were raised whenever the colonists were met with a situation involving a legislative violation of due process of law. So overwhelming is the proof of the importance of this protection in this regard that it is difficult to understand how there would have been any serious question regarding it when the courts considered it a half century later.[210]

This reader vainly searched for some, let alone "overwhelming," pre-1789 evidence to that effect. It would serve no useful purpose to collate still other instances of Mott's substitution of wishful thinking for hard analysis. On the most charitable view, he was overwhelmed by the mountain of facts he had assembled, and did not really appreciate their significance.[211] The evidence, in my judgment, rebuts his attempt to give substantive due process deep historical roots.

CONCLUSION

There is no basis in the pre-1787 historical materials for the proposition that "due process of law" comprehended judicial power to test legislation for reasonableness. To the contrary, Magna Carta, from which due process was derived, was aimed exclusively at arbitrary action by the king, not at a rudimentary parliament of which the barons, for the most part, were themselves members. When due process appeared on the scene in the fourteenth century, it plainly was designed only

---

[207]*Id.* at 160.

[208]*Id.* at 161.

[209]*Id.* (emphasis added).

[210]*Id.* at 142.

[211]Mott "has been unable to master the vast amount of material which he has gathered. Rather we suspect that the material has mastered him." Brown, *supra* note 8, at 802. "The reviewer has sampled some of the authorities cited for particular propositions, and has frequently found them to lack that accuracy which lawyers are accustomed to demand. . . . Statements are frequently made that are based on references wrung from their context." Rottschaefer, *supra* note 8, at 482.

to ensure that a defendant would be given the opportunity to appear in court to answer by service of proper process in due course.

The "law of the land" in early English law, it is safe to say, referred to the customs and laws of the realm; the phrase was not designed to fashion a paramount test for the validity of such customs and laws, for the barons were well content with the protection they afforded. What the barons wanted was a hearing in court prior to judgment, and to be charged with violation of some existing custom or law, without which a trial would be a farce. Chapter 39, we are assured by competent authority, from which I found no dissent, was never regarded in England as a limitation upon the legislature. A number of colonies even more plainly differentiated between due process as the service of proper process in due course and "the law of the land" for which they substituted "the law of the province," thereby cutting the ground from resort to either phrase for the invalidation of legislation.

Reliance for judicial review in part was placed on the pre-1787 state cases, but not one attempted to substitute judicial for legislative judgments; all proceeded from legislative infractions of some constitutional provision or violation of a treaty. A few poorly reasoned post-1787 cases in South Carolina, North Carolina, Massachusetts, and New York reached out for power to override legislation; the better-reasoned New Hampshire and Virginia cases correctly pointed out that Magna Carta had never been applied to override statutes, and that power to make law and policy had been vested in the legislature alone. Unhappily, as Gresham noted in the field of coinage, bad cases in course of time crowded out the good, being congenial to the deep-seated greed for power from which judges, alas, are not immune. And by dint of repetition, what was manifest usurpation became clothed in respectability. To say this is to utter a commonplace; what bears emphasis is the fact that such judicial claims can find no warrant in Magna Carta nor Anglo-American constitutional history, that it is a perversion of "due process" or of the "law of the land" to apply either for the judicial overthrow of legislation.[212]

---

[212]Maitland stated that the "process by which old principles and old phrases are charged with a new content is from the lawyer's [judge's] point of view an evolution of the true intent and meaning of the old law; from the historian's point of view it is almost of necessity a process of perversion and misunderstanding." 3 P. GAY & V. WEXLER, HISTORIANS AT WORK 301–02 (1975) (quoting F. Maitland, Inaugural Lecture at Cambridge (1888)).

CHAPTER VIII

The Fourteenth Amendment: Light from the Fifteenth

> *[L]egal history still has its claims.*
>
> *Justice Frankfurter* *

The framers of the fourteenth amendment, my prior studies led me to conclude, intended to exclude suffrage and segregation from its scope.[1] Those findings were not novel. Justice Harlan's demonstration that suffrage was excluded,[2] said an activist critic of my view, Professor Louis Lusky, is "irrefutable and unrefuted."[3] Another activist, Professor Nathaniel Nathanson, agrees and adds that Alexander Bickel "conclusively" demonstrated that segregation likewise was excluded, and that "Berger's independent research and analysis confirms and adds weight to those conclusions."[4] A number of reviewers, including activist critics, concur that the proof on this score is compelling.[5]

With this history I coupled documentation of Justice Harlan's statement that "when the Court disregards the express intent and understanding of the Framers, it has invaded the realm of the political process to which the amending power was committed, and it has violated the constitutional structure which it is its highest duty to protect."[6] That coupling, wrote Professor Michael Perry, "necessarily involves a call for a revolution in constitutional doctrine."[7] Not so; it merely calls for reassessment of a very recent "revolution."[8] Prior to the 1940s, one of my activist critics, Professor Stanley Kutler, tells us, academe was wont to criticize the federal judiciary for "frustrating desirable social policies," for arrogating "a policymaking function unwarranted by the Constitution," thereby "negating the basic principles of representative government." Came a new day and "[m]ost of the judiciary's longtime critics suddenly found a new faith"; now an "activist judiciary" promoted "preferred freedoms" that matched the "new libertarianism."[9] For Kutler and his like, the test of "arrogation" has become "whose ox is gored." For me, the issue is: since the framers unmistakably

---

*Federal Power Comm'n v. Natural Gas Pipeline Co., 315 U.S. 575, 609 (1942) (Frankfurter, J., concurring).

[1] R. Berger, Government by Judiciary: The Transformation of the Fourteenth Amendment (1977).

[2] Reynolds v. Sims, 377 U.S. 533, 590–91 (1964) (Harlan, J., dissenting).

[3] Lusky, *"Government by Judiciary": What Price Legitimacy?,* 6 Hastings Const. L.Q. 403, 406 (1979).

[4] Nathanson, Book Review, 56 Tex L. Rev. 579, 580–81 (1978).

[5] Alfange, *On Judicial Policymaking and Constitutional Change: Another Look at the "Original Intent" Theory of Constitutional Interpretation,* 5 Hastings Const. L.Q. 603, 606–07 (1978); Kommers, *Role of the Supreme Court,* 40 Rev. of Pol. 409, 413 (1978); Beloff, Book Review, The Times (London), Apr. 7, 1978, (Higher Educ. Supp.), at II; Bridwell, Book Review, 1978 Duke L.J. 801, 803, 806, 807 n.32; Perry, Book Review, 78 Colum. L. Rev. 685, 687, 691 (1978).

[6] Oregon v. Mitchell, 400 U.S. 112, 203 (1970) (Harlan, J., concurring in part and dissenting in part).

[7] Perry, *supra* note 5, at 694.

[8] Alfred Kelly wrote that the Warren Court was determined "to carry through a constitutional equalitarian revolution." Kelly, *Clio and the Court: An Illicit Love Affair,* 1965 Sup. Ct. Rev. 119, 159.

[9] Kutler, *Raoul Berger's Fourteenth: A History or Ahistorical,* 6 Hastings Const. L.Q. 511, 514 (1979). To the same effect, R. Berger, *supra* note 1, at 312 (quoting Sutherland, *Privacy in Connecticut,* 64 Mich. L. Rev. 283, 284 (1965)).

excluded suffrage, whence does the Court derive power to reverse that decision by its "one-person-one-vote" doctrine?

The importance of that issue[10] led me to round out my study by a search of the records of the several Civil War and Reconstruction Congresses, in which sat some of the leading *dramatis personae* of the debates on the fourteenth amendment. Those records fortify my conclusions and confirm that racism and attachment to states' rights played a prominent role throughout, helping to explain why black entry into a white society was so incompletely realized.[11] As William Gillette, whose words bear the imprimatur of Professor David Donald,[12] a leading Reconstruction historian, wrote, "Most congressmen apparently did not intend to risk drowning by swimming against the treacherous current of racial prejudice and opposition to Negro suffrage"; "white Americans resented and resisted" it, and "Negro voting in the North—was out of the question."[13]

INTENT OF THE FRAMERS

In employing statements made by members of the Reconstruction Congresses,[14] the primary evidence is of course what was said in the Thirty-ninth Congress during the debates on the fourteenth amendment and the immediately related Civil Rights Act of 1866.[15] Next come utterances of the framers in subsequent Congresses which confirm their earlier statements. Subsequent utterances in conflict therewith are discounted on the premise that a later shift of opinion cannot contradict the earlier representations made to influence their fellows to adopt the amendment. Statements of nonframers, often in reliance on the earlier history, carry weight as contemporary constructions. While there was a division of opinion subsequent to the Thirty-ninth Congress, the utterances that confirm the earlier history considerably outnumber, on crucial points, those that take an opposing view. For some, political exigencies altered cases. Then there are statements that are *in pari materia,* for example, respecting the identical "Congress shall enforce" provisions

[10]Professor Philip Kurland stated that "the most immediate constitutional crisis of our present time [is] the usurpation by the judiciary of general governmental powers on the pretext that its authority derives from the Fourteenth Amendment." Letter from Philip Kurland to Harvard University Press (Aug. 15, 1977). In 1937 Professor Felix Frankfurter wrote to President Roosevelt that "the Supreme Court for about a quarter of a century has distorted the power of judicial review into a revision of legislative policy, thereby usurping powers belonging to the Congress and to the legislatures of the several States." ROOSEVELT AND FRANKFURTER: THEIR CORRESPONDENCE 384 (M. Freedman ed. 1967). The Warren Court went further still: it reversed the decisions of the framers and ratifiers of the fourteenth amendment.

[11]"Negrophobia tended to hold even the sparse Reconstruction institutions that the nation created at low throttle, and played a part in Reconstruction's incompleteness." H. HYAMN, A MORE PERFECT UNION 447 (1973). "The Republican platform of 1868 has carefully left the question of suffrage in the northern states up to the states themselves. It was evident, however, that when the issue was placed on the ballot in the various northern states, it was likely to be voted down." A. GRIMES, DEMOCRACY AND THE AMENDMENTS OF THE CONSTITUTION 53 (1978).

It needs to be remembered that ratification of the fourteenth amendment was made a condition of readmission to the Union, that in "June 1868, Arkansas, North Carolina, South Carolina, Georgia, Louisiana, Alabama and Florida were readmitted to the Union," and that these states were needed "to make the amendment valid as part of the Constitution." *Id.* at 50–51. "Ratification of the Fifteenth as well as of the Fourteenth Amendment was made a condition of readmission to the Union for Georgia, Texas, Virginia, and Mississippi. Without the required ratifications of these states, the Fifteenth Amendment would have failed. . . ." *Id.* at 58. In less polite terms, Northern opposition was circumvented by a compulsory Southern vote. Presumably, it was this that led Kenneth Stampp to write that neither the fourteenth nor the fifteenth amendments "could have been adopted under any other circumstances, or at any other time, before or since. . . ." *Id.* at 55 (quoting Stampp, *The Tragic Legend of Reconstruction,* in RECONSTRUCTION: AN ANTHOLOGY OF REVISIONIST WRITINGS 11–12 (K. Stampp & Litwack eds. 1968)). *But see* Walter Murphy, text accompanying note 17 *infra.*

[12]W. GILLETTE, THE RIGHT TO VOTE: POLITICS AND THE PASSAGE OF THE FIFTEENTH AMENDMENT 15 (1965). His "mentor" Professor "Donald read early drafts, weighed every word, and practically tested every piece of evidence." *Id.*

[13]*Id.* at 25, 27, 32.

[14]I confine myself almost entirely to statements by Republicans, excluding the Democratic opposition.

[15]Civil Rights Act of 1866, ch. 31 §§ 1-10, 14 Stat. 27 (codified at 42 U.S.C. §§ 1981–1982 (1976)).

of the fourteenth's section 5 and fifteenth's section 2 frequently made by men who participated in framing both.

Influence of Racism

It needs immediately to be stressed that the influence of racism and attachment to states' rights merely furnish the background of my earlier study; they help to explain the attitude of the framers. Reliance was placed rather upon their *statements* that suffrage and segregation were to be excluded. John Hart Ely, however, insists that adoption of the fifteenth amendment "only two years later" is "fatal . . . to Berger's general claim of the dominance of 'Negrophobia.'"[16] And Walter Murphy states that "Berger probably overestimates the prevalence of that neurosis among leaders of the Republican party."[17] But a Reconstruction historian, Morton Keller, observes that "most congressional Republicans were aware of (and shared) their constituents' hostility to black suffrage."[18] Let us descend from Murphy's "gossamery guesses" to some "brute facts."[19] In the midst of the Civil War a delegation of Negro leaders called on Lincoln, and he told them:

> There is an unwillingness on the part of our people, harsh as it may be, for you free colored people to remain with us . . . even when you cease to be slaves, you are far removed from being placed on an equality with the white man . . . I cannot alter it if I would. It is a fact.[20]

Lest this seem an aberrant utterance by a sadly harassed President, upon whose Gettysburg Address Chief Justice Warren later relied,[21] it needs to be shown that it was but a reflection of predominant Northern sentiment.

Francis Blair of Missouri referred to Lincoln's program for "separation of the races" by colonization.[22] A Report by the House Select Committee on Emancipation, July 16, 1862, proposed "an amount of twenty millions of dollars . . . for the purposes of colonization," and explained that

> [m]uch of the objection to emancipation arises from the opposition of a large portion of our people to the intermixture of the races, and from the association [*i.e.,* feared competition] of white and black labor. The committee would do nothing to favor such a policy; apart from the antipathy which nature has ordained, the presence of a race among us who cannot, and ought not to, be admitted to our social and political privileges, will be a perpetual source of injury and inquietude to both.
>
> . . . .
>
> . . . Without this equality of political and social privileges . . . the emancipation of the slaves . . . will be but adding a new burden to their wretchedness. . . . [I]n proportion as the legal barriers established by slavery have been removed by emancipation, the prejudice of caste becomes stronger, and public opinion more intolerant to the negro race.
>
> . . . How, then, can the separation of the races after emancipation be accomplished? Colonization appears to be the only mode in which this can be done. . . . Hayti and others of the West India islands,

---

[16]Ely, *Constitutional Interpretivism: Its Allure and Impossibility,* 53 IND. L.J. 399, 436 n.133 (1978) (emphasis omitted); Gibbons, Book Review, 31 RUTGERS L. REV. 839, 845 (1978). *See* notes 31–39 and accompanying text *infra.*

[17]Murphy, Book Review, 87 YALE L.J. 1752, 1768 n.81 (1978). Nevertheless, those leaders bowed to public opinion in the Republican platform of 1868, leaving suffrage in the North to the states. A. GRIMES, note 11 *supra.*

[18]R. BERGER, *supra* note 1, at 105 (quoting M. KELLER, AFFAIRS OF STATE 67 (1977)). *See* W. GILLETTE, notes 12–13 and accompanying text *supra.*

[19]Murphy wrote, "The *message* of this review is that Berger's argument relies far less on 'brute facts' about whatever it was the framers intended and more on incomplete research and gossamery guesses about what they had in mind." Murphy, *supra* note 17, at 1768 n.81 (emphasis added). For Murphy's feet of clay, see Berger, *The Scope of Judicial Review and Walter Murphy,* 1979 WIS. L. REV. 341, 343.

[20]R. BERGER, *supra* note 1, at 12 (quoting C. WOODWARD, THE BURDEN OF SOUTHERN HISTORY 81 (1960)).

[21]*Id.* at 85 (quoting Reynolds v. Sims, 377 U.S. 533, 558 (1964) (quoting Gray v. Sanders, 372 U.S. 368, 381 (1963))).

[22]CONG. GLOBE, 37th Cong., 2d Sess. 1633 (1862) (remarks of Rep. Blair), *reprinted in* VIRGINIA COMM'N ON CONSTITUTIONAL GOVERNMENT, THE RECONSTRUCTION AMENDMENTS' DEBATES 36 (A. AVINS ed. 1967) [hereinafter cited as A. AVINS]. The Avins compilation is a compendious and convenient reprint of almost all of the relevant debates.

Central America and the upper portions of South America and Liberia, are all interesting fields of inquiry in relation to the future of the liberated negroes of the United States.[23]

In the Senate, James Doolittle of Wisconsin, and Orville Browning and Lyman Trumbull of Illinois spoke up for colonization.[24] But Senator John Hale of New Hampshire and others pointed out that such schemes were utterly impractical, that the transportation of millions of Negroes would require an astronomical shipping fleet. As Hale remarked, "[T]he whole Navy of the United States could not carry off the annual increase."[25] Then too, Glenni Scofield of Pennsylvania emphasized, it was impossibly costly to transport them to a foreign shore.[26] Senator Timothy Howe of Wisconsin reminded the Senate that a similar effort to transport "emancipated Negroes of the District of Columbia to Haiti" failed utterly; the colony returned.[27] So colonization was discarded, but the intractable prejudice it evidenced remained. The Indiana Radical, George Julian, had told the House in the Thirty-ninth Congress which framed the fourteenth amendment, "the real trouble is *we hate the Negro*," a remark echoed by others.[28] In the Senate, John Sherman of Ohio said, "[W]e do not like Negroes. We do not conceal our dislike."[29]

During the debates on the fifteenth amendment, Senator Henry Wilson, a Radical Republican from Massachusetts, stated, "There is not to-day a square mile in the United States where the advocacy of the equal rights and privileges of those colored men has not been . . . and is not now unpopular."[30] And Senator Sherman prophesied that "no change" was "likely to excite so much popular feeling as this proposed change to extend to the negro race in Ohio the elective franchise."[31]

[23]H.R. REP. No. 148, 37th Cong., 2d Sess. 13–16 (1862), *reprinted in* A. AVINS, *supra* note 22, at 30–31. Tocqueville had noticed in the North that "the prejudice which repels the negroes seems to increase in proportion as they are emancipated." R. BERGER, *supra* note 1, at 11 (quoting 1 A. DE TOCQUEVILLE, DEMOCRACY IN AMERICA 365 (1900)). Fear that the emancipated slaves would flock north in droves alarmed the North. *Id.* at 12 (quoting C. WOODWARD, THE BURDEN OF SOUTHERN HISTORY127–28, 131–32 (1960)). The policy was "to protect white labor." *Id.* at 12 n.37 (quoting CONG. GLOBE, 39th Cong., 1st Sess. 2939 (1866) (remarks of Sen. Hendricks)).

Samuel Cox, a Democrat of Ohio, stated on June 3, 1962, that "[t]he last Legislature of Ohio, by their committee" reported that "[t]he negro race is looked upon by the people of Ohio as a class . . . to be debarred of social intercourse with the whites. . . ." CONG. GLOBE, 37th Cong., 2d Sess. app. 245 (1862) (remarks of Rep. Cox), *reprinted in* A. AVINS, *supra* note 22, at 42. In 1867 Senator John Sherman of Ohio said, "[W]e do not like Negroes. We do not conceal our dislike." R. BERGER, *supra* note 1, at 233 (quoting Woodward, *Seeds of Failure in Radical Racial Policy*, in NEW FRONTIERS OF THE AMERICAN RECONSTRUCTION 128 (H. Hyman ed. 1966)).

[24]CONG. GLOBE, 37th Cong., 2d Sess. 1191 (remarks of Sen. Doolittle), 1520 (remarks of Sen. Browning), 1604 (remarks of Sen. Trumbull) (1862), *reprinted in* A. AVINS, *supra* note 22, at 32, 34, 35.

[25]*Id.* at 1605 (remarks of Sen. Hale), *reprinted in* A. AVINS, *supra* note 22, at 35.

[26]CONG. GLOBE, 39th Cong., 1st Sess. 178 (1866) (remarks of Rep. Scofield,) *reprinted in* A. AVINS, *supra* note 22, at 102.

[27]CONG. GLOBE, 40th Cong., 2d Sess. 883 (1868) (remarks of Sen. Howe), *reprinted in* A. AVINS, *supra* note 22, at 290.

[28]R. BERGER, *supra* note 1, at 13 (quoting CONG. GLOBE, 39th Cong., 1st Sess. 257 (1866) (remarks of Rep. Julian) (emphasis in original)). *See also id.* at 233 (quoting CONG. GLOBE, 39th Cong., 1st Sess. 739 (remarks of Sen. Lane), 911 (remarks of Rep. Cullom), 2799 (remarks of Sen. Stewart) (1866)).

[29]*Id.* at 233 (quoting C. WOODWARD, THE BURDEN OF SOUTHERN HISTORY 128 (1960)). *See note 23 supra.*

[30]CONG. GLOBE, 40th Cong., 3d Sess. 672 (1869) (remarks of Sen. Wilson), *reprinted in* A. AVINS, *supra* note 22, at 340. Adverting to the 1867 fall elections, Senator Sherman said the Republicans submitted the "rugged issue" of suffrage to the Ohio electorate but "[i]t was an unpopular issue . . . upon which all the prejudices of the people could be rallied against us." CONG. GLOBE, 40th Cong., 2d Sess. 877 (1868) (remarks of Sen. Sherman), *reprinted in* A. AVINS, *supra* note 22, at 289. Senator Wilson said of that election, "The defeat of manhood suffrage in several of the States . . . is another evidence of the melancholy fact" that all Republicans "have not conquered their prejudices." *Id.* at 40 (remarks of Sen. Wilson), *reprinted in* A. AVINS, *supra* note 22, at 285. Gillette characterizes it as a "devastating defeat." W. GILLETTE, *supra* note 12, at 32.

[31]CONG. GLOBE, 40th Cong., 3d Sess. 1039 (1869) (remarks of Sen. Sherman), *reprinted in* A. AVINS, *supra* note 22, at 387. During the debate on the Civil Rights Act of 1875, Senator Aaron Sargent of California stated on May 22, 1874, that "a powerful prejudice exists in every part of the country." 2 CONG. REC. 4172 (1874) (remarks of Sen. Sargent), *reprinted in* A. AVINS, *supra* note 22, at 705. For an encapsulated account of the passage of the fifteenth amendment, see A. GRIMES, *supra* note 11, at 51–59.

Writing of the "fight for ratification" of the fifteenth amendment, William Gillette stated: "[P]ublic opinion strongly opposed Negro rights, and the state legislatures who outraged this consensus would commit political suicide."[32]

The fifteenth amendment, therefore, does not testify to abatement of racial prejudice; instead, it was a response to shifting political exigencies. The primary goal, Gillette concluded, was enfranchisement of Negroes "outside the deep South," in order to obtain the necessary swing vote of Negroes in the North. A secondary objective, he wrote, "was to protect the southern Negro against future disfranchisement,"[33] for it had become apparent that military occupation must come to an end and continued control must rest on Negro voters, again aimed to perpetuate Republican ascendancy.[34] Whether the Northern or Southern vote played a greater role in Republican calculations is for present purposes of no moment; it suffices that the drive for the fifteenth amendment was political in origin. Thaddeus Stevens, leader of the Radicals, began drafting the amendment "to save the Republican party from defeat. . . ."[35] Senator Oliver Morton of Indiana, who had opposed Negro suffrage, now embraced it "as a political necessity."[36] With Negro votes the Republicans could hope to stay in power, *the* primary aim from the very beginning.[37] The motivation, in short, was "largely political, not humanitarian, in origin."[38]

Suffrage Was Left to the States

Proof in Section 2 of the Fourteenth.—In addition to the framers' statements of their intention to exclude suffrage, the structure of the amendment affords telling proof. Section 2, roughly speaking, provided that if suffrage was denied on racial grounds, the state's representation in the House should be reduced accordingly. Manifestly this left suffrage in the hands of the states, subject to reduction of representation for its discriminatory denial.[39] Interesting light on the genesis of

[32]W. GILLETTE, *supra* note 12, at 80. *See also* A. GRIMES, *supra* note 11, at 88, 146.

[33]W. GILLETTE, *supra* note 12, at 46–47, 49–50.

[34]For reliance on the Northern Negro, see the statements of Stevens and Boutwell of Massachusetts quoted in *id.* at 35, 47. See also the remarks of Senator Charles Sumner. CONG. GLOBE, 40th Cong., 1st Sess. 439 (1867), *reprinted in* A. AVINS, *supra* note 22, at 273; CONG. GLOBE, 40th Cong., 3d Sess. 904 (1869), *reprinted in* A. AVINS, *supra* note 22, at 359.

Respecting Southern votes, Halbert Paine of Wisconsin stated, "We saw there was no safety . . . except upon the solid rock of reconstruction; that to such loyal reconstruction loyal majorities were indispensable; . . . [that we] must either have black votes or not have the majorities." CONG. GLOBE, 40th Cong., 2d Sess. 578 (1868) (remarks of Rep. Paine), *reprinted in* A. AVINS, *supra* note 22, at 288. Senator James Patterson of New Hampshire declared, "[Y]ou must either give them indefinite military rule . . . or you must create a black voting population." *Id.* at 2899, *reprinted in* A. AVINS, *supra* note 22, at 327. *See id.* at 1408, *reprinted in* A. AVINS, *supra* note 22, at 296. For remarks of a similar tenor, see generally CONG. GLOBE, 42d Cong. 1st Sess. 349 (1871) (remarks of Sen. Morton), *reprinted in* A. AVINS, *supra* note 22, at 503; CONG. GLOBE, 40th Cong., 2d Sess. 4142 (1868) (remarks of Rep. Van Horn), *reprinted in* A. AVINS, *supra* note 22, at 334; *id.* at app. 166 (remarks of Rep. Benton), *reprinted in* A. AVINS, *supra* note 22, at 298; *id.* at 1969 (remarks of Rep. Beaman), *reprinted in* A. AVINS, *supra* note 22, at 305; *id.* at 725–26 (remarks of Sen. Morton), *reprinted in* A. AVINS, *supra* note 22, at 288–89. Samuel Shellabarger of Ohio "stated the widespread view that the loyal state governments in the South would collapse without loyal negro voters to support such governments, . . ." W. GILLETTE, *supra* note 12, at 50.

Similarly, measures to curb the Ku Klux Klan sprang in no inconsiderable part from the fear that the Klan intimidated Republican voters and sought ascendancy of the Democratic party. CONG. GLOBE, 42d Cong., 1st Sess. 321 (1871) (remarks of Rep. Stoughton), *reprinted in* A. AVINS, *supra* note 22, at 500; *id.* at 412–13 (remarks of Rep. Roberts), *reprinted in* A. AVINS, *supra* note 22, at 520–21. Senator Morton stated that the Klan "proposes to gain the supremacy by driving Republicans into submission or silence. . . ." *Id.* at app. 253 (remarks of Sen. Morton), *reprinted in* A. AVINS, *supra* note 22, at 525. *See also id.* at 459 (remarks of Rep. Coburn), *reprinted in* A. AVINS, *supra* note 22, at 534.

[35]W. GILLETTE, *supra* note 12, at 34.

[36]*Id.* at 57.

[37]*Id.* at 87, 90, 99. *See* CONG. GLOBE, 40th Cong., 2d Sess. 706 (1868) (remarks of Sen. Doolittle), *reprinted in* A. AVINS, *supra* note 22, at 288; R. BERGER, *supra* note 1, at 16 (quoting CONG. GLOBE, 39th Cong., 1st Sess. 74 (1865) (remarks of Rep. Stevens)); *id.* at 52–53 (quoting CONG. GLOBE, 39th Cong., 1st Sess. app. 94 (1865) (remarks of Sen. Williams)).

[38]W. GILLETTE, *supra* note 12, at 146.

[39]R. BERGER, *supra* note 1, at 64–68.

this provision was cast by Senator William Fessenden of Maine, Chairman of the Joint Committee on Reconstruction. On February 9, 1869, he read extracts from the Journal of the Committee, showing he had proposed that denials of suffrage on account of race should be "inoperative and void."[40] But the hard-nosed, realistic Radical leader, Thaddeus Stevens, moved that such discrimination should merely be followed by reduction of representation, true to his candid avowal that the main goal was to perpetuate Republican ascendancy.[41] "Consequently," Fessenden recounted, he "was directed to report [that representation] amendment, which . . . does recognize most distinctly the power, which nobody at the time denied, of the States to regulate suffrage. . . ."[42] Senator Jacob Howard, a member of the committee, had explained to the Thirty-ninth Congress that "[t]he Second section leaves the right to regulate the elective franchise with the States. . . ."[43] The draftsman of the fourteenth amendment, John Bingham of Ohio, said in the House, "The amendment does not give, as the [second] section shows, the power of regulating suffrage in the several States."[44] So the Report of the Joint Committee on Reconstruction confirms.[45] That Report, widely distributed,[46] was, as Howard stated in May, 1870, "accepted throughout the loyal part of the United States and by the Republican party universally and without dissent."[47] Except for a few, like George Boutwell of Massachusetts, who had signed the Report, but suffered a lapse of memory when this history was recalled to him,[48] the members of Congress confirmed that section

[40]CONG. GLOBE, 40th Cong., 3d Sess. 1032–33 (1869) (remarks of Sen. Fessenden), *reprinted in* A. AVINS, *supra* note 22, at 381.

[41]R. BERGER, *supra* note 1, at 16. *See* note 35 *supra*. Speaking to such a proposal in the Thirty-ninth Congress, Stevens said:

I hold that the States have the right . . . to fix the elective franchise within their own States. And I hold that this [§ 2] does not take it from them. . . . How many [states] would allow Congress to come within their jurisdiction to fix the qualification of their voters? . . . [Y]ou could not get five in this Union.

R. BERGER, *supra* note 1, at 62 (quoting CONG. GLOBE, 39th Cong., 1st Sess. 536 (1866) (remarks of Rep. Stevens)). For similar Stevens statements see *id.* at 109, 420, 422–23 (quoting THE JOURNAL OF THE JOINT COMMITTEE OF FIFTEEN ON RECONSTRUCTION 350 (B. Kendrick comp. 1914)); CONG. GLOBE, 39th Cong., 1st Sess. 428 (1866) (remarks of Reps. Higby and Stevens).

And he signed the Report of the Joint Committee which stated that suffrage was left with the states. R. BERGER, *supra* note 1, at 84. *See* note 45 *infra*. Against this, his statement on March 18, 1868, that the fourteenth amendment "settles the whole question and places every American on a perfect equality" so that "suffrage throughout this nation is impartial and universal" offers a sad commentary on political morality. CONG. GLOBE, 39th Cong., 2d Sess. 1966–67 (1868), *reprinted in* A. AVINS, *supra* note 22, at 304–05.

[42]CONG. GLOBE, 40th Cong., 3d Sess. 1033 (1869) (remarks of Sen. Fessenden), *reprinted in* A. AVINS, *supra* note 22, at 381.

[43]R. BERGER, *supra* note 1, at 65–66 (quoting CONG. GLOBE, 39th Cong., 1st Sess. 2766 (1866) (remarks of Sen. Howard)).

[44]*Id.* at 65 (quoting CONG. GLOBE, 39th Cong., 1st Sess. 2542 (1866) (remarks of Rep. Bingham)).

[45]S. REP. NO. 112, 39th Cong., 1st Sess. 7 (1866) (Report of the Joint Committee on Reconstruction), *reprinted in* A. AVINS, *supra* note 22, at 94 [hereinafter cited as JOINT COMMITTEE REPORT].

[46]A. AVINS, *supra* note 22, at vi.

[47]CONG. GLOBE, 41st Cong., 2d Sess. 3614 (1870) (remarks of Sen. Howard), *reprinted in* A. AVINS, *supra* note 22, at 448.

[48]JOINT COMMITTEE REPORT, *supra note 45, at 1, reprinted in* A. AVINS, *supra* note 22, at 94. When Boutwell was twitted by John Nicholson, a Delaware Democrat, whether he had not conceded "[t]hat this fourteenth article would not confer political rights" upon blacks, he replied, "I have no recollection of anything of that sort. . . ." CONG. GLOBE, 40th Cong., 3d Sess. 559 (1869) (remarks of Reps. Nicholson and Boutwell), *reprinted in* A. AVINS, *supra* note 22, at 336. But in the Thirty-ninth Congress he had stated, "The proposition in the matter of suffrage falls far short of what I desire . . . I demand the franchise for all loyal male citizens. . . ." R. BERGER, *supra* note 1, at 68 n.70 (quoting CONG. GLOBE, 39th Cong., 1st Sess. 2508 (1866) (remarks of Rep. Boutwell)); and he signed the Joint Committee Report stating that suffrage had been left with the states. JOINT COMMITTEE REPORT, *supra* note 45, at 1, *reprinted in* A. AVINS, *supra* note 22, at 94. He later said that the purpose of the fifteenth amendment was "to secure to the slave class the right to vote." CONG. GLOBE, 40th Cong., 3d Sess. 1225 (1869) (remarks of Rep. Boutwell), *reprinted in* A. AVINS, *supra* note 22, at 390; and said "there is a very general agreement that it is desirable to submit an amendment to the Constitution . . .," *i.e.*, the fifteenth. *Id.* at 725, *reprinted in* A. AVINS, *supra* note 22, at 349.

2 left suffrage with the states. Because Justice Brennan questioned this history, in particular the meaning of section 2,[49] the overwhelming refutation of such views contained in the debates on the fifteenth amendment deserves to be recorded in some detail.

Senator Howard declared on February 8, 1869, that "this is the first time it ever occurred to me that the right to vote was to be derived from the fourteenth article." That construction, he said, "is plainly and flatly contradicted by what follows in the second section . . . a plain, indubitable recognition and admission on the very face and by the very terms of this fourteenth amendment of the right and power of each State to regulate the qualification of voters."[50] Senator Charles Sumner immediately responded. "The Senator is aware that that was denied at that time, and it would not have passed had anybody attributed to it that meaning. That I am able to say. It could not have passed in the Senate."[51] It is such arrant misrepresentations that vitiate Sumner's credibility. Responding to such views, Senator Aaron Cragin of New Hampshire declared:

[W]hen I remember that it was announced upon this floor by more than one gentleman, and contradicted and denied by no one so far as I recollect, that [the fourteenth] amendment did not confer the right of voting upon anybody, I say I am surprised that such a position should be taken at this late hour in the debate. There is no doubt upon the question. It was the understanding of Congress and of the people of this country that the amendment did not confer and did not seek to confer any right to vote upon citizen. . . .[52]

After reading section 2, Senator Henderson said that the fourteenth amendment "clearly permits the State to exclude, for any reason whatever, the male inhabitants of the State from the suffrage."[53] Similar views were expressed by other framers, Senators Roscoe Conkling of New York and James Dixon of Connecticut, James Doolittle of Wisconsin, Frederick Frelinghuysen of New Jersey, Oliver Morton of Indiana, and Lyman Trumbull of Illinois.[54] Senator Daniel Norton of Minnesota "supposed the report of the committee and the amendment they proposed left suffrage with the States," to which the chairman of the committee, Senator William Fessenden, replied, "The Senator is perfectly correct in his supposition."[55]

In the House, Fernando Beaman of Michigan, likewise a framer, declared that section 2 "left it entirely in the power of those white rebels to say whether or not the negro is a man and entitled to use the ballot, subject only to the condition that if they should decide adversely, he should not be represented."[56] Even that far-out radical, William Higby of California, upon whom reliance for an activist construction has been placed,[57] said of section 2, "Clearly there is an implied authority in the States, from the reading of this section to control in a greater or less degree the right of

[49]Oregon v. Mitchell, 400 U.S. 112, 255–56 (Brennan, J., concurring in part and dissenting in part). *See* R. BERGER, *supra* note 1, at 90–98.

[50]CONG. GLOBE, 40th Cong., 3d Sess. 1003 (1869) (remarks of Sen. Howard), *reprinted in* A. AVINS, *supra* note 22, at 373.

[51]*Id.*

[52]*Id.* at 1004 (remarks of Sen. Cragin). This is borne out by the history of § 2. *See* R. BERGER, *supra* note 1, at 64–68.

[53]CONG. GLOBE, 40th Cong., 2d Sess. 2606 (1868) (remarks of Sen. Henderson), *reprinted in* A. AVINS, *supra* note 22, at 322.

[54]*Id.* at 2665, 2698, 2699 (remarks of Sens. Conkling, Doolittle, and Trumbull), *reprinted in* A. AVINS, *supra* note 22, at 323; *id.* at 725 (remarks of Sen. Morton), *reprinted in* A. AVINS, *supra* note 22, at 289; *id.* at app. 238 (remarks of Sen. Dixon), *reprinted in* A. AVINS, *supra* note 22, at 299; CONG. GLOBE, 40th Cong., 3d Sess. 979 (1879) (remarks of Sen. Frelinghuysen), *reprinted in* A. AVINS, *supra* note 22, at 364–65.

[55]CONG. GLOBE, 40th Cong., 3d Sess. 1033 (1869) (remarks of Sens. Norton and Fessenden), *reprinted in* A. AVINS, *supra* note 22, at 382.

[56]CONG. GLOBE, 40th Cong., 2d Sess. 1969 (1868) (remarks of Rep. Beaman), *reprinted in* A. AVINS, *supra* note 22, at 305.

[57]R. BERGER, *supra* note 1, at 79–80, 420.

suffrage. . . ." Of section 1 he said, "It would seem that every right pertaining to citizenship was conferred, and yet the language of the second section implies that a State may deny or abridge the right of a citizen to vote."[58] Similar statements were made by Burton Cook of Illinois, James Ashley of Ohio, and George Miller of Pennsylvania.[59] Such views were given formal expression in a Senate Judiciary Committee Report of January 25, 1872, addressed to a petition for women's suffrage: "It is evident from the second section of this amendment above quoted that the States are considered to possess the power of excluding a portion of their male citizens from the right to vote, upon grounds or reasons to be determined by themselves. . . ."[60]

Confirmation in the Fifteenth Amendment.—A few years after ratification of the fifteenth amendment the Supreme Court held it testified that suffrage was not conferred by the fourteenth.[61] No doubt was left by the framers of the fifteenth that it was conceived to fill the gap. So, Senator Frelinghuysen could not "conclude that the fourteenth amendment confers on Congress the right to regulate suffrage. We want a further amendment."[62] The proposed amendment, said Senator Dixon, "is acknowledged by every Senator who has participated in the debate, to be a most important change in the policy of this Government. Heretofore the question of suffrage has been left wholly to the States."[63] Consequently, said Senator Timothy Howe of Wisconsin, "The great purpose is to strip from [the states] the power to exclude from the right of suffrage men who happen to be colored. . . ."[64] The proposed amendment, Senator Howard observed, "is the only attempt which has been made since the foundation of the government to interfere with this right of the States to prescribe the qualifications of voters. . . ."[65] Later, Senator Morton declared, "It was well understood in the adoption of the fourteenth amendment that it was not intended to extend or to cover the right of suffrage. . . . Then we come to the fifteenth amendment. That was

---

[58]Cong. Globe, 40th Cong., 3d Sess. app. 294 (1869) (remarks of Rep. Higby), *reprinted in* A. Avins, *supra* note 22, at 417.

[59]Cong. Globe, 40th Cong., 2d Sess. 2402 (1868) (remarks of Rep. Cook), *reprinted in* A. Avins, *supra* note 22, at 313; Cong. Globe, 40th Cong., 3d Sess. app. 92 (remarks of Rep. Miller), *reprinted in* A. Avins, *supra* note 22, at 341. James Ashley of Ohio said, "I voted with great reluctance for the amendment submitted by the Thirty Ninth Congress because it did not secure the ballot but left the question to the States with a kind of coercive, bribing, penal clause, which seemed to me unworthy of the Congress." Cong. Globe, 40th Cong., 2d Sess. 117 (1867) (remarks of Rep. Ashley), *reprinted in* A. Avins, *supra* note 22, at 286. He overlooked that the Republicans regarded it as more important to maintain Republican ascendancy than to confer black suffrage. *See* note 41 and accompanying text *supra*; R. Berger, *supra* note 1, at 66 (quoting Cong. Globe, 40th Cong., 1st Sess. 141 (1866) (remarks of Rep. Blaine)).

Similar remarks were made by Senator Henry Corbett of Oregon, Cong. Globe, 40th Cong., 3d Sess. 938 (1869) (remarks of Sen. Corbett), *reprinted in* A. Avins, *supra* note 22, at 363; James Dixon of Connecticut, Cong. Globe, 40th Cong., 2d Sess. app. 238 (1868) (remarks of Sen. Dixon), *reprinted in* A. Avins, *supra* note 22, at 299; George Edmunds of Vermont ("want of power" to pass a suffrage bill), Cong. Globe, 40th Cong., 1st Sess. 614 (1867) (remarks of Sen. Edmunds), *reprinted in* A. Avins, *supra* note 22, at 276.

Reconstructing the debates in the Thirty-ninth Congress, Senator Richard Yates of Illinois observed, "It was said that the African . . . had no right to vote. And after a long debate it was decided by the Senate upon that interpretation," an interpretation opposed to his own, but he was ready to "secure by a constitutional amendment [the fifteenth] what I have failed to secure. . . ." Cong. Globe, 40th Cong., 3d Sess. 1004 (1869) (remarks of Sen. Yates), *reprinted in* A. Avins, *supra* note 22, at 374.

[60]S. Rep. No. 21, 42d Cong., 2d Sess. 3 (1872), *reprinted in* A. Avins, *supra* note 22, at 572.

[61]Minor v. Haperstett, 88 U.S. (21 Wall.) 162, 175 (1874).

[62]Cong. Globe, 40th Cong., 3d Sess. 979 (1869) (remarks of Sen. Frelinghuysen), *reprinted in* A. Avins, *supra* note 22, at 365. *See* note 59 *supra*, remarks of Senator Yates. Senator Morton had maintained that "suffrage in the States could not be controlled by Congress, and that it was this conviction upon the part of a majority in this body that led subsequently to the adoption of the fifteenth amendment." Cong. Globe, 41st Cong., 2d Sess. app. 275 (1870) (remarks of Sen. Morton), *reprinted in* A. Avins, *supra* note 22, at 435. *See also id.* at 3571, *reprinted in* A. Avins, *supra* note 22, at 442.

[63]Cong. Globe, 40th Cong., 3d Sess. 1030 (1869) (remarks of Sen. Dixon), *reprinted in* A. Avins, *supra* note 22, at 380.

[64]*Id.* at 1040 (remarks of Sen. Howe), *reprinted in* A. Avins, *supra* note 22, at 388; to the same effect Senator Conkling, *id.* at 1315, *reprinted in* A. Avins, *supra* note 22, at 404.

[65]*Id.* at 985 (remarks of Sen. Howard), *reprinted in* A. Avins, *supra* note 22, at 367.

found to be necessary."[66] Similar utterances during the fifteenth amendment debates were made by Senators Waltman Willey of West Virginia, Richard Yates of Illinois, and James Nye of Nevada.[67] Dissent was negligible. When Senator Edmunds opined that section 1 of the fourteenth amendment conferred the right to vote, Senator Charles Drake of Missouri immediately replied that the proposition was unsound.[68] Senator Wilson was of a mixed mind. At first he said, "I have not the shadow of a doubt that we have the right" under the fourteenth amendment to confer "universal suffrage,"[69] but subsequently noted that the fourteenth amendment clothed freedmen with "civil rights" and that the proposed fifteenth amendment denied "to States the power to withhold suffrage on account of race," reiterating that he would vote "for securing suffrage."[70]

The vastly preponderant view that the fifteenth amendment was required to fill a gap likewise found expression in the House. As John Broomall of Pennsylvania stated, "The proposition before the House is so to change the Constitution of the United States that no State shall hereafter discriminate among citizens of the United States with respect to the right of suffrage. . . ."[71] Benjamin Butler of Massachusetts proposed, "Let us take away that power of disfranchisement by the States by constitutional amendment. . . ."[72] So far as I could find, there was little or no dissent but, rather, abundant confirmation. So William Higby stated, "The amendment proposed . . . insures certain rights . . . not expressed in any part of the Constitution."[73] Were it adopted, Bingham said, "it would be henceforth out of the power of any State of the Union to discriminate. . . ."[74] There were similar statements by Samuel Shellabarger of Ohio and Glenni Scofield.[75] George Boutwell declared, "There is a very general agreement that it is desirable to submit an amendment. . . ."[76]

In sum, the history of the fifteenth amendment confirms beyond a doubt that no suffrage was conferred by the fourteenth. For this we have the testimony of framers which corroborates the views they or their confreres expressed in the Thirty-ninth Congress; the nonframers' utterances carry weight as contemporary constructions that do not contradict but confirm the history of the fourteenth amendment. Is it too much to hope that this detailed documentation will serve to still further useless debate on this score so that academe may focus on the more important issues raised by this history?

State Power over Apportionment

Related to the subject of suffrage is the problem of malapportionment, which gave rise to the "one-person-one-vote" doctrine, a doctrine some would defend because the subject "was not even

---

[66]2 CONG. REC. app. 359 (1874) (remarks of Sen. Morton), *reprinted in* A. AVINS, *supra* note 22, at 684.

[67]CONG. GLOBE, 40th Cong., 3d Sess. 911 (1869) (remarks of Sen. Willey), *reprinted in* A. AVINS, *supra* note 22, at 361; *id.* at 1006 (remarks of Sen. Yates), *reprinted in* A. AVINS, *supra* note 22, at 374; *id.* at 1306 (remarks of Sen. Nye), *reprinted in* A. AVINS, *supra* note 22, at 400.

[68]*Id.* at 1000 (remarks of Sens. Edmunds and Drake), *reprinted in* A. AVINS, *supra* note 22, at 371. Charles Sumner "opposed any amendment on the subject as being both unnecessary and politically inexpedient." A. GRIMES, *supra* note 11, at 56. But Sumner was almost always out of step with his Republican colleagues. *See* text accompanying notes 98–108 *infra*.

[69]CONG. GLOBE, 40th Cong., 1st Sess. 440 (1867) (remarks of Sen. Wilson), *reprinted in* A. AVINS, *supra* note 22, at 273.

[70]CONG. GLOBE, 40th Cong., 3d Sess. app. 153 (1869) (remarks of Sen. Wilson), *reprinted in* A. AVINS, *supra* note 22, at 370.

[71]*Id.* at app. 102 (remarks of Rep. Broomall), *reprinted in* A. AVINS, *supra* note 22, at 353.

[72]*Id.* at 725 (remarks of Rep. Butler), *reprinted in* A. AVINS, *supra* note 22, at 348.

[73]*Id.* at app. 294 (remarks of Rep. Higby), *reprinted in* A. AVINS, *supra* note 22, at 417.

[74]*Id.* at 1225 (remarks of Rep. Bingham), *reprinted in* A. AVINS, *supra* note 22, at 391.

[75]*Id.* at app. 99 (remarks of Rep. Shellabarger), *reprinted in* A. AVINS, *supra* note 22, at 348; *id.* at 725 (remarks of Rep. Scofield), *reprinted in* A. AVINS, *supra* note 22, at 349.

[76]*Id.* at 725 (remarks of Rep. Boutwell), *reprinted in* A. AVINS, *supra* note 22, at 349.

mentioned in the debates,"[77] from which it allegedly follows that history does not foreclose the use of the fourteenth amendment to reapportion. Nonmention is a feeble justification for reading "general" words to invade traditional state control of suffrage in the teeth of the tenth amendment's reservation of powers not delegated. Not content to rest on that presumption, my study set forth materials showing acceptance of malapportionment as a settled practice.[78] A number of confirmatory facts may here be added. Bingham, who was to draft the fourteenth amendment, said in 1862 that "*all* political rights must be controlled by the majority," and that the "Federal Government has no power to *regulate* the elective franchise in any State. . . ."[79] In the Thirty-ninth Congress, Senator Trumbull stated that the Civil Rights Bill of 1866, regarded without dissent as "identical" with the fourteenth amendment,[80] had "nothing to do with the right of suffrage, or any other political right. . . ."[81]

In March, 1867, Senator Drake quoted a complaint in the House by a Maryland representative that 150,000 whites in fifteen counties had fifteen members of the state senate, whereas the remaining 500,000 whites had only nine so that the majority did not rule. On these facts, said Drake, Maryland did not enjoy a republican form of government,[82] a view rejected by the Senate Judiciary Committee with respect to similar apportionment in Florida.[83] More important, Drake did not say that these facts conflicted with the fourteenth amendment. Similar practices in an adjoining "little State" (Delaware) under the aegis of the Democratic party were arraigned by Washington Townsend of Pennsylvania, in the hope that "the sovereign people of that State will not permit themselves to suffer much longer this grievous wrong,"[84] recognition that the remedy was for the state, not the federal government.

Such views reflected a deep-seated attachment to states' rights, once more recently noticed by Professor Don Fehrenbacher, a "widespread and tenacious resistance to the interventionism federalism aggressively embodied"[85] in the Reconstruction program. That this "resistance" was a very important factor in confining the fourteenth amendment to a narrow compass has been widely recognized.[86] Here it may be useful to note that it persisted and found frequent utterance in the subsequent debates. So, Senator Lot Morrill rightly declared in 1872, "This Government of ours is dual in its character, national and State. The national is derived; it has no more power than is expressly given and what results from obvious implication. The rest is with the people,"[87] under the tenth amendment. One who unlike Morrill read the fourteenth amendment broadly, Senator Frelinghuysen, in 1871 agreed:

[t]he fourteenth Amendment must . . . not be used to make the General Government imperial. It *must be read . . . together with the tenth amendment.* . . . Thus reading the fourteenth amendment . . . I do

---

[77]Clark, Book Review, 56 TEX. L. REV. 947, 953 (1978).

[78]R. BERGER, *supra* note 1, at 72–74.

[79]CONG. GLOBE, 37th Cong., 2d Sess. 1639 (1862) (remarks of Sen. Bingham) (emphasis added), *reprinted in* A. AVINS, *supra* note 22, at 37.

[80]R. BERGER, *supra* note 1, at 22–23 (quoting Fairman, *Does the Fourteenth Amendment Incorporate the Bill of Rights?* 2 STAN. L. REV. 5, 44 (1949)).

[81]*Id.* at 29 (quoting CONG. GLOBE, 39th Cong., 1st Sess. 599 (1866) (remarks of Sen. Trumbull)).

[82]CONG. GLOBE, 40th Cong., 1st Sess. 440 (1867) (remarks of Sen. Drake), *reprinted in* A. AVINS, *supra* note 22, at 273.

[83]R. BERGER, *supra* note 1, at 74.

[84]CONG. GLOBE, 42d Cong., 2d Sess. 794 (1872) (remarks of Rep. Townsend), *reprinted in* A. AVINS, *supra* note 22, at 605.

[85]D. FEHRENBACHER, THE DRED SCOTT CASE: ITS SIGNIFICANCE IN AMERICAN LAW AND POLITICS 581 (1978).

[86]*See* R. BERGER, *supra* note 1, at 63 n.50, 64, 155 (quoting H. HYMAN, A MORE PERFECT UNION 426 (1973); Kelly, *Comment on Harold M. Hyman's Paper, in* NEW FRONTIERS OF THE AMERICAN RECONSTRUCTION 55 (H. Hyman ed. 1966); P. PALUDAN, A COVENANT WITH DEATH 52 (1975)). *See also id.* at 60–64.

[87]CONG. GLOBE, 42d Cong., 2d Sess. app. 5 (1872) (remarks of Sen. Morrill), *reprinted in* A. AVINS, *supra* note 22, at 593.

not consider it now expedient for the General Government to assume a general municipal jurisdiction over crimes in the States.[88]

Said Charles Willard of Vermont:

What the General Government might do was plainly set forth in the Constitution . . . outside of that the people and the States had all the power. . . . The internal affairs of a State, its police regulations for the protection of society or the person and property of individuals against lawless violence, are matters of State concern, and entirely outside of any power conferred upon the General Government.[89]

Federal intervention was limited by the fourteenth amendment to *discrimination* on ground of race; the Constitution, Willard continued, "secured . . . equality of rights and immunities . . . and . . . we could only punish by United States laws a denial of that equality."[90] I would not suggest that the majority, by which the Civil Rights Act of 1875 was enacted, did not in part swallow such scruples; what is important is to note that they existed. The feebleness of the constitutional arguments made in favor of the invasion of states' rights will hereinafter appear.

Segregation in the Schools

Little mention of desegregation of the schools is to be found in the debates on the fourteenth amendment. As said by Alexander Bickel, "It was preposterous to worry about unsegregated schools . . . when hardly a beginning had been made at educating Negroes at all and when obviously special efforts, suitable only for the Negroes, would have to be made. . . ."[91] Even so, James Wilson, Manager of the Civil Rights Bill of 1866, which the framers were repeatedly told was "identical"

---

[88]CONG. GLOBE, 42d Cong., 1st Sess. 501 (1871) (remarks of Sen. Frelinghuysen) (emphasis added), *reprinted in* A. AVINS, *supra* note 22, at 542. Trumbull likewise rejected a federal "right to pass a general criminal code for the states. . . ." *Id.* at 579 (remarks of Sen. Trumbull), *reprinted in* A. AVINS, *supra* note 22, at 551.

[89]*Id.* at app. 187 (remarks of Rep. Willard), *reprinted in* A. AVINS, *supra* note 22, at 539. Judge Robert Hale of New York had warned the House "that there are other liberties as important as the liberties of the individual citizen, and those are the liberties and rights of the States," notwithstanding states' rights had been pressed too far by the South. CONG. GLOBE, 39th Cong., 1st Sess. 1065 (1866) (remarks of Rep. Hale), *reprinted in* A. AVINS, *supra* note 22, at 155. Senator Oliver Morton of Indiana found it necessary to say in 1868 that "I still recognize the doctrine of State rights. There are rights that belong to the States, secured by the same Constitution that secures the rights of this Government, and therefore they are equally sacred." CONG. GLOBE, 40th Cong., 2d Sess. 2742 (1868), *reprinted in* A. AVINS, *supra* note 22, at 324. In the House, John Farnsworth of Illinois, who had been a proponent of the fourteenth amendment, said, "I do not believe in centralization of the power of Government, nor in abolishing the State lines or State governments or abridging their powers." CONG. GLOBE, 42d Cong., 1st Sess. app. 117 (1871) (remarks of Rep. Farnsworth), *reprinted in* A. AVINS, *supra* note 22, at 508. And James Moore, Republican of Illinois, objected in 1871 that an act for enforcement of the fourteenth amendment:

looks very like the prescribing of a criminal code for the punishment and redress of private wrongs in the States. . . .

. . .[T]he whole machinery of the State governments is superseded. . . . I am sure that I am not by any means alone among the Republican members of the House in views I have taken of this provision of the bill.

Id. at app. 112 (remarks of Rep. Moore), *reprinted in* A. AVINS, *supra* note 22, at 516. His Illinois colleague, John Hawley, added that this was "a monstrous doctrine." *Id.* at 382 (remarks of Rep. Hawley), *reprinted in* A. AVINS, *supra* note 22, at 517. For a careful survey of the 1866 debate, see *id.* at app. 150–52 (remarks of Rep. Garfield), *reprinted in* A. AVINS, *supra* note 22, at 526–28.

[90]CONG. GLOBE, 42d Cong., 1st Sess. app. 188 (remarks of Rep. Willard), *reprinted in* A. AVINS, *supra* note 22, at 540.

[91]R. BERGER, *supra* note 1, at 100 (quoting R. KLUGER, SIMPLE JUSTICE 654 (1976)). Compare the remarks that because of the pernicious influence of slavery the blacks were unfit for suffrage: Senator Edgar Cowan of Pennsylvania, CONG. GLOBE, 38th Cong., 1st Sess. 2140 (1864), *reprinted in* A. AVINS, *supra* note 22, at 70; Thaddeus Stevens, R. BERGER, *supra* note 1, at 58 (quoting F. BRODIE, THADDEUS STEVENS: SCOURGE OF THE SOUTH 211 (1959)); Senator James Harlan of Iowa, CONG. GLOBE, 38th Cong., 1st Sess. 2240 (1864), *reprinted in* A. AVINS, *supra* note 22, at 72; Senator Lafayette Foster of Connecticut, *id.*, *reprinted in* A. AVINS, *supra* note 22, at 72; Senator Morton Wilkinson of Minnesota, *id.* at 2241, *reprinted in* A. AVINS, *supra* note 22, at 73; Senator Stewart of Nevada, CONG. GLOBE, 39th Cong., 1st Sess. 110 (1865), *reprinted in* A. AVINS, *supra* note 22, at 98; Senator Morton of Indiana, CONG. GLOBE, 40th Cong., 1st Sess. 69 (1867), *reprinted in* A. AVINS, *supra* note 22, at 269.

with the amendment, felt constrained to assure them that it did not comprehend mixed schools.[92] The roots of such sentiments were laid bare by Senator James Harlan of Iowa, when the District of Columbia schools were under discussion in April, 1860:

> I know there is an objection to the association of colored children with white children in the same schools. This prejudice exists in my own State. It would be impossible to carry a proposition in Iowa to educate the few colored children that now live in that State in the same school-houses with white children. It would be impossible, I think, in any one of the States in the Northwest.[93]

Hence it was proposed to provide "for the education of all the children of the District—the white children in separate schools, and the colored children in separate schools."[94] Such a bill passed the Senate in July, 1862.[95]

One man, Senator Charles Sumner, unflaggingly sought to turn the tide. As early as 1849 he had failed to persuade Chief Justice Lemuel Shaw that segregated schools were unlawful.[96] Rising indomitably from defeat after defeat[97] he almost succeeded in prevailing on the Senate to include a school provision in the Civil Rights Act of 1875, but his unlucky absence at a critical juncture left the field to opponents, who not only reflected contemporary racism, but also detested Sumner.[98] Of his idealism there can be no question; but he was self-righteous, could brook no compromise and gave the rough side of his tongue to those of his allies who would. For example, Senator Matthew Carpenter of Wisconsin, who sought to amend a Sumner proposal that he favored, felt the lash and protested bitterly:

> [H]ow ought . . . [the] Senator to have treated this difference of opinion? Certainly with a candid and decent respect for the doubts of others. A great leader of a dominant party, aware that one of its members entertained an honest scruple, ought certainly with kindness and forbearance to have dealt with the doubt, and condescended to illumine the darkness of a weak brother's mind.[99]

Small wonder that Charles Francis Adams concluded, "[A]t no moment of his career did he show any proof of high practical wisdom of a Statesman. He could never cooperate to gain an end because he never admitted of difference of opinion."[100] Senator Stewart corroborated that Sumner "is not a practical man . . . he has failed utterly to help us to get practical measures."[101] That said, it will

[92]R. BERGER, *supra* note 1, at 27 (quoting CONG. GLOBE, 39th Cong., 1st Sess. 1117 (1866) (remarks of Rep. Wilson)).

[93]CONG. GLOBE, 36th Cong., 1st Sess. 1680 (1860) (remarks of Sen. Harlan), *reprinted in* A. AVINS, *supra* note 22, at 22.

[94]*Id.* at 1684 (remarks of Sen. Harlan), *reprinted in* A. AVINS, *supra* note 22, at 26.

[95]CONG. GLOBE, 37th Cong., 2d Sess. 2020 (1862), *reprinted in* A. AVINS, *supra* note 22, at 43.

[96]Roberts v. Boston, 59 Mass. (5 Cush.) 198 (1849).

[97]Sumner vainly sought to attach to the fifteenth amendment a provision that "there shall be no discrimination in any rights on account of race or color." CONG. GLOBE, 40th Cong., 3d Sess. 1008 (1869) (remarks of Sen. Sumner), *reprinted in* A. AVINS, *supra* note 22, at 375. For rejection of other Sumner efforts, see CONG. GLOBE, 42d Cong., 2d Sess. 245 (1871), *reprinted in* A. AVINS, *supra* note 22, at 578; *id.* at 821–22 (1872), *reprinted in* A. AVINS, *supra* note 22, at 610. For example, Senator Morrill commented that Sumner "knows that that committee [on the Judiciary] were unanimously opposed to his bill. . . ." *Id.* at 370, *reprinted in* A. AVINS, *supra* note 22, at 599.

[98]CONG. GLOBE, 42d Cong., 2d Sess. 3737 (1872) (remarks of Sen. Sumner), *reprinted in* A. AVINS, *supra* note 22, at 655. *See also* Senator Morrill's comment, *id.* at 11, *reprinted in* A. AVINS, *supra* note 22, at 657; R. BERGER, *supra* note 1, at 235–36.

[99]CONG. GLOBE, 42d Cong., 2d Sess. 826 (1872) (remarks of Sen. Carpenter), *reprinted in* A. AVINS, *supra* note 22, at 612. Carpenter also said, "I came not cracking whips over other men's shoulders, nor did I attempt to enforce or invoke party discipline against reluctant consciences; I appealed to no one's prejudice or passion. . . ." *Id.*

[100]W. GILLETTE, *supra* note 12, at 177. Senator Fessenden called Sumner a "heated controversialist." CONG. GLOBE, 39th Cong., 1st Sess. 1281 (1866) (remarks of Sen. Fessenden).

[101]CONG. GLOBE, 41st Cong., 2d Sess. 1183 (1870) (remarks of Sen. Stewart), *reprinted in* A. AVINS, *supra* note 22, at 424. *See also* the statements of Senator Nye, CONG. GLOBE, 40th Cong., 3d Sess. 1306 (1869), *reprinted in* A. AVINS, *supra* note 22, at 400; and Senator Trumbull, R. BERGER, *supra* note 1, at 236 (quoting M. BENEDICT, A COMPROMISE OF PRINCIPLE 36 (1975)).

forever redound to his credit that, sailing on a stormy sea of prejudice, he was the conscience of the Senate, unflinchingly holding it to the noblest ideals. Unfortunately, the nation was not ready to apply them to the blacks.

But Sumner would have been at home with the "activists" of today. His "great rule of interpretation conquered at Appomattox . . . [was] a new rule of interpretation for the Constitution, according to which . . . it is to be interpreted uniformly for human rights."[102] When pressed for specifics, he invariably turned to the Declaration of Independence, insisting:

> [T]he Constitution must be interpreted by the Declaration. I insist that the Declaration is of equal and coordinate authority with the Constitution itself. . . . Show me any words in the Constitution applicable to human rights, and I invoke at once the great truths of the Declaration as the absolute guide in determining their meaning.[103]

But the acknowledged leader of the radicals, Thaddeus Stevens, declared, "[W]hile the Declaration clearly proved what the intention *then* was, the action of the Convention in framing the Constitution . . . bartered away . . . some of those inalienable rights. . . ."[104] By the time the Convention was convened, political currents had shifted sharply. By then, said Samuel Eliot Morison and Henry Steele Commager, "the democratic movement was in abeyance, a 'thermidorean reaction' was in full swing. . . . Hence the Federal Constitution put a stopper to those levelling and confiscatory demands of democracy. . . ."[105]

To Sumner's flights of eloquence, Senator Morrill of Maine made apt reply:

> [A]n appeal to the moral forces of the age should not be sufficient to justify the action of a Senator when action under the Constitution is in question. . . . If the Senator from Massachusetts cannot put his finger on the provision of the Constitution which warrants this measure, these impassioned appeals to these high considerations should have no weight. . . . Let the voice of the Senator from Massachusetts ring through the land . . . to give him the authority he invokes here. . . .[106]

During the course of the debates on the fifteenth amendment, on February 8, 1869, Sumner proposed to add a phrase outlawing "discrimination in *any* rights on account of race," correctly insisting that "*if the Fourteenth is inadequate to protect persons in their . . . right to vote, it is inadequate to protect them in anything.*"[107] That proposal, as the face of the fifteenth discloses, fell to the ground. Another attempt by Sumner, in May, 1872, to achieve "complete equality before the law," led Senator Morrill to say:

> There is no doubt as to how he feels on that subject; but the misfortune, after all, is that the Senate has never agreed with him upon that subject. He has pressed it . . . with great zeal . . . and still he has never

---

[102]CONG. GLOBE, 42d Cong., 2d Sess. 727 (1872) (remarks of Sen. Sumner), *reprinted in* A. AVINS, *supra* note 22, at 596. Senator Morrill dismissed this "new interpretation," saying that thereunder "you can do what you please. In other words, there is no limitation upon your power." *Id.* at 730 (remarks of Sen. Morrill), *reprinted in* A. AVINS, *supra* note 22, at 599. For him "Appomatox" was no source of constitutional power. The Senate Judiciary Committee reported adversely on the bill. *Id.* at 731 (remarks of Sen. Edmunds), *reprinted in* A. AVINS, *supra* note 22, at 600.

[103]*Id.* at 728 (remarks of Sen. Sumner), *reprinted in* A. AVINS, *supra* note 22, at 597. Senator Carpenter commented, Sumner "is not trammeled by the Constitution. He ascends into the higher, serener, more general atmosphere of the Declaration of Independence." *Id.* at 827 (remarks of Sen. Carpenter), *reprinted in* A. AVINS, *supra* note 22, at 613.

[104]CONG. GLOBE, 40th Cong., 2d Sess. 1967 (1868) (remarks of Rep. Stevens), *reprinted in* A. AVINS, *supra* note 22, at 305. *See also* R. BERGER, *supra* note 1, at 88.

[105]S. MORISON & H. COMMAGER, THE GROWTH OF THE AMERICAN REPUBLIC 300 (1950).

[106]CONG. GLOBE, 42d Cong., 2d Sess. app. 1–2 (1872) (remarks of Sen. Morrill), *reprinted in* A. AVINS, *supra* note 22, at 590. Justice Holmes wrote, "[N]othing but confusion of thought can result from assuming that the rights of man in a moral sense are equally rights in the sense of the constitution and the laws." O.W. HOLMES, COLLECTED LEGAL PAPERS 171–72 (1920).

[107]CONG. GLOBE, 40th Cong., 3d Sess. 1008 (1869) (remarks of Sen. Sumner), (emphasis added), *reprinted in* A. AVINS, *supra* note 22, at 375.

got a recognition of the bill, either from the committee or the Senate. So far as the action of the Senate has been concerned . . . it has been against the bill.[108]

In fact, however, sentiment among the Republicans was divided, as Benjamin Butler and Julius Burrows of Michigan noted.[109] And, said Senator Boutwell, "a great portion of the people" would say that separate but equal schools would furnish "equal facilities."[110] The drive to include equal access to the schools in the Civil Rights Act of 1875, where initially it was placed on the same footing with equal accommodations in inns, public conveyances, theaters, and cemeteries,[111] was wrecked on the shoals of insurmountable prejudice. Senator Sargent of California urged that the common school proposal would reinforce "what may be perhaps an unreasonable prejudice, but a prejudice nevertheless—a prejudice powerful, permeating every part of the country, and existing more or less in every man's mind. . . . I say that the powerful prejudice exists in every part of the country."[112] In the House, Barbour Lewis of Tennessee made a similar statement;[113] and William Phelps of New Jersey added, "You are trying to legislate against human prejudice, and you cannot do it. No enactment will root out prejudice, no bayonet will prick it. You can only educate away prejudice. . . ."[114]

The arguments that were made on behalf of a requirement of mixed schools were without solid constitutional footing. One such was the guarantee of a "republican form of government,"[115] as to which Trumbull justly commented that all the writers "speak of the guarantee clause, as only admitting an interference to maintain a government which previously existed of a republican form, and never was thought of giving Congress power to enter a State to interfere with its school system."[116] That both the Founders and the framers of the fourteenth amendment conceived the clause to guarantee maintenance of an existing republican form of government as contrasted, for example, with a dictatorship, can hardly be doubted.[117] Senator Frelinghuysen read the *Slaughterhouse Cases*,[118] of all things, to dispel "doubt that legal equality is now a privilege of United States citizenship," notwithstanding the holding that only a pitifully meager list of privileges, which he himself enumerated, were incident to "United States citizenship."[119] "It is true," he said, "the language of the court is that it was 'the existence of laws [the Black Codes] which discriminated with gross injustice and hardship against the class,' that was the evil to be remedied." But, he continued, "There is no significance in the words 'gross injustice and hardship.' Any discrimination is injustice and hardship."[120] Manifestly, this substitutes wishful thinking for a decision that

[108]CONG. GLOBE, 42d Cong., 2d Sess. 11 (1872) (remarks of Sen. Morrill), *reprinted in* A. AVINS, *supra* note 22, at 657.

[109]2 CONG. REC. 1005 (1875) (remarks of Rep. Butler), *reprinted in* A. AVINS, *supra* note 22, at 730; *id.* at 999 (remarks of Rep. Burrows), *reprinted in* A. AVINS, *supra* note 22, at 727.

[110]3 CONG. REC. 4168 (1874) (remarks of Sen. Boutwell), *reprinted in* A. AVINS, *supra* note 22, at 703.

[111]CONG. GLOBE, 42d Cong., 1st Sess. 21 (1871), *reprinted in* A. AVINS, *supra* note 22, at 484.

[112]3 CONG. REC. 4172 (1874) (remarks of Sen. Sargent), *reprinted in* A. AVINS, *supra* note 22, at 705. *See* text accompanying note 93 *supra*, remarks of Senator Harlan.

[113]"The prejudices of the whites against allowing the blacks to attend their schools in many portions of our country are intense and honest, though perhaps greatly mistaken and wrong." 3 CONG. REC. 998 (1875) (remarks of Rep. Lewis), *reprinted in* A. AVINS, *supra* note 22, at 726.

[114]*Id.* at 1002 (remarks of Rep. Phelps), *reprinted in* A. AVINS, *supra* note 22, at 729.

[115]CONG. GLOBE, 41st Cong., 2d Sess. 1180 (1870) (remarks of Sen. Sumner), *reprinted in* A. AVINS, *supra* note 22, at 424.

[116]*Id.* at 1365 (remarks of Sen. Trumbull), *reprinted in* A. AVINS, *supra* note 22, at 425.

[117]R. BERGER, *supra* note 1, at 77–81.

[118]83 U.S. (16 Wall.) 36 (1873).

[119]3 CONG. REC. 3453 (1874) (remarks of Sen. Frelinghuysen), *reprinted in* A. AVINS, *supra* note 22, at 674.

[120]*Id.* Justice Miller had recapitulated some of the evils of the Black Codes—these were "the evil to be remedied." 83 U.S. (16 Wall.) at 81. *See* text accompanying note 188 *infra*, remarks of Senator Trumbull and text accompanying note 208, *infra*, comment of Senator Frelinghuysen.

severely limited, indeed aborted, the few rights conferred by the fourteenth amendment.[121] Not Frelinghuysen, but Trumbull more truly spoke for the framers of the amendment. Lyman Trumbull had been Chairman of the Senate Judiciary Committee, draftsman and sponsor of the 1866 bill, and therefore was preeminently qualified to know the meaning of "civil rights"—originally part of an introductory clause that was deleted because it was considered too "latitudinarian" and "oppressive."[122] Now (May, 1872), he iterated that "the right to go to school is not a civil right and never was," but is "a matter to be regulated by the localities."[123] This it was that had led James Wilson, Chairman of the House Judiciary Committee and Manager of the Civil Rights Bill of 1866, to assure the Thirty-ninth Congress that mixed schools were not within the compass of the bill,[124] which was represented as "identical" with the fourteenth amendment. In the upshot, the Civil Rights Act of 1875 was shorn of desegregation in schools and cemeteries,[125] although the faulty logic which underlay equality for accommodations in transport, inns, and theaters no less required desegregated schools and cemeteries. Logic, however, had to yield to insurmountable racism. Even party needs had to give way, for as Senator William Stewart, an ardent proponent of unsegregated schools, stated of the school clause, "I do not believe that but for the eight hundred thousand [Negro] votes there would be ten votes, or even five votes, in this Chamber for this particular clause."[126]

The Language of the Constitution

Although the *Slaughterhouse Cases* had thrown their shadow over the debates on the Civil Rights Act of 1875,[127] it is one of the oddities of constitutional law that the *Civil Rights Cases* of 1883,[128] which set the Act aside, made no reference to the earlier holding and found it unnecessary to pass on the scope of "privileges or immunities." Instead, Justice Bradley held that the fourteenth amendment only permitted Congress to "adopt appropriate legislation for *correcting* the effects of such prohibited state law and state acts"; that the amendment "does not authorize Congress to create a code of municipal law for the regulation of private rights"; and that "civil rights, such as are guaranteed by the Constitution against state agression [*sic*], cannot be impaired by the wrongful acts of individuals, unsupported by state authority in the shape of laws, customs, or judicial or

---

[121]R. BERGER, *supra* note 1, at 37–51.

[122]*See id.* at 119–20, 122.

[123]CONG. GLOBE, 42d Cong., 2d Sess. 3189, 3190, 3426 (1872) (remarks of Sen. Trumbull), *reprinted in* A. AVINS, *supra* note 22, at 641, 642, 654. While the fourteenth amendment was up for ratification, in February, 1868, Senator Stewart said that § 1 "secures to every citizen in the United States the protection of the laws in his civil rights," protection of "person and property," a reading immediately echoed by Senator Morrill, CONG. GLOBE, 40th Cong., 2d Sess. 931 (1868) (remarks of Sen. Morrill), *reprinted in* A. AVINS, *supra* note 22, at 290, both members of the Thirty-ninth Congress.

[124]R. BERGER, *supra* note 1, at 27 (quoting CONG. GLOBE, 39th Cong., 1st Sess. 1117 (1866) (remarks of Rep. Wilson)).

[125]18 Stat. 335.

[126]2 CONG. REC. 4169 (1874) (remarks of Sen. Stewart), *reprinted in* A. AVINS, *supra* note 22, at 704.

[127]Senator Carpenter reminded the Senate of the *Slaughterhouse* holding, that the "privileges or immunities" clause referred only to those of a citizen of the United States, not of a state. 3 CONG. REC. 1862 (1875) (remarks of Sen. Carpenter), *reprinted in* A. AVINS, *supra* note 22, at 737. That was likewise stated by Senator Thurman. *Id.* at 1791–92 (remarks of Sen. Thurman), *reprinted in* A. AVINS, *supra* note 22, at 731, and given reluctant credence as "the law of the case" by Senator Boutwell. *Id.* (remarks of Sen. Boutwell).

It is paradoxical that Trumbull, who reminded Congress that the Civil Rights Act of 1866 had been enacted in order to curb the serfdom to which the Black Codes would return the freedmen, providing "that the rights of the colored people should be the same as those conceded to white people in certain respects," there enumerated, should in the same breath, anticipating *Slaughterhouse*, insist that the fourteenth amendment only conferred upon a citizen of the United States rights "of a national character," *e.g.*, protection abroad, not protection "in his rights of person and property." CONG. GLOBE, 42d Cong., 1st Sess. 575, 577 (1871) (remarks of Sen. Trumbull), *reprinted in* A. AVINS, *supra* note 22, at 548, 550. He was immediately controverted by Senator Carpenter. *Id.* at 577 (remarks of Sen. Carpenter), *reprinted in* A. AVINS, *supra* note 22, at 550.

[128]109 U.S. 3 (1883).

executive proceedings,"[129] that is, "under color of law." Although such decisions, as Professor Don E. Fehrenbacher observed, "virtually stripped the Negro of federal protection against private acts of oppression and against public discrimination indirectly imposed,"[130] it must be said in justice to the Court that its reading of "No State shall" has support in the debates on the fourteenth amendment. Samuel Shellabarger, explaining the antecedent Civil Rights Bill of 1866, which the amendment embodied, said, "[T]he violation of citizens' rights, which are reached and punished by this bill are those which are inflicted under 'color of law,' &c. The bill does not reach mere private wrongs, but only those done under color of State authority. . . ."[131] Speaking to the final form of the fourteenth amendment, its draftsman, John Bingham, stated that it supplied protection "from unconstitutional State enactments. . . . That is the extent that it hath; no more."[132] There are similar statements by Thaddeus Stevens and Senator Howard.[133]

Confronted, however, by the outrages of the Ku Klux Klan in the 1870s which threatened Republican control of the South,[134] Congress was not minded to limit penalties to offenses under "color of law."[135] In process, Bingham and Howard shifted their positions.[136] Senator Howard conceded that the fifteenth amendment

> does not, in terms, relate to the conduct of mere individuals, and a very "strict construction" court of justice might, as I can well conceive, refuse to apply the real principles of the amendment to the case of individuals who themselves, as mere individuals . . . should undertake to deny or prevent a colored man the exercise of his right of suffrage. . . .[137]

This "narrow construction," he asserted, "is not in harmony with the advocates and friends of the amendment. . . ."[138] Any statements by advocates of the amendment on behalf of sanctions against individuals escaped my notice.[139] Howard's own views on the similar fourteenth amendment

---

[129]*Id.* at 11, 17. Ten years earlier Justice Bradley had held on circuit "that there can be no constitutional legislation of Congress for directly enforcing the privileges and immunities . . . where the State has passed no laws adverse to them. . . ." United States v. Cruikshank, 25 F. Cas. 707, 714 (C.C.D. La. 1874) (No. 14,897). The debates bear him out. R. BERGER, *supra* note 1, at 183–92.

[130]D. FEHRENBACHER, *supra* note 85, at 582.

[131]CONG. GLOBE, 39th Cong., 1st Sess. 1294 (1866) (remarks of Rep. Shellabarger), *reprinted in* A. AVINS, *supra* note 22, at 189. *See also* Jeremiah Wilson of Indiana, CONG. GLOBE, 42d Cong., 1st Sess. 481 (1871) (remarks of Rep. Wilson), *reprinted in* A. AVINS, *supra* note 22, at 537; Horatio Burchard of Illinois, *id.* at app. 314–15, *reprinted in* A. AVINS, *supra* note 22, at 545; and note 89 *supra*, remarks of Representative Moore.

[132]CONG. GLOBE, 39th Cong., 1st Sess. 2543 (1866) (remarks of Rep. Bingham), *reprinted in* A. AVINS, *supra* note 22, at 218.

[133]Stevens said the fourteenth amendment "allows Congress to correct the unjust legislation of the States. . . ." R. BERGER, *supra* note 1, at 185 (quoting CONG. GLOBE, 39th Cong., 1st Sess. 2459 (1866) (remarks of Rep. Stevens)). Senator Howard stated § 5 "enables Congress, in case the States shall enact laws in conflict with the principles of the amendment, to correct that legislation by a formal congressional enactment." *Id.* at 228 (quoting CONG. GLOBE, 39th Cong., 1st Sess. 2768 (1866) (remarks of Sen. Howard)).

[134]*See* note 34 *supra.*

[135]By a vote of 41 to 9, the Senate rejected Vickers's clarifying proposal that the Act be aimed only at persons acting "by color of State authority." CONG. GLOBE, 41st Cong., 2d Sess. 3684 (1870) (remarks of Sen. Thurman), *reprinted in* A. AVINS, *supra* note 22, at 456. Yet is approved the bill, § 17 of which provided that "any person who, under color of any law. . . ." *Id.* at 3689–90, *reprinted in* A. AVINS, *supra* note 22, at 458.

[136]Bingham said the fourteenth amendment protects against "individuals in States." CONG. GLOBE, 42d Cong., 1st Sess. app. 83 (1871) (remarks of Rep. Bingham), *reprinted in* A. AVINS, *supra* note 22, at 509.

[137]CONG. GLOBE, 41st Cong., 2d Sess. 3655 (1870) (remarks of Sen. Howard), *reprinted in* A. AVINS, *supra* note 22, at 448.

[138]*Id.*

[139]On the other hand, Benjamin Butler proposed, "Let us take away that power of disfranchisement by the States by constitutional amendment. . . ." CONG. GLOBE, 40th Cong., 3d Sess. 725 (1869) (remarks of Rep. Butler), *reprinted in* A. AVINS, *supra* note 22, at 348. Senator Ferry called for abolishing "disfranchisement." *Id.* at 855 (remarks of Sen. Ferry), *reprinted in* A. AVINS, *supra* note 22, at 353. *See* remarks of Senator Howard, *id.* at 985, *reprinted in* A. AVINS, *supra* note

provision were to the contrary.[140] James Garfield quoted Shellabarger's and Bingham's earlier views and commented that Bingham "can make but cannot unmake history."[141]

If, however, as Ely maintains, *"the most important datum bearing on what was intended is the constitutional language itself,"*[142] how is "No State shall" to be converted into "No individual shall"? For as Justice Bradley observed, "It is State action of a particular character that is prohibited. Individual invasion of individual rights is not the subject."[143] Not by the remotest stretch of the imagination can "No State shall" be viewed as "general" words "inviting" the Court to import extraconstitutional considerations.

LIGHT ON THE TEXT OF THE FOURTEENTH AMENDMENT

The activists' chief reliance for expanded review is that the words of section 1 of the fourteenth amendment are allegedly "general," "open-ended," an "invitation" to the courts to adapt the amendment to present day needs.[144] The focus of inquiry, however, should be not what *we* choose to have the words mean today, but what they meant to the framers who employed them.[145]

Due Process of Law

"Due process" was not general; it was a term of fixed historical content both in 1791 and in 1866. Summing up 400 years of history, Hamilton said, "The words 'due process' have a precise technical import, and are only applicable to the process and proceedings of the courts of justice;

22, at 367. The purpose of the fifteenth amendment, said Senator Timothy Howe, was "to strip from [the state] the power to exclude from suffrage" on account of race. *Id.* at 1040 (remarks of Sen. Howe), *reprinted in* A. AVINS, *supra* note 22, at 388. The fifteenth amendment, said Bingham, would put it beyond the "power of any State . . . to discriminate against" blacks. *Id.* at 1225 (remarks of Rep. Bingham), *reprinted in* A. AVINS, *supra* note 22, at 391.

[140]*See* note 133 *supra.*

[141]CONG. GLOBE, 42d Cong., 1st Sess. app. 151 (1871) (remarks of Rep. Garfield), *reprinted in* A. AVINS, *supra* note 22, at 527. Horatio Burchard of Illinois likewise reminded Bingham of his limiting statement, "That is the extent . . . it hath, it hath no more." *Id.* at app. 315 (remarks of Rep. Burchard), *reprinted in* A. AVINS, *supra* note 22, at 545–46. Republicans who clung to "under color of law" were Senator Sherman, CONG. GLOBE, 41st Cong., 2d Sess. 3663 (1870) (remarks of Sen. Sherman), *reprinted in* A. AVINS, *supra* note 22, at 454, and James Blair of Missouri, CONG. GLOBE, 42d Cong., 1st Sess. app. 208 (1871) (remarks of Rep. Blair), *reprinted in* A. AVINS, *supra* note 22, at 518.

Garfield asserted, however,

[I]t is undoubtedly within the power of Congress to provide by law for the punishment of all persons, official or private, who shall invade these rights, and who by violence, threats or intimidation shall deprive any citizen of their fullest enjoyment. This is a part of that general power vested in Congress to punish the violation of its law.

Id. at app. 153 (remarks of Rep. Garfield), *reprinted in* A. AVINS, *supra* note 22, at 529. But he added:

In so far as this section punishes persons who under color of any State law shall deny or refuse to others the equal protection of the laws I give it my cheerful support; but when we provide by congressional enactment to punish a mere violation of a State law, we pass the line of constitutional authority.

Id. at 154, *reprinted in* A. AVINS, *supra* note 22, at 530.

[142]Ely, *supra* note 16, at 418 (emphasis in original). Nevertheless, both Justice Holmes and Judge Learned Hand emphasized the judicial duty to effectuate the intent in the teeth of the text. Johnson v. United States, 163 F. 30, 32 (1st Cir. 1908). Cawley v. United States, 272 F.2d 443, 445 (2d Cir. 1959): if the legislative purpose is "manifest," it "overrides even the explicit words used." How, moreover, would Ely account for the transformation of the textual "No State shall" into "No individual shall"? Certainly not by resort to "legislative history [that] is in unusual disarray," Ely, *supra* note 16, at 418, for on this score the history confirms the text.

[143]The Civil Rights Cases, 109 U.S. 3, 11 (1883).

[144]For discussion of this "open-ended" phraseology theory, see R. BERGER, *supra* note 1, at 99–116; Berger, *Government by Judiciary: John Hart Ely's "Invitation,"* 54 IND. L.J. 277 (1979).

[145]"We must learn, not from modern theorists, but from contemporaries of the events we are studying." We should not impose "upon the past a creature of our own imagining." Richardson & Sayles, *Parliament and Grand Councils in Medieval England,* 77 LAW Q. REV. 213, 224 (1961). Miller & Howell, *The Myth of Neutrality in Constitutional Adjudication,* 27 U. CHI. L. REV. 661, 673 (1960), label it an "historicist fallacy" to "appraise a former historical era by the criteria of values that have become important since."

they can never be referred to an act of legislature."[146] With but a couple of "aberrational" exceptions which exerted no influence, due process continued to be so regarded through the Civil War.[147] When I combed the 1866 debates, I found that all references to due process were in procedural terms.[148] Judge William Lawrence of Ohio, who had been a member of the Thirty-ninth Congress and the scholarly adviser of the Managers of the House in the impeachment of Andrew Johnson,[149] quoted the Hamilton definition in 1871.[150] Another member of the Thirty-ninth Congress, James Garfield, stated in 1871 that the due process clause of the fourteenth amendment "is copied from" the fifth, differing in that it applied to the states; he defined it as an impartial trial according to the laws of the land."[151] Two members of the 1866 Senate, Lyman Trumbull of Illinois and George Edmunds of Vermont, who differed in other matters, agreed in 1871 that the due process of the fourteenth was like that of the fifth.[152] The latter undeniably referred "only" to judicial procedure, "never" to legislation.[153] Nowhere in the debates from 1866 through 1875 did I encounter a contrary definition. So far as the meaning of due process in the fourteenth amendment is concerned, it is safe to say that the framers gave those words their accepted common law procedural meaning, without the slightest intimation that the framers meant to confer judicial power to displace legislative policymaking. Such a grant, in fact, was at war with their abiding distrust of the courts and, as will appear, it is contradicted by the history of section 5 of the amendment.

Equal Protection of the Laws

Unlike "due process," the phrase "equal protection of the laws" had no prior historical content and was first introduced by John Bingham. So, as Charles Sumner stated in the Thirty-ninth Congress, with respect to words of "no fixed signification . . . we turn to the framers. . . ."[154] In 1856 Bingham had tied "equality to protection of life, liberty, and property,[155] code words for protection of personal security and personal liberty, *i.e.,* freedom of locomotion, later embodied in the Civil Rights Act of 1866 phrase, "equal benefit of all laws for security of person and property."[156] In 1859 Bingham distinguished "political equality" from equality "in the enjoyment of the rights of life, liberty and property," that is, that "no one shall be deprived of life or liberty, but as punishment for crime, nor of his property. . . ."[157] In 1864, the radical leader, Thaddeus

---

[146]R. BERGER, *supra* note 1, at 194 (quoting THE PAPERS OF ALEXANDER HAMILTON 35 (H. Syrett & J. Cooke eds. 1962)). *See also* Berger, *"Law of the Land" Reconsidered,* 74 NW. U.L. REV. 1 (1979).

[147]Ely, *supra* note 16, at 417, 420. *See* Corwin, *The Doctrine of Due Process of Law Before the Civil War,* 24 HARV. L. REV. 366, 375–76 (1911). In the Thirty-eighth Congress, Chilton White of Ohio said, " 'Due process of law' . . . imports day in court and trial by jury." CONG. GLOBE, 38th Cong., 2d Sess. 215 (1865) (remarks of Rep. White), *reprinted in* A. AVINS, *supra* note 22, at 83.

[148]R. BERGER, *supra* note 1, at 201–08.

[149]R. BERGER, IMPEACHMENT: THE CONSTITUTIONAL PROBLEMS 268 (1973).

[150]CONG. GLOBE, 41st Cong., 3d Sess. 1245 (1871) (remarks of Rep. Lawrence), *reprinted in* A. AVINS, *supra* note 22, at 479.

[151]*See* CONG. GLOBE, 42d Cong., 2d Sess. 153 (1871) (remarks of Rep. Garfield), *reprinted in* A. AVINS, *supra* note 22, at 529.

[152]CONG. GLOBE, 42d Cong., 1st Sess. 577 (1871) (remarks of Sen. Trumbull), *reprinted in* A. AVINS, *supra* note 22, at 550; *id.* at 697 (remarks of Sen. Edmunds), *reprinted in* A. AVINS, *supra* note 22, at 563. A Democrat, Senator George Vickers, was of the same opinion. *Id.* at 660 (remarks of Sen. Vickers), *reprinted in* A. AVINS, *supra* note 22, at 559.

[153]Charles Curtis stated that when the framers put due process "into the Constitution, its meaning was as fixed and definite as the common law could make a phrase. . . . It meant a procedural due process. . . ." Curtis, *Review and Majority Rule,* in SUPREME COURT AND SUPREME LAW 170, 177 (E. Cahn ed. 1954).

[154]R. BERGER, *supra* note 1, at 372 (quoting CONG. GLOBE, 39th Cong., 1st Sess. 677 (1866) (remarks of Sen. Sumner)).

[155]CONG. GLOBE, 34th Cong., 3d Sess. app. 140 (1857) (remarks of Rep. Bingham), *reprinted in* A. AVINS, *supra* note 22, at 12.

[156]R. BERGER, *supra* note 1, at 21–22, 179.

[157]CONG. GLOBE, 35th Cong., 2d Sess. 985 (1859) (remarks of Rep. Bingham), *reprinted in* A. AVINS, *supra* note 22, at 18.

Stevens, disclaimed adherence to the "doctrine of negro equality" and he distinguished "equality in all things" from equality "before the laws";[158] the latter he later explained as equal "punishment" and "equal protection" of the black man as expressed in the Civil Rights Bill of 1866.[159]

The words again appear in explaining the scope of that Bill. It barred discrimination with respect to ownership of property, the right to contract and to have access to the courts—rights, the framers stressed, that were carefully enumerated.[160] Throughout the debates on the Bill, the framers interchangeably referred to "equality," "equality before the law," and "equal protection," but always in the circumscribed context of the enumerated rights. For example, Samuel Shellabarger told the House that the Bill secures "equality of protection in the enumerated rights."[161] Leonard Myers of Pennsylvania stated that the change "from slavery to freedom" required that "each State shall provide for equality before the law, equal protection of life, liberty and property, equal rights to sue and to be sued, to inherit, make contracts, and give testimony," rights theretofore denied to blacks.[162] Act and amendment proceeded on parallel tracks at the same session, and they are *in pari materia*. As Charles Willard of Vermont stated in 1871, the Act "was enacted by the same Congress which recommended the adoption of the fourteenth amendment, and is therefore the best possible statement of what the amendment was intended to secure."[163] The uncontroverted evidence is that the amendment was designed to "embody" the Act; they were regarded as "identical."[164] Every reasonable intendment favors giving the words "equal protection" the same meaning in the amendment that they had been given in discussing the Act, or as Senator Trumbull stated, section 1 of the amendment "is but a copy of the civil rights act."[165] The Supreme Court has held that where

---

[158]CONG. GLOBE, 38th Cong., 1st Sess. 124 (1864) (remarks of Rep. Stevens), *reprinted in* A. AVINS, *supra* note 22, at 81.

[159]R. BERGER, *supra* note 1, at 172.

[160]*Id.* at 24, 28, 170.

[161]*Id.* at 169–70 (quoting CONG. GLOBE, 39th Cong., 1st Sess. 1293 (1866) (remarks of Rep. Shellabarger)). *See also id.* at 172.

[162]CONG. GLOBE, 39th Cong., 1st Sess. 1622 (1866) (remarks of Rep. Myers), *reprinted in* A. AVINS, *supra* note 22, at 193. Senator Daniel Clark of New Hampshire stated that because blacks were subjected to "oppressive indignities, barbarous cruelties," it was necessary to give them "protection of the laws." CONG. GLOBE, 39th Cong., 1st Sess. 833 (1866) (remarks of Sen. Clark). Willard stated in 1871 that "[t]he negroes . . . had always been denied equality of right with white persons to life, liberty and property by the laws in many States of the Union. The Republican party demanded that equality, and adopted the fourteenth amendment to make it finally and forever secure. . . ." CONG. GLOBE, 42d Cong., 1st Sess. app. 189 (1871) (remarks of Rep. Willard), *reprinted in* A. AVINS, *supra* note 22, at 540.

[163]CONG. GLOBE, 42d Cong., 1st Sess. app. 188 (1871) (remarks of Rep. Willard), *reprinted in* A. AVINS, *supra* note 22, at 540. Without resort to the legislative history, Justice Bradley earlier held: "[T]he civil rights bill was enacted at the same session, and but shortly before the presentation of the fourteenth amendment; . . . was in pari materia; and was probably intended to reach the same object. . . . [T]he first section of the bill covers the same ground as the fourteenth amendment. . . ." Livestock Dealers' & Butchers' Ass'n v. Crescent City Livestock & Slaughterhouse Co., 15 F. Cas. 649, 655 (C.C.D. La. 1870) (No. 8,408).

[164]Charles Fairman stated, "Over and over in this debate [on the amendment] the . . . provisions of the one are treated as though they were essentially identical with those of the other." R. BERGER, *supra* note 1, at 22–23 (quoting Fairman, *Does the Fourteenth Amendment Incorporate the Bill of Rights?* 2 STAN. L. REV. 5, 44 (1949)). The activist Howard Jay Graham said, "Virtually every speaker in the debates . . . said or agreed that the Amendment was designed to embody or incorporate the Civil Rights Act." *Id.* at 23 (quoting H. GRAHAM, EVERYMAN'S CONSTITUTION 291 n.73 (1968)). Harry Flack wrote that "nearly all said it was but an incorporation of the Civil Rights Bill . . . there was no controversy as to its purpose or meaning." *Id.* at 23 n.13 (quoting H. FLACK, THE ADOPTION OF THE FOURTEENTH AMENDMENT 81 (1908). George R. Latham of West Virginia explained that the Civil Rights Act "covers exactly the same ground as this amendment." *Id.* at 23 (quoting CONG. GLOBE, 39th Cong., 1st Sess. 2883 (1866) (remarks of Rep. Latham)). *See also* text accompanying notes 190–92 *infra*.

[165]CONG. GLOBE, 42d Cong., 1st Sess. 575 (1871) (remarks of Sen. Trumbull), *reprinted in* A. AVINS, *supra* note 22, at 548.

"[b]oth acts are *in pari materia* it will be presumed that if the same word be used in both, and a special meaning were given it in the first act, that it was intended it should receive the same interpretation in the latter act, in the absence of anything to show a contrary intention.[166]

Alexander Bickel, who searched the debates on the amendment, concluded that the moderate leadership, which prevailed, had in mind a limited and well-defined meaning . . . a right to equal protection in the literal sense of benefiting from the laws for the security of person and property."[167] That no more was intended is confirmed by the repeated rejection of attempts to abolish *all* distinctions.[168] As Senator Fessenden, Chairman of the Joint Committee on Reconstruction, explained to the Thirty-ninth Congress, "We cannot put into the Constitution, owing to existing prejudices and existing institutions, an entire exclusion of all class distinctions. . . ."[169]

Recognition of these views is found in the debates that followed submission of the amendment for ratification. Senator William Stewart, a member of the Thirty-ninth Congress, stated in 1868 that section 1 of the fourteenth amendment secures protection to every citizen, "protection of the laws in his civil rights."[170] He explained in 1870 that a bill reported by the Judiciary Committee, which extended the "original civil rights bill" of 1866 to aliens, was a bill to secure "to all persons equal protection of the laws," that is, protection of "their ordinary civil rights," relying on the "equal protection" clause of the amendment.[171] A fellow member of the Thirty-ninth Congress, Senator Lot Morrill of Maine, recalled that "under the laws of the southern States there was no such thing as protection to person or property or redress for grievance for colored men, no courts in which the negro could be permitted to tell the truth in vindication of his own rights," and the Civil Rights Bill of 1866 was introduced "to protect him in his civil rights."[172] Speaking to the fourteenth amendment in 1868, Bingham said, "I desire equality of right, equality of civil right," and in 1871 he said that "equal protection of the laws" was to be enforced "to the extent of securing to all the guarantees of life, liberty and property."[173]

The several broadened appeals to "equal protection" during the debates on the Civil Rights Act of 1875 are bare assertions that "equal protection" means freedom from all discrimination, taking no heed of the limited purposes of the Thirty-ninth Congress, its association of "equal protection" with those aims, and its repeated rejection of attempts to ban all distinctions. Thus, Senator Edmunds read the Civil Rights Act of 1866 as providing that "the colored man should have a right to stand on an equality with the white citizen as it respected *all* rights of citizenship," though he acknowledged that "we . . . only sought to carry . . . what we could carry by a two-thirds vote" to override President Johnson's veto of the 1866 Act.[174] Senator Oliver Morton maintained that "equal

---

[166]Reiche v. Smythe, 80 U.S. (13 Wall.) 162, 165 (1871). A "rather heavy load rests on him who would give different meanings to the same word or the same phrase when used a plurality of times in . . . Acts which are *in pari materia* with each other." United States v. Montgomery Ward & Co., 150 F.2d 369, 377 (7th Cir.), *vacated as moot*, 326 U.S. 690 (1945).

[167]R. BERGER, *supra* note 1, at 170 n.20 (quoting A. BICKEL, THE LEAST DANGEROUS BRANCH 56 (1962)).

[168]*Id.* at 163–64.

[169]*Id.* at 99 (quoting CONG. GLOBE, 39th Cong., 1st Sess. 705 (1866) (remarks of Sen. Fessenden)).

[170]CONG. GLOBE, 40th Cong., 2d Sess. 931 (1868) (remarks of Sen. Stewart), *reprinted in* A. AVINS, *supra* note 22, at 290. *See* text accompanying note 92 *supra*.

[171]CONG. GLOBE, 41st Cong., 2d Sess. 1536, 3658 (1870) (remarks of Sen. Stewart), *reprinted in* A. AVINS, *supra* note 22, at 428, 449. In 1870, Senator John Pool, a Republican from North Carolina, stated that § 1 of the fourteenth amendment "made all men equal before the law, made them equal in civil rights." *Id.* at 2720 (remarks of Sen. Pool), *reprinted in* A. AVINS, *supra* note 22, at 436. *See* note 190 *infra*.

[172]CONG. GLOBE, 40th Cong., 2d Sess. app. 114 (1868) (remarks of Sen. Morrill), *reprinted in* A. AVINS, *supra* note 22, at 291. *See* note 162 *supra;* R. BERGER, *supra* note 1, at 201.

[173]CONG. GLOBE, 40th Cong., 2d Sess 2463 (1868) (remarks of Rep. Bingham), *reprinted in* A. AVINS, *supra* note 22, at 316; CONG. GLOBE, 42d Cong., 1st Sess. 83 (1871) (remarks of Rep. Bingham), *reprinted in* A. AVINS, *supra* note 22, at 509.

[174]CONG. GLOBE, 42d Cong., 2d Sess. 900 (1872) (remarks of Sen. Edmunds) (emphasis added), *reprinted in* A. AVINS, *supra* note 22, at 628.

protection" was not limited to protection from violence and destruction, but was "intended to promote equality in the States, and to take from the States the power . . . to create inequality among their people."[175] So, too, William Lawrence stated that the object was "to make men equal before the law," that "equal protection" meant that "the equal benefit . . . of *all* laws is to be extended to all citizens," "all rights which exist under law," but his appeal to the history of the amendment offers him no support.[176]

Elsewhere I pointed out that the three clauses of section 1 of the fourteenth amendment were facets of one and the same concern: to ensure that there would be no discrimination against the freedmen with respect to "fundamental rights."[177] Roughly speaking, the substantive rights were subsumed in the "privileges or immunities" clause; the "equal protection" clause was to bar legislative discrimination with respect to those rights; and the judicial machinery to secure them was to be supplied by nondiscriminatory due process of the states. In a word, equal protection was an *adjective* right to protect the substantive "privileges or immunities."[178] To read "equal protection" substantively to embrace the rights comprehended in "privileges or immunities" is to render the latter superfluous, whereas the draftsmen "are presumed to have used no superfluous words."[179] One may agree with Lawrence that equality "of all rights which exist under law, is simple justice,"[180] but this is to substitute what ought to be for the framers' rejection of repeated attempts to abolish all distinctions. The fact is that the undeniable exclusion of suffrage from the fourteenth amendment constituted a great breach in the argument for blanket equality, and, as Sumner insisted, if that had to be cured by the fifteenth amendment, an explicit constitutional provision for mixed schools was equally necessary. Other arguments pointed up the gap. Addressing himself to the clause of the 1875 bill that would permit Negroes to serve as jurors, Senator Matthew Carpenter flatly denied that "equal protection" had any application, arguing that "women and infants . . . are excluded from service as jurors in every State in the Union . . . no one pretends or claims that . . . they are deprived of . . . the equal protection of the laws."[181] Others pointed out that the states provided separate schools for females and that the constitutionality of such separation was hardly questionable.[182]

[175]*Id.* at 847 (remarks of Sen. Morton), *reprinted in* A. AVINS, *supra* note 22, at 621–22.

[176]2 CONG. REC. 412–13 (1874) (remarks of Rep. Lawrence) (emphasis added), *reprinted in* A. AVINS, *supra* note 22, at 662–63. He notes Stevens's explanation that the object was to "ingraft it [Civil Rights Act] on the Constitution in principle and effect," *id.*, and forgets how narrow were the aims of the Act. *See* notes 187–90 and accompanying text *infra*.

[177]*See* R. BERGER, *supra* note 1, at 21–22, 25. *See also* text accompanying notes 188–96 *infra*.

[178]R. BERGER, *supra* note 1, at 18–19, 209–11. Justice Harlan correctly stated, "Since the Privileges and Immunities Clause was expected to be the primary source of substantive protection, the Equal Protection and Due Process Clauses were relegated to a secondary role, as the debates and other contemporary materials make clear." Oregon v. Mitchell, 400 U.S. 112, 164 (1970) (Harlan, J., concurring in part and dissenting in part). For Stevens "equal protection" meant equal "means of redress," the "same punishment." The ' "civil rights bill secures the same thing." ' R. BERGER, *supra* note 1, at 172 (quoting CONG. GLOBE, 39th Cong., 1st Sess. 2459 (1866) (remarks of Rep. Stevens)). *See* note 90 and accompanying text *supra;* notes 187–92 and accompanying text *infra*, especially the remarks of Charles Willard. For the Act of 1866, see R. BERGER, *supra* note 1, at 24.

[179]Platt v. Union Pac. R.R., 97 U.S. 48, 58, 59 (1878); Adler v. Northern Hotel Co., 175 F.2d 619, 621 (7th Cir. 1949). In 1791 Jefferson wrote, "It is an established rule of construction where a phrase will bear either of two meanings to give it that which will allow some meaning to the other parts of the instrument, and not that which would render all others useless." 3 M. FARRAND, RECORDS OF THE FEDERAL CONVENTION OF 1787, at 363 (1911).

[180]2 CONG. REC. 414 (1874) (remarks of Rep. Lawrence), *reprinted in* A. AVIS, *supra* note 22, at 663. *See also id.* at 3452–53 (remarks of Sen. Frelinghuysen), *reprinted in* A. AVINS, *supra* note 22, at 674.

[181]2 CONG. REC. 1861 (1875) (remarks of Sen. Carpenter), *reprinted in* A. AVINS, *supra* note 22, at 737. Carpenter suggested that equal transportation accommodations "might be sustained as a regulation of commerce if confined to that commerce over which Congress has the power of regulation. . . ." *Id.*

[182]CONG. GLOBE, 42d Cong., 2d Sess. 3190 (1872) (remarks of Sen. Ferry), *reprinted in* A. AVINS, *supra* note 22, at 641; 2 CONG. REC. 4171–72 (1874) (remarks of Sen. Sargent, *reprinted in* A. AVINS, *supra* note 22, at 705. *See also* remarks of

Until the very recent past "equal protection" played a negligible role, being all but dormant. Its resurrection may be viewed as an escape from "the hostility to substantive due process," largely due, as Professor Gerald Gunther explained, to the "Supreme Court fishing out of thin air its own predilections. . . ."[183] With economic due process discredited, as the Supreme Court itself acknowledges, it was convenient to resort to words that carried no taint.[184] But as Professor Herbert Packer put it, "the new 'substantive equal protection' has under a different label permitted today's justices to impose their prejudices in much the same manner as the Four Horsemen [of the pre-1937 Court] once did,"[185] and with no more constitutional justification. In short "the new equal protection is the old substantive due process,"[186] bent to goals closer to the activist heart.

Privileges or Immunities

No one could speak more authoritatively about the meaning of "privileges or immunities" than Senator Lyman Trumbull, for it was he, Chairman of the Senate Judiciary Committee, who had drafted the Civil Rights Bill of 1866 and who explained that the terms "civil rights and immunities" were drawn from the "privileges and immunities" of article IV, as judicially construed.[187] He reminded Congress in 1871 that the bill had been enacted because of the Black Codes "which denied to persons of color the ordinary and fundamental rights which were conceded to white citizens."[188] He recalled that the Act declared the rights of blacks "should be the same as those conceded to whites *in certain respects,* which were *named in the act,*" stating that section 1 of the fourteenth amendment "is but a copy of the civil rights act. . . ."[189] The fourteenth amendment clause, he reiterated, "is but a repetition of a provision in the Constitution as it before existed."[190]

Senator Thurman, former Chief Justice of the Ohio Supreme Court and a Democrat. CONG. GLOBE, 42d Cong., 2d Sess. app. 26 (1872), *reprinted in* A. AVINS, *supra* note 22, at 618.

[183]*Symposium—Equal Protection and the Burger Court,* 2 HASTINGS CONST. L.Q. 645, 664 (1975) [hereinafter cited as HASTINGS *Symposium*].

[184]R. BERGER, *supra* note 1, at 265–66.

[185]*Id.* at 191–92 (quoting Packer, *The Aims of Criminal Law Revisited: A Plea for a New Look at Substantive Due Process,* 44 S. CAL. L. REV. 490, 491 (1971)).

[186]Kurland, HASTINGS *Symposium, supra* note 183, at 661.

[187]R. BERGER, *supra* note 1, at 29 (quoting CONG. GLOBE, 39th Cong., 1st Sess. 600 (1866) (remarks of Sen. Trumbull)).

[188]CONG. GLOBE, 42d Cong., 1st Sess. 575 (1871) (remarks of Sen. Trumbull), *reprinted in* A. AVINS, *supra* note 22, at 548. Charles Willard explained:

> The negroes in this country had always been denied equality of right with white persons to life, liberty and property. . . . The Republican party demanded that equality, and adopted the fourteenth amendment to make it finally and forever secure. . . .
>
>   . . . [T]he character of that citizenship, its privileges and immunities, were in no way changed, or enlarged, or limited. . . .

Id. at app. 189, *reprinted in* A. AVINS, *supra* note 22, at 540.

[189]*Id.* at 575 (remarks of Sen. Trumbull) (emphasis added), *reprinted in* A. AVINS, *supra* note 22, at 548. Senator Frelinghuysen, a broad constructionist, recognized that the "privileges and immunities" of article IV "were only fundamental rights, and not such as were incident to residence." 2 CONG. REC. 3454 (1874) (remarks of Sen. Frelinghuysen), *reprinted in* A. AVINS, *supra* note 22, at 675. Samuel Shellabarger observed that the "privileges or immunities" clause had reference to those "which are in their nature 'fundamental,' " and referred further to Corfield v. Coryell, 6 F. Cas. 546 (C.C.E.D. Pa. 1823) (No. 3, 230). CONG. GLOBE, 42d Cong., 1st Sess. app. 69 (1871) (remarks of Rep. Shellabarger), *reprinted in* A. AVINS, *supra* note 22, at 494.

[190]Trumbull stressed that the Act was "confined exclusively to civil rights and nothing else, no political and no social rights," that it was enacted because the freedmen "had no right to buy or sell, to go or come, to contract . . . to enforce contracts." CONG. GLOBE, 42d Cong., 2d Sess. 901 (1872) (remarks of Sen. Trumbull), *reprinted in* A. AVINS, *supra* note 22, at 628–29. Senator Morrill stated that "privileges or immunities," as in the case of article IV, were the privileges "to enter another State, to make contracts, to sell, hold . . . inherit property, and to be protected in person and property." Never, he said, were the "privileges . . . more concisely or authoritatively stated than in the civil rights bill" of 1866; he emphasized that "it does not mean all the rights that belong to man." *Id.* at app. 3–4 (remarks of Sen. Morrill), *reprinted in* A. AVINS, *supra* note 22, at 591–92.

A broad constructionist, Senator Oliver Morton, directed attention to the fact that the privileges and immunities of article IV were treated in the *Slaughterhouse Cases* "as being identical with the privileges of citizens of the United States under the fourteenth article, and the judge read from the case of [Corfield v.] Coryell to show that those rights were identical in character."[191]

In the House, James Garfield, who emphasized that he "not only heard the whole debate at the time, but I have lately read over, with scrupulous care, every word of it as recorded in the Globe"—and indeed quoted copiously therefrom—stated:

> In the long debate which followed, this section [section 1] of the amendment was considered as equivalent to the first section of the civil rights bill, except that a new power was added [equal protection clause]. . . .
> It was throughout the debate, with scarcely an exception, spoken of as a limitation of the power of the States to legislate unequally for the *protection of life and property*.[192]

The substance of the "privileges or immunities" clause, he stated, "is in the main text of the Constitution [article IV], and has again and again been interpreted by the courts."[193] It was this which led Michael Kerr, a Democrat of Indiana, and a well-schooled lawyer as his every speech attests, to say in 1871 of "privileges and immunities" that, "These words are historic. They may be said almost to have become words of art, and to be crystallized in our fundamental law. They have very often received the most careful and deliberate judicial interpretation."[194] Of one of these cases, *Corfield v. Coryell*,[195] cited in 1871 as in 1866, Charles Willard of Vermont observed:

> There is, however, a far higher and better authority for and definition of the rights which belong to a citizen of the United States in the first section of the 'civil rights bill' [of 1866]. . . .
> This section, it should be remembered, was enacted by the same Congress which recommended the adoption of the fourteenth amendment, and is, therefore, the best possible statement of what that amendment was intended to secure. . . .[196]

An 1871 Report of the House Committee on the Judiciary, adopted by the House, stated that the "privileges or immunities" clause of the fourteenth amendment "does not . . . refer to privileges and immunities . . . other than those privileges and immunities embraced in the original text of the Constitution, article 4, section 2. The fourteenth amendment, it is believed, did not add to the privileges or immunities before mentioned. . . ."[197]

In contrast to such faithful representations of the legislative history, the broad constructionists often contradict it squarely. Thus, Senator George Boutwell read the "privileges or immunities"

---

[191] 2 Cong. Rec. 4087 (1874) (remarks of Sen. Morton), *reprinted in* A. Avins, *supra* note 22, at 679.

[192] Cong. Globe, 42d Cong., 1st Sess. app. 151 (1871) (remarks of Rep. Garfield) (emphasis added), *reprinted in* A. Avins, *supra* note 22, at 527.

[193] *Id.* at app. 152 (remarks of Rep Garfield), *reprinted in* A. Avins, *supra* note 22, at 528. *See* R. Berger, *supra* note 1, at 32–34.

[194] Cong. Globe, 42d Cong., 1st Sess. app. 47 (1871) (remarks of Rep. Kerr), *reprinted in* A. Avins, *supra* note 22, at 497.

[195] 6 F. Cas. 546 (C.C.E.D. Pa. 1823) (No. 3,230).

[196] Cong. Globe, 42d Cong., 1st Sess. app. 189 (1871) (remarks of Rep. Willard), *reprinted in* A. Avins, *supra* note 22, at 540. Horatio Burchard stated in 1871:

> What some of the privileges and immunities . . . are the contemporaneous legislation—the civil rights bill, passed at the same session by the same Congress that proposed this [fourteenth] amendment—enumerates. The meaning of those words, as used in the Constitution before the adoption of this amendment, has been discussed by writers upon elementary law and defined, to some extent, by courts and judges.

Id. at app. 313 (remarks of Rep. Burchard), *reprinted in* A. Avins, *supra* note 22, at 544. He justly preferred the decision of the Massachusetts court in Abbott v. Bayley, 23 Mass. (6 Pick.) 92 (1827) to the loose "obiter dictum of a single circuit judge" in Corfield v. Coryell. *Id.*

[197] H.R. Rep. No. 22, 41st Cong., 3d Sess. 2 (1871) (Report of the Committee on the Judiciary), *reprinted in* A. Avins, *supra* note 22, at 466. *See also* 2 Cong. Rec. 384 (1874) (remarks of Rep. Mills), *reprinted in* A. Avins, *supra* note 22, at 659.

clause as "a comprehensive inhibition upon the States," applying to "any privilege" which "any other citizen may enjoy" including "the right to vote [as] one of the privileges of the citizen."[198] Senator Edmund Ross of Kansas likewise regarded suffrage as "a most important privilege" within the "privileges or immunities" clause, as did Senator Edmunds in 1869.[199] But as Senator Henry Wilson of Massachusetts noted, "perhaps a large majority . . . of the Republicans of the country entertain serious doubts of the right to secure suffrage by congressional legislation,"[200] doubts that before long found expression in adoption of the fifteenth amendment. Senator Trumbull had assured the Senate in 1866 that the Civil Rights Bill "has nothing to do with the right of suffrage, or any other political right,"[201] and there are many statements to the same effect—that suffrage was not conferred by the fourteenth amendment.[202] When Boutwell was reminded by John Nicholson, a Delaware Democrat, of such statements, he replied, "I have no recollection of anything of the sort. . . . I cannot say but that some members on this side of the House may have disavowed that construction, but I was not one of them."[203] This was false. He was a member of the Joint Reconstruction Committee and signed its report stating that the whole question of suffrage was "left with the people of each State."[204] In 1871 Trumbull reiterated that privileges or immunities "have nothing to do with voting. They refer to civil rights . . . not political rights. . . ."[205] A Report of the Senate Judiciary Committee, submitted in 1870 by Edmunds himself, stated that "[t]he 'privileges and immunities' . . . mentioned in the petition [by women] as secured by the fourteenth amendment, do not include the right of suffrage."[206] The several misrepresentations by Boutwell

[198]CONG. GLOBE, 40th Cong., 3d Sess. 558 (1868) (remarks of Rep. Boutwell), *reprinted in* A. AVINS, *supra* note 22, at 335. In 1874 Boutwell maintained, "[O]f course one of the first rights . . . of the citizen of the United States, is that in the State in which he chooses to reside he shall be the equal of any other citizen in that State. That is his first immunity, his first privilege. . . ." 2 CONG. REC. 4116 (1874) (remarks of Sen. Boutwell), *reprinted in* A. AVINS, *supra* note 22 at 686. Yet he had stated, "The proposition in the matter of suffrage falls short of what I desire. . . . I demand . . . the full franchise for all loyal male citizens. . . ." R. BERGER, *supra* note 1, at 68 n.70 (quoting CONG. GLOBE, 39th Cong., 1st Sess. 2508 (1866)). But he voted for the fourteenth amendment. Almost alone, he later read § 2 as imposing a "penalty . . . for doing that which in the first section it is declared the State had no right to do." CONG. GLOBE, 40th Cong., 3d Sess. 559 (1869) (remarks of Rep. Boutwell), *reprinted in* A. AVINS, *supra* note 22, at 336. *See* notes 37–65 and accompanying text *supra*.

[199]CONG. GLOBE, 40th Cong., 3d Sess. 982 (1869) (remarks of Sen. Ross), *reprinted in* A. AVINS, *supra* note 22, at 366; *id.* at 1000 (remarks of Sen. Edmunds), *reprinted in* A. AVINS, *supra* note 22, at 370–71. Yet in 1871 Edmunds stated, "[E]verybody agrees that that privilege and that immunity is the very same thing mentioned in the next clause—the privilege of life, the privilege of liberty, the privilege of the acquirement of property." CONG. GLOBE, 42d Cong., 1st Sess. 697 (1871) (remarks of Sen. Edmunds), *reprinted in* A. AVINS, *supra* note 22, at 563. Switching again, he averred in 1872 that the Civil Rights Act of 1866 provided that "the colored man should have a right to stand on an equality with the white citizen as it respected *all* rights of citizenship. . . ." notwithstanding repeated assurances to the Thirty-ninth Congress that it did not cover all rights but only those enumerated. CONG. GLOBE, 42d Cong., 2d Sess. 900 (1872) (remarks of Sen. Edmunds) (emphasis added), *reprinted in* A. AVINS, *supra* note 22, at 628. *See* R. BERGER, *supra* note 1, at 27–30.

[200]CONG. GLOBE, 40th Cong., 3d Sess. app. 154 (1869) (remarks of Sen. Wilson), *reprinted in* A. AVINS, *supra* note 22, at 370.

[201]R. BERGER, *supra* note 1, at 30 (quoting CONG. GLOBE, 39th Cong., 1st Sess. 599 (1866) (remarks of Sen. Trumbull)).

[202]R. BERGER, *supra* note 1, at 30–31, 58–60.

[203]CONG. GLOBE, 40th Cong., 3d Sess. 559 (1869) (remarks of Reps. Nicholson and Boutwell), *reprinted in* A. AVINS, *supra* note 22, at 336. Eric McKitrick described Boutwell as one of "as baleful a trio of buzzards as ever perched in the House." E. McKITRICK, ANDREW JOHNSON AND RECONSTRUCTION 492 (1960).

[204]R. BERGER, *supra* note 1, at 84.

[205]CONG. GLOBE, 42d Cong., 1st Sess. 576 (1871) (remarks of Sen. Trumbull), *reprinted in* A. AVINS, *supra* note 22, at 549. In 1872 Trumbull repeated that the Civil Rights Bill was

confined exclusively to civil rights and nothing else, no political and no social rights. Here were millions . . . who . . . had been made free men. They had no right to buy or sell, to go or come, to contract . . . to enforce contracts. . . . [W]e were bound to give them the rights of men.

CONG. GLOBE, 42d Cong., 2d Sess. 901 (1872) (remarks of Sen. Trumbull), *reprinted in* A. AVINS, *supra* note 22, at 628–29.

[206]S. REP. NO. 187, 41st Cong., 2d Sess. 1–2 (1870) (Report of the Committee on the Judiciary), *reprinted in* A. AVINS, *supra* note 22, at 464.

and Edmunds respecting suffrage illustrate the extent to which sentiment caused libertarians to turn a blind eye to incontrovertible historical fact.

Such views were carried over to "equal accommodations" by Senator Frelinghuysen: "[I]t is one of the privileges of a citizen of the United States . . . not to be discriminated against on account of race or color by the law of a State relating to inns, schools &c. . . ."[207] Yet he noticed that the Supreme Court had recounted in the *Slaughterhouse Cases* that

> the fourteenth amendment was passed because States "imposed upon their colored race onerous disabilities [Black Codes]," and "curtailed their right to the pursuit of life, liberty and property"; that it was passed for the "protection of the newly made citizen from the oppression of those who had formerly exercised unlimited dominion over him.[208]

He also acknowledged that the "privileges or immunities" of article IV "were only fundamental rights, and not such as were incident to residence,"[209] apparently unaware that those "fundamental rights," were the protection of person and property. More faithful to the legislative history, Trumbull declared that "[t]he right to go to school is not a civil right and never was";[210] in fact, the Chairman of the House Judiciary Committee, James Wilson, had explained to the Thirty-ninth Congress that the words "civil rights" did not mean that "children shall attend the same schools."[211] I have detailed this history because, like James Garfield, "I am unwilling that the interpretation which some gentlemen have given of the constitutional power of Congress shall stand as the uncontradicted history of this legislation."[212] And having, like Garfield, pored over the 1866 debates, I am convinced that Trumbull, Garfield, and others far more accurately described the intentions of the Thirty-ninth Congress than did Edmunds, Sumner, and Frelinghuysen.

Incorporation of the Bill of Rights

Justice Black's argument that the fourteenth amendment incorporated the Bill of Rights, rested on remarks by John Bingham and Senator Howard in the Thirty-ninth Congress, was convincingly refuted by Charles Fairman, as I learned, when I followed in his path through the debates.[213] Alexander Bickel stated that Fairman "conclusively disproved Black's contention, at least such is the weight of opinion among disinterested observers."[214] That opinion is shared by a number of activist adherents such as Dean Alfange and Michael Perry.[215]

In 1871, Bingham explained that when he belatedly read the *Barron v. Baltimore*[216] holding that the Bill of Rights applied solely to the federal government, not to the states, he determined to correct that deficiency, stating that "the privileges and immunities of a citizen of the United

---

[207]2 CONG. REC. 3454 (1874) (remarks of Sen. Frelinghuysen), *reprinted in* A. AVINS, *supra* note 22, at 674.

[208]*Id.*

[209]*Id., reprinted in* A. AVINS, *supra* note 22, at 675.

[210]CONG. GLOBE, 42d Cong., 2d Sess. 3189 (1872) (remarks of Sen. Trumbull), *reprinted in* A. AVINS, *supra* note 22, at 641.

[211]R. BERGER, *supra* note 1, at 27 (quoting CONG. GLOBE, 39th Cong., 1st Sess. 1117 (1866) (remarks of Rep. Wilson)).

[212]CONG. GLOBE, 42d Cong., 1st Sess. app. 153 (1871) (remarks of Rep. Garfield), *reprinted in* A. AVINS, *supra* note 22, at 529.

[213]*See* R. BERGER, *supra* note 1, at 134–56.

[214]*Id.* at 137 n.17 (quoting A. BICKEL, THE LEAST DANGEROUS BRANCH 102 (1962)).

[215]Alfange, *supra* note 5, at 607; Perry, *supra* note 5, at 689. On the other hand, Ely, *supra* note 16, at 432 maintains:
[A]lthough neither the ratified language nor what is known of the intentions that generated it fairly compels the conclusion that the provisions of the Bill of Rights were to be counted among the privileges and immunities of citizens, there is at the same time nothing in that language or those intentions that should preclude that result.
Let such inconclusiveness be assumed, the tenth amendment reservation of all rights not granted creates a burden to prove that the states surrendered control of the area covered by the Bill of Rights, a burden not met by inconclusive evidence. *See also* Perry, *supra* note 5, at 689–90.

[216]32 U.S. (7 Pet.) 243 (1833).

States, as contradistinguished from a citizen of a State, are chiefly defined in the first eight amendments. . . . These eight articles . . . never were limitations upon the power of the States, until made so by the fourteenth amendment."[217] Apparently he had forgotten that a couple of months earlier he had submitted a Report of the Committee on the Judiciary, stating:

> The clause of the fourteenth amendment, "No State shall make or enforce any law which shall abridge the privileges or immunities of citizens of the United States," *does not* in the opinion of the committee, *refer* to the privileges and immunities of citizens of the United States *other* than privileges and immunities embraced in the original text of the Constitution, article 4, section 2. The fourteenth amendment, it is believed, *did not add to* the privileges or immunities before mentioned, but was deemed necessary for their enforcement as an express limitation upon the powers of the States.[218]

Self-evidently, the "privileges and immunities" of article IV, which preceded the drafting of the Bill of Rights by two years, could not have comprehended the latter. It has earlier been noted that Senators Trumbull and Morrill, and James Garfield, considered that the two clauses were identical[219] and that its content, in the words of Morrill, had been "defined" by the Civil Rights Act of 1866.[220] And Trumbull, who had explained the antecedent "civil rights and immunities," flatly declared in 1871 that the fourteenth amendment did not "enlarge" the provision "as it before existed," that it "is but a repetition of the provision in the Constitution as it before existed."[221] That earlier provision manifestly did not include the Bill of Rights.

Striking confirmation is furnished by an amendment proposed by James Blaine in 1875, in a Congress which included twenty-three members of the Thirty-ninth Congress, among them Blaine. Prior thereto he had written a letter published by the *New York Times* indicating that the fourteenth amendment did not forbid states from establishing official churches or maintaining sectarian schools. Consequently he proposed that "No State shall make any law respecting an establishment of religion or prohibiting the free exercise thereof."[222]

> Not one of the several Representatives and Senators who spoke on the proposal even suggested that its provisions were implicit in the amendment ratified just seven years earlier. . . . Remarks of Randolph, Christiaincy, Kernan, White, Bogy, Eaton and Morton give confirmation to the belief that none of the legislators in 1875 thought the Fourteenth Amendment incorporated the religious provisions of the First."[223]

[217]CONG. GLOBE, 42d Cong., 1st Sess. app. 84 (1871) (remarks of Rep. Bingham), *reprinted in* A. AVINS, *supra* note 22, at 510. For Garfield's tart comments on Bingham's version of his 1866 remarks, see *id.* at app. 151 (1871) (remarks of Rep. Garfield), *reprinted in* A. AVINS, *supra* note 22, at 527. *See also id.* at app. 116 (remarks of Rep. Farnsworth), *reprinted in* A. AVINS, *supra* note 22, at 507. Senator Howard did not reiterate his 1866 reference to the Bill of Rights, but his renewed assertion that suffrage was excluded from the fourteenth amendment and left to the states (see text accompanying note 47 *supra*) raises the question why the states were readier to surrender their control over local criminal administration.

Bingham, however, had gathered a few adherents: Senator Joseph Fowler of Tennessee, CONG. GLOBE, 41st Cong., 2d Sess. 515 (1870) (remarks of Sen. Fowler), *reprinted in* A. AVINS, *supra* note 22, at 420; Horace Maynard of Tennessee, CONG. GLOBE, 42d Cong., 1st Sess. app. 310 (1871) (remarks of Rep. Maynard), *reprinted in* A. AVINS, *supra* note 22, at 503; who assumed without explaining that the "privileges or immunities" clause comprehended one or the other of the Bill of Rights.

[218]H.R. REP. No. 22, 41st Cong., 3d Sess. 1 (1871) (Report of the Committee on the Judiciary) (emphasis added), *reprinted in* A. AVINS, *supra* note 22, at 466.

[219]*See* notes 186 (remarks of Sen. Trumbull), 173 (remarks of Sen. Morrill), 189 (remarks of Rep. Garfield) and accompanying text *supra*.

[220]Referring to the Civil Rights Bill, he stated here "is defined what is meant by privileges and immunities." CONG. GLOBE, 42d Cong., 2d Sess. app. 3 (1872) (remarks of Sen. Morrill), *reprinted in* A. AVINS, *supra* note 22, at 591.

[221]CONG. GLOBE, 42d Cong., 1st Sess. 576 (1871) (remarks of Sen. Trumbull), *reprinted in* A. AVINS, *supra* note 22, at 549.

[222]J. McCLELLAN, JUSTICE STORY AND THE AMERICAN CONSTITUTION 154 (1971).

[223]F. O'BRIEN, JUSTICE REED AND THE FIRST AMENDMENT 116 (1958), *quoted at* J. McCLELLAN, *supra* note 222, at 154.

To cling to the Bingham-Howard remarks on which Justice Black relied for his incorporation doctrine is obstinately to ignore the facts showing they were not generally shared and were untenable.

THE OPEN-ENDED THEORY

From the foregoing it is safe to conclude that, for the framers of the fourteenth amendment, the words "due process" had a fixed, historical meaning; that "privileges and immunities" was drawn from article V, as judicially construed, by way of the Civil Rights Act of 1866; and that "equal protection" was associated by them with the rights enumerated in that Act, that is, with the protection of person and property, and was not conceived to overthrow *all* distinctions. However that be, those terms cannot be construed to embrace the suffrage and segregation which the framers unmistakably excluded from the amendment. A Radical extremist, William Higby, said of section 1, "It would seem that every right pertaining to citizenship was conferred, and yet the language of the second section implies that a State may deny or abridge the right of a citizen to vote."[224] A clearly expressed intention to exclude cannot be less effective. The theory that the framers employed "open-ended"[225] terms in order to enable the courts to reverse their choice improbably premises that they employed words to defeat their purposes.[226] Let it be assumed that such was the concealed purpose of a coterie of framers—for which there is not an iota of evidence in the record—it was not ratified because it was not disclosed to the people. Ratification requires disclosure, whereas in fact the people were led to believe that the amendment did not confer suffrage.[227] And the theory posits that the framers gave a blank check to the Justices to curtail the rights reserved to the states by the tenth amendment and to which they repeatedly expressed their attachment. Curtailment of that reservation cannot rest on speculation. The presumption is all the other way, as is confirmed by the repeated emphasis on the narrow scope of the Civil Rights Act of 1866 and its identity with the fourteenth amendment.

No activist critic of my views has attempted to explain how Bingham, who insisted on deletion of the words "civil rights" because they were too sweeping and "oppressive," or as translated by James Wilson, too "latitudinarian,"[228] came to embrace even more sweeping jurisdiction in the guise of "general," "open-ended" words, which Ely regards as an "invitation" to exercise "untethered" discretion.[229] One of Bingham's statements in the Thirty-ninth Congress looks the other

[224]*See* text accompanying note 58 *supra*. Robert Bork wrote, "If the legislative history revealed a consensus about segregation in schools and all the other relations in life, I do not see how the Court could escape the choices revealed and substitute its own, even though the words are general and conditions have changed." R. BERGER, *supra* note 1, at 214 (quoting Bork, *Neutral Principles and Some First Amendment Problems,* 47 IND. L.J. 1, 13 (1971)).

[225]R. BERGER, *supra* note 1, at 99–116. For a critique of a recent attempt to rationalize the theory, see Berger, *"Government by Judiciary"; John Hart Ely's "Invitation,"* 54 IND. L.J. 277 (1979).

[226]Charles Sumner, the foremost libertarian, declared that resort should be had to the original intention, precisely where the language had no "fixed" meaning, that is, was "general." R. BERGER, *supra* note 1, at 372 (quoting CONG. GLOBE, 39th Cong., 1st Sess. 677 (1866) (remarks of Sen. Sumner)).

[227]R. BERGER, *supra* note 1, at 115, 153. *See* text accompanying notes 43–47, 52 *supra*.

[228]*See* note 120 *supra*.

[229]*See* note 14 *supra*. Perry, *supra* note 5, at 695–96, wrote:

Berger's historical inquiry has, in my view, devastated the notion that the framers of the fourteenth amendment . . . intended it to be "open-ended. . . ." There is no historical evidence supporting the assumption that the founding fathers contemplated, much less intended, that the Supreme Court would frustrate majoritarian policymaking by rendering its own expansive readings of the Constitution.

The evidence is all the other way. *See* R. BERGER, *supra* note 1, at 300–11. *See also* text accompanying notes 282–87 *infra*.

Consider too Hamilton's utterances: (1) "The judiciary . . . can take no active resolution whatever. It may truly be said to have neither *force* nor *will,* but merely judgment . . ." that is, it cannot initiate policy. THE FEDERALIST No. 78, at 504 (Mod. Lib. ed. 1938) (emphasis in original). (2) There "is no liberty, if the power of judging be not separated from the

way: "I should remedy that not by an arbitrary assumption of power, but by amending the Constitution . . . expressly prohibiting the States from any such abuse of power."[230] The reluctance of the framers to go beyond the needs of the moment is illustrated by other remarks. In 1869, Senator James Patterson of New Hampshire, one of the framers, said in response to some proposal, "Let us meet this evil, and not in attempting to meet it provide others that we know not of."[231] That thought was more forcefully expressed by Senator Orris Ferry of Connecticut:

> [W]hen we propose to amend the Constitution we should carry our action just so far as the evil extends, the necessity for remedying which exists, and that we should not project beyond that into theoretical amendments. . . . If a new evil shall develop itself in any future step of the history of the nation then it will be time enough to meet that.[232]

On another note, made familiar by present day activists, Senator Matthew Carpenter of Wisconsin, one of the noted lawyers of the period commented,

> We are told in substance, that whatever Congress in its wisdom [substitute Court] deems advisable to be done, that it has the undoubted power to do; and any man who indulges in constitutional scruple stands in the way of modern progress, and is hostile to the rights of man. . . .
>
> Why, sir, what is the meaning of all this wild talk about the Constitution being construed in the light of modern progress and new American ideas? . . . Does the Senator from Massachusetts seriously maintain that Congress has the power to amplify its jurisdiction according to the generous theory of a court of chancery, to meet any case, which, in its judgment, calls for a remedy? . . .
>
> . . . .
>
> . . . This loose method of construction, this utter contempt of the Constitution, bodes evil to our country, and nothing but evil.[233]

legislative and executive powers." *Id.* (3) Quoting Montesquieu, "Of the three [departments] the judiciary is next to nothing." *Id.* (4) The courts may not "on the pretense of a repugnancy . . . substitute their own pleasure to the constitutional intentions of the legislature." *Id.* at 507. (5) "To avoid an arbitrary discretion in the courts, it is indispensable that they should be bound down by strict rules and precedents. . . ." *Id.* at 510. (6) He assured the Ratifiers in FEDERALIST No. 81 that the judges could be impeached for "deliberate usurpations on the authority of the legislature." *Id.* at 526–27.

[230] CONG. GLOBE, 39th Cong., 1st Sess. 1291 (1866) (remarks of Rep. Bingham) (emphasis added). In 1871 Senator John Pool of North Carolina stated, "Contemporaneous history will show that at the time" the fourteenth amendment was under discussion:

> an amendment was proposed which should affirmatively confer a right of interference with the States and insist upon individual rights within the States, but it was rejected by Congress . . . it is neither just nor honest to attempt now to torture words that were well weighed . . . and give them a meaning which was refused at the time the question was under discussion.

CONG. GLOBE, 42d Cong., 1st Sess. app. 243 (1871) (remarks of Sen. Pool), *reprinted in* A. AVINS, *supra* note 22, at 552. Pool is confirmed by Congress's repeated rejection of attempts to abolish all restrictions. R. BERGER, *supra* note 1, at 163–64.

In the lengthy debates after submission of the fourteenth amendment some argued that "equal" meant equality across the board; no one, so far as I found, argued that the framers purposely chose "general" terms so that future courts might work their will.

[231] CONG. GLOBE, 40th Cong., 3d Sess. 1009 (1869) (remarks of Sen. Patterson), *reprinted in* A. AVINS, *supra* note 22, at 376.

[232] *Id.* at 1008 (remarks of Sen. Ferry), *reprinted in* A. AVINS, *supra* note 22, at 375. A week later, Ferry stated, "It is only wise and safe to change constitutions according to the exigencies which arise demanding a change." He preferred "perspicuous language . . . free from capability of being perverted and misapprehended." *Id.* at 1309 (remarks of Sen. Ferry), *reprinted in* A. AVINS, *supra* note 22, at 402. I would not read such remarks back into the minds of the 1866 framers, but the fact that they were uttered at a time when political exigencies prompted Republicans to embrace less grudging measures suggests that any hint of an "open-ended" phraseology in 1866 would at least have provoked an outcry in some quarters. Compare the rejection by the Thirty-ninth Congress of a proposal to confer suffrage as of July 4, 1876. R. BERGER, *supra* note 22, at 93.

[233] CONG. GLOBE, 41st Cong., 2d Sess. 2425 (1870) (remarks of Sen. Carpenter), *reprinted in* A. AVINS, *supra* note 22, at 433. *See also* text accompanying note 106 *supra* (remarks of Senator Morrill).

In the House, David Lowe said in 1871 that "there is no evil so great but that the obligations of the Constitution are paramount to any necessity."[234] Such was the view Washington expressed in his Farewell address:

> [L]et there be no change by usurpation; for though this, in one instance, may be the instrument of good, it is the customary weapon by which free governments are destroyed. The precedent must always greatly overbalance in permanent evil any partial or transient benefit which the use can at any time yield.[235]

SECTION FIVE: CONGRESS SHALL ENFORCE

Enforcement by Legislation

One of the most significant though least noticed provisions of the fourteenth amendment which, if my analysis is valid, poses a formidable obstacle to contemporary judicial activism, is section 5: "The Congress shall have power to enforce by appropriate legislation the provisions of this article." In 1879, the Supreme Court declared:

> It is not said that the judicial power of the general government shall extend to enforcing the prohibitions and to protecting the rights and immunities guaranteed. It is not said that branch of the government shall be authorized to declare void any action of a State in violation of the prohibitions. It is the power of Congress which has been enlarged.[236]

My earlier study showed that this preference for Congress sprang from a lively distrust of the courts, that the inferior courts had not enjoyed "arising under" jurisdiction until the Civil Rights Act conferred some in 1866, and that the framers regarded Congress as the primary agent for enforcement of the fourteenth amendment.[237] Telling confirmation of these views is furnished by the records of the several Reconstruction Congresses.

Distrust of the courts derived in considerable part from the disastrous *Dred Scott*[238] decision. How lasting was its impression may be gathered from statements in the years that followed. So, Senator James Harlan of Iowa said in 1870 that the decision "has done more to shake the confidence of the American people in the integrity of that high tribunal than all other decisions it has ever rendered."[239] Senator James Nye of Nevada, a member of the Thirty-ninth Congress, stated that the "decision was an outrage upon the Constitution, a defiant outrage upon the rights of the people."[240] More pointedly, Senator Howard added,

> It was a partisan, political decision, the purpose of which was to establish by judicial decision . . . for all time to come the legality, the rightfulness, and even the piety of slavery. . . . The comment made upon that great wrongful judicial decision is to be seen in the dreadful war through which we have passed.[241]

Given such sentiments, the framers were little likely to entrust to the courts enforcement of their efforts to liberate the freedmen. For this we need not resort to conjecture.

---

[234]CONG. GLOBE, 42d Cong., 1st Sess. 374 (1871) (remarks of Rep. Lowe), *reprinted in* A. AVINS, *supra* note 22, at 516.

[235]R. BERGER, *supra* note 1, at 299 (quoting 35 G. WASHINGTON WRITINGS 228–29 (J. Fitzpatrick ed. 1940)).

[236]*Id.* at 221 (quoting *Ex parte* Virginia, 100 U.S. 339, 345 (1879) (emphasis omitted)).

[237]*Id.* at 221–29.

[238]Dred Scott v. Sandford, 60 U.S. (19 How.) 393 (1857).

[239]CONG. GLOBE, 41st Cong., 2d Sess. 598 (1870) (remarks of Sen. Harlan), *reprinted in* A. AVINS, *supra* note 22, at 421. In the midst of the Civil War (1862), William Dunn of Indiana bluntly stated, "I am not willing to trust this court in this question of slavery, because very much of the trouble in which we are now involved may be attributed to the fact that we had a proslavery judiciary." CONG. GLOBE, 37th Cong., 2d Sess. 1792 (1862) (remarks of Rep. Dunn), *reprinted in* A. AVINS, *supra* note 22, at 38.

[240]CONG. GLOBE, 41st Cong., 2d Sess. 1513 (1870) (remarks of Sen. Nye), *reprinted in* A. AVINS, *supra* note 22, at 428.

[241]*Id.* at 1543 (remarks of Sen. Howard), *reprinted in* A. AVINS, *supra* note 22, at 429.

Senator Oliver Morton adverted in 1872 to the "great fact" that "the remedy for the violation of the fourteenth and fifteenth amendments [section 2 of the fifteenth employed the terms of section 5 of the fourteenth] was expressly *not left to the courts.* The remedy was legislative, because in each the amendment itself provided that it shall be enforced by legislation on the part of Congress."[242] If, said Senator Howard in 1869, a Southern state

> shall see fit to divest the colored man there of his right to vote. . . ., the *only mode* in which the right to vote could be restored . . . would be under the subsequent clause in this [fifteenth] amendment giving to Congress power to carry out and effectuate this clause by appropriate legislation. . . .[243]

Of the rights secured by the fourteenth amendment, Senator Matthew Carpenter declared, "[T]hey are not left to be disposed of by the courts as the cases should arise between man and man, but Congress is clothed with the affirmative power and jurisdiction to correct the evil."[244] Speaking to the offenses of the Ku Klux Klan, Senator Daniel Pratt of Indiana said, "[W]e are charged with the duty of devising the mode and manner of stopping these outrages."[245] Senator Morton said in 1874, "Who shall be the judge of what is the appropriate legislation? Congress only. It is not for the courts to judge and determine whether the legislation is appropriate. . . . Congress is made the judge of the character of the means to be employed in the enforcement of the [fourteenth] amendment."[246]

Neither the fourteenth nor the fifteenth amendments were regarded as self-executing. Referring to holdings by the California courts, Senator Sherman stated that the language of the fifteenth "at least" implied "that *before it shall be enforced in the courts* some legislation should be passed by Congress."[247] How, asked Benjamin Butler, can a citizen "avail himself of those constitutional guarantees" of the fourteenth amendment "if Congress cannot pass laws to make them operative?"[248] The very enactment of the Civil Rights Act of 1875 testifies to the prevailing view that the amendment was not self-executing. Such jurisdiction as the courts had was conferred by Congress. This was immediately perceived by Justice Bradley: by section 5 Congress would "have the right to authorize the federal courts to take jurisdiction of cases of this sort. . . . Congress has

---

[242]CONG. GLOBE, 42d Cong., 2d Sess. 525 (1872) (remarks of Sen. Morton) (emphasis added), *reprinted in* A. AVINS, *supra* note 22, at 588. Speaking to the fifteenth amendment in 1870, Morton said, "We know that the second section was put there for the purpose of enabling Congress itself to carry out the provisions . . . for the purpose of enabling Congress to take every step that might be necessary to secure the colored man in the enjoyment of these rights." CONG. GLOBE, 41st Cong., 2d Sess. 3670 (1870) *reprinted in* A. AVINS, *supra* note 22, at 455. Morton also called attention in 1874 to a statement in the Slaughterhouse Cases that "If, however, the States did not conform their laws to its requirements, then by the fifth section of the article [fourteen] of amendment Congress was authorized to enforce it by suitable legislation." 2 CONG. REC. app. 358 (1874) (remarks of Sen. Morton), *reprinted in* A. AVINS, *supra* note 22, at 683.

In one form or another, the proposition, to use Bingham's words, that "Congress is invested with express authority to enforce the limitation," was repeated by Charles Willard, Senator Pool, and Senator Frelinghuysen. CONG. GLOBE, 40th Cong., 3d Sess. 727 (1869) (remarks of Rep. Bingham), *reprinted in* A. AVINS, *supra* note 22, at 350; CONG. GLOBE, 42d Cong., 1st Sess. app. 188–89 (1871) (remarks of Rep. Willard), *reprinted in* A. AVINS, *supra* note 22, at 540; *id.* at 604 (remarks of Sen. Pool), *reprinted in* A. AVINS, *supra* note 22, at 551; 2 CONG. REC. 3452 (1874) (remarks of Sen. Frelinghuysen), *reprinted in* A. AVINS, *supra* note 22, at 674.

[243]CONG. GLOBE, 40th Cong. 3d Sess. 1625 (1869) (remarks of Sen. Howard) (emphasis added), *reprinted in* A. AVINS, *supra* note 22, at 411. *See also* note 113 *supra.*

[244]CONG. GLOBE, 42d Cong., 1st Sess. 577 (1871) (remarks of Sen. Carpenter), *reprinted in* A. AVINS, *supra* note 22, at 550.

[245]*Id.* at 505 (remarks of Sen. Pratt), *reprinted in* A. AVINS, *supra* note 22, at 542.

[246]2 CONG. REC. 358 (1874) (remarks of Sen. Morton), *reprinted in* A. AVINS, *supra* note 22, at 683. In the House, Jeremiah Wilson of Indiana averred in 1871, "[O]f what is necessary to this end Congress alone must be the judge." CONG. GLOBE, 42d Cong., 1st Sess. 483 (1871) (remarks of Rep. Wilson), *reprinted in* A. AVINS, *supra* note 22, at 538.

[247]CONG. GLOBE, 41st Cong., 2d Sess. 3568 (1870) (remarks of Sen. Sherman) (emphasis added), *reprinted in* A. AVINS, *supra* note 22, at 441.

[248]CONG. GLOBE, 42d Cong., 1st Sess. 448 (1871) (remarks of Rep. Butler), *reprinted in* A. AVINS, *supra* note 22, at 532.

neglected to pass an additional law for carrying the fourteenth amendment into effect, the civil rights bill [of 1866] being regarded as having already supplied the necessary provisions for that purpose."[249] James Garfield pointed out that Congress was empowered to provide "that cases arising under . . . these amendments may be carried up on appeal from the State tribunals to the courts of the United States. . . ." The Civil Rights Act of 1866 and the Enforcement Act of 1870, he continued, "opens" the federal courts to those who are denied the equal rights of white men.[250] David Lowe of Kentucky described as "appropriate legislation" to "enforce" the fourteenth amendment, a bill throwing "open the doors of the United States courts to those whose rights under the Constitution are denied or impaired."[251] As said by Senator Carpenter, "We must legislate *and then commit the enforcement* of our laws to the Federal tribunals. . . ."[252]

Almost alone, Senator Trumbull went counter to the current; he considered that the enforcement section added nothing to Congress's authority "to make all laws which shall be necessary and proper for carrying into execution the foregoing powers."[253] But Senator Edmunds pointed out a sound distinction: it was one thing to enforce *powers* granted to the *federal* government and something else again to enforce prohibitions, *denials* of power, against the states.[254] Trumbull apparently had forgotten that *Kentucky v. Dennison*[255] denied the existence of "implied power to exercise any control over a state's officers and agencies,"[256] a lack of power emphasized by Bingham, and which led him to propose the grant to Congress of the power to enforce the guarantees of the fourteenth amendment.[257]

Power Over Jurisdiction

Not less important is the need to reexamine the congressional power over the jurisdiction of the courts in light of section 5. That the jurisdiction of the inferior federal courts rests within the complete discretion of Congress was long since held in *Sheldon v. Sill*:[258] "[H]aving a right to prescribe, Congress may withhold . . . jurisdiction of any of the enumerated controversies."[259] Section 5 may be regarded as a particularized provision to the same effect, for history indicates it was contemplated that Congress "would commit" to the courts "enforcement" of the laws it enacted

---

[249]Livestock Dealers' & Butchers' Ass'n v. Crescent City Livestock & Slaughterhouse Co., 15 F. Cas. 649, 654 (C.C.D. La. 1870) (No. 8,408). Apparently he was unaware that the Act of May 31, 1870, 16 Stat. 140, had been signed.

[250]Cong. Globe, 42d Cong., 1st Sess. app. 153 (1871) (remarks of Rep. Garfield), *reprinted in* A. Avins, *supra* note 22, at 529.

[251]*Id.* at 376 (remarks of Rep. Lowe), *reprinted in* A. Avins, *supra* note 22, at 516.

[252]Cong. Globe, 42d Cong., 2d Sess. 897 (1872) (remarks of Sen. Carpenter) (emphasis added), *reprinted in* A. Avins, *supra* note 22, at 626.

[253]Cong. Globe, 42d Cong., 1st Sess. 577 (1871) (remarks of Sen. Trumbull), *reprinted in* A. Avins, *supra* note 22, at 550. Ulysses Mercur of Pennsylvania was of divided counsels; he thought that courts set aside deprivations of privileges or immunities, and state infringements of due process, but that "equal protection" must be enforced by "appropriate legislation." *Id.* at app. 182 (remarks of Rep. Mercur), *reprinted in* A. Avins, *supra* note 22, at 543. Section 5, however, grants to Congress power to enforce "the *provisions* of this article." U.S. Const. amend. XIV, § 5 (emphasis added).

[254]Cong. Globe, 42d Cong., 1st Sess. 696 (1871) (remarks of Sen. Edmunds), *reprinted in* A. Avins, *supra* note 22, at 562. Senator Howard explained in the Thirty-ninth Congress that the restraints of § 1 of the fourteenth amendment "are not powers granted to Congress, and therefore it is necessary, if they are to be effectuated and enforced . . . that additional power should be given to Congress to that end. This is done by the fifth section . . . a power not found in the Constitution." Cong. Globe, 39th Cong., 1st Sess. 2766 (1866) (remarks of Sen. Howard), *reprinted in* A. Avins, *supra* note 22, at 220.

[255]65 U.S. (24 How.) 66 (1860).

[256]R. Berger, *supra* note 1, at 226–27 (quoting Frantz, *Congressional Power to Enforce The Fourteenth Amendment Against Private Acts*, 73 Yale L.J. 1353, 1357 (1964)).

[257]*Id.* at 227. Justice Story had written to John Berrien, Chairman of the Senate Judiciary Committee, respecting the return of fugitive slaves, "State magistrates now generally refuse to act, and cannot be compelled to act." J. McClellan, *supra* note 222, at 262 n.94.

[258]49 U.S. (8 How.) 441 (1850).

[259]*Id.* at 449. *See* C. Wright, A Handbook on the Law of Federal Courts 24 (1963).

to "enforce" the fourteenth amendment. What it confers it may withdraw. While state court jurisdiction originally was not subject to congressional control, section 5 may have altered the situation so far as concerns the fourteenth amendment. Impetus for a federal judicial remedy derived in considerable part, as said by Senator Henry Lane, from fear that the "emancipated slaves would not have their rights in the courts of the slave States."[260] It would be anomalous if the federal courts were compelled to wait on congressional legislation before "declar[ing] void any action of a State" under the fourteenth amendment,[261] while the distrusted state courts remained free to proceed without regard thereto. If section 5 makes congressional action a prerequisite to judicial review of rights "arising under" the amendment, as the foregoing history indicates, state court jurisdiction of such cases, I suggest, must likewise wait on such action. Otherwise, "Congress shall enforce" would be converted into "The states shall enforce."

What is the extent of Congress's power over the Supreme Court's appellate jurisdiction? Article III, section 2 renders the appellate jurisdiction subject "to such exceptions and under such regulations as Congress shall make." It is therefore not surprising that, given such specific and unequivocal terms, Professor Herbert Wechsler should write in 1965, "Congress has the power by enactment of a statute to strike at what it deems judicial excess by delimitation of the jurisdiction of the lower courts and of the Supreme Court's appellate jurisdiction."[262] The Founders, he wrote, contemplated that "Congress would decide from time to time how far the federal judicial institution should be used without the limits of the federal judicial power."[263] Article III, Justice Harold Burton stated, constitutes the "Achilles heel of the Supreme Court's right of judicial review."[264] In advocacy of an amendment which would shield the appellate jurisdiction, Justice Owen Roberts asked, "[W]hat is there to prevent Congress taking away, bit by bit, all the appellate jurisdiction of the Supreme Court?"[265] The view that article III gives Congress power that "may be uncontrollable" to limit the Court's appellate jurisdiction is echoed in many decisions.[266] No exception from its terms is provided for appeals from state courts. A generation that exalts the "general" terms of the fourteenth amendment over the unmistakable choice of the framers can hardly refuse to give effect to the *specific* power to carve out "exceptions." For, as activist Ely stresses, *The most important datum bearing on what was intended is the constitutional language itself.*"[267]

Long accustomed, however, to look behind the text for light on the legislative intention, I sought in 1969 to learn what the draftsmen of the "exceptions" clause were seeking to accomplish and concluded, as had Professor H.J. Merry before me,[268] that they merely meant to prevent the Court from revising the findings of a jury. Trial by jury was, for the Founders, a central pillar of the democratic structure, not to be tampered with. But the widely varying state practices respecting jury trial compelled the framers to delegate detailed regulation for its protection to Congress.[269] The Merry-Berger findings caused scarcely a ripple in academe; and in light of its current contempt for the legislative intention, academe cannot well complain if Congress chooses to give literal effect to the plain terms of article III. Whatever the effect of article III—and nothing I have read leads

---

[260]R. BERGER, *supra* note 1, at 201–02 (quoting CONG. GLOBE, 39th Cong., 1st Sess. 602 (1866) (remarks of Sen. Lane)).

[261]*See* note 236 and accompanying text *supra*.

[262]Wechsler, *The Courts and the Constitution,* 65 COLUM. L. REV. 1001, 1005 (1965).

[263]*Id.*

[264]R. BERGER, CONGRESS V. THE SUPREME COURT 3 (1969) (quoting Burton, *Two Significant Decisions: Ex parte* Milligan and *Ex Parte* McArdle, 41 A.B.A.J. 124, 176 (1955)).

[265]*Id.* (quoting Roberts, *Fortifying The Supreme Court's Independence,* 35 A.B.A.J. 1, 3–4 (1949)).

[266]*Id.* at 1.

[267]Ely, *supra* note 16, at 418 (emphasis in original). And he states, "[T]he only reliable evidence of what 'the ratifiers' thought they were ratifying is obviously the language of the provision they approved." *Id.* at 419.

[268]Merry, *Scope of the Supreme Court's Appellate Jurisdiction: Historical Basis,* 47 MINN. L. REV. 53, 68 (1962).

[269]R. BERGER, *supra* note 264, at 285–96. For the place of the jury in the colonial scheme, see R. BERGER, *supra* note 1, at 399.

me to alter the views I expressed about the legislative history of the article—it is superseded, so far as respects review of state laws falling within the scope of the fourteenth amendment, by the later enforcement clause of section 5.[270] In conferring jurisdiction to enforce the amendment on Congress, not the courts, the framers did not exempt the Supreme Court. In fact, section 5 sprang from the enduring sense of outrage *Dred Scott* had inspired.[271] A remedy that was "expressly not left to the courts" could not be taken over by the Supreme Court when appeals were filed from state courts.

Those to whom the unfamiliar immediately condemns itself would do well to remember that the Court declared 100 years ago, in a "contemporaneous" construction, that section 5 does *not* provide "that the judicial power . . . shall extend to enforcing" the amendment's guarantees, nor that "it shall be authorized to declare void" state violations of its prohibitions.[272]

This history calls upon proponents of judicial activism to justify the judicial takeover of functions reserved to Congress, and to act before Congress has adopted the requisite enactments. For the meaning of section 5 is that it is for Congress, not the Court, to take the leading oar.

RULES OF CONSTRUCTION AND ORIGINAL INTENTION

The rules of documentary construction represent the deposit of centuries of experience and, as Jean Monnet said of "rules of action" for the Common Market, they "substitute an enduring collective memory for fleeting and fragmented . . . experience"[273] of individual judges. In addition, Hamilton assured the ratifiers that "to avoid arbitrary discretion in the courts, it is indispensable that they should be bound down by strict rules and precedents, which serve to define and point out their duty in every particular case that comes before them,"[274] a far cry from academe's current insistence that the Court must enjoy freewheeling power. That view has made it the fashion to regard rules of construction as archaic;[275] but they were the familiar tools of the 1866 framers and may be considered to be among the presuppositions they brought to the task of framing, rules that would prevent the courts from altering the aims they had in mind. Thus Samuel Shellabarger, a member of the Thirty-ninth Congress, addressing himself in 1869 to a bill to secure the "privileges or immunities" of the fourteenth amendment, referred to the "well known and universally recognized principle of law, *expressio unius exclusio alterius,*" that which is expressed excludes the nonmentioned,[276] a common sense description of the fact that a deed granting a farm to a son does

---

[270]Ignorant, like the rest of my brethren, of the impact of § 5 on the power of Congress to bar all judicial review under the fourteenth amendment, I expressed the view that such action lay beyond its powers. R. BERGER, *supra* note 264, at 282–84. That view required reconsideration in light of § 5.

[271]R. BERGER, *supra* note 264, at 228–30.

[272]*See* note 236 and accompanying text *supra.*

[273]J. MONNET, MEMOIRS 457 (1978).

[274]R. BERGER, *supra* note 1, at 308 (quoting Horwitz, *The Emergence of an Instrumental Conception of American Law, 1780–1820,* in 5 PERSPECTIVES IN AMERICAN HISTORY 287, 309–26 (1971)). Not long after Kent said that without the comparable precedents that constitute the common law, "the courts would be left to a dangerous discretion to roam at large in a trackless field of their own imagination." 1 J. KENT, COMMENTARIES ON AMERICAN LAW 373 (5th ed. 1858). And Justice Story asked, "How is it [a federal statute] to be interpreted? Are the rules of the common law to furnish the proper guide, or is every court and department to give it any interpretation it may please, according to its own arbitrary will?" J. MCCLELLAN, *supra* note 222, at 173.

Rules of construction continue to be applied by the Court: T.I.M.E. Inc. v. United States, 359 U.S. 464, 471 (1959); Virginia v. Tennessee, 148 U.S. 503, 519 (1893); United States v. Arrendondo, 31 U.S. (6 Pet.) 691, 725 (1832).

[275]Alfange, *supra* note 5, at 618–19. *But see* Berger, *Comment on Professor Dean Alfange Jr.'s Article,* 6 HASTINGS CONST. L.Q. 613 (1979).

[276]CONG. GLOBE, *40th Cong., 3d Sess. app. 98 (1869) (remarks of Rep. Shellabarger), reprinted in* A. AVINS, *supra* note 22, at 347.

not vest it in a daughter. Senator Howard referred to it as "an ancient maxim of the law," which had to be taken into account in drafting,[277] a proposition in which Senator Nye joined.[278]

The effort to nullify the intention of the framers also leads activists to argue that a constitution is not to be construed after the fashion of a statute.[279] Yet, Senator Howard, speaking to a proposed amendment, stated, "[L]ook at it with the eye of a lawyer, of a person accustomed to explain and interpret statutes, and you can come to no other conclusion."[280] On what ground indeed are we freer to disregard the unmistakable intention of the framers, for example, to exclude suffrage from the fourteenth amendment, than that of a legislature expressed in a statute. If anything, the will of the framers, particularly when ratified by the people, is paramount to that of the legislators who are merely their delegates.

On that score the members of the several Reconstruction Congresses have left no doubt. In the midst of the session that was framing the fourteenth amendment, Senator Charles Sumner, well aware that the majority of the Senate were uttering sentiments opposed to his own, yet stated:

> Every Constitution embodies the principles of its framers. It is a transcript of their minds. If its meaning in any place is open to doubt, or if words are used which seem to have no fixed signification [e.g., equal protection], we cannot err if we turn to the framers; and their authority increases in proportion to the evidence which they have left on the question.[281]

This was confirmed by confreres who also sat in the Thirty-ninth Congress; so, in 1871, John Farnsworth of Illinois, said of the fourteenth amendment, "Let us see what was understood to be its meaning at the time of its adoption by Congress. . . ."[282] James Garfield rejected an interpretation of the amendment that went far "beyond the intent and meaning of those who framed and those who amended the Constitution."[283] Such sentiments were summarized in 1872 by "a unan-

[277]Id. at 1304 (1869) (remarks of Sen. Howard), reprinted in A. AVINS, supra note 22, at 399.

[278]Id. at 1306 (remarks of Sen. Nye), reprinted in A. AVINS, supra note 22, at 400.

[279]Alfange, supra note 5, at 609; Miller, The Elusive Search for Values in Constitutional Interpretation, 6 HASTINGS CONST. L.Q. 487 (1979); Murphy, supra note 17, at 1761. But Julius Goebel states that the Founders were accustomed to "resort to the accepted rules of statutory interpretation to settle the intent and meaning of constitutional provisions. . . ." 1 J. GOEBEL, HISTORY OF THE SUPREME COURT OF THE UNITED STATES 128 (1971). To the same effect, Corwin, The "Higher Law" Background of American Constitutional Law, 42 HARV. L. REV. 149, 370–71 (1928).

Senator Richard Yates, who was a framer of the fourteenth amendment, said with respect to the word "citizen" therein, "so far as the intention of the Legislature was concerned, (and that is one rule of determining the meaning of a statute or enactment,) . . . so far as the intention of Congress at the time was concerned . . . it was decided against us" on the suffrage issue. CONG. GLOBE, 40th Cong., 3d Sess. 1005 (1869) (remarks of Sen. Yates), reprinted in A. AVINS, supra note 22, at 374.

Another attempt to discredit resort to legislative intention is exemplified by activist assertions that a constitution is not to be construed like a contract. Alfange, supra note 5, at 609. Yet a Senate Judiciary Committee Report of 1872 took precisely that course: "The Constitution, like a contract between private parties, must be read in the light of the circumstances which surrounded those who made it." S. REP. No. 21, 42d Cong., 2d Sess. 2 (1872) (Report of the Committee on the Judiciary), reprinted in A. AVINS, supra note 22, at 571. For whatever the document, "The end which interpretation aims at," said Thomas Rutherforth, a commentator known to the Founders, "is to find out what was the intention of the writer. . . ." R. BERGER, supra note 1, at 366 (quoting 2 T. RUTHERFORTH, INSTITUTE OF NATURAL LAW 307 (1754–1756)).

[280]CONG. GLOBE, 40th Cong., 3d Sess. 1301 (1869) (remarks of Sen. Howard), reprinted in A. AVINS, supra note 22, at 397.

[281]R. BERGER, supra note 1, at 372 (quoting CONG. GLOBE, 39th Cong., 1st Sess. 677 (1866) (remarks of Sen. Sumner)).

[282]CONG. GLOBE, 42d Cong., 1st Sess. app. 115 (1871) (remarks of Rep. Farnsworth), reprinted in A. AVINS, supra note 22, at 506.

[283]Id. at app. 152 (remarks of Rep. Garfield), reprinted in A. AVINS, supra note 22, at 528. Garfield cautioned his colleagues to bear in mind that "[n]ot only the words which we put into the law, but what shall be said here in the way of defining and interpreting the meaning of the clause . . . may go far to settle the meaning of the clause. . . ." Id. at app. 149, reprinted in A. AVINS, supra note 22, at 526. Of the fourteenth amendment, Horatio Burchard said, "The interpretation given to it by gentlemen who then debated it, and especially by those who advocated its passage, has almost an authority in construing its meaning equal to that of the writings of Madison and Hamilton in the Federalist pending the adoption of

imous Senate Judiciary Committee report, signed by senators who had voted for the Thirteenth, Fourteenth, and Fifteenth Amendments in Congress":[284]

> In construing the Constitution [*i.e.*, the fourteenth] we are compelled to give it such interpretation as will secure the result which was intended to be accomplished by those who framed it and the people who adopted it. A construction which should give the phrase . . . a meaning differing from the sense in which it was understood and employed by the people when they adopted the Constitution, would be as unconstitutional as a departure from the plain and express language of the Constitution in any other particular. This is the rule of interpretation adopted by all commentators on the Constitution, and in all judicial expositions of that instrument; and your committee is satisfied of the entire soundness of this principle. A change in the popular use of any word employed in the Constitution cannot retroact upon the Constitution, either to enlarge or limit its provisions.[285]

The attempts of John Wofford and Leonard Levy to read into the framers' words whatever meaning the courts choose[286] represent a forlorn effort to rationalize otherwise insupportable decisions. Be it said to the credit of the Court, it has never openly repudiated the original intention as an index of constitutional meaning; instead, as Jacobus tenBroek, an early activist, wrote, the Court "has insisted with almost uninterrupted regularity that the end and object of constitutional construction is the discovery of the intention of those persons who formulated the instrument. . . ."[287]

EPILOGUE

For about twenty-five years, adherents of the "new faith" have been rationalizing what Louis Lusky frankly describes as "the Court's new and grander conception of its own place in the governmental scheme," its "assertion of power to revise the Constitution, bypassing the cumbersome amendment procedure prescribed by Article V,"[288] what Alfred Kelly called a "constitutional revolution."[289] Against this I urged with Hamilton that "an agent cannot new model his commission;"[290] that the Court is not authorized to "bypass the cumbersome amendment procedure," not empowered to set aside the clearly discernible intention of the framers to exclude suffrage and segregation from the fourteenth amendment. That approach, by no means novel, derives from a long tradition that Thomas Grey, an activist, acknowledges "is one of great power and compelling

the original Constitution." *Id.* at app. 315 (remarks of Rep. Burchard), *reprinted in* A. Avins, *supra* note 22, at 545. Senator Morton said, "If we read the history of the [fourteenth] amendment we shall understand precisely what was meant by it. . . ." Cong. Globe, 42d Cong., 2d Sess. 847 (1872) (remarks of Sen. Morton), *reprinted in* A. Avins, *supra* note 22, at 622. For another appeal to the "history of the amendments," see William Lawrence of Ohio. 2 Cong. Rec. 412 (1874) (remarks of Rep. Lawrence), *reprinted in* A. Avins, *supra* note 22, at 662.

[284]A. Avins, *supra* note 22, at ii.

[285]S. Rep. No. 21, 42d Cong., 2d Sess. 2 (1872) (Report of the Committee on the Judiciary), *reprinted in* A. Avins, *supra* note 22, at 571–72.

[286]R. Berger, *supra* note 1, at 370 (citing Wofford, *The Blinding Light: The Uses of History in Constitutional Interpretation,* 31 U. Chi. L. Rev. 502 (1964) and L. Levy, Judgments: Essays of American Constitutional History (1972)).

[287]TenBroek, *Use by the United States Supreme Court of Extrinsic Aids in Constitutional Construction,* 27 Calif. L. Rev. 399 (1939). *See* Bork, note 346 *infra.*

[288]Lusky, *supra* note 3, at 406. Compare this with Montesquieu's "Of the three powers . . . the judiciary is next to nothing," quoted by Hamilton in The Federalist No. 78, at 504 (Mod. Lib. ed. 1938), an assurance meant to allay suspicion of the novel judicial review.

[289]Kelly, note 8 *supra.*

[290]6 A. Hamilton, Works 166 (Letters of Camillus) (H. Lodge ed. 1904). "In all free states, the constitution is fixed; it is from thence, that the legislative derives its autority; therefore it cannot change the constitution without destroying its own foundation." Letter of Massachusetts House to the Earl of Shelburne, *reprinted in* H. Commager, Documents of American History 65 (7th ed. 1963).

simplicity . . . deeply rooted in our history . . . and . . . in our formal constitutional law."[291] So obscured by the recent overlay of activist apologetics is this tradition that it will be instructive to recall a few illustrations.

In the Convention it had been proposed to make the Justices members of a Council of Revision that would assist the President in exercising the veto power, on the ground that "laws may be . . . dangerous . . . and yet not be so unconstitutional as to justify judges in refusing to give them effect."[292] The proposal was rejected because, as Elbridge Gerry declared, "It was quite foreign from the nature of ye office to make them judges of the policy of public measures."[293] Nathaniel Gorham chimed in that judges "are not to be presumed to possess any peculiar knowledge of the mere policy of public measures;" and Rufus King added that judges "ought not to be legislators."[294] This history bars the way to a judicial takeover of policymaking. It is reflected in one of the earliest and strongest decisions to lay claim to the power of judicial review, *Kamper v. Hawkins.*[295] Judge Henry held:

> The judiciary from the nature of the office . . . could never be designed to determine upon the equity, necessity or usefulness of a law; that would amount to an express interfering with the legislative branch. . . . [N]ot being chosen immediately by the people, nor being accountable to them . . . they do not, and ought not, to represent the people in framing or repealing any law.[296]

Even less was it conceived that the courts would amend the Constitution, for the concept of a "fixed Constitution," to which the Founders were attached,[297] contemplated that the provision it contained for amendment "was expected to be the only form of change. . . ."[298] What departures the federal courts made from such constitutional limits were *sub rosa;* my critics point to no naked judicial claim of power to "revise" the Constitution. Chief Justice Marshall, as we shall see, explicitly disclaimed a power to "change" the Constitution.[299]

My further documentation of these undeniable facts was met by a torrent of distortion, misrepresentation, and challenges to my credibility, revealing that I have touched a raw nerve and

---

[291]Grey, *Do We Have an Unwritten Constitution?* 27 STAN. L. REV. 703, 705 (1975). Ely, *supra* note 16, at 412, agrees that it is a view which "stretches back" to Hamilton and Marshall and "seems to enjoy virtually universal contemporary acceptance. . . ." *See also* Justice Harlan, note 6 and accompanying text *supra.*

[292]R. BERGER, *supra* note 1, at 301 (quoting 2 M. FARRAND, THE RECORDS OF THE FEDERAL CONVENTION OF 1787, at 73 (1911) (emphasis added)).

[293]*Id.* (quoting 1 M. FARRAND, THE RECORDS OF THE FEDERAL CONVENTION OF 1787, at 97–98 (1911)).

[294]*Id.* at 301–02 (quoting 1 M. FARRAND, THE RECORDS OF THE FEDERAL CONVENTION OF 1787, at 108 (1911) and 2 *id.* at 73)).

[295]3 Va. (1 Va. Cas.) 20 (1793).

[296]*Id.* at 47. In the same case Judge St. George Tucker quoted Vattel: the legislators "ought to consider the fundamental laws as sacred, if the nation has not *in express terms* given them power to change them." *Id.* at 76 (emphasis added). Of the courts he stated, their duty is "declaring what the law is, and not making a new law," *id.* at 96, much less "to change" the "fundamental laws."

Peter Duponceau, one of the foremost lawyers of his period, questioned in 1824 whether the "Federal courts have a right . . . to mould the Constitution as they please, and to extend their own jurisdiction beyond the limits preserved by the National Compact." P. DUPONCEAU, A DISSERTATION ON THE NATURE AND EXTENT OF THE JURISDICTION OF THE COURTS OF THE UNITED STATES i (1824). In 1819 Chief Justice Marshall disclaimed "a right to change the constitution." *See* note 372 and accompanying text *infra. See also* Berger, *"Law of the Land" Reconsidered,* 74 NW. U.L. REV. 1, 14–27 (1979).

[297]P. KURLAND, WATERGATE AND THE CONSTITUTION 7 (1978). *See also* note 290 *supra.*

[298]P. KURLAND, *supra* note 297, at 7. Elbridge Gerry, erstwhile President of the Continental Congress and a framer, stated in the First Congress, "The people have" directed a "particular mode of making amendments, which we are not at liberty to depart from." R. BERGER, *supra* note 1, at 317–18 (quoting 1 ANNALS OF CONG. 503 (1789, Gayles & Seaton eds. 1836) (print bearing running head "History of Congress"). *See also* Hawke v. Smith, 253 U.S. 221, 227 (1920); Oregon v. Mitchell, 400 U.S. 112, 203 (1970) (Harlan, J., concurring in part and dissenting in part).

[299]*See* notes 369–74 and accompanying text *infra.*

betraying incapacity to bring dispassionate judgment to evaluation of my proof.[300] Rancor clouds judgment. For instance, Paul Brest wrote that Berger "persistently distorted [the historical data] to support his thesis."[301] Only one who is willfully blind can disregard the proof, further documented in these pages, that the framers excluded suffrage and segregation from the fourteenth amendment. I challenge Brest to cite chapter and verse for his opprobrious charge.[302] Similarly, Walter Murphy makes it *"the message* of [his] review . . . that Berger's argument relies far less on 'brute facts' about whatever it was the framers intended and more on incomplete research and gossamery guesses about what they had in mind,"[303] this about the exclusion of suffrage and segregation! If more "complete research" would disclose facts that confute my demonstration, Murphy owes his scholarly profession a duty to produce them in support of his charges. In truth, the exclusion of suffrage, which is the core of my study, is now so widely accepted that Murphy's charge may be viewed as splenetic. It would be tedious to recapitulate similar charges by Dean Alfange, Stanley Kutler, and Arthur Miller.[304] One and all they illustrate Robert Jastrow's observation: "[W]hen our beliefs are in conflict with the evidence . . . we become irritated, we pretend the conflict does not exist, or we paper it over with meaningless phrases."[305]

What is to be learned from my critics? For Laurence Tribe, constitutional history is beside the point; indeed, he opined that "Berger mistakes historical digging for scholarship."[306] By that remarkable distinction, the Leakeys presumably are mere gravediggers rather than anthropologists. For Justice Horace Gray, however, "all questions of constitutional construction" were "largely a historical question."[307] That follows from considerations of enduring importance. Ours is a government "founded on the consent of the governed." "The people," declared James Iredell, one of the ablest of the Founders, "have chosen to be governed under such and such principles. They have not chosen to be governed or promised to submit upon any other."[308] Any light upon what they consented to, what the words in which that consent was expressed mean, is therefore of the utmost importance. Gripped by fear of the greedy expansiveness of power, the framers steered by a leading principle—to crib and confine all delegated power.[309] Words were employed to limit the

[300]"Berger's uncomfortable and unfashionable analysis is an important one. It will not do, as some have already done, to brush it aside in a peremptory manner." Monaghan, *The Constitution Goes to Harvard,* 13 Harv. C.R.-C.L. Rev. 117, 124 (1978). "Regrettably, fewer constitutional scholars and theorists than one might think seem prepared to acknowledge the serious challenge Berger's argument poses." Perry, *supra* note 5, at 694. If "the Supreme Court's purpose is to establish justice without reference to the original intent of the framers, then what remains to circumscribe judicial power? Berger's critics have given singularly unsatisfactory answers to this question." Kommers, *Role of the Supreme Court,* 40 Rev. of Pol. 409, 413 (1978).

[301]Brest, N.Y. Times, Dec. 11, 1977, § 7 (Book Review), at 10, col. 3.

[302]Brest's undocumented charge was without further ado described by Laurence Tribe as the exposure by a "careful scholar" of the "flaws in Berger's history." Boston Globe, Mar. 20, 1978, § 1 at 14, col. 6. On the other hand, Michael Perry, whose review indicates a painstaking examination of the evidence, wrote that Brest's "is a grave charge, and I cannot myself see the basis for it." Perry, *supra* note 5, at 689 n.14.

[303]Murphy, note 17 and accompanying text *supra* (emphasis added).

[304]For my comments on the Miller, Kutler, and Alfange critiques, see 6 Hastings Const. L.Q. 576, 590, 613 (1979).

[305]Jastrow, *Have Astronomers Found God?* N.Y. Times, June 25, 1978, § 6 (Magazine), at 19, col. 1. Richard Kay writes of the desegregation and reapportionment decisions, "These doctrines have now become almost second nature to a generation of lawyers and scholars. Thus it is hardly surprising that the casting of a fundamental doubt on such basic assumptions should produce shock, dismay, and sometimes anger." Kay, Book Review, 10 Conn. L. Rev. 801, 801 (1978).

[306]Quoted in Shrum, *How Supreme the Court?* New Times, Nov. 11, 1977, at 8. *See also* note 302 *supra.*

[307]R. Berger, *supra* note 1, at 367 n.22 (quoting Sparf v. United States, 156 U.S. 51, 169 (1895) (Gray, J., dissenting)). *See* tenBroek, note 287 *supra.*

[308]R. Berger, *supra* note 1, at 295–96 (quoting 2 Life and Correspondence of James Iredell 146 (G. McRee ed. 1857)).

[309]Bernard Bailyn tells us that the colonists interminably dwelt on the problem of power, "its endlessly propulsive tendency to expand itself beyond legitimate boundaries." B. Bailyn, The Ideological Origins of the American Revolution 56 (1967). *See also* R. Berger, *supra* note 264, at 8–18.

power they so jealously delegated—what Jefferson called "the chains of the Constitution";[310] hence, a written constitution is subverted by a theory that leaves the Justices free to jettison the meaning attached by the framers to their words in favor of their own.[311]

Tribe espouses what he acknowledges is "the most controversial" of his views, "an active judicial posture in giving life to the Constitution"—a euphemism for rewriting it. He relies on "the Framers' *deliberate* choice of broad terminology," *i.e.,* "equal protection" and "due process,"—"open-textured" phrases—"when narrower alternatives were at hand," a way of "inviting growth."[312] He posits, as Michael Perry notes, that "the Constitution is an *intentionally* incomplete, often *deliberately* indeterminate structure for the participatory evolution of political ideals and governmental practices."[313] To label "due process" as an "indeterminate" vehicle for "evolution of political ideals" is to prefer a crystal ball to evidence that due process, both in 1791 and 1866, was applicable only to judicial proceedings.[314] Where is the evidence that the framers of the fourteenth amendment "intentionally and deliberately" left its terms "incomplete and indeterminate?" To the contrary, the uncontroverted evidence, confirmed in these pages, is that the framers repeatedly stated that the amendment and the Civil Rights Act of 1866 were "*identical*";[315] the face of the Act exhibits its narrow, enumerated aims.[316] That "identity" alone rebuts a "deliberately indeterminate structure." The framers did not at one and the same time identify the amendment with the enumerated objectives of the Act and then, by the use of "general" words, "invite" the Court to frustrate the "identical" purpose. It is not a little remarkable that it took academe almost 100 years to discover that "invitation."

By way of confirmation, I showed in three fact-packed chapters that "privileges or immunities," "equal protection," and "due process" had a restricted, "determinate" meaning for the framers who employed the terms,[317] as is further corroborated in these pages,[318] proof that is not met by bare assertion to the contrary. Moreover, men do not use words to defeat their purpose, *e.g.,* their all but indisputable intention to exclude suffrage, a fact which underlies the decisions of Justice Holmes and Judge Learned Hand that the "manifest" intent must "override even the explicit words used."[319] If we may discard the meaning attached to their words by the framers, we enter the world of Humpty Dumpty,[320] or the chill close of George Orwell's *Animal Farm,* where all animals are

---

[310]R. BERGER, *supra* note 1, at 252 (quoting 4 DEBATES IN THE SEVERAL STATE CONVENTIONS OF THE ADOPTION OF THE FEDERAL CONSTITUTION 446 (J. Elliott comp. 1836)).

[311]That was articulated by Madison: if "the sense in which the Constitution was accepted and ratified by the Nation . . . be not the guide in expounding it, there can be no security for . . . a faithful exercise of its powers." R. BERGER, *supra* note 1, at 3 (quoting 9 THE WRITINGS OF JAMES MADISON 191 (G. Hunt ed. 1900–1910)). Jefferson pledged as President to administer the Constitution "according to the safe and honest meaning contemplated by the plain understanding of the people at the time of its adoption—a meaning to be found in the explanations of those who advocated . . . it." *Id.* at 366–67 (quoting 4 DEBATES IN THE SEVERAL STATE CONVENTIONS ON THE ADOPTION OF THE FEDERAL CONSTITUTION 446 (J. Elliot comp. 1836)). No contemporary utterances to the contrary have come to my attention.

[312]L. TRIBE, AMERICAN CONSTITUTIONAL LAW 1–2 (Supp. 1979) (emphasis added). He would not permit "the racial bigotry of many who wrote or ratified the Fourteenth Amendment . . . to bring into question the legitimacy . . . of Brown v. Board of Education." *Id.* at 2. In plain words, the framers' intention is of no moment. Compare his theorizing with the facts, R. BERGER, *supra* note 1, at 99–116, and *see* text accompanying notes 224–32 *supra*.

[313]Perry, *supra* note 5, at 695 (quoting L. TRIBE, AMERICAN CONSTITUTION LAW iii (1978) (emphasis added)).

[314]*See* notes 146–53 and accompanying text *supra; R.* BERGER, *supra* note 1, at 193–220; Berger, note 296 *supra*.

[315]*See* note 164 and text accompanying notes 189, 192, 196 *supra*.

[316]R. BERGER, *supra* note 1, at 24 (quoting Civil Rights Act of 1866, ch. 31, § 1, 14 Stat. 27 (codified at 42 U.S.C. § 1981 (1976))). *See id.* at 24–29.

[317]*Id.* at 20–36, 166–220.

[318]*See* notes 144, 212, 224–31 and accompanying text *supra*.

[319]*See* note 142 *supra*.

[320]"When I use a word," Humpty Dumpty said, "it means just what *I* choose it to mean." L. CARROL, THROUGH THE LOOKING GLASS 163 (Norton ed. 1971) (emphasis in original).

equal but some are more equal than others.[321] And when traditional state powers are invaded, it is not enough that the "general" words are capable of a broad meaning; the reservation by the tenth amendment to the states of powers not delegated to the federal government calls for a clear showing that the successor amendment was designed to curtail those reserved powers.[322] The "open-textured" theory, put forth by Alexander Bickel in 1955 as a possible hypothesis,[323] represents an untenable attempt to sustain a decision, *Brown v. Board of Education*,[324] which Bickel himself demonstrated was contrary to the framers' intention.[325] That is what is meant by "giving life to the Constitution."

What seems "decisive" to Tribe, what "expose[s] the inherent subjectivity" of my "supposedly objective approach," is "leaving in place just those decisions which [I] think wrong but whose overruling even [I] find unthinkable."[326] This misrepresents my views. Although I found that segregation was excluded from the fourteenth amendment, I concluded that it would be "probably impossible to undo the past. . . . But to accept thus far accomplished ends is not to condone the continued employment of the unlawful means."[327] What is "subjective" about acknowledging that, like poured concrete, events have hardened, that the *status quo ante* cannot be restored merely by "overruling" a past decision? But that does not justify the *continued* exercise of usurped jurisdiction in decisions that wring protests even from fervid activists.[328]

The "open-ended" theory—the activists' mainstay—is further developed by John Hart Ely. He recognizes that "untethered" discretion is "undemocratic," that though "[an] untrammeled majority is indeed a dangerous thing . . . it will require a heroic inference" to deduce that "[judicial] enforcement . . . of an 'unwritten constitution' is an appropriate response in a democratic republic;"[329] more baldly, that the people have surrendered majoritarian government to the Court. He draws that "heroic inference" from the terms of the fourteenth amendment whereby the framers allegedly issued "open and across-the-board invitations to import into the constitutional decision process considerations that will not be found in the amendment nor even, at least in any obvious sense, elsewhere in the Constitution."[330] But even Ely finds the "invitation" "frightening," and concludes that "[i]f a principled approach to judicial enforcement of the Constitution's open-ended provisions cannot be developed [he undertakes to develop it] . . . , whatever the framers may have been assuming, the courts should stay away from them."[331] A marvelous theory! The 1866

[321]G. ORWELL, ANIMAL FARM 148 (1954).

[322]A recent analogy was furnished by Pierson v. Ray, 386 U.S. 547 (1967). After adverting to the common law immunity of judges for acts performed in their official capacity, the Court held:
We do not believe that this settled principle was abolished by § 1983, which makes liable "every person" who under color of law deprives another of his civil rights. . . . The immunity of judges . . . [is] well established and we presume that Congress would have specifically so provided had it wished to abolish the doctrine.
Id. at 554–55. Thus the *express* "every person" yielded to a common law immunity; the tenth amendment demands an even more exacting standard before "general" words reduce the constitutionally reserved powers of the states.

[323]R. BERGER, *supra* note 1, at 101–02, 104 (quoting A. BICKEL, THE LEAST DANGEROUS BRANCH 60–61, 100 (1962)).

[324]347 U.S. 483 (1954).

[325]R. BERGER, *supra* note 1, at 100–01. *See* note 4 and accompanying text *supra*.

[326]L. TRIBE, *supra* note 312, at 2.

[327]R. BERGER, *supra* note 1, at 412–13.

[328]*See* notes 329–40 and accompanying text *infra*. *See also* R. BERGER, *supra* note 1, at 428–29 (quoting Cox, *The New Dimensions of Constitutional Adjudication*, 51 WASH. L. REV. 791, 802, 814–15 (1976)). "Suppose . . . that certain undeniably subconstitutional decisions are too tightly woven into the fabric of law and society to be called into question. It does not follow from their existence that the mode of decision which produced those holdings should become standard operating procedure in the future." Shrock & Welsh, *Reconsidering the Constitutional Commom Law,* 91 HARV. L. REV. 1117, 1126 n.59 (1978).

[329]Ely, *supra* note 16, at 404, 411.

[330]*Id.* at 415.

[331]*Id.* at 425, 448.

framers, who admittedly distrusted the courts,[332] extended an "invitation," which at the distance of 100 years still "frightens" Ely, to exercise "untethered" discretion, to set aside their determination to exclude suffrage, content to wait for Ely to develop limiting principles! It may confidently be assumed that a Court which was undeterred by the framers' intention to withhold control of suffrage will be no more discouraged by Ely's limiting principles from exercising the "untethered" discretion with which academe has endowed it. It bears repetition that one will vainly search the records of the Court for a claim that the fourteenth amendment "invited" it to exercise illimitable discretion.

Ely is not alone among activists in seeking to "limit" the genie they have released from the bottle.[333] "Of course," writes Dean Alfange, "judges ought not to be free to manipulate [the Constitution's] words at will to arrive at whatever results their personal inclinations commended to them."[334] Does not "one-person-one-vote" in the face of the framers' exclusion of suffrage exemplify precisely such manipulation? It is only when judicial inclinations do not coincide with their own that activists are moved to protest. Thus, although Louis Lusky praises "the tremendously valuable work" the Court "has done in the past third of a century," he condemns the post-1968 "string of school desegregation decisions" because they have "led to grotesquely destructive results" and "wantonly . . . wreck[ed] a number of public school systems and outrage[d] the communities they serve."[335] For Henry Abraham, *Brown v. Board of Education* was "constitutionally permissible," but he rejects the decisions that followed in its train: "[T]he Court had no constitutional mandate to turn itself . . . into a combination of national school board, transportation expert, disciplinarian, employment manager and administrative director. . . ."[336] So too, he is critical of the abortion cases:[337] the "Court should not view itself as a 'social reform agency,'" as "when it in effect wrote the Federal Abortion Code."[338] What was the desegregation decision but a revolutionary "social reform" measure? The debates in the Thirty-ninth Congress show that segregation was excluded from the fourteenth amendment, as Abraham agrees,[339] but not a reference was made to abortion. Surely the Court does not have more power in the face of express exclusion than of silence. Manifestly Lusky and Abraham draw the line where their own predilections stop short.[340]

The identification of their predilections with constitutional warrant is more nakedly made by Robert Cover and Paul Brest. Proceeding from my recognition that the results of the desegregation decision cannot be undone, Cover concludes that "[i]t is in this recognition of the practical, present and future-looking consequences of constitutional symbols that a proper beginning point for a book on constitutional law must lie."[341] In other words an attractive result implies constitutional power to accomplish it; constitutional *limits* on delegated power are reduced to "constitutional symbols." He thrusts aside "the self-evident meaning of the Constitution," let alone "the

---

[332]*Id.* at 448.

[333]Abraham, *"Equal Justice Under Law" or "Justice at Any Cost,"* 6 HASTINGS CONST. L.Q. 467 (1979); Alfange, *supra* note 5, at 625–26.

[334]Alfange, *supra* note 5, at 629.

[335]Lusky, *supra* note 3, at 424.

[336]Abraham, *supra* note 333, at 480. *See* R. BERGER, *supra* note 1, at 428–29 (quoting Cox, *The New Dimensions of Constitutional Adjudication,* 51 WASH. L. REV. 791, 802, 814–15 (1976)).

[337]Doe v. Bolton, 410 U.S. 179 (1973); Roe v. Wade, 410 U.S. 113 (1973).

[338]Abraham, *supra* note 333, at 479–80. *See also* Ely, *The Wages of Crying Wolf: A Comment on Roe v. Wade,* 82 YALE L.J. 920 (1973).

[339]Abraham, *supra* note 333, at 480.

[340]Thus Lusky urges the Court to repudiate "its misinterpretation of the Fourteenth Amendment in the 1873 Slaughter House Cases," but maintains that the judicial decisions of the last 25 years are "irreversible," that "we cannot turn back the clock." Lusky, *supra* note 3, at 421–23.

[341]Cover, Book Review, NEW REPUBLIC, Jan. 14, 1978, at 26, 27.

intention of the framers," in favor of an "ideology" framed by a nonelected, life-tenured bench[342] which, as Judge Henry early noted, is not accountable to the electorate. The Constitution, Cover explains, is of no moment because "we" have decided to "entrust" judges with forming an "ideology" by which legislative action can be measured, and it may be added, the framers' choices can be supplanted.[343] Of course, he does not point to the source of this decision to "entrust" judges with the ultimate power to frame our "ideology," but equates the wishes of the academic illuminati with the will of "We, the people."[344] But where is the referendum in which *they* have spoken?

Brest dresses the Cover theory in "general" words rhetoric: "[B]road constitutional guarantees require the Court to discern, articulate, and apply values deeply held by our society. . . . The ultimate touchstone . . . is not the people long since dead, but the consent of the living. The process of appointing judges and carrying out their decisions tends to secure this assent."[345] Appointment of new judges hardly signifies assent to decisions of those replaced. And they are sworn to "support," not to revise, the Constitution. The people, moreover, cannot assent to what is not disclosed; they have never been told that the Court is engaged in amending the Constitution, but to the contrary have been assured that its decisions are rooted in the instrument. As Robert Bork wrote, "[V]alue choices are attributed to the Founding Fathers, not to the Court."[346] Were the contrary true, Brest would have ratification of judicial amendment by popular inertia, thus circumventing the provision for amendment pursuant to article V.[347]

Of another proponent of judicial amendment, Arthur S. Miller,[348] Randall Bridwell has written that he trots out "all the shopworn cliches . . . in favor of government action to cure whatever ails us . . . with the nonanalytical, rhetorical exuberance that has become the hallmark of the . . . result-oriented advocate of judicial reform."[349] Since Miller is one of the "philosophers" *cum*

---

[342]"Surely utter indifference to the constitutional text or its history makes the Constitution relatively meaningless." Bridwell, *supra* note 5, at 910.

[343]Cover explains further:

[A] reading of the Constitution must stand or fall not upon the Constitution's self-evident meaning, nor upon the intentions of 1787 or 1866 framers. . . . [I]t is for *us,* not the framers, to decide whether that end of liberty is best served by entrusting to judges a major role in defining our governing political ideas and in measuring the activity of the primary actors in majoritarian politics against that ideology.

Cover, *supra* note 341, at 27 (emphasis added). Cover draws a distinction, "intelligible to most pre-adolescents—between the direction 'Do what you want' and 'Do *what you think is right* or just.'" *Id.* (emphasis added). Doubtless Justice Peckham did what *he* thought "right or just" in Lochner v. New York, 198 U.S. 45 (1905), but that decision has yet to find favor with libertarians. Barbara Tuchman noted "the sense of right that supreme office breeds." B. Tuchman, A Distant Mirror 525 (1978). And John Stuart Mill cautioned against entrusting power to those who know what is best for the rest of us. R. Berger, *supra* note 1, at 413 n.20 (quoting Furman v. Georgia, 408 U.S. 238, 467 (1972) (Rehnquist, J., dissenting) (quoting J. Mill, On Liberty 28 (1885))).

[344]As Joseph Bishop, Cover's more sagacious colleague at Yale, wrote:

Those who favor abortion, busing . . . and who oppose capital punishment . . . obviously have no faith whatever in the wisdom or will of the great majority of the people, who are opposed to them. They are doing everything possible to have these problems resolved by a small minority in the courts or the bureaucracy.

Symposium—What Is a Liberal—Who Is a Conservative? Commentary, Sept. 1976, at 47.

[345]Brest, *supra* note 301, at 44.

[346] R. Berger, *supra* note 1, at 319 (quoting Bork, *Neutral Principles and Some First Amendment Problems,* 47 Ind. L.J. 1, 3–4 (1971)). Bork states, "The Supreme Court regularly insists that its results . . . do not spring from the mere will of the Justices . . . but are supported, indeed compelled, by a proper understanding of the Constitution. . . ." *Id.* Young enthusiasts like Brest and Cover have outrun the object of their solicitude.

[347] In The Federalist No. 78, at 509 (Mod. Lib. ed. 1938), Hamilton stated, "Until the people have, by some solemn and authoritative act, annulled or changed the established form, it is binding . . . and no presumption, or even knowledge, of their sentiments, can warrant their representatives in a departure from it, prior to such an act." Presumed or tacit "assent" was not for Hamilton.

[348]Miller, *The Elusive Search for Values in Constitutional Interpretation,* 6 Hastings Const. L.Q. 487 (1979). Only one who wears activist blinders would find the framers' clearly discernible intention to exclude suffrage from the fourteenth amendment "elusive."

[349]Bridwell, *The Federalist Judiciary: America's Recently Liberated Minority,* 30 S.Car. L. Rev. 471 n.11 (1979).

jurisprudes who grind out activist theory, it may not be amiss to consider some of his lucubrations. In a massive accumulation of data from all quarters, he proved that all decisionmaking involves discretion, the making of choices.[350] To an "ex-Washington lawyer turned historian,"[351] that smacks of proof of the obvious: whether to turn left or right, to go by plane or train, requires choice. Ignored by Miller was that the necessity of choosing does not empower the Court to *displace the choices of the framers.* For, as a fellow activist, Judge Skelly Wright has written, the framers have already made the choices, and judicial "value choices are to be made only within the parameters" of those choices.[352] Such is the analysis that Miller derides as "filio-pietistic," "puerile," and "false."[353] Consider too his charge that his opponents invoke the shades of the framers because, "[I]f we pretend that the framers had a special sort of wisdom, then perhaps we do not have to think too hard about how to solve pressing social problems,"[354] when the real issue is whether the solution of those "pressing social problems" was confided to the judiciary.[355] Finally, his "The Founding Fathers . . . cannot rule us from their graves"[356] consigns the Constitution, text and all, to the scrap heap. In thrusting aside the dead hands of the framers, he thrusts aside the Constitution.[357] But that decision was left not to academe, but to the people, and the people, as Professor Hans Linde indicated, prefer the Constitution to the Justices.[358]

Theorizing that rests on such specious reasoning is not confined to Miller. So Stanley Kutler wrote, "Judicial policymaking fills a vacuum created when politically accountable legislators . . . abdicate their proper policy roles."[359] The Supreme Court has held, however, that a constitutional

---

[350]Miller & Howell, *The Myth of Neutrality in Constitutional Adjudication,* 27 U. CHI. L. REV. 561 (1960).

[351]So Miller sneeringly referred to me in *Do The Founding Fathers Know Best?* Wash. Post, Nov. 13, 1977, § E (Book World), at 5, col. 1. Of the same order is his statement that Berger "discovered' that the Supreme Court has been making law wholesale through a freewheeling interpretation of the Fourteenth Amendment"; "Berger thus has reinvented the wheel." *Id.* Throughout derision and denigration are made to serve in place of analytical refutation. Compare Justice Harlan's opinion in Oregon v. Mitchell, 400 U.S. 112, 203 (1970) (Harlan, J., concurring and dissenting in part).

[352]R. BERGER, *supra* note 1, at 322 (quoting Wright, *Professor Bickel, The Scholarly, Tradition, and the Supreme Court,* 84 HARV. L. REV. 769, 785 (1971)).

[353]Miller & Howell, *supra* note 350, at 683. *See* notes 348–51 *supra.* Miller's solution is, "Should modern decisionmaking be frozen in time? Hardly." Miller, *supra* note 351, at E5.

[354]R. BERGER, *supra* note 1, at 364–65 (quoting Miller, *An Inquiry into the Relevance of the Intentions of the Founding Fathers, With Special Emphasis Upon the Doctrine of Separation of Powers,* 27 ARK. L. REV. 583, 596 (1973)). Another misrepresentation is Miller's statement that "Berger, who a decade ago maintained that judicial review, although not mentioned in the Constitution, was nevertheless constitutionally proper, has now decided that . . . the Supreme Court [has] gone too far in interpreting the fourteenth amendment," thus charging me with inconsistency. Miller, *supra* note 348, at 487. My CONGRESS V. THE SUPREME COURT (1969) was addressed to the *legitimacy* of judicial review, *i.e.,* was such jurisdiction conferred. My GOVERNMENT BY JUDICIARY (1977) asks the next question—if it was conferred what, for purposes of the fourteenth amendment, is its *scope. See* R. BERGER, *supra* note 264, at 337–46. These are quite distinct problems.

Consider too his Berger "asserts that an 1879 decision permitting Negroes to serve as jurors was wrongly decided—because the 39th Congress *did not consider* the question." Miller, *supra* note 351, at E1 (emphasis added). In fact, I quoted assurances by several framers that blacks could not serve as jurors. R. BERGER, *supra* note 1, at 27, 163 (quoting CONG. GLOBE, 39th Cong., 1st Sess. 1117, app. 156–57 (1866) (remarks of Rep. Wilson)). A critic who would discredit another on the basis of such misstatements is unworthy of trust.

[355]The "real issue," Willard Hurst observed, "is who makes the policy choices in the twentieth century: judges or the combination of legislature and electorate that makes constitutional amendments." R. BERGER, *supra* note 1, at 315 (quoting Hurst, *Discussion,* in SUPREME COURT AND SUPREME LAW 75 (E. Cahn ed. 1954)).

[356]Miller, *supra* note 351, at E1.

[357]In 1872 a Senate Judiciary Committee Report on the fourteenth amendment declared that "[a] construction which should give the phrase . . . a meaning differing from the sense in which it was understood and employed by the people when they adopted the Constitution, would be as unconstitutional as a departure from the plain and express language of the Constitution in any other particular." S. REP. NO. 21, 42d Cong., 2d Sess. 2 (1872) (Report of the Committee on the Judiciary), *reprinted in* A. AVINS, *supra* note 22, at 571. More fully quoted at note 285 and accompanying text *supra.*

[358]R. BERGER, *supra* note 1, at 320 n.28 (quoting Linde, *Judges, Critics, and the Realist Tradition,* 82 YALE L.J. 227, 256 (1972)).

[359]Kutler, *supra* note 9, at 525. To the same effect, Lusky, *supra* note 3, at 405.

power may not be "abdicated."[360] And one of the framers, Charles Pinckney, stated in the House of Representatives in 1798 that their object was "that the powers of Government should be distributed among the different departments, and that they ought not to be assigned or relinquished."[361] What may not be relinquished by Congress may not be taken over by the judiciary. John Adams's 1780 Massachusetts Constitution made the separation of power explicit, forbade each branch to exercise the powers of another, and particularized that the "judiciary should never exercise the legislative power . . . so that this may be a government of laws and not of men."[362] Consequently, legislative power, the power of making policy, is not transferred to the judiciary because Congress neglects to exercise it. Discretion when to exercise a power is vested in the branch to whom the power is confided.[363]

Again, activists dispose of the reservation of the amendment power to the people by article V— a power that on its face is exclusive, and was said to be such by a preeminent framer, Elbridge Gerry—[364] on the plea that it is cumbersome. In the genteel phraseology of Myres McDougal, because "the process of amendment is *politically* difficult, other modes of change have emerged";[365] or as Stanley Kutler puts it, "the path for amendment is often blocked by inertia or irresponsibility."[366] It does not follow, however, that because it is difficult, and sometimes impossible, to obtain the assent of the people "politically," that their servants may amend the Constitution without consulting them.[367] Difficulty of amendment does not authorize a judicial takeover of a function unmistakably reserved to the people. Who would maintain that the Court may confer the equality women seek by the Equal Rights Amendment if it fails of ratification?

But it is Marshall's famous dictum in *McCulloch v. Maryland*[368] that serves the activists as a never-failing incantation; it is their Rock of Ages, a refuge from the rigors of analysis: "[We] must never forget that it is *a constitution* we are expounding . . . a constitution intended to endure for ages to come, and, consequently, to be adapted to . . . human affairs."[369] At best the dictum represents a self-serving claim of judicial power to amend the Constitution. And, as Justice Black observed, "[T]he Founders wisely provided the means for that endurance: changes in the Constitution . . . are to be proposed by Congress or conventions and ratified by the States."[370] In fact, Marshall repudiated the activist reading of his *McCulloch v. Maryland* dictum. When the case

---

[360]United States v. Morton Salt Co., 338 U.S. 632, 647 (1950). In the Jay Treaty debate, Mr. Havens "laid it down as incontrovertible maxim that neither of the branches of the government could, rightfully or constitutionally, divest itself of any powers . . . by a neglect to exercise those powers that were granted to it by the Constitution." 5 ANNALS OF CONG. 486 (1796). To the same effect, the statements of Senator Nichols. *Id.* at 447.

[361]3 M. FARRAND, RECORDS OF THE FEDERAL CONVENTION of 1787, at 376 (1911).

[362]B. POORE, THE FEDERAL AND STATE CONSTITUTIONS, COLONIAL CHARTERS AND OTHER ORGANIC LAWS OF THE UNITED STATES 960 (1878). For the same utterance by Madison, see 1 ANNALS OF CONG. 435, 436 (1789, Gayles & Seaton eds. 1836) (print bearing running head "History of Congress"). The contemporary view is exemplified by the 1767 statement of Chief Justice Hutchinson of Massachusetts: "[T]he *Judge* should never be the *Legislator:* Because then the Will of the Judge would be the Law and this tends to a State of Slavery." R. BERGER, *supra* note 1, at 307 (emphasis in original).

[363]Decatur v. Paulding, 39 U.S. (14 Pet.) 497 (1840); Marbury v. Madison, 5 U.S. (1 Cranch) 137, 169–70 (1803).

[364]*See* note 298 *supra. See, e.g.,* T.I.M.E. Inc. v. United States, 359 U.S. 464, 471 (1959); Wisconsin Cent. R.R. v. Price County, 133 U.S. 496, 504 (1890).

[365]McDougal & Lans, *Treaties and Congressional-Executive or Presidential Agreements: Interchangeable Instruments of National Policy,* 54 YALE L.J. 181, 293 (1954) (emphasis added).

[366]Kutler, *supra* note 9, at 525.

[367]*See* Hamilton, note 347 *supra.* The cumbersomeness and difficulty of amendment, Randall Bridwell justly comments, furnishes an "equally good argument *against* unrestrained judicial rulemaking at the constitutional level, since we would be hard-pressed to gain relief from their decisions." Bridwell, *supra* note 349, at 472 n.12.

[368]17 U.S. (4 Wheat.) 316 (1819).

[369]*Id.* at 407, 415 (emphasis in original); Alfange, *supra* note 5, at 624, 629–30; Ely, *supra* note 16, at 456; Kutler, *supra* note 9, at 516; Lusky, *supra* note 3, at 405; Nathanson, *supra* note 4, at 1133.

[370]R. BERGER, *supra* note 1, at 375 (quoting Bell v. Maryland, 378 U.S. 226, 342 (1964) (Black, J., dissenting)).

came under attack, Marshall rose to its defense, stating that it "does not contain the most distant allusion to any extension by construction of the powers of congress. Its sole object is to remind us that a constitution cannot possibly *enumerate the means* by which the powers of government are to be carried into execution."[371] Again and again he repeated this repudiation, and concluded by stating that the judicial power "cannot be the assertion of a right to change that instrument," i.e., the Constitution.[372] Gerald Gunther, who discovered Marshall's "Defense of *McCulloch v. Maryland,*" commented, "[I]f virtually unlimited congressional [or judicial] discretion is indeed required to meet twentieth century needs, candid argument to that effect, rather than ritual invoking of Marshall's authority, would seem to me more closely in accord with the Chief Justice's stance."[373] What better illustrates the poverty of the activist case than continued reliance on this exploded dictum? Such reasoning richly deserves the denunciation of earlier samples by a disinterested British political scientist: "The quite extraordinary contortions that have gone into proving the contrary [of the traditional view] make sad reading for those impressed by the high quality of American legal-historical scholarship."[374]

Today it is the fashion to approach decisionmaking in terms of available "options." The several activist justifications for "untethered" judicial review are demonstrably untenable. "Refutation of an argument," Chief Justice Thomas McKean told the Pennsylvania Ratification Convention, "begets a proof."[375] In other words, the hollowness of activist argumentation urges us to prefer the other option: to give effect to the clearly discernible, unmistakable intention of the framers to exclude suffrage from the scope of the fourteenth amendment. That responds to a centuries-old tradition of documentary interpretation which the Founders lost no time in applying to constitutional construction. It is preferable to the "untethered" discretion which "frightens" one of its staunchest advocates and is confessedly opposed to our system of democratic government. For the power of making the grand policy choices was reserved to the people and their representatives in the legislatures. It is one of the least admirable activist traits that, with rare exceptions,[376] they refuse plainly to acknowledge that they seek to transfer policymaking from the people and their elected representatives to a nonelected, unaccountable judicial oligarchy,[377] and even worse, to delude the people into thinking that they have surrendered self-government to the Court.

[371]*Id.* at 377 (quoting John Marshall's Defense of *McCulloch v. Maryland* 209 (G. Gunther ed. 1969) (emphasis added)).
[372]*Id.*
[373]*Id.* at 378 n.19 (quoting John Marshall's Defense of McCulloch v. Maryland 20–21 (G. Gunther ed. 1969)).
[374]Beloff, *supra* note 5.
[375]2 Debates in the Several State Conventions on the Adoption of the Federal Constitution 541 (J. Elliot comp. 1836).
[376]Forrester, *Are We Ready for Truth in Judging?* 63 A.B.A.J. 1212 (1977).
[377]*See* note 344 *supra.*

CHAPTER IX

The Ninth Amendment

The Forgotten Ninth Amendment Bennett Patterson entitled his little book in 1955,[1] hardly anticipating that the amendment would be invoked in more than a thousand cases[2] after Justice Goldberg rescued it from obscurity[3] in his concurring opinion in *Griswold v. Connecticut*,[4] the 1965 contraceptive case. Justice Goldberg was not alone, being joined by Chief Justice Warren and Justice Brennan;[5] in the opinion of the Court, Justice Douglas included the ninth amendment among the provisions in the Bill of Rights that have "penumbras formed by emanations from [those] guarantees."[6] Thus inspired, litigants have invoked the ninth to assert the inherent rights of schoolboys to wear long hair,[7] challenge school textbooks,[8] prevent imprisonment in a maximum security section,[9] protect against conscription,[10] immunize the transportation of lewd materials in interstate commerce,[11] and claim a right to a healthful environment.[12]

Justice Goldberg declared that "[t]he language and history of the Ninth Amendment reveal that the Framers of the Constitution believed that there are additional fundamental rights, *protected* from governmental infringement, which exist alongside those fundamental rights specifically mentioned in the first eight constitutional amendments."[13] Who is to protect undescribed rights?

---

[1]B. Patterson, The Forgotten Ninth Amendment (1955). One hundred thirty-two pages are devoted to appendices and a reprint of the legislative history. Most of the 85-page discussion is a hymn to "individual inherent rights," that are unenumerated and independent of constitutional grant.

[2]A Lexis computer search in September, 1980 located 1,296 cases after 1965 from the "General Federal" and "States" libraries. Lexis is a registered trademark of Mead Data Central, Inc.

[3]Prior to Griswold v. Connecticut, 381 U.S. 479 (1965), the Court had few occasions to probe the meaning of the ninth amendment. In United Public Workers v. Mitchell, 330 U.S. 75, 95 (1947), a case challenging the Hatch Act prohibition against political activities by federal employees, the Court fleetingly referred to "the freedom of the civil servant under the First, Ninth and Tenth Amendments," but held that they interposed no obstacle to federal regulation where constitutional power is granted. Earlier, the Court had rejected an appeal to the ninth amendment as a restraint on government action because it "does not withdraw the rights which are expressly granted to the Federal Government." Ashwander v. TVA, 297 U.S. 288, 330–31 (1936).

[4]381 U.S. 479, 486 (1965).

[5]Justices Harlan and White separately concurred in the judgment. *Id.* at 499, 502. Justices Black and Stewart dissented. *Id.* at 507, 527.

[6]381 U.S. at 484. Justice Douglas did not win a plurality for his interpretation. And he has since wavered. In Olff v. East Side Union High School Dist., 404 U.S. 1042, 1044 (1972), he dissented from a denial of certiorari in a case involving regulation of schoolboy hairstyle, saying "[t]he word 'liberty' [in the fourteenth amendment] . . . includes at least the fundamental rights 'retained by the people' under the Ninth Amendment." On the other hand, concurring in Doe v. Bolton, 410 U.S. 179, 210 (1973), in which the Court found Georgia's abortion law unconstitutional, he declared that "[t]he Ninth Amendment obviously does not create federally enforceable rights."

[7]Freeman v. Flake, 405 U.S. 1032 (1972) (denial of certiorari) (although four circuits upheld and four struck down regulations of schoolboy hair style).

[8]Williams v. Board of Educ., 388 F. Supp. 93 (S.D.W. Va. 1975).

[9]Burns v. Swenson, 430 F.2d 771 (8th Cir. 1970).

[10]United States v. Uhl, 436 F.2d 773 (9th Cir. 1970).

[11]United States v. Orito, 413 U.S. 139 (1973).

[12]Tanner v. Armco Steel Corp., 340 F. Supp. 532 (S.D. Tex. 1972).

[13]381 U.S. at 488 (emphasis added).

Justice Goldberg would transform the ninth amendment into a bottomless well in which the judiciary can dip for the formation of undreamed of "rights" in their limitless discretion, a possibility the Founders would have rejected out of hand.[14] And, as Professor Robert Bork points out, an imputed authorization judicially "to develop new individual rights . . . correspondingly create[s] new disabilities for democratic government;"[15] it disables the states from governing in those areas. Whatever the meaning of the ninth amendment, one thing it clearly did not contemplate—encroachment on state control of local matters except as the Constitution otherwise authorized. It is undisputed that such a claim had not been made by the Court in the more than 150 years since the adoption of the Bill of Rights.[16] Justice Stewart remarked in his dissent that "to say that the Ninth Amendment has anything to do with this case is to turn somersaults with history."[17]

The ninth amendment provides that "[t]he enumeration in the Constitution, of certain rights, shall not be construed to deny or disparage others retained by the people."[18] Paired with it is the tenth: "The powers not delegated to the United States by the Constitution, nor prohibited by it to the States, are reserved to the States respectively, or to the people."[19] The two are complementary: the ninth deals with *rights* "retained by the people," the tenth with *powers* "reserved" to the states or the people. As Madison perceived, they are two sides of the same coin. During the debates on ratification of the Bill of Rights in Virginia, he wrote to Washington:

> If a line can be drawn between the powers granted and the rights retained, it would seem to be the same thing, whether the latter be secured by declaring that they shall not be abridged, or that the former shall not be extended. If no such line can be drawn, a declaration in either form would amount to nothing.[20]

Understanding the ninth amendment is aided by appreciation of the background from which it emerged. The Founders were deeply attached to their local governments: these were the tried and true, whereby they had resisted the impositions of royal governors and judges.[21] That attachment constituted a formidable obstacle to the adoption of the Constitution;[22] there was widespread distrust of the remote newcomer, a federal government removed by vast distances from the

---

[14]*See* text accompanying notes 122, 125 *infra.*

[15]Bork, *The Impossibility of Finding Welfare Rights in the Constitution,* 1979 WASH. U. L.Q. 695, 697.

[16]Griswold v. Connecticut, 381 U.S. at 491 n.6 (Goldberg, J., concurring); *id.* at 520 (Black, J., dissenting); *id.* at 529–30 (Stewart, J., dissenting).

[17]*Id.* at 529.

[18]U.S. CONST. amend. IX.

[19]U.S. CONST. amend. X.

[20]Letter from James Madison to George Washington (Dec. 5, 1789) *reprinted in* 5 THE WRITINGS OF JAMES MADISON 432 (G. Hunt ed. 1904).

[21]In his 1791 Philadelphia lectures, Justice James Wilson, who had been a leading architect of the Constitution, explained that before the Revolution

the executive and the judicial powers of government . . . were derived from . . . a foreign source . . . [and] were directed to foreign purposes. Need we be surprised, that they were objects of aversion and distrust? . . . On the other hand, our assemblies were chosen by ourselves: they were the guardians of our rights, the objects of our confidence, and the anchor of our political hopes. . . .

Even at this time [1791], people can scarcely devest themselves of those opposite prepossessions. . . .

But it is high time that we should chastise our prejudices.

J. WILSON, *Of Government,* in 1 WORKS OF JAMES WILSON 292–293 (R. McCloskey ed. 1967).

[22]Madison acknowledged this "habitual attachment of the people." 1 M. FARRAND, THE RECORDS OF THE FEDERAL CONVENTION OF 1787 at 284 (1911). It was condemned by Gouverneur Morris: "State attachments, and State importance have been the bane of this Country," *id.* at 530, but the current ran strongly the other way. *See* R. BERGER, CONGRESS v. THE SUPREME COURT 260–64 (1969). It was to "state Governments," Oliver Ellsworth said at the Convention, that he "turned his eyes . . . for the preservation of his rights." 1 M. FARRAND, *supra,* at 492. There, Elbridge Gerry asked, "[w]ill any man say that liberty will be safe in the hands of eighty or a hundred men taken from the whole continent, as in the hands of two or three hundred taken from a single State?" 2 *id.* at 386. James Wilson told the Pennsylvania Ratification Convention that "the framers of [the Constitution] were particularly anxious . . . to preserve the state governments unimpaired." 3 *id.* at

governed, wherein large states might outvote the small, and in which there would be clashing sectional interests.[23] The measure of that distrust may be gathered from the fact that after providing for "inferior" federal courts, the First Congress committed the initial enforcement of constitutional issues to the state courts,[24] where it remained for the next seventy-seven to eighty-six years.[25] Allied to this was insistence on a government of limited powers arising from a pervasive fear of "despotic government";[26] hence the outcries against unlimited power. As Jefferson said, "[i]t is jealousy and not confidence which prescribes limited constitutions to bind down those whom we are obliged to trust with power."[27]

The drive for the Bill of Rights was fed by such distrust. At the outset of the deliberations in the First Congress, Madison, who drafted the proposed Bill of Rights, averred that "the abuse of the powers of the General Government may be guarded against in a more secure manner than is now done."[28] Elbridge Gerry alluded to the "great body of our constituents opposed to the Constitution as it now stands, who are apprehensive of the enormous powers of Government," and added, "[t]he ratification of the Constitution in several States would never have taken place, had they not been assured that the objections would have been duly attended to by Congress."[29] Madison recalled to the House that the proposed amendments were "most strenuously required by the opponents to the constitution" in the state ratification conventions.[30] A number of states accompanied their ratifications with proposed amendments.[31] Toward the close of the First Congress Gerry said, "This declaration of rights, I take it, is intended to secure the people against the mal-administration of the [federal] Government."[32]

Even stronger evidence that the Bill of Rights was to have no application to the states is furnished by the fate of the first sentence of Madison's fifth resolution: "*No State* shall violate the equal rights of conscience, or the freedom of the press, or the trial by jury in criminal cases."[33] Madison explained that "every Government should be disarmed of powers which trench upon *those particular rights.* . . . [T]he State Governments are as liable to attack *these* invaluable privileges as the General Government is, and therefore ought to be as cautiously guarded against."[34] When the clause came before the Committee of the Whole, Madison urged that this provision was "the most valuable amendment in the whole list," and that it was "equally necessary" that "*these* essential rights" should be "secured against the State Governments."[35] As Professor Norman Redlich observed,

---

144. Madison assured the Ratifiers that the jurisdiction of the proposed government "extends to certain enumerated objects only, and leaves to the several States a residuary and inviolable sovereignty over all other objects." The Federalist No. 39 (J. Madison) 249 (Mod. Lib. ed. 1937).

[23]R. Berger, *supra* note 22, at 31–33.

[24]*Id.* at 263, 273.

[25]C. Wright, Handbook of the Law of Federal Courts 3–4 (3d ed. 1976). Appeals to the Supreme Court were not defended on the ground that the Court must be enabled to rewrite state legislation, but because, in Hamilton's words, "Thirteen independent courts of final jurisdiction over the same causes, arising upon the same laws, is a hydra in government from which nothing but contradiction and confusion can proceed." The Federalist No. 80 (A. Hamilton) 516 (Mod. Lib. ed. 1937). The password was "uniformity." R. Berger, *supra* note 22, at 272. Even so, there were those like Gerry who feared that "the judicial department will be oppressive." 3 M. Farrand, *supra* note 22, at 128.

[26]H. Adams, John Randolph 38 (1882).

[27]C. Warren, Congress, The Constitution, and the Supreme Court 153 (1925). *See* R. Berger, *supra* note 22, at 13. *See also* H. Adams, *supra* note 26, at 8–14..

[28]1 Annals of Cong. 432 (Gales & Seaton eds. 1836) (printing bearing running title "History of Congress").

[29]*Id.* at 446–47.

[30]*Id.* at 746. *See also id.* at 661 (remarks of Rep. Page).

[31]*See, e.g.,* 3 J. Elliot, Debates in the Several State Conventions on the Adoption of the Federal Constitution 657–63 (2d ed. 1876) (Virginia); *cf. 2 id.* at 542–46 (Pennsylvania); 2 *id.* at 177 (Massachusetts); 2 *id.* at 413–14 (New York).

[32]1 Annals of Cong., *supra* note 28, at 749.

[33]*Id.* at 435 (emphasis added).

[34]*Id.* at 441 (emphasis added).

[35]*Id.* at 755 (emphasis added).

"When Madison intended an amendment to restrict the states in his proposal to prevent the states from abridging free speech or press, he was quite specific."[36] The clause was adopted by the House but rejected by the Senate,[37] underscoring that the Founders well knew how to limit state authority, as is again evidenced by their reference in the tenth amendment to power not "prohibited by [the Constitution] to the States."

The words "rights retained by the people" in the ninth amendment expressed a political postulate explained by Jefferson: "the purposes of society do not require a surrender of all our rights to our ordinary governors," and it followed that there remained reserved to the people an area of unsurrendered rights.[38] Opponents of a Bill of Rights had urged that it was unnecessary because, as Washington wrote Lafayette, "the people evidently retained every thing which they did not in express terms give up."[39] In the words of Hamilton, quoted by Justice Goldberg, "why declare that things shall not be done which there is no power to do?" instancing "no power is given by which restrictions [on "liberty of the press"] may be imposed."[40] Madison admitted that the amendments "may be deemed unnecessary; but there can be no harm in making such a declaration."[41] Thus viewed, the Bill of Rights added nothing,[42] but was merely declaratory.

---

[36]Redlich, *Are There "Certain Rights" . . . Retained by the People?*, 37 N.Y.U. L. REV. 787, 805 n.87 (1962).

[37]*See* Warren, *The New "Liberty" Under the Fourteenth Amendment*, 39 HARV. L. REV. 431, 433–35 (1926). Redlich concluded, "It would be unrealistic to attribute to the Senate an intent to impose ill-defined legally enforceable restraints on the states in light of this rejection." Redlich, *supra* note 36, at 806. Thus, the records of the First Congress confirm Chief Justice Marshall's holding in Barron v. Mayor of Baltimore, 32 U.S. (7 Pet.) 243 (1833), that the Bill of Rights did not apply to the states.

[38]E. DUMBAULD, THE BILL OF RIGHTS 145 (1957). *See also* G. WOOD, THE CREATION OF THE AMERICAN REPUBLIC 1776–1787 at 293–94 (1969). For Thomas Cooley, the ninth amendment affirmed "the principle that constitutions are not made to create rights in the people, but in recognition of, and in order to preserve them." T. COOLEY, THE GENERAL PRINCIPLES OF CONSTITUTIONAL LAW IN THE UNITED STATES OF AMERICA 31–35 (2d ed. 1891). The ninth amendment "was an affirmation of the principle that, as rights in the United States are not created by government, so they are not to be diminished by government, unless by the appropriate exercise of an express power." Dunbar, *James Madison and the Ninth Amendment*, 42 VA. L. REV. 627, 638 (1956).

[39]29 THE WRITINGS OF GEORGE WASHINGTON 478 (Fitzpatrick ed. 1939). In his letter to Lafayette, Washington referred to James Wilson's assurance to the Pennsylvania Ratification Convention that by the Constitution the citizens dispense "a part of their original power in what manner and what proportion they think fit. They never part with the whole; and they retain the right of recalling what they part with. . . . To every suggestion concerning a bill of rights, the citizens of the United States may always say, WE reserve the right to do what we please." 2 J. ELLIOT, *supra* note 31, at 437.

C. C. Pinckney told the South Carolina House of Representatives that "by delegating express powers, we certainly reserve to ourselves every power and right not mentioned." 3 M. FARRAND, *supra* note 22, at 256. In the First Congress, Rep. Hartley observed that "it had been asserted in the convention of Pennsylvania, by the friends of the Constitution, that all the rights and power that were not given to the Government were retained by the States and the people thereof. This was also his own opinion." 1 ANNALS OF CONG., *supra* note 28, at 732.

[40]381 U.S. at 489 n.4 (quoting THE FEDERALIST No. 84 (A. Hamilton) 558–59 (Mod. Lib. ed. 1937)).

[41]1 ANNALS OF CONG., *supra* note 28, at 441.

[42]Dumbauld justly sums up: "The Ninth Amendment was not intended to add anything to the meaning of the remaining articles in the Constitution. . . . [It] was designed to obviate the possibility of applying the maxim *expressio unius exclusio alterius* in interpreting the Constitution. It was adopted in order to eliminate the grant of powers by implication." E. DUMBAULD, *supra* note 38, at 63. Earlier, Justice Story wrote that the ninth amendment "was manifestly introduced to prevent any perverse or ingenious misapplication of the well-known maxim, that an affirmation in particular cases implies a negation in all others." J. STORY, COMMENTARIES ON THE CONSTITUTION OF THE UNITED STATES § 1905 (5th ed. 1891). *See also* note 43 *infra*.

Parenthetically, this confutes those who argue that the rules of statutory construction should not apply to interpretation of the Constitution, and those like Professor Dean Alfange, who ridicule the application of a canon of construction as an authoritative guide to constitutional interpretation. *See* Alfange, *On Judicial Policymaking and Constitutional Change: Another Look at the "Original Intent" Theory of Constitutional Interpretation*, 5 HASTINGS CONST. L. Q. 603, 618–19 (1978). *See also* Berger, *"Government by Judiciary": Judge Gibbons Argument Ad Hominem*, 59 B.U. L. REV. 783, 805 (1977).

Others, however, were deeply concerned by the effect of the maxim *expressio unius est exclusio alterius:* what is expressed excludes what is not.[43] They feared that an enumeration of some rights might deliver those not enumerated into the hands of the federal government. Madison's response to such fears is quoted by Justice Goldberg:

> It has been objected also against a bill of rights, that, by enumerating particular exceptions to the grant of power, it would disparage those rights which were not placed in that enumeration; and it might follow by implication, that those rights which were not singled out, were intended *to be assigned* into the hands of the General Government, and were consequently insecure. This is one of the most plausible arguments I have ever heard urged against the admission of a bill of rights into this system; but, I conceive, that *it may be guarded against.* I have attempted it, as gentlemen may see by turning to the last clause of the fourth resolution [the ninth amendment].[44]

As Justice Black pointed out, "th[is] very material . . . shows that the Ninth Amendment was intended to protect against the idea that 'by enumerating particular exceptions to the grant of power' to the Federal Government, 'those rights which were not singled out, were intended to be assigned into the hands of the General Government.'"[45] Madison, in short, meant to bar the implication that unenumerated rights were "assigned" to the federal government, for enforcement or otherwise, returning to the theme he had sounded at the outset: "[T]he great object in view is to limit and qualify the powers of Government, by excepting out of the grant of power those cases in which the *Government ought not to act,* or to act only in a particular mode."[46]

Justice Goldberg neglected to turn "to the last clause of the fourth resolution" in order to learn how Madison proposed that the undesirable implication "may be guarded against." That last clause, the progenitor of the ninth amendment, provided:

> The exceptions here or elsewhere in the constitution, made in favor of particular rights, shall *not* be so construed as to diminish the just importance of other rights retained by the people, or as *to enlarge the powers* delegated by the constitution; but either as *actual limitations* of such powers, or as inserted merely for greater caution.[47]

Madison's disclaimer of intention "to enlarge the powers delegated by the constitution" by non-enumeration of "other rights" and his emphasis upon enumeration as "actual limitations" on such powers bars a construction which would endow the federal government with the very powers that were denied. It is incongruous, moreover, to read the text of the ninth amendment as expanding *federal* powers at the very moment that the tenth was reserving to the states or the people all

---

[43]James Wilson assured the Pennsylvania Convention that "everything not expressly mentioned will be presumed to be purposely omitted." 3 M. FARRAND, *supra* note 22, at 144. Chief Justice Thomas McKean also assured that Convention that congressional power, being enumerated in the Constitution "and *positively* granted, can be no other than what this positive grant conveys." 2 J. ELLIOT, *supra* note 31, at 540. For a similar expression in South Carolina by C. C. Pinckney, see 3 M. Farrand, *supra* note 22, at 256. Rep. Jackson of Georgia alluded to the maxim in the First Congress, 1 ANNALS OF CONG., *supra* note 28, at 442.

[44]381 U.S. at 489–90 (quoting 1 ANNALS OF CONG., *supra* note 28, at 439 (emphasis added)).

[45]*Id.* at 519 (Black, J., dissenting). *See* note 42 *supra.*

[46]1 ANNALS OF CONG., *supra* note 28, at 437 (emphasis added). Leslie Dunbar observes that Madison "seems to have thought of rights under two main headings. One, as stipulating agreed upon methods by which in particular cases the government shall exercise its powers. . . . Secondly, he thought of another class of rights as declarations of areas *totally outside the province of government.*" Dunbar, *supra* note 38, at 635 (emphasis added). Madison's intention was "to define those fields into which *powers do not extend at all.*" *Id.* at 636 (emphasis added). Even prior to *Griswold,* Justice Black concluded that the ninth amendment merely "emphasize[d] the limited nature of the Federal Government." Black, *The Bill of Rights,* 35 N.Y.U. L. REV. 865, 871 (1960).

[47]1 ANNALS OF CONG., *supra* note 28, at 435 (emphasis added). On October 17, 1788, Madison wrote to Jefferson that he favored a Bill of Rights "provided it be so formed *as not to imply powers not* to be included *in the enumeration.*" 5 THE WRITINGS OF JAMES MADISON, *supra* note 20, at 271.

"powers not delegated."[48] Then too, because the federal government may not "deny" unenumerated rights, it does not follow that it may *enforce* them against the states.

In fact, enforcement was to be confined to expressly "stipulated rights." "[T]he great mass of the people who opposed [the Constitution]," said Madison, "disliked it because it did not contain effectual provisions against encroachments *on particular rights.*"[49] Hence, Madison explained, if the Bill of Rights were

> incorporated into the Constitution, independent tribunals of justice will consider themselves in a peculiar manner the guardians of *those rights;* they will be an impenetrable bulwark against every assumption of power in the legislative or executive [not the states]; they will be naturally led to resist every encroachment upon rights *expressly stipulated* for in the constitution by the declaration of rights.[50]

For present purposes, the relevant provision of article III, section two, clause one, which enumerates the various categories of federal court jurisdiction, is "all cases . . . arising under this Constitution."[51] A right "retained" by the people is not embodied in the Constitution, and a suit brought on such a right does not "arise" thereunder, as Madison made plain in stressing judicial protection for "particular" rights "expressly stipulated." It does violence to the historical record to construe the ninth amendment to give the courts a roving commission to enforce a catalog of unenumerated rights against the will of the states.[52] What the Constitution expressed was the will of the people to reserve unto themselves all powers not delegated and all unenumerated rights,[53] a will likewise articulated in the article V provision for amendment. With Leslie Dunbar, I would hold that the ninth amendment "is an affirmation that rights exist independently of government, that they constitute an area of no-power."[54]

How does Justice Goldberg meet these materials? On the one hand he states. "I do not mean to imply that the Ninth Amendment is applied against the States by the Fourteenth. Nor do I mean to state that the Ninth Amendment constitutes an independent source of rights protected from infringement by either the States or the Federal Government."[55] On the other hand, he argues that "the Ninth Amendment is relevant in a case dealing with a *State's* infringement of a fundamental right. While the Ninth Amendment—and indeed the entire Bill of Rights—originally concerned restrictions upon *federal* power, the subsequently enacted Fourteenth Amendment prohibits the States as well from infringing fundamental personal liberties."[56] Justice Goldberg goes on to explain that

> the Ninth Amendment, in indicating that not all such liberties are specifically mentioned in the first eight amendments, is surely relevant in showing the *existence* of other fundamental personal rights, now *protected* from state, as well as federal, infringement. In sum, the Ninth Amendment simply lends

---

[48]As the Court held in Holmes v. Jennison, 39 U.S. (14 Pet.) 540, 587 (1840): "so far from the states which insisted upon these amendments contemplating any restraint or limitation by them on their own powers; the very cause which gave rise to them, was a strong jealousy on their part of the power which they had granted in the Constitution."

[49]1 ANNALS OF CONG., *supra* note 28, at 433 (emphasis added).

[50]*Id.* at 440 (emphasis added). Leslie Dunbar comments. "[T]he practical effect of enumeration is the enlistment of the protection of positive law, spoken through the courts, for rights which otherwise could be defended only through political action." Dunbar, *supra* note 38, at 643.

[51]U.S. CONST. art III, sec. 2.

[52]"Had Congress engaged in the extraordinary occupation of improving the constitutions of the several states by affording the people additional protection from the exercise of power by their own governments in matters which concerned themselves alone, they would have declared this purpose in plain and intelligible language." Barron v. Mayor of Baltimore, 32 U.S. (7 Pet.) 243, 250 (1833). See text accompanying notes 117–18 *infra*.

[53]*See* note 39 *supra*.

[54]*See* Dunbar, *supra* note 38, at 641. *See also* Redlich, *supra* note 36, at 807 (quoted at text accompanying note 103 *infra*); note 46 *supra*.

[55]381 U.S. at 492 (concurring opinion).

[56]*Id.* at 493.

strong support to the view that the "liberty" protected by the Fifth and Fourteenth Amendments from infringement by the Federal Government or the States is not restricted to rights specifically mentioned in the first eight amendments.[57]

Justice Goldberg leaps too lightly from the "existence of rights" retained by the people to a federal power to *protect* them. That no such power was conferred is disclosed by Madison's disavowal of any implication that the enumerated rights were "assigned into the hands of the General Government," least of all for diminution of States' rights, his affirmation that there was no intention to enlarge but rather to limit the delegated powers, and his demarcation of "cases in which the Government ought not to act."[58]

Goldberg's appeal to the "liberty" of the fifth amendment's due process clause for authority to "protect" the unspecified rights retained by the people under the ninth amendment implies that what the ninth plainly withheld was conferred under the rose by the fifth. But why should the Founders take pains to exclude federal power with regard to the unenumerated right of the ninth if they were simultaneously conferring it *sub silentio* by the fifth? That is inexplicable. In fact, the Founders fenced off "cases in which the Government ought not to act," and it requires evidence that those fences were torn down by the fifth. Then too, the "liberty" of the fifth amendment on which Goldberg relies referred to freedom from imprisonment and freedom of locomotion,[59] which with fine casuistry the Court, overturning a maximum hours law in *Lochner v. New York*,[60] perverted into "liberty of contract"—the "liberty" of a bakery worker to contract for sixty hours of labor a week. Notwithstanding his caustic dissent in *Lochner*, Justice Holmes later drew on this "liberty" for a better cause: free speech "must be taken to be included in the Fourteenth Amendment, *in view of* the scope that has been given to the word 'liberty.' "[61] Thus "liberty" has been expanded in our own time from a shrivelled root. Then too, the due process clause of the fifth amendment was meant only to protect against deprivation of "liberty" without judicial proceedings, not to endow the courts with visitorial powers over legislation.[62] Not a glimmer of intention exists in the history of the fourteenth amendment to alter that meaning and deliver the last word on state legislation to federal judges.[63] James Wilson, chairman of the House Judiciary Committee during the fourteenth amendment debates, indicated that the due process clause furnished a "remedy" to secure the "fundamental rights" enumerated in the Civil Rights Act of 1866[64]—a law

---

[57]*Id.* (emphasis added).

[58]*See* text accompanying notes 44, 46, & 47.

[59]*See* Shattuck, *The True Meaning of the Term "Liberty" in those Clauses in the Federal and State Constitutions Which Protect "Life, Liberty, and Property,"* 4 HARV L. REV. 365 (1891); Warren, *The New "Liberty" Under the Fourteenth Amendment,* 39 HARV. L. REV. 431, 442–45 (1926). *See generally* R. BERGER, GOVERNMENT BY JUDICIARY: THE TRANSFORMATION OF THE FOURTEENTH AMENDMENT 270 (1977).

Blackstone defined "the personal liberty of individuals" as consisting "in the power of locomotion . . . or moving one's person to whatsoever place one's own inclination may direct, without imprisonment of restraint, unless by due course of law." 2 W. BLACKSTONE, COMMENTARIES *134. During the debates about the fourteenth amendment, James Wilson read Blackstone to the House. CONG. GLOBE, 39th Cong., 1st Sess. 1118 (1866).

[60]198 U.S. 45 (1905).

[61]Gitlow v. New York, 268 U.S. 652, 672 (1925) (Holmes, J. dissenting) (emphasis added).

[62]On the eve of the Federal Convention, Hamilton stated in the New York assembly: "The words *"due process"* have a precise technical import, and are only applicable to the process and proceedings of the courts of justice; they can never be referred to an act of legislature." 4 PAPERS OF ALEXANDER HAMILTON 35 (Syrett and Cooke eds. 1962). He summarized 400 years of history. *See* Berger, *"Law of the Land" Reconsidered,* 74 Nw. U. L. REV. 1 (1979).

[63]*See* BERGER, *supra* note 59, at 201–06. *See also* Ely, *Constitutional Interpretivism: Its Allure and Impossibility,* 53 IND. L.J. 399, 416 (1978).

[64]CONG. GLOBE, 39th Cong., 1st Sess. 1294–95 (1866).

considered by the framers to be "exactly" like the fourteenth amendment.[65] Those "fundamental rights" are far removed from Goldberg's ambitious catalog. In the words of the draftsman of the Act, Senator Lyman Trumbull, chairman of the Senate Judiciary Committee, they were "the right to acquire property, the rights to go and come at pleasure [freedom of locomotion], the right to enforce rights in the courts, [and] to make contracts. . . ."[66] It took the wonder-working Warren Court to transform the fourteenth amendment into a cornucopia of "rights" *excluded* by the framers.[67]

Possibly I do not appreciate the subtle differentiation between "incorporation" of the ninth amendment in the fourteenth and enforcement of the unspecified rights "retained" under the ninth by resort to the "liberty" of the fourteenth, but to my mind the distinction is purely semantic. Let me therefore reiterate that the argument that the Bill of Rights was incorporated in the fourteenth amendment is without historical warrant, as Charles Fairman demonstrated, and as is widely acknowledged.[68] Since it must draw upon the due process clause,[69] and since "due process" in the fifth and fourteenth amendments is identical, the argument makes nonsense of the Bill of Rights. For incorporation of the "first eight" amendments into the "due process" of the fifth renders all the rest superfluous. The framers' attachment to state sovereignty[70] led the Thirty-ninth Congress to limit federal intrusion to the ban on discrimination with respect to the "fundamental rights" enumerated by Trumbull.[71] In particular, Chairman Wilson emphasized, "[w]e are not making a

[65]*See* R. BERGER, *supra* note 59, at 22–23. Justice Bradley declared: "[T]he civil rights bill was enacted at the same session, and but shortly before the presentation of the fourteenth amendment; . . . [it] was in pari materia; and was probably intended to reach the same object. . . . [T]he first section of the bill covers the same ground as the fourteenth amendment." Live-Stock Dealers' & Butchers Ass'n v. Crescent City Live-stock Landing & Slaughterhouse Co., 15 F. Cas. 649, 655 (C.C. La. 1870) (No. 8,408).

[66]CONG. GLOBE, 39th Cong., 1st Sess. 475 (1866). This was a paraphrase of the terms of the Civil Rights Bill. *See* R. BERGER, *supra* note 59, at 24.

[67]*See* R. BERGER, *supra* note 59, at 52–68, 117–33. *See also,* Berger, *supra* note 42, at 793–94. Senator William Fessenden, Chairman of the Joint Committee on Reconstruction of both Houses, stated, "[w]e cannot put into the Constitution, owing to existing prejudices and existing institutions, an entire exclusion of all class distinctions. . . ." CONG. GLOBE, 39th Cong., 1st Sess. 705 (1866). Time and again attempts to ban *all* discriminations were defeated. *See* R. BERGER, *supra* note 59, at 163–64.

[68]*See* Fairman, *Does the Fourteenth Amendment Incorporate the Bill of Rights?*, 2 STAN. L. REV. 5 (1949); Morrison, *Does the Fourteenth Amendment Incorporate the Bill of Rights?*, 2 STAN. L. REV. 140 (1949). *See also* R. BERGER, *supra* note 59, at 137; A. BICKEL, THE LEAST DANGEROUS BRANCH 102 (1962). Professor Dean Alfange, an activist, wrote, "it is all but certain that the Fourteenth Amendment was not intended to incorporate the Bill of Rights and thus to revolutionize the administration of criminal justice in the states." Alfange, *supra* note 42, at 607. Professor Charles E. Merriam noted that the Founders believed government must be limited in many ways:

it must be checked at every possible point; it must be at all times under suspicion. . . . Too much emphasis cannot well be laid upon the fear which the 'Fathers' had of government. To them the great lesson of history was, that government always tends to become oppressive, and it was the greatest foe of individual liberty.

C. MERRIAM, A HISTORY OF AMERICAN POLITICAL THEORIES 76–77 (1903). Let one bit of contemporary evidence suffice. The Kentucky Resolutions of 1798, drafted by Jefferson, stated that "limited constitutions [are designed] to bind down those whom we are obliged to trust with power," to bind them "down from mischief by the chains of the Constitution." 4 J. ELLIOT, *supra* note 31, at 543.

Professor Philip Kurland wrote of the Court's decisions that the due process clause of the fourteenth amendment made the religion clauses of the first amendment applicable to the states: "Of course, nothing in the history of the fourteenth amendment suggests that this was among its purposes or goals. The transmogrification occurred solely at the whim of the Court. An attempt to pass a constitutional amendment providing for the application of the religion clauses to the states, the Blaine amendment, failed in 1876, eight years after effectuation of the fourteenth amendment." Kurland, *The Irrelevance of the Constitution: The Religion Clauses of the First Amendment and the Supreme Court*, 24 VILL. L. REV. 3, 9–10 (1978) (citations omitted).

[69]R. BERGER, *supra* note 59, at 139–41.

[70]*See* CONG. GLOBE, 39th Cong., 1st Sess. 358 (1866) (remarks of Rep. Conkling); *id.* at 1292–93 (remarks of Rep. Bingham). *See generally,* R. BERGER, *supra* note 59, at 60–64.

[71]*See* note 66 and accompanying text *supra.*

general criminal code for the States."[72] The last thing the framers had in mind was to vest the distrusted judiciary[73] with the power of controlling state administration of local matters. Thus, the Court's long journey from the fifth amendment through the fourteenth to the ninth amendment exemplifies the unremitting expansion of judicial usurpation, from what is first disputed to what becomes Holy Writ and is then further dilated.[74] In a crowning irony, Justice Black who fathered the "incorporation" doctrine, at last cried "halt":

> [F]or a period of a century and a half no serious suggestion was ever made that the Ninth Amendment, enacted to protect state powers against federal invasion, could be used as a weapon of federal power to prevent state legislatures from passing laws they consider appropriate to govern local affairs. Use of any such broad, unbounded judicial authority would make of this Court's members a day-to-day constitutional convention.[75]

This is not, as Justice Goldberg argued, "to give . . . [the ninth amendment] no effect whatsoever."[76] Ample effect, overlooked by Goldberg, was commonsensically furnished by Dean Roscoe Pound: "Those [rights] not expressly set forth are not forever excluded but are, if the Ninth Amendment is read with the Tenth, left to be secured by the states or by the people of the whole land by constitutional change, as was done, for example, by the Fourteenth Amendment."[77] In "retaining" the unenumerated rights, the people reserved to themselves power to add to or subtract from the rights enumerated in the Constitution by the process of amendment exclusively confided to them by article V. If this be deemed supererogatory, be it remembered that according to Madison the ninth amendment itself "inserted merely for greater caution."

Bennett Patterson

It is tempting to dismiss Patterson's *The Forgotten Ninth Amendment* out of hand.[78] But the fact that it has Roscoe Pound's encomium[79]—although his own conclusions were diametrically opposed to those of Patterson—and that it has been cited by others[80] calls for more considered judgment.[81] Although more than half of Patterson's 217 pages are devoted to a reprint of the debates in the First Congress on the Bill of Rights, he gleans little therefrom. He mentions Gerry's unsuccessful

---

[72]Cong. Globe, 39th Cong., 1st Sess. 1120 (1866).

[73]*See* R. Berger, *supra* note 59, at 222–23; Berger, *The Fourteenth Amendment: Light From the Fifteenth*, 74 Nw. U. L. Rev. 311, 350–51 (1979).

[74]Thus the Court has fulfilled the colonists' fear of power's "endlessly propulsive tendency to expand itself beyond legitimate boundaries." B. Bailyn, The Ideological Origins of the American Revolution 56 (1967).

[75]381 U.S. at 520 (Black, J., dissenting). *See also* note 52 *supra*.

[76]381 U.S. at 491 (Goldberg, J., concurring). In this error Goldberg had been anticipated by Patterson. *See* B. Patterson, *supra* note 1, at 24.

[77]Pound, *Foreword to* B. Patterson, *supra* note 1, at iv. Pound reiterated: "[T]hese reserved rights may be defined and enforcement of them may be provided by the states, except as may be precluded by the Fourteenth Amendment, or may be defined and acquire secured enforcement by the people of the United States by constitutional amendment." *Id.* at vi.

[78]Patterson's unreliability may be quickly illustrated. He states:
"We believe that the law should grow and our Constitution should be interpreted in the light of current history, as was stated by one of the eminent courts of last resort of one of the States, [quoting] 'The law should be construed in reference to the habits of business prevalent in the country *at the time it was enacted. The law . . . as then known* to exist.' "
Id. at 56 (emphasis added). Patently, the case expresses exactly the opposite of Patterson's proposition that "the law should grow."

[79]Pound, *Foreword to* B. Patterson, *supra* note 1, at vi–vii.

[80]*See, e.g.*, 381 U.S. at 490 n.9 (Goldberg, J. concurring); E. Dumbauld, *supra* note 38, at 138; Redlich, *supra* note 36, at 805 n.87.

[81]"The flaccid acceptance of shoddy work ha[s] long been a scandal of scholarly and literary journals." O. Handlin, Truth in History 149 (1973).

proposal to change the word "disparage" in the ninth to "impair";[82] and sets out the "last clause of Madison's fourth resolution,"

> The exceptions here or elsewhere in the Constitution, made in favor of particular rights, shall not be so construed as to diminish the just importance of other rights retained by the people, or as to enlarge the powers delegated by the Constitution; but either as actual limitations of such power, or as inserted merely for greater caution.[83]

Instead of noticing this disclaimer of intention "to enlarge," but rather to impose "actual limitations" on the powers "delegated by the Constitution," Patterson seizes on the words "the exceptions *here or elsewhere* in the Constitution."[84] From this he concludes that the language "definitely demonstrates that the clause was intended as a *general* declaration of human rights . . . a general clause relating to the entire Constitution, and not a specific clause relating only to the proposed amendments."[85] Without doubt it "related to any other rights *enumerated* . . . in the Constitution,"[86] but it is a nonsequitur to conclude that these words constitute "a general declaration of human rights." The specific is not the "general."

Patterson also construes a proposed Senate preamble to the Bill of Rights recognizing state desires to "prevent misconstruction or abuse of [the granted] powers" by adding "further *declaratory* and restrictive clauses"[87] to mean that the ninth and tenth amendments are a "declaration of principles" rather than "restrictive clauses."[88] The word "declaratory" means to declare the law or rights as they stand, rather than a "declaration" of new law or rights.[89] Thus, the Framers regarded the proposed amendments as merely declaring what was implicit: unenumerated powers are not granted.[90]

True it is that the Constitution is not to "be construed as a *grant* to the individual of inherent rights or liberties;"[91] rather, as Hamilton said of a "declaration of rights," it is a "limitation . . . of the power of the government itself."[92] But it was the federal government, not the states, that was so limited.[93] Patterson finds it "impossible to believe that human rights and individual liberties" had been fought for "only to be surrendered up to State governments where they could be destroyed by the sovereign people acting en masse."[94] He forgets that the Bill of Rights issued out of state

---

[82]B. PATTERSON, *supra* note 1, at 16.

[83]*See* text accompanying note 47 *supra*.

[84]B. PATTERSON, *supra* note 1, at 13. He also set forth Madison's response to the "assignment" objection to a Bill of Rights, *see* text accompanying note 44 *supra*, without comment on its significance.

[85]B. PATTERSON, *supra* note 1, at 13 (emphasis added).

[86]*Id.* (emphasis added).

[87]*Id.* at 17.

[88]*Id.* at 18.

[89]So far as the amendments were not "actual limitations," said Madison, they were "inserted merely for greater caution." *See* text accompanying note 47 *supra*. *See also* text accompanying note 41 *supra*.

[90]*See* notes 42, 43 *supra*. Justice Stone stated that the tenth "amendment states but a truism that all is retained which has not been surrendered." It was merely "declaratory" of the existing relationship between state and federal governments; its purpose was to "allay fears that the new federal government might seek to exercise powers not granted, and that the states might not be able to exercise fully their reserved powers." United States v. Darby, 312 U.S. 100, 124 (1941).

[91]B. PATTERSON, *supra* note 1, at 19 (emphasis added).

[92]THE FEDERALIST No. 84 (A. Hamilton) at 558 (Mod. Lib. ed. 1937).

[93]It needs constantly to be remembered that

the sovereign powers vested in the State governments, by their respective constitutions, remained unaltered and unimpaired, except so far as they were granted to the government of the United States.

. . . .

The government, then, of the United States, can claim no powers which are not granted to it by the constitution, and the powers actually granted, must be such as are expressly given, or given by necessary implication.

Martin v. Hunter's Lessee, 14 U.S. (1 Wheat.) 304, 325–26 (1816) (Story, J.).

[94]B. PATTERSON, *supra* note 1, at 36–37.

distrust of the powers of the general government. "In an age where men looked to the states as the chief guardians of individual rights," Professor Redlich observed, "it was not surprising that the barrier of the Ninth and Tenth Amendments was erected against only the federal government."[95] Patterson would fetter the "sovereign people" themselves, although the ninth amendment provides that unenumerated rights are "retained by the people," not by some superior body that will protect against them.

The bulk of Patterson's discussion is beside the point—a sustained panegyric to "inherent natural rights of the individual."[96] Be they as wide as all outdoors,[97] he assumes rather than proves that the enforcement of unenumerated rights "retained by the people" was handed over to the General Government by the ninth amendment. His insistence that "[t]here is no provision in the Constitution which shall prevent the Government of the United States from protecting inherent rights"[98] overlooks the elementary fact that the federal government has only such powers as are granted.[99] His is the error in rejecting the proposition that "in order to protect a native human or inherent right, we must find the source of its protection in the Constitution."[100]

Professor Norman Redlich

More sophisticated than Patterson, Professor Redlich appreciates the import of the legislative history: "the sketchy legislative history would seem to support the holding in *Barron v. Baltimore* that it was intended to restrict only the federal government."[101] He considers that "[i]t would be unrealistic to attribute to the Senate," which had added to the tenth amendment the words "or to the people," and "intent to impose ill-defined legally enforceable restraints on the states."[102] Those

last four words of the Tenth Amendment must have been added to conform its meaning to the Ninth Amendment and to carry out the intent of both—that as to the federal government there were rights,

---

[95]Redlich, *supra* note 36, at 808. *see* note 22 *supra*. Patterson infers from the statement in Eilenbecker v. District Court of Plymouth County, 134 U.S. 31, 34 (1890), that "the first eight articles of the amendments to the Constitution have reference to powers *exercised* by the government of the United States and not to those of the States," that the ninth amendment did not contain such limitation. B. PATTERSON, *supra* note 1, at 28 (emphasis added). *Eilenbecker* considered challenges under the fifth, sixth, and eighth amendments, and the Court had no occasion to wander beyond the first eight. In addition, it was the "exercise," not the "reservation" of rights or powers that was at issue. It would take more than *Eilenbecker* to translate the ninth's *retention* of rights by the states or the people into *limits* upon the states, let alone that history precludes the Patterson differentiation.

[96]B. Patterson, *supra* note 1, at 19. Throughout he exalts the status of the individual over the collective. But to the Revolutionists of 1776, "individual rights, even the basic civil liberties that we consider so crucial, possessed little of their modern theoretical relevance when set against the will of the people." G. WOOD, *supra* note 38, at 63.

The individual with whom Patterson, a member of a Houston law firm, B. PATTERSON, *supra* note 1, at 99, was concerned is the capitalist, who must be shielded from the "sentimental over-generosity and assistance that will in short time weaken our people by doing for them the things which they should be able and willing to do for themselves, and thus stifle genius and destroy their stamina."

"[S]ome of us," he counsels, "will have greater material wealth than others and none of our people can permit themselves to rankle and become bitter, because it is a part of our system to believe in private ownership of property." *Id.* at 84.

[97]The sovereign people's power to create "rights" knows no bounds: "The other rights 'retained by the people' may be, of course, justified by derivation from natural law theory; but they could just as well be ascribed . . . to the consensus of the American people." Dunbar, *supra* note 38, at 640.

[98]B. PATTERSON, *supra* note 1, at42.

[99]*See* notes 43, 93 *supra*.

[100]B. PATTERSON, *supra* note 1, at 45. Like Patterson, Knowlton Kelsey jumps to his conclusion without prior demonstration that it is compelled by text or history: "[The ninth] must be a positive declaration of existing, though unnamed rights, which may be vindicated under the authority of the Amendment whenever and if ever any governmental authority shall aspire to ungranted power in contravention of "unenumerated rights." Kelsey, *The Ninth Amendment of the Federal Constitution,* 11 IND. L.J. 309, 323 (1936).

[101]Redlich, *supra* note 36, at 805–06 (footnote omitted).

[102]*Id.* at 806.

not enumerated in the Constitution, which were 'retained . . . by the people,' and that because the people possessed such rights there were *powers* which *neither* the federal government nor the States possessed.[103]

These remarks, plus his observation that the Founders "looked to the states as the chief guardians of individual rights" and consequently that the "barrier of the Ninth and Tenth Amendments was erected against only the federal government,"[104] require the conclusion that the ninth amendment has no application to the states. It is therefore puzzling to read that the ninth and tenth amendments "might be peculiarly suited to meet the unique and important problems suggested by the Connecticut birth control law case."[105]

The starting point for Redlich is a "strong historical argument" that the ninth and tenth amendments "were intended to apply in a situation where the asserted right appears to the Court as fundamental to a free society but is, nevertheless, not specified in the Bill of Rights."[106] Apparently Redlich assumes that the Court is to be the enforcer of these "not specified" rights.[107] That role apparently is premised in his statement that the ninth and tenth amendments "appear to have been designed" for "the protection of individual rights not specified in the Constitution."[108] But it is incompatible with his statement that "because the people possessed such [retained] rights, there were *powers* which *neither* the federal government nor the States *possessed*."[109] Among such "no-powers" is the "protection" of those retained rights.

Anticipating Justice Goldberg, Redlich attempts to bridge this chasm by invoking the fourteenth amendment to provide "the framework for applying these restrictions against the states, even though they may have been originally intended to apply only against the United States."[110] First, he suggests that those Justices "who consider the Fourteenth Amendment as having embodied either or all the major portions of the Bill of Rights could appropriately consider the Ninth and Tenth Amendments as 'incorporated' or 'absorbed' into the first paragraph of the Fourteenth Amendment."[111] Thus the discredited "incorporation" doctrine is to serve as the vehicle of yet another arrogation, a result on which even the apostle of "incorporation," Justice Black, gagged. Redlich would have the tenth amendment, which reserves powers not delegated, and against which all "general" delegations are to be read, swallowed up by the fourteenth![112] Next, Redlich turns to "those Justices who have viewed the Fourteenth Amendment as limited only to 'fundamental' rights unrelated to the specific provisions of the Bill of Rights [who] should have no difficulty in adopting a Constitutional provision which appears to have been almost custom-made for this approach."[113] This collides with his conclusion that the retention of rights was accompanied by the withholding of correlative power.

[103]*Id.* at 807 (emphasis added). For present purposes there is no need to inquire whether the reservation of powers not delegated to the federal government also operates against the states. The Founders feared federal, not state power, as Redlich himself recognizes. *See* text accompanying note 95 *supra*.

[104]Redlich, *supra* note 36, at 808.

[105]*Id.* at 804.

[106]*Id.* at 808.

[107]It is not only such judicially recognized "fundamental" rights, but *all* unenumerated rights which are "retained by the people."

[108]Redlich, *supra* note 36, at 808.

[109]*Id.* at 807 (emphasis added).

[110]*Id.* at 806.

[111]*Id.* at 808.

[112]Senator Frederick Frelinghuysen, a framer who construed the fourteenth amendment broadly, said in 1871 that "the Fourteenth Amendment must . . . not be used to make the General Government imperial. It must be read . . . together with the Tenth Amendment." CONG. GLOBE, 42nd Cong., 1st Sess. 501 (1871). In a more innocent decade (1957), Professor Dumbauld wrote, "The Ninth and Tenth Amendments, being reservations for the benefit of the states, of course give no occasion for raising the question whether they are made applicable against the states by the Fourteenth Amendment." E. DUMBAULD, *supra* note 38, at 138.

[113]Redlich, *supra* note 36, at 808.

John Hart Ely

Stamping Chief Justice Warren's holding in *Bolling v. Sharpe* "that the Due Process Clause of the Fifth Amendment incorporates the Equal Protection Clause of the Fourteenth Amendment" as "gibberish both syntactically and historically," [114] Professor John Hart Ely turns to the ninth amendment, asserting that "such an open-ended provision is appropriately read to include an 'equal protection' component."[115] Indeed, he considers that "the conclusion that the Ninth Amendment was intended to signal the existence of federal constitutional rights beyond those specifically enumerated in the Constitution is the only conclusion its language seems comfortably able to support."[116]

If I do not mistake his meaning, Ely confines his invocation of the ninth amendment to the federal domain. We are agreed that "[i]t is quite clear that the original framers and ratifying conventions intended the Bill of Rights to control only the actions of the federal government."[117] It therefore bears emphasis that Ely's "federal constitutional rights" can be asserted only against the federal government and not the states, for he does not here call on incorporation into the fourteenth amendment.

Ely's reference to the "existence of federal constitutional rights" requires explication. Both the rights expressed in the Bill of Rights and the unspecified rights retained by the people "exist," but only the former are "constitutional rights." To my mind, a right "retained" by the people and not described has not been embodied in the Constitution. Madison made clear that the retained rights were not "assigned" to the federal government: to the contrary, he emphasized that they constitute an area in which the "Government ought not to act." This means, in my judgment, that the courts have not been empowered to enforce the retained rights against either the federal government or the states.

Ely himself observes, "One thing we know to a certainty from the historical context is that the Ninth Amendment was not designed to grant Congress authority *to create* additional rights, to amend Article I, Section 8 by *adding a general power* to protect rights."[118] Without protection, a "right" is empty. And he justly points out that the phrase " 'others retained by the people' [is not] an apt way of saying 'others Congress may create.' "[119] That power of creation equally was withheld from the courts; the Founders did not regard the courts as "creators," or lawmakers, but as discoverers of law.[120] For them, the separation of powers, as Madison said in the First Congress, was a "sacred principle"[121] reinforced by a "profound fear" of judicial discretion.[122] It does not, therefore, advance the case for judicial enforcement of the ninth amendment that "[t]here was at the time of the original Constitution little legislative history indicating that *any* particular provision was to receive judicial enforcement: the Ninth Amendment was not singled out one way or the other."[123] All the presuppositions the Founders brought to the task militate against a blank check

---

[114]J. ELY, DEMOCRACY AND DISTRUST 32 (1980).

[115]*Id.* at 33.

[116]*Id.* at 38.

[117]*Id.* at 37.

[118]*Id.*

[119]*Id.*

[120]"[J]udges conceived of their role as merely that of discovering and applying preexisting legal rules." Horwitz, *The Emergence of an Instrumental Conception of American Law 1780–1820,* in 5 PERSPECTIVES IN AMERICAN HISTORY 287, 297 (1971).

[121]1 ANNALS OF CONG., *supra* note 28, at 596–97 (Gerry referring to Madison's argument).

[122]G. WOOD, *supra* note 38, at 298. In 1769 Chief Justice Hutchinson of Massachusetts declared: "*the judge* should never be the *Legislator:* Because, then the will of the Judge would be the Law: and this tends to a State of Slavery." Horwitz, *supra* note 120, at 292.

[123]J. ELY, *supra* note 114, at 40.

to that branch which Hamilton assured them "was next to nothing."[124] Ely himself remarks that "read for what it says the Ninth Amendment seems open-textured enough to support almost anything one might wish to argue, and that thought can get pretty scary."[125] "[T]hat thought," I venture, would have scared the Founders out of their wits. It runs against Madison's explanation that the Bill of Rights would impel the judiciary "to resist encroachments upon rights expressly stipulated for . . . by the declaration of rights,"[126] and reinforces the conclusion that courts were not empowered to enforce the retained and unenumerated rights.

Ely finds Madison's explanation of the ninth amendment separating "the question of unenumerated powers from the question of unenumerated rights"[127] confused: "the possibility that unenumerated rights will be disparaged is seemingly made to do service as an intermediate premise in an argument that unenumerated powers will be implied. . . ."[128] This "confusion" he attributes to "what we today would regard as a category mistake, a failure to recognize that rights and powers are not simply the absence of one another but that rights can cut across or 'trump' powers."[129] But whether the Founders were mistaken in logic is of no moment if they acted on that mistaken view.[130] That the Framers premised that rights and powers were two sides of the same coin is hardly disputable. The exceptions "made in favor of particular *rights,*" Madison stated, were to be regarded as "actual limitations on such *powers.*"[131] The "great object" of a Bill of Rights, he said, was to limit . . . the *powers* of Government, *by excepting out* of the grant of power those cases in which the Government ought not to act, or could act only in a particular mode."[132] As Ely observes, "[w]hat is important" is that Madison "wished to forestall *both* the implication of unexpressed powers *and* the disparagement of unenumerated rights," employing the tenth amendment for the one and the ninth for the other.[133] By what logic do we derive "unexpressed powers" to enforce "unenumerated rights" in the teeth of Madison's purpose to "foreclose . . . the implication of unexpressed powers," and his emphasis that the enumeration of "particular rights" was not to be construed to "enlarge the powers delegated by the Constitution," but rather "as actual limitations of such powers?"[134] Is it conceivable that Madison meant to confer "open-ended" power by "unenumerated rights" while limiting power by the enumeration of "particular rights?" Ely's

---

[124]THE FEDERALIST No. 78 (A. Hamilton) at n.* (Mod. Lib. ed. 1937) (quoting C. MONTESQUIEU, THE SPIRIT OF THE LAWS (1748)) *See also* J. WILSON, *supra* note 21.

[125]J. ELY, *supra* note 114, at 34.

[126]1 ANNALS OF CONG., *supra* note 28, at 457 (quoted at text accompanying note 50 *supra*).

[127]J. ELY, *supra* note 114, at 35.

[128]*Id.* at 36.

[129]*Id.* Citing Hamilton's reply to the argument that the power of taxation could be used to inhibit freedom of expression. THE FEDERALIST No. 84 (A. Hamilton) 560 n.* (Mod. Lib. ed. 1937), Ely concludes that "the possibility of a governmental act's being supported by one of the enumerated powers and at the same time violating one of the enumerated rights is one our forebears were capable of contemplating." J. ELY, *supra* note 114, at 202 n.86. Hamilton rejected the notion that "the imposition of duties upon publications" would be impeded by express "declarations in the State constitutions, in favor of the freedom of the press." He argued in support of his conclusion "that newspapers are taxed in Great Britain and yet it is notorious that the press nowhere enjoys greater liberty than in that country." THE FEDERALIST No. 84 (A. Hamilton) 560 n.* (Mod. Lib. ed. 1937).

Whether an *enumerated* power might override an "exception" in favor of an *enumerated* right need not presently concern us, although it is worth noting Madison's emphasis that *enumerated* rights were "excepted" "out of the grant of power"— that they were to be regarded "as actual limitations of such powers." Here the issue is whether there is an "unexpressed power" to enforce *unenumerated* rights "retained by the people."

[130]C. HUGHES, THE SUPREME COURT OF THE UNITED STATES 186 (1928).

[131]1 ANNALS OF CONG., *supra* note 28, at 435 (quoted at text accompanying note 47 *supra*) (emphasis added).

[132]1 ANNALS OF CONG., *supra* note 28, at 437 (quoted at text accompanying note 46 *supra*) (emphasis added). *See also* 3 M. FARRAND, *supra* note 22, at 256 (remarks of Rep. Pinckney) (quoted at note 39 *supra*).

[133]J. ELY, *supra* note 114, at 36.

[134]1 ANNALS OF CONG., *supra* note 28, at 435 (quoted at text accompanying note 47 *supra*).

conclusion also collides with his affirmation that the ninth amendment was not designed to add to article I, section eight "a general power to protect rights."

Finally Ely concludes, "[i]f a principled approach to judicial enforcement of . . . open ended provisions cannot be developed, one that is not hopelessly inconsistent with our nation's commitment to representative democracy, responsible commentators must consider seriously the possibility that courts simply should stay away from them."[135] The notion that the Framers, so fearful of the greedy expansiveness of power,[136] would make an "open-ended," *i.e.* unlimited, grant, which after the lapse of almost two hundred years is so "scary" that Ely would condemn it unless limited by a "principled" approach, verges on the "incredible."[137] Little less strange is the assumption that a Court which employed the allegedly "open-ended" terms of the fourteenth amendment[138] in disregard of the framers' unmistakable intention to exclude suffrage from its scope[139] will show greater respect for the self-denying "principles" which Ely now proffers.

CONCLUSION

The ninth amendment demonstrably was not custom-made to enlarge federal enforcement of "fundamental rights" in spite of state law; it was merely declaratory of a basic presupposition: all powers not "positively" granted are reserved to the people. It added no unspecified rights to the Bill of Rights; instead it demarked an area in which the "General Government" has no power whatsoever. To transform it into an instrument of control over state government by recourse to the fourteenth amendment blatantly perverts the meaning of the framers, both in 1789 and in 1866.

The newly discovered "meaning" of the ninth amendment is but another facet of the unremitting effort to rationalize the judicial take-over of government in areas which have found favor with activists. It was not ever thus. The shift has been described by an activist, Professor Stanley Kutler: through the late 1930s, academe "critized vigorously the abusive powers of the federal judiciary" for "frustrating desirable social policies" and "arrogat[ing] a policymaking function not conferred

[135]J. ELY, *supra* note 114, at 41.

[136]*See* note 74 and accompanying text *supra.*

[137]I borrow the pejorative from Ely's description of my views. *See* J. ELY, *supra* note 114 at 198 n.66.

[138]For a critique of this theory, see R. BERGER, GOVERNMENT BY JUDICIARY: THE TRANSFORMATION OF THE FOURTEENTH AMENDMENT 300–11 (1977). Ely has it that the framers of the fourteenth amendment issued "open and across-the-board *invitations* to import into the constitutional decision process considerations that will not be found in the amendment nor even . . . elsewhere in the Constitution." Ely, *supra* note 63, at 415 (emphasis added). For a critique of this view, *see* Berger, *Government by Judiciary: John Hart Ely's "Invitation,"* 54 IND. L.J. 277 (1979).

The claim that the 1789 framers issued such an "invitation" through the medium of "open-ended" terms runs counter to Ely's own analysis. He remarks that the founders "certainly didn't have natural law in mind when the Constitution's various open-ended delegations to the future were inserted and approved." J. ELY, *supra* note 114, at 39. He notes that "you can invoke natural law to support anything you want." *Id.* at 50. His "open-ended" theory would permit the imposition of personal, extra-constitutional values that found no favor in the shape of natural law.

The founders, as Professor Philip Kurland observed, and as is well attested, were attached to a "written Constitution"— one of "fixed and unchanging meaning," except as changed by amendment. P. KURLAND, WATERGATE AND THE CONSTITUTION 7 (1978). They conceived the judge's role as *policing* constitutional boundaries, not as taking over legislative functions within those boundaries, and still less as revision of the Constitution. *See* Berger, *Government by Judiciary: John Hart Ely's "Invitation," supra,* at 287. As Elbridge Gerry stated, "[i]t was quite foreign from the nature of [the] office to make them judges of the policy of public measures." 1 M. FARRAND, *supra* note 22, at 97–98. *See* 2 M. FARRAND, *supra* note 22, at 75. "Vague and uncertain laws, and more especially Constitutions," wrote Samuel Adams, "are the very instruments of slavery." 3 S. ADAMS, WRITINGS OF SAMUEL ADAMS 262 (H. Cushing ed. 1904) (quoted in Berger, *Government by Judiciary: John Hart Ely's "Invitation," supra,* at 288).

Such were the presuppositions that underlie Madison's reference to judicial protection of "stipulated rights." Ely's acknowledgment that the ninth amendment did not empower Congress to "create" additional rights, or add "a general power to protect rights" is at war with his view that the amendment is "open-ended."

[139]*See* notes 144, 145, and accompanying text *infra.*

upon them by the Constitution."[140] After 1937, these critics "suddenly found a new faith," a "new libertarianism promoting 'preferred freedoms' " protected by an "activist judiciary."[141] Now another activist, Professor Louis Lusky, defends "the Court's new and grander conception of its own place in the governmental scheme"[142] resting on "basic shifts in its approach to constitutional adjudication [including] . . . assertion of the power to *revise* the Constitution, *bypassing* the cumbersome amendment procedure prescribed by article V."[143] That "new and grander" role—conferred by the Court on the Court—pays little heed to the intention of the Framers. When confronted by Justice Harlan's "irrefutable" demonstration that the fourteenth amendment was not intended to "authorize Congress to set voter qualifications"[144]—it is safe to say that suffrage was *unmistakably excluded*[145]—Justices Brennan, White and Marshall "could not accept this thesis even if it were supported by historical evidence."[146] and Justice Douglas dismissed it as "irrelevant."[147] This repudiated the traditional canon of construction reiterated by Justice Holmes: when a legislature "has intimated its will, however indirectly, that will should be recognized and obeyed. . . . [I]t is not an adequate discharge of duty for courts to say: We see what you are driving at, but you have not said it."[148] Still less is that will to be disobeyed when the Framers have spoken with unmistakable clarity, any more than the Court may "revise" the express text. Posterity will honor Justice Harlan's comment:

> When the Court disregards the express intent and understanding of the Framers, it has invaded the realm of the political process to which the amending power was committed, and it has violated the constitutional structure which it is its highest duty to protect.[149]

Even the express text is thrust aside by one super-heated activist, Professor Robert Cover:

> [A] reading of the Constitution must stand or fall not upon the Constitution's *self-evident meaning,* nor upon the intentions of the 1787 or 1866 framers . . . [I]t is for *us,* not the framers, to decide whether that end of liberty is best served by *entrusting* to judges a major role in defining our governing political ideas and in measuring the activity of the primary actors in majoritarian politics against that ideology.[150]

Of course Cover does not—and cannot—point to the source of this decision to "entrust" judges with the ultimate power to frame our "ideology"; he chooses instead to equate the wishes of the academic illuminati with the will of "We, the people." Widespread resistance to busing, as well as

---

[140]Kutler, *Raoul Berger's Fourteenth Amendment: A History or Ahistorical?,* 6 HASTINGS CONST. L.Q. 511–12 (1979).

[141]*Id.* at 513.

[142]Lusky, *"Government by Judiciary": What Price Legitimacy?,* 6 HASTINGS CONST. L.Q. 403, 408 (1979).

[143]*Id.* at 406 (emphasis added).

[144]Oregon v. Mitchell, 400 U.S. 112, 350 (1970).

[145]Looking back in *Griswold,* Justice Harlan justly remarked that the reapportionment interpretations were "made in the face of irrefutable and still unanswered history to the contrary." 381 U.S. at 501 (Harlan, J., concurring). *See* R. BERGER, *supra* note 59, at 52–98. Lusky considers that Harlan's demonstration is "irrefutable and unrefuted." Lusky, *supra* note 142, at 406. *See generally* Berger, *supra* note 42, at 794.

[146]Oregon v. Mitchell, 400 U.S. 112, 251 (1970).

[147]*Id.* at 140. Little wonder that Professor Paul Brest challenges the assumption "that judges and other public officials were bound by the text or original understanding of the Constitution." Brest *The Misconceived Quest for the Original Understanding,* 60 B.U.L. Rev. 204, 224 (1980).

[148]Johnson v. United States, 163 F. 30, 32 (1st Cir. 1908) (quoted in Keifer & Keifer v. R.F.C., 306 U.S. 381, 391 n.4 (1939)). Judge Learned Hand stated in 1959 that "the purpose may be so manifest as to override even the explicit words used." Cawley v. United States, 272 F.2d 443, 445 (2d Cir. 1959). "The intention of the lawmaker is the law." Hawaii v. Mankichi, 190 U.S. 197, 212 (1903) (quoting Smythe v. Fiske, 90 U.S. (23 Wall.) 374, 380 (1874)). Those who dismiss out of hand the application of canons of statutory construction to constitutional interpretation are probably unaware that Justice Story, Edward Corwin, Julius Goebel and Harry Jones are to the contrary. *See* Berger, *supra* note 42, at 805.

[149]Oregon v. Mitchell, 400 U.S. 112, 203 (1970) (Harlan, J., concurring).

[150]Cover, Book Review, NEW REPUBLIC, Jan. 14, 1978, at 27 (emphasis added). *See also* Brest, *The Misconceived Quest for the Original Understanding,* 60 B.U. L. REV. 204, 224 (1980).

dissatisfaction with affirmative action, the Court's restrictions on death penalties, and State criminal law enforcement testify that the identification is imaginary. Were the values of the Justices superior to those of the commonality,[151] they would yet represent those of "Big Brother" and recall Robespierre: "If Frenchmen would not be free and virtuous voluntarily, then he would force them to be free and cram virtue down their throats."[152]

It is against this background that the Goldbergian resort to the ninth amendment is to be viewed; another bit of legal legerdemain whose purpose is to take from the people their right to self-government and put it in the hands of the Justices.[153]

---

[151]Professor G. Edward White asks, "[W]hy should [the Court] not openly acknowledge that the source of [newly-invented] rights is not the constitutional text but the enhanced seriousness of certain values in American society?" White, *Reflections on the role of the Supreme Court: the Contemporary Debate and the "Lessons" of History,* 63 JUDICATURE 162, 168 (1979). *See also* Forrester, *Are We Ready for Truth in Judging?,* 63 A.B.A.J. 1212 (1977).

[152]2 C. BRINTON, J. CHRISTOPER & R. WOLFF, A HISTORY OF CIVILIZATION 115 (1st ed. 1955).

[153]Alfred Kelly, a devout activist, wrote that the Warren Court was "apparent[ly] determin[ed] to carry through a constitutional . . . revolution." Kelly, *Clio and the Court: An Illicit Love Affair,* 1965 SUP. CT. REV. 119, 158.

CHAPTER X

Residence Requirements for Welfare and Voting: A Post-Mortem

I. INTRODUCTION

In the wake of *Shapiro v. Thompson*[1]—residence requirements for migrant welfare recipients are unconstitutional—Professor Margaret Rosenheim wrote, "*Shapiro* stands as a high-water mark of judicial indignation over a discrimination which betrays the meanness and inhumanity of public assistance. The traditions of six hundred years have been dealt a mortal blow."[2] Those traditions were rooted in pre-Elizabethan law and custom, in colonial enactments[3] and at the time of the decision were expressed in the statutes of forty or more States.[4] "Judicial indignation" did not, therefore, represent the "moral" sense of the American people on which activists customarily rely for judicial revision of the Constitution,[5] but rather, as Chief Justice Hughes had advised a newcomer, Justice Douglas, it constituted an "emotional" reaction for which the "rational part of us supplies the reasons for supporting our predilections." In Douglas' homelier terms, "the 'gut' reaction of a judge at the level of constitutional adjudication . . . [was] the main ingredient of his decision."[6] Are the "gut reactions" of the Justices an adequate basis for setting aside the continuing objections of the American people to contributing to the immediate support of migrants?

---

[1]394 U.S. 618 (1969) (Warren, C.J., Black & Harlan, J.J., dissenting).

[2]Rosenheim, Shapiro v. Thompson: *"The Beggars Are Coming To Town,"* 1969 SUP. CT. REV. 303, 345–46. Chief Justice Marshall said with respect to the slave trade that "this Court must not yield to feelings which might seduce it from the path of duty. . . ." The Antelope, 23 U.S. (10 Wheat.) 66, 114 (1825). Justice Holmes wrote that "nothing but confusion of thought can result from assuming that the rights of man in a moral sense are equally rights in the sense of the Constitution and the law" O.W. HOLMES, *The Path of the Law*, in COLLECTED LEGAL PAPERS 167, 171–72 (1920).

[3]The "English Law of Settlement and Removal of 1662 . . . and the earlier Elizabethan Poor Law of 1601 were the models adopted by the American Colonies." Shapiro v. Thompson, 394 U.S. 618, 628 n.7 (1969). For an instructive panorama of English, colonial and early State laws, with copious citations to the literature, *see* Riesenfeld, *The Formative Era of American Public Assistance Law*, 43 CALIF. L. REV. 175 (1955).

[4]Shapiro v. Thompson, 394 U.S. 618, 639–40, 676 n.36 (1969). The Court noted that "[i]n the Congress, sponsors of federal legislation to eliminate all residence requirements have been consistently opposed by representatives of state and local welfare agencies who have stressed the fears of the States that elimination of the requirements would result in a heavy influx of individuals into States providing the most generous benefits." *Id.* at 628. Chief Justice Warren alluded to "the apprehensions of many States that an increase in benefits without minimal residence requirements would result in an inability to provide an adequate welfare system. . . ." *Id.* at 651 (dissenting; Black & Harlan, JJ., concurring). Justice Harlan noted that "a previous Congress had already enacted a one-year residence requirement with respect to aid for dependent children in the District of Columbia." *Id.* at 664. Under its "plenary" power over commerce, Prudential Ins. Co. v. Benjamin, 328 U.S. 408, 425 (1946), Congress should have the last word. Once more the Court rushed in where Congress had refrained, branding as an "unreasonable burden" on free travel a practice to which the English and American people had been wedded for 600 years! 394 U.S. 618, 629 (1969).

[5]For citations to and a critique of such views *see* Ely, *Foreword: On Discovering Fundamental Values*, 92 HARV. L. REV. 5 (1978). On the other hand, Justice Holmes stated that "this Court always had disavowed the right to intrude its judgment upon questions of policy or morals." Hammer v. Dagenhart, 247 U.S. 251, 280 (1918) (dissenting opinion; Brandeis, Clark & McKenna, JJ., concurring). He was anticipated by Madison: "[Q]uestions relating to the general welfare being questions of policy and expediency, are unsusceptible of judicial cognizance and decision." Veto of Internal Improvement Bill (1817), 1 J.D. RICHARDSON, MESSAGES AND PAPERS OF THE PRESIDENTS 584, 585 (1897).

[6]W. DOUGLAS, THE COURT YEARS 1939–1975, at 8 (1981). *See* note 197 *infra*. *See also* Kurland quotation, note 198 *infra*.

"We do not doubt," said Justice Brennan, "that the one-year waiting period is well-suited to discourage the influx of poor families in need of assistance." But the "nature of our Federal Union and our constitutional concepts of personal liberty unite to require that all citizens be free to travel throughout the length and breadth of our land. . . ."[7] Be that assumed, and it is a manifest *non sequitur* to insist that a right to travel entitles a migrant to support at the terminus.[8] One recalls Justice Holmes' analogous "[t]he petitioner may have a constitutional right to talk politics, but he has no constitutional right to be a policeman,"[9] an apothegm that is peculiarly relevant because the "right to travel" was for 600 years limited by a sovereign right to exclude paupers.[10]

A luminous study by a migrant sympathizer, Professor Zechariah Chafee, asks "Should a law enacted by a sovereign State [one of forty or more] be nullified unless it contravenes a specific clause of the Constitution?"[11] "[T]here is," he states, "a queer uncertainty about what clause in the Constitution establishes this right" to travel.[12] Justice Harlan regarded it as "nebulous";[13] and the *Shapiro* majority noted that the " 'right finds no explicit mention in the Constitution,' " but found "no occasion to ascribe the source of this right to travel interstate to a particular constitu-

---

[7]Shapiro v. Thompson, 394 U.S. 618, 629 (1969).

[8]To be sure, the Court does not baldly formulate its conclusions in this manner. It argues that a State may not "chill the assertion of constitutional rights by penalizing those who choose to exercise them." *Id.* at 631. To penalize is to impose a penalty, and a penalty imposes a "loss or disadvantage." OXFORD UNIVERSAL DICTIONARY 1462 (3d ed. 1955). Thus the Court tacitly premises that the traveler is *entitled* to support at his destination merely because he must be "free to travel." 394 U.S. 618, 629 (1969). To deny this is to impose a "disadvantage." It is "unreasonable" to brand as an "unreasonable burden" on the right to travel, *id.*, a practice that has been embodied in law for 600 years. *See* note 10 *infra*.

Another branch of *Shapiro* relies on the equal protection clause: "any classification which *serves to penalize* the exercise" of the right to travel is unconstitutional "unless shown to be necessary to promote a *compelling* governmental interest." 394 U.S. 618, 634 (1969) (emphasis added.) Again this postulates that a migrant has a right to support because it is given a resident. The equal protection argument is discussed in text accompanying notes 153–71 *infra*. Here it may be noted, as Chief Justice Warren pointed out, that many States were apprehensive "that an increase in benefits without minimal residence requirements would result in an inability to provide an adequate welfare system." *Id.* at 651.

Opposing President Reagan's idea of "making welfare a state responsibility," Governor Lee S. Dreyfus of Wisconsin "warned that states 'that try to do a better job' in their welfare programs would suffer a flood of poor migrants," N.Y. Times, May 17, 1981, at 32, col. 1. The other side of the coin is illuminated by the Puerto Rican Commissioner's protest that Reagan's proposed cutbacks would "send a wave of up to 500,000 people to the United States mainland," N.Y. Times, March 12, 1981, at 1, col. 5, who would, of course, look to the given State for support, as when a wave of Cuban refugees recently descended on Florida. Of course, a State may abandon its welfare system and thus obviate the discriminatory classification, but what is this but coercion to accept a migrant's "right to support," conjured up by the Court only yesterday.

[9]McAuliffe v. Mayor of New Bedford, 155 Mass. 216, 200, 29 N.E. 517, 517 (1892).

[10]"If a thing has been practiced for two hundred years by common consent, it will need a strong case for the Fourteenth Amendment to affect it. . . ." Jackman v. Rosenbaum Co., 260 U.S. 22, 31 (1922). "A procedure customarily employed, long before the Revolution, . . . and generally adopted by the States . . . cannot be deemed inconsistent with due process of law. . . ." Ownbey v. Morgan, 256 U.S. 94, 111 (1921). Schick v. Reed, 419 U.S. 256, 261–62 (1974): "At the time of the drafting and adoption of our Constitution it was considered elementary that the prerogative of the English Crown could be exercised upon conditions. . . . The history of our executive pardoning power reveals a consistent pattern of adherence to the English common law practice." Duncan v. Louisiana, 391 U.S. 145, 160 (1968): "So-called petty offenses were tried without juries both in England and in the Colonies and have always been held to be exempt from the otherwise comprehensive language of the Sixth Amendment's jury trial provisions. There is no substantial evidence that the Framers intended to depart from this established common-law practice." *See also* United States v. Wong Kim Ark, 169 U.S. 649, 658 (1898). By the Court's own criteria, its overturn of the 600 year old practice in *Shapiro* is indefensible.

[11]Z. CHAFEE, THREE HUMAN RIGHTS IN THE CONSTITUTION OF 1787, at 190 (1956) [hereinafter cited as CHAFEE].

[12]*Id.* at 188. And he concludes, "Freedom of Movement is a valuable human right, but is it in the Constitution? Only part way. Freedom to live where one pleases inside the United States is in it somewhere, as the Supreme Court has established. . . ." *Id.* at 209. "The 'right to travel' from state to state has been a favorite of both the Warren and Burger Courts. The Constitution makes no mention of any such right. By now we know that that cannot be determinative, but we are entitled to some sort of explanation of why the right is appropriately attributable. In recent years the Court has been almost smug in its refusal to provide one." J. ELY, DEMOCRACY AND DISTRUST 177 (1980).

[13]United States v. Guest, 383 U.S. 745, 771 (1966) (concurring in part and dissenting in part).

tional provision," content that it "has been firmly established"[14]—by the Court, a judicial Cloud Nine unencumbered by constitutional moorings. Such nebulosity underlines the admonition in John Adams' 1780 Massachusetts Constitution: "A frequent recurrence to the fundamental principles of the constitution . . . [is] absolutely necessary to preserve the advantages of liberty and to maintain a free government,"[15] particularly when the Court, as Justice Harlan charges, has engaged in "contriving new constitutional principles."[16]

Before searching for the "right to travel" on which *Shapiro* rests, it will be instructive to note a few historical aspects of English and colonial treatment of welfare for migrants that represent an "established" qualification of the right to travel and mirror present-day concerns. To Rosenheim, the "durational residence requirement" had "seemed to be permanent"; derived from the Elizabethan Poor Law, it "had been part of the states' poor relief laws from the beginning"[17] That Poor Law was grounded on three principles: (1) local responsibility, (2) settlement (domicile) and removal (of migrants), and (3) primary family responsibility, a trinity which, Professor Stefan Riesenfeld observed, "influenced colonial development profoundly."[18] Imposition of local responsibility resulted in "vigorous attempts to reduce the relief burden as much as possible," in large part by preventing "strangers" from adding to the burden of relief.[19] For example, in 1629, the Judges of Assize at Lancaster entered an order reciting that whereas the Manchester inhabitants

> from time to time have made great provisions for the poor of said town which good actions and the want of execution of some convenient course to restrain poor people, that come from several places to inhabit and in short time chargeable unto the said town, has been such a motive and invitation of strangers that are poor and weak in estate as the town is at this present so pestered and overburdened as the native poor is wronged. . . .[20]

Consequently the court restrained "persons from settling in the town without sufficient security to prevent their becoming public charges."[21]

"It was exactly this state of affairs," wrote Riesenfeld, "which the colonists transplanted to the new country."[22] Thus, a Massachusetts Bay statute of 1665 provided that "all such persons as shall be brought into any such town without the consent and allowance of the prudential men, shall not be chargeable to the town where they dwell, but, if necessity shall require, shall be relieved and maintained by those that were the cause of their coming. . . ."[23] Similarly, the 1655 New Haven Code "ordered that any person who had lived for a whole year . . . in any plantation should be counted as an inhabitant of that plantation and neither be sent back nor be chargeable to any other plantation," and that "nobody should be received as a new settler without consent of the majority of the freemen."[24] There is no need to recapitulate numerous other examples collated by Riesenfeld; as Jacobus tenBroek wrote, Riesenfeld showed how the English Poor Law system, "step by step, settlement by settlement, and colony by colony," became "deeply imbedded in community life and legal order."[25]

---

[14]Shapiro v. Thompson, 394 U.S. 618, 630 (1969) (quoting United States v. Guest, 383 U.S. 745, 758 (1966)).

[15]Article XVIII, 1 B. Poore, Federal and State Constitutions, Colonial Charters 959 (1878). For similar provisions, *see* New Hampshire (1784), Article XXXVIII, *id.* at 1283; North Carolina (1776) Article XXI, *id.* at 1410; Pennsylvania (1776), Article XIV, *id.* at 1542; Vermont (1777), Article XVI, *id.* at 1860.

[16]Shapiro v. Thompson, 394 U.S. 618, 677 (1969).

[17]Rosenheim, Shapiro v. Thompson: *"The Beggars Are Coming to Town,"* 1969 Sup. Ct. Rev. 303, 304.

[18]Riesenfeld, *The Formative Era of American Public Assistance Law,* 43 Calif. L. Rev. 175, 178 (1955).

[19]*Id.* at 181.

[20]*Id.* at 194.

[21]*Id.* at 191.

[22]*Id.* at 198.

[23]*Id.* at 207.

[24]*Id.* at 211.

[25]TenBroek, *California's Dual System of Family Law: Its Origin, Development and Present Status,* 16 Stan. L. Rev.

Very early the constitutional validity of State law reflecting these practices was recognized by the Court. In *New York v. Miln* (1837)[26] the issue was whether the commerce power overrode the New York statute. The Court held that "the object of the legislation was, to prevent New York from being burdened by an influx of persons brought thither in ships, either from foreign countries, or from other of the states. . . . [T]he necessary steps might be taken . . . to prevent them from becoming chargeable as paupers."[27] Alluding to New York's purpose to "prevent her citizens from being oppressed by the support of multitudes of poor persons, who come from foreign countries without possessing the means of supporting themselves," the Court stated that "[t]here can be no mode in which the power to regulate internal police could be more appropriately exercised";[28] and that since the power "undeniably existed at the formation of the Constitution," it "was [not] taken from the states" by the commerce power.[29] Although Justice Story filed a dissenting opinion, he "admitted" that the States "have a right to pass poor laws, and laws to prevent the introduction of paupers. . . ."[30] As a participant in *Gibbons v. Ogden*,[31] who now cited the case for the exclusive commerce power of Congress,[32] Story was eminently qualified to affirm that the said power left the right to exclude paupers untouched.

These views were reiterated in seriatim opinions in the 1849 *Passenger Cases*,[33] all being in agreement as to the right to exclude paupers. Justice Woodbury observed that "[s]uch legislation commenced in Massachusetts early after our ancestors arrived at Plymouth. It first empowered the removal of foreign paupers"; and he cited Justice Story's "admission" that States "have a right . . . to prevent the introduction of paupers into the States. . . ."[34] Justice McLean referred to the "unquestionable power in the State to protect itself from foreign paupers and other persons who would be a public charge."[35] Justice Wayne averred that paupers are "not within the regulating power which the United States have over commerce. Paupers . . . never have been subjects of rightful national intercourse. . . . The States may . . . prevent them from entering their territories, may carry them out or drive them off."[36] Justice Grier stated that "[t]his right of the States has its foundation in the sacred law of self-defense, which no power granted to Congress can restrain or annul. It is admitted by all. . . ."[37] And Chief Justice Taney rejected the notion that a "mass of pauperism and vice may be poured out upon the shores of a State in opposition to its laws, and the State authorities are not permitted to resist or prevent it," for he too regarded it as "a power

257, 291 (1964). In the eighteenth century, Riesenfeld found, "[r]emoval provisions specifically applying to unsettled paupers became a ubiquitous feature of the poor laws." Riesenfeld, *The Formative Era of American Public Assistance Law,* 43 CALIF. L. REV. 175, 224 (1955).

[26]36 U.S. (11 Pet.) 102 (1837).

[27]*Id.* at 133.

[28]*Id.* at 141.

[29]*Id.* at 132. The Court cited *Federalist No.* 45: "[T]he powers reserved to the several states, will extend to all the objects, which in the ordinary course of affairs, concern the lives, liberties and properties of the people; and the internal order, improvement, and prosperity of the state." *Id.* at 133. Madison stated in *Federalist No.* 14, the Government's "jurisdiction is limited to certain *enumerated* objects [e.g., war and treaty making], which concern all the members of the republic, but which are not to be attained by the separate provisions of any," THE FEDERALIST No. 14, at 82 (J. Madison) (Mod. Lib. ed. 1937) (emphasis added).

[30]36 U.S. (11 Pet.) 102, 156 (1837).

[31]22 U.S. (9 Wheat.) 1 (1824).

[32]36 U.S. (11 Pet.) 102, 155 (1837). Story later repeated, "We entertain no doubt whatever that the States, in virtue of their general police power" may exclude or remove "vagabonds and paupers." Prigg v. Pennsylvania, 41 U.S. (16 Pet.) 539, 625 (1842).

[33]48 U.S. (7 How.) 283 (1849).

[34]*Id.* at 519, 526.

[35]*Id.* at 402.

[36]*Id.* at 426. Wayne likewise stated, "The States have also reserved the police right to turn off from their territories paupers. . . ." *Id.* at 425.

[37]*Id.* at 457. Justice Catron concurred with Grier. *Id.* at 464.

of self-preservation," that "was never intended to be surrendered."[38] These principles were reaffirmed in *Railroad Co. v. Husen* (1877):[39]

> We admit that the deposit in Congress of the power to regulate foreign commerce and commerce among the States was not a surrender of that which may properly be denominated police power. . . . Under it a State may legislate to . . . exclude from its limits convicts, paupers . . . and persons likely to become a public charge . . . a right founded as intimated in *The Passenger Cases* . . . by Mr. Justice Greer [*sic*] [and Chief Justice Taney], in the sacred law of self-defense.[40]

A word, too, about what Justice Rutledge reminded us Chief Justice Marshall declared was "a grant to Congress of plenary and supreme authority" over commerce.[41] By the Act of March 3, 1891, Congress mandated the exclusion of "paupers or persons likely to become a public charge."[42] The Act was challenged in the *Japanese Immigrant Case* (1903)[43] as in violation of a treaty with Japan, which called for "full liberty to enter, travel or reside . . . but not to affect the laws . . . with regard to . . . police and public security. . . ."[44] Justice Harlan the elder held that the treaty "expressly excepts from its operation any ordinance or regulation relating to 'police and public security.' A statute excluding paupers or persons likely to become a public charge is manifestly one of police and public security,"[45] precisely as the Court had held with respect to cognate State exclusions.

In sum, the right of a State to exclude paupers in the exercise of its police power was repeatedly recognized by the Court and was not questioned until 1941 in *Edwards v. California*.[46] There Justice Byrnes, referring to the "contention that the limitation upon State power to interfere with the interstate transportation of persons is subject to an exception in the case of 'paupers'," remarked of earlier judicial references to such migrants as a "moral pestilence" that this "language has been casually repeated in numerous later cases up to the turn of the century," and then he even more casually overruled the earlier uninterrupted string of cases on the ground that "it will [not] now be seriously contended that because a person is without employment and without funds he constitutes a 'moral pestilence.' "[47] Indigence need not be regarded as a "moral pestilence" in order to justify the rejection by forty States of the burden of supporting migrants. Compare Byrnes' indignation with Justice Story's application in a similar case of long "established" canons of construction: "[S]uch long acquiescence in it, such contemporaneous construction of it, and such extensive and uniform recognition [and here embodiment in long-standing State law] of it . . . would . . . entitle the question to be considered at rest."[48] This is not to exalt stare decisis—though

---

[38]*Id.* at 472, 470. Justices Daniels and Nelson concurred with Taney. *Id.* at 515, 518. *Shapiro v. Thompson* quotes from this opinion of Taney:

> For all the great purposes for which the Federal Government was formed, we are one people, with one common country. We are all citizens of the United States; and, as members of the same community, must have the right to pass and repass through every part of it without interruption, as freely as in our own States.

394 U.S. 618, 630 (1969). But it ignores Taney's qualification which is decisive of the *Shapiro* issue: the States reserved the right to exclude migrant paupers.

[39]95 U.S. 465 (1877).

[40]*Id.* at 470–71.

[41]Prudential Ins. Co. v. Benjamin, 328 U.S. 408, 423 (1946). Justice Frankfurter considered that under the commerce clause jurisdiction, "judgments denying power to the States are subject to Congressional revision." A. BICKEL, THE SUPREME COURT AND THE IDEA OF PROGRESS 30 (1978).

[42]Ch. 551, § 1,26 STAT. 1084 (1891) (the exclusion of paupers appears in the current statutes at 8 U.S.C. § 1182 (1976)).

[43]189 U.S. 86 (1903).

[44]*Id.* at 96.

[45]*Id.* at 97. Similar statutes went unquestioned in Gegiow v. Uhl, 239 U.S. 3 (1915), per Justice Holmes. *See also* note 4 *supra*.

[46]314 U.S. 160 (1941).

[47]*Id.* at 176–77.

[48]Prigg v. Pennsylvania, 41 U.S. (16 Pet.) 539, 621 (1842). Justice Catron said in a seriatim opinion in The License

Justices Thurgood Marshall and Brennan cried out in 1973 at a fancied departure from the "well-established principles" of *Shapiro v. Thompson* (1969)[49]—but rather to ask whether present-day Justices have been given a dazzling revelation that was denied to Justices who were closer in time to the Founders and whose views reflect the "600 year tradition." Justice Jackson reminded the Brethren, "We are not final because we are infallible, but we are infallible only because we are final."[50]

More is involved, however, than unbroken "practice." That long usage gives meaning to the terms the Framers employed. Such terms, the Court held, must be interpreted with reference "to British institutions as they were when the instrument was framed and adopted."[51] Whatever the scope of "commerce" and "liberty," they cannot comprehend what English and colonial law and practice so plainly excluded. Who would have maintained in 1787 that since "commerce" and "liberty"[52] comprehended the "right to travel," they included an indigent's right to be supported at his destination? Of those terms we may say, as did Chief Justice Marshall of "treason," "It is scarcely conceivable that the term was not employed by the framers of our constitution in the sense which had been affixed to it by those from whom we borrowed it."[53] In fact, the one time the Founders specifically dealt with the right of "ingress and regress" in the Articles of Confederation, they expressly *excepted* "paupers" therefrom,[54] evidencing their respect for colonial and State exclusion of indigent migrants. To read current judicial "interpretations" back into the constitutional terms is to transform the meaning they had for the Founders.[55] A departure from the governing principles of 1787 to "a principle never before recognized," declared Chief Justice Marshall, "should be expressed in plain and explicit terms."[56] That can hardly be claimed for a right to support that finds no mention in the constitutional text or its history.

Present-day Justices have not, however, felt constrained by historical meaning. Dissenting in a death-penalty case, Justice Douglas said, "The Court has history on its side—but history alone."[57] Justice Brennan even more flatly stated that history was not binding on the Court.[58] On the other hand, Chief Justice Taney emphasized that "[i]f in this court we are at liberty to give old words new meanings when we find them in the Constitution, there is no power which may not, by this mode of construction, be conferred on the general government and denied to the States."[59] That is precisely what activists unabashedly advocate; but let us be clear that it cannot be rooted in

---

Cases, 46 U.S. (5 How.) 504, 607 (1847), that "[i]f long usage, general acquiescence, and the absence of complaint can settle the interpretation . . . then it should be deemed as settled in conformity with the usage by the courts." For similar expression by Justice Holmes, see note 10 *supra*, and by Chief Justice White, see text accompanying note 106 *infra*. See also Walz v. Tax Comm'r, 397 U.S. 664, 678 (1970).

[49]Vlandis v. Kline, 412 U.S. 441, 455 (1973) (concurring opinion).

[50]Brown v. Allen, 344 U.S. 443, 540 (1953) (concurring opinion).

[51]*Ex parte* Grossman, 267 U.S. 87, 108–09 (1925). For example, "the word 'jury' and the words 'trial by jury' were placed in the Constitution . . . with reference to the meaning affixed to them in the law as it was in this country and in England at the adoption of that instrument. . . ." Thompson v. Utah, 170 U.S. 343, 350 (1898). *See also* R. BERGER, GOVERNMENT BY JUDICIARY 403 (1977).

[52]In Kent v. Dulles, 357 U.S. 116, 125 (1958), the Court held that "[t]he right to travel is a part of the 'liberty' of which the citizen cannot be deprived without due process of law under the Fifth Amendment."

[53]United States v. Burr, 25 F. Cas. 55, 159 (C.C.Va. 1807) (No. 14,693).

[54]*See* text accompanying note 83 *infra*.

[55]*See* Justice Black quotation at text accompanying note 64 *infra*.

[56]United States v. Burr, 25 F. Cas. 55, 165 (C.C.Va. 1807) (No. 14,693), *See also* Pierson v. Ray, 386 U.S. 547 (1967).

[57]McGautha v. California, 402 U.S. 183, 241 (1971) (dissenting opinion). On the other hand, the Court, per Justice Harlan, held that "it requires a strong showing to upset this settled practice of the Nation on constitutional grounds," *Id.* at 203.

[58]Oregon v. Mitchell, 400 U.S. 112, 251 (1970) (dissenting and concurring in part): "We could not accept [Justice Harlan's] thesis even if it were supported by historical evidence far stronger than anything adduced here today."

[59]The Passenger Cases, 48 U.S. (7 How.) 283, 478 (1849).

constitutional warrant but rather represents a claim to judicial power to revise the Constitution.[60]

Consider how Justice Byrnes, in *Edwards v. California*,[61] the first interstate indigent nonresident case, replied to the argument that such State restraints enjoy "a firm basis in English and American history": "[T]he theory of the Elizabethan poor laws no longer fits the facts" in light of "a growing recognition that in an industrial society the task of providing assistance to the needy has ceased to be local in character."[62] That "recognition" had not, however, prompted the forty States to repeal their residence requirements, and therefore merely represented the moral sentiments of the Court, but another example of what Justice Douglas described as "the evolving gloss of civilized standards which this Court . . . *has been reading into*" the Constitution.[63] In a similar case Justice Black accused the Court of giving a constitutional phrase "a new meaning which it believes represents a better governmental policy."[64] That policy may be highly desirable and nonetheless constitute an arrant arrogation of power to amend the Constitution. Change is for the people themselves, through the machinery of article V.[65]

II. THE RIGHT TO TRAVEL

Since the Court hung the indigent migrant's constitutional claim to immediate support on the right to travel, it will profit us to retrace the search for its roots, a search which perplexed Zechariah Chafee, an eminent protagonist of the right.[66] "Although," said Justice Stewart, "there have been recurring differences in emphasis within the Court as to the source of the constitutional right of interstate travel, there is no need here to canvass those differences further. All have agreed that

---

[60]Professor Louis Lusky pays tribute to "the Court's new and grander conception" of its role, its "assertion of power to revise the Constitution, bypassing the cumbersome amendment procedure prescribed by article V." Lusky, Book Review, 6 HASTINGS CONST. L.Q. 403, 406, 408 (1979). On such reasoning a break-in through a window may be defended because entry through the barred door was "cumbersome." *See also* text accompanying notes 199–200 *infra*.

[61]314 U.S. 160 (1941).

[62]*Id.* at 174–75. Consider the reasoning of Justice Douglas in a similar case: "We agree, of course, with Mr. Justice Holmes that the Due Process clause of the Fourteenth Amendment 'does not enact Mr. Herbert Spencer's Social Statics'. . . . Likewise the Equal Protection Clause is not shackled to the political theory of a particular era." Harper v. Virginia Bd. of Elections, 383 U.S. 663, 669 (1966). Douglas perverted Holmes' meaning. Holmes objected to reading Spencer's *Social Statics* into the Constitution. By parity of reasoning, Douglas should not read *his* social predilections into the clause. As Justice Harlan observed, the clause does not "rigidly impose upon America an ideology of unrestrained egalitarianism." *Id.* at 686 (dissenting opinion). The framers left us a record of the limited scope they contemplated for equal protection. *See* text accompanying notes 160–66 *infra*.

When, however, a particular ruling displeased him, Douglas denounced it as "such a serious invasion of state sovereignty protected by the Tenth Amendment that it is in my view not consistent with our constitutional federalism." Maryland v. Wirtz, 392 U.S. 183, 201 (1968) (dissenting opinion). At issue was the application of the Fair Labor Standards Act to State hospitals and schools, requiring outlays that fell far short of the burdens imposed by migrant paupers. But then Douglas stated that constitutional decision making is largely determined by the judges' "gut reactions." *See* text accompanying note 6 *supra*.

[63]McGautha v. California, 402 U.S. 183, 241 (1971) (dissenting opinion) (emphasis added). *Cf.* Justice Cardozo:

The constitution and statutes and judicial decisions of the Commonwealth of Massachusetts are the authentic forms through which the sense of justice of the People of that Commonwealth expresses itself in law. We are not to supersede them on the ground that they deny the essentials of a trial because opinions may differ as to their policy of fairness. Not all the precepts of conduct precious to the hearts of many of us are immutable principles of justice. . . .

Snyder v. Massachusetts, 291 U.S. 97, 122 (1934).

[64]Harper v. Virginia Bd. of Elections, 383 U.S. 663, 672 (1966) (dissenting opinion).

[65]Time and again Justice Black hammered the point home, dismissing "rhapsodical strains, about the duty of this Court to keep the Constitution in tune with the times. The idea is that the Constitution must be changed from time to time and that this Court is charged with the duty to make those changes. . . . The Constitution makers knew the need for change and provided for it" by the amendment process of Article V. Griswold v. Connecticut, 381 U.S. 479, 522 (1965) (Black, J., dissenting opinion).

[66]*See* text accompanying notes 10 & 12 *supra*; text accompanying note 134 *infra*.

the right exists."[67] The Justices' "recurring differences," however, render it "uncertain" that it can be located in the Constitution, where, Justice Harlan properly insisted, it "must be found."[68] What is in issue is the constitutional warrant for the Court's overthrow of centuries-old residence restrictions on migrant welfare, and that cannot be settled by the Court's self-serving declarations.[69]

A. The Commerce Clause

The first judicial invocation in the premises of the commerce clause was that of Justice William Johnson, who held on circuit in 1823 that State seizure of a British Negro seaman who temporarily entered South Carolina offended the clause.[70] When the clause came before the Supreme Court in 1837, the Court held that "goods are the subject of commerce, . . . persons are not,"[71] a conclusion echoed about 100 years later by Justice Jackson in *Edwards v. California:* "[T]he migrations of a human being . . . do not fit easily into my notions of what is commerce."[72] So it seemed to the Framers for, as Chafee notes, "[t]hough much was said about barriers at State-lines against goods, nobody spoke of barriers against persons,"[73] presumably because the Framers justifiably assumed that such barriers had been razed by the "privileges and immunities" clause of article IV.[74] The 1837 *Miln* view, however, was apparently abandoned by the Court in *The Passenger Cases* (1849),[75] in which several Justices considered "transportation of passengers [to be] a part of commerce,"[76] but, as has been noted, all adhered to the traditional exception for paupers as an exercise of power reserved to the States. The Court eschewed reliance on the commerce clause in the much-cited *Crandall v. Nevada* (1867).[77] And as Chafee asked, "[A]re human beings engaged in commerce when they are not on business trips but traveling from state to state on pleasure bent or in search of new homes?"[78] But the commerce clause was again invoked in *Henderson v. Mayor of New York* (1875).[79]

B. The "Privileges and Immunities" of Article IV

Not the least singular aspect of the Court's search for roots is its relative indifference to the "privileges and immunities" clause of article IV, section 2, although it most clearly discloses the Founders' commitment to the right of interstate travel. *Paul v. Virginia* (1868)[80] noted in passing

[67]United States v. Guest, 383 U.S. 745, 759 (1966). *Shapiro v. Thompson* repeats that the right "has been firmly established." 394 U.S. 618, 630 (1969). The fact that the Justices cannot agree on the constitutional source of the right, note 9 *supra*, suggests that "firmly established" refers to a judicial construct rather than a constitutional right.

[68]United States v. Guest, 383 U.S. 745, 763 (1966) (concurring and dissenting in part). Justice Douglas remarked, "[I]t is apparent that this right is not specifically granted by the Constitution." Edwards v. California, 314 U.S. 160, 178 (1941) (concurring opinion).

[69]Bork, *The Impossibility of Finding Welfare Rights in the Constitution,* 1979 Wash. U.L.Q. 695, 698.

[70]Elkinson v. Deliesseline, 8 F. Cas. 493 (C.C.S.C. 1823) (No. 4,366).

[71]New York v. Miln, 36 U.S. (11 Pet.) 102, 136 (1837).

[72]314 U.S. 160, 182 (1941) (concurring opinion). *See also id.* at 177 (Douglas, J., concurring opinion).

[73]Chafee, *supra* note 11, at 186. On the other hand, Charles Pinckney referred to the commerce clause as "the measure of regulating trade." 3 M. Farrand, Records of the Federal Convention of 1787, at 116 (1911); and Madison explained that the clause "grew out of the abuse of the power by the importing States in taxing the non-importing. . . ." *Id.* at 478. Professor Ernest Brown noted that the predominant usage of "commerce" at the adoption of the Constitution was the "exchange of merchandise." Brown, Book Review, 67 Harv. L. Rev. 1439, 1448 (1954).

[74]*See* text accompanying note 83 *infra*.

[75]48 U.S. (7 How.) 283 (1849).

[76]*Id.* at 401. Apparently Justice Wayne was of the same opinion. *Id.* at 413, 426.

[77]73 U.S. (6 Wall.) 35, 43 (1867): "[I]t is not easy to maintain . . . that [the tax] violates" the commerce clause. Chief Justice Chase and Justice Clifford, concurring, rested on the clause. For further discussion, *see* text accompanying notes 130–40 *infra*.

[78]Chafee, *supra* note 11, at 189.

[79]92 U.S. 259, 270 (1875); but the Court did not decide whether the States can "protect themselves against actual paupers." *Id.* at 275.

[80]75 U.S. (8 Wall.) 168 (1868).

that it gives citizens of States "the right of free ingress into other States."[81] as *United States v. Wheeler* (1920) again recognized.[82] Article IV was borrowed from the antecedent article IV of the Articles of Confederation. The latter provided that

> [t]he better to secure and perpetuate mutual friendship and intercourse among the people of the different States in this Union, the free inhabitants of each of these States, *paupers . . . excepted,* shall be entitled to all privileges and immunities of free citizens in the several States; and the people of each State shall have *free ingress and regress* to and from any other state. . . .[83]

Thus, "privileges and immunities" were defined to include "ingress" into a sister State, "paupers excepted."

Article IV, section 2 of the Constitution provided that "[t]he citizens of each State shall be entitled to all Privileges and Immunities of Citizens in the several States." Justice Harlan commented that "free ingress and regress' was eliminated . . . without discussion" because "it was so obviously an essential part of our federal structure that it was necessarily subsumed under more general clauses of the Constitution."[84] But where? To my mind, ingress into a sister State was implicit in "privileges and immunities." How could a citizen of one State fully enjoy the privileges of a sister State without entry therein, particularly since the prime purpose of the antecedent Articles of Confederation clause was to secure "mutual friendship and intercourse among the people of the different States in this Union. . . ."[85] Thirty of the fifty-five Framers had been members of the Continental Congress that drafted the Articles of Confederation,[86] and it is not a little remarkable that in both the Articles and the Constitution "privileges and immunities" was the subject of the same article, article IV. To borrow from Chief Justice Taney, "[T]hey ought not to be supposed to have used familiar words in a new or unusual sense."[87] To the contrary, the Framers presumably employed the phrase "in the sense which had been affixed to it by those from whom we borrowed it."[88]

Chafee's exegesis of article IV takes a restrictive view: the "trade and commerce" of the Articles of Confederation, he considers, "can be regarded as embraced" in the commerce clause,[89] disregarding that "commerce" had been associated with goods, not people, whereas "privileges and immunities" had specifically dealt with the "ingress" of people, going beyond "trade and commerce" to promote "mutual friendship and intercourse" among them. Chafee himself noted that commerce would not embrace the pleasure trip or search for a new home[90] comprehended by article IV's promotion of mutual "intercourse and friendship." No adequate explanation has been offered for abandoning the familiar ingress-egress connotation of privileges and immunities in favor of transplantation to the "commerce" or "due process" clauses with which they had not theretofore been

---

[81]*Id.* at 180.

[82]254 U.S. 281 (1920), discussed in text accompanying notes 94–96 & 105–08 *infra*.

[83]*Id.* at 294 (emphasis added).

[84]United States v. Guest, 383 U.S. 745, 764 (1966).

[85]United States v. Wheeler, 254 U.S. 281, 294 (1921). Chief Justice White commented on the argument that since a State may deprive its own citizens of the right of "free ingress thereto and egress therefrom" that such legislation is "incompatible with its existence as a free government and destructive of the fundamental rights of its citizens. . . ." *Id.* at 299. There is no need for such generalities because article IV of the Articles of Confederation declared that its purpose was to serve "mutual friendship and intercourse among the people of the different States" by granting "free ingress and regress to and from any other State" to "the free inhabitants of *each* of these States," *Id.* at 294 (emphasis added). That purpose would be defeated if any State could bar its own citizens from egress "to any other State."

[86]For list of dual members, *see* R. Berger, Executive Privilege 127 n.51 (1974).

[87]The Passenger Cases, 48 U.S. (7 How.) 283, 477 (1849).

[88]*See* text accompanying note 53 *supra, Cf.* Yates v. United States, 354 U.S. 298, 319 (1957), in which Justice Harlan stated, "[We] should not assume that Congress . . . used the words 'advocate' and 'teach' in their ordinary dictionary meanings when they had already been construed as terms of art carrying a special and limited connotation."

[89]Chafee, *supra,* note 11, at 185.

[90]*See* text accompanying note 78 *supra.*

associated. Moreover, to locate "ingress and egress" in the commerce clause would amputate the qualifying exception for paupers, an unexplained rejection of the centuries-old English and colonial practice so carefully preserved by the Articles of Confederation.[91] It seems more logical, therefore, to conclude that the Framers left "ingress" and the qualifying exception for paupers where those Articles had placed them—in the privileges and immunities clause.[92] Throughout, the Framers sought to pare each phrase of the extensive Constitution to its barest essentials. Aware that the Continental Congress had defined privileges and immunities in terms of ingress subject to the exception for paupers, the Framers might safely rely on the familiar connotation.[93] This was taken for granted by the Supreme Court. In *United States v. Wheeler*[94] Chief Justice White repeated the statement in the *Slaughter House Cases*[95] respecting the article IV provisions of the Articles of Confederation and of the Constitution: "There can be but little question that the purpose of both these provisions is the same, and that the privileges and immunities intended are the same in each."[96]

Before we leave article IV, it needs to be emphasized that it was framed in terms of the right the "Citizens of each *State*" would enjoy. Notwithstanding, the Court has persistently spoken in terms of a right of "citizens of the United States." Thus, Justice Harlan stated that "[b]ecause of the close proximity of the right of ingress and regress to the Privileges and Immunities Clause of the Articles of Confederation it has long been declared that the right is a privilege and immunity of national citizenship under the Constitution."[97] But the stated object of the Articles of Confederation was to promote "mutual intercourse among the people of the different states," and it accorded privileges and immunities to the "free inhabitants of *each* of these States," not to "citizens of the United States." The latter concept was yet to be born. Before the Constitution, said Chief Justice Marshall in *Gibbons v. Ogden*,[98] the States "were sovereign, were completely independent, and were connected with each other only by a league,"[99] as the Articles immediately attest. Article II recited, "Each State retains its sovereignty, freedom and independence"; article III provided, "The said States hereby severally enter into a firm league of friendship with each other. . . ."[100]

---

[91]That article IV, § 2 left no room for the claim that ingress was accompanied by a right to "welfare relief" may be gathered from an early construction by Justice Bushrod Washington on circuit in Corfield v. Coryell, 6 F. Cas. 546, 522 (C.C.E. Pa. 1823) (No. 3,230): "The oyster beds belonging to a State may be abundantly sufficient for the use of the citizens of that State, but might be totally exhausted if the legislature could not . . . exclude the citizens of other States from taking them. . . ." *Cited in* Blake v. McClung, 172 U.S. 239, 249–50 (1898). *See also* McReady v. Virginia, 94 U.S. 391, 394–95 (1876).

[92]*Cf.* Woodruff v. Parham, 75 U.S. (8 Wall.) 123, 136 (1868): "The only allusion to imports in the Articles of Confederation is clearly limited to duties on goods imported from foreign States."

[93]For example, Madison sought expressly to limit "cases and controversies" "to cases of a Judiciary Nature," but was turned down, "it being generally supposed that the jurisdiction given was constructively limited to cases of a Judiciary nature." 2 M. FARRAND, RECORDS OF THE FEDERAL CONVENTION OF 1787, at 430 (1911). In the First Congress, Abraham Baldwin, a Framer, commenting on a proposed amendment said that such minute regulation "would have swelled [the Constitution] to the size of a folio volume." 1 ANNALS OF CONG. 581 (Gales & Seaton eds. 1836) (print bearing running title "History of Debates in Congress"). Chief Justice Taney observed. "[N]o word was unnecessarily used or needlessly added. . . . Every word appears to have been weighed with the utmost deliberation, and its force and effect to have been fully understood." Holmes v. Jennison, 39 U.S. (14 Pet.) 540, 571 (1840).

[94]254 U.S. 281 (1920).

[95]83 U.S. (16 Wall.) 36 (1872).

[96]United States v. Wheeler, 254 U.S. 281, 296 (1920).

[97]United States v. Guest, 383 U.S. 745, 746 (1966) (concurring and dissenting in part).

[98]22 U.S. (9 Wheat.) 1 (1824).

[99]*Id.* at 187. In later years Madison pointed out that article II "emphatically declares 'that each State *retains* its *sovereignty* freedom & independence and every power &c, which is not expressly delegated to the U.S. in Congs. assembled.' " 3 M. FARRAND, RECORDS OF THE FEDERAL CONVENTION OF 1787, at 522 (1911). *See also* R. BERGER, EXECUTIVE PRIVILEGE 103–05 (1974).

[100]H. COMMAGER, DOCUMENTS OF AMERICAN HISTORY 111 (7th ed. 1963).

Until the Court struck out on a new path in 1941, it had adhered to the traditional view, as Justice Douglas acknowledged: "To be sure, there are expressions in the cases that this right of free movement of persons is an incident of *state* citizenship. . . ."[101] Thus, *Twining v. United States*[102] explained an early construction of article IV in terms of rights "which belong to the citizens of States as such and are under the sole care and protection of the state governments."[103] As late as 1921, Chief Justice White, speaking for a Court graced by Justices Holmes and Brandeis, noted that article IV of the Articles of Confederation secured uniformity "not by lodging power in Congress to deal with the subject, but, while reserving in the several States authority which they had theretofore enjoyed, yet subjecting such authority to a limitation inhibiting the power from being used to discriminate."[104] He went on to say that "the text of Article IV, [section] 2 of the Constitution, makes manifest that it was drawn with reference to the corresponding clause of the Articles of Confederation and was intended to perpetuate its limitations. . . ,"[105] including, it may be added, the "exception" for "paupers." The "continued possession by the States of the reserved power to deal with free residence, ingress and egress. . . ," he declared, "has been so conclusively settled as to leave no room for controversy."[106] And he concluded that the article IV reservation "to the several States" excluded "federal authority" except where invoked "to enforce the limitation,"[107] and dismissed the view that "the privilege of passing from State to State is an attribute of national citizenship."[108] This in a case that held United States citizenship "confers no immunity against being run out of Arizona by a mob"![109] For Justice Douglas all this was of no moment because "the thrust of the *Crandall* [*v. Nevada*] case is deeper,"[110] preferring judicial improvisation to constitutional footing.

C. The "Privileges or Immunities" of the Fourteenth Amendment

Before examining *Crandall,* let us consider Justice Jackson's appeal to the "privileges or immunities" of the fourteenth amendment: "No State shall . . . abridge the privileges or immunities of citizens of the United States. . . ."[111] Justice Jackson did not go behind what he termed "these general and abstract words"[112] but, he besought the Court to give them "real meaning," notwith-

---

[101]Edwards v. California, 314 U.S. 160, 180 (1941) (concurring opinion).

[102]211 U.S. 78 (1908).

[103]*Id.* at 94. Justice Bradley declared in the Slaughter-House Case, 15 F. Cas. 649, 652 (C.C.D. La. 1870) (No. 8,408), "The 'privileges and immunities' secured by the original constitution, were only such as each State gave to its own citizens." On a number of occasions, the Court emphasized that article IV did not "profess to control the power of the state governments over the rights of its own citizens. Its sole purpose was to declare . . . that whatever" rights it granted to them, "the same, neither more nor less, shall be the measure of the rights of citizens of other States. . . ." Blake v. McClung, 172 U.S. 239, 252 (1898).

[104]United States v. Wheeler, 254 U.S. 281, 294 (1920).

[105]*Id.*

[106]*Id.*

[107]*Id.* at 298. White emphasized that but for the prohibition against discrimination, "the entire domain of the privileges and immunities of citizens of the States . . . lay within the constitutional and legislative powers of the . . . States . . . , and without that of the Federal Government." *Id.* at 298–99.

[108]*Id.* at 299.

[109]CHAFEE, *supra* note 11, at 191. In "any State every citizen of any other State is to have the same privileges and immunities which the citizens of that State enjoy. The section, in effect, prevents a State from discriminating against citizens of other States in favor of its own." Hague v. C.I.O., 307 U.S. 496, 511 (1939).

[110]Edwards v. California, 314 U.S. 160, 180 (1941) (concurring opinion).

[111]*Id.* at 182. Justice Stewart, on the other hand, considers that "[t]he right to travel from State to State finds constitutional protection that is quite independent of the Fourteenth Amendment." Shapiro v. Thompson, 394 U.S. 618, 643 (1969) (concurring opinion). But he does not identify any particular clause as source of the right. The text of the fourteenth amendment, "[n]o State shall make or enforce any law which shall abridge the privileges or immunities of citizens of the United States," poses the question whether the federal government was left free to do so. (Emphasis added).

[112]Edwards v. California, 314 U.S. 160, 183 (1941) (concurring opinion).

standing that "[f]or nearly three-quarters of a century this Court rejected every plea to the privileges and immunities clause."[113] The words were not, however, "general and abstract" for the Framers. In its origin the fourteenth amendment was not concerned with migrants, but with conferring on *resident* Negroes the rights secured by article IV to migrant citizens of sister States.[114] The terms "privileges or immunities" were not, of course, picked out of the air but were plainly borrowed from the article IV phrase. In its inception, the Civil Rights Bill of 1866, which was temporally coterminous with the fourteenth amendment, which the latter was designed to constitutionalize and place beyond danger of repeal and was in fact regarded as "identical" with the Bill,[115] banned "discrimination in civil rights or immunities," and went on to particularize and identify them: the right to contract, to own property and to have access to the courts.[116] Although the words "ingress and egress" were not mentioned, employment of the article IV phrase carried its attributes with it.[117] Aware, moreover, of southern restrictions on the mobility of the freedmen,[118] the framers, in the words of Senator Lyman Trumbull, chairman of the Senate Judiciary Committee and draftsman of the Bill, meant to leave them free "to go and come at pleasure,"[119] thus reinforcing the implications flowing from use of the article IV phraseology on which the "civil rights or immunities" of the Bill avowedly was patterned.[120] Nowhere in the debates of the Thirty-ninth Congress is there a reference to the freedman's right to support. Rather, Thaddeus Stevens, the leader of the radical Republicans, vainly sought a homestead for the black man,[121] repeating in his valedictory of defeated hopes while urging adoption of the fourteenth amendment, "Forty acres of land and a hut would be of more value to him than the immediate right to vote."[122] A North that was loath to confiscate the land of vanquished rebels for distribution to the freedmen was little likely to welcome support of blacks who migrated to the North. Indeed, the very possibility of such migration was regarded with dismay.[123] Nothing is gained by invoking the words "citizen of the United States," for his rights, as Trumbull explained, were those conferred by the parallel article

---

[113]*Id.* at 182, 183. Chafee cautioned that "exclusive reliance on the Fourteenth Amendment leads to the unbelievable result that the Philadelphia Convention did nothing at all to preserve the vital assurance, in the Articles of Confederation of 'free ingress and regress to and from any other State.' " CHAFEE, *supra* note 11, at 191–92. In my judgment, the Founders did something by article IV. *See* text accompanying notes 81–88 *supra*.

[114]For details, *see* R. BERGER, GOVERNMENT BY JUDICIARY 41–42 (1977).

[115]For citations, *see id.* at 22–23. Justice Bradley held in 1870 that "the civil rights bill was enacted at the same session, and but shortly before the presentation of the fourteenth amendment; was reported by the same committee; . . . [it] was in pari materia, and was probably intended to reach the same object . . . the first section of the bill covers the same ground as the fourteenth amendment. . . ." Live Stock Dealers & Butchers' Ass'n v. Crescent City Live-Stock Landing & Slaughterhouse Co., 15 F. Cas. 649, 655 (C.C. La. 1870) (No. 8,408).

[116]The bill is quoted in R. BERGER, GOVERNMENT BY JUDICIARY 24 (1977).

[117]For example, the ratifiers of the Constitution were frequently assured that the words "trial by jury" embraced all their attributes, such as the right to challenge jurors. *Id.* at 403. So too, the Court found that "the power of inquiry . . . was regarded and employed as a necessary and appropriate attribute of the power to legislate" in England, and hence was an attribute of Congress' "legislative functions." McGrain v. Daugherty, 273 U.S. 135, 175 (1927).

[118]*See* CONG. GLOBE, 39th Cong., 1st Sess. 474 (1866).

[119]*Id.* at 475. Explaining the fourteenth amendment to the electorate in Cincinnati, Senator John Sherman said that "everybody . . . should have the right to go from county to county, and from State to State. . . ." Fairman, *Does the Fourteenth Amendment Incorporate the Bill of Rights?*, 2 STAN. L. REV. 5, 77 (1949).

[120]CONG. GLOBE, 39th Cong., 1st Sess. 474 (1866).

[121]F. BRODIE, THADDEUS STEVENS: SCOURGE OF THE SOUTH 211, 303 (1959).

[122]CONG. GLOBE, 39th Cong., 1st Sess. 2459 (1866).

[123]Fear that the emancipated slaves would flock North in droves alarmed the North. R. BERGER, GOVERNMENT BY JUDICIARY 12 (1977). Senator John Sherman of Ohio said in the Senate, "[W]e do not like Negroes. We do not disguise our dislike." Woodward, *Seeds of Failure in Radical Race Policy,* in NEW FRONTIERS OF THE AMERICAN RECONSTRUCTION 128 (H. Hyman ed. 1966). In an article published in THE NATION, August 2, 1866, Thomas G. Shearman wrote, "The members from Indiana and Southern Illinois well knew that their constituents had barely overcome their prejudices sufficiently to tolerate even the residence of negroes among them, and that any greater liberality would be highly repulsive to them. . . ." *Quoted in* 6 C. FAIRMAN, HISTORY OF THE SUPREME COURT 1283 n.246 (1971).

IV clause.[124] The Court itself said in 1872, comparing article IV and the fourteenth amendment, "There can be but little question that . . . the privileges and immunities intended are the same in each [case]."[125] Be it assumed that, as Justice Jackson said, it should be a privilege of United States citizens "to enter any State of the Union,"[126] the 1866 debates furnish no basis for repudiation of the established States' right to exclude indigent migrants.[127] It begs the question to reiterate that "[t]he constitutional right to travel from one State to another . . . has been firmly established and repeatedly recognized,"[128] for the States' right to exclude indigent migrants had been even more "firmly established and repeatedly recognized,"[129] and it had the living sanction of the people as expressed in the legislation of forty or more States.

D. Crandall v. Nevada

Chief reliance is placed by expansionist Justices on *Crandall v. Nevada* (1867).[130] Justice Douglas considers it decided that the right to travel is "fundamental to the national character of our Federal government";[131] Justice Stewart asserts that it "firmly established" the right.[132] It is, however, a strange case on which to erect the superstructure of no-residence-restrictions-on-welfare. The case involved a Nevada tax on any person *leaving* the State by common carrier. Confessedly it did not rest on the commerce clause as urged by Chief Justice Chase and Justice Clifford.[133] Instead it held that citizens must have free access to the nation's capital for federal purposes. Justice Miller, Chafee observed, "found that somewhere between the lines of the Constitution there was a right of citizens to leave a state in order to go to the national capital, although there was no evidence in the case that any stagecoach passenger was bound for Washington."[134] Consequently the federal access theory represents the veriest dictum, violating the canon reemphasized by Justice Brandeis: "The Court will not 'formulate a rule of constitutional law broader than is required by the precise facts to which it is to be applied.' "[135] And as Chafee points out,

---

[124]CONG. GLOBE, 39th Cong., 1st Sess. 474 (1866). In 1871, Senator Trumbull, draftsman of the Civil Rights Bill, explained that the "privileges or immunities" clause is "a repetition of a provision [article IV] as it before existed. . . . The protection which the government affords to American citizens under the Constitution as it was originally formed is precisely the protection it now affords under the Constitution as it now exists. The fourteenth amendment has not extended the rights and privileges of citizens one iota." CONG. GLOBE, 42d Cong., 1 Sess. 576 (1871).

[125]Slaughter House Cases, 83 U.S. (16 Wall.) 36, 75 (1872).

[126]Edwards v. California, 314 U.S. 160, 183 (1941) (concurring opinion).

[127]For that we should require, in Justice Miller's words, "language which expresses such a purpose too clearly to admit of doubt." Slaughter House Cases, 83 U.S. (16 Wall.) 36, 78 (1872).

[128]Shapiro v. Thompson, 394 U.S. 618, 642 (1969) (concurring opinion) (quoting United States v. Guest, 383 U.S. 745, 757 (1966). Chafee remarks that "[d]espite inspiring statements in all the opinions, *Edwards v. California* leaves me somewhat troubled." CHAFEE, *supra* note 11, at 191. Little wonder that he concluded, "Freedom of movement is a valuable human right, but is it in the Constitution? . . . [It] is in it somewhere, *as the Supreme Court has established.*" *Id.* at 209 (emphasis added). Divided judicial counsels are no substitute for a constitutional grant.

[129]*See* text accompanying notes 17–44 *supra.*

[130]73 U.S. (6 Wall.) 35 (1867).

[131]Edwards v. California, 314 U.S. 160, 178 (1941) (concurring opinion).

[132]United States v. Guest, 383 U.S. 745, 757 (1966).

[133]Justice Miller reviewed the prior decisions and said that "in view of the principles on which those cases were decided" it was "not easy to maintain" that the tax violates the commerce clause. 73 U.S. (6 Wall.) 35, 43 (1867). For Clifford's insistence (joined by Chief Justice Chase) on the commerce clause, *see id.* at 49.

Justice Douglas could not "accede to the suggestion . . . that the commerce clause is the appropriate explanation of *Crandall v. Nevada.*" Edwards v. California, 314 U.S. 160, 179 (1941) (concurring opinion).

[134]CHAFEE, *supra* note 11, at 189. Justice Douglas commented, "[T]here is not a shred of evidence in the record of the *Crandall* case that the persons there involved were en route on any such mission. . . ." Edwards v. California, 314 U.S. 160, 178 (1941) (concurring opinion).

[135]Ashwander v. Tennessee Valley Authority, 297 U.S. 288, 347 (1936) (concurring opinion).

"Justice Miller's fanciful desire to facilitate trips to Washington would not help a Texan driving to California."[136]

Whatever the meaning *Crandall* holds for present innovative Justices, it did not in the eyes of the Court contemporary with it repudiate the States' right to exclude indigent migrants. In 1877 the Court declared in *Railroad Co. v. Husen*,[137] "We admit that the deposit in Congress of the power to regulate foreign commerce and commerce among the States was not a surrender of that which may properly be denominated police power. . . . Under it a State . . . may exclude from its limits convicts, paupers . . . and persons likely to become a public charge."[138] And in 1873 the self-same Justice Miller who wrote the *Crandall* opinion referred to the recently adopted fourteenth amendment and said in *Bartemeyer v. Iowa*[139] that "the most liberal advocate of the rights conferred by that amendment have contended for nothing more than that the rights of citizens *previously existing,* and dependent wholly on State laws for their recognition, are now placed under the protection of the Federal government. . . ."[140] There was no "previously existing" right of an indigent migrant to support in a sister State. It is scarcely conceivable that what the commerce clause and the amendment did not accomplish was achieved by *Crandall,* which had nothing whatsoever to do with the *entry* of a migrant. The logical inference is that for the Court *Crandall* had no relevance to welfare restrictions, then and thereafter an unchallenged State's right.

E. Due Process of Law

Justice Harlan found more "solid ground" for the right to travel in the "liberty" of which "the citizen cannot be deprived without due process of law";[141] but Professor Chafee noted the English pre-colonial practice of excluding migrant paupers, a recognized qualification on "freedom of movement."[142] Then, too, the words "due process of law," as Hamilton explained on the eve of the Convention, "have a precise technical import, and are applicable only to the process and proceedings of the courts of justice; they can never be referred to an act of the legislature."[143] This was an accurate summary of the preceding 400 years of English and colonial law.[144] The identity of the due process terminology of the fifth amendment with that of the fourteenth bespeaks an

---

[136]CHAFEE, *supra* note 11, at 192.

[137]95 U.S. 465 (1877).

[138]*Id.* at 470–71.

[139]85 U.S. (18 Wall.) 129 (1873).

[140]*Id.* at 133 (emphasis added).

[141]United States v. Guest, 383 U.S. 745, 770 (1966) (concurring and dissenting in part). *See also* CHAFEE, *supra* note 11, at 192. In justice to Professor Chafee, he made no comment on the historic content of due process but urged instead that the several decisions the Court had used to "safeguard" racial rights freely to choose places of residence "inside a state" be expanded to "assure the right to live in any state one desires. . . ." *Id.* at 192.

Justice Jackson remarked that the "Court has not been timorous about giving concrete meaning to such obscure and vagrant phrases as 'due process.' " Edwards v. California, 314 U.S. 160, 183 (1941) (concurring opinion). But the obscurity is of the Court's own making. Charles Curtis, an admirer of judicial "adaptation" of the Constitution, wrote that when the Framers put due process into the Constitution, "its meaning was as fixed and definite as the common law could make a phrase. . . . It meant a procedural due process. . . ." C. CURTIS, REVIEW AND MAJORITY RULE IN SUPREME COURT AND SUPREME LAW 170, 177 (E. Cahn ed. 1954). It is the Court that made due process an obscurantist phrase. R. BERGER, GOVERNMENT BY JUDICIARY 258–60 (1977).

[142]CHAFEE, *supra* note 11, at 164. "A procedure customarily employed, long before the Revolution in . . . England, and generally adopted by the States . . . cannot be deemed inconsistent with due process of law." Ownbey v. Morgan, 256 U.S. 94, 111 (1921).

[143]4 THE PAPERS OF ALEXANDER HAMILTON 35 (H. Syrette & J. Cooke, eds. 1962).

[144]Berger, *"Law of the Land" Reconsidered,* 74 Nw. U. L. REV. 1 (1979). Justice Story wrote that the due process clause "in effect affirms the right of trial according to the process and proceedings of the common law." 3 J. STORY, COMMENTARIES ON THE CONSTITUTION OF THE UNITED STATES § 1783 (1833). In the Japanese Immigrant Case, 189 U.S. 86, 100 (1903), Justice Harlan referred to "the fundamental principle that inhere[s] in 'due process of law' as understood at the time of adoption of the Constitution."

identity of content.[145] My study of the 1866 debates convinced me that the framers viewed the words in terms of judicial proceedings;[146] Professor John Hart Ely arrived at the same view.[147] The substantive content given to the words in the 1890s in order to overturn socio-economic legislation was a feat of the wonder-working Court.[148] It has since cried *mea culpa*,[149] recalling the "era when the Court thought the Fourteenth Amendment gave it power to strike down state laws 'because they may be unwise, improvident, or out of harmony with a particular school of thought'. . . . That era has long ago passed into history"[150]—regrettably only partly. The Court has confined its abjuration to "economic" due process; substantive due process continues to be employed to overturn social legislation,[151] though to differentiate between "liberty and property," equally governed by "due process," requires a logic that escapes the ordinary mind, and even baffled the extraordinary mind of Judge Learned Hand.[152] To extract from the ban against deprivation of "liberty" without due process of law a prohibition of *legislative* limitations on a migrant's access to relief is to do violence to the historical meaning attached to the term due process by both the Founders and the framers of the fourteenth amendment.

III. "EQUAL PROTECTION OF THE LAWS"

In *Shapiro v. Thompson,* the Court, Justice Harlan considered, "basically relies upon the equal protection ground."[153] It found that the classification between residents and migrants was a violation of the equal protection clause, that "the purpose of deterring the immigration of indigents cannot serve as a justification for the classification created by the one-year waiting period, since that purpose is constitutionally impermissible."[154] It cast the issue in moral terms: mothers who move into a State to obtain public assistance are not therefore the less deserving. That is not the issue: the issue is whether taxpayers of that State must be burdened with the cost of supporting the "deserving" migrant. As this is being written the Bahamas feel threatened by a flood of Haitian

---

[145]James Garfield, a framer of the fourteenth amendment, stated in 1871 that its due process clause "is copied from the Fifth Amendment"; he defined it as "an impartial trial according to the laws of the land." CONG. GLOBE, 42d Cong., 1st Sess. App. 153 (1871).

[146]R. BERGER, GOVERNMENT BY JUDICIARY 201–06 (1977).

[147]Ely wrote that the debates are "devoid of any reference that gives the provision more than a procedural connotation." J. ELY, DEMOCRACY AND DISTRUST 15 (1980). Wallace Mendelson stated that due process meant in the fourteenth amendment what it meant in the fifth, that "[t]o incorporate the words is to incorporate their traditional meaning, and no more. . . ." namely, "a fair hearing." Mendelson, Book Review, 6 HASTINGS CONST. L.Q. 437, 453 (1979).

[148]Ely. *Constitutional Interpretivism: Its Allure and Impossibility,* 53 IND. L.J. 399, 415–16 (1978).

[149]R. BERGER, GOVERNMENT BY JUDICIARY 258–59 (1977).

[150]Dandridge v. Williams, 397 U.S. 471, 485 (1970).

[151]Ely deplores "the unfortunate resurrection" of the doctrine in Roe v. Wade, 410 U.S. 113 (1973), the abortion case. Ely, *Constitutional Interpretivism: Its Allure and Impossibility,* 53 IND. L.J. 399, 422 (1978). In the contraceptive case, Griswold v. Connecticut, 381 U.S. 479, 482 (1965), Justice Douglas stated, "We do not sit as a super-legislature to determine the wisdom, need, and propriety of laws that touch economic problems . . . or social conditions. . . . This law, however, operates directly on an intimate relation of husband and wife." As Alpheus Thomas Mason points out, the inarticulate premise is that "the Court *does sit* as a super-legislature in safeguarding the penumbral right of privacy." Mason, *The Burger Court in Historical Perspective,* 47 N.Y.ST.B.J. 87, 89 (1975).

In one such case Justice Black declared, "By the use of the due process formula the Court does not . . . abstain from interfering with congressional policy. It actively enters that field with no standards except its own conclusion as to what is 'arbitrary' and what is 'rational.' " Flemming v. Nestor, 363 U.S. 603, 626 (1960) (dissenting opinion).

[152]Judge Learned Hand observed that the current reading of the fifth amendment as imposing "severer restrictions as to Liberty than Property" is a "strange anomaly." "There is no constitutional basis," he declared, "for asserting a larger measure of judicial supervision over" liberty than property. L. HAND, THE BILL OF RIGHTS 50, 51 (1958).

[153]Shapiro v. Thompson, 394 U.S. 618, 657 (1969) (dissenting opinion).

[154]*Id.* at 631.

refugees that strain its financial fabric;[155] the deluge in 1980 of 100,000 Cubans has overtaxed the capacity of Miami to care for them.[156] An exclusory practice, which has the weight of 600 years of English, colonial, and continued State laws behind it, was too lightly dismissed as constitutionally "impermissible." Certainly the equal protection clause furnishes no warrant for the view that it repudiated that practice.

Recourse to the equal protection clause is a relatively recent phenomenon, not long since referred to by Justice Holmes as "the usual last resort of constitutional arguments."[157] With due process discredited, equal protection provided an untarnished alternative, "permit[ting] today's Justices," as Professor Herbert Packer explained, "under a different label . . . to impose their prejudices in much the same manner as the Four Horsemen once did."[158] But what did the words mean to the framers who employed them, the test Senator Charles Sumner, archradical of the Thirty-ninth Congress, commended to the framers: "[I]f words are used which seem to have no fixed signification, we cannot err if we turn to the framers."[159]

They began with the Civil Rights Bill of 1866, which proceeded on a parallel track with the fourteenth amendment in the Thirty-ninth Congress. It secured to blacks the *same* right to contract, to hold property, and to sue as whites enjoyed.[160] At that time whites enjoyed no right to support by a sister State. In describing their aims, the framers interchangeably referred to "equality," "equality before the law," and "equal protection," but always in the circumscribed context of the rights enumerated in the Bill, so that it is reasonable to infer that the framers regarded the terms as synonymous.[161] For example, a leading radical, Samuel Shellabarger of Ohio, said of the Civil Rights Bill, "[W]hatever rights *as to each of these enumerated* civil (not political) matters *the State may confer* upon one race . . . shall be held by all races in equality. . . . It secures . . . *equality of protection in those enumerated* civil rights. . . ."[162] Attempts to abolish *all* distinctions repeatedly were rejected;[163] suffrage and segregation were plainly excluded from the scope of the fourteenth

[155]N.Y. Times, Jan. 23, 1981, at 2. Professor Rosenheim wrote, "Immigration of low-income groups produces great strains on public education, public housing, law enforcement, and criminal justice." Rosenheim, Shapiro v. Thompson: "*The Beggars Are Coming To Town*," 1969 SUP. CT. REV. 303, 355 n.133. One may conjecture that such strains contributed to the near bankruptcy of some urban centers.

John V. Lindsay, former mayor of New York, writes that the federal government must "relieve states and local governments of the fiscal burdens that are brought to their doorsteps by the migrating poor. . . . Urban areas, which have become the repositories of the poorest of the nation's poor, will never be able to deliver essential services . . . as long as they are oppressed by such Federal mandates as welfare and Medicaid." N.Y. Times, Feb. 5, 1981, at A23, col. 5. In Edwards v. California, 314 U.S. 160, 173 (1941). Justice Byrnes noted. "The State asserts that the huge influx of migrants into California in recent years has resulted in problems of health, morals, and especially finance, the proportions of which are staggering." His comment was that "we do not conceive it our function to pass upon 'the wisdom, need or appropriateness' of the legislative efforts of the States to solve such difficulties." *Id.* In fact, however, he was overturning a State effort to deal with the problem because he deemed it "inappropriate," though he sought to clothe his judgment in constitutional terms that repudiated the Court's own utterances going back 100 years.

[156]Puerto Rico's Resident Commissioner predicted in Washington that President Reagan's cutbacks "would cause a loss of 30,000 jobs [in Puerto Rico], send a wave of up to 500,000 people to the United States mainland. . . ." N.Y. Times, March 12, 1981, at 1. Most of the migrants would head for New York and Massachusetts.

[157]Buck v. Bell, 274 U.S. 200, 208 (1927).

[158]Packer, *The Aims of the Criminal Law Revisited: A Plea for a New Look at Substantive Due Process.* 44 S.CAL. L. REV. 490, 491–92 (1967).

[159]CONG. GLOBE, 39th Cong., 1st Sess. 677 (1866). Such sentiments were summarized in 1872 by "a unanimous Senate Judiciary Committee Report, signed by Senators who had voted for the Thirteenth, Fourteenth, and Fifteenth Amendments in Congress." A. AVINS, THE RECONSTRUCTION DEBATES ii (1967). "In construing the Constitution we are compelled to give it such interpretation as will secure the result which was intended . . . by those who framed it and the people who adopted it." *Id.* at 571.

[160]CONG. GLOBE, 39th Cong., 1st Sess. 474 (1866).

[161]For citations, *see* R. BERGER, GOVERNMENT BY JUDICIARY 169–71 (1977).

[162]CONG. GLOBE, 39th Cong., 1st Sess. 1293 (1866) (emphasis added).

[163]For citations *see* R. BERGER, GOVERNMENT BY JUDICIARY 163–64 (1977).

amendment,[164] because as the chairman of the Joint Committee on Reconstruction of both Houses, Senator William Fessenden, explained, "We cannot put into the Constitution, owing to existing prejudices and *existing institutions* [e.g., existing exclusion of migrant paupers], an entire exclusion of all class distinctions."[165] Where terms have been given a meaning in a prior act (the Civil Rights Act) that is *in pari materia,* the Supreme Court has held, that meaning will be given the terms in a later act (the amendment).[166] Bearing in mind that there was not the slightest intimation in the debates that either whites or blacks were entitled to support at the end of their travels and that Stevens' attempt to give the freedmen forty acres in their own States failed, it is sheer fantasy to read into equal protection a migrant's immediate right to support in a sister State.

Even within the framework of the Court's own decisions, *Shapiro,* as Justice Harlan observed, represented "an expansion of the comparatively new constitutional doctrine that some state statutes will be deemed to deny equal protection of the laws unless justified by a 'compelling' " governmental interest, a "doctrine of relatively recent vintage."[167] Prior thereto the rule had been that there is no denial of equal protection if the statute "is rationally related to a legitimate governmental objective."[168] Chief Justice Burger commented that "no state law has ever satisfied this seemingly insurmountable ["compelling"] standard,"[169] a twentieth century Procrustean bed. The "compelling state interest" is merely a vehicle for overturning legislation with which the Justices disagree; it is one of what Justices White and Thurgood Marshall describe as "a spectrum of standards in reviewing discrimination allegedly violative of the Equal Protection Clause,"[170] That "spectrum" means shifting standards at the service of uncurbed discretion.[171]

IV. VOTING AND RESIDENCE RESTRICTIONS

"Every breach of the fundamental laws," Hamilton observed, "forms a precedent for other breaches,"[172] as the Court demonstrated by quickly extending the "compelling interest" test to overthrow State restrictions on a migrant's immediate right to vote. State residence restrictions on voting had been "well-established." By way of explaining article IV, *Blake v. McClung* (1898)[173] stated that a State may "require residence within its limits for a given time before a citizen of another State who becomes a resident thereof shall exercise the right of suffrage. . . ."[174] *Pope v. Williams* (1904)[175] sustained a Maryland requirement of one-year residence for the privilege to vote, and declared that

[t]he privilege to vote in any State is not given by the Federal Constitution, or by any of its amendments. It is not a privilege springing from citizenship of the United States. . . . In other words, the privilege to vote in a State is within the jurisdiction of the State itself, to be exercised as the State may direct, . . .

absent discrimination in violation of the federal constitution.[176] As late as 1965, *Carrington v.*

---

[164]*Id.* at 52–68, 117–33. *See also* Berger, *The Fourteenth Amendment: Light From the Fifteenth,* 74 Nw. U. L. Rev. 311, 326–31 (1979).

[165]Cong. Globe, 39th Cong., 1st Sess. 705 (1866).

[166]Reiche v. Smythe, 80 U.S. (13 Wall.) 162, 165 (1871). *See also* Taney. C.J., in text accompanying note 87 *supra. See also* note 88 *supra.*

[167]Shapiro v. Thompson, 394 U.S. 618, 655, 658 (1969) (dissenting opinion).

[168]*Id.* at 658.

[169]Dunn v. Blumstein, 405 U.S. 330, 363–64 (1962) (dissenting opinion).

[170]Vlandis v. Kline, 412 U.S. 441, 458 (1973) (concurring opinion).

[171]*See* Justice Black quotation at text accompanying note 196 *infra.*

[172]The Federalist No. 25, at 158 (A. Hamilton) (Mod. Lib. ed. 1937).

[173]172 U.S. 299 (1898).

[174]*Id.* at 256.

[175]193 U.S. 621 (1904).

[176]*Id.* at 632.

Rash[177] cited *Pope* for the proposition that a State has "unquestioned power" to impose reasonable residence restrictions on the right to vote.[178]

A new day dawned in *Dunn v. Blumstein:*[179] "Durational residence laws penalize those persons who have traveled from one place to another," and the State showed no "compelling reason for imposing durational residence requirements."[180] Justice Blackmun, on the other hand, contended that "clearly" the "state does have a profound interest in the purity of the ballot box and an informed electorate and is entitled to take appropriate steps to assure those ends."[181] I would not insist that decisions aged in the wood are to be preferred to those of very recent vintage, but maintain rather that the older decisions effectuated the Framers' design, the traditional canon of constitutional construction from which activists now avert their countenances.

To begin with the original Constitution, Justice James Wilson, a leading architect of the Constitution, said in his 1791 Philadelphia Lectures that article I, section 2 "intrusts to . . . the several states, the very important power of ascertaining the qualifications" of the electors.[182] He was well aware, for example, that Connecticut authorized exclusion of freemen "according to the sentiments which others entertain concerning their conversation and behavior . . . a power of a very extraordinary nature,"[183] but notwithstanding bowed to State control. Although the Court based its "one-person-one-vote" rule on the fourteenth amendment, history, as Justice Harlan justly maintained, is "irrefutably" to the contrary,[184] as a few facts out of many speedily show. Between 1865 and 1868, "17 or 19" Northern States had rejected suffrage for blacks.[185] Consequently, Roscoe Conkling, a member of the Joint Committee on Reconstruction, which drafted the amendment, stated that it would be "futile to ask three quarters of the States to do . . . the very thing most of them have already refused to do. . . ."[186] Another member of the Committee, Senator Jacob Howard, spoke to the same effect.[187] Senator Fessenden, Chairman of the Joint Committee, said of a suffrage

---

[177]380 U.S. 89 (1965).

[178]*Id.* at 91. *See also* Drueding v. Devlin, 380 U.S. 125 (1965), *aff'g* 234 F. Supp. 721 (D. Md. 1964) (without opinion); Starns v. Malkerson, 326 F. Supp. 234 (D. Minn. 1970), *summarily aff'd,* 401 U.S. 985 (1971), *cited in* Vlandis v. Kline, 412 U.S. 441, 452 n.9 (1973).

[179]405 U.S. 330 (1972).

[180]*Id.* at 334, 335.

[181]*Id.* at 362 (concurring opinion).

[182]1 JAMES WILSON, WORKS 407 (R. McCloskey ed. 1967).

[183]*Id.* at 409. Although *Federalist No.* 52 noted that the "definition of the right of suffrage is very justly regarded as a fundamental article of republican government . . . ," it concluded that the right must be left to the States because "the different qualifications in the different States [could not be reduced] to one uniform rule." THE FEDERALIST NO. 52, at 341–42 (A. Hamilton or J. Madison) (Mod. Lib. ed. 1937). And alluding to the allocation of representatives according to the numbers of inhabitants, *Federalist No.* 54 added that "the right of choosing this alloted number in each State is to be exercised by such part of the inhabitants as the State itself may designate. . . . In every State, a certain proportion of inhabitants are deprived of this right by the constitution of the State." THE FEDERALIST NO. 54, at 356 (A. Hamilton) (Mod. Lib. ed. 1937).

[184]Griswold v. Connecticut, 381 U.S. 479, 501 (1965) (Harlan, J., concurring in judgment): the reapportionment interpretations were "made in the face of irrefutable and still unanswered history to the contrary."

[185]Oregon v. Mitchell, 400 U.S. 112, 256 (1970) (Brennan, White & Marshall, JJ., dissenting in part).

[186]CONG. GLOBE, 39th Cong., 1st Sess. 358 (1866).

[187]*Id.* at 2766. Another member of the Joint Committee, Senator George W. Williams of Oregon, stated:

[T]he people of these United States are not prepared to surrender to Congress the absolute right to determine as to the qualifications of voters in the respective States, or to adopt the proposition that all persons, without distinction of race or color, shall enjoy political rights and privileges equal to those now possessed by the white people of the country. Sir, some of the States have lately spoken upon that subject. Wisconsin and Connecticut, northern, loyal, and republican States, have recently declared that they would not allow the negroes within their own borders political rights; and is it probable that of the thirty-six States more than six, at the most, would at this time adopt the constitutional amendment proposed by the gentleman? . . . Put it before the country and commit the Union party to it, the amendment will be defeated and the Union party overwhelmed in its support—and the control of the government would pass into the hands of men who have more or less sympathized with the rebellion; and I say that it is of more consequence, in my judgment,

proposal that there is not "the slightest possibility that it will be adopted by the States. . . ."[188] The Report of the Joint Committee doubted that "the States would consent to surrender a power they had exercised, and to which they were attached," and therefore thought it best to "leave the whole question with the people of each State."[189] That such was the vastly preponderant opinion is confirmed by a remarkable fact: during the pendency of ratification, radical opposition to readmission of Tennessee because its Constitution excluded negro suffrage was voted down in the House by 125 to 12; Senator Charles Sumner's related proposal was rejected by 34 to 4.[190] A bevy of activist commentators concur that suffrage was excluded.[191] Former Solicitor General Robert Bork sums up: "Chief Justice Warren's opinions in [the state reapportionment] cases are remarkable for their inability to muster a single respectable supporting argument. The principle of one man, one vote . . . runs counter to the text of the fourteenth amendment, the history surrounding its adoption and ratification and the political practice of Americans from colonial times up to the day the Court invented the new formula."[192] Warren's "legislators represent people, not trees or acres"[193] substitutes rhetoric for adverse historical fact. By comparison with judicial arrogation of control over reapportionment, the annulment of State residence requirements for voting is innocuous. History even more deeply etches the States' reserved power over suffrage than over exclusion of indigent migrants, so that *Dunn v. Blumstein* illustrates afresh that power grows by what it feeds on.

Let me call to witness the whilom idol of the activists, Justice Black. In overruling *Breedlove v. Suttles*[194] (poll taxes are valid), the Court, he stated, did not proceed from "the original meaning of the Equal Protection Clause" but gave it "a new meaning which it believes represents a better governmental policy."[195] He condemned use of the due process clause as

that the control of the Government should remain in the hands of the men who stood up for the Union during the late war than that any constitutional amendment should be adopted by which the right of suffrage should be extended to any person or persons not now enjoying it. CONG. GLOBE, 39th Cong., 1st Sess. S. App. 95–96 (1866).

[188]*Id.* at 704. For additional citations, *see* R. BERGER, GOVERNMENT BY JUDICIARY 58–60 (1977).

[189]*Reprinted in* A. AVINS, THE RECONSTRUCTION AMENDMENTS DEBATES 94 (1967).

[190]For details *see* R. BERGER, GOVERNMENT BY JUDICIARY 56, 59–60, 79 (1977). Little wonder that a dyed-in-the-wool activist, Justice Thurgood Marshall, asked in a moment of truth: "I would like to know where the Constitution guarantees . . . the right to vote." Vlandis v. Kline, 412 U.S. 441, 458 (1973) (dissenting opinion).

[191]Lusky, Book Review, 6 HASTINGS CONST. L.Q. 403, 406 (1979), refers to "Justice Harlan's irrefutable and unrefuted demonstration in dissent that the Fourteenth Amendment was not intended to protect the right to vote. . . ."*See also* Abraham, Book Review, 6 HASTINGS CONST. L.Q. 467, 467–68 (1979); Alfange, *On Judicial Policymaking and Constitutional Change: Another Look at the "Original Intent" Theory of Constitutional Interpretation,* 5 HASTINGS CONST. 603, 622 (1978); Mendelson, Book Review, 6 HASTINGS CONST. L.Q. 437, 452–53 (1979); Nathanson, Book Review, 56 TEX. L. REV. 579, 581 (1978); Perry, Book Review, 78 COLUM. L. REV. 685, 687 (1978).

Professor Gerald Gunther wrote, "The ultimate justification for the [Reynolds v. Sims, 377 U.S. 533 (1964)] ruling is hard, if not impossible, to set forth in constitutionally legitimate terms. It rests, rather, on the view that courts are authorized to step in when injustices exist and other institutions fail to act. That is a dangerous—and I think illegitimate—prescription for judicial action." Gunther, *Some Reflections on the Judicial Role: Distinctions, Roots and Prospects,* 1979 WASH. U.L.Q. 817, 825.

[192]Bork, *Neutral Principles and Some First Amendment Problems,* 47 IND. L.J. 1, 18 (1971). Ward Elliot justly stated that in Reynolds v. Sims, 377 U.S. 533 (1964), the Court fabricated a "fundamental principle of 'one person, one vote' that was exactly the reverse of the text and stated intent of the equal protection clause." W. ELLIOT, THE RISE OF A GUARDIAN DEMOCRACY 129 (1974).

[193]Reynolds v. Sims, 377 U.S. 533, 562 (1964). Justice Harlan justifiably charged in Carrington v. Rash, 380 U.S. 89, 97 (1965) (dissenting opinion), that "the Court totally ignores . . . all the history of the Fourteenth Amendment and the course of judicial decisions which together plainly show that the Equal Protection Clause was not intended to touch State electoral matters."

[194]302 U.S. 277 (1937).

[195]Harper v. Virginia Bd. of Elections, 383 U.S. 663, 672 (1966).

though it provided a blank check to alter the meaning of the Constitution as written so as to add to it substantive constitutional changes which a majority of the Court at any given time believes are needed to meet present day problems. . . . If basic changes as to the respective powers of the State and national governments are needed, I prefer to let these changes be by amendment as Article V of the Constitution provides. For a majority of this Court to undertake that task, whether purporting to do so under the Due Process or on the Equal Protection Clause amounts, in my judgment, to an exercise of power the Constitution makers with foresight and wisdom refused to give the Judicial Branch of the Government.[196]

V. CONCLUSION

The source of the constitutional right to travel has unnecessarily been wrapped in "uncertainty," for the Founders considered that the "privileges and immunities" of article IV embraced "ingress and egress," as is indeed implicit in its text. How else can a citizen of one State enjoy the privileges of a sister State? But that right was qualified by the States' reserved right to exclude indigent migrants, a reservation expressly written into the antecedent "privileges and immunities" of the Articles of Confederation, giving effect to centuries of English, colonial and State law and custom. If the legislation of more than forty States may serve as an index, it continued to represent the will of the American people until it was overthrown by *Shapiro v. Thompson*. Be it assumed that it is mean and inhumane, as Professor Rosenheim labelled it, to condition relief to migrants on one-year residence, the Court is not empowered to supplant the morality of the people by its own.[197]

Although this is a thrice-told tale, federal Judge Irving R. Kaufman still incants exploded cliches: "We are not the arbiters of what, in our view, should be. We are the interpreters of what is. . . . When faced with a contrary legal mandate, a judge has no choice but to put aside his personal policy preferences."[198] Contemporary academicians are less naive. Professor Robert Cover thrusts aside "the self-evident meaning of the Constitution," let alone "the intentions of the framers," explaining that the Constitution is of no moment because "we" have decided to "entrust" judges

---

[196]*Id.* at 675–76. Similarly, Justice Harlan declared, "When the Court disregards the express intent and understanding of the Framers, it has invaded the realm of the political process to which the amending power was committed, and it has violated the constitutional structure which it is its highest duty to protect." Oregon v. Mitchell, 400 U.S. 112, 203 (1970) (concurring and dissenting in part).

[197]Crane Brinton wrote of Robespierre, "If Frenchmen would not be free and virtuous voluntarily then he would force them to be free and cram virtue down their throats." 2 C. BRINTON, S. CHRISTOPHER & R. WOLFF, A HISTORY OF CIVILIZATION 115 (1955). W.H. Auden noted that "under the Protectorate, Englishmen learned that the dangers of arbitrary power were not necessarily removed simply by the abolition of the Crown, for the claims of self-appointed saints to know by divine inspiration what the good life should be and to have the right to impose their notions on the ungodly could be as great a threat as the divine right of kings." Auden, *Introduction* to THE SELECTED WRITINGS OF SIDNEY SMITH at xvi (1956).

Presumably awareness of such historical experience inspired Justice Holmes to advise Justice Harlan Stone: "Young man about 75 years ago I learned that I was not God. And so, when the people . . . want to do something I can't find anything in the Constitution expressly forbidding them to do, I say, whether I like it or not, 'Goddamit, let 'em do it.'" C. CURTIS, LIONS UNDER THE THRONE 281 (1947). In stark contrast stands the eagerness of contemporary activist Justices—our "self-appointed saints"—to "cram" their moral sentiments "down the throats" of the American people. *See* R. BERGER, GOVERNMENT BY JUDICIARY 328 n. 56 (1977).

[198]N.Y. Times, Jan. 24, 1981, at 23, col. 6. For a more realistic appraisal, *see* the dissent of four of his brethren in Turpin v. Mailet, 579 F.2d 152, 171 (1978) (dissenting opinion by Circuit Judge Van Graafeiland). Contrast with Judge Kaufman's the following comment on *Dunn v. Blumstein* by Professor Philip Kurland:

The judgment was based on the invocation of two slogans as though they were reasons: "the right to travel" was one and the "lack of a compelling state interest to overcome a suspect classification" was the other. A "compelling state interest" like "a suspect classification" and "the right to travel" remain subjective determinations dependent on the personal proclivities of each of the Justices.

. . . .

The transmogrification of welfare from a concept of charity to one of constitutional right received a strong push in *Shapiro v. Thompson*. . . .

Kurland, *1971 Term: The Year of the Stewart-White Court*, 1972 SUP. CT. REV. 181, 206, 255.

with forming an "ideology" whereby legislation may be measured, and it may be added, the Framers' choices discarded.[199] Of course, Cover does not tell us where the *people* "entrusted" such power to judges; it is simply a grant by academic illuminati. Professor Paul Brest lets the cat out of the bag, challenging the "assumption" that "judges and other public officials are bound by the text or original understanding of the Constitution."[200] Why should the people be more bound by the Constitution than the judges, who have sworn "to support this Constitution"?

It is the purpose of this article, one of a number of other case studies,[201] to flesh out what Professor Philip Kurland described as "the usurpation by the judiciary of general governmental powers on the pretext that its authority derives from the fourteenth amendment."[202] Only when the people understand that it is the Justices, not the Constitution,[203] that require bussing, affirmative action and the like will they be moved to reassert their right to self-government.

[199] Cover, Book Review, THE NEW REPUBLIC, Jan. 14, 1978, at 26, 27.

[200] Brest, *The Misconceived Quest for the Original Understanding*, 60 B.U.L. REV. 204, 224 (1980; *see also* Forrester, *Are We Ready For Truth in Judging?*, 63 A.B.A.J. 1212 (1977).

[201] Elsewhere I demonstrated that the Court read suffrage and desegregation of schools into the fourteenth amendment, notwithstanding their having been excluded by the framers, R. BERGER, GOVERNMENT BY JUDICIARY 52–68, 117–133 (1977); that it converted the prohibition of Bills of Attainder—confessedly associated at the adoption of the Constitution with legislative condemnations to death, Berger, *Bills of Attainder: A Study of Amendment by the Court*, 63 CORNELL L. REV. 355 (1978)—to strike down noncapital, even civil, "penalties." Similarly I examined the Court's six-man jury decision which toppled the twelve-man jury "sacred" to the Founders and considered by them to be a central pillar of their democratic edifice. R. BERGER, GOVERNMENT BY JUDICIARY 397, 399–400 (1977). Soon, however, the Court decreed that a five-man jury is unconstitutional, on the ground, three Justices considered, that "a line has to be drawn somewhere." Ballew v. Georgia, 435 U.S. 223, 239, 246 (1978). Why could it not be drawn where the Framers reverently left it? To an irreverent observer there is a striking similarity to George Orwell's ANIMAL FARM 47 (1946), where the sheep were taught to bleat: "Four legs good, two legs bad."

[202] Letter to Harvard University Press, August 15, 1977. *See also* Gunther quotation, note 191 *supra*.

[203] At the height of the Court Packing campaign Professor Felix Frankfurter advised President Roosevelt:

People have been taught to believe that when the Supreme Court speaks it is not they who speak but the Constitution, whereas, of course, in so many vital cases, it is *they* who speak and *not* the Constitution. And I verily believe that that is what the country needs most to understand.

ROOSEVELT AND FRANKFURTER: THEIR CORRESPONDENCE, 1928–1945, at 383 (M. Freedman ed. 1967).

CHAPTER XI

Insulation of Judicial Usurpation: A Comment on Lawrence Sager's "Court-Stripping" Polemic

I. INTRODUCTION

Lawrence Sager's seventy-page, densely packed assault upon "court-stripping,"[1] which he labels as an attempt to "neuter"[2] (*i.e.*, castrate) the Court, is written in an "icily abstract"[3] vacuum, virtually ignoring the ongoing debate[4] about what activist Louis Lusky admiringly describes as the Court's "assertion of the power to revise the Constitution," and to repudiate "the limits on judicial review."[5] Although Sager recognizes that "court-stripping" proposals "are the product of deep hostility . . . [in] the nation"[6] to the school prayer, mandatory busing and similar decisions, he lamely renders the impetus for this development as differences with the Court's "erroneous interpretations of the Constitution,"[7] when they involve nothing less, as Philip Kurland wrote, than the Court's "usurpation of general governmental powers on the pretext that its authority derives from the Fourteenth Amendment."[8] Instead, therefore, of an attempted rape of a vestal virgin, the "stripping" measures constitute the sovereign people's attempt to "curb a judiciary run amok"[9] and to restore their right to self-government—for example, to reinstate their unrestricted right to enact death penalties, a right that never had been questioned prior to 1972.[10] This it is that Sager condemns as a "tawdry precedent [for] sabotaging the integrity of the judicial process."[11]

---

[1]Sager, *The Supreme Court, 1980 Term—Foreword: Constitutional Limitations on Congress' Authority to Regulate the Jurisdiction of the Federal Courts*, 95 HARV. L. REV. 17 (1981). For a critique of the article, see Redish, *Constitutional Limitations on Congressional Power to Control Federal Jurisdiction: A Reaction to Professor Sager*, 77 NW. U.L. REV. 143 (1982).

[2]Sager, *supra* note 1, at 20.

[3]*Id.* at 72.

[4]Some of the articles are collated in Perry, *Interpretivism, Freedom of Expression, and Equal Protection*, 42 OHIO ST. L.J. 261, 285 n. 100 (1981). For evaluation of the debate, see Bridwell, *The Scope of Judicial Review: A Dirge for the Theorists of Majority Rule?* 31 S.C.L. REV. 617 (1980); Gangi, *Judicial Expansionism: An Evaluation of the Ongoing Debate*, 8 OHIO N.U.L. REV. 1 (1981).

[5]Lusky, Book Review, 6 HASTINGS CONST. L.Q. 403, 406 (1979).

[6]Sager, *supra* note 1, at 18.

[7]*Id.*

[8]Letter to Harvard University Press (August 15, 1977) (available in Ohio State University Law Library).

[9]Sager, *supra* note 1, at 38.

[10]R. BERGER, DEATH PENALTIES: THE SUPREME COURT'S OBSTACLE COURSE 1–2 (1982) [hereinafter cited as R. BERGER, DEATH PENALTIES]. Of the same nature is Shapiro v. Thompson, 394 U.S. 618 (1969), cited by Sager, *supra* note 1, at 70 n.159. There the Court, overturning a centuries old practice, held that the "right to travel" entitles an indigent-migrant to immediate support at the terminus. An advocate of an unrestricted right to travel, Zechariah Chafee, said, "[T]here is a queer uncertainty about what clause in the Constitution established this right." Z. CHAFEE, THREE HUMAN RIGHTS IN THE CONSTITUTION OF 1787, at 188 (1956). For 600 years the "right to travel" had been limited by a sovereign right to exclude paupers, recognized in the prior decisions of the Court. Berger, *Residence Requirements for Welfare and Voting: A Post-Mortem,* 42 OHIO ST. L.J. 853 (1982).

[11]Sager, *supra* note 1, at 89.

Respect for the "integrity of the judicial process," however, requires that the Court stay within the confines the Framers contemplated, for "integrity" is defined as "uncorrupted condition; original perfect state."[12] More than "integrity of the judicial process" is involved. At issue is the integrity of our democratic system, whereunder the people have delegated law-making power to elected, accountable officials, not to life-tenured judges who are all but unaccountable,[13] reserving to themselves the power to amend the Constitution. In short, Sager has performed Hamlet without the Dane.

Lest the reader too hastily conclude that the foregoing is the product of an overheated imagination, let me adduce some activist statements. Michael Perry concluded that "[t]here is no plausible textual or historical justification for constitutional policymaking by the judiciary."[14] Although Chief Justice Warren declared that the "provisions of the Constitution" are "the rules of government"[15] and that "[w]e cannot push back the limits of the Constitution . . . [but] must apply those limits as the Constitution prescribes them,"[16] his worshipful biographer and former clerk, G. Edward White, tells us that "Warren was never concerned with constitutional text or intention. Rather, he believed that his job as judge lay in discovering and articulating the 'ethical imperatives' *he felt* were (or *should be*) embedded in the Constitution."[17] Paul Brest, a flaming apostle of activism, boldly challenged the assumption that "judges . . . [are] bound by the text or the original understanding of the Constitution,"[18] notwithstanding they are sworn to support it.[19] But he has since adjured academe "simply to acknowledge that most of our writings [about judicial review] are not political theory but advocacy scholarship—amicus briefs ultimately designed to persuade the Court to adopt our various notions of the public good."[20] Of all this, and of activist scrambling to rationalize the Court's exercise of extraconstitutional power and policy making,[21] there is scarcely an intimation in Sager's article.

---

[12] 5 THE OXFORD ENGLISH DICTIONARY 368 (Murray ed. 1933).

[13] We "are philosophically [and historically] committed," Perry observes, to the "principle that governmental policymaking . . . ought to be subject to control by persons accountable to the electorate." This principle is "axiomatic; it is judicial review, not the principle, that requires justification." M. PERRY, THE CONSTITUTION, THE COURTS, AND HUMAN RIGHTS 9 (1982) (footnotes omitted).

[14] *Id.* at 24. In the face of pronouncements such as Kurland's, *see supra* text accompanying note 8, of Perry, and of a broad activist consensus that modern "constitutional rights" of individuals have no constitutional footing, *see infra* note 44. Sager refers to "*allegedly* erroneous decisions that [Senator Jesse Helms] regards as judicial usurpation of power." Sager, *supra* note 1, at 19 n.5 (emphasis added). An ardent activist, Paul Brest now acknowledges that "[f]undamental rights adjudication is open to the criticisms that is not *authorized* and not *guided* by the text and original history of the Constitution." Brest, *The Fundamental Rights Controversy: The Essential Contradictions of Normative Constitutional Scholarship,* 90 YALE L.J. 1063, 1082 (1981) (emphasis in original).

[15] Trop v. Dulles, 356 U.S. 86, 103 (1958).

[16] *Id.* at 104.

[17] McDowell, Book Review, Wall St. J., Aug. 26, 1982, at 20, col. 3 (emphasis added). This is Gary McDowell's summary of White's exposition. It is richly confirmed by White's narrative. *See* G. WHITE, EARL WARREN: A PUBLIC LIFE (1982). *See also infra* text accompanying notes 219–97.

[18] Brest, *The Misconceived Quest for the Original Understanding,* 60 B.U.L. REV. 204, 224 (1980).

[19] Chief Justice Marshall asked, "Why does a judge swear to discharge his duties agreeably to the constitution of the United States, if that constitution forms no rule for his government?" Marbury v. Madison, 5 U.S. (1 Cranch) 137, 180 (1803).

[20] Brest, *supra* note 14, at 1109.

[21] *See Symposium: Judicial Review Versus Democracy,* 42 OHIO ST. L.J. 1 (1981); *Symposium: Constitutional Adjudication and Democratic Theory,* 56 N.Y.U.L. REV. 259 (1981). Mark Tushnet considers that the academicians seek to "superimpose a facade of rationality on the Court's decisions." Tushnet, *Truth, Justice, and the American Way: An Interpretation of Public Law Scholarship in the Seventies,* 57 TEX. L. REV. 1307, 1325 (1979). After examining "seven representative scholars who favor one or another form of fundamental rights adjudication," Brest indicates that their

Sager notices that there are opponents of his view, among them Herbert Wechsler, a seminal scholar in the field, who deserves more than mere mention in a footnote.[22] Wechsler concluded that "Congress has the power by enactment of a statute to strike at what it deems judicial excess by delimitations of the jurisdiction" of the federal courts.[23] The constitutional plan, he added, "was quite simply that the Congress would decide from time to time how far the federal judicial institution should be used within the limits of the federal judicial power."[24] To this may be added the comment of a redoubtable activist, Charles Black: "I am not sure that I could defend, as consistent with the postulates of democracy, a system which really did put nine men, with life tenure, in an absolutely invulnerable position of final power,"[25] a view in which Michael Perry concurs.[26] Black could avouch Alexander Hamilton who, in *Federalist No. 81*,[27] rejected the argument that the "usurpations of the Supreme Court . . . will be uncontrollable and remediless" as based upon "false reasoning."[28] He went on to declare that "usurpations on the authority of the legislature" could be checked by impeachment.[29] But the fact that impeachment provides an alternate remedy does not reduce the provisions of article III to surplusage, particularly because, as James Bryce observed, impeachment is so heavy a "piece of artillery" as "to be unfit for ordinary use"[30]—a good reason for giving effect to the unequivocal provisions of article III.

Congressional control of the courts' jurisdiction under article III has the sanction of the First Congress, draftsmen of the Judiciary Act of 1789,[31] and of an unbroken string of decisions stretching from the beginning of the Republic.[32] Such control of the Supreme Court's appellate jurisdiction derives from the article III provision that it shall be subject to "such exceptions and under such

conclusions derived from their particular predilections. Brest, *supra* note 14, at 1089. Of elaborate efforts to construct such a theory, Sanford Levinson, a dedicated activist, wrote, "[i]t is naive to pretend that the construction will be an easy task or that we can so easily shed the view of the Constitution, and its limits, articulated by Berger." Levinson, Book Review, 236 NATION 250 (1983). *See also infra* note 40.

[22]Sager, *supra* note 1, at 21 n.10.

[23]Wechsler, *The Courts and the Constitution*, 65 COLUM. L. REV. 1001, 1005 (1965).

[24]*Id.* Michael Perry considers that "congressional power over the jurisdiction of the federal judiciary, including the appellate jurisdiction of the Supreme Court, is not disputed." Perry, *Noninterpretive Review in Human Rights Cases: A Functional Justification*, 56 N.Y.U. L. REV. 278, 332 (1981). Louis Lusky refers to Congress' "undoubted authority to strip away virtually all power of the federal courts to engage in judicial review." Lusky, Book Review, 6 HASTINGS CONST. L.Q. 403, 412 (1979). Sanford Levinson is "inclined to accept the view that Congress indeed has power, subject to extremely few constraints, to determine federal jurisdiction however it sees fit." Levinson, *The Turn Toward Functionalism in Constitutional Theory*, 8 U. DAYTON L. REV. 567, 575 (1983). To my mind the cases abundantly justify such views, as will appear.

[25]Black, *The Presidency and Congress*, 32 WASH. & LEE L. REV. 841, 847 (1975). Scharpf likewise insists "that judicial review in a democracy remains defensible only to the extent that the Court itself will be defenseless against the processes through which the community may assert and enforce its own considered understanding of its basic code." Scharpf, *Judicial Review and the Political Question: A Functional Analysis*, 75 YALE L. J. 517, 589 (1966).

[26]*See* M. PERRY, *supra* note 13, at 138.

[27]THE FEDERALIST No. 81 (A. Hamilton).

[28]*Id.* at 523–24 (Mod. Libr. ed. 1937).

[29]*Id.* at 526–27.

[30]1 J. BRYCE, THE AMERICAN COMMONWEALTH 212 (new ed. 1914) (discussing relations between Congress and the President).

[31]Act of Sept. 24, 1789, ch. 20, 1 Stat. 73. Charles Warren considered that the First Congress was "almost an adjourned session" of the Constitutional Convention. C. WARREN, CONGRESS, THE CONSTITUTION AND THE SUPREME COURT 99 (1925). Sager notes that 19 Framers, including Oliver Ellsworth, Elbridge Gerry, James Madison, William Paterson and Roger Sherman, were members of the First Congress. Sager, *supra* note 1, at 31 n. 37. To these may be added many who had participated in the state ratification conventions.

[32]*See, e.g.,* Glidden Co. v. Zdanok, 370 U.S. 530, 567–68 (1962); *Ex parte* McCardle, 74 U.S. (7 Wall.) 506 (1869); Cary v. Curtis, 44 U.S. (3 How.) 236 (1845); Wiscart v. Dauchy, 3 U.S. (3 Dall.) 321 (1796). *See infra* text accompanying notes 74–93.

regulations as the Congress shall make." William Van Alstyne considers that "[t]he power to make exceptions to Supreme Court appellate jurisdiction is a plenary power. It is given in express terms and without limitation."[33] Sager himself observes that "[i]t seems odd—indeed inappropriate—to find in as barren an expression as 'with such Exceptions . . . as the Congress shall make' the existence of some category of jurisdiction beyond Congress' reach."[34] For activists, according to John Hart Ely, *the most important datum bearing on what was intended is the constitutional language itself,*[35] adding that "the only reliable evidence of what 'the ratifiers' thought they were ratifying is obviously the language of the provisions they approved."[36] It is therefore refreshing to find Sager so frequently turning to the legislative history,[37] for in their efforts to undergird the desegregation, reapportionment and Bill of Rights decisions, activists have consigned legislative history to the outermost bounds of limbo.[38] Let Paul Brest speak:

> [M]any scholars and judges reject Berger's major premise, that constitutional interpretation should depend chiefly on the intent of those who framed and adopted such a provision. . . . [W]hatever the framers' expectations may have been, broad constitutional guarantees require the Court to discern, articulate and apply values that are widely and deeply held by our society.[39]

Activists cannot have it both ways; resort to legislative history must be evenhanded. Were effect given to the history of the fourteenth amendment, the motivation for "court-stripping" would disappear. The history of the fourteenth amendment, more and more activists agree, shows that jurisdiction over suffrage and segregation was withheld and the Bill of Rights was not incorporated therein,[40] thereby undermining the Court's desegregation, reapportionment, school prayer and like decisions—areas Sager would shield from "stripping."[41]

---

[33]Van Alstyne, *A Critical Guide to* Ex Parte McCardle, 15 Ariz. L. Rev. 229, 260 (1973).

[34]Sager, *supra* note 1, at 45.

[35]Ely, *Constitutional Interpretivism: Its Allure and Impossibility,* 53 Ind. L.J. 399, 418 (1978) (emphasis in original).

[36]*Id.* at 419.

[37]But he notes the argument that "[t]he broad license that article III gives Congress to limit the jurisdiction of the Supreme Court . . . is beyond restraints spun from threads as slender as perceptions about intent of the framers." Sager, *supra* note 1, at 44. He tells us that the

> "exceptions and regulations" language . . . was adopted by the Convention . . . without a ripple of recorded debate, concern, or explication. In light of this quiescence, it is hard to imagine that the framers were consciously adopting a provision that could completely unravel one of the most basic aspects of the constitutional scheme to which they had committed themselves.

Id. at 51 (footnotes omitted); *see also id.* at 42. This is an extraordinary interpretive approach: *silence* authorizes the curtailment of an express, unmistakable text! The First Congress (*see supra* note 24) speedily embodied in the Judiciary Act of 1789 the very unravelling provision—on a grand scale—that Sager condemns; federal question jurisdiction was made the exclusive province of the state courts subject to limited review by the Supreme Court. And even more "basic" was the mandate that every branch comply with constitutional limits. R. Berger, Death Penalties, *supra* note 10, at 77–79; *see infra* text accompanying notes 282–87.

[38]*See, e.g.,* Brest, *The Misconceived Quest for the Original Understanding,* 60 B.U.L. Rev. 204 (1980); Alfange, Book Review, 5 Hastings Const. L.Q. 603, 608–15, (1978).

[39]Brest, Book Review, N.Y. Times, Dec. 11, 1977, § 7 (Book Rev.), at 44. For comment on "values that are widely and deeply held," *see infra* text accompanying notes 218–42.

[40]An activist, Nathaniel Nathanson, wrote about my conclusion that segregation and suffrage were excluded by the framers from the fourteenth amendment: "These are not surprising historical conclusions. The first was quite conclusively demonstrated by Alexander Bickel . . . ; the second was also quite convincingly demonstrated by . . . Mr. Justice Harlan . . . Mr. Berger's independent research and analysis confirms and adds weight to those conclusions." Nathanson, Book Review, 56 Tex. L. Rev. 579, 581 (1978). Perry observed, "The framers of the fourteenth amendment did not intend to ban state-ordered racial segregation, and yet the Supreme Court has done so." M. Perry, *supra* note 13, at 92. For additional citations see Perry, *Interpretivism, Freedom of Expression, and Equal Protection,* 42 Ohio St. L.J. 261, 285 n.100 (1981),

Against this background, Sager's repeated emphasis on the Court's duty to safeguard "constitutional rights"[42] begs the question. "Constitutional rights" are those created by the Constitution, not those pulled out of thin air by the Court without constitutional warrant.[43] Increasingly, activists agree that most modern "rights" are not specified in the Constitution, but have been fashioned by the Court.[44] Perry understands Sager to doubt "that very much modern constitutional doctrine regarding human rights can be grounded in the *written* Constitution."[45] For present purposes it may be assumed that congressional control of jurisdiction does not extend to "rights" specified in the Constitution.[46] The issue, rather, is whether such control may be exercised to curb judicial arrogation of power that proceeds in despite of the Constitution. In *Federalist No. 83* Hamilton wrote that the judicial authority extended to "certain cases *particularly specified.* The expression

who adds that my finding that the fourteenth amendment was not intended to make the Bill of Rights applicable to the States "is amply documented and widely accepted." *Id.* at 286.

[41]*See* Sager, *supra* note 1, at 17–18, 88–89.

[42]*Id.* at 68, 70, 72, 77, 79.

[43]In his classic post-Civil War commentary on the Constitution, Chief Justice Thomas Cooley stated that a court cannot "declare a statute unconstitutional and void, solely on the ground of unjust and oppressive provisions, or because it is supposed to violate the natural, social, or political rights of the citizen, unless it can be shown that such injustice is prohibited or such rights guaranteed or protected by the Constitution." T. COOLEY, A TREATISE ON THE CONSTITUTIONAL LIMITATIONS 341 (8th ed. 1927). Similar sentiments were uttered by the Framers in rejecting the Council of Revision. R. BERGER, GOVERNMENT BY JUDICIARY: THE TRANSFORMATION OF THE FOURTEENTH AMENDMENT 301 (1977) [hereinafter cited as R. BERGER, GOVERNMENT BY JUDICIARY.] For Chief Justice Warren's flagrant disregard of such canons, see *infra* text accompanying notes 218–42.

[44]Perry observes that since "there is neither a textual nor a historical justification . . . for noninterpretive review in human rights cases, [unless there is a functional justification] virtually all of constitutional doctrine regarding human rights fashioned by the Supreme Court in this century must be judged illegitimate." M. PERRY, *supra* note 13, at 91. It "becomes virtually impossible to justify the Court's actions [in providing 'vigorous protection for constitutional rights of minorities'] on the ground that it is doing no more than 'finding' the law of the Constitution and fulfilling the intention of its framers." J. CHOPER, JUDICIAL REVIEW AND THE NATIONAL POLITICAL PROCESS 137 (1980). Terrance Sandalow emphasizes the difference between "two quite different problems"—(1) "the protection of individual and minority rights," and (2) "the definition of the rights that individuals and minorities *should* have." He questioned "what mandate courts can claim for exercising powers to determine what the rights of individuals and minorities *should* be, especially since decisions regarding those rights will have an important impact upon the interests of others." Sandalow, *The Distrust of Politics,* 56 N.Y.U. L. REV. 446, 460 (1981) (emphasis added.) Gary C. Leedes considers that "[t]he framers did not intend article III to empower a federal judge to invalidate legislation simply because he decides that, beyond its limitations, the Constitution should protect a claimant's rights." Leedes, *The Supreme Court Mess,* 57 TEX. L. REV. 1361, 1385 (1979). *See also* Berger, *Paul Brest's Brief for an Imperial Judiciary,* 40 MD. L. REV. 1, 18–22 (1981). Perry considers that a person's claim that his "human rights" have been violated is "really a claim about what human rights he *ought* to be deemed to have . . . when no value judgment constitutionalized by the framers is determinative." M. PERRY, *supra* note 13, at 112 (emphasis added). Sager affirms that "[a]bsent a cognizable body of rights, the justification for judicial review is all but conclusively dissipated." Sager, *Rights Skepticism and Process-Based Responses,* 56 N.Y.U. L. REV. 417, 420 (1981) (footnotes omitted.) Gary C. Leedes also considers that there are "no extra-constitutional minority rights." Leedes, *Supra,* at 1385.

When Ira Lupu writes that "Perry's noninterpretivism removes most modern constitutional protection of the individual from the written Constitution," he assumes that "modern" individual rights were *in* the written Constitution, when as activists now acknowledge, they are extraconstitutional constructs without roots in the "written Constitution." Lupu, *Constitutional Theory and the Search for the Workable Premise,* 8 U. DAYTON L. REV. 579, 608 (1983). A recent acknowledgement of the fact is that of Larry Alexander: "There is no power delegated to Congress under article I or the enforcement provisions of the Civil War Amendments to enact legislation enforcing values not constitutionalized." Alexander, *Painting Without Numbers: Noninterpretive Judicial Review,* 8 U. DAYTON L. REV. 447, 458 (1983).

Centuries ago Dante noted that the "usurpation of a right does not create a right." W. DURANT, THE AGE OF FAITH 1063 (1950).

[45]M. PERRY, *supra* note 13, at 231 (emphasis in original). Notwithstanding, Sager refers only to "highly controversial federal court decisions recognizing individual rights." Sager, *supra* note 1, at 68.

[46]For the factors implicated in that assumption, see Berger, *Michael Perry's Functional Justification for Judicial Activism,* 8 U. DAYTON L. REV. 466, 511–12 (1983).

of those cases marks the *precise limits,* beyond which the federal courts cannot extend their jurisdiction."[47] Consequently, the specification of cases "arising under this Constitution" excludes cases not "arising" thereunder but drawn from external sources.[48] And if, as Hamilton stated, Congress was confined to laws passed "in pursuance of their just and constitutional powers of legislation,"[49] the Court equally was bound to stay within its "just and constitutional powers" of adjudication.[50]

Sager stresses "the firm commitment to federal supervision of the states reflected in the history and logic of the Constitution."[51] But that is only half of the story. The states' rights advocates at the Constitutional Convention, as Sager notes, "were most concerned with bridling the federal government" and "least supportive of a substantial judiciary."[52] Their unrelenting pressure left a deep imprint on the structure and powers of that judiciary. Because many, like William Grayson of Virginia, felt that state courts were "the principal defence of the states,"[53] their stubborn insistence on state court arbitrament of federal-state conflicts persisted and soon was expressed in the Judiciary Act of 1789.[54] The supremacy clause, Hamilton wrote in *Federalist No. 33,* "*expressly* confines this supremacy to laws made *pursuant to the Constitution;*"[55] federal acts which are not pursuant thereto but "*are invasions of the residuary powers* of the smaller societies . . . will be merely acts of usurpation and will deserve to be treated as such."[56] His condemnation

---

[47]THE FEDERALIST NO. 83, at 541 (A. Hamilton) (Mod. Libr. ed. 1937) (emphasis added).

[48]"[A]rticle III grants the federal courts power to decide cases 'arising under the Constitution,' but it does not grant the power to decide cases involving extra-constitutional value judgments." Alexander, *Painting Without the Numbers: Non-interpretive Judicial Review,* 8 U. DAYTON L. REV. 447, 458 (1983).

[49]THE FEDERALIST NO. 80, at 515 (A. Hamilton) (Mod. Libr. ed. 1937).

[50]The Founders were more attached to the legislatures than to the courts. Of the three branches, Hamilton assured the ratifiers, the judiciary is next to nothing. THE FEDERALIST NO. 78, at 504 n.* (A. Hamilton) (Mod. Libr. ed. 1937) (quoting MONTESQUIEU, THE SPIRIT OF LAWS). In his 1791 lectures, Justice James Wilson admonished America that it was time "to chastise our prejudices" (*i.e.,* courts had been "objects of aversion and distrust"). 1 THE WORKS OF JAMES WILSON 292–93 (R. McCloskey ed. 1967).

[51]Sager, *supra* note 1, at 45.

[52]8 *Id.* at 58. For discussion of the Founders' passionate attachment to state sovereignty, see R. BERGER, CONGRESS V. THE SUPREME COURT 261–63 (1969) [hereinafter cited as R. BERGER, CONGRESS].

[53]3 DEBATES IN THE SEVERAL STATE CONVENTIONS ON THE ADOPTION OF THE FEDERAL CONSTITUTION 563 (J. Elliott ed. 1827–30 & photo. reprint 1941). In the North Carolina Convention Spencer declared, "[T]he state governments are the basis of our happiness, security and prosperity." A. MASON, THE STATES RIGHTS DEBATE: ANTI-FEDERALISM AND THE CONSTITUTION 161 (2d ed. 1972). Contrast with Grayson's observations Sager's remark that all congressional control can accomplish is to "take Congress out of the grip of the federal courts and put it in the grip of state judiciaries." Sager, *supra* note 1, at 41. That choice was made by the First Congress and it remains for Congress to make it. So far as Congress invades the sovereignty over local matters reserved to the states, the Framers made the state courts the first resort.

[54]*See supra* note 31 and accompanying text.

[55]THE FEDERALIST NO. 33, at 202 (A. Hamilton) (Mod. Libr. ed. 1937) (emphasis in original).

[56]*Id.* (emphasis added); R. BERGER, CONGRESS, *supra* note 52, at 13–16, 266–67. The Constitution's restrictions on federal jurisdiction are discussed *infra,* text accompanying notes 279–97. Against this Sager argues,

It is hard to imagine that total congressional control of Supreme Court jurisdiction was deliberately embraced by the same body that had worried for months about restraint of the states, had fought to a compromise over the structure of Congress, and had engaged in a tug-of-war over congressional control of judicial appointment until the final hour of its deliberations.

Sager, *supra* note 1, at 52 (footnotes omitted). The great "compromise," which assured the states equal representation in the Senate, responded to the states rights proponents' fears that "[p]roportional representation would strike 'at the existence of the lesser States.'" A. MASON, *supra* note 53, at 37. A states' rights leader, William Paterson, "virtually equated state sovereignty with equal state representation." *Id.* at 40. Alpheus Thomas Mason concluded that "[e]nemies of a strong national government, as well as friends of the small states, had good reason to hail the Connecticut Compromise as a victory. The term 'compromise' is a misnomer." *Id.* at 49. Another victory was scored when the final compromise left

of usurpation extended to judicial arrogation.[57] Madison assured the ratifiers in *Federalist No. 39* that federal jurisdiction "extends to certain enumerated objects only, and leaves to the several States a residuary and *inviolable* sovereignty over all other objects."[58] He particularized in *Federalist No. 45* that federal powers "will be exercised principally on *external* objects, as war, peace, negotiation and foreign commerce. . . . The powers reserved to the several States will extend to all the objects which . . . concern . . . the *internal order* . . . of the State."[59] To Madison and Hamilton, Garry Wills observes, "it seemed inconceivable . . . that a central authority would want to descend to the enforcement of local laws."[60] Their assurances to the ratifiers were calculated to allay intense fears that the federal government would invade or swallow up the sovereignty of the States.[61]

The basic issue, therefore, is whether the people may protect themselves from a judicial takeover of local government that was reserved to the states. Instead of meeting that issue, Sager asserts that "if Congress were able to free the States from federal judicial supervision, the constitutional

creation of inferior courts in the discretion of Congress, and the First Congress then left federal jurisdiction exclusively with the state courts with spotty appeals to the Supreme Court. The nationalists "were convinced that they had suffered fatal defeats." *Id.* at 58.

[57]*See* THE FEDERALIST NO. 33, at 201–02 (A. Hamilton) (Mod. Libr. ed. 1937). Sager observes that the jurisdiction of the Court "was consciously tailored to the role of supervising the enforcement of the supremacy clause," Sager, *supra* note 1, at 51, but fails to note that it did not extend to invasions of the residuary powers of the states. Justice James Iredell stated, "The question then under this [supremacy] clause, will always be whether congress has exceeded its authority. If it has not exceeded it we must obey, otherwise not." A. MASON, *supra* note 53, at 165. And he said, "If Congress, under pretence of exercising the power delegated to them, should in fact, by the exercise of any other power, usurp upon the rights of the different [State] Legislatures, . . . [i]t would be an act of tyranny." *Id.* at 128.

[58]THE FEDERALIST NO. 39, at 249 (J. Madison) (Mod. Libr. ed. 1937) (emphasis added). *See also* comments of A. Hamilton, *infra* text accompanying notes 157–58.

[59]THE FEDERALIST NO. 45, at 303 (J. Madison) (Mod. Libr. ed. 1937) (emphasis added). Madison proposed "complete authority in all cases where uniform measures are necessary." A. MASON, *supra* note 53, at 62. Wilson likewise emphasized that federal power extends to matters "to the direction of which no state is competent," *id.* at 15, which "extend beyond the bounds of the particular States," *id.* at 76, therefore not embracing, for example, local control of education or criminal law enforcement. Iredell assured the North Carolina Ratification Convention that "[w]ith the mere internal concerns of a State, Congress are to have nothing to do." *Id.* at 127. Chief Justice Marshall, who in the Virginia Ratification Convention had vigorously defended judicial review to curb action in excess of constitutional bounds, stated in *Gibbons v. Ogden* that the federal powers applied

to all the external concerns of the nation, and to those internal concerns which affect the States generally; but not to those which are completely within a particular State, which do not affect other States, and with which it is not necessary to interfere, for the purpose of executing some of the general powers of the government.

22 U.S. (9 Wheat.) 1, 195 (1824).

Contrast this with Sager's view that

[f]ederal judicial supervision of state conduct is particularly important because of the daily impact of state and local government on the lives of individuals. . . . States or their municipal constituents register voters, run public schools, control access to speech opportunities, employ the police personnel with whom citizens regularly have contact, regulate the use of land, license professionals, and regulate families.

Sager, *supra* note 1, at 55 n.112. In short, Sager would have Big Brother take over administration of local matters which Madison assured the Framers were left to the states, to be forever "inviolable." *See* THE FEDERALIST NO. 39, at 249 (J. Madison) (Mod. Libr. ed. 1937). This is the mainspring of Sager's attack on congressional curtailment of jurisdiction to continue on this path.

[60]G. WILLS, *Introduction* to THE FEDERALIST at xiv (1982). Oliver Ellsworth stated in the Convention, "The Nat[iona]l Gov[ernmen]t could not descend to the local objects on which this [individual rights] depended. It could only embrace objects of a general nature. He turned his eyes therefore for the preservation of his rights to the State Gov[ernmen]ts." 1 THE RECORDS OF THE FEDERAL CONVENTION OF 1787, at 492 (M. Farrand ed. 1911). "In the Convention and later, states rights—not individual rights—was the real worry." A. MASON, *supra* note 53, at 78.

[61]R. BERGER, CONGRESS, *supra* note 52, at 261–62.

order would be badly wrenched,"[62] when in truth it has been "badly wrenched" by the Court's arrogation of jurisdiction withheld. One can agree that "the framers put critical restraints on state autonomy into the Constitution itself"[63] and yet reject the non sequitur that states are equally bound by restraints imported by the Court that the Framers did not put into the Constitution. The federal courts, Hamilton stated, were to overrule state laws that "might be in *manifest contravention* of the articles of Union";[64] that was the scope of the "firm commitment" to federal supervision of state courts relied on by Sager.[65] It is not breached when Congress intervenes to deprive the Court of jurisdiction to enter decisions that manifestly deprive states of rights reserved to them by the Constitution.

Current assaults on the long-recognized congressional power are without historical or judicial warrant; they are simply, as activist Michael Perry wrote, "attacks, by those enthusiastic about the modern Court's activist work product."[66] Such academicians, having cheered on the Court in the realization of their social aspirations, now seek to barricade the way to correction of the Court's excesses.

II. THE CASES

Sager's discussion of the cases is replete with remarkable readings of what they held. He finds "ambiguous statements in early decisions,"[67] but concludes that "article III itself contains a direct, self-executing grant of jurisdiction" to the Court,[68] a matter "well established"[69] when Chief Justice Taney wrote for the Court in *Barry v. Mercein*.[70] Taney apparently was unaware that it was "well established," for he held that "[b]y the constitution . . . the Supreme Court possesses no appellate power in any case, *unless conferred* upon it by act of Congress."[71] Congress, moreover, Sager notes, "has never chosen to act as though the Supreme Court's jurisdiction were self-executing. From the Judiciary Act of 1789 on, Congress has assumed the statutory voice of affirmatively *granting* the Court jurisdiction."[72] Regarding Congress' power to "subtract legal issues" from the Court's jurisdiction, he observes that "[t]he Court itself has shared this understanding. In no opinion has the Court taken a contrary view. Indeed, . . . the Court displays an almost unseemly

---

[62]Sager, *supra* note 1, at 45. He insists that to conclude that "Congress can sweep aside the entire federal judicial establishment in order to facilitate state court repudiation of Supreme Court doctrine . . . seems at war with our commitment to national constitutional government." *Id.* at 74. That commitment was to *limited* national government, to state sovereignty over local matters; it did not contemplate shelter for lawless judicial infringements of that sovereignty. Justices as diverse as Chief Justice Burger and Justices Douglas and Frankfurter insist on looking at the Constitution for themselves, never mind what their predecessors said about it. *See* R. BERGER, GOVERNMENT BY JUDICIARY, *supra* note 43, at 297 & n.57. The right of the sovereign people is no more limited.

[63]Sager, *supra* note 1, at 46.

[64]THE FEDERALIST NO. 80, at 516 (A. Hamilton) (Mod. Libr. ed. 1937) (emphasis added).

[65]*See* Sager, *supra* note 1, at 45–57.

[66]M. PERRY, *supra* note 13, at 138.

[67]Sager, *supra* note 1, at 23.

[68]*Id.* at 23–24.

[69]*Id.* at 24 n.16.

[70]46 U.S. (5 How.) 103 (1847).

[71]*Id.* at 119 (emphasis added).

The pivotal language . . .—to the effect that the Court possesses no jurisdiction unless Congress has conferred it—is ambiguous; it may do no more than restate the practical result of the rule of Durousseau v. United States, 10 U.S. (6 Cranch) 307 (1810); . . . that purportedly positive grants of jurisdiction by Congress are to be read to exclude the jurisdiction not granted. Sager, *supra* note 1, at 23 n.16. What is ambiguous about restating that in the absence of a positive grant there is no jurisdiction? The unequivocal terms of the exceptions clause speak for themselves.

[72]Sager, *supra* note 1, at 24–25 (emphasis added) (footnotes omitted).

enthusiasm in discussing Congress' power to lop off diverse heads of the Court's article III jurisdiction."[73] Thus, in defending the Court against "stripping," Sager is more royalist than the king.

Among the allegedly "ambiguous statements" Sager finds is that of *Wiscart v. Dauchy,*[74] in which Chief Justice Ellsworth held that, "[i]f Congress has provided no rule to regulate our proceedings, we cannot exercise an appellate jurisdiction"[75]—a tolerably unambiguous statement that in the absence of congressional action the Court has no appellate jurisdiction. Ellsworth had been a draftsman of the exceptions clause as a member of the Committee on Detail, and of the Judiciary Act of 1789[76] in the First Congress, and therefore was presumably familiar with the Framers' intentions as well as those of the First Congress. His statement is to be read against that background. Sager notes that in the Judiciary Act, after excluding federal question jurisdiction from the purview of the inferior courts—an exclusion that survived until 1875—"a Congress familiar with the drafting of article III withheld from the Court *large portions* of section 2 jurisdiction. This was no oversight, to be corrected in short order, but the forging of an enduring pattern,"[77] so that some exclusions remained for 125 years or more.[78]

Little wonder that *Cary v. Curtis*[79] declared, "[T]he judicial power of the United States, although it has its origin in the Constitution, is . . . dependent for its distribution . . . entirely upon the action of Congress."[80] *Daniels v. Railroad Co.*[81] repeated, "[I]t is for Congress to determine how far . . . appellate jurisdiction shall be *given,* and when *conferred,* . . . it is wholly the creature of legislation."[82] And in 1892, after Congress had granted it jurisdiction in criminal cases, the Court held, "The appellate jurisdiction of this court *rests wholly* on the acts of Congress."[83] Even Chief Justice Warren, that paragon of activist judges, stated, "It is axiomatic, as a matter of history as well as doctrine, that the *existence* of appellate jurisdiction in a specific federal court over a given type of case is *dependent* upon authority expressly *conferred* by statute."[84]

All this is burlesqued by Sager: "Congress acts as though it were giving the Court jurisdiction in measured statutory doses, and ordinarily the Court has no occasion to take umbrage at this *pretense.*"[85] And he states that "[t]he judiciary has never had the occasion to rule decisively on

---

[73]*Id.* at 32 (footnotes omitted). In J.W. Hampton, Jr. & Co. v. United States, 276 U.S. 394 (1927), the unanimous Court declared, "This Court has repeatedly laid down the principle that a contemporaneous legislative exposition of the Constitution when the founders of our Government and framers of our Constitution were actively participating in public affairs, long acquiesced in, fixes the construction to be given its provisions." *Id.* at 412 (citations omitted).

[74]3 U.S. (3 Dall.) 321 (1796).

[75]*Id.* at 327.

[76]Act of Sept. 24, 1789, ch. 20, 1 Stat. 73

[77]Sager, *supra* note 1, at 31 (emphasis added) (footnotes omitted). The First Congress' withholding was confirmed by the Court: "[W]hole classes of cases [may] be kept out of the jurisdiction altogether." The "Francis Wright," 105 U.S. 381, 386 (1882). *The "Francis Wright"* is cited by Sager for the proposition that article III "contains a direct, self-executing grant of jurisdiction." Sager, *supra* note 1, at 24 n.17.

[78]Sager observes that "[t]he First Judiciary Act was not especially generous to the Court, and for a number of years there remained some rather surprising gaps in the Court's jurisdiction." Sager, *supra* note 1, at 52–53. For example, the "Court was not granted general power to review major federal criminal cases until 1891." *Id.* at 53 n.105. Compare with this Sager's assertion that "[a]n 'exception' implies a minor deviation from a surviving norm; it is a nibble, not a bite. And there is reason to believe that this sense of the term was, if anything, clearer at the time the Constitution was drafted than now"! *Id.* at 44.

[79]44 U.S. (3 How.) 236 (1845).

[80]*Id.* at 245.

[81]70 U.S. (3 Wall.) 250 (1866).

[82]*Id.* at 254 (emphasis added).

[83]United States v. Sanger, 144 U.S. 310, 319 (1892) (emphasis added).

[84]Carroll v. United States, 354 U.S. 394, 399 (1957) (emphasis added).

[85]Sager, *supra* note 1, at 25 (emphasis added).

such incursions into federal jurisdiction."[86] *Ex parte McCardle*[87] is to the contrary. Henry Hart, no friend of "court-stripping," wrote of *McCardle*,

> [I]n perhaps the most spectacular of historic examples a unanimous Court recognized the power of Congress to frustrate a determination of the constitutionality of the post-Civil War reconstruction legislation by withdrawing, during the very pendency of an appeal, its jurisdiction to review decisions of the federal circuit courts in habeas corpus.[88]

McCardle, Sager comments, "endorse[d] the broad power of Congress to *tamper* with [the Court's] jurisdiction."[89] But he speculates that *McCardle* might be decided differently today; among other things, "the Court did not address itself to issues of equal protection and due process—which is not surprising in view of the fact that the fourteenth amendment had not yet been passed."[90] But the due process clause of the fifth amendment was available because a federal act was involved, although the distorted version of due process that characterized the laissez-faire Court was yet unborn. Without pausing to consider such possibilities, the Court approved *McCardle* in *Glidden Co. v. Zdanok*.[91] And the continuing vitality of *McCardle* was recognized by no less an activist than Justice Douglas: "As respects our appellate jurisdiction, Congress may largely fashion it as Congress desires by reason of the express provisions of § 2, Art. III. See *Ex parte McCardle* . . . ."[92] Justice Frankfurter, a pioneer student of federal jurisdiction, stated, "Congress need not give this Court any appellate power; it may withdraw appellate jurisdiction once conferred and it may do so even while a case is *sub judice*. *Ex parte McCardle*."[93] So far as the cases go, therefore, Sager patently has a hard row to hoe.

He is not helped by *United States v. Klein*[94] to which he repeatedly turns:[95] "When Congress manipulates jurisdiction in an effort to deny recognition and judicial enforcement of constitutional rights, it has deliberately set itself against the Constitution as the Court understands that document. . . . *Klein* stands for nothing less."[96] The *Klein* decision merely rejected a congressional attempt "to prescribe a rule for the decision of a cause in a particular way," explaining that "this is not an exercise of the acknowledged power of Congress to make exceptions and prescribe regulations to the appellate power."[97] Much later, *Glidden Co. v. Zdanok*[98] stated that in *Klein* "the claimant had already been adjudged entitled to recover by the Court of Claims"; hence

---

[86]*Id.* at 19.

[87]74 U.S. (7 Wall.) 506 (1869).

[88]Hart, *The Power of Congress to Limit the Jurisdiction of Federal Courts: An Exercise in Dialectic*, 66 HARV. L. REV. 1362, 1362–63 (1953). In Oregon v. Mitchell, 400 U.S. 112 (1970), Justices Brennan, White and Marshall stated, "Radical disenchantment with decisions of this Court had led . . . to the Act of March 27, 1868, . . . withdrawing our appellate jurisdiction over certain habeas corpus cases. See *Ex parte McCardle*. . . ." *Id.* at 275 n.43 (citation omitted) (Brennan, J., concurring and dissenting).

[89]Sager, *supra* note 1, at 54 (emphasis added).

[90]*Id.* at 77 n.187.

[91]370 U.S. 530, 567–68 (1962).

[92]Flast v. Cohen, 392 U.S. 83, 109 (1968) (citation omitted).

[93]National Mut. Ins. Co. v. Tidewater Transfer Co., 337 U.S. 582, 655 (1949) (citation omitted) (Frankfurter, J., dissenting on other grounds). Louis Lusky refers to Congress "undoubted authority to strip away virtually all power of the federal courts to engage in judicial review." Lusky, Book Review, 6 HASTINGS CONST. L.Q. 403, 412 (1979) (footnotes omitted).

[94]80 U.S. (13 Wall.) 128, 146 (1872).

[95]Sager, *supra* note 1, at 70, 71, 72, 73, 76–77.

[96]*Id.* at 76–77. Among Sager's citations is Shapiro v. Thompson, 394 U.S. 618 (1969), an excellent example of how "the Court understands" the Constitution. There the Court found that the "right to travel," as to whose provenance no two Justices agreed, entitled an indigent migrant to immediate support at the terminus! See Berger, *Residence Requirements for Welfare and Voting: A Post-Mortem*, 42 OHIO ST. L.J. 853 (1981); *see also supra* note 10.

[97]80 U.S. (13 Wall.) 128, 146 (1872).

[98]370 U.S. 530 (1962).

application of the statute was rejected as "an unconstitutional attempt to invade the judicial province by prescribing a rule of decision in a pending case,"[99] and therefore distinguishable from *McCardle,* wherein the Court was deprived of jurisdiction. Sager's failure to perceive the difference between the two is of a piece with his insistence that since Congress cannot *reverse* a particular decision, it cannot withdraw the Court's jurisdiction to decide.[100] But as Michael Perry points out, article III "gives Congress the jurisdiction-limiting power, but not the power legislatively to reverse."[101] That distinction was drawn by Hamilton in *Federalist No. 81:* although a "legislature . . . cannot reverse a determination once made in a particular case,"[102] "usurpations [by] the Supreme Court . . . will [not] be uncontrollable and remediless."[103] In the very same *No. 81* Hamilton declared that the Court's appellate jurisdiction will be "subject to any *exceptions* and *regulations* which may be thought advisable,"[104] thus distinguishing the power to reverse from the power to control jurisdiction. Sager's failure to perceive this distinction leads him to say that "there is no indication that the framers saw Congress' power over jurisdiction as a way to manipulate federal jurisdiction."[105] Time and again he insists that "Congress cannot use jurisdiction to undermine the decisions of the Supreme Court,"[106] that it cannot "undo the Supreme Court's constitutional doctrine by simple legislative fiat, and it should not be able to accomplish the same end by manipulating federal jurisdiction."[107] But impeachment for judicial usurpation might equally be labelled manipulation of federal doctrine, yet the ratifiers were assured by Hamilton that impeachment would furnish the cure;[108] article III merely furnishes an alternate remedy.

III. SAGER'S LIMITATION ARGUMENTS

Sager observes that "while Congress does enjoy great discretion in molding federal jurisdiction, serious restrictions nevertheless limit congressional authority to enact" the current jurisdiction withdrawal bills.[109] In undertaking to limit jurisdiction Congress, he asserts, "is fully bound by the constitutional limitations that ordinarily constrain its behavior."[110] But he notices that "from Supreme Court dicta and academic commentary there occasionally emerges a sense that Congress is immune from full constitutional scrutiny when the distribution of jurisdiction is at stake."[111] The burden is on Sager to demonstrate that the plenary, unequivocal terms of the exceptions clause mean less than they say. In *McCardle,* he tells us, "[t]he Court implicitly followed Chief Justice Marshall's view that these enumerated powers should be construed broadly."[112] Early on, Justice James Wilson's view in dissent that "a positive restriction" by Congress would have to yield

---

[99]*Id.* at 568.

[100]For a discussion of his statement to that effect see *infra* text accompanying notes 106–07.

[101]M. PERRY, *supra* note 11, at 135.

[102]THE FEDERALIST NO. 81, at 526 (A. Hamilton) (Mod. Libr. ed. 1937).

[103]*Id.* at 523.

[104]*Id.* at 533 (emphasis in original).

[105]Sager, *supra* note 1, at 42 n.71.

[106]*Id.* at 38. "One starts with the observation that Congress cannot override the constitutional decisions of the Supreme Court by a simple legislative act." *Id.* at 39. He notes without differentiating that "[a] proposal that the 'judicial power shall be *exercised in such manner* as the Legislature shall direct' was repulsed." *Id.* at 49 (quoting 2 THE RECORDS OF THE FEDERAL CONVENTION OF 1787, at 425, 431 (M. Farrand ed. 1911) (emphasis added) (footnotes omitted).

[107]*Id.* at 68 (footnotes omitted).

[108]*See infra* text accompanying note 158.

[109]Sager, *supra* note 1, at 21–22.

[110]*Id.* at 37.

[111]*Id.*

[112]*Id.* at 77 n.187.

to the "superior authority"[113] of the Constitution was rejected by the Court in *Wiscart v. Dauchy*.[114] Sager's bill of particulars fails to make out his case.

A. Congressional Discretion

Sager argues that "[a]rticle III does not say 'Congress shall withhold such jurisdiction as it may deem appropriate.'"[115] That hardly squares with his view that "Congress does enjoy great discretion."[116] Moreover, such exceptions "as Congress shall make" patently leaves the judgment of what is appropriate to Congress. Hamilton said in *Federalist No. 81* that the exceptions clause "will enable the government to modify [appellate jurisdiction] in such a manner as will best answer the ends of public justice and security"[117]—a judgment necessarily left in the discretion of Congress, who could make "*any* exceptions and regulations which may be *thought advisable*."[118] A vigorous advocate of adoption of the Constitution, Justice James Iredell, declared that given a grant of power to the legislature, action within the grant "only exercise[s] a discretion expressly confided to them by the constitution."[119] A grant of power carries with it discretion how to exercise it. So the Supreme Court held in the present context in *Daniels v. Railroad Co.*[120] that "it is for Congress to determine how far . . . appellate jurisdiction shall be given."[121] When Sager appeals to a Committee report for the proposition that "such open discretion was rejected by the framers,"[122] he overlooks that the proposal—"'the judicial power shall be *exercised in such manner* as the Legislature shall direct'"[123]—sought congressional control of *how* a court shall decide as distinguished from curtailment of its jurisdiction to decide, a power exercised and accepted from the beginning.

Congressional discretion is attacked by Sager from another angle under the heading "The Vice of Selective Deprivation of Jurisdiction"; current bills, he urges, "deprive federal courts of jurisdiction in a highly selective way."[124] What could be more selective than the Norris-LaGuardia Act's withdrawal of federal jurisdiction to issue injunctions in labor disputes?[125] Yet the Act was sustained

---

[113]3 U.S. (3 Dall.) 321, 325 (1796) (Wilson, J., dissenting).

[114]*Id.* at 327. *See supra* text accompanying notes 74–75. As an example of "patently unconstitutional limitation" on federal court jurisdiction of federal questions under existing statutes. Sager instances "a provision restricting jurisdiction to plaintiffs of a particular . . . religion." Sager, *supra* note 1, at 26. Federal jurisdiction over religion was first claimed by the Court in the mid-twentieth century, resting on the alleged incorporation of the Bill of Rights in the fourteenth amendment, which activists increasingly agree is historically untenable. *See, e.g.*, Brest, *The Misconceived Quest for the Original Understanding*, 60 B.U.L. REV. 204 (1980); Alfange, Book Review, 5 HASTINGS CONST. L.Q. 603 (1978); for citations see Perry, *Interpretivism, Freedom of Expression, and Equal Protection*, 42 OHIO ST. L.J. 261, 285–86 (1981). As late as 1922 the Court held that the first amendment does not apply to the states. Prudential Ins. Co. of Am. v. Cheek, 259 U.S. 530, 538 (1922). The Court's subsequent decisions to the contrary do not settle the issue when the authority of the Court itself is being challenged.

[115]Sager, *supra* note 1, at 44.

[116]*Id.* at 21.

[117]THE FEDERALIST NO. 81, at 532–33 (A. Hamilton) (Mod. Libr. ed. 1937).

[118]*Id.* at 533 (emphasis added).

[119]Ware v. Hylton, 3 U.S. (3 Dall.) 199, 266 (1796). Control of executive discretion also lies beyond the judicial function. Marbury v. Madison, 5 U.S. (1 Cranch) 137, 169–70 (1803); Decatur v. Paulding, 39 U.S. (14 Pet.) 497, 515 (1840).

[120]70 U.S. (3 Wall.) 250 (1866).

[121]*Id.* at 254. Justice Stone declared many years later than "[w]hen the action of a legislature is within the scope of its power, fairly debatable questions as to its reasonableness, wisdom and propriety are not for the determination of courts, but for the legislative body." South Carolina State Highway Dept. v. Barnwell Bros., 303 U.S. 177, 190–91 (1938).

[122]Sager, *supra* note 1, at 44 (footnote omitted). *See also id.* at 50.

[123]*Id.* at 50 n.95 (emphasis added) (quoting 2 THE RECORDS OF THE FEDERAL CONVENTION OF 1787, at 425, 431 (M. Farrand ed. 1911)); *see supra* text accompanying notes 94–108.

[124]Sager, *supra* note 1, at 68.

[125]29 U.S.C. §§ 101, 115 (1976).

by the Court.[126] So too, as Sager notes, the 1789 Judiciary Act left "surprising gaps in the Court's jurisdiction."[127] In contrast with his strident charge that control advocates are engaged in "tawdry . . . sabotag[e of] the integrity of the judicial process"[128] he understates the congressional concern, shared by more and more activists, that has been "provoked by highly controversial federal court decisions recognizing individual rights."[129] Despite the "highly controversial" character of these decisions, Sager dwells on "the vice of selectively depriving the federal courts of jurisdiction over discrete and disfavored claims of *constitutional right.*"[130] But rights drawn by the Court *dehors* the Constitution are *not* constitutional rights, and Congress' exercise of power under an unequivocal and, in terms, unlimited grant to curb such "discrete" judicial arrogations can hardly be dismissed as "tawdry sabotage." The current proposals, he states, "are plainly efforts to undermine the enforcement of prevailing constitutional doctrine in order to facilitate other, favored substantive outcomes."[131] Thus, he assumes that "prevailing constitutional doctrine" is legitimate; that it must be shielded at all costs; that opposing "substantive outcomes" are merely a matter of taste rather than based on the fundamental principle that the Court, like the other branches, must stay within constitutional limits; that it is not free to revise the Constitution by importing values the Framers excluded. For him, the "argument against such legislation is simple: Congress ordinarily cannot undo the Supreme Court's constitutional doctrine by simple legislative fiat, and it should not be able to accomplish the same end by manipulating federal jurisdiction."[132] He "simply" will not perceive the distinction, drawn by Hamilton, between the power to *reverse* a decision, which was not granted, and the power to withdraw jurisdiction to decide, which was conferred.[133] Sager experiences no difficulty in concluding that the existence of inferior courts "was left to the discretion of Congress," under the article III provision for "such inferior Courts *as the Congress may* from time to time ordain and establish."[134] What distinguishes "such exceptions . . . *as the Congress shall make*"?[135] Why is the former discretionary and the latter not?

B. Cure by Amendment

Sager points out that amendment requires a two-thirds vote as does the override of a veto, and that "[c]ontrol of jurisdiction as a majoritarian check on the judiciary does not fit easily into this

---

[126]Lauf v. E.G. Shinner & Co., 303 U.S. 323, 329–30 (1938).

[127]Sager, *supra* note 1, at 53.

[128]*Id.* at 89. An example of Sager's loaded rhetoric: "If . . . Congress removes slices of federal jurisdiction in order to insulate *federal* conduct from disfavored constitutional challenges," it "will be insulating its own unconstitutional conduct. . . ." *Id.* at 69. Consider this against the Court's invalidation of the Child Labor Law in Hammer v. Dagenhart, 247 U.S. 251 (1918), generally regarded as a mere reflection of the Court's laissez-faire prepossessions, having no constitutional warrant. Would Congress' withdrawal of jurisdiction of such cases justly be regarded as "insulating its own unconstitutional conduct"? Such are the perils of "icily abstract" analysis.

And if Congress may not insulate "its own unconstitutional conduct," why does the Court stand higher? Of the three branches, Hamilton assured the ratifiers, "the judiciary is next to nothing." THE FEDERALIST NO. 78, at 504 n.* (A Hamilton) (Mod. Libr. ed. 1937). Madison wrote in *Federalist No. 51*, "In republican government, the legislative authority necessarily predominates." THE FEDERALIST NO. 51, at 338 (J. Madison) (Mod. Libr. ed 1937). Justice Brandeis referred to the deepseated conviction of the English and American people that they "must look to representative assemblies for the protection of their liberties." Myers v. United States, 272 U.S. 52, 294–95 (1926) (dissenting opinion in which Justice Holmes concurred). Elbridge Gerry expressed similiar views in the First Congress. *See* 1 THE RECORDS OF THE FEDERAL CONVENTION OF 1787, at 97–98 (M. Farrand ed. 1911); and 2 *id.* at 75.

[129]Sager, *supra* note 1, at 68.

[130]*Id.* at 70 (emphasis added). Since even some activists consider that these decisions have no constitutional warrant, *see supra* note 44, they are justly disfavored.

[131]Sager, *supra* note 1, at 68.

[132]*Id.* (footnotes omitted).

[133]*See supra* text accompanying notes 94–108.

[134]Sager, *supra* note 1, at 48; U.S. CONST. art. III, § 1 (emphasis added).

[135]U.S. CONST. art. III, § 2, cl. 2 (emphasis added).

institutional setting," so that "it makes no sense to single out one rather bizarre form of legislation to which no supermajority requirement attaches and make it the last democratic hurrah."[136] The short answer is that the First Congress read article III in just that "bizarre" fashion. And what is "bizarre" about giving effect to the express, unequivocal terms of article III when Sager swallows the Court's continuous amendment of the Constitution, which is without express sanction?[137]

The proper procedure, Sager suggests, is to amend.[138] Activists defend the Court's extraconstitutional forays on the ground that resort to amendment is too cumbersome. So, Louis Lusky refers to the Court's "assertion of the power to revise the Constitution, bypassing the cumbersome amendment procedure prescribed by Article V."[139] If it is too cumbersome to seek popular consent to judicial alteration of the Constitution, it is too cumbersome to require the people to reverse judicial usurpation by amendment.[140] Resort to statutory "exceptions" to correct the Court's unconstitutional excesses has express constitutional authorization; activist judicial review has none.

C. Hart's "Essential Function"

Sager considers that removal of jurisdiction "to hear or review constitutional challenges to State conduct," such as school prayer legislation, "would be subject to a substantial constitutional objection"—it undercuts the constitutional objective of "ensur[ing] state compliance with federal constitutional *norms*,"[141] again begging the question of judicial authority to outlaw school prayer legislation. He notes that this is "a narrowed form of the 'essential function' view of the Supreme Court's appellate jurisdiction"[142] formulated by Henry Hart: " 'exceptions must not be such as will destroy the essential role of the Supreme Court in the Constitutional plan.' "[143] That plan did not contemplate judicial revision of the Constitution in order to invade state sovereignty over local matters reserved to the states.[144] As Michael Perry observes, it is "self-serving in the extreme to suppose" the essential role to be "anything more than to enforce the value judgments constitutionalized by the framers."[145]

Viewing "essentially" in the frame of *federal* conduct, Sager recognizes that "the sources . . . are more equivocal when review of federal conduct is at stake."[146] He notes that "Hart never gave clear shape to his view of the essential function premise,"[147] that there was a large, clear "hole in the Supreme Court's jurisdiction: for much of the nineteenth century, the Supreme Court could

[136]Sager, *supra* note 1, at 39–40.

[137]"When the Court disregards the express intent and understanding of the Framers [as with suffrage and segregation], it has invaded the realm of the political process to which the amending power was committed, and it has violated the constitutional structure which it is its highest duty to protect." Oregon v. Mitchell, 400 U.S. 112, 203 (1970) (Harlan, J., concurring in part and dissenting in part).

[138]"Congress can attack Supreme Court decisions by presenting a constitutional amendment to the States for ratification." Sager, *supra* note 1, at 39.

[139]Lusky, Book Review, 6 HASTINGS CONST. L.Q. 403, 406 (1979); *see also* Kutler, Book Review, 6 HASTINGS CONST. L.Q. 511, 525; P. BREST, PROCESSES OF CONSTITUTIONAL DECISIONMAKING: CASES AND MATERIALS 978–79 (1975).

[140]Charles Black, a dyed-in-the-wool activist, observes that an amendment "can be thwarted by thirty-four senators out of a hundred, or by states containing as few as nine million people." He is "staggered by the implied assertion, or assumption, that such a position can be consonant with the root-ideas and greater sayings of democracy." C. BLACK, DECISION ACCORDING TO LAW 38 (1981) (footnotes omitted).

[141]Sager, *supra* note 1, at 43 (emphasis added).

[142]*Id.*

[143]*Id.* (quoting Hart, *The Power of Congress to Limit the Jurisdiction of Federal Courts: An Exercise in Dialectic,* 66 HARV. L. REV. 1362, 1365 (1953)).

[144]*See supra* text accompanying notes 56–61.

[145]M. PERRY, *supra* note 13, at 133.

[146]Sager, *supra* note 1, at 57.

[147]*Id.* at 57 n.114.

not directly review federal criminal cases," that the remedy by habeas corpus was "decidedly restricted" and had its own jurisdictional complications.[148] He concludes that "[i]f the essential function claim is understood to require that the Supreme Court itself be able to review all cases that require federal judicial review, then the Court's toleration of *this hole* in its jurisdiction places the claim in jeopardy."[149] To bolster the "federal conduct version of the essential function claim," he therefore resorts to the farfetched analogy furnished by "the constitutional limitation on giving article III business to a non-article-III tribunal," a "point of departure" that he rightly anticipates will raise his "reader's hackles."[150] Since "Congress' ability to give article III business to federal tribunals whose judges do not enjoy article III security is limited," Sager argues, "Congress should be similarly limited in its ability to relegate article III cases to the state courts, whose judges do not and cannot enjoy article III security."[151] Precisely such a relegation en masse was made by the First Congress in excluding federal courts from federal question jurisdiction, which was left to the state courts.[152] Legislative courts, moreover, are not mentioned in the Constitution; they are a judicial construct and are therefore subject to court-imposed limitations on their own creation. Congressional control stands on higher ground because the Framers gave it express sanction without a hint that it might be curtailed in the interest of tenure-salary protection. Let us consider Sager's explanation under the head of "judicial independence."

D. Judicial Independence

The keystone of Sager's "essential function" argument is that "[t]he tenure and compensation provisions of article III manifest a clear commitment to judicial independence."[153] Let that be admitted, and the question arises: independence for what? Independence is essential to protect judges who enforce constitutional limitations, but it does not constitute a commission to ride roughshod over rights reserved to the states by the tenth amendment.[154] Hamilton wrote that independence was necessary so that judges could act as "faithful guardians . . . [against] legislative invasions" of the Constitution.[155] Little did the Framers contemplate that the judges were free to substitute their own "invasions" for those of the legislature. To the contrary, the Supreme Court declared that the judicial power was "indispensible, not merely to maintain the supremacy" of federal law "but also to *guard the States* from any *encroachment* upon their reserved rights by the General Government."[156] The Framers did not mean the "guardians" to behave after the fashion of a fox guarding a chicken yard—quite the contrary. The courts, Hamilton states, may not, "on the pretense of a repugnancy, . . . substitute their own pleasure to the constitutional intentions of the legislature";[157] and by the same token, they may not override the powers reserved to the states

[148]*Id.* at 60 (footnotes omitted).
[149]*Id.* (emphasis added) (footnotes omitted).
[150]*Id.*
[151]*Id.* at 63 (footnotes omitted).
[152]"For 125 years, the Supreme Court lacked jurisdiction over state cases upholding federal claims of right; for ninety-six of these years, the lower federal courts lacked federal question jurisdiction. During this period, it was thus impossible for many cases to reach any federal court." *Id.* at 36 (footnotes omitted). Contrast Sager's statement: "Unrestricted use of the state courts as the exclusive forum for article III business is as inconsistent with the constitutional commitment to a radically independent federal judiciary as would be unrestricted use of article I tribunals." *Id.* at 64–65. How is this to be reconciled with the Founders' exclusive commitment of federal question jurisdiction to the state courts, with large gaps in appellate review?
[153]*Id.* at 61.
[154]Hamilton affirmed that "every act of a delegated authority, contrary to the tenor of a commission [*e.g.,* desegregation] under which it is exercised, is void." THE FEDERALIST NO. 78, at 505 (A. Hamilton) (Mod. Libr. ed. 1937).
[155]*Id.* at 509.
[156]Ableman v. Booth, 62 U.S. (21 How.) 506, 520 (1859) (emphasis added).
[157]THE FEDERALIST NO. 78, at 507 (A. Hamilton) (Mod. Libr. ed. 1937).

without clear constitutional warrant. He assured the ratifiers that judges could be impeached for "deliberate usurpations on the authority of the legislature,"[158] and a fortiori for setting aside the will of the Framers. Independence, in short, was not intended to be a shield for judicial usurpation.

Sager argues that "[t]he framers did not intend to put in article III two major premises at war with one another."[159] The "war" between the tenure-salary provisions and congressional control of jurisdiction is a figment of his imagination. The First Congress withheld "large portions" of the Court's appellate jurisdiction and all federal question jurisdiction from the inferior courts,[160] utterly oblivious to the alleged incompatibility with judicial independence. Independence requires that judges be left free to *decide* causes committed to them; it has no relevance to what jurisdiction must be conferred upon them. It is late in the day to argue, for example, that removal of jurisdiction by the Norris-LaGuardia Act to issue labor injunctions undermined judicial independence. That argument had to wait for Sager.

He observes that "[t]he point of the article III compromise was to give Congress discretion over the size and shape of the subordinate federal judiciary, and the tenure and salary provisions should not be read to swallow up this clear understanding."[161] The unequivocal grant of power to make "exceptions" is no less clear and no more "swallowed up" by those provisions. As long as courts remain free to *decide* cases that are confided to them, their independence is not "swallowed up." Whether they should be vested with jurisdiction to decide cases arising in any given jurisdictional area was left to Congress, as the Court repeatedly has recognized, with never an intimation that judicial independence was threatened in the slightest.

E. Uniformity

Sager also attaches great weight to the need for preserving the Court's appellate jurisdiction in the interest of uniformity: "With the courts of fifty states ruling independently on the constitutionality of challenged federal programs, the frequent result would be chaos of a magnitude that we have thus far been unable to produce in our legal system."[162] If a choice had to be made between preservation of uniformity and shielding the Court from congressional correction of its invasion of rights reserved to the states, there can be little doubt that the Framers would have sacrificed uniformity. That they did not regard uniformity as indispensable is evidenced by the following: (1) the Judiciary Act "authorized review of only certain types of state cases 'arising under' federal law";[163] (2) "The Court was not granted general powers to review major criminal federal cases until 1891";[164] (3) the First Congress withheld "large portions of section 2 jurisdiction" from the Court;[165] (4) Hamilton, who had perceived the need for uniformity in *Federalist No. 22*,[166] nevertheless rejected the argument that the " 'usurpations of the Supreme Court . . . will be uncontrollable and remediless.' "[167]

Sager himself states that "[i]n the context of state court rulings on the constitutionality of *state* conduct, I think that the need for uniformity is very much overstated."[168] This takes in most of the areas—segregation, suffrage, death penalties, school prayer—in which judicial interference

---

[158]THE FEDERALIST NO. 81, at 527 (A. Hamilton) (Mod. Libr. ed. 1937).

[159]Sager, *supra* note 1, at 67.

[160]*See supra* note 152.

[161]Sager, *supra* note 1, at 65.

[162]*Id.* at 40 (footnotes omitted).

[163]Sager, *supra* note 1, at 53 n.105.

[164]*Id.*

[165]*Id.* at 31. *See supra* text accompanying note 77.

[166]THE FEDERALIST NO. 22, at 138–39 (A. Hamilton) (Mod. Libr. ed. 1937).

[167]THE FEDERALIST NO. 81, at 523 (A. Hamilton) (Mod. Libr. ed. 1937).

[168]Sager, *supra* note 1, at 40 n.67 (emphasis in original).

has engendered hostility, and where the Court, in the absence of federal legislation, interposed to strike down "state conduct."[169] With respect to review of federal conduct, Sager states that "uniformity and institutional self-defense were matters that could have been safely entrusted to the discretion of Congress."[170] Finally, he states that the Court need not "itself review state court decisions that repudiate constitutional claims against state conduct" and that it would suffice to provide "effective supervision of state conduct by employing the existing lower federal judiciary."[171] Hamilton was more specific: "instead of being carried to the Supreme Court, [appeals] may be made to lie from the State courts to district courts of the Union."[172] The decisions of the district courts are by no means uniform.

F. Due Process

Sager considers that "divestiture of both state and federal jurisdiction would create fatal due process problems."[173] Although he regards the due process clause as "vague and abstract,"[174] he does not pause to inquire how rights expressly reserved to the states by the tenth amendment can be curtailed under cover of "vague" language. The Founders scarcely contemplated that the fifth amendment would constitute an instrument for emasculating the tenth. Rather, the fifth was meant to apply to delegated powers and "constitutional" rights, not to those created by the Court without constitutional warrant. In truth, the clause is "vague" only for those whose purposes are served by vagueness. Summarizing 400 years of English history, Hamilton stated on the eve of the Convention that "[t]he words *due process* have a precise technical import, and are only applicable to the process and proceedings of the courts of justice; they can never be referred to an act of legislature."[175] Charles P. Curtis, whose *Lions Under the Throne*[176] is a paean to the Justices, said that the meaning of due process in the fifth amendment "was as fixed and definite as the common law could make a phrase. . . . It meant a procedural due process. . . ."[177] The meaning of due process in the fourteenth amendment is the same as in the fifth.[178] Consequently, the Court may not in the name of due process invalidate a statute. The Court itself declared in *Davidson v. New*

---

[169]*See supra* note 59.

[170]Sager, *supra* note 1, at 57.

[171]*Id.* at 56.

[172]THE FEDERALIST NO. 82, at 538 (A. Hamilton) (Mod. Libr. ed. 1937).

[173]Sager, *supra* note 1, at 41 n.70. I was of the same opinion in 1969; but more extended research and reflection led me to change my view. For detailed explanation see. R. BERGER, DEATH PENALTIES, *supra* note 10, at 158–72.

Sager also invokes "the equal protection tradition of the fifth amendment's due process clause." Sager, *supra* note 1, at 78. That "tradition" was born in Bolling v. Sharpe, 347 U.S. 497 (1954), wherein Chief Justice Warren, his biographer tells us, said that segregation "was being outlawed because its continuance was 'unthinkable' after the outlawing of segregation in the states in *Brown*. That argument made sense primarily as an ethical proposition." G. WHITE, *supra* note 17, at 227. In terms of constitutional analysis it compounded the rape of the fourteenth amendment, from which the framers had excluded segregation, by reading into the fifth amendment the equal protection of the fourteenth. An ardent admirer and former clerk of Warren, John Hart Ely, condemned this as "gibberish both syntactically and historically." J. ELY, DEMOCRACY AND DISTRUST 32 (1980). Some tradition!

[174]Sager, *supra* note 1, at 44.

[175]4 THE PAPERS OF ALEXANDER HAMILTON 35 (H. Syrett & J. Cooke eds. 1962) (emphasis in original); *see generally* Berger, *"Law of the Land" Reconsidered,* 74 NW. U.L. REV. 1 (1979).

[176]C. CURTIS, LIONS UNDER THE THRONE (1947).

[177]Curtis, *Review and Majority Rule,* in SUPREME COURT AND SUPREME LAW 170, 177 (E. Cahn ed. 1954). The Court itself confessed error, referring to "our abandonment of the 'vague contours' of the Due Process Clause to nullify laws which a majority of the Court believed to be economically unwise." Ferguson v. Skrupa, 372 U.S. 726, 731 (1963) (footnotes omitted). "We have returned," it said, "to the original constitutional principle that courts do not substitute their social and economic beliefs for the judgment of the legislative bodies, who are elected to pass laws." *Id.* at 730.

[178]*See* Hurtado v. California, 110 U.S. 516, 535 (1884).

Orleans,[179] per Justice Miller, that the Barons did not by Magna Carta's "law of the land" intend to "protect themselves against the enactment of laws" by Parliament.[180] They sought protection against arbitrary deprivations by King John without the shelter of judicial proceedings under standing law. One who was brought to trial had to be charged with violation of a "standing law" and to have a fair trial of the issues posed by that law; but a change in the "standing law" after trial nowise violated due process.[181] There is not the faintest historical foundation for an argument that Magna Carta rendered Parliament powerless to change "standing law."

An attempt to insulate decisions that unconstitutionally[182] strike down state statutes on the ground that a claimant is entitled to a fair trial on such issues is the sheerest bootstrap lifting. To insist that a claimant of a right created by judicial arrogation must be given a judicial hearing for assertion of that right is to maintain that the Court must be allowed to pass on its own violation of the Constitution, to be the judge in its own cause for the insulation of judicial wrongdoing.

Whatever may be the limitations of congressional power under article III, so far as rights are asserted against the states under the fourteenth amendment, they are subject to section 5, which, as "the last expression of the will of the lawmaker, prevails over an earlier one."[183] Section 5 provides, "*Congress* shall have power to enforce . . . the provisions of this article."[184] Giving effect to the negative pregnant, the Court emphasized in *Ex parte Virginia*[185] that this power was given to Congress, not the courts,[186] as a number of Justices have reemphasized.[187] Judicial enforcement against the will of Congress would convert "Congress shall" into "the Court shall," usurping a power withheld, for discretion to enforce was left to Congress. Section 5 does not provide that "Congress *shall* enforce," but rather that "Congress *shall have power* to enforce."[188] Elsewhere I have collected the historical evidence that the framers meant to exclude the Court from making "political decisions."[189] Commenting on section 2 of the fifteenth amendment, the analogue of section 2 of the fourteenth, Senator Oliver Morton, a framer of the fourteenth, stated that "the remedy for the violation of the fourteenth and fifteenth amendments *was expressly not left to the courts,*" but was to "be enforced by legislation on the part of Congress."[190] Senator Matthew Carpenter said, "We must legislate, and *then commit* the enforcement of our laws to the Federal tribunals. . . ."[191] What Congress "commits" it can withdraw.

Moreover, the due process clause, like other provisions of section 1, is governed by section 5.

---

[179]96 U.S. 97 (1877).

[180]*Id.* at 102.

[181]*See* Berger, *"Law of the Land" Reconsidered,* 74 Nw. U.L. Rev. 1, 2–5, 29–30 (1979).

[182]In Erie R.R. v. Tompkins, 304 U.S. 64 (1938), the Court, per Justice Brandeis, branded the doctrine of Swift v. Tyson, 41 U.S. (16 Pet.) 1 (1842), as an " 'unconstitutional assumption of powers by courts of the United States which no lapse of time or respectable array of opinion should make us hesitate to correct.' " 304 U.S. 64, 79 (1938) (quoting Black & White Taxicab & Transfer Co. v. Brown & Yellow Taxicab & Transfer Co., 276 U.S. 518, 533 (1928) (Holmes, J., dissenting)).

[183]Schick v. United States, 195 U.S. 65, 68–69 (1904).

[184]U.S. Const. amend. XIV, § 5 (emphasis added).

[185]100 U.S. 339 (1879).

[186]*Id.* at 345.

[187]*See, e.g.,* Harper v. Virginia Bd. of Elections, 383 U.S. 663, 678–79 (1966) (Black, J., dissenting); United States v. Guest, 383 U.S. 745, 783 n.7 (1966) (Brennan, J., dissenting, joined by Warren, C.J., and Douglas, J.).

[188]U.S. Const. amend. XIV, § 5 (emphasis added). In Oregon v. Mitchell, 400 U.S. 112 (1970) (separate opinion), Justice Douglas declared that "[t]he manner of enforcement involves discretion; but that discretion is largely [in fact, entirely] entrusted to the Congress, not to the courts." *Id.* at 143. Justice Iredell stated that where the legislators "only exercise a discretion expressly confided to them by the constitution . . . [i]t is a discretion no more controulable . . . by a Court . . . than a judicial determination is by them. . . ." Ware v. Hylton, 3 U.S. (3 Dall.) 199, 266 (1796).

[189]*See* R. Berger, Death Penalties, *supra* note 10, at 169–70.

[190]Cong. Globe, 42nd Cong., 2d Sess. 525 (1872) (emphasis added).

[191]*Id.* at 879 (emphasis added).

The clause is one of the "provisions" that "Congress shall have power to enforce." Consequently, even the due process clause comes into play only after Congress exercises that "power" and "commits" enforcement of the clause to the courts. To require a judicial trial against the will of Congress would be to take over the power granted to Congress alone, thereby depriving section 5 of its intended effect. In short, the due process clause of the fourteenth amendment is subordinate to section 5, for the framers left it in the discretion of Congress whether to provide an enforcement proceeding.[192]

G. Jurisdiction to Decide Jurisdiction

"Courts and commentators," Sager notes, "agree that Congress' discretion in granting jurisdiction to the lower federal courts implies that those courts take jurisdiction from Congress and not from article III."[193] The "lower federal courts do not have a constitutional grant of jurisdiction on which to fall back. Still, this structural embarrassment does not render the lower courts as vulnerable to congressional bullying as one might suppose."[194] His escape hatch is "jurisdiction to decide jurisdiction."[195] Recognizing that a court "cannot generate its own jurisdiction," that "jurisdiction has to come from some external source—typically the relevant constitution or legislature"[196]—he considers that the "court's responsibilities as a court within our constitutional scheme would require it to invalidate a restriction on its capacity to measure its grants of jurisdiction against the Constitution."[197] This he deduces from the postulate that "[a]s long as the district court continues to exist as a court, it enjoys jurisdiction to determine whether it has jurisdiction. Without such pump-priming jurisdiction, a court could not function. . . ."[198] But a district court "exists as a court" by the grace of Congress; such existence does not generate its own jurisdiction.[199] "Jurisdiction to decide jurisdiction," Sager recognizes, is "not self-generated; it is implicit in the grant or grants of jurisdiction upon which the court is founded."[200] How can an "implicit" grant survive the withdrawal of the express grant from which it is derived? It is part and parcel of the express grant and falls with it. Otherwise the "implicit" grant would authorize the court to defeat withdrawal of the express grant.[201] Although the 1789 Judiciary Act withheld all federal question jurisdiction, no district court ever questioned the constitutionality of that withholding (which stands on the same plane as a withdrawal) by virtue of its jurisdiction to decide jurisdiction. Sager overlooks what *McCardle* held:

> What, then, is the effect of the repealing act upon the case before us? We cannot doubt as to this. Without jurisdiction the court *cannot proceed at all* in any cause. Jurisdiction is power to declare the law, and when it ceases to exist, the only function remaining to the court is that of announcing the fact and dismissing the cause.[202]

---

[192][T]he jurisdiction having been conferred [by Congress on the inferior courts] may, at the will of Congress, be taken away in whole or in part; and if withdrawn . . . all pending cases through cognizable when commenced must fall. A right which thus comes into existence only by virtue of an act of Congress, and which may be withdrawn by an act of Congress after its exercise has begun, cannot well be described as a constitutional right.
Kline v. Burke Constr. Co., 260 U.S. 226, 234 (1922) (citations omitted).

[193]Sager, *supra* note 1, at 25 (footnote omitted).

[194]*Id.* at 26.

[195]*Id.* at 22.

[196]*Id.*

[197]*Id.* at 27.

[198]*Id.* at 26.

[199]Sager observes that the "existence" of the inferior courts "was left to the discretion of Congress." *Id.* at 48 (footnote omitted).

[200]*Id.* at 22.

[201]*See supra* note 192.

[202]*Ex parte* McCardle, 74 U.S. (7 Wall.) 506, 514 (1869) (emphasis added); *see also supra* note 192.

Next Sager turns to "the possibility that the lower courts can fall back on the statutory grants of jurisdiction that they enjoyed before Congress employed the limitation."[203] Assuming that Congress "does not intend to dismantle the federal judiciary,"[204] he argues that the

> strong likelihood that the pre-existing general grants of jurisdiction would survive an unconstitutional attempt to limit them . . . enables the lower courts to strike down the offending limitation and to hear the excluded case in exercise of their surviving jurisdiction. This is in fact what took place in the wake of *United States v. Klein.*[205]

Klein, we have seen, merely rejected Congress' attempt to "prescribe a rule for the decision of a cause in a particular way"[206] for a case that had already been decided; it did not involve a withdrawal of jurisdiction.[207] On Sager's reasoning, once a grant of general jurisdiction is made, Congress is powerless to withdraw particular subject matters except with the consent of the courts. That would undo Congress' plenary power over the jurisdiction of the inferior federal courts; and it conflicts with the holding of *McCardle* and of *Kline v. Burke Construction Co.*[208] "Surviving jurisdiction" allows the district courts to decide subject matter cases that Congress left untouched, not to resist particular withdrawals from the general grant.

IV. CONCLUSION

Sager's attack on Congress' control of federal jurisdiction is a tapestry of cobwebs. In essence, he urges that the unequivocal terms of article III cannot mean what they say.[209] The legislative history lends him cold comfort; from its silence he would wrest an inference that the Framers could not so drastically have altered their scheme of judicial review,[210] overlooking that the Framers regarded the proposed federal judiciary with far more apprehension than does Sager[211] and at most authorized it to police the constitutional boundaries,[212] not to redraw them. The Judiciary Act of 1789, enacted by the First Congress, which was privy to the Framers' intention, stands like a roadblock before every branch of Sager's arguments. It withheld the entire "arising under" jurisdiction from the lower courts and, by Sager's own testimony, left large gaps and gaping holes in the appellate jurisdiction of the Supreme Court.[213] The few particularized removals proposed by current bills do not remotely approach the 1789 Act's wholesale withholding. Manifestly, the First Congress did not consider that it was "unravel[ling] one of the most basic aspects of the constitutional scheme."[214] Its construction was immediately accepted by the Court, and in no case has the Court repudiated its unbroken line of decisions. A prior attempt to distinguish those cases

---

[203]Sager, *supra* note 1, at 27.

[204]*Id.* at 28.

[205]*Id.* at 29 (footnote omitted).

[206]United States v. Klein, 80 U.S. (13 Wall.) 128, 146 (1872).

[207]*See supra* text accompanying notes 94–104.

[208]*See supra* notes 202 & 192 and accompanying text.

[209]*See* Sager, *supra* note 1, at 42, 44–45.

[210]*See supra* note 37.

[211]*See supra* note 50. The exclusion of the lower courts from the federal question jurisdiction is one item of evidence. Another is Hamilton's assurance that of the three branches "the judiciary is next to nothing." THE FEDERALIST No. 78, at 504 n.* (A. Hamilton) (Mod. Libr. ed. 1937).

[212]R. BERGER, CONGRESS, *supra* note 52, at 13–16. For John Marshall's statement in the Virginia Ratification Convention, see *id.* at 16 n.39.

[213]*See supra* note 78, and text accompanying note 149.

[214]Sager, *supra* note 1, at 51.

dismissed them as "dicta";[215] but 175 years of dicta by respected Justices, in which a unanimous Court joined, may be preferred to Sager's novel and palpably untenable readings. He has journeyed far afield for analogies, but in vain; the cases simply are not to be shrivelled by his theorizing. He concedes that "two hundred years of consistent behavior by Congress and the Supreme Court" indicate that Congress has "at least some power to limit the Court's jurisdiction."[216] What are the boundaries of that power? Sager's attempts to frame limitations on the plenary grant to Congress are, in my judgment, fruitless.

By all but exclusively focusing on the proposed congressional cure while resolutely shutting his eyes to the disease, Sager recalls a comment by a member of the House of Commons in 1742 (when it was considering an inquiry into the fallen regime of Robert Walpole): "Would not a Physician be a Madman, to prescribe to a Patient, without first examining into the State of his Distemper, the Causes from which it arose."[217] Sager has not paused to inquire into the causes which led Congress to propose its cure—the substitution by the Justices of their predilections for the Framers' choices. That is the cardinal problem going to the roots of our democratic system—the right of the people, however misguided, to govern themselves.

Now we have a study which lays bare with startling clarity what hitherto has only been a subject of inference and surmise—the process whereby Chief Justice Warren, that beau ideal of activist Justices, identified his personal beliefs with constitutional mandates. It has been noted that Warren "was never concerned with constitutional text or intention. Rather he believed that his job as a judge lay in discovering and articulating the 'ethical imperatives' he felt were (or should be) embedded in the Constitution for what it provided or its Framers intended."[218] That substitution is catalogued by his worshipful biographer, G. Edward White, in fascinating detail, and because it is rarely acknowledged by most academicians and generally concealed from the public,[219] it deserves to be highlighted. Warren's lip service to "the limits of the Constitution" was at odds with his actions, as *Trop v. Dulles*[220] exemplifies. While purporting to "apply those limits as the Constitution prescribes them,"[221] he was in fact rewriting them to fit his private notions of "the dignity of man."[222]

At issue was the constitutionality of an act expatriating a citizen for desertion of the armed forces in time of war. For Warren, citizenship was "man's basic right,"[223] though, as White notes, it had no "support in the case law," and "there was no indication in the Constitution that citizenship was a specially protected right that could not be divested, let alone that it was a fundamental

---

[215]Ratner, *Congressional Power over the Appellate Jurisdiction of the Supreme Court,* 109 U. PA. L. REV. 157. 173–83 (1960). *But see supra* note 73.

[216]Sager, *supra* note 1, at 33.

[217]13 THE HISTORY AND PROCEEDINGS OF THE HOUSE OF COMMONS 85 (R. Chandler ed. 1743).

[218]*See supra* note 17.

[219]In the midst of Franklin Roosevelt's Court-packing plan (1937), Professor Felix Frankfurter wrote him: "People have been taught to believe that when the Supreme Court speaks it is not they who speak but the Constitution, whereas, of course, in so many vital cases, it is *they* who speak and *not* the Constitution." ROOSEVELT AND FRANKFURTER: THEIR CORRESPONDENCE 1928–1945, at 383 (M. Freedman ed. 1967) (emphasis in original). *See also* Kauper. *The Supreme Court: Hybrid Organ of State,* 21 Sw. L.J. 573, 579–80 (1967). Michael Perry remarks, "After all, it is a radical thing to say, and a thing not often said, that the source of judgment is the judge's own values." M. PERRY, *supra* note 13, at 123. Martin Shapiro wrote, "It would be fantastic indeed if the Supreme Court, in the name of sound scholarship, were to disavow publicly the myth on which its power rests." M. SHAPIRO, LAW AND POLITICS IN THE SUPREME COURT 27 (1964). It is not "scholarship," but obedience to constitutional limitations that calls for candid renunciation of unauthorized practices.

[220]356 U.S. 86 (1958).

[221]*Id.* at 104. *See supra* text accompanying notes 14–16.

[222]356 U.S. 86, 100 (1958). For detailed discussion of *Trop v. Dulles* see R. BERGER, DEATH PENALTIES, *supra* note 10, at 116–22.

[223]Perez v. Brownell, 356 U.S. 44, 64 (1958) (Warren, C.J., dissenting).

right."[224] Since "five justices had rejected his view of citizenship," he invoked the eighth amendment: expatriation was a cruel and unusual punishment.[225] But banishment had been a staple of English law and that of the Revolutionary American states.[226] Warren reasoned, however, that expatriation destroyed the "political existence"[227] of the individual, though as White remarks, the language of the Constitution

> suggested that a political existence could be restricted to qualified persons. . . . Warren, in short, had made no serious effort . . . to analyze the doctrinal history or the current doctrinal status of the Eighth Amendment. He had *simply asserted* that since citizenship was man's most basic right, involuntary expatriation was necessarily a cruel and unusual punishment.[228]

Thus he substituted what he felt the law should be for the unvarying English and American law to the contrary.

Warren's most spectacular decision—*Brown v. Board of Education,*[229] the desegregation case— was to serve as his inspiration for future forays. That decency called for an end to the detestable practice must not obscure the fact that the Constitution does not authorize the Court to strike it down.[230] Judicial revision of the Constitution for benign purposes is not its own justification. Addressing a judge's resort to his "individual sense of justice," Cardozo wrote, "That might result in a benevolent despotism if the judges were benevolent men. It would put an end to the reign of law."[231] Our system is committed to "Equal Justice *Under* Law" not to "Justices Above the Law." They were not authorized to revise the Constitution in the interests of "justice."

Two of the most practiced constitutional lawyers on the Court, Justices Frankfurter and Jackson, "were hard pressed to find an adequate rationale for overruling *Plessy [v. Ferguson].*"[232] Frankfurter had suggested that "nothing in the Fourteenth Amendment prevented racial segregation in the states,"[233] a view that even activist academicians have now been constrained to accept.[234] Warren began with rejecting the "premise that blacks were inferior to whites" and hence "was prepared to invalidate segregation."[235] As Warren saw it, "The practice of racial segregation in the public schools . . . was immoral and therefore wrong; the Court's duty was to eradicate it. . . . [I]f the doctrinal analysis offended, he would modify it or delete it"[236]—a short and easy way with constitutional obstacles. The *Brown* opinion, White remarks, "declared racial segregation unconstitutional through appeal to contemporary social perceptions rather than to constitutional doctrine."[237] But that approach had been rejected at the very outset by Hamilton: "Until the people have, by some solemn and authoritative act [amendment], annulled or changed the established form, it is

[224]G. WHITE, *supra* note 17, at 233–34.

[225]*Id.* at 232.

[226]*See* R. BERGER, DEATH PENALTIES, *supra* note 10, at 117.

[227]356 U.S. 86, 101 (1958).

[228]G. WHITE, *supra* note 17, at 233 (emphasis added).

[229]347 U.S. 483 (1954).

[230]*See supra* note 43.

[231]B. CARDOZO, THE NATURE OF THE JUDICIAL PROCESS 136 (1921). Lord Mansfield said that "[w]hatever doubts I may have in my own breast with respect to the policy and expedience of this law, . . . I am bound to see it executed according to its meaning." Pray v. Edie, 99 Eng. Rep. 1113, 1114 (1786).

[232]G. WHITE, *supra* note 17, at 162.

[233]*Id.* at 166.

[234]*See supra* note 40.

[235]G. WHITE, *supra* note 17, at 165.

[236]*Id.* at 228. On the other hand, Chief Justice Marshall declared that "the constitution . . . was not intended to furnish the corrective for every abuse of power which may be committed by the state governments." Providence Bank v. Billings, 29 U.S. (4 Pet.) 514, 563 (1830).

[237]G. WHITE, *supra* note 17, at 170.

binding . . . and no presumption, or even knowledge, of their sentiments, can warrant their representatives in a departure from it, prior to such an act."[238]

The "social perceptions" were Warren's, not those of the people for whom he purported to speak, as is illustrated in the Court's rejection of Jackson's plea that they tell the people they were "declaring new law for a new day"[239] well knowing that such an admission would raise a fire storm. Activists acknowledge that in 1954 it would have been impossible to procure an amendment barring segregation in the schools;[240] since then racism has been exacerbated.[241] White states, "The ideal behind *Brown*—the intuitive justice of equality of opportunity—was an ideal not explicitly codified in the Constitution."[242] That is a masterly understatement, for the framers of the fourteenth amendment restricted equality to a very narrow category of rights: to contract, own property, and have access to the courts.[243] Senator William Fessenden, Chairman of the Joint Committee on Reconstruction, said, "[W]e cannot put into the Constitution, owing to existing prejudices and existing institutions, an entire exclusion of all class distinctions. . . ."[244] So too, Thaddeus Stevens, the implacable opponent of discrimination, lamented that he had hoped so to remodel "all our institutions as to have freed them from every vestige of . . . inequality of rights, . . . [so] that no distinction would be tolerated. . . . This bright dream has vanished. . . ."[245] Thus the leaders confessed that complete equality was legislatively unattainable, as in fact the repeated rejection of attempts to ban all discrimination attested.[246] That is a deplorable, but nonetheless undeniable, historical fact. It is open to the people to alter it by an amendment—the course activists so blithely recommend to proponents of congressional control of jurisdiction. No power of amendment was granted to the Court.

What Warren regarded as the jewel in his crown,[247] the reapportionment decision,[248] proceeded in the teeth of the framers' incontrovertible exclusion of suffrage from the fourteenth amendment.[249] White notes that "the right to vote was sharply qualified at the time of the framing of the Constitution,"[250] and adds, "If the states were not prohibited by the Constitution from restricting

---

[238]THE FEDERALIST NO. 78, at 509 (A. Hamilton) (Mod. Libr. ed. 1937). For the Framers this was a basic postulate. *See infra* text accompanying note 282.

[239]R. KLUGER, SIMPLE JUSTICE 681 (1976). In a file memorandum Jackson wrote, "[D]espite my personal satisfaction with the Court's [forthcoming] judgment, I simply can not find, in surveying all the usual sources of law, anything which warrants me in saying that it is required by the original purpose and intent of the Fourteenth or Fifth Amendment." *Id.* at 689.

[240]Brest, *The Misconceived Quest for the Original Understanding*, 60 B.U.L. Rev. 204, 237 (1980). Edmond Cahn stated that "as a practical matter it would have been impossible to secure adoption of a constitutional amendment to abolish 'separate but equal.' " Cahn, *Jursiprudence*, 30 N.Y.U. L. REV. 150, 156 (1955).

[241]For citations see R. BERGER, GOVERNMENT BY JUDICIARY, *supra* note 43, at 327–28.

[242]G. WHITE, *supra* note 17, at 170.

[243]For the massive evidence, see R. BERGER, GOVERNMENT BY JUDICIARY, *supra* note 43, at 117–33.

[244]CONG. GLOBE, 39th Cong., 1st Sess. 705 (1866).

[245]*Id.* at 3148.

[246]*See* R. BERGER, GOVERNMENT BY JUDICIARY, *supra* note 43, at 163–64.

[247]G. WHITE, *supra* note 17, at 238.

[248]Baker v. Carr, 369 U.S. 186 (1962).

[249]Justice Harlan reminded the Court that its reapportionment decisions were "made in the face of irrefutable and still unanswered history to the contrary." Griswold v. Connecticut, 381 U.S. 479, 501 (1965) (concurring opinion). Activist Louis Lusky refers to Harlan's "irrefutable and unrefuted demonstration" to that effect. Lusky, Book Review, 6 HASTINGS CONST. L.Q. 403, 406 (1979). *See also* Abraham, Book Review, *id.* at 467–68; Mendelson, Book Review, *id.* at 453; Nathanson, Book Review, 56 TEX. L. REV. 579, 581 (1978). Gerald Gunther wrote,

The ultimate justification for the *Reynolds* ruling is hard, if not impossible, to set forth in constitutionally legitimate terms. It rests, rather, on the view that courts are authorized to step in when injustices exist and other institutions fail to act. That is a dangerous—and I think illegitimate—prescription for judicial action.

Gunther, *Some Reflections on the Judicial Role: Distinctions, Roots and Prospects*, 1979 WASH. U.L.Q. 817, 825.

[250]G. WHITE, *supra* note 17, at 236.

the right to vote itself . . . it would seem to suggest that 'the right to vote freely' was not initially regarded as something essential to a representative form of government."[251] Warren, however, asserted "that a constitutional right to have one's vote counted equally existed" and that a denial of that right violates ' "the essence of a democratic society.' "[252] White comments,

> Warren had based his purported usurpation of legislative prerogatives on an interpretation of the Constitution that was neither faithful to its literal text nor consistent with the context in which it had been framed. He had substituted homilies such as '[c]itizens, not history or economic interests, cast votes' for doctrinal analysis.[253]

The "history" Warren dismissed was the framers' determination to exclude suffrage from the fourteenth amendment. Let White sum up: "[I]n none of the leading activist Warren Court decisions was a constitutional mandate obvious. *Brown v. Board of Education* reversed a long-established precedent on the basis of social science evidence. *Baker v. Carr* found a judicial power to review the political judgments of legislators where none had previously existed."[254] He concludes, "[W]hen one divorces Warren's opinions from their ethical premises, they evaporate. . . . [T]hey are individual examples of [Warren's own] beliefs leading to judgments."[255]

His thinking was colored by yet another high-handed notion—that the meaning of constitutional terms changes with the times. "The Bill of Rights *needed revision* with time. 'We will pass on,' Warren said, a 'document [that] will not have exactly the same meaning it had when we received it from our fathers.' "[256] Thereby he laid claim to the prerogative of Humpty-Dumpty: "When *I* use a word, . . . it means just what I choose it to mean."[257] A judge who pours his own meaning into constitutional terms lays claim to power to amend the Constitution, as Chief Justice Taney perceived: "If in this court we are at liberty to give old words new meanings . . . , there is no power which may not, by this mode of construction, be conferred on the general government and denied to the States."[258] In this he echoed Madison and Jefferson.[259] And it remained the view of the

---

[251]*Id.* at 238.

[252]*Id.* (quoting Reynolds v. Sims, 377 U.S. 533, 555 (1964)).

[253]G. WHITE, *supra* note 17, at 239 (footnote omitted) (quoting Reynolds v. Sims, 377 U.S. 533, 580 (1964)).

[254]G. WHITE, *supra* note 17, at 357.

[255]*Id.* at 367.

[256]*Id.* at 223 (emphasis added). His friend Justice Black tartly dismissed "rhapsodical strains, about the duty of the Court to keep the Constitution in tune with the times. . . . The Constitution makers knew the need for change and provided for it" by the amendment process of article V. Griswold v. Connecticut, 381 U.S. 479, 522 (1965) (dissenting opinion). In a 1784 pamphlet Thomas Tudor Tucker of South Carolina wrote that the Constitution "should prescribe the limits of all delegated power. It should be declared to be . . . unalterable by any authority but the express consent of a majority of the citizens collected by such regular mode as may be therein provided." G. WOOD, THE CREATION OF THE AMERICAN REPUBLIC 1776–1787, at 281 (1969). Wood commented that this "remarkable" pamphlet "summed up what Americans had done in two decades to the conception of a constitution. . . . It was a conclusive statement that has not essentially changed in two hundred years." *Id.* at 280–81.

In the Convention, George Mason said, "The plan now to be formed will certainly be defective. . . . Amendments therefore will be necessary, and it will be better to provide for them, in an easy, regular and Constitutional way. . . ." 1 THE RECORDS OF THE FEDERAL CONVENTION OF 1787, at 202–03 (M. Farrand ed. 1911). He considered article V dangerous because the amendment process required initiation by Congress, so that "the whole people of America can't make, or even propose alterations to it." 2 *id.*, at 629 n.8. Activists would endow the Court with a power denied to the people themselves without congressional intervention.

[257]L. CARROLL, THROUGH THE LOOKING GLASS 163 (Norton ed. 1971) (emphasis in original). John Hart Ely considers that we are not "free to make the Constitution mean whatever we please." Ely, *The Supreme Court 1977 Term—Foreword: On Discovering Fundamental Values*, 92 HARV. L. REV. 5 (1978).

[258]Smith v. Turner (The Passenger Cases), 48 U.S. (7 How.) 283, 478 (1849).

[259]If "the sense in which the Constitution was accepted and ratified by the nation . . . be not the guide in expounding it, there can be no security . . . for a faithful exercise of its powers." 9 THE WRITINGS OF JAMES MADISON 191 (G. Hunt ed. 1900–1910). Jefferson pledged as President to administer the Constitution "according to the safe and *honest* meaning contem-

Reconstruction Congress. In 1872 a unanimous Senate Judiciary Committee Report, signed by Senators who had voted for the fourteenth amendment, stated, "A construction which should give the phrase . . . a meaning differing from the sense in which it was understood and employed by the people when they adopted the Constitution, would be as unconstitutional as a departure from the plain and express language of the Constitution. . . ."[260]

Warren strikingly verifies Douglas' frank avowal that in constitutional adjudication "the 'gut' reaction of a judge . . . was the main ingredient of his decision."[261] In White's words, "[t]he ethical imperatives that guided Warren as a judge reflected his personal morality":[262] his "justifications for a result were often conclusory statements of what he perceived to be ethical imperatives."[263] Often those imperatives were at war with those of the people.[264] The idiosyncratic, nakedly personal nature of his imperatives is revealed by *Marchetti v. United States*,[265] in which he decided that gamblers should not receive the protection accorded other taxpayers by the fifth amendment's self-incrimination clause. "[T]here is no evidence," White correctly comments, that the clause "was designed to protect only innocent persons, only some guilty persons, or the disclosure of only some 'incriminating' activities."[266] "It is hard to see," he says, why the law should not "be the same for gamblers as for other taxpayers."[267] "At a point," White comments, "Warren's concern with ethical imperatives comes so close to what appears to be an apology for subjective preferences in judging as to be unsupportable."[268] For, White observes, a judge has not been appointed "with an expectation that he will simply use his power to do what he thinks is fair and just."[269] In the past, liberals derisively compared such adjudication to a caliph dispensing justice under a tree. "On the contrary," White continues, "a judge is expected to 'follow the law,' 'uphold the Constitution,' [he is *sworn* to do so] and otherwise subordinate his personal preferences to some more legitimized body of wisdom."[270] When he fails to do so, he may be said to be "betraying a trust."[271] Thus, White has richly confirmed Anthony Lewis' early evaluation of Warren: " '[T]he closest thing the United States has had to a Platonic Guardian, dispensing law from a throne without any

---

plated by the *plain understanding of the people at the time of its adoption.*" 4 DEBATES IN THE SEVERAL STATE CONVENTIONS ON THE ADOPTION OF THE FEDERAL CONSTITUTION 446 (J. Elliott ed. 1827–30 & photo. reprint 1941) (quoted by John Rutledge) (emphasis in original). Such was also Chief Justice Marshall's view: if a word was understood in a certain sense "when the constitution was framed. . . . [t]he convention must have used it in that sense," and it is that sense which is to be given judicial effect. Gibbons v. Ogden, 22 U.S. (9 Wheat.) 1, 190 (1824).

[260] S. REP. NO. 21, 42nd Cong., 2d Sess. 2 (1872), *reprinted* in THE RECONSTRUCTION AMENDMENTS' DEBATES 571 (A. Avins ed. 1967).

[261] W. DOUGLAS, THE COURT YEARS, 1939–1975, at 8 (1981).

[262] G. WHITE, *supra* note 17, at 218.

[263] *Id.* at 230. Philip Kurland had made the point in 1977: " 'History may yet decide' that Warren's chief justiceship was essentially one where 'political power, including judicial power, was . . . exercised for the advancement of what was "*right* and *good*" as [Warren's] personal ideolog[y] defined those . . . terms.' " *Id.* at 220 (quoting Kurland, Book Review, 87 Yale L.J. 225, 233 (1977) (emphasis in original)).

[264] School prayer and busing, for example.

[265] 390 U.S. 39 (1968).

[266] G. WHITE, *supra* note 17, at 361.

[267] *Id.* at 365.

[268] *Id.* at 362. "The difficulty is that an approach based on ethics seems inevitably to lead one to justification of one's ethical stance. . . ." *Id.* at 365. Ely has convincingly demonstrated that a divorce between a judge's personal values and the social consensus is delusory, that what he is "really . . . 'discovering' . . . are his own values." Ely, *The Supreme Court, 1977 Term—Foreword: On Discovering Fundamental Values,* 92 HARV. L. REV. 5, 16 (1978). Ely notes that " 'Lenin used to claim this godlike gift of divination of the people's "real" interests.' " *Id.* at 51 n.198. (quoting H. MAYO, AN INTRODUCTION TO DEMOCRATIC THEORY 97 (1960)).

[269] G. WHITE, *supra* note 17, at 364.

[270] *Id.* at 364–65.

[271] *Id.* at 365.

sensed limits of power except what was seen [by him] as the good of society.' "[272] Warren's judicial conduct violated Cardozo's precept: a judge "is not a knight-errant, roaming at will in pursuit of his own ideal of beauty or of goodness. He is to draw his inspiration from consecrated principles."[273] Even less is he to overturn constitutional text or the unmistakable intention of the Framers because they do not conform to his "ethical imperatives."

Finally, a brief comment on White's approach to these facts. He is to be warmly commended for his forthright appraisal of what Warren was doing. But he errs, in my judgment, in regarding doubts about Warren's course as merely a matter of taste, a choice between opposing doctrinal premises: "In an area as open-ended and susceptible to change as constitutional interpretation, who can say that Warren's approach, which settled on the ethically dictated result first and derived traditional justifications later, is less sound than an approach conditioning results on the emergence of 'principled' reasoning?"[274] That antiseptic statement obscures that Warren displaced the framers' choices with his own; that he overturned their determination, for example, to leave suffrage to the states, a course that cannot be "derived" from traditional justifications." White also instances a "line of influential critics in the twentieth century" who rejected *Brown v. Board of Education* because "its reasoning was illegitimate. . . . No one wanted to defend 'separate but equal' segregation on moral grounds, but nothing in the Fourteenth Amendment's Equal Protection Clause prevented the practice; to invalidate it on the basis of dubious empirical research was the essence of unbridled judicial glossing of the Constitution," an example of flawed "reasoning."[275] Warren proceeded in the opposite direction, seeking to determine "the ethically required resolution of a given case."[276] White observes that "if one deplores Warren's choice, one might question what empowers him to pick and choose,"[277] or more concretely, to ignore the constitutional text or proceed in spite of the unmistakable intention of the framers to exclude suffrage and segregation from the fourteenth amendment. That is the issue, not "whether ignoring the established jurisprudential canons of judicial performance . . . constitutes 'bad' judicial reasoning."[278] The issue is whether judges are indeed, as Paul Brest asserts, not "bound by the text or original understanding of the Constitution."[279] That is far more than a matter of taste in jurisprudential canons or "principled reasoning"; it involves the Court's violation, in the words of Justice Harlan, of the very "constitutional structure [of government] which it is its highest duty to protect."[280] Since that lesson apparently has been lost on Sager as well as White, I may be indulged for rehearsing a few elementary constitutional facts.

Fearful of power, the Founders resorted to a written Constitution in order to define and limit it.[281] Their presuppositions were well summarized by Philip Kurland:

> The concept of the written constitution is that it defines the authority of government and its limits, that government is the creature of the constitution and cannot do what it does not authorize. . . . *A priori,* such a constitution could only have a fixed and unchanging meaning, if it were to fulfill its function. For

---

[272]*Id.* at 359 (quoting Lewis, *Earl Warren,* in 4 The Justices of the United States Supreme Court 1789–1969, at 2726 (1969)).

[273]B. Cardozo, The Nature of the Judicial Process 141 (1921).

[274]G. White, *supra* note 17, at 363–64.

[275]*Id.* at 360–61.

[276]*Id.* at 361.

[277]*Id.* at 365.

[278]*Id.* at 236.

[279]Brest, *The Misconceived Quest for the Original Understanding,* 60 B.U.L. Rev. 204, 224 (1980).

[280]Oregon v. Mitchell, 400 U.S. 112, 203 (1970) (Harlan, J., concurring and dissenting).

[281]"Out of this fear of absolute power arose a revolutionary contribution to the idea of establishing constitutions, i.e. from 1776 on constitutions were to be written." Sisson, *The Idea of Revolution in the Declaration of Independence and the Constitution,* in Constitutional Government in America 411 (R. Collins ed. 1980).

changed conditions, the instrument itself made provision for amendment which, in accordance with the concept of a written constitution, was expected to be the only form of change. . . .[282]

First and last, the "limited" Constitution was meant to "bind down" our delegates "from mischief by the chains of the Constitution."[283] Very early, Chief Justice Marshall, who had been a proponent of judicial review in the Virginia Ratification Convention, declared that a written constitution was designed to define and limit power; he asked, "To what purpose are powers limited, . . . if these limits may, at any time, be passed by those intended to be restrained?"[284] Among those to be restrained he included the courts,[285] later specifically disclaiming a judicial "right to change [the] instrument."[286] As we have seen, even Warren affirmed that "[w]e must apply those limits as the Constitution prescribes them."[287]

In turning his back on those limits in the interest of his personal morality, Warren fell within Justice Harlan's charge that "when the Court disregards the express intent and understanding of the Framers, it has invaded the realm of the political process to which the amending power was committed, and it has violated the constitutional structure which it is its highest duty to protect."[288] That had much earlier been forcibly stated by Justice Story:

> Nor should it ever be lost sight of, that the government of the United States is one of limited and enumerated powers, and that a departure from the true import and sense of its powers is *pro tanto* the establishment of a new constitution. It is doing for the people what they have not chosen to do for themselves. It is usurping the functions of a legislator. . . .[289]

In the upshot, White concludes, "the choices made by Warren and other advocates of judicial liberalism [i.e., revisionism] appear less as ordained principles of justice and more as *vulnerable policy judgments*"[290]—judgments the Constitution reserved to the people and their legislative representatives.

To remain attached to these fundamental principles of our democratic system is not to be "encumbered with professional cant";[291] to condemn Warren's reversal of the framers' exclusion

---

[282]P. Kurland, Watergate and the Constitution 7 (1978) (emphasis added). Justice William Paterson, a leading Framer, declared, "The constitution is certain and fixed; . . . and can be revoked or altered only by the authority that made it." Van Horne v. Dorrance, 28 F. Cas. 1012, 1014 (C.C.D. Pa. 1795) (No. 16, 857). *See also* S. Adams, *Massachusetts Circular Letter, February 11, 1768* in Documents of American History 66 (H. Commager, 7th ed. 1963).

[283]4 Debates in the Several State Conventions on the Adoption of Federal Constitution 543 (J. Elliott ed. 1827–30 & photo. reprint 1941).

[284]Marbury v. Madison, 5 U.S. (1 Cranch) 137, 176 (1803). *See also* Loan Ass'n v. Topeka, 87 U.S. (20 Wall.) 655 (1874): "The theory of our governments . . . is opposed to the deposit of unlimited power anywhere." *Id.* at 663.

[285]Marbury v. Madison, 5 U.S. (1 Cranch) 137, 179–80 (1803).

[286]John Marshall's defense of *McCulloch v. Maryland* 209 (G. Gunther ed. 1969).

[287]Trop v. Dulles, 356 U.S. 86, 104 (1958).

[288]Oregon v. Mitchell, 400 U.S. 112, 203 (1970). It needs to be remembered, as Justice Daniel vigorously stated in the License Cases, 46 U.S. (5 How.) 504 (1847), that "whether the decision of the court in such cases be itself binding . . . must depend upon its conformity with, or its warrant from, the constitution. It cannot be correctly held, that a decision, merely because it be by the Supreme Court, is to override alike the constitution and the laws both of the States and of the United States." *Id.* at 613 (Daniel, J., concurring). (For similar remarks by Justices Douglas, Frankfurter, and Chief Justice Burger, see R. Berger, Government by Judiciary, *supra* note 43, at 297 n.57.) One hundred years later Justice Brandeis, borrowing the words of Justice Holmes, branded the doctrine of Swift v. Tyson, 41 U.S. (16 Pet.) 1 (1842), an " 'unconstitutional assumption of powers by courts of the United States which no lapse of time or respectable array of opinion should make us hesitate to correct.' " Erie R.R. v. Tompkins, 304 U.S. 64, 79 (1938) (quoting Black & White Taxicab & Transfer Co. v. Brown & Yellow Taxicab & Transfer Co., 276 U.S. 518, 533 (1928) (Holmes, J., dissenting)).

[289]1 J. Story, Commentaries on the Constitution of the United States, § 426 (5th ed. 1891).

[290]G. White, *supra* note 17, at 349 (emphasis added).

[291]"Warren kept his eye on the essentials of a case—the essential facts, the essential justice of the situation—and in so doing reminded us that when the law gets encumbered with professional cant, it ceases to approximate reality and loses

of suffrage and segregation is not "professional cant." Although White concedes that Warren's ideal of "equality of opportunity" was not "explicitly codified in the Constitution"[292]—in fact it was repeatedly rejected by the framers of the fourteenth amendment—he concludes that "[t]he most eloquent statement of a white supremacist interpretation of the equal protection clauses could not be likely to gain much current acceptance. . . . [T]he premise would be considered flawed."[293] Those whose attachment to integrity of the Constitution overrides their social aspirations are not to be kissed off as "white supremacists."[294] Nor is a demand that the Court observe constitutional "limits" a "flawed premise." Would busing or the bar against school prayer "gain much current acceptance"? At bottom, White and Sager advocate judicial squatter sovereignty; having preempted territory that is not theirs, the Court's preemption is irreversible.[295]

It is unfortunate that the struggle against the substitution of the Justices' personal predilections for the text and original understanding of the framers has fallen to Senator Jesse Helms and his ilk. But scripture is not discredited because it is cited by the devil. It is a reproach to the liberal academicians, for whom the rule of law had been central, that they have abandoned their standard. For myself, I insist with Charles McIlwain that "[t]he two fundamental correlative elements of constitutionalism for which all lovers of liberty must yet fight are the legal limits to arbitrary power and a complete political responsibility of government to the governed."[296] Warren was contemptuous of such limits, and the life-tenured Justices are virtually unaccountable. Sager would make them invulnerable.[297]

V. APPENDIX

In a symposium[298] on Michael Perry's recent book,[299] which appeared after this article was in the hands of the editors, one activist referred to "existing constitutional doubt about jurisdiction removals."[300] Another stated that the legitimacy of the congressional power "is opposed by the substantial weight of scholarly opinion."[301] Neither referred to the unbroken string of Supreme

---

its reason for being." *Id.* at 367. By such statements White renders vain his disclaimer that his "attempt to elucidate Warren's jurisprudence should not be taken as an attempt to defend it in any particular." *Id.* at 230.

[292]*Id.* at 170.

[293]*Id.* at 364. Taking issue with Michael Perry's statement—"Certainly not many would take issue with . . . the Court's . . . disestablishment of laws and other official practices aimed at maintaining racial segregation"—, Ira Lupu tartly comments, "It requires the rosiest or most disingenuous distortion to make such an assertion in the face of the turbulence of school desegregation efforts since 1954." Lupu, *Constitutional Theory and the Search for the Workable Premise*, 8 U. DAYTON L. REV. 579, 593 (1983). See also Berger, *The Scope of Judicial Review: An Ongoing Debate*, 6 HASTINGS CONST. L.Q. 527, 583 (1979).

[294]In 1942 I wrote of a decision that responded to my predilections that I liked it no better when the Court read them into the Constitution than when the Four Horsemen read in theirs. Berger, *Constructive Contempt: A Post-Mortem*, 9 U. CHI. L. REV. 602, 604–05, 642 (1942).

[295]For some salty comments on such views, see Bridwell, *The Scope of Judicial Review: A Dirge for the Theorists of Majority Rule*, 31 S.C.L. REV. 617, 632–35, 653 (1980).

[296]C. MCILWAIN, CONSTITUTIONALISM: ANCIENT AND MODERN 146 (rev. ed. 1947).

[297]*But see supra* text accompanying note 25.

[298]*Judicial Review and the Constitution—the Text and Beyond*, 8 U. DAYTON L. REV. 443 (1983).

[299]M. PERRY, *supra* note 13.

[300]Lupu, *supra* note 293, at 616.

[301]Tushnet, *Legal Realism, Structural Review, and Prophecy*, 8 U. DAYTON L. REV. 809, 813 (1983). Tushnet proffers no count of noses. Among those who recognize the congressional power are Charles Black, Michael Perry, and Herbert Wechsler. *See* Berger, *Michael Perry's Functional Justification for Judicial Activism*, 8 U. DAYTON L. REV. 465, 503 (1983); Wechsler, *The Courts and the Constitution*, 65 COLUM. L. REV. 1001, 1005 (1965); Lusky, Book Review, 6 HASTINGS CONST. L.Q. 403, 406, 412 (1979); Leedes, *The Supreme Court Mess*, 57 TEX. L. REV. 1361, 1442–43 (1979); R. BERGER, DEATH PENALTIES, *supra* note 10, at 153–72.

Court pronouncements, stretching from 1796 to the present day,[302] that recognize the plenary power of Congress. Instead, a commentator cited a 1953 article by Henry Hart,[303] overlooking that in 1962 the Court approved *Ex parte McCardle* unmoved by Hart's theorizing.[304] Activists are defending the Court in contradiction of its own pronouncements. Disregard of the long line of precedents is the more remarkable given Ira Lupu's emphasis that Perry introduces "the possibility of radical discontinuity," departing "from the principles that have previously governed analogous [here the very same] matters," a "rip in the seamless web."[305] What could be more radically discontinuous than the Court's resort in 1972 to the cruel and unusual punishments clause in the teeth of universal attachment for 183 years before *Furman v. Georgia*[306] to death penalties for murder and rape;[307] or the Court's saddling upon a state support of out-of-state indigents immediately upon their arrival, thereby scrapping the contrary practice of 600 years;[308] or its substitution in 1970 of the six-man jury for the twelve-man jury to which the Founders were attached and that was rooted in centuries-old English tradition.[309] The "web," in truth, is being "ripped" by "those enthusiastic about the modern Court's work product,"[310] a part of the activist drive "to protect the legacy of the Warren Court."[311]

A significant portion of that "legacy" is the extraconstitutional rights created by the Court, which activists acknowledge are without constitutional warrant.[312] In Perry's words, "there is neither a textual nor a historical justification . . . for noninterpretivist review in human rights cases."[313] Lupu therefore begs the question in urging that jurisdiction withdrawal "is designed to prohibit the exercise of rights which the Supreme Court has been willing to protect, and to deprive those who seek to exercise such rights of any judicial forum for their vindication."[314] That the Court is "willing to protect" such rights does not confer upon the Court power that was withheld in the Constitution.[315] Nor is it opprobrious to deprive the Court of jurisdiction to enforce such unconstitutional constructs. The specification in article III of cases "arising under this Constitution" excludes cases drawn outside its bounds, for as Hamilton explained, the judicial authority extends to "certain cases particularly specified," marking "the precise limits, beyond which the federal courts cannot extend their jurisdiction."[316] One may agree with Lupu that the "arising

---

[302]Berger, *Michael Perry's Functional Justification for Judicial Activism*, 8 U. Dayton L. Rev. 465, 504–05 (1983).

[303]Alexander, *Painting Without the Numbers: Noninterpretive Judicial Review*, 8 U. Dayton L. Rev. 447, 455 (1983).

[304]Glidden Co. v. Zdanok, 370 U.S. 530, 567–68 (1962). Later Justice Douglas stated in Flast v. Cohen, 392 U.S. 83 (1968), "As respects our appellate jurisdiction, Congress may largely fashion it as Congress desires by reason of the express provisions of § 2, Art. III. See *Ex parte McCardle*. . . ." *Id.* at 109 (citation omitted).

[305]Lupu, *supra* note 293, at 616.

[306]408 U.S. 238 (1972).

[307]R. Berger, Death Penalties, *supra* note 10, at 1, 4. Hamilton wrote, "Experience is the oracle of truth; and where its responses are unequivocal, they ought to be conclusive and sacred." The Federalist No. 20, at 124 (A. Hamilton) (Mod. Libr. ed. 1937).

[308]Berger, *Residence Requirements for Welfare and Voting: A Post-Mortem*, 42 Ohio St. L.J. 853 (1981).

[309]R. Berger, Government by Judiciary, *supra* note 43, at 397–06.

[310]M. Perry, *supra* note 13, at 138.

[311]Tushnet, *supra* note 301, at 811. Paul Brest adjured his activist brethren "simply to acknowledge that most of our writings [about judicial review] are not political theory but advocacy scholarship—amicus briefs ultimately designed to persuade the Court to adopt our various notions of the public good." Brest, *supra* note 14, at 1109.

[312]*See supra* note 44 and accompanying text; *see also* Berger, *Michael Perry's Functional Justification for Judicial Activism*, 8 U. Dayton L. Rev. 465, 466 n.12 (1983).

[313]M. Perry, *supra* note 13, at 91.

[314]Lupu, *supra* note 293, at 617.

[315]"The framers did not intend article III to empower a federal judge to invalidate legislation simply because he decides that, beyond its limitations, the Constitution should protect a claimant's rights." Leedes, *The Supreme Court Mess*, 57 Tex. L. Rev. 1361, 1385 (1979).

[316]The Federalist No. 81, at 541 (A. Hamilton) (Mod. Libr. ed. 1937).

under" jurisdiction is "coterminous with the enumeration of sources of 'supreme law' in article VI. If decisional products of noninterpretivist review are not 'law' for supremacy clause purposes, they cannot be 'law' for purposes of permitting an article III court to hear disputes arising out of interpretation of those decisional products."[317] Precisely. Hamilton wrote in *Federalist No. 33* that the clause "*expressly* confines this supremacy to laws made *pursuant to the Constitution*"; federal acts which are not pursuant thereto but are "invasions of the residuary powers of the smaller societies . . . will be merely acts of usurpation, and will deserve to be treated as such."[318] Acts of usurpation by the judiciary, the branch which Hamilton noted was "less than nothing,"[319] would hardly stand higher than those of the legislative branch.

Lupu urges that for "state courts to ignore the entire corpus of American obscenity law, as a response to an act of congressional jurisdiction control, would simply be lawless,"[320] overlooking that federal imposition of first amendment requirements on the states is itself "lawless,"[321] and that under *Erie Railroad v. Tompkins*[322] it is never too late so to hold. Notwithstanding a congressional removal of jurisdiction, Lupu urges state court review of a school prayer law to avoid, among other things, "the corrosive pressures on state courts to move with the popular tide rather than remain bound by authoritative national precedent."[323] A precedent that arrogates unconferred power should not be regarded as "authoritative." Popular majority will is to be thwarted only when the Constitution so demands. Given nationwide resistance to the school prayer decisions,[324] why should state courts cram Supreme Court predilections down the throat of an unwilling people after Congress withdraws its jurisdiction to do so?

Lupu argues that considerations of "supremacy and uniformity" require state courts to follow the Supreme Court decisions, notwithstanding withdrawal of jurisdiction to decide such cases in the future. There is no need to recapitulate the facts, set forth in the body of this article, that undermine the "uniformity" argument.[325] They demonstrate that the Framers themselves departed from uniformity and did not regard it as indispensable. I would add that as between judicial usurpation and "uniformity" the Framers would have chosen to keep the Court within bounds at the cost of uniformity.[326] For nothing exceeded the Founders' dread of unrestrained power.[327] In the context of the Court's death penalty, school prayer, and obscenity decisions, it may be expected that the state courts, relieved of Supreme Court appellate coercion, will pretty uniformly return to the thwarted state policies, thus achieving the much extolled "uniformity." Moreover, the power of Congress to exclude state courts from decisions of federal matters has long been accepted. From

[317]Lupu, *supra* note 293, at 615.

[318]THE FEDERALIST No. 33, at 202 (A. Hamilton) (Mod. Libr. ed. 1937) (emphasis in original).

[319]THE FEDERALIST No. 78, at 504 n.* (A. Hamilton) (Mod. Libr. ed. 1937).

[320]Lupu, *supra* note 293, at 613.

[321]Perry considers that Berger's "finding that the fourteenth amendment was not intended to make the Bill of Rights . . . applicable to the states—which is confirmatory of earlier findings to the same effect by such eminent historians as Charles Fairman . . . is amply documented and widely accepted." Perry, *Interpretivism, Freedom of Expression, and Equal Protection,* 42 OHIO ST. L.J. 261, 285–86 (1981) (footnotes omitted). For detailed discussion see R. BERGER, DEATH PENALTIES, *supra* note 10, at 10–28.

[322]304 U.S. 64 (1938). There the Court, following Holmes, branded the doctrine of Swift v. Tyson, 41 U.S. (16 Pet.) 1 (1842), " 'an unconstitutional assumption of power by courts of the United States which no lapse of time . . . should make us hesitate to correct.' " 304 U.S. 64, 79 (1938) (quoting Black & White Taxicab & Transfer Co. v. Brown & Yellow Taxicab & Transfer Co., 276 U.S. 518 (1928) (Holmes, J., dissenting)).

[323]Lupu, *supra* note 293, at 614.

[324]This does not jibe with Lupu's warning against "the undermining of a sense of shared national experience." *Id.*

[325]*See supra* text accompanying notes 163–72.

[326]*Compare supra* text accompanying note 163.

[327]The colonists were unceasingly concerned with the aggressiveness of power, "its endlessly propulsive tendency to expand itself beyond legitimate boundaries." B. BAILYN, THE IDEOLOGICAL ORIGINS OF THE AMERICAN REVOLUTION 56 (1967).

the beginning, Charles Alan Wright wrote, Congress has "provided that in certain instances the jurisdiction of the federal courts shall be exclusive of the courts of the several states."[328] One such instance is the provision of section 3 of the Civil Rights Act of 1866 that "the district courts . . . shall have, exclusively of the courts of the several States, cognizance of all crimes and offences committed against the provisions of this act."[329] Such precedents are buttressed by section 5 of the fourteenth amendment—"*Congress* shall have power to enforce" the provisions of the amendment.[330] Were state courts to proceed in despite of Congress' omission to delegate enforcement power to, or to withdraw it from, the federal and state courts, they would take over power conferred upon Congress alone.

By virtue of the binding force of the supremacy clause, state judges are bound by the Constitution and the laws pursuant thereto. But in the New York Convention Hamilton assured the ratifiers that "the laws of Congress are restricted to a certain sphere, and when they depart from this sphere, they are no longer supreme and binding."[331] Judicial grafts of extraconstitutional claims on the Constitution stand no higher than statutory invasions of the states' "residuary powers." The legislature, not the courts, was the darling of the Founders;[332] it is the Constitution, not judicial encrustations, that bind state judges.[333] The Framers hardly contemplated that the Court could bind states by unconstitutional decisions. Judicial review was conceived in terms of curbing excesses by the other branches,[334] policing the constitutional boundaries,[335] not as a warrant for excesses by the Court itself. Of what use were Hamilton's assurances that the " 'usurpations of the Supreme Court . . . will [not] be uncontrollable and remediless,' " that it could be impeached for "usurpations on the authority of the legislature,"[336] and a fortiori for the even graver invasion of rights reserved to the states, if the decisions which gave rise to removal of jurisdiction would continue to bind the states. They sought protection against encroachment on their reserved rights, not merely removal of offenders while leaving the harm in place.

Who shall decide whether a Supreme Court decision is extraconstitutional? Manifestly, the

---

[328]C. WRIGHT, HANDBOOK OF THE LAW OF FEDERAL COURTS 26 (3d ed. 1976). "As a general matter, Congress may restrict the jurisdiction of, and remedies available in, the lower federal courts and may similarly restrict state courts in matters of federal concern." P. BREST, PROCESSES OF CONSTITUTIONAL DECISIONMAKING: CASES AND MATERIALS 1314–15 (1975).

[329]Civil Rights Act of 1866, ch. 31, 14 Stat. 27 (1866).

[330]For detailed discussion of section 5 see R. BERGER, DEATH PENALTIES, *supra* note 10, at 167–72. For the effect of the due process clause of the fourteenth amendment see *id.* at 171–72.

[331]2 DEBATES IN THE SEVERAL STATE CONVENTIONS ON THE ADOPTION OF THE FEDERAL CONSTITUTION 362 (J. Elliott ed. 1827–30 & photo. reprint 1941).

[332]1 THE WORKS OF JAMES WILSON 292 (R. McCloskey ed. 1967).

[333]Gary C. Leedes considers that there "is no reason, which is based on the Constitution, that suggests why the executive branch ought to obey an extra-constitutional decision." Leedes, *A Critique of Illegitimate Noninterpretivism*, 8 U. DAYTON L. REV. 533, 561 (1983). Given the tenth amendment, there is less reason for state courts to do so. After the breakup of the Four Horsemen, then Solicitor General Robert H. Jackson compared the emergence of the constitutional text from beneath a laissez-faire gloss to the rediscovery of an Old Master after the retouching brushwork of succeeding generations has been removed. Jackson, *Back to the Constitution*, 25 A.B.A. J. 745 (1939). Justices as diverse as Douglas, Frankfurter and Chief Justice Burger have claimed the right to look beneath the gloss of their predecessors to the Constitution itself. See R. BERGER, DEATH PENALTIES, *supra* note 10, at 12 n.8. Are states less entitled to do so?

[334]R. BERGER, CONGRESS, *supra* note 52, at 8–16.

[335]James Bradley Thayer and Judge Learned Hand, cited in R. BERGER, GOVERNMENT BY JUDICIARY, *supra* note 43, at 305. It is worth noting that the Court's appellate jurisdiction was explained as serving the interests of uniformity rather than supremacy. R. BERGER, CONGRESS, *supra* note 52, at 272–73; see also Martin v. Hunter's Lessee, 14 U.S. (1 Wheat.) 304, 351 (1816). "In the early years of our national history when state's rights fervor was strong, the Supreme Court had some difficulty in establishing its right to reverse a decision of the highest court of a state." A. SAYE, AMERICAN CONSTITUTIONAL LAW: CASES AND TEXT 35 (2d ed. 1979).

[336]THE FEDERALIST No. 81, at 523, 527 (A. Hamilton) (Mod. Libr. ed. 1937).

Court should not sit as judge of its own derelictions. But in *Cooper v. Aaron*[337] the Court, citing *Marbury v. Madison*, stressed that "the federal judiciary is supreme in the exposition of the law of the Constitution," that "the interpretation of the Fourteenth Amendment enunciated . . . in the *Brown* case is the supreme law of the land, and Art. VI of the Constitution makes it of binding effect on the States," and that state officials are "solemnly committed by oath . . . 'to support of this Constitution.' "[338] *Marbury* is not a happy citation; Chief Justice Marshall declared that if the Constitution is not "unchangeable by ordinary means . . ., then written constitutions are absurd attempts, on the part of the people, to limit a power, in its own nature illimitable."[339] That judicial revision was an "ordinary means" is evidenced by his statement that the judicial power "cannot be the assertion of a right to change that instrument."[340] Then too, in holding that Congress may not enlarge the "original" jurisdiction of the Court, *Marbury* was enforcing the unambiguous text of the Constitution, not a judicial importation, whereas *Brown* overturned the framers' plain intention to leave segregation to the states;[341] and as Warren's disciple, G. Edward White, attests, he grafted on the fourteenth amendment his own sentiments, having no roots in the Constitution and in despite of popular sentiment.[342] As regards the "oath" to "support the Constitution," that does not require respect for judicial action which, in defiance of the Constitution, invades the states' "residuary powers." Whatever the case, when a state, standing alone, resists a Supreme Court mandate, as in *Cooper*, congressional removal of the Court's jurisdiction alters the situation and, in my judgment, fortifies the state.

In essence, activists would bind the state courts to enforce unconstitutional and unpopular policies which Congress, as authorized by article III, has disabled the Court from enforcing. Neither the supremacy clause nor considerations of uniformity constrain state courts to do so. Obedience to the Court flowed from its power of compulsion on review. With that no longer operative, state courts may return to effectuation of state policy in local matters. As regards jurisdiction, the last word is for Congress. Sanford Levinson is "willing to assign Congress the last word" because "[d]emocratic theory requires . . . that the stopping point be the most democratic branch of the polity, unless special reasons can be offered to defend a different theory."[343] Where Levinson relies upon political theory, I would summon the terms of article III, which, in conferring upon Congress power over jurisdiction of the federal courts, gave it the last word.[344] No activist speculations have persuasively diminished the unequivocal text.

Several symposiasts, as if to show the absurdity of the jurisdiction removal power, argue that if

---

[337]358 U.S. 1 (1958).

[338]*Id.* at 18 (quoting U.S. CONST. art. VI, cl. 3).

[339]Marbury v. Madison, 5 U.S. (1 Cranch) 137, 177 (1803).

[340]JOHN MARSHALL'S DEFENSE OF *McCulloch v. Maryland* 209 (G. Gunther ed. 1969). For discussion see R. BERGER, GOVERNMENT BY JUDICIARY, *supra* note 43, at 373–78.

[341]The legislative history of the fourteenth amendment clearly discloses that "the framers did not mean for the amendment to have any effect on segregated schooling." M. PERRY, *supra* note 13, at 68. "The framers . . . did not intend to ban state-ordered racial segregation, and yet the Supreme Court has done so." *Id.* at 92; *see also id.* at 1, 33, 105. For the evidence see R. BERGER, GOVERNMENT BY JUDICIARY, *supra* note 43, at 117–33. For citations to activists who accept these findings see R. BERGER, DEATH PENALTIES, *supra* note 10, at 184 n.14.

[342]*See supra* text accompanying notes 236–42 & 254–55. Tushnet observes that "the most significant decisions of [the Warren] Court overturned legislation that substantial local, and probably national, majorities supported both in theory . . . and in practice." Tushnet, Book Review, 57 TEX. L. REV. 1295, 1303 (1979). Philip Kurland wrote, "There is . . . no showing that the judiciary's notion of fundamental values originating outside the Constitution bears any resemblance to the values preferred by the majority of the people." Kurland, *Curia Regis: Some Comments on the Divine Right of Kings and Courts "To Say What the Law Is,"* 23 ARIZ. L. REV. 581, 589 (1981).

[343]Levinson, *The Turn Toward Functionalism in Constitutional Theory*, 8 U. DAYTON L. REV. 567, 577 n.41 (1983).

[344]See the discussion of Perry's and Charles Black's positions in Berger, *Michael Perry's Functional Justification for Activist Review*, 8 U. DAYTON L. REV. 465, 503, 513 (1983).

it can remove jurisdiction it should be able to revise the decisions of the Court as well.[345] The Court itself, however, drew a distinction between those two powers in *United States v. Klein*.[346] Sanford Levinson observes that one "might feel differently if the text stated explicitly that Congress shall have no authority to revise Constitution-based judgments of the Supreme Court, but, of course, there is no such patch of text."[347] It would be superfluous. The powers of the federal government are only those that have been granted; what was not granted was reserved to the states.[348] In addition, there is the implication that the express grant of authority to control jurisdiction excludes powers not mentioned. Then too, Hamilton stated in *Federalist No. 81* that a "legislature . . . cannot reverse a determination once made in a particular case,"[349] noting, however, in the same *No. 81* that "usurpations by the Supreme Court . . . will [not] be uncontrollable and remediless."[350] Such distinctions were appreciated by Daniel Webster, who argued in *Gibbons v. Ogden* that

> [i]f Congress were to pass an act expressly revoking or annulling this New-York grant, such an act would be wholly useless and inoperative. If the New-York grant be . . . inconsistent with, any constitutional power which Congress has exercised, then, . . . the grant is nugatory and void, necessarily, and by reason of the supremacy of the law of Congress.[351]

One who argues from a power of removal to a congressional power to revise decisions could equally maintain that because a state statute is inconsistent with a congressional power, Congress may annul it. Professor Felix Frankfurter, a leading student of constitutional law and federal jurisdiction, proposed an amendment that would authorize Congress to overrule Supreme Court decisions under certain circumstances,[352] recognizing thereby that article III does not authorize such revision. Perhaps such "niceties" carry little weight with activists, who measure all things by the result. But limits on power remain important to those of us who cling to a democratic system.

---

[345]Alexander, *Painting Without the Numbers: Noninterpretivist Judicial Review*, 8 U. DAYTON L. REV. 447, 456 (1983); Levinson, *supra* note 343, at 575.

[346]*See supra* text accompanying notes 94–99.

[347]Levinson, *supra* note 343, at 576.

[348]James Wilson assured the Pennsylvania ratifiers that in contrast with the states, federal power is to be "collected, not from tacit implication, but from the positive grant expressed in the instrument of the union. . . . [E]verything which is not given is reserved." A. MASON, *supra* note 53, at 129. In Martin v. Hunter's Lessee, 14 U.S. (1 Wheat.) 304, 326 (1816), Justice Story declared that the federal government "can claim no powers which are not granted to it by the constitution, and the powers actually granted must be such as are expressly given, or given by necessary implication."

[349]THE FEDERALIST NO. 81, at 526 (A. Hamilton) (Mod. Libr. ed. 1937).

[350]*Id.* at 523.

[351]Gibbons v. Ogden, 22 U.S. (9 Wheat.) 1, 30 (1824).

[352]Levinson, *supra* note 343, at 577.

CHAPTER XII

The Activist Legacy of the New Deal Court

> *However the Court may interpret the provisions of the*
> *Constitution, it is still the Constitution which*
> *is the law, not the decisions of the Court.*
>
> Charles Warren*

The activist legacy of the New Deal Court was free-wheeling adjudication. It sprang from the Four Horsemen's obdurate identification of their economic and social predilections with constitutional mandates, halting the Rooseveltian reform measures in their tracks, and bringing on the Court-Packing Plan.[1] Although the Plan failed, it was followed by a shake-out resulting in the "reconstructed Court,"[2] a Court that had learned from its predecessors how to manipulate the Constitution, albeit for a new set of goals. The transition was aptly described by Stanley Kutler, an ardent admirer of judicial activism:

> From the early twentieth century through the late 1930s, academic and liberal commentators . . . criticized vigorously the abusive powers of the federal judiciary . . . consistently frustrating desirable social policies. . . . [T]he judges had arrogated a policymaking function not conferred upon them by the Constitution . . . negat[ing] the basic principles of representative government . . . in favor of the interests of a privileged few.
>
> . . . .
>
> . . . After 1937, most of the judiciary's longtime critics suddenly found a new faith. . . . The judges themselves pointed the way of the true faith as they rationalized a minimal judicial role for superintending economic legislation while championing civil rights and civil liberties to the maximum.[3]

Tactics that were anathema to the True Believers when employed by the earlier Court now gained an odor of sanctity because the Warren Court satisfied their aspirations,[4] never mind that

---

*3 C. WARREN, THE SUPREME COURT IN UNITED STATES HISTORY 470 (1922). Chief Justice Burger rejected the "thesis that what the Court said lately controls over the Constitution." L. LEVY, AGAINST THE LAW: THE NIXON COURT AND CRIMINAL JUSTICE 29 (1974). Like Burger, Justices Douglas and Frankfurter claimed the right to look at the Constitution rather than what the Court had said about it. Graves v. New York *ex rel.* O'Keefe, 306 U.S. 466, 491–92 (1939) (Frankfurter, J., concurring) ("the ultimate touchstone of constitutionality is the Constitution itself and not what we have said about it"); Douglas, *Stare Decisis* 49 COLUM. L. REV. 735, 736 (1949).

[1] "The actions of the [pre-New Deal] Court were attacked as being those of men consciously or unconsciously biased in favour of capital against labour, and giving a blind allegiance to the economic doctrine of *laissez-faire.*" M. BELOFF, THE AMERICAN FEDERAL GOVERNMENT 56, 57 (1959). The Court "sent the whole edifice of government intervention toppling." *Id.* at 58.

[2] So described by Justice Frankfurter in Graves v. New York *ex rel.* O'Keefe, 306 U.S. 466, 487 (1939) (Frankfurter, J., dissenting).

[3] Kutler, *Raoul Berger's Fourteenth Amendment: A History or Ahistorical?* (Book Review), 6 HASTINGS CONST. L.Q. 511, 512–13 (1979). "Only a third of a century ago, most liberal Americans were much more concerned with cutting down the Supreme Court's power than with preserving it." Sutherland, *All Sides of the Question—Felix Frankfurter and Personal Freedom,* in FELIX FRANKFURTER—THE JUDGE 109, 152 (W. Mendelson ed. 1964).

[4] Thus, Fred Rodell exulted that Chief Justice Warren "brush[ed] off pedantic impediments to the results he felt were right," and that he was "almost unique" in his "dependence on the present day results of separate schools." Rodell, *It Is*

it "arrogated a policy making function not conferred upon it by the Constitution." "[W]hoever places emphasis upon the product rather than the process," wrote Sidney Hook, "upon an all-sanctifying end rather than upon the means of achieving it, is opening the doors of anarchy."[5] The Court itself has repudiated its "use of the 'vague contours' of the Due Process Clause to nullify laws which a majority of the Court believed to be *economically* unwise."[6] But it continues to frustrate the will of the people when it considers their *social* choices unwise.[7]

What warrant does it have for reading "liberty" to serve its social predilections? Neither the fifth nor the fourteenth amendment draws a distinction between "liberty" and "property"; the Framers, Learned Hand remarked, would have regarded the current reading of the fifth amendment as "constitut[ing] severer restrictions as to Liberty than Property" as a "strange anomaly." "[T]here is no constitutional basis," he averred, "for asserting a larger measure of judicial supervision over [liberty than property]."[8] In fact, civil liberties did not loom large in the thinking of the Founders; they were more concerned with the interests of the collective society.[9] It was property rather than

the Earl Warren Court, N.Y. Times Magazine, Mar. 13, 1966, at 30. For similar activist remarks, see R. Berger, Government by Judiciary: The Transformation of the Fourteenth Amendment 286 n.13 (1977).

[5]S. Hook, Philosophy and Public Policy 36 (1980).

[6]Ferguson v. Skrupa, 372 U.S. 726, 731 (1963).

[7]Judge Learned Hand wrote that judges "wrap up their veto [of legislation] in a protective veil of adjectives such as 'arbitrary,' . . . 'inherent,' 'fundamental,' or 'essential,' whose office usually . . . is to disguise what they are doing and impute to it a derivation far more impressive than their personal preferences, which are all that in fact lie behind the[ir] decision[s]." L. Hand, The Bill of Rights 70 (1958). We need to remember that "there still remains a distinction between a constitution which . . . provides that the law shall be whatever the supreme court thinks fit, and the actual constitution of the United States." H. Hart, The Concept of Law 141 (1961).

Lest the reader consider that in focusing on due process I am beating a dead horse when present-day emphasis is on the equal protection clause, I would call attention to Herbert Packer's statement that "the new 'substantive equal protection' has under a different label permitted today's justices to impose their prejudices in much the same manner as the Four Horsemen once did." Packer, *The Aim of the Criminal Law Revisisted: A Plea for a New Look at "Substantive Due Process,"* 44 S. Cal. L. Rev. 490, 491–92 (1971). Philip Kurland likewise concluded that "The new equal protection . . . is the old substantive due process." *Forum: Equal Protection and the Burger Court,* 2 Hastings Const. L.Q. 645, 661 (1975) (remarks of Philip Kurland). For the narrow scope of equal protection as conceived by the framers, see *infra* text accompanying notes 178–82.

[8]L. Hand, *supra* note 7, at 50–51. "The great and chief end . . . of men," John Locke wrote, "[in] putting themselves under government, is the preservation of their property. . . ." *Quoted in* J. Randall, The Making of the Modern Mind 342 (1940) (quoting J. Locke. II Treatise on Civil Government, ch. 2). For the Founders, property "was the basic liberty, because until a man was secure in his property . . . life and liberty could mean little." 1 P. Smith, John Adams 272 (1962). Hence they "warmly endorsed John Adams' deep-seated conviction that 'property is as sacred as the laws of God.' " Mason, *The Burger Court in Historical Perspective,* 47 N.Y. St. B.J. 87, 91 (1975). In the convention Gouverneur Morris said, "Life and liberty were generally said to be of more value, than property. An accurate view of the matter would nevertheless prove that property was the main object of Society." 1 M. Farrand, The Records of the Federal Convention Of 1787, 533 (1911). Madison also considered that "[t]he primary objects of civil society are the security of property and public safety." 1 M. Farrand, *supra* at 147. For similar sentiments of John Rutledge, Rufus King, and Pierce Butler, see 1 M. Farrand, *supra,* at 534, 541, 542. "[T]he dichotomy between personal liberties and property rights is a false one. . . . In fact, a fundamental interdependence exists between the personal right to liberty and the personal right in property. Neither could have meaning without the other." Lynch v. Household Fin. Corp., 405 U.S. 538, 552 (1972). John Hart Ely also rejects the differentiation of "economic rights" from "human rights." Ely, *The Wages of Crying Wolf: A Comment on Roe v. Wade,* 82 Yale L.J. 920, 938 (1973). They have been "essentially read as a unit." Ely, *Constitutional Interpretivism: Its Allure and Impossibility,* 53 Ind. L.J. 399, 421 (1978).

[9]For the Founders, "individual rights, even the basic civil liberties that we consider so crucial, possessed little of their modern theoretical relevance when set against the will of the peoples." G. Wood, The Creation of the American Republic. 1776–1787, at 63 (1969). "In the Convention and later, states rights and not individual rights were the real worry." A. Mason, The States Rights Debate: Antifederalism and the Constitution 75 (1964). Those who insisted on a Bill of Rights, as Cecelia Kenyon noted, "were primarily preoccupied with the failure of the Constitution to lay down the precious and venerable common-law rules of criminal procedure." Kenyon, *Men of Little Faith: The Anti-Federalists on the Nature of Representative Government,* XII Wm. & Mary Q., 3d series, 3, 19 (1955). Even today, "[f]or most men, to be deprived . . .

civil liberties which they regarded as sacred. But the "reconstructed" Court, as will appear, was little impeded by the presuppositions and intentions of the Framers. Under the leadership of Chief Justice Warren, this judicial revolution[10] resulted in "usurpation of general governmental powers on the pretext that its authority derives from the Fourteenth Amendment."[11]

As the Court progressively realized the social aspirations of sundry academicians (which I share), they rose to new heights in its defense. So, Paul Brest challenged the assumption that judges are bound by the Constitution.[12] Another activist knight-errant, Robert Cover, thrust aside "the Constitution's self-evident meaning" in favor of an "ideology" framed by a non-elected, life-tenured, virtually unaccountable bench. The Constitution, he asserted, is of no moment because "we" have decided to "entrust" judges with forming an "ideology" by which legislative action can be measured[13] and, it may be added, the Framers' choices supplanted. Cover, of course, did not explain where "we, the people" had spoken, whether in constitutional text, conventions or referenda. A few drastically summarized case studies will enable us to measure the effects of this revolution, described by an activist admirer, Louis Lusky, as an "assertion of the power to revise the Constitution, bypassing the cumbersome amendment procedure prescribed by article V," and as a "repudiation of the limits on judicial review that are implicit in the orthodox doctrine of *Marbury v. Madison*,"[14] and in fact are explicit in the constitutional history.

Preliminarily, it needs to be recalled that application of the Bill of Rights to the states is without constitutional foundation. Chief Justice Marshall pointed out in *Barron v. Baltimore* that the Bill applied only to the federal government,[15] as the legislative history plainly confirms.[16] Justice Black's theory that the Bill of Rights was "incorporated" in the fourteenth amendment[17] was vigorously rejected by the Court.[18] But it accomplished piecemeal incorporation under what has come to be known as "selective incorporation." In what remains the most searching study, Louis Henkin wrote: "Selective incorporation finds no support in the language of the [fourteenth] amendment, or in the history of its adoption," and it is truly "more difficult to justify than Justice Black's position that the Bill of Rights was wholly incorporated."[19] Judge Henry Friendly, one of our ablest jurists, wrote, "it appears undisputed that the selective incorporation theory has [no historical support]."[20] Thus, the Court's invocation of this or the other provisions of the Bill of Rights

---

of private property would be a far greater and more deeply felt loss . . . than to be deprived of the right to speak freely." M. OAKESHOTT, RATIONALISM IN POLITICS 44 (1962).

[10]Alfred Kelly stated that the Warren Court was determined "to carry through a constitutional equalitarian revolution." Kelly, *Clio and the Court: An Illicit Love Affair*, 1965 SUP. CT. REV. 119, 159.

[11]Letter from Philip Kurland to Harvard University Press (Aug. 15, 1977).

[12]Brest, *The Misconceived Quest for the Original Understanding*, 60 B.U.L. REV. 204, 224 (1980).

[13]Cover, Book Review, NEW REPUBLIC, Jan. 14, 1978, at 26, 27.

[14]Lusky, *"Government by Judiciary": What Price Legitimacy?* (Book Review), 6 HASTINGS CONST. L.Q. 403, 406 (1979). The Court itself rejected the notion that the Constitution may be "amended by judicial decision without action by the designated organs in the mode by which alone amendments can be made." McPherson v. Blacker, 146 U.S. 1, 36 (1892); *see also* Hawke v. Smith, 253 U.S. 221, 227 (1920).

[15]32 U.S. (7 Pet.) 243 (1833).

[16]For citations see R. BERGER, DEATH PENALTIES: THE SUPREME COURT'S OBSTACLE COURSE 13–14 (1982).

[17]Adamson v. California, 332 U.S. 46, 68 (1947) (Black, J., dissenting).

[18]Speaking for the Court in Bartkus v. Illinois, 359 U.S. 121, 124 (1959), Justice Frankfurter stated:
We have held from the beginning and uniformly that the Due Process Clause of the Fourteenth Amendment does not apply to the States any of the provisions of the first eight amendments as such. The relevant historical materials have been canvassed by this Court and by legal scholars. These materials demonstrate conclusively that Congress and the members of the legislatures of the ratifying States did not contemplate that the Fourteenth Amendment was a short-hand incorporation of the first eight amendments making them applicable as explicit restrictions upon the States.

[19]Henkin, *"Selective Incorporation" in the Fourteenth Amendment*, 73 YALE L.J. 74, 77 (1963).

[20]Friendly, *The Bill of Rights as a Code of Criminal Procedure*, 53 CALIF. L. REV. 929, 934, 935 (1965). To my mind, rejection of incorporation en masse entails rejection of piecemeal incorporation. The whole includes the part. The verbal justifications are most unsatisfying. *See* R. BERGER, *supra* note 16, at 16–18. Paul Bator observed, "the way we arrived at

constitutes the threshold usurpation. Activists shrug this off under what appears to be a doctrine of judicial squatter sovereignty—usurpation is legitimated by long-continued repetition.

I. CASE STUDIES: JUDICIAL REVISION OF THE CONSTITUTION

A. *Bridges v. California*

The watershed case was *Bridges v. California,*[21] a five-to-four decision, in which Justice Frankfurter dissented, joined by Chief Justice Stone and Justices Roberts and Byrnes. Bridges, a labor leader, had virtually threatened to call a strike if a then-pending decision was enforced. In a companion case, the Los Angeles Times editorially advised the judge that he would "make a serious mistake" to grant probation rather than a severe sentence to certain labor "gorillas." Both were summarily held in contempt of court for these out-of-court utterances. Reversing, 150 years after adoption of the Bill of Rights, Justice Black discovered that the long-recognized summary power of courts over contemptuous publications was curtailed by the first amendment and then by the fourteenth. Liberals, myself included, heartily detested the strike-breaking use of the contempt power. But the fact remains that this power was deeply rooted in the common law and our own practice for 150 years. My study of the history of the first amendment convinced me that it was not designed to cut down summary contempts.[22]

In barest outline, the first amendment provides that "*Congress* shall make no law."[23] Neither the amendment nor its history refers to a ban on the courts. By the Judiciary Act of 1789 the First Congress, an authoritative interpreter of the Constitution,[24] conferred upon the courts power to punish "contempts,"[25] a technical term, the meaning of which courts sought in English law and practice. Blackstone, regarded by the colonists as the oracle of the common law, stated that "liberty of the press . . . consists in laying no *previous* restraints upon publications, and not in freedom from censure for criminal matter when published."[26] In the Pennsylvania Ratification Convention James Wilson, a leading member of the Philadelphia Convention, said, "what is meant by the liberty of the press is, that there should be no antecedent restraint upon it."[27] Thomas McKean, Chief Justice of the Supreme Court of Pennsylvania, who vigorously advocated adoption of the Constitution in the Pennsylvania Ratification Convention, declared in *Respublica v. Oswald,* an attachment for contemptuous publication: "Could not this be done in England? Certainly it could. . . . [T]here is nothing in the constitution of this state, respecting the liberty of the press, that has not been authorized by the constitution of that kingdom for near a century past."[28] Shortly

---

incorporation was intellectually shoddy. It was just announced, as though it were a *coup d' etat;* suddenly we had incorporation." Bator, *Some Thoughts on Applied Federalism,* 6 HARV. J.L. & PUB. POL'Y 51, 58 (Special Issue, 1982).

[21] 314 U.S. 252 (1941).

[22] Berger, *Constructive Contempt: A Post-Mortem,* 9 U. CHI. L. REV. 602 (1942).

[23] "Insofar as the semantics of the eighteenth and early nineteenth centuries are concerned, the word 'laws' did not include decisions but was limited to legislative enactments." Teton, *The Story of Swift v. Tyson,* 35 ILL. L. REV. 519, 537 (1941).

[24] In this first Congress sat many members of the Constitutional Convention of 1787. This Court has repeatedly laid down the principle that a contemporaneous legislative exposition of the Constitution when the founders of our Government and framers of our Constitution were actively participating in public affairs long acquiesced in fixes the construction to be given its provisions.
Hampton & Co. v. United States, 276 U.S. 394, 412 (1928) (quoting Myers v. United States, 272 U.S. 52 (1926)).

[25] Judiciary Act of 1789, ch. 20, § 17, 1 STAT. 83 (1789).

[26] 4 W. BLACKSTONE, COMMENTARIES ON THE LAWS OF ENGLAND 151 (1765–1769).

[27] J. MCMASTER & F. STONE, PENNSYLVANIA AND THE FEDERAL CONSTITUTION 308 (1888). All "that the earlier sages of the Revolution had in view" was to erect "barriers against any previous restraints upon publication." 1 J. KENT, COMMENTARIES ON AMERICAN LAW 627 (7th ed. 1851).

[28] 1 Dall. 319, 322 (Pa. 1788).

thereafter Chancellor Kent employed the summary power in *People v. Freer.*[29] Chief Justice Hughes referred in *Near v. Minnesota* to the "conceded authority of courts to punish for contempt when publications directly tend to prevent the proper discharge of judicial functions,"[30] as Justice Holmes earlier stated in *Patterson v. Colorado.*[31] The cases upholding the summary power are legion.[32] The fourteenth amendment, as Justice Black observed, did not go beyond the first.[33] But in *Bridges,* Justice Black, in my judgment, simply molded history to rationalize a result with which I sympathize but nonetheless is extra-constitutional.

B. The Reapportionment Cases

What Warren regarded as the jewel in his crown,[34] the reapportionment decision, proceeded in the teeth of what Justice Harlan justly described as the framers' "irrefutable and unrefuted" exclusion of suffrage from the fourteenth amendment.[35] In a nutshell, Justice Brennan observed that seventeen of nineteen Northern States had rejected black suffrage between 1865 and 1868.[36] Consequently, Roscoe Conkling, a member of the Joint Committee on Reconstruction of both Houses, stated it would be "futile to ask three quarters of the States to do . . . the very thing which most of them have already refused to do."[37] Another member of that Committee, Senator Jacob Howard, said "three fourths of the States of this Union could not be induced to vote to grant the right of suffrage."[38] The chairman of the Committee, Senator William Fessenden, said of a suffrage proposal that "there [is not] the slightest probability that it will be adopted by the States."[39] The unanimous report of the Committee doubted that "the States would consent to surrender a power they had always exercised, and to which they were attached," and therefore thought it best to "leave the whole question with the people of each State."[40] That such was the vastly preponderant opinion is confirmed by a remarkable fact. During the pendency of ratification, radical opposition to the readmission of Tennessee because its constitution excluded Negro suffrage was voted down in the House 125-to-12. Senator Charles Sumner's parallel proposal was rejected 34-to-4.[41] The fifteenth amendment was later adopted, its framers stated, to fill the gap left by the failure of the fourteenth to ban discriminatory exclusion from suffrage.[42] His own masterly collection of the historical facts led Justice Harlan to conclude that the argument for reapportionment flew "in the face of irrefutable and still unanswered history to the contrary."[43] My independent study of the

[29] 1 Cai. R. 518 (N.Y. 1804).

[30] 283 U.S. 697, 715 (1931).

[31] 205 U.S. 454, 462–63 (1907) (citing Respublica v. Oswald, 1 Dall. 319 (Pa. 1788)).

[32] For citations, see Berger, *supra* note 22, at 620 n.129.

[33] Bridges v. California, 314 U.S. 252, 268 (1941); *see* Berger, *supra* note 22, at 625 n.165.

[34] G. WHITE, EARL WARREN: A PUBLIC LIFE 238 (1982). Paul Bator stressed the need for "rooting the language of the Fourteenth Amendment within some limits of historical purpose—that is, of trying to understand the language in the context of the legal culture of its framers and the purposes they were trying to achieve." Bator, *Some Thoughts on Applied Federalism,* 6 HARV. J. PUB. POL. 53, 54 (1982).

[35] *See infra* text accompanying note 43.

[36] Oregon v. Mitchell, 400 U.S. 112, 256 (1970) (Brennan, White, and Marshall, JJ., dissenting in part).

[37] CONG. GLOBE 358, 39th Cong., 1st Sess. (1866).

[38] *Id.* at 2766.

[39] *Id.* at 704.

[40] Report of the Joint Committee on Reconstruction, S. REP. NO. 112, 39th Cong., 1st Sess. (1866), *reprinted in* THE RECONSTRUCTION AMENDMENTS' DEBATES 94 (A. Avins ed. 1966) [hereinafter cited as RECONSTRUCTION AMENDS.].

[41] For details, see Berger, *supra* note 4, at 56, 59–60, 79.

[42] For citations, see Berger, *The Fourteenth Amendment: Light From the Fifteenth,* 74 NW. U.L. REV. 311, 321–23 (1979). A Court contemporary with the fifteenth amendment declared that before adoption of that amendment a state could "exclude citizens of the United States from voting on account of race. . . . [T]he Amendment has invested citizens of the United States with a new constitutional right." United States v. Reese, 92 U.S. 214, 217–18 (1876).

[43] Griswold v. Connecticut, 381 U.S. 479, 501 (1965) (Harlan, J., concurring). Louis Lusky considers that Harlan's demonstration is "irrefutable and unrefuted." Lusky, *supra* note 14, at 406.

history richly confirmed Harlan.[44] Gerald Gunther wrote that "most constitutional lawyers agree" that "the 'one person-one vote' ruling . . . lacks all historical justification."[45] Summing up, Robert Bork stated: "The principle of one man, one vote . . . runs counter to the text of the fourteenth amendment, the history surrounding its adoption and ratification and the political practice of Americans from colonial times up to the day the Court invented the new formula."[46] Warren's worshipful biographer and former law clerk commented:

> Warren had based his purported usurpation of legislative prerogatives on an interpretation of the Constitution that was neither faithful to its literal text nor consistent with the context in which it had been framed. He had substituted homilies such as "[c]itizens, not history or economic interests, cast votes" for doctrinal analysis.[47]

The history Warren dismissed was the framers' determination to exclude suffrage from the fourteenth amendment, thereby reversing the choice they made. As G. Edward White further stated, "*Baker v. Carr* found a judicial power to review the political judgments of legislators where none had previously existed."[48]

C. The Desegregation Decision: *Brown v. Board of Education*

Little less convincing is the case for exclusion of segregation from the fourteenth amendment. Richard Kluger, author of a laudatory history of *Brown v. Board of Education,* asked: "Could it be reasonably claimed that segregation had been outlawed by the Fourteenth when the yet more basic emblem of citizenship—the ballot—had been withheld from the Negro under that amendment?"[49] The temper of the times is disclosed by Senator James Harlan's remarks when desegregation of the District of Columbia schools was under discussion in April, 1860:

> I know there is an objection to the association of colored children with white children in the same schools. This prejudice exists in my own State [Iowa]. It would be impossible to carry a proposition in Iowa to educate the few colored children that now live in that State in the same schoolhouses with the white children.[50]

To have upended segregated schools, Charles Fairman considers, "would have exposed the [Civil Rights] bill to active opposition in the North."[51] Cognizant of such sentiments, James Wilson, Chairman of the House Judiciary Committee, assured the House that the terms of the Civil Rights Bill, which it was the purpose of the fourteenth amendment to incorporate, did not mean that the children of "all citizens" shall attend the same schools.[52] The framers' pervasive assumption, recorded in the debates, was that black children would attend separate schools,[53] if only, as

---

[44]Berger, *supra* note 4, at 52–68; Nathanson, Book Review, 56 TEX. L. REV. 579, 581 (1978).

[45]Gunther, Book Review, Wall St. J., Nov. 25, 1977, at 4, col. 5.

[46]Bork, *Neutral Principles and Some First Amendment Problems,* 47 IND. L.J. 1, 18 (1971).

[47]G. WHITE, *supra* note 34, at 239.

[48]*Id.* at 357.

[49]R. KLUGER, SIMPLE JUSTICE 635 (1976).

[50]CONG. GLOBE, 36th Cong., 1st Sess. 1680 (1860).

[51]C. FAIRMAN, HISTORY OF THE SUPREME COURT OF THE UNITED STATES 1179 (1971). An Indiana Radical, George Julian, told the House, "the real trouble is that *we hate the negro,*" CONG. GLOBE, 39th Cong., 1st Sess. 257 (1866), a remark echoed by Senator Lane, *id.* at 739, Representative Cullom, *id.* at 911, and Senator Stewart, *id.* at 2799. Senator John Sherman of Ohio said, "We do not like negroes. We do not disguise our dislike." Woodward, *Seeds of Failure in Radical Race Policy,* in NEW FRONTIERS OF THE AMERICAN RECONSTRUCTION 128 (H. Hyman ed. 1966). William Gillette wrote, "public opinion strongly opposed Negro rights, and the state legislators who outraged this consensus would commit political suicide." W. GILLETTE, THE RIGHT TO VOTE: POLITICS AND THE PASSAGE OF THE FIFTEENTH AMENDMENT 80 (1965).

[52]CONG. GLOBE, 39th Cong., 1st Sess. 1117 (1866). A number of contemporaneous constructions of the fourteenth amendment by northern courts are to the same effect. *See infra* Appendix.

[53]Berger, *supra* note 4, at 125–27.

Alexander Bickel explained, because "It was preposterous to worry about unsegregated schools, for example, when hardly a beginning had been made at educating Negroes at all and when obviously special efforts, suitable only for Negroes, would have to be made."[54] As late as 1875, Senator Sumner, who had pressed increasingly for mixed schools, could not persuade the Senate, prepared to accept equal accommodations in inns and transportation, to include schools. Senator Sargent of California urged that the common school proposal would reinforce "a prejudice powerful, permeating every part of the country, and existing more or less in every man's mind."[55] A similar statement was made in the House by Barbour Lewis of Tennessee.[56] More and more activist commentators agree that the framers of the fourteenth amendment excluded segregation.[57] Consequently the desegregation decision represents a square reversal of the will of the framers. Warren's biographer concludes that "when one divorces Warren's opinions from their ethical premises, they evaporate. . . . [T]hey are individual examples of [Warren's own] beliefs leading to judgments."[58]

Let it be assumed that segregation necessitated a breakout from constitutional limits; the trouble is, as Hamilton presciently noted in *The Federalist*, that "every breach of the fundamental laws, though dictated by necessity . . . forms a precedent for other breaches where the same plea of necessity does not exist at all."[59] What "necessity," what evil condemned by many, required the court to cut down the hallowed twelve-man jury, to saddle the States with the duty immediately to support out-of-state indigent migrants, to curtail death penalties? Of these in turn.

D. *Williams v. Florida:* The Twelve-Man Jury

The twelve-man jury, Coke wrote, was "very ancient."[60] Usage, Matthew Bacon's *Abridgment* stated, called for a "petit jury of twelve, and can be neither more nor less," as Chief Justice Matthew Hale had earlier declared.[61] Trial by jury, this "most transcendent privilege," Blackstone observed, required a jury of twelve.[62] The South Carolina Constitution provided, for example, that "trial by jury, as heretofore used . . . shall be forever inviolably preserved.[63] In *Holmes v. Walton,* a statute

---

[54]R. Kluger, Simple Justice 654 (1976).

[55]See Reconstruction Amends, *supra* note 40, at 705. In 1883 the New York court, passing on an 1864 statute providing for separate schools for blacks, stated, "The attempt to enforce social intimacy and intercourse between the races, by legal enactments, would probably tend only to embitter the prejudices . . . which exist between them." People *ex rel.* King v. Gallagher, 93 N.Y. 438, 448 (1883).

[56]Reconstruction Amends., *supra* note 40, at 726.

[57]Nathaniel Nathanson wrote about my demonstration that the fourteenth amendment "would not require school desegration or negro suffrage. These are not surprising historical conclusions. The first was quite conclusively demonstrated by Alexander Bickel. . . . Berger's independent research and analysis confirms and adds weight to those conclusions." Nathanson, *supra* note 44, at 581; *see also* Abraham, Book Review, 6 Hastings Const. L.Q. 467, 467–68 (1979); Alexander, *Modern Equal Protection Theories: A Metatheoretical Taxonomy and Critique*, 42 Ohio St. L.J. 3, 6 (1981); Levinson, *The Turn Toward Functionalism in Constitutional Theory*, 8 U. Dayton L. Rev. 567, 578 (1983); Perry, *Interpretivism, Freedom of Expression and Equal Protection*, 42 Ohio St. L.J. 261, 285–86 n.100, 292 (1981).

[58]G. White, *supra* note 34, at 367.

[59]The Federalist No. 25, at 158 (Mod. Lib. ed. 1941).

[60]1 T. Coke, Institutes of the Laws of England 155b (1628–1641).

[61]5 M. Bacon, A New Abridgment of the Laws of England, *Juries* (A) at 234 (3d ed. 1768); 2 M. Hale, History of the Pleas of the Crown 161 (1736).

[62]3 W. Blackstone, *supra* note 26, at 379; *see also id.* at 358, 365.

[63]Article IX, § 6; *see* 2 B. Poore, Federal and State Constitutions, Colonial Chapters 1633 (1877). Seven states enacted statutes providing that the petit jury must be composed of 12 men: New Hampshire: Act of Jan. 17, 1777, Acts and Laws of New Hampshire 65 (1780); New York: Act of April 19, 1786, Article XVI, Laws of New York 266 (Greenleaf ed. 1792); North Carolina: Act of November 10, 1779, Chapter VI, Laws of North Carolina 388 (Iredell ed. 1791); Pennsylvania: Act of March 19, 1785, § 9, Laws of Pennsylvania 262–265 (Dallas ed. 1793); Rhode Island: Session of March 18, 1776, p. 316; South Carolina: Act of August 20, 1731, Public Laws of South Carolina 125 (Grimke ed. 1790); Virginia: Session of October 20, 1777, Chapter XVII, Art. XI, Collection of Public Acts 1776–1783 (1785).

providing for a six-man jury was held contrary to the 1776 New Jersey Constitution which preserved the "inestimable right of trial by jury."[64] In the Virginia Ratification Convention, Governor Edmund Randolph stated: "There is no suspicion that less than twelve jurors will be thought sufficient."[65] The Court itself held in *Patton v. United States* that it "is not open to question . . . that the jury should consist of twelve men, neither more nor less."[66]

All this was thrown into the discard by *Williams v. Florida*[67] as "a historical accident, unrelated to the great purposes which gave rise to the jury in the first place," dismissing "superstitious insights into the significance of '12.' "[68] "Superstitions" cherished by the hard-headed Chief Justice Coke and which for 600 years have been embodied in law and practice are not so easily dismissed. As the Court held per Justice Holmes: "If a thing has been practiced for two hundred years by common consent, it will need a strong case for the Fourteenth Amendment to affect it. . . ."[69] The idiosyncratic nature of the six-man decision is pointed up by the subsequent *Burch v. Louisiana*, rejecting a five-man jury, though ruefully admitting that "the line between six members and five was not altogether easy to justify."[70] The line drawn at "twelve" for 600 years needed no justification. The governing criterion was voiced anew by Chief Justice Burger in the recent "legislative chaplain" case: "Clearly the men who wrote the First Amendment Religion Clause did not view paid legislative chaplains and opening prayers as a violation of that Amendment, for the practice of opening sessions with prayer has continued without interruption ever since that early session of Congress."[71] By that unimpeachable test the twelve-man jury, death penalties, and out-of-state indigent decisions, cannot stand up. Rather, they illustrate that constitutional decisions are a product of the Justices' "gut" reactions.[72]

E. *Shapiro v. Thompson:* Migrant Indigents' Right To Support

Resting on the "right to travel," *Shapiro v. Thompson*[73] struck down state requirements of one year of residence before an indigent migrant would be eligible for "welfare" aid. An advocate of the unrestricted right to travel, Zechariah Chafee, wrote, "[T]here is a queer uncertainty about what clause in the Constitution establishes this right" to travel.[74] Justice Harlan stamped it a

---

[64]The case, not officially reported, is discussed in C. HAINES, THE AMERICAN DOCTRINE OF JUDICIAL SUPREMACY 92–95 (1932).

[65]3 DEBATES IN THE SEVERAL STATE CONVENTIONS ON THE ADOPTION OF THE FEDERAL CONSTITUTION 467 (J. Elliot ed. 18jj). Julius Goebel adverted to "popular sensitivity regarding any tampering with the 'inestimable' right of jury trial," and concluded that "[a]ny suggestion that the jury system as then entrenched might be amended in any detail was beyond tolerance." 1 J. GOEBEL, HISTORY OF THE SUPREME COURT OF THE UNITED STATES 141, 493 (1971).

[66]281 U.S. 276, 288 (1930); *see also* Thompson v. Utah, 170 U.S. 343, 350 (1898) ("the words 'trial by jury' were placed in the Constitution . . . with reference to the meaning affixed to them in the law as it was in this country and in England at the time of the adoption of that instrument)."

[67]399 U.S. 78 (1970).

[68]*Id.* at 88, 89–90. On the other hand, Justice Holmes said, "A common-law judge could not say, 'I think the doctrine of consideration a bit of historical nonsense and shall not enforce it. . . .' " Southern Pac. Co. v. Jensen, 244 U.S. 205, 221 (1917) (Holmes, J., dissenting).

[69]Jackman v. Rosenbaum Co., 260 U.S. 22, 31 (1922); *see also* Hampton & Co. v. United States, 276 U.S. 394, 412 (1928); Prigg v. Pennsylvania, 41 U.S. (16 Pet.) 539, 621 (1842) (Story, J., delivering opinion of the Court, as quoted *infra* text accompanying note 86); T. COOLEY, CONSTITUTIONAL LIMITATIONS 67 (1883) (quoted *infra* note 86).

[70]441 U.S. 130, 137 (1979). One is reminded of the chant in George Orwell's *Animal Farm* 38 (1946): "FOUR LEGS GOOD, TWO LEGS BAD."

[71]Marsh v. Chambers, 103 S. Ct. 3330, 3334 (1983). In Townsend v. Sain, 372 U.S. 293, 311 (1963), the Court stated that the "historic conception of the writ [of habeas corpus], anchored in the ancient common law and in our Constitution . . . has remained constant to the present day."

[72]Justice Douglas disclosed that "the 'gut' reactions, of a judge at the level of constitutional adjudications, dealing with the vagaries of due process . . . was the main ingredient of his decision." W. DOUGLAS, THE COURT YEARS, 1939–1975, at 8 (1980); *see also supra* note 7.

[73]394 U.S. 618 (1969). Chief Justice Warren and Justices Black and Harlan dissented.

[74]Z. CHAFEE, THREE HUMAN RIGHTS IN THE CONSTITUTION OF 1787, at 188 (1956).

"nebulous judicial construct";[75] and the *Shapiro* majority noted that the "right finds no explicit mention in the Constitution," but found "no occasion to ascribe the source of this right to travel interstate to a particular constitutional provision," content that it "has been firmly established"— by the Court.[76] But such self-serving statements do not dispense with the necessity of finding constitutional footing for curtailment of long-settled states' rights. Assuming the existence of a "right to travel," it is a manifest non sequitur to insist that it entitles a migrant to immediate support at the terminus.[77]

For 600 years the law and practice were to the contrary, reaching back to pre-Elizabethan custom and law, picked up by colonial enactments and, at the time of *Shapiro*, expressed in the statutes of forty or more States.[78] As Margaret Rosenheim, an admirer of *Shapiro*, wrote, the " 'durational residence requirement' had 'seemed to be permanent'; derived from the Elizabethan Poor Law, it 'had been part of the states' poor relief laws from the beginning.' "[79] English and colonial communities excluded pauper-strangers from support in order to reduce the burden of relief. In providing for the "privileges and immunities" to be extended to residents of sister States, Article IV of the Articles of Confederation declared that the "people of each State shall have *free ingress* and *regress* to and from any other state . . . *paupers . . . excepted.*"[80] Just as the "privileges or immunities" of the fourteenth amendment were "intended [to be] the same" as those of Article IV,[81] so the latter carried all the "limitations" of the predecessor Articles of Confederation phrase.[82] So there is good reason to conclude that the exclusion of paupers has constitutional sanction.

Very early the constitutional validity of state law reflecting these practices was recognized by the Court in *Mayor of New York v. Miln.*[83] Although Justice Story dissented, he "admitted" that the States "have a right to pass poor laws, and laws to prevent the introduction of paupers,"[84] all being in agreement as to the right to exclude paupers.[85] As Justice Story remarked in a similar case, "such long acquiescence in it, such contemporaneous expositions of it, and such extensive and uniform recognition [and embodiment in State law of it] . . . would . . . entitle the question to be considered at rest."[86] Were the issue doubtful, the welfare of indigent migrants should be

[75]Oregon v. Mitchell, 400 U.S. 112, 216 (1970) (Harlan, J., concurring in part and dissenting in part).

[76]Shapiro v. Thompson, 394 U.S. 618, 630 (1969).

[77]*See* Berger, *Residence Requirements for Welfare and Voting: A Post-Mortem,* 42 Ohio St. L.J. 853, 854 n.8 (1981).

[78]*Id.* at 854–66.

[79]*Id.* at 855.

[80]*Id.* at 862.

[81]*Slaughter-House Cases,* 83 U.S. (16 Wall.) 36, 75 (1873).

[82]"[T]he text of article 4, § 2, of the Constitution, makes manifest that it was drawn with reference to the corresponding clause of the Articles of Confederation and was intended to perpetuate its limitations. . . ." United States v. Wheeler, 254 U.S. 281, 294 (1920).

[83]36 U.S. (11 Pet.) 102 (1837).

[84]*Id.* at 156 (Story, J., dissenting).

[85]*See also* Railroad Co. v. Husen, 95 U.S. 465, 470–71 (1877); The Passenger Cases, 48 U.S. (7 How.) 283, 406 (1849).

[86]Prigg v. Pennsylvania, *supra* note 69; for similar utterances, see Berger, *supra* note 77, at 859 n.48. Contemporaneously with the adoption of the fourteenth amendment, Chief Justice Thomas Cooley, with Justice Story a preeminent commentator of the Constitution, wrote:

A constitution is not to be made to mean one thing at one time, and another at some subsequent time when the circumstances may have so changed as perhaps to make a different rule in the case seem desirable. A principal share of the benefit expected from written constitutions would be lost if the rules they established were so flexible as to bend to circumstances or be modified by public opinion. . . . [A] court or legislature which should allow a change in public sentiment to influence it in giving construction to a written constitution a construction *not warranted by the intention of the founders,* would be justly chargeable with reckless disregard of official oath and public duty; and if its course could become a precedent, these instruments would be of little avail.

T. Cooley, *supra* note 69, at 67 (emphasis added). So taken for granted was the "original understanding" rule, that another contemporary court could say without troubling to cite cases that "[o]ne of the cardinal rules of construction is, that courts shall give effect to the intent of the framers of the instrument." Cory v. Carter, 48 Ind. 327, 342 (1874).

balanced against the burden upon local taxpayers of supporting them. The recent deluge of 100,000 Cubans has overtaxed the capacity of Miami to provide needed services and support.[87] For 600 years English, colonial, and state law protected ratepayers from support of indigent migrants. When the Court outlawed such laws in 1969, it disregarded established criteria of constitutionality.

F. The Death Penalty Cases

A final example of unwarranted manipulation of constitutional terms is furnished by the Court's intrusion into the field of death penalties. Hamilton had assured the Ratifiers in *Federalist No. 17* that "[t]here is one transcendent advantage belonging to the province of the State governments . . . the ordinary administration of criminal and civil justice."[88] Nevertheless the Court, under cover of "selective incorporation," has held that a death penalty for rape[89] or for a murderer's accomplice violates the "cruel and unusual punishments" clause of the eighth amendment.[90] And under that banner it has required unprecedented "standards" for jury sentencing that have enabled it to overturn convictions of undoubted murderers.[91] For 300 years, from 1689 when the English Bill of Rights first employed the phrase, until 1972 when the Court belatedly discovered that it curtailed the right to punish by death, such penalties had been employed without let or hindrance. Before that discovery, Hugo Bedau, an impassioned opponent of death penalties, stated, "No death sentence had ever been voided as a violation of due process, equal protection" or "cruel and unusual punishment."[92] "Until fifteen years ago," he wrote, "save for a few mavericks, no one gave any credence to the possibility of ending the death penalty by judicial interpretation of constitutional law. . . . Save for a few eccentrics and visionaries," he remarked, the death penalty was "taken for granted by all men . . . as a bulwark of the social structure."[93] To borrow from the Court's 1983 "legislative chaplain" decision, a practice that "has continued without interruption ever since [the earliest] session of Congress"[94] cannot be deemed a "cruel and unusual punishment." That particular Congress had drafted the eighth amendment, and it enacted a statute which made murder, robbery, and other offenses punishable by death; and to safeguard the penalty it prohibited resort to "benefit of clergy" as an exemption from capital punishment.[95] Further evidence that the Framers did not intend to bar death penalties is furnished by the face of the Constitution, what another "opponent of death penalties," Sanford Levinson, considers a "devastating" fact: "[B]oth the Fifth and Fourteenth Amendments specifically acknowledge the possibility

---

[87]John V. Lindsay, former Mayor of New York, wrote that the federal government must relieve states and local governments of the fiscal burdens that are brought to their doorsteps by the migrating poor. . . . Urban areas, which have become the repositories of the poorest of the nation's poor, will never be able to deliver the essential services . . . as long as they are oppressed by such Federal mandates as welfare and Medicaid. N.Y. Times, Feb. 5, 1981, at A-23.

[88]THE FEDERALIST No. 17 at 103 (Mod. Lib. ed. 1941). He repeated in the New York Ratification Convention, "the states have certain independent powers, in which their laws are supreme; for example, in making and executing laws concerning the punishment of certain crimes, such as murder, theft, etc., the states cannot be controlled." 2 ELLIOTT, *supra* note 65, at 362.

[89]Coker v. Georgia, 433 U.S. 584 (1977).

[90]Enmund v. Florida, 458 U.S. 782 (1982).

[91]R. BERGER, DEATH PENALTIES: THE SUPREME COURT'S OBSTACLE COURSE 128–42 (1982).

[92]H. BEDAU, THE COURTS, THE CONSTITUTION AND CAPITAL PUNISHMENT 81–83 (1977).

[93]*Id.* at 118, 120.

[94]Marsh v. Chambers, 103 S. Ct. 3330, 3334 (1983). Commenting on a construction by the First Congress, confirmed by a practice of 40 years, Madison stated, "No novel construction, however ingeniously devised . . . can withstand the weight of such authorities, or the unbroken current of so prolonged and universal a practice." 4 ELLIOT, *supra* note 65, at 602.

[95]Act of April 30, 1790, ch. 9, 1 Stat. 115, 119. This exemption was first afforded to the clergy and then to such of the laity as could read. M. RADIN, ANGLO-AMERICAN LEGAL HISTORY 230–31 (1936). *See* Hampton Co. v. United States, *supra* note 24.

of a death penalty. They require only that due process of law be followed before a person can be deprived of life." And he reluctantly concedes that "Berger easily shows that the various framers did not regard infliction of death as cruel or unusual."[96]

Fourteen months before the split Court in *Furman v. Georgia*[97] demanded "standards" for the guidance of juries, it declared in *McGautha v. California:* "we find it quite impossible to say that committing to the untrammeled discretion of the jury the power to pronounce life or death in capital cases is offensive to anything in the Constitution."[98]

That conclusion, I found, is confirmed by the historical materials;[99] to cite only the summation by Chief Justice Thomas Cooley, who said of an attempt

> to surround the jury with arbitrary rules as to the weight they shall allow the evidence [which is at the heart of the Court-imposed "standards"] . . . no such arbitrary rules are admissible . . . [T]he jury must be left to weigh the evidence by their own tests. They cannot properly be furnished for this purpose with balances which leave them no discretion.[100]

"Cruel and unusual punishment" left this discretion untouched, for it applied only to the *nature* of the punishment, not to the *process* whereby it was decreed. The "untrammeled discretion" enjoyed for centuries by the jury was an "attribute" of the "trial by jury"[101] secured by the Constitution and therefore protected from judicial control.[102] It follows that the "standards" requirement—which has resulted in a wilderness of confusion[103] and a death row log-jam—is "unconstitutional."[104]

In revising the meaning that "cruel and unusual" had for the Framers, the Court followed in the footsteps of Robespierre: "If Frenchmen would not be free and virtuous voluntarily, then he would force them to be free and cram virtue down their throats."[105] Be it assumed that death penalties are a savage survival, the Court is not empowered to cram its morals down the throats of the American people. They were not deprived by the Constitution of the right to make their own moral choices. Jealously rationing power, circumscribing it at every step, the Framers resorted to familiar

[96]Levinson, *Wrong But Legal?,* Nation, Feb. 26, 1983, at 248–49.

[97]408 U.S. 238 (1972).

[98]402 U.S. 183, 207 (1971).

[99]R. Berger, *supra* note 91, at 133–39.

[100]People v. Garbutt, 17 Mich. L. Rev. 9, 27–28 (1868). The Founders placed their faith in juries, not in judges. R. Berger, *supra* note 91, at 133–34. As said by Herbert Storing, "the jury trial provided the people's safeguard at the bottom, administrative level." 1 H. Storing, The Complete Anti-Federalist 19 (1981) (quoting the *Federal Farmer:* " 'by holding the jury's right to return a general verdict in all cases sacred, we secure to the people at large, their just and rightful control in the judicial department' ").

[101]For assurances by John Marshall, Edmund Randolph, and Edmund Pendleton that "trial by jury" embraced all its "attributes," see J.J. Elliot, Debates in the Several Conventions on the Adoption of the Federal Constitution 464, 546, 549, 559 (2d ed. 1846).

[102]Trial by jury is mentioned several times in the Constitution; judicial review not at all. In the Convention, Elbridge Gerry "urged the necessity of Juries to guard [against] corrupt Judges." 2 M. Farrand, *supra* note 8, at 587. Insistence on "standards" for jury verdicts runs counter to Wilson's praise in the Pennsylvania Ratification Convention of "another advantage annexed to the trial by jury; the jurors may indeed return a mistaken, or ill founded verdict, but their errors cannot be systematical." J. McMaster & F. Stone, *supra* note 27, at 404. *See,* H. Storing, *supra* note 100. The Founders had in mind jury *control of judges,* not judicial control of juries.

[103]R. Berger, *supra* note 91, at 139–52.

[104]In Erie Ry. v. Tompkins, 304 U.S. 64, 79 (1938), the Court, per Justice Brandeis, quoting Justice Holmes, branded the doctrine of Swift v. Tyson, 41 U.S. (16 Pet.) 1 (1842) an "unconstitutional assumption of powers by the Courts of the United States which no lapse of time . . . should make us hesitate to correct."

[105]1 C. Brinton, J. Christopher & R. Wolff, A History of Civilization 115 (1960). From "their experiences under the Protectorate, Englishmen learned that . . . the claims of self-appointed saints to know by divine inspiration what the good life should be and to have the right to impose their notions on the ungodly could be as great a threat as the divine right of kings." Auden, *Introduction* to S. Smith, Selected Writings at xvi (W. Auden ed. 1956).

common law terms to prick out those limits. If the Court is free to substitute its own meaning for the established content of the constitutional terms, it obliterates those limits and substitutes its own predilections.[106] In turning its back on the practice that obtained at the adoption of the Constitution and persisted for another 181 years, the Court assumed power to amend the Constitution, a power that was reserved to the people.

II. ACTIVIST JUSTIFICATIONS OF JUDICIAL REVISIONISM

Activist writings, Mark Tushnet observes, are "plainly designed to protect the legacy of the Warren Court,"[107] and to that end activists are busily spinning theories whose only merit is novelty.[108]

A. The "Original Intention"

Activist attacks on the original intention rule are a very recent phenomenon, inspired by the need to protect the desegregation and reapportionment decisions which demonstrably are contrary to the framers' intention. Typical is Paul Brest:

> [M]any scholars and judges reject Berger's major premise, that constitutional interpretation should depend chiefly on the intent of those who framed and adopted a provision. . . . [W]hatever the framers' expectations may have been, broad constitutional guarantees require the Court to discern, articulate and apply values that are widely and deeply held by our society. . . .[109]

"Widely and deeply held" cannot be said of the school prayer, abortion, and death penalty decisions. And among the judges who do not share Brest's view was his "beloved mentor,"[110] Justice Harlan: "When the Court disregards the express intent and understanding of the Framers, it has invaded the realm of the political process to which the amending power was committed. . . ."[111] In truth, activists seek to jettison a doctrine of which Jacobus tenBroek, a critic of the rule, said "[the Court] has insisted, with almost uninterrupted regularity, that the end and object of constitutional construction is the discovery of the intention of those persons who formulated the instrument. . . ."[112]

1. Common Law Terms

It will be illuminating first to discuss the Framers' cognate employment of common law terms. The Founders resorted to a written constitution the more clearly to limit delegated power, to

---

[106]See *infra* text accompanying note 126; *and cf.* Hampton & Co. v. United States, 276 U.S. 394 (1928), quoted *supra* note 24.

[107]Tushnet, *Legal Realism, Structural Review and Prophecy*, 8 U. DAYTON L. REV. 809, 811 (1983).

[108]Brest adjures academe "simply to acknowledge that most of our writings [about judicial review] are not political theory but advocacy scholarship—amicus briefs ultimately designed to persuade the Court to adopt our various notions of the public good." Brest, *The Fundamental Rights Controversy: The Essential Contradictions of Normative Scholarship*, 90 YALE L.J. 1063, 1109 (1981). See also his rejection of the rationalizations of "seven representative scholars," *id.* at 1067–89.

[109]Brest, Book Review, N.Y. Times, Dec. 11, 1977, at 11 col. 2. But Brest blows hot and cold on the issue. When he attacks congressional control of federal jurisdiction, in the face of an unequivocal grant by article III, he does not scruple to call upon the "intention" of the Framers. P. BREST, PROCESSES OF CONSTITUTIONAL DECISIONMAKING: CASES AND MATERIALS 1329 (1975).

[110]So Harlan is identified in Brest's dedication of his casebook. P. BREST, *supra* note 109, at 1329.

[111]Oregon v. Mitchell, 400 U.S. 112, 203 (1970) (Harlan, J., concurring in part and dissenting in part); *see also supra* note 80.

[112]tenBroek, *Use by the Supreme Court of Extrinsic Evidence in Constitutional Construction: The Intent Theory of Constitutional Construction*, 27 CALIF. L. REV. 399 (1939).

establish a "fixed" constitution alterable only by amendment.[113] A key means for accomplishment of that purpose was their use of common law terms of established and familiar meaning.[114] Doubtless, the Framers were aware of the long-settled rule of construction expressed in Matthew Bacon's *Abridgment:* "If a statute makes use of a Word the meaning of which is well known at the Common Law, the Word shall be understood in the same sense it was understood at the Common Law."[115] Chief Justice Marshall applied the rule in *Gibbons v. Ogden,* stating that if a word was understood in a certain sense "when the Constitution was framed . . . the convention must have used it in that sense," and it is that sense that is to be given judicial effect.[116] A procession of judges followed in his path.[117] And in 1925 the Court explained:

> The language of the Constitution cannot be interpreted safely except by reference to the common law and to British institutions as they were when the instrument was framed and adopted. The statesmen and lawyers of the Convention . . . were born and brought up in the atmosphere of the common law, and thought and spoke in its vocabulary. . . . [W]hen they came to put their conclusions into the form of fundamental law in a compact draft, they expressed them in terms of the common law, confident that they could be shortly and easily understood.[118]

Examples of such terms are bills of attainder, ex post facto, habeas corpus, and trial by jury. To express all that was implicated in "trial by jury," for example, would have required prolix detail unsuited to a "compact draft." Hence, when anxious delegates inquired whether they would have the prized right to challenge jurors, they were assured that it was an "attribute" of trial by jury.[119] So rooted was the presupposition that English law would apply that the First Congress prohibited resort to "benefit of clergy" as an exemption from capital punishment.[120] Consequently, as Justice Story stated in 1820, the common law "definitions are necessarily included, as much *as if they stood in the text* of the act."[121]

Activists counter that over the years words change their meaning.[122] But it does not follow that we may saddle the Framers with *our* meaning.[123] Even Humpty Dumpty did not carry it so far as

---

[113]P. KURLAND. WATERGATE AND THE CONSTITUTION 7 (1983). Justice William Paterson, a leading Framer, declared, "The constitution is certain and fixed . . . and can be revoked or altered only by the authority that made it." Van Horne v. Dorrance, 28 F. Cas. 1012, 1014 (1795) (No. 16,857). Chief Justice Marshall, who had been a proponent of judicial review in the Virginia Ratification Convention, declared that a written constitution was designed to define and limit power, and asked, "To what purpose are powers limited . . . if those limits may, at any time, be passed by those intended to be restrained." Marbury v. Madison, 5 U.S. (1 Cranch) 137, 176 (1803).

Justice Story emphasized that:

the government of the United States is one of limited and enumerated powers; and that a departure from the true import and sense of its powers is *pro tanto* the establishment of a new constitution. It is doing for the people, what they have not chosen to do for themselves. It is usurping the functions of a legislator.

1 J. STORY, COMMENTARIES ON THE CONSTITUTION OF THE UNITED STATES § 426 (5th ed. 1905).

[114]For a detailed discussion, see R. BERGER, *supra* note 91, at 59–76.

[115]4 M. BACON, *supra* note 61, at (1), (4).

[116]22 U.S. (9 Wheat.) 1, 190 (1824); *see also* Thompson v. Utah, 170 U.S. 343, 350 (1898).

[117]For citations, see Berger, *Bills of Attainder: A Study of Amendment by the Court,* 64 CORNELL L. REV. 355, 361, 362–63 n. 55 (1978).

[118]*Ex parte* Grossman, 267 U.S. 87, 108–09 (1925).

[119]3 ELLIOT, *supra* note 65, at 467–68, 546, 556–59. Justice Bushrod Washington stated, "The right of challenge was a privilege highly esteemed and anxiously guarded at the common law. . . ." United States v. Johns, 26 F. Cas. 616, 617 (C.C.D. Pa. 1806) (No. 15,481).

[120]*See supra* note 95.

[121]United States v. Smith, 18 U.S. (5 Wheat.) 153, 160 (1820) (emphasis added).

[122]*E.g.* Wofford, *The Blinding Light: The Uses of History in Constitutional Interpretation,* 31 U. CHI. L. REV. 502, 523 (1964); *cf.* L. LEVY, JUDGMENTS: ESSAYS ON AMERICAN CONSTITUTIONAL HISTORY 71 (1972).

[123]In his casebook, Brest wrote:

Suppose that the Constitution provided that some acts were to be performed "bi-weekly." At the time of the framing of the Constitution, this meant only "once every two weeks"; but modern dictionaries, bowing to pervasive misuse, now

to insist that when Alice "used" a word *he* could dictate what *she* meant. The beau ideal of activists, Chief Justice Warren, said, "[t]he provisions of the Constitution" are "the rules of government."[124] By changing the meaning of the words in which they were framed the Court changes the rules, thereby reducing written limits on power to ropes of sand. Chief Justice Taney perceived that "[i]f in this Court we are at liberty to give old words new meanings . . . there is no power which may not, by this mode of construction, be conferred on the general government and denied to the States."[125] That constitutional terms must mean what they meant to the Framers was categorically stated by the Court.[126] With Willard Hurst, I would underscore that "[i]f the idea of a document of superior legal authority"—the "fixed Constitution" dear to the Framers—"is to have meaning, terms which have a precise, history-filled content to those who draft and adopt the document or to which they attach a clear meaning must be held to that precise meaning."[127]

2. The Framers' Intention

For Hurst, the terms to which the Framers attached clear meaning[128] were no more alterable than common law words of established meaning. Common sense demands no less. Why should words which are defined by external common law practice weigh more heavily than those clearly explained by the draftsmen themselves? Respect for their intention goes back to medieval days, as the Court noted, saying "the books are full of authorities to the effect that the intention of the lawmaking power will prevail, even against the letter of the statute. . . . 'The intention of the lawmaker is the law.' "[129] That was the established rule at the framing of the Constitution. In a treatise known to colonists, Thomas Rutherforth assimilated the interpretation of statutes to that of contracts and wills, and stated that "[t]he end, which interpreters aim at, is to find out what was the intention *of the writer* to clear up the meaning of his words."[130] On the heels of the Convention, Justice James Wilson, second only to Madison as an architect of the Constitution, said, "[t]he first and governing maxim in the interpretation of a statute is, to discover the meaning

report "twice a week" (i.e., semi-weekly) as an acceptable definition. To construe the provision now to mean "semi-weekly" would certainly be a change of meaning (and an improper one at that).

P. BREST, *supra* note 109, at 146 n. 38. That has been the accepted view:

The Constitution is a written instrument. As such its meaning does not alter. That which it meant when adopted it means now. . . . "Any other rule of construction would abrogate the judicial character of this court, and make it a mere reflex of the popular opinions or passion of the day."

South Carolina v. United States, 199 U.S. 437, 448, 449 (1905). Activists seek to bend the Court to their own passions, *See supra* note 108, often at war with those of the people.

[124]Trop v. Dulles, 356 U.S. 86, 103 (1958). Warren's comment reveals his constitutional naivete, for in this very case he was engaged in rewriting the "rules." R. BERGER, *supra* note 91, at 116–22.

[125]The Passenger Cases, 48 U.S. (7 How.) 283, 478 (1849) (Taney, C.J. dissenting). Madison stated, if "the sense in which the Constitution was accepted and ratified by the nation . . . be not the guide in expounding it, there can be no security . . . for a faithful exercise of its powers." 9 J. MADISON, WRITINGS 191 (G. Hunt ed. 1900–1910).

[126]*See* South Carolina v. United States, *supra* note 116; and Marshall, C.J. *supra* text accompanying note 116.

[127]Hurst, *The Process of Constitutional Construction,* in SUPREME COURT AND SUPREME LAW 55, 57 (E. Cahn ed. 1954).

[128]It needs emphasis that I did not treat *ambiguous* legislative history but confined myself to the framers' *unmistakable* intention to exclude suffrage and segregation from the ambit of the fourteenth amendment.

[129]Hawaii v. Mankichi, 190 U.S. 197, 212 (1903).

[130]T. RUTHERFORTH, INSTITUTES OF NATURAL LAW 307 (1754–1756). Rutherforth's INSTITUTES, said Justice Story, "contain a very lucid exposition of the general rules of interpretation." 1 STORY, *supra* note 113, § 403 n. 1, at 285. Justice Robert Yates of the New York Supreme Court and a delegate to the Convention, wrote under the pseudonym "Brutus" that the Constitution is to be explained "according to the rules laid down for construing a law." C. KENYON, THE ANTIFEDERALISTS 337 (1966).

Recognition of the writer's intention is the very essence of communication. As Walter Benn Michaels observes, "no one treats sounds or marks as words unless he or she thinks of them as speech acts expressing the intentions of some agent. No one would even try to interpret the Constitution if everyone thought it had been put together by a tribe of monkeys with quills." Michaels, Book Review, 61 TEX. L. REV. 765, 774 (1982) (footnote omitted).

of those, who made it."[131] The reason was made clear by Justice Story, asking how a federal statute is to be interpreted. "Are the rules of the common law to furnish the proper guide, or is every court and department to give it any interpretation it may please, according to its own arbitrary will?"[132] The Founders preferred rules, in the words of Chancellor Kent, to "a dangerous discretion . . to roam at large in the trackless field of [the judges'] own imagination."[133]

In a "blinding" flash of insight, Judge John Gibbons of the Third Circuit Court of Appeals[134] rejected the application "to constitutional history of the inadequate tools of statutory interpretation."[135] Are judges to enjoy greater discretion in seeking the will of the Framers than they do in the case of mere legislators? Why indeed should we be willing to effectuate the will of a testator and deny effect to the unmistakable intention of the Framers? Gibbons overlooked that the common law proceeds by analogy, from wills to statutes, from statutes to constitutions. Since the common law knew no written constitutions, judges had to turn, as did Marshall, to rules pertaining to "other legal documents."[136] Edward Corwin observed that our early judges adapted "the numerous [common law] rules for construction of written instruments . . . to the business of constitutional construction."[137] Julius Goebel likewise noted that the Founders were accustomed to "resort to the accepted rules of statutory interpretation to settle the intent and meaning of constitutional provisions."[138] Other commentators concur.[139]

Gibbons' ill-considered foray can draw comfort from the reigning idol of jurisprudes, Ronald Dworkin, who flatly asserts that "there is no such thing as the intention of the Framers waiting to be discovered."[140] He is refuted by what Justice Harlan justly described as the "irrefutable and . . . unanswered" evidence[141] for the framers' exclusion of suffrage from the fourteenth amendment. The pervasive hostility to Negro suffrage is strikingly exemplified by the 112-to-12 and 34-to-4 votes in the House and Senate, rejecting attempts to compel Tennessee to embody Negro suffrage in its Constitution.[142] Here are indubitable "intentions."

Weighing the alternatives, Mark Tushnet observed that the interpretivist view that "we are indeed better off being bound by the dead hand of the past then being subjected to the whims of

---

[131]THE WORKS OF JAMES WILSON 75 (R. McCloskey ed. 1967). Justice Holmes observed, "Of course, the purpose of written instruments is to express some intention or state of mind of those who write them, and it is desirable to make that purpose effectual. . . ." O. HOLMES, COLLECTED LEGAL PAPERS 206 (1920).

[132]1 J. STORY, supra note 113, § 158 n. 2, at 112.

[133]1 J. KENT, COMMENTARIES ON AMERICAN LAW 373 (9th ed. 1858).

[134]Gibbons charged me with discerning the original intention "with blinding clarity in the stygian darkness of the records of the 39th Congress." Gibbons, Book Review, 31 RUTGERS L. REV. 839, 840 (1978). This is about the "irrefutable" exclusion of suffrage from the fourteenth amendment!

[135]Id. at 847. President Washington, however, appealed to the original understanding in maintaining that a treaty did not require consent of the House. Washington said that in the Journal of the Convention it appeared " 'that no Treaty should be binding on the United States which was not ratified by a law,' and that the proposition was explicitly rejected." 3 M. FARRAND, supra note 8, at 371. Although Madison considered that the meaning of the Constitution was to be sought in the records of the Ratification Convention rather than in those of the Federal Convention, id. at 518, he nevertheless turned to the understanding of the Framers, id. at 458, 464, 473, 534.

Activists attack the "original intention" because it thwarts their free-wheeling interpretations. Paul Bator remarks on "the total triumph of a kind of reductionist legal realism, that leads people to believe that you are entitled to put anything you want in the Constitution." Bator, supra note 20, at 53.

[136]Tushnet, Following the Rules Laid Down: A Critique of Interpretivism and Neutral Principles, 96 HARV. L. REV. 781, 786 (1983).

[137]Corwin, The "Higher Law" Background of American Constitutional Law, 42 HARV. L. REV. 149, 371 (1938).

[138]1 JULIUS GOEBEL, HISTORY OF THE SUPREME COURT 128 (1971).

[139]E.g., Jones, The Common Law in the United States: English Themes and American Variations, in POLITICAL SEPARATION AND LEGAL CONTINUITY 101, 102, 134 (H. Jones ed. 1976).

[140]Dworkin, The Forum of Principle, 56 N.Y.U.L. REV. 469, 477 (1981).

[141]Supra text accompanying note 43.

[142]Supra text accompanying note 41.

willful judges trying to make the Constitution live . . . [is] 'fairly powerful.' "[143] Feeble are the arguments to the contrary. As said by Justice Harlan, "[w]hen the Court disregards the express intent and understanding of the Framers [as with segregation and suffrage], it has invaded the realm of the political process to which the amending power was committed, and it has violated the constitutional structure which is its highest duty to protect."[144] Activists may flatter themselves that they have buried the "intention" doctrine, but the corpse sprang to life in the Court's recent "legislative chaplain" case: "Clearly the men who wrote the First Amendment religion clause did not view paid legislative chaplains and opening prayers as a violation of that amendment."[145]

B. General Language

Activists rely heavily on the "general" terms employed in the Constitution as an "invitation" to judicial legislation. The argument will be considered first in the 1787 setting and then in the 1866 setting of the fourteenth amendment.

1. 1787

Amongst the "circumstantial evidence that the framers authorized interpreters of the Constitution to make value judgments that are not necessarily analogous to the framers' own particular value judgments," Gary Leedes points to Carl Friedrich's statement that in the eighteenth century norms were considered "the more important and valuable, the more general they were."[146] Yet Samuel Adams wrote that "[v]ague and uncertain laws, and more especially constitutions, are the very instruments of slavery."[147] One of the Framers, Rufus King, told the Massachusetts Convention that the Federal Convention sought "to use those expressions that were . . . least equivocal in their meaning. . . . We believe that the powers are clearly defined, the expressions as free from ambiguity as the Convention could form them. . . ."[148] Understandably, Madison wrote that "it exceeds the possibility of belief, that the known advocates in the Convention for a jealous grant & cautious definition of federal powers, should have silently permitted the introduction of words or phrases in a sense rendering fruitless the restrictions & definitions elaborated by them."[149] Men do not use words to defeat their purpose.[150]

Nevertheless, John Hart Ely regards the ninth amendment as an open-ended provision, "intended to signal the existence of federal constitutional rights beyond those specifically enumerated in the Constitution."[151] "[R]ead for what it says," he avers, "the Ninth Amendment seems open-textured enough to support almost anything one might wish to argue, and that thought can get pretty scary."[152] An "open-ended" grant that scares Ely across the gap of 200 years can hardly be laid at the door of the Founders, to many of whom the federal courts were suspect.[153] The ninth amend-

---

[143]Tushnet, *supra,* note 136, at 787. The theory, interpretivism, that the Court is not empowered to revise the Constitution, says Thomas Grey, a devout activist, is "of great power and compelling simplicity . . . deeply rooted in our history and . . . in our formal constitutional law . . . the theory upon which judicial review was founded in *Marbury v. Madison.*" Grey, *Do We Have an Unwritten Constitution?* 27 STAN L. REV. 703, 705 (1975).

[144]Oregon v. Mitchell, 400 U.S. 112, 203 (1970) (dissenting in part). Henry Monaghan insists "that any theory of constitutional interpretation which renders unimportant or irrelevant questions as to the original intent, *so far as that intent can be fairly discerned,* is not, given our tradition, politically or intellectually defensible." Monaghan, *The Constitution Goes to Harvard,* 13 HARV. C.R., C.L. L. REV. 117, 124 (1978).

[145]Marsh v. Chambers, 103 S. Ct. 3330, 3334 (1983).

[146]Leedes, *A Critique of Illegitimate Noninterpretivism,* 8 U. DAYTON L. REV. 533, 552, 553 (1983).

[147]3 S. ADAMS, WRITINGS 262 (H. Cushing ed. 1904).

[148]3 M. FARRAND, *supra* note 8, at 268.

[149]*Id.* at 488.

[150]United States v. Classic, 313 U.S. 299, 316 (1941).

[151]J. ELY, DEMOCRACY AND DISTRUST 38 (1980).

[152]*Id.* at 34.

[153]R. BERGER, CONGRESS V. THE SUPREME COURT 263–64 (1969).

ment provides, "[t]he enumeration in the Constitution of certain rights shall not be construed to deny or disparage others retained by the people." Madison made clear that the retained rights were not "assigned" to the federal government, emphasizing that they constitute an area in which the "[g]overnment ought not to act."[154] Ely himself observes, "[o]ne thing we know to a certainty from the historical context is that the Ninth Amendment was not designed to grant Congress authority to *create* additional rights, to amend Article I, Section 8 by adding a *general power to protect* rights," pointing out that the phrase "others retained by the people" is not "an apt way of saying 'others Congress may create.' "[155] What Congress may not "create" also lies outside the judicial province. Madison left no doubt that the "great object" of a Bill of Rights was to "limit and qualify the powers of Government, by *excepting out* of the grant of power those cases in which the Government ought not to act or to act only in a particular mode."[156] It perverts meaning to read the *retention* of unenumerated rights as a grant of "open-ended" power.

2. 1866

Instead of meeting the undeniable exclusion of suffrage, for example, activists rely on the generality of the fourteenth amendment's language. Thus Gary Leedes considers that "[t]he loose language of the fourteenth amendment . . . was a standing invitation for innovative interpretation."[157] So too, Ely asserts that its framers issued "open and across-the-board invitations to import into the constitutional decision process considerations that will not be found in the amendment nor [sic] even . . . elsewhere in the Constitution."[158] For him the "Privileges or Immunities" clause is "inscrutable," and the "Equal Protection" clause no more forthcoming.[159] He is aware, moreover, that "vague and untethered standards inevitably lend themselves to the virtually irresistible temptation to intervene when one's political or moral sensitivities are sufficiently affronted."[160] His attribution to the framers of an intention to issue such an invitation to the Court is at war with his recognition that the *Dred Scott* (and fugitive slave cases) had "spilled over into a general distrust of the institution of judicial review."[161] In truth, the framers bitterly resented the Court's intrusion into "settlement of political questions which," said John Bingham, "it has no more right to decide for the American people than has the Court of St. Petersburg."[162] In consequence, they confided enforcement of the amendment to Congress, not the Court; section 5 provides "*Congress* shall have power to enforce. . . ." This is incompatible with a free rein to read judicial predilections into the amendment. Now to examine the several clauses.

[154] 1 ANNALS OF CONG. 439, 437 (Gales & Seaton eds. 1836) (print bearing running title "History of Congress").

[155] J. ELY, *supra* note 144, at 37.

[156] 1 ANNALS OF CONG., *supra* note 154, at 437. What the Supreme Court said of the tenth amendment equally applies to the ninth; the Framers intended that:
[i]f in the future further powers seemed necessary they should be granted by the people in the manner they had provided for amending that [organic] act.

. . . .

. . . [A]fter making provision for an amendment to the Constitution by which any needed additional powers would be granted, they reserved to themselves all powers not so delegated.
Kansas v. Colorado, 206 U.S. 46, 90 (1907).

[157] Leedes, *supra* note 146, at 556. But compare Justice Harlan: "The general statements by Bingham and Stevens to the effect that the Amendment was designed to achieve equality . . . do not weaken the force of the statements specifically addressed to the suffrage question." Oregon v. Mitchell, 400 U.S. 112, 186 n.54 (1970). The specific governs the general.

[158] Ely, *Constitutional Interpretivism: Its Allure and Impossibility*, 53 IND. L.J. 399, 415 (1978). Such theorizing is dismissed by Larry Alexander, as "some dubious invitation from the Framers to transcend the specific values [and limitations] they embodied in various constitutional clauses." Alexander, *Painting Without the Numbers: Noninterpretive Judicial Review*, 8 U. DAYTON L. REV. 447 (1983).

[159] J. ELY, *supra* note 151, at 98.

[160] Ely, *supra* note 158, at 403.

[161] *Id.* at 448.

[162] 6 C. FAIRMAN, HISTORY OF THE SUPREME COURT OF THE UNITED STATES 462 (1971).

a. Due Process

Leedes' reference to the "loose language" of the amendment is paralleled by others who label the due process clause, for instance, as "vague."[163] To the extent that it is "vague," it is because the Court has made it so. On the eve of the Convention, Hamilton stated that "[t]he words, 'due process' have a precise technical import, and are only applicable to the process and proceedings of the courts of justice."[164] Charles Curtis, an admirer of the Court's transformation of due process, wrote that the meaning of the fifth amendment's due process of law "was as fixed and definite as the common law could make a phrase. . . . It meant a procedural process."[165] In the fourteenth amendment the words were "used in the same sense and with no greater extent,"[166] as the legislative history confirms. Ely found no references that gave the fourteenth's clause "more than a procedural connotation."[167] The framers did not view "due process" as a "vague" term but one of fixed and narrow meaning.[168]

b. Privileges or Immunities

The words "privileges and immunities" are first met in article IV of the Articles of Confederation: "the people of the different states . . . shall be entitled to all privileges and immunities of free citizens in the several states," specifying "all the privileges of trade or commerce."[169] For the Founders, the enumerated "privileges of trade or commerce" qualified the general words "privileges and immunities."[170] The latter words were picked up by article IV of the Constitution, and very early the courts of Maryland and Massachusetts construed them in terms of trade and commerce.[171] The words came into the fourteenth amendment via the Civil Rights Bill of 1866, which referred to "*civil rights* and immunities."[172] After reading from the cases, Senator Lyman Trumbull,

---

[163]F. FRANKFURTER, MR. JUSTICE HOLMES AND THE SUPREME COURT 19 (2d. ed. 1961): "phrases like 'due process of law' [are] . . . of 'convenient vagueness.' "

[164]4 THE PAPERS OF ALEXANDER HAMILTON 35 (H. Syrett & J. Cooke eds. 1962). Two English scholars who presumably are familiar with English legal institutions are in accord with Hamilton. Lord Beloff wrote, due process of law "was transformed from an apparently procedural limitation into one of substance . . . from a statement that some things should be done only in a particular way [judicial proceedings] to a statement that some things could not be done at all even by legislation." M. BELOFF, *supra* note 1, at 48. Denis Brogan referred to the "astonishingly wide meaning given to 'due process of law,' " which "has come to mean anything that a majority of the Court has found contrary to its sense of natural justice and enlightened reason." D. BROGAN, THE CRISIS OF AMERICAN FEDERALISM 32 (1944) (footnotes omitted). For a study of English antecedents see Berger, *"Law of the Land" Reconsidered,* 74 Nw. U.L. REV. 1 (1979). In a classic work, Charles G. Haines wrote that due process of law "referred in England to a method of procedure in criminal trials," and that when the term was "inserted in the American state constitutions it was accepted with the usual English significance" and "chiefly used as a protection to individuals against summary and arbitrary executive action," and "not regarded as a check on legislative authority." C. HAINES, THE AMERICAN DOCTRINE OF JUDICIAL SUPREMACY 410 (1959).

[165]Curtis, *Review and Majority Rule,* in SUPREME COURT AND SUPREME LAW 170, 177 (E. Cahn ed. 1954). "When the Fifth Amendment was added to the Constitution in 1792, no one . . . had ever suggested that the term 'due process of law' had any other than its anciently established and self-evident meaning of correct procedure. . . ." E. CORWIN, THE TWILIGHT OF THE SUPREME COURT 95 (1934). The "modern doctrine of due process of law . . . could never have been laid down except in defiance of history." *Id.* at 118–19.

[166]Hurtado v. California, 110 U.S. 516, 535 (1884).

[167]Ely, *supra* note 158, at 288. R. BERGER, *supra* note 4, at 201–06.

[168]James Garfield, a framer of the fourteenth amendment, explained in 1871 that due process of law meant "an impartial trial according to the law of the land." CONG. GLOBE, 42d Cong., 1st Sess. 152–53 (1871).

[169]H. COMMAGER, DOCUMENTS OF AMERICAN HISTORY 111 (7th ed. 1963).

[170]Madison wrote:
[F]or what purpose could the enumeration of particular powers be inserted, if these and all others were meant to be included in the preceding general power? Nothing is more natural nor common than first to use a general phrase, and then to explain and qualify it by a recital of particulars.
THE FEDERALIST No. 41, at 269 (Mod. Lib. ed. 1941).

[171]Campbell v. Morris, 3 H.&McH. 535 (Md. 1797); Abbot v. Bayley, 6 Pick. 89 (Mass. 1827).

[172]Section 1 of the bill is set out in CONG. GLOBE, 39th Cong., 1st Sess. 474 (1866).

chairman of the Senate Judiciary Committee, stated that "[t]he great fundamental rights set forth in this bill [are] the right to acquire property, the right to . . . make contracts, and to inherit and dispose of property,"[173] the very rights the Black Codes denied.[174] Even so, John Bingham, draftsman of the amendment, protested that "civil rights and immunities" was "oppressive" and so broad as to encroach on the province of the states.[175] So the phrase was deleted in order to obviate a "construction going beyond the specific rights named in the section," a "latitudinarian construction not intended."[176] In substituting the narrower word "privileges" for "rights" in the amendment, Bingham hardly embraced the "latitudinarian construction" he had denounced.[177] Justice Bradley declared in 1870 that "the first section of the bill covers the same ground as the fourteenth amendment."[178] That ground, the Supreme Court stated, was narrow.[179]

By virtue of judicial construction, recognized by the framers, the words "privileges and immunities" had become words of art. Judge William Lawrence, regarded by his congressional fellows as a scholarly lawyer, observed that "the courts have by construction limited the words 'all privileges' to mean only 'some privileges.' "[180] On the basis of much thinner evidence, the Court, per Justice Harlan, declared, "we should not assume that Congress . . . used the words 'advocate' and 'teach' in their ordinary dictionary meanings when they had already been construed as terms of art carrying a special and limited connotation."[181]

c. Equal Protection of the Laws

Unlike its companion clauses, "equal protection of the laws" had no antecedents. In such a case, Senator Charles Sumner counselled the framers that if the meaning of the Constitution is "in any place open to doubt, or if words are used which seem to have no fixed significance, we cannot err if we turn to the framers."[182] Such were the views of his fellows in the Reconstruction Congress, summarized by a "unanimous Senate Judiciary Report, signed by Senators who had voted for the Thirteenth, Fourteenth and Fifteenth Amendments,"[183] the subject being the fourteenth:

---

[173]*Id.* at 475.

[174]The Black Codes "excluded blacks from voting, owning land, making contracts, securing access to the courts, working without a license, travelling without a pass, or engaging in certain trades." Dimond, *Strict Construction and Judicial Review of Racial Discrimination Under the Equal Protection Clause: Meeting Raoul Berger on Interpretivist Grounds*, 80 MICH. L. REV. 462, 474 (1982).

[175]CONG. GLOBE, 39th Cong., 1st Sess. 1291 (1866).

[176]*Id.* at 1366, 1367.

[177]CONG. GLOBE, 39th Cong., 1st Sess. 1034 (1866). Justice Harlan pointed out that in the Joint Committee on Reconstruction, Bingham was "successful in replacing § 1 of Owen's proposal, which read: 'No discrimination . . . as to the civil rights' with the . . . 'abridge the privileges or immunities of citizens' " avowedly borrowed from article IV. Oregon v. Mitchell, 400 U.S. 112, 172 (1970).

[178]Live-Stock Dealers' & Butchers' Ass'n v. Crescent City Live-Stock Landing & Slaughter House Co., 15 F. Cas. 649, 655 (C.C.D. La. 1870) (No. 8,408).

[179]The legislative history of the 1866 Act clearly indicates that Congress intended to protect a limited category of rights. . . . [T]he Senate bill did contain a general provision forbidding "discrimination in civil rights or immunities," preceding the specific enumeration of rights. . . . Objections were raised in the legislative debates to the breadth of the rights of social equality that might be encompassed by a prohibition so general. . . . [A]n amendment was accepted [in the House] striking the phrase from the bill.
Georgia v. Rachel, 384 U.S. 780, 791–92 (1966).

[180]CONG. GLOBE, 39th Cong., 1st Sess. 1835 (1866).

[181]Yates v. United States, 354 U.S. 298, 391 (1957). Chief Justice Taney stated, "The members of the Convention unquestionably used the words they inserted in the Constitution in the same sense in which they used them in their debates." The Passenger Cases, 48 U.S. (7 How.) 283, 477 (1849) (Taney, J., dissenting). *See also* Marshall, *supra* text accompanying note 116, and Thompson v. Utah, 170 U.S. 343, 350 (1898).

[182]CONG. GLOBE, 39th Cong., 1st Sess. 677 (1866).

[183]RECONSTRUCTION AMENDS., *supra* note 40, at ii.

A construction which should give the phrase . . . a meaning different from the sense in which it was understood and employed by the people when they adopted the Constitution, would be as unconstitutional as a departure from the plain and express language of the Constitution . . . This is the rule of interpretation adopted by all commentators on the Constitution, and in all judicial expositions of that instrument.[184]

Mark that the Report considered the framers' intention as weighty as the text, and, as Chief Justice Marshall had laid down, the meaning the words had for the framers was to be given effect.[185] That meaning is scarcely open to doubt; emphatically it was not expressive of uncircumscribed, boundless equality. Time and again the framers had rejected proposals to ban *all* discrimination.[186] Throughout the debates on the Civil Rights Bill—which proceeded on a parallel track with the amendment, which it was an object of the amendment to incorporate and shield from repeal, and which without dissent was *regarded* as identical with the amendment[187]—the framers associated equal protection with the narrow group of rights the bill enumerated. One example must suffice: Samuel Shellabarger of Ohio said, "whatever rights as to each of the enumerated civil (not political) matters the States may confer upon one race . . . shall be held by all races in equality . . . It [the bill] secures *equality of protection in those enumerated* civil rights."[188] If two acts are in *pari materia*, the Court held, "it will be presumed that if the same word be used in both, and a special meaning were given to it in the first act, that it was intended that it should receive the same interpretation in the latter act, in the absence of anything to show a contrary intention."[189] The repeated rejection of proposals to bar all discrimination forecloses a "contrary intention." It strains credulity to impute to Bingham, draftsman of the amendment, the "oppressive" breadth he had condemned in the bill.

Activists turn their back on such facts and instead descant on the framers' choice of "general" words in place of the enumerated rights of the bill. This recalls Henry Hart's scathing comment that William Crosskey "is a devotee of that technique of interpretation which reaches its apogee of persuasiveness in the triumphant question, 'If that's what they meant, why didn't they say so?' "[190] Enumeration, as Bickel noted, would conduce to the prolixity of a code.[191] Moreover, the framers could rely on the rule that the words they used would be construed as they understood them.[192] The issue was summed up in 1974 by Robert Bork:

> The words are general but surely that would not permit us to escape the framers' intent if it were clear. If the legislative history revealed a consensus about segregation in schooling. . . . I do not see how the

---

[184]S. REP. No. 21, 42d Cong., 2d Sess. 2 (1872), *reprinted in* RECONSTRUCTION AMENDS., *supra* note 40, at 571.

[185]*See supra* note 116 and accompanying text.

[186]R. BERGER, *supra* note 4, at 163–65.

[187]*Id.* at 22–23; *see also* Justice Bradley, *supra* text accompanying note 178.

[188]2 CONG. GLOBE, 39th Cong., 1st Sess. 1293 (1866); for other citations see R. BERGER, *supra* note 4, at 169–71; *see also* The Passenger Cases, 48 U.S. (7 How.) 283, 483 (1849) (Taney, C.J., dissenting) (quoted *supra* note 181).

[189]Reiche v. Smythe, 80 U.S. (13 Wall.) 162, 165 (1871).

[190]Hart, Book Review, 67 HARV. L. REV. 1456, 1462 (1954). Justice Holmes held that when a legislature "has intimated its will, however indirectly, that will should be recognized and obeyed. . . . [I]t is not an adequate discharge of duty for courts to say 'We see what you are driving at, but you have not said it.' " Johnson v. United States, 163 F. 30, 32 (1st Cir. 1908), *quoted in* Keifer & Keifer v. Reconstruction Fin. Corp., 306 U.S. 381, 391 n.4 (1939). Activists, moreover, reverse the burden of proof. Given that by "inscrutable" words they would diminish the rights reserved to the states by the tenth amendment (*see infra*, text accompanying notes 191–99) it is incumbent upon them to prove the intention to curtail. *See infra* text accompanying notes 193–94.

[191]The "specific and exclusive enumeration of rights as appeared in section 1 of the Civil Rights Act" presumably was considered inappropriate in a constitutional provision. Bickel, *supra* note 54, at 61. A similar proposal in the First Congress led Abraham Baldwin, a Framer, to say that such minute regulation "would have swelled [the Constitution] to the size of a folio volume." 1 ANNALS OF CONG. *supra* note 154, at 559.

[192]*Supra* text accompanying note 116; The Passenger Cases, 48 U.S. (How.) 283, 477 (1849) (Taney, C.J., dissenting) (quoted *supra* note 181).

Court could escape the choices revealed and substitute its own, even though the words are general and conditions have changed.[193]

Judge Learned Hand said of the desegregation decision, "I have never been able to understand on what basis it does or can rest except as a *coup de main*."[194] The soundness of such views is attested by a remarkable fact: in an early version of the amendment, provision was made for both "the same political rights and privileges; and . . . equal protection in the enjoyment of life, liberty, and property," testimony that "equal protection" was not deemed to comprehend "political rights and privileges."[195] When the latter words were deleted, at the instance of John Bingham, its draftsman,[196] leaving "equal protection" standing alone, the latter patently did not include the elided "political privileges." Now to insist that "equal protection" includes what unmistakably was excluded, namely suffrage and segregation, is, in the words of Justice Story, to commit "a fraud" upon the people.[197]

Yet another formidable hurdle confronts the "general" words school—the tenth amendment: "The powers not delegated to the United States . . . are reserved to the States respectively, or to the people." These rights are not to be curtailed under cover of "vague," "inscrutable" words, allegedly justifying judicial intrusion into what was the established province of the States, e.g., suffrage. As Roscoe Conkling, a member of the Joint Committee on Reconstruction of both Houses, stated, "[t]he proposition to prohibit States from denying civil or political rights to any class of persons, encounters a great objection on the threshold. It trenches upon the principle of existing local sovereignty" and "meddles with a right reserved to the States."[198] An intention, said Chief Justice Marshall, "to establish a principle never before recognized, should be expressed in plain and explicit terms."[199] That requirement was applied to the fourteenth amendment by Justice Miller, who refused to "embrace a construction" of the amendment that would subject the states' local concerns to "the control of Congress . . . in the absence of language which expresses such a purpose too clearly to admit of doubt."[200] In short, an intention to diminish rights reserved by the tenth amendment must be clearly expressed.

Michael Perry considers, however, that reliance on the tenth amendment is historically unsound, since as Justice Brennan indicated in dissent:

> The amendment states but a truism that all is retained which has not been surrendered. There is nothing in the history of its adoption to suggest that it was more than *declaratory* of the relationship between the national and state governments as it had been *established* by the Constitution before the amendment. . . .[201]

A truism is a proposition that "is so obviously true as not to require discussion."[202] Brennan failed to take into account that the tenth was adopted to put the obvious beyond peradventure; he overlooked that Justice Stone, from whom he borrowed the quotation, went on to say that its

---

[193]Bork, *supra* note 46, at 13.

[194]L. HAND, THE BILL OF RIGHTS 55 (1962).

[195]Bickel, *supra* note 54, at 31.

[196]Bingham's instrumentality was noted by Justice Harlan in Oregon v. Mitchell, 400 U.S. 112, 171 (1970).

[197]"If the Constitution was ratified under the belief sedulously propagated, that such protection was offered, would it not now be a fraud upon the whole people to give it a different construction." 2 J. STORY, *supra* note 113, § 1084.

[198]CONG. GLOBE, 39th Cong., 1st Sess. 358 (1866).

[199]United States v. Burr, 25 F. Cas. 55, 165 (C.C.D. Va. 1807) (No. 14,693); *see also* Pierson v. Ray, 386 U.S. 547, 554–55 (1967).

[200]Slaughter-House Cases, 83 U.S. (16 Wall.) 36, 78 (1872). Justice Frankfurter said this case "has the authority that comes from contemporaneous knowledge of the purposes of the Fourteenth Amendment." Louisina *ex rel.* Francis v. Resweber, 329 U.S. 459, 467 (1947) (Frankfurter, J., concurring).

[201]M. PERRY, CONSTITUTION, THE COURTS, AND HUMAN RIGHTS 188 n. 47 (1982) (emphasis added).

[202]OXFORD UNIVERSAL DICTIONARY (1955).

purpose was "to allay fears that the new national government might seek to exercise powers not granted."[203] In Alpheus Thomas Mason's more graphic terms, the opposition "had conjured up the image of a national colossus, destined to swallow up or destroy the defenseless states. To quiet these fears, Madison proposed the Tenth Amendment."[204] The reservation, the Court stated, was "made absolutely certain by the Tenth Amendment" to forestall federal exercise of "powers which had not been granted."[205] Consequently, reliance on the tenth as a shield against federal encroachments is strengthened rather than weakened by the fact that the Founders took the precaution to put into express terms what had rested on assurances and implications.[206]

C. Open-Ended Terms

Alexander Bickel conceived a subtle variant of the "general" words and "change of meaning" theories: the framers meant to leave posterity free to read into the amendment the suffrage and desegregation they had excluded. This escaped rejection of the framers' intention by attributing to them a theretofore undreamed of intention, an intention that has no factual foundation. As clerk to Justice Frankfurter, Bickel had informed him that "it is *impossible* to conclude that the Thirty-ninth Congress intended that segregation be abolished, impossible also to conclude that they *foresaw it might be,* under the language they were adopting."[207] What they did not foresee they did not authorize.

In a memorandum for his files, Justice Frankfurter, who had concluded that "in all likelihood, the framers of the amendment had not intended to outlaw segregation,"[208] asserted that constitutional terms must accommodate "change in men's feelings,"[209] so that equal protection could mean one thing in 1868 and the very opposite in 1954. Writing after his clerkship, Bickel framed a tentative hypothesis: might not "equal protection" be read to exhibit receptiveness "to 'latitudinarian' construction?" Bickel concluded that "[n]o one made the point with regard to this particular clause."[210] Noting that Republicans drew back from a "formulation dangerously vulnerable to attacks pandering to the prejudices of the people [which they themselves shared],"[211] he speculated that the framers might have resorted to language which they could "defend against damaging alarms raised by the opposition, but which at the same time was sufficiently elastic to permit reasonable future advances?"[212] More bluntly, Bickel hypothesized that the framers concealed the future objectives they dared not avow lest the whole enterprise be imperilled. There is not a shred of evidence that the framers employed double-talk to hoodwink the ratifiers. If they

---

[203]United States v. Darby, 312 U.S. 100, 124 (1941).

[204]Mason, *The Bill of Rights: An Almost Forgotten Appendage,* in THE FUTURE OF OUR LIBERTIES 47 (S. Halpern ed. 1982).

[205]Kansas v. Colorado, 206 U.S. 46, 89–90 (1907).

[206]Patrick Henry exclaimed in the Virginia Ratification Convention: "What do they tell us? That our rights are reserved. Why not say so?" 3 ELLIOT, *supra* note 65, at 448.

[207]R. KLUGER, *supra* note 9, at 654.

[208]*Id.* 598.

[209]*Id.* 685. *But see* Chief Justice Cooley, *supra* note 86. "Men's feelings" had not changed. Derrick Bell, a black academician, wrote in 1975: "Today opposition to desegregation is, if anything, greater than it was in 1954." Bell, *The Burden of Brown on Blacks: History Based on Observation of a Landmark Decision,* 7 N.C. CENTRAL L.J. 25, 25 (1975). Another black, Roy Wilkins, stated in 1978 that "the attitude of whites toward blacks is basic in this county. And that has changed for the worse." Wilkins, *Racial Outlook: Lack of Change Disturbs Blacks,* N.Y. Times, March 3, 1978, at A-26, col. 1.

[210]Bickel, *supra* note 54, at 61 (emphasis added). *But compare supra* text accompanying note 176.

[211]Senator John Sherman of Ohio said in the Senate in 1862, "We do not like negroes. We do not disguise our dislike." C. Woodward, *supra* note 51. George Julian, a radical from neighboring Indiana, told the House in 1866, "the real trouble is that *we hate the Negro,*" CONG. GLOBE, 39th Cong., 1st Sess. 257 (1866).

[212]Bickel, *supra* note 54, at 61.

did, there was no ratification, because "If the material facts be either suppressed or unknown, the ratification is treated as invalid."[213]

Attribution of such intentions to the framers overlooks that as late as 1875, a Reconstruction Congress, at last ready to bar discrimination in hotels and transportation facilities, rejected mixed schools because they would excite prejudice.[214] No one mentioned that allegedly concealed authorization in the "open-ended" language. To postulate that in such an atmosphere of ingrown prejudice the 1866 framers tucked away in the amendment an authorization to do *in futuro* what they themselves could not stomach in the present is sheer fantasy. Bickel's followers overlook that in 1970 Bickel wrote, "[t]he Framers of the Fourteenth Amendment explicitly rejected the option of an open-ended grant of power to Congress freely to meddle with conditions within the states, so as to render them equal in accordance with Congress's own notions."[215] This denial of "open-ended" authority to future Congresses is at odds with its incorporation in the amendment. Congress well knew that its successors also could enact amendments, as the fifteenth speedily proved. Proof, not speculation, is required that the framers departed from the article V path and authorized posterity to interpret their determination to exclude suffrage and segregation as authority to reverse this exclusion. It remains to be said that a candid activist, seeking to clear away the underbrush of "theories," wrote that Berger "devastated the notion that the framers of the fourteenth amendment . . . intended it to be 'open-ended.' "[216]

D. The Constitution Must Grow

The "truly difficult question," Michael Perry considers, is "whether the original understanding of important power limiting provisions like the first and fourteenth amendments—the plainly narrow original understandings—ought, as a matter of constitutional theory, to be deemed the only legitimate sources of norms for constitutional adjudication." And he cites Gerald Lynch's argument for "institutional growth beyond the original understanding."[217] This bland rhetoric masks a plea for judicial power to erase constitutional limits. Very early Justice Marshall declared that a written Constitution was designed to limit power and asked: "To what purpose are powers limited . . . if these limits may, in any time be passed by those intended to be restrained?"[218] Later he specifically disclaimed a judicial right to change the instrument.[219] The notion that a Constitution so limited could be made to "grow" by the judiciary is refuted by the evidence, which here can only be summarized: (1) The Founders' belief in a fixed Constitution of unchanging meaning, alterable only by the people through the process of amendment; (2) the avowedly inferior place of the judiciary in the federal scheme, deriving from suspicion of the innovative judicial review by judges who theretofore had been regarded with "aversion;" (3) the Founders' profound distrust of judicial discretion; (4) their attachment to the separation of powers and their insistence that courts should not engage in policymaking but rather act solely as interpreters, not makers, of the law; (5) Hamilton, foremost advocate of judicial review, iterated that there "is no liberty, if the power of judging be not separated from the legislative and executive powers." That he did not mean to authorize the judiciary to take over legislative functions is demonstrated by his statement that courts may not "on pretense of a repugnancy . . . substitute their own pleasure for the

---

[213]Owings v. Hull, 34 U.S. (9 Pet.) 607, 629 (1835) (Story, J.).

[214]Senator Aaron Sargent of California said the common school proposal would reinforce "a prejudice powerful, permeating every part of the country." 3 CONG. REC. 4172 (1874). For similar remarks in the House by Barbour Lewis of Tennessee, see 3 CONG. REC. 998 (1875), and William Phelps of New Jersey, *id.* at 1002.

[215]A. BICKEL, THE SUPREME COURT AND THE IDEA OF PROGRESS 48 (1977).

[216]Perry, Book Review, 78 COLUM. L. REV. 685, 695 (1978).

[217]Perry, *Noninterpretive Review in Human Rights Cases: A Functional Justification*, 56 N.Y.U.L. REV. 278, 311 (1981).

[218]Marbury v. Madison, 5 U.S. (1 Cranch) 137, 176 (1803).

[219]JOHN MARSHALL'S DEFENSE OF McCULLOCH V. MARYLAND 185 (G. Gunther ed. 1969). *See also* J. STORY, *supra* note 113.

constitutional intentions of the legislature." James Iredell, himself a powerful advocate of judicial review, put the matter unequivocally: within their constitutional boundaries legislatures are not controllable by the courts. And Hamilton assured the Ratifiers that judges could be impeached for deliberate usurpations on the authority of the legislature; and (6) The Founders' jealous attachment to states' rights and suspicion of federal courts, evidenced by the First Congress' grant of exclusive "arising under" jurisdiction to the state courts, is incompatible with the theory that courts could make the Constitution grow at the cost of the states' reserved rights.[220]

The foregoing greatly telescoped review of activist arguments should persuade that they are merely a facade concocted, as Leonard Levy observed, "to rationalize a growing satisfaction with judicial review among liberal intellectuals and scholars,"[221] a satisfaction growing out of the Court's gratification of desires the people would not satisfy.[222] The contra-activist doctrine—interpretivism, to borrow from Raymond Aron, "justifies itself by the falseness of the beliefs that oppose it."[223]

E. The Role of The Court

No activist has cited a constitutional provision that authorizes the Court to revise the Constitution, in Justice Black's scornful phrase, to keep it "in tune with the times."[224] Such an authorization, Perry justly observes, "would have been a remarkable delegation for politicians to grant an institution like the Supreme Court, given the electorates' longstanding commitment to policymaking . . . by those accountable, unlike the Court, to the electorate."[225] It would also have been an unexplained departure from the long judicial tradition excluding judges from lawmaking. Samuel Thorne tells us that Bracton wrote his treatise in 1250 because there had been found judges "who decide cases according to their own will rather than by the authority of the laws."[226] Hundreds of years later Francis Bacon counselled judges "to remember that their office is to interpret the law, and not to make it."[227] Just before our Revolution, Blackstone condemned "arbitrary judges" whose decisions are "regulated only by their own opinions, and not by any fundamental principles of law" which "judges are bound to observe."[228]

Recognition of those bounds is evidenced by the statement of Justice James Wilson in his 1791 Philadelphia Lectures: the judge "will remember, that his duty and his business is, not to make

---

[220]For detailed discussion and citations, see Berger, *Michael Perry's Functional Justification for Judicial Activism*, 8 U. DAYTON L. REV. 465, 523–27 (1983).

[221]JUDICIAL REVIEW AND THE SUPREME COURT 24 (L. Levy ed. 1967). Mark Tushnet notes that activists are "eager to superimpose a facade of rationality on the Court's decisions." Tushnet, *Truth, Justice and the American Way: An Interpretation of Public Scholarship in the Seventies*, 57 TEX. L. REV. 1307, 1325 (1979). Federalism implies "a legally immutable constitution." A. DICEY, INTRODUCTION TO THE STUDY OF THE CONSTITUTION 142 (7th ed. 1903), as is confirmed by the article V provision that "no state . . . shall be deprived of its equal suffrage in the Senate."

[222]See Bishop, *infra* text accompanying note 255.

[223]Aron, Pensees, N.Y. Times, October 23, 1983 at E-19, col. 1. Interpretivism, unlike activism, was not recently fabricated to rationalize the Court's illegitimate decisions, but as activist Thomas Grey wrote it is "deeply rooted in our history and in our shared principles of political legitimacy. It has equally deep roots in our formal constitutional law. . . ." Grey, *Do We Have an Unwritten Constitution?*, 27 STAN. L. Rev. 703, 705 (1975). Grey recognizes that the opposing view is more difficult to justify. *Id.* at 708.

[224]Griswold v. Connecticut, 381 U.S. 479, 522 (1965) (Black, J., dissenting).

[225]M. PERRY, *supra* note 201, at 20. Perry considers that the principle of electorally accountable policymaking is "axiomatic; it is judicial review, not that principle, that requires justification." *Id.* at 9.

[226]BRACTON, ON THE LAWS AND CUSTOMS OF ENGLAND 19 (S. Thorne, translator, 1968).

[227]J. DRINKER, LEGAL ETHICS 327 (1953).

[228]1 W. BLACKSTONE, *supra* note 26, at 269. Chief Justice Mansfield stated, "Whatever doubts I may have in my own breast with respect to the policy and expediency of this law . . . I am bound to see it executed according to its meaning." Pray v. Edie, 99 E.R. 1113, 1114 (1786).

the law, but to interpret and apply it."[229] Policymaking was emphatically considered out of judicial bounds as is evidenced by the Framers' rejection of the Justices' participation in a Council of Revision. It had been proposed that they should assist the President in exercising the veto power on the ground that "[l]aws may be . . . unwise, may be dangerous . . . and yet not be so unconstitutional as to justify the Judges in refusing to give them effect."[230] But Elbridge Gerry objected: "It was quite foreign from the nature of ye office to make them judges of the policy of public measures."[231] Nathaniel Gorham said judges "are not to be presumed to possess any peculiar knowledge of . . . public measures;"[232] and John Dickinson stated that judges "ought not to be legislators."[233] As Edward Corwin concluded, "The first important step in the clarification of the Convention's ideas with reference to the doctrine of judicial review is marked, therefore, by its rejection of the Council of Revision idea on the basis of the principle . . . '[T]hat the power of *making* ought to be kept distinct from that of *expounding* the law.' "[234] A leading activist, Charles Black, confirms that for the colonists, "The function of the judge was thus placed in sharpest antithesis to that of the legislator," who alone was concerned "with what the law ought to be."[235]

Two other factors fed into this dichotomy. The Founders had a "profound fear of judicial independence and discretion,"[236] given colorful utterance by Chief Justice Hutchinson of Massachusetts: "*the Judge* should never be the *Legislator:* Because, then the Will of the Judge would be the Law: and this tends to a State of Slavery."[237] Such sentiments were inspired by some sorry English history, epitomized by Lord Camden: "The discretion of a judge is the law of tyrants . . . In the best of times it is often caprice . . . in the worst, it is every vice, folly and passion, to which human nature is liable."[238] Then there was the fact that colonial judges, often unsympathetic to expanding democratarianism, were saddled on the colonists by the Crown, so that Justice Wilson did not find it surprising in 1791 that judges "were objects of aversion and distrust."[239] To give the last word on policy to judges, therefore, would not only have been a "remarkable delegation," it would have required a repudiation of established and cherished tradition. Instead, as Hamilton assured the Ratifiers, judicial authority was confined to "certain cases *particularly specified.* The expression of those cases marks the *precise limits* beyond which the federal courts cannot extend their jurisdiction. . . ."[240] Concretely, jurisdiction of cases "arising under" the Constitution implicitly excludes cases that do not "arise" thereunder, for instance, cases in which the Court has fashioned rights *not* conferred by the Constitution, thereby taking over powers reserved to the

---

[229]2 James Wilson, Works 502 (R. McCloskey ed. 1967). That was often repeated by the Court: "It is the province of a court to expound the law, not to make it." Luther v. Borden, 48 U.S. (7 How.) 1, 41 (1849) (Taney, C.J.); Minor v. Happersett, 88 U.S. (21 Wall.) 162, 178 (1874) ("Our province is to decide what the law is, not to declare what it should be") (Waite, C.J.). In Houston v. Moore, U.S. (5 Wheat.) 1, 48 (1820), Justice Story emphasized, "[W]e are not at liberty to add one jot of power to the national government beyond what the people have granted by the constitution. . . ."

[230]2 M. Farrand, *supra* note 8, at 73.

[231]1 M. Farrand, *supra* note 8, at 97–98.

[232]2 M. Farrand, *supra* note 8, at 73.

[233]1 M. Farrand, *supra* note 8, at 108.

[234]E. Corwin, The Doctrine of Judicial Review 42 (1963).

[235]C. Black, The People and the Court 160 (1960); *compare also supra* text accompanying notes 227–33. *See also* R. Berger, Congress v. The Supreme Court, Index "Expounding the Law" (1969).

[236]Wood, *supra* note 9, at 298.

[237]Horwitz, *The Emergence of an Instrumental Conception of American Law, 1780–1820,* in 5 Perspectives in American History 287, 292 (1971). Hutchinson echoed Montesquieu, the oracle of the Founders, who had written that if the judges were to be the Legislators, "the life and liberty of the subject would be exposed to arbitrary control." de Montesquieu, *The Spirit of the Laws,* in 38 Great Books of the Western World 70 (R. Hutchins ed. 1952).

[238]*Quoted by* Justice Brennan in McGautha v. California, 402 U.S. 183, 257 (1971).

[239]1 James Wilson, Works 292 (R. McCloskey ed. 1967).

[240]The Federalist No. 83 at 541 (Mod. Lib. ed. 1941) (emphasis added).

States.[241] Similarly, the article V provision for amendment by the people according to prescribed procedure[242] precludes amendment by the Court. Even the legislature, darling of the Founders—in contrast to the judiciary which, Hamilton assured the Ratifiers, "was next to nothing"[243]—cannot change the Constitution, for as Madison said, "it would be a novel & dangerous doctrine that a Legislature could change the constitution under which it held its existence."[244] Its attempt to do so was rejected in *Marbury v. Madison*: Congress is not empowered to enlarge the jurisdiction of the Court: "[N]o organ of the government may alter [the Constitution's] terms."[245]

The traditional rule was reiterated by Chief Justice Taney: "It is the province of the court to expound the law, and not to make it," as Chief Justice Waite later reaffirmed.[246] Robert Bork pointedly commented: "The Supreme Court regularly insists that its results . . . do not spring from the mere will of the Justices in the majority but are supported, indeed compelled, by a proper understanding of the Constitution. . . . Value choices are attributed to the Founding Fathers, not to the Court."[247] Even Chief Justice Warren piously intoned that "[t]he provisions of the Constitution . . . are vital, living principles that authorize and limit governmental power. . . . They are the rules of government."[248] The activists' extravagant rationalizations on its behalf have never been voiced by the Court. In a similar context, Bork wrote, "It should give theorists of the open-ended Constitution pause . . . that not even the most activist courts have ever grounded their claims for legitimacy" on such arguments.[249] I cannot improve on Brest's plea to academe "simply to acknowledge that most of our writings [about judicial review] are not political theory but advocacy scholarship—amicus briefs ultimately designed to persuade the court to adopt our various notions of the public good."[250]

III. CONCLUSION

The argument for judicial activism—resort to extra-constitutional values—is fundamentally flawed: it is counter-majoritarian, hence, as Perry observed, "the recurring embarrassment of the noninterpretivists: majoritarian democracy is, they know, the core of our entire system. . . ."[251] Earlier academe was deeply imbued with faith in majorities, but as Arthur Sutherland explained with admirable candor, a "change of political theory developed" deriving from "Hitler's popularity among the German people, public support of the Un-American Activities Committee and the

---

[241]For citations see Berger, *Insulation of Judicial Usurpation: A Comment on Lawrence Sager's "Court-Stripping" Polemic*, 44 OHIO ST. L.J. 611, 615 n.44 (1983).

[242]Article V was the "mode preferred by the convention" for alterations. THE FEDERALIST No. 43 at 286 (Mod. Lib. ed. 1941). James Wilson noted that the parallel Pennsylvania Constitution "cannot be amended by any other mode than that which it directs. . . ." 2 ELLIOT, *supra* note 65, at 457. In the Massachusetts Ratification Convention, Jarvis observed that article V furnishes "an adequate provision for all the purposes of political reformation." *Id.* at 116. That Article, Richard Law said in Connecticut, "provides a remedy for whatever defects [the Constitution] may have." *Id.* at 200. "It is not the function of courts or legislative bodies . . . to alter the method [for change] which the Constitution has fixed." Hawke v. Smith, 253 U.S. 221, 227 (1920); *see also supra* note 155. Louis Lusky, an admirer of the activist Court, observes that the Court asserts the "power to revise the Constitution, bypassing the cumbersome amendment procedure prescribed by article V." Lusky, *supra* note 14, at 406.

[243]THE FEDERALIST No. 78 at 504 (Mod. Lib. ed. 1941) (quoting Montesquieu).

[244]2 M. FARRAND, *supra* note 8, at 92, 93.

[245]E. CORWIN, THE TWILIGHT OF THE SUPREME COURT 110 (1934) (emphasis added).

[246]*See supra* note 228.

[247]Bork, *supra* note 46, at 3–4.

[248]Trop v. Dulles, 356 U.S. 86, 103 (1958). That said, he proceeded to upend the rules; *see* Berger, *supra* note 91, at 116–22.

[249]Bork, *The Impossibility of Finding Welfare Rights in the Constitution*, 1979 WASH U.L.Q. 695, 697.

[250]Brest, *supra* note 108, at 1109.

[251]M. PERRY, *supra* note 201, at 125 (quoting J. ELY, DEMOCRACY AND DISTRUST: A THEORY OF JUDICIAL REVIEW).

McCarthy hearings" and the like. "[V]otaries of unreviewed majoritarianism" suddenly realized that "unrestricted majorities could be as tyrannical as wicked oligarchs . . . *We* could not say in plain terms that occasionally *we* have to select wise and able people and give them the constitutional function of countering the democratic process. . . ."[252] Again a gift from the omnipresent "we"![253] But as Myres McDougal wrote some years ago, "Government by a self-designated elite—like that of benevolent despotism of Plato's philosopher kings—may be a good form of government for some peoples, but it is not the American way."[254]

No intellectual can but from time to time be disappointed by the vox populi, but as Winston Churchill remarked, the alternatives to democracy are even worse. Activism, it needs to be underscored, must be understood as a flight from democratic self-government. As Joseph Bishop wrote, "those who favor abortion, busing . . . and oppose capital punishment . . . have no faith whatever in the wisdom or will of the great majority of the people, who are opposed to them."[255]; Hence, their appeal to the courts. Because the course of Demos is at times mistaken, even woefully wrong, it does not follow that the Court is empowered to save the people from themselves. A seminal constitutional scholar, James Bradley Thayer, considered that the Court "cannot rightly attempt to protect the people, by undertaking a function not its own."[256] A judge, wrote Cardozo, "is not a knight-errant roaming at will in pursuit of his own ideal of beauty or of goodness."[257] In saltier terms, Holmes said, "if my country wants to go to hell, I am here to help it."[258] With Lincoln, I cling to faith in the ultimate good sense of the people; I cannot subscribe to the theory that America needs a savior in the shape of nine—ofttimes only five—Platonic Guardians.

The "very notion of the rule of law," Tushnet rightly states, is "at issue."[259] "[W]e generally agree," said Philip Kurland, that "we are all to be governed by the same preestablished rules and not by the whim of those charged with executing those rules. . . . [F]rom the beginning [the Court] assumed the role . . . of keeper of the rule of law as embodied in the Constitution."[260] Governance by whim[261] is freshly illustrated by the Court's recent "legislative chaplain" decision. "Clearly," Chief Justice Burger stated, "the men who wrote the First Amendment Religion Clause did not view paid legislative chaplains and opening prayers as a violation of that Amendment, for the practice of opening sessions with prayer has continued without interruption ever since that early session of Congress."[262] By parity of reasoning, the Court's resort to the "cruel and unusual punishments"

---

[252]Sutherland, *Privacy in Connecticut*, 64 MICH. L. REV. 283, 283–84 (1965) (emphasis added). Earlier, "the Progressive realists viewed the policy-making function of judges as deviant in a democratic society . . . they preferred policy evolved through the political process." A. BICKEL, THE SUPREME COURT AND THE IDEA OF PROGRESS 22–23 (1970).

[253]*See* Cover, *supra* text accompanying note 13.

[254]McDougal & Lans, *Treaties and Congressional-Executive or Presidential Agreements: Interchangeable Instruments of National Policy*, 54 YALE L.J. 181, 578 (1945).

[255]Bishop, *What is a Liberal—Who is a Conservative?*, 62 COMMENTARY 47 (1976). Richard Kluger, an admiring chronicler of *Brown v. Board of Education*, noted that "the whole issue of segregation came to the courts because the other parts of government, and certainly our private society, were unwilling to face it," *quoted in* M. PERRY, *supra* note 201, at 211 n.91. Jefferson wrote Madison on December 20, 1783, "it is my principle that the will of the majority should always prevail." Mason, *supra* note 9, at 169. It is not, wrote Dean Charles E. Clark, "a sound and practical theory . . . suited to an independent people, to hold that control and direction of its future should be committed to an aloof judicial tribunal." E. CORWIN, THE TWILIGHT OF THE SUPREME COURT xix (1934).

[256]J. THAYER, JOHN MARSHALL 109 (1901).

[257]B. CARDOZO, THE NATURE OF THE JUDICIAL PROCESS 141 (1921).

[258]F. BIDDLE, JUSTICE HOLMES, NATURAL LAW AND THE SUPREME COURT 9 (1961).

[259]Tushnet, *supra* note 107, at 811.

[260]Kurland, *Curia Regis: Some Comments on the Divine Right of Kings and Courts "To Say What the Law Is"*, 23 ARIZ L. REV. 581, 582–83 (1981). To "engage in result-oriented adjudication," Leonard Levy wrote, is to leave "far behind the idea of the rule of law enforced by impersonal and impartial judges." L. LEVY, AGAINST THE LAW: THE NIXON COURT AND CRIMINAL JUSTICE 438 (1974).

[261]*See* Tushnet, *supra* text accompanying note 143.

[262]Marsh v. Chambers, 103 S. Ct. at 3334.

clause for its strictures on death penalties is untenable. From 1689 when the English employed the phrase in their Bill of Rights, through 1789 when it was incorporated in the Eighth Amendment, through 1976 when the Court first discovered that death penalties violated the phrase, such penalties, with not a single exception, were not deemed to be within "cruel and unusual punishments."[263] Nevertheless the Court overturned the centuries-old practice but now exalts the identical 200-year old chaplain practice on the very grounds which dictated hands off death penalties.

Who are the demigods to whom activists would turn over our governance? For the most part they are political accidents, as was Chief Justice Warren himself, ranging, with a few exceptions, from mediocre to competent,[264] who, a perfervid activist states, have not been prepared "for the task of constitutional interpretation." He states that few have "broad-gauged approach and knowledge" essential "to search for and identify the values that should be sought in constitutional adjudication."[265] Another activist, Owen Fiss, explains that judges "are lawyers, but in terms of personal characteristics they are no different from successful businessmen or politicians. Their capacity to make a special contribution to our social life derives not from any personal knowledge, but *from the definition of the office* in which they find themselves and through which they exercise power."[266] Elevation to the Bench thus resembles the medieval anointment with Holy Oil that clothed the emperor with "a mandate from heaven." "Time has proved," wrote then Solicitor General Robert H. Jackson, that the Court's "judgment was wrong on the most outstanding issues upon which it has chosen to challenge the popular branches."[267] Terrance Sandalow, an activist, wrote that the developments of 200 years have "strength[ened] belief in the wisdom of the framers' intentions,"[268] whereas already, even to the eyes of his admiring biographer, Chief Justice Warren's choices "appear less as ordained principles of justice and more as vulnerable policy judgments,"[269] judgments the Constitution left to the people's elected legislative representatives, or to the people themselves.

Let it be assumed that the morals of a high-minded Court are superior to those of the commonality;[270] it is nevertheless not authorized to cram them down the throats of the people, as is the case with death penalties, school prayer and the like. When the Court does for the people "what they have not chosen to do for themselves," Justice Story declared, "[i]t is usurping the function of a legislator,"[271] and as Justice Harlan underscored, "it has violated the constitutional structure which it is its highest duty to protect."[272] And it has sanctified the deplorable example of the pre-1937 Court, an endorsement activists may yet have cause to regret. They have forgotten Cardozo's wise caution: the judges' "individual sense of justice . . . might result in a benevolent despotism if the judges were benevolent men. It would put an end to the reign of law."[273]

An excellent homily, encapsulating the points I have been making, was recently delivered by the court in an opinion by Chief Justice Burger. True, it is addressed to *Congress'* use of the legislative veto, but its principles apply equally to the Court itself: the Framers divided the

---

[263]*Supra* text accompanying notes 92–100.

[264]For citations see Berger, *supra* note 220, at 480–81.

[265]Miller, *The Elusive Search for Values in Constitutional Interpretation*, 6 HASTINGS CONST. L.Q. 487, 507 (1979).

[266]Fiss, *Foreword: The Forms of Justice*, 93 HARV. L. REV. 1, 12 (1979) (emphasis added).

[267]R. JACKSON, THE STRUGGLE FOR JUDICIAL SUPREMACY 37 (1941). For academicians' concurrence, see Berger, *supra* note 4, at 331 n.66.

[268]Sandalow, *Constitutional Interpretation*, 79 MICH. L. REV. 1033, 1062 (1981).

[269]G. WHITE, *supra* note 34, at 349.

[270]The philosopher Thomas Nagel observes that "a radical division of opinion" (e.g. about abortion, dealth penalties), indicates that we have "a case of basic moral uncertainty." Nagel, *The Supreme Court and Political Philosophy*, 56 N.Y.U.L. REV. 519, 523–24 (1981).

[271]1 J. STORY, *supra* note 113, at § 426.

[272]Oregon v. Mitchell, 400 U.S. 112, 203 (1970).

[273]B. CARDOZO, *supra* note 257, at 136.

government "into three defined categories . . . to assure, as nearly as possible, that each Branch of government would confine itself to its assigned responsibility." The "carefully defined limits on the power of each branch must not be eroded." And he emphasized, "we have not yet found a better way to preserve freedom than by making the exercise of power subject to the carefully crafted restraints spelled out in the Constitution."[274] Physician, heal thyself.[275]

---

[274]Immigration & Naturalization Serv. v. Chadha, 103 S. Ct. 2764 (1983).

[275]In 1934 Edward Corwin adjured the Court "to give over attempting to supervise national legislative policies on the basis of a super-constitution which, in the name of the Constitution, repeals and destroys that historic document." E. CORWIN, *supra* note 245, at 182. That admonition may be underscored today, particularly as regards the Court's invasion of rights to control local concerns which the tenth amendment reserves to the States.

CHAPTER XIII

The Constitution and the Rule of Law

In his article, *The Specious Morality of the Law*,[1] Professor Sanford Levinson[2] brands various calls for maintenance of the rule of law under the Constitution a "ritualistic incantation" and deplores the divorce of law from moral norms.[3] He maintains that a law that is merely identified with majority "will" is not, in terms of moral integrity, worthy of respect, because the majority "notion of justice" may be "perceived as manifest tyranny by someone else." Why should "those who feel tyrannized by the existing legal order . . . recognize it as legitimate?"[4] Add his emphasis that "[l]iberty has come to focus on freedom from the community or the State,"[5] and Levinson verges on an invitation to disregard for law, at a time, as even he acknowledges, when except "reverence for law . . . there is no other basis for uniting a nation of so many disparate groups."[6] His counsel to resist "the call for new faith in an old gospel"[7] requires more solid footing than he has furnished.

I

Levinson begins by dismissing Barbara Jordan's "total" commitment to the Constitution in the course of the House Judiciary Hearings on the impeachment of President Nixon as incomprehensible because "presumably" she would not have thought the original Constitution which "protected slavery . . . worthy of veneration."[8] One may as well reject the great cultural achievements of the Greeks because the Athenians were slaveholders, and a slave was heartlessly defined by Aristotle as "a tool with life in it."[9] Each society must be judged by standards of its own time and historical context. To transport Barbara Jordan back 200 years in time—when a nation aborning compromised with slaveholding states the better to face a hostile world—is not nearly so fruitful as to view the world in which she lives, where in the Africa where she has her roots Idi Amin slaughters thousands of fellow blacks in Uganda and is regarded admiringly by many Africans. Well might she prefer to live under a constitution that secures her against such horrors, even though it falls short of perfection.

Philosophers, William James said, devote themselves to study of those residual questions on which people are unable to agree, among them the nature of "law."[10] The thin air of philosophy is

---

[1]S. Levinson, *The Specious Morality of the Law*, HARPER'S, May, 1977, at 35.
[2]Professor Levinson is a lawyer and teaches in the department of politics at Princeton University.
[3]S. Levinson, *supra* note 1, at 36.
[4]*Id.* at 38, 40.
[5]*Id.* at 36.
[6]*Id.* at 41.
[7]*Id.* at 35.
[8]*Id.* at 35, 36.
[9]1 C. BRINTON, J. CHRISTOPHER, & R. WOLFF, A HISTORY OF CIVILIZATION 67 (1960).
[10]Singer, *A Discipline Examining Nature's Ultimate Reality*, N.Y. Times, May 8, 1977, § 4 (Week in Review), at 20, col. 1.

not for an earthbound lawyer, so I shall attempt in more mundane fashion first to examine what the Constitution and the rule of law meant to the Founders, and why that meaning remains vitally important for us today.

After a long and bitter struggle, the Founders had succeeded in throwing off the shackles of an "omnipotent parliament" and hereditary monarch.[11] Now they proclaimed that the *people* were sovereign and that all power was delegated by them to their "servants and agents." Schooled in the insatiable greed for power of those given to rule, the Founders grudgingly enumerated the granted powers and repeatedly stressed that those grants were "limited."[12] Their fear of arbitrary power led them to insist on standing laws, not, as the 1780 Massachusetts Constitution emphasized, laws passed after the fact which retroactively made a nonproscribed act criminal.[13] They wanted no personal justice administered after the fashion of Caliph Haroun-al-Rashid, but rather the administration of known laws with an absolute minimum of discretion. As Jefferson graphically put it, the Founders sought to bind man down with "the chains of the Constitution" because they had no confidence in rulers.[14] They regarded the Constitution with "sacred reverence," in Hamilton's words, because they considered that it constituted the "bulwark" of their liberties.[15]

This is what John Adams meant by "a government of laws and not of men," not, as Levinson would have it, a linkage with "moral norms."[16] Adams' biographer, Page Smith, confirms that Adams meant by that phrase that "men are secured in their rights to life, liberty and property by clear and fair laws, falling equally on all . . . justly administered," differentiating a society where a king bestows rights at "whim" as "a society of men, not of laws."[17] When one affirms the continuing indispensability of this structure, he does not, as Levinson charges, "embrace the rule of law as an answer to the problems of modern governance."[18] No structure of government can supply the "answer," it can only furnish a framework within which each generation can strive for a peaceable solution of clashing aims. Surely this generation need not be reminded that uncurbed power, abandonment of the rule of law, returns us to the law of the jungle or, worse, the crematoria of Auschwitz and Belsen. It is easy enough for one sheltered by the rule of law blithely to dismiss it, but the Indians who lived for a time without its protection under Indira Ghandi have recently greeted its return with jubilation.[19]

II

Levinson maintains that most pre-nineteenth century adherents of the rule of law viewed law as being linked with moral norms.[20] For this postulate, Levinson relies on Adams and traces the lineage back to the medieval jurist, Bracton, who linked law to God. Law was defined by the medievalist as the "natural reason [natural law] given by God," or "as the commands of political leaders ordained by God and therefore given the right to rule."[21] Adams, however, flatly repudiated monarchical rule by divine right.[22] His 1780 Massachusetts Constitution described the body politic

---

[11]*See* R. BERGER, CONGRESS V. THE SUPREME COURT 34–35 (1969).

[12]*Id.* at 13–16.

[13]Bill of Rights, Article 24, *reprinted in* H. S. COMMAGER, DOCUMENTS OF AMERICAN HISTORY 109 (7th ed. 1962).

[14]R. BERGER, *supra* note 11, at 13 (quoting C. WARREN, CONGRESS 153 (1935)).

[15]THE FEDERALIST No. 25, at 158 (Mod. Lib. ed. 1937).

[16]S. Levinson, *supra* note 1, at 36.

[17]1 P. SMITH, JOHN ADAMS 246 (1962).

[18]S. Levinson, *supra* note 1, at 36.

[19]Borders, *India's Courts Welcome Back 'Rule of Law,'* N.Y. Times, June 14, 1977, § L, at 2, col. 2.

[20]*See* text accompanying note 16 *supra*.

[21]S. Levinson, *supra* note 1, at 36.

[22]*See* 2 P. SMITH, *supra* note 17, at 692–93.

as "a social compact" whereby the whole people covenant with each citizen that "all shall be governed by certain [known] laws for the common good," in order that "every man may . . . find his security in them."[23] So too, natural law, like the "mandate from heaven" of Chinese emperors, which was known only to them, collides with Adams' commitment to "clear laws," known to all.[24] This commitment is underscored by his lengthy Bill of Rights in the 1780 Constitution, which particularizes *rights* to be *protected against* the government or community. The ban on the quartering of soldiers in private homes,[25] for example, reflects a practical rather than a moral concern.

It is true that Adams referred to the duty of the state to inculcate a common morality. Nevertheless, he wrote, "It is certain . . . that the only moral foundation of government is the consent of the people."[26] While he was attached to the "moral basis of life, the need for religion,"[27] Adams maintained that "[g]ood laws and orderly government alone would protect 'lives, liberties, religion, property, and characters.' "[28] He had long been convinced that "neither philosophy, nor religion, nor morality . . . will ever govern nations. . . . Nothing but force in the form of soundly drawn constitutions and firm laws could restrain men."[29] His were not counsels of a heavenly city of moral perfectibility, but a hard-headed response to man's inherent selfishness.

Not that Adams' views are for present purposes crucial, for Levinson himself notes that Jefferson believed that it "was the will of the nation which makes the law obligatory."[30] In this belief Jefferson was joined by James Wilson, second only to Madison as an architect of the Constitution. "[P]opular sovereignty, rooted in will rather than in a common moral order," Levinson recognizes, "was to become the motif of the new American polity."[31] This view, that *positive* law, expressed in constitutions and laws, represented the will of the people, was shared by Adams, Hamilton, Madison, and Wilson.[32] It was later reformulated by Justice Holmes and remains, as Levinson notes, "the dominant view" of American constitutional law.[33] It *was* a radical shift from Bracton's notions of law, but those medieval notions had little or no place in the thinking of the Founders, including Adams.

Those of us who are firmly convinced that Richard Nixon was properly forced out of office because of impeachable offenses cannot concur with Levinson that the "rule of law . . . provided an *ostensibly* apolitical rationale for driving from office a scoundrel who richly deserved his fate."[34] Such a result-oriented judgment would be a reproach to American justice. As one who searched the history of the constitutional impeachment provisions before the Nixon impeachment rose on the horizon,[35] I am convinced that by established standards Nixon committed impeachable offenses.

Levinson intimates that the impeachment leaders were not viewed as "subordinate to general conceptions of public morality," and cites the contention of the ten Republican dissenters on the House Judiciary Committee that there "was no specific law prohibiting 'abuse of power,' " the

---

[23]H. S. Commager, *supra* note 13, at 107.

[24]*See* R. Berger, Government by Judiciary: The Transformation of the Fourteenth Amendment 251–52 (1977).

[25]Bill of Rights, Article 27, *reprinted in* H. S. Commager, *supra* note 13, at 109.

[26]1 P. Smith, *supra* note 17, at 258.

[27]*Id.* at 274.

[28]2 P. Smith, *supra* note 17, at 690.

[29]*Id.* at 274.

[30]S. Levinson, *supra* note 1, at 37.

[31]*Id.*

[32]R. Berger, *supra* note 24, at 252.

[33]S. Levinson, *supra* note 1, at 37–38.

[34]*Id.* at 36 (emphasis added).

[35]*See* Berger, *Impeachment for "High Crimes and Misdemeanors,"* 44 S.C.L. Rev. 395 (1971).

offense with which Nixon was charged.[36] But "abuse of power" was a classic rubric of "high crimes and misdemeanors," and since it therefore had constitutional warrant it needed no statutory sanction. When the Republican dissenters argued that an "abuse of power" could not merely be what seems improper "in the *subjective* view of a *temporary majority* of legislators," a view apparently shared by Levinson,[37] they equally impugned the time-worn judicial and jury function of determining what conduct was "unreasonable" under the circumstances. No legal formula, be it "restraint of trade," "negligent conduct," or "abuse of power," can do more than pose the particular case for judgment. Each Congress, like each judge or jury, must independently decide whether the facts at bar make out the charge. Agreed that the Senate, sitting in judgment, should consult the precedents of the past—of which the English, from where the terms "high crimes and misdemeanors" were drawn, are more important than the post-Constitution Senate precedents— and that it should not arbitrarily label a trivial act as an "abuse." But the recalcitrant Republicans fought tooth and nail to prevent the issue from going to the Senate. To cast them in the role of paladins of "public morality" is little short of grotesque.

At bottom Levinson objects to majority rule. "[A]bsolute acquiescence in the decisions of the majority," said Jefferson, is a "vital principle of republics."[38] Where would we be after a bitterly fought election if the defeated minority took to the streets to reject the will of the majority? For the protection of minorities, certain rights were placed in the Constitution beyond majority reach. Like all human endeavors, this is not a perfect shield. The reconciliation of minority and majority interests, as Arthur Schlesinger, Jr. wrote, presents an insoluble problem.[39] Certainly it is not likely to be solved by invoking "moral norms." One can say of "moral norms" what David Hume said of "natural law": "The word natural is commonly taken in so many senses, and is of so loose a signification, that it seems vain to dispute whether justice be natural or not."[40] Conceptions of what is "moral" have differed from time to time, from country to country. For the Inquisition, morality demanded that heretics be burned at the stake; southern ministers preached that slavery was divinely ordained. "[S]o much that was thought [to be] wisdom," said Bertrand Russell, "turned out to be folly."[41] Levinson acknowledges that insistence on a "linkage between law and moral norms . . . assume[s] a moral consensus which no longer exists. . . ."[42] Where, then, are we to derive moral norms? Few will be prepared to look for them in some Platonic absolute about which philosophers will forever dispute. Justice Holmes, that most philosophical of jurists, wrote, "[N]othing but confusion of thought can result from assuming that the rights of man in a moral sense are equally rights in the sense of the constitution and the laws."[43]

III

As an offshoot of his "moral norms," Levinson differentiates between current "moral pluralism" and the halcyon community sharing "a common religious or moral order."[44] In truth that community was more divided than we are today. Roger Williams did not flee Massachusetts because he shared a "common religious order." Whether Quakers and Mennonites of Pennsylvania shared

---

[36]S. Levinson, *supra* note 1, at 38.
[37]*Id.* (emphasis in original).
[38]A. Schlesinger, Jr., The Age of Jackson 401 (1947).
[39]*Id.* at 421.
[40]*Quoted in* R. Cover, Justice Accused: Antislavery and the Judicial Process 23 (1975).
[41]B. Russell, Portraits From Memory 197 (1956).
[42]S. Levinson, *supra* note 1, at 99.
[43]O. Holmes, Jr., Collected Legal Papers 171–72 (1920).
[44]S. Levinson, *supra* note 1, at 36.

that "order" with Catholics of Maryland, or the Scotch-Irish nonconformists with the Tidewater Episcopal establishment of Virginia, may be doubted.

A "community sharing a common moral vision"[45] in terms of the federal Constitution, to which Levinson's discussion is directed, romanticizes the facts. In 1787 the people viewed a remote, centralized federal government with suspicion rather than as an expression of a "common vision." Such distrust was bred in the bone of those who had fled from European tyranny and oppression. Sent to Congress in Philadelphia from Georgia in 1785, William Houstoun "thought of himself as leaving his 'country' to go to a strange land among Strangers."[46] Madison said, "[O]f the affairs of Georgia I know as little as those of Kamskatska."[47] The Southern States feared that they would be oppressed by the North; small states were fearful of the large; the interests of importing and non-importing states diverged; there were quarrels over fisheries; a state imposed imposts on vessels that came from or went to another as if it were a foreign nation.[48] Above all there was a vital lack of power to deal with commerce and defense on a national scale. It was such worldly considerations, not a "common moral vision," which led to the creation of the national "community." Early America, in sum, was not "tied together" by shared "moral norms" but rather, as Tocqueville perceived, "by the common pursuit of individual interests."[49]

In primeval America, Adams, according to Levinson, believed individuals were "willing to subordinate their selfish personal interest in behalf of a 'common good,'" ready "to recognize primary obligation to the community," whereas today "most of us certainly believe that our primary duties are to ourselves and our families. Liberty has come to focus on freedom *from* the community or the state rather than the realization of a common vision *through* the community. . . ."[50] Preoccupation with the self is nothing new. Adams considered that only "force in the form of . . . constitutions" would restrain the beast.[51] A wise government, said Jefferson, would "restrain men from injuring one another" and "leave them otherwise free to regulate their own pursuits."[52] Government was instituted, said Hamilton in THE FEDERALIST No. 51, "because the passions of men will not conform to the dictates of reason and justice, without restraint."[53] "What is government itself," asked THE FEDERALIST No. 51, "but the greatest of all reflections on human nature? If men were angels no government would be necessary."[54] In short, that "old devil," selfish personal interest, was no less present in 1787 than it is today.

With the passage of 200 years, men have turned to the "community" in a manner originally undreamed of, for welfare, subsidies, and other contributions. How is this reconcilable with "freedom from the community"? At no time has the majority been as ready to help minorities as today; it taxes itself heavily to aid the helpless. And what but a "moral vision of the community" can account for the billions of dollars in food and aid America has sent to foreign nations? To make the test of "moral vision" turn on the treatment of minorities is to ignore that racial discrimination is a stubborn, worldwide phenomenon with which "law" may be inadequate to deal. It is no reproach to the Constitution that it has not remade man. It could only impose such restraints as he would accept and provide a framework in which he could work out his own destiny.

---

[45]*Id.*
[46]R. BERGER, *supra* note 11, at 33.
[47]*Id.*
[48]*See* S. E. MORISON, THE OXFORD HISTORY OF THE AMERICAN PEOPLE 304 (1965).
[49]S. RATNER, AMERICAN TAXATION 47 (1942).
[50]S. Levinson, *supra* note 1, at 36 (emphasis in original).
[51]*See* note 29 *supra* and accompanying text.
[52]H. C. HOCKETT, POLITICAL AND SOCIAL HISTORY OF THE UNITED STATES, 1492–1828, at 272 (1931).
[53]THE FEDERALIST No. 15, at 92 (Mod. Lib. ed. 1937).
[54]*Id.* at 337.

Levinson denies the existence of "an enduring, timeless Constitution" because its meaning has changed over time, and concludes that "A faith whose premises change radically over time is scarcely the rock upon which to rely for support. . . ."[55] It would be more accurate to say that over the years the Supreme Court has undertaken to *revise* the Constitution, to read into it preferences of a given majority of the Court, even in flat contradiction of the meaning attached to the terms by the Framers. In Levinson's words, the Court has "suppl[ied] new meanings."[56]

A quick example of these "new meanings" is furnished by the words "due process of law." At the adoption of the Constitution, Alexander Hamilton, reflecting historical usage, declared that these words "are only applicable to the process and proceedings of the *courts* of justice; they can *never* be referred to an act of *the legislature*."[57] The records of the several Conventions and of the First Congress which drafted the fifth amendment contain no evidence to the contrary, and Hamilton's view was also that of the framers of the fourteenth amendment.[58] Notwithstanding, in the 1890s the Court transformed due process into an instrument for the overthrow of socio-economic *legislation*, thereby substituting its own will for that of the people, and giving rise to an "unwritten constitution." No admirer of such judicial "change" has ever pointed to the constitutional warrant for this revisory function; instead there is solid ground for the conclusion that such authority was withheld from the Court. Hamilton branded such judicial action an impeachable "usurpation."[59] Here Levinson, however, echoes conventional approval of judicial "change." But Justices as diverse as Chief Justice Burger, Justice Douglas, and Justice Frankfurter are agreed that the touchstone of constitutionality is the Constitution itself, not what the Court has said about it.[60]

"Can we accept a definition of 'the law,' " asks Levinson, "as anything other than that which is declared by the Supreme Court . . .?"[61] The Constitution is not an inscrutable mystery which yields its secrets only to a black-robed priesthood. Time and again the Court has rejected its own earlier constitutional decisions. For decades commentators, and eminent jurists, Holmes, Brandeis, Stone, Learned Hand, refused to accept the Court's identification of its *laissez-faire* prepossessions with constitutional dogma whereby it blocked social and economic reform. Ultimately that educational process led the Court to acknowledge error.[62] Unfortunately, similar scholarly criticism of the Court's subsequent identification of its libertarian predilections with constitutional mandates,[63] for the most part, has been lacking because the judicial course now corresponded with the aspirations of academe and led it to mute its criticism. "Scholarly exposure of the Court's abuse of its powers," said Justice Frankfurter, would "bring about a shift in the Court's viewpoint."[64] Heightened public awareness rather than "self-help"—" 'taking the law into our own hands' upon recognizing that established officials [Nixon or the Court] are unwilling to follow 'the law' "[65]—

---

[55]S. Levinson, *supra* note 1, at 36, 42.

[56]*Id. See generally* R. BERGER, *supra* note 24, at 370–72.

[57]R. BERGER *supra* note 24, at 194 (emphasis added).

[58]*Id.* at 201–06.

[59]THE FEDERALIST No. 81, at 526–27 (Mod. Lib. ed. 1937).

[60]R. BERGER, *supra* note 24, at 297 n. 57.

[61]S. Levinson, *supra* note 1, at 36.

[62]R. BERGER, *supra* note 24, at 258 n. 39.

[63]In 1945, Chief Justice Stone wrote, "My more conservative brethren in the old days [read their preferences] into the Constitution . . . [H]istory is repeating itself. The Court is now in as much danger of becoming a legislative and Constitution-making body, enacting into law its own predilections, as it was then." A. T. MASON, SECURITY THROUGH FREEDOM: AMERICAN POLITICAL THOUGHT AND PRACTICE 145–46 (1955). In 1976, Archibald Cox stated that "the Warren Court behaved even more like a Council of Wise Men and less like a court than the *laissez faire* Justices," A. COX, THE ROLE OF THE SUPREME COURT IN AMERICAN GOVERNMENT 50 (1976).

[64]R. BERGER, *supra* note 24, at 415 n. 28.

[65]S. Levinson, *supra* note 1, at 36.

appears to me a better alternative. After the "Saturday Night Massacre," an aroused public repudiated Nixon's excesses and drove him from the White House. The Court, Professor Charles Black wrote, would not have "the strength to prevail in the face of resolute public repudiation of its legitimacy," or of the legitimacy of its decisions.[66]

V

Levinson glides over the problems presented by judicial "change," among them government by judiciary, and draws instead on a number of presidential acts to show that the "imperatives of the Constitutional system" have not "remained constant since the establishment of the Constitutional system in 1789."[67] These, he avers, "present problems for anyone seeking an unequivocal American tradition against which to measure political leadership and define the rule of law."[68]

Levinson begins with "Jefferson's questionable expansion of Presidential power in the decision to purchase Louisiana from France in 1803."[69] Jefferson laid no claim to "expanded" power. As Schlesinger described it, "Congress set up a clamor for Louisiana, confirmed the envoys who negotiated the purchase, appropriated the funds for the purchase, ratified the treaty consummating the purchase and passed statutes authorizing the President to receive the purchase. . . ."[70] Even so, Jefferson entertained grave doubts concerning the constitutional authority of *both* Congress and the President to annex new territory, but was dissuaded from seeking an amendment.[71] Napoleon was an unpredictable expansionist neighbor who could block the Mississippi, and Congress and Jefferson acted before the mercurial Bonaparte could change his mind. With good reason did Jefferson say, "The legislature . . . must . . . throw themselves on their country for doing for them unauthorized, what we know [the people] would have done for themselves had they been in a situation to do it."[72] Jefferson did not regard this as a "precedent" for unconstitutional executive acts. Months after the purchase he wrote, "I had rather ask an enlargement of power from the nation, where it is found necessary, than to assume it by a construction which would make our powers boundless."[73] This was for him the "constant."

Next, Levinson refers to Lincoln's "putative disobedience of constitutional provisions relating to habeas corpus."[74] Immediately after the firing on Fort Sumter, while the Union was crumbling, Lincoln suspended the writ of habeas corpus to prevent armed secessionists from operating in Maryland. Maryland was swarming with them and secessionist control might have isolated Washington.[75] Article I of the Constitution provides that the writ may be suspended "when in cases of rebellion or invasion the public safety may require it."[76] It does not say who may suspend, though inferably Congress was to do so because the power appears in the "legislative" article. Lincoln might have invoked the analogy of the impeachment of Justices notwithstanding that the provision for impeachment of "officers" is contained in the "executive" article. Should Lincoln have waited

---

[66]C. BLACK, THE PEOPLE AND THE COURT 209 (1960).

[67]S. Levinson, *supra* note 1, at 41.

[68]*Id.*

[69]*Id.*

[70]A. SCHLESINGER, JR., THE IMPERIAL PRESIDENCY 23 (1973).

[71]*Id.* at 24; S. E. MORISON, *supra* note 48, at 366. *See also* 4 J. ELLIOT, DEBATES IN THE SEVERAL STATE CONVENTIONS ON THE ADOPTION OF THE FEDERAL CONSTITUTION 450 (2d ed. 1836).

[72]A. SCHLESINGER, *supra* note 70, at 24.

[73]Letter from Thomas Jefferson to W. D. Nicholas (Sept. 7, 1803), *reprinted in* 8 THE WRITINGS OF THOMAS JEFFERSON 247 (P. L. Ford ed. 1897).

[74]S. Levinson, *supra* note 1, at 42.

[75]H. C. HOCKETT, THE CONSTITUTIONAL HISTORY OF THE UNITED STATES, 1826–1876, at 280–81 (1939); S. E. MORISON, *supra* note 48, at 612.

[76]U.S. CONST. art. I, § 9.

to convene Congress, then not in session? Even today one cannot dismiss Lincoln's evaluation of the imminent danger. When Congress assembled in July it accepted Lincoln's measures willy-nilly. It was in these circumstances that Lincoln asked, "Are all the laws, *but one,* to go unexecuted, and the government itself to go to pieces, lest that one be violated?"[77] Lincoln's "suspension" furnishes the only genuine illustration in our history for Jefferson's 1810 statement, after he left the presidency, that the laws "of self-preservation, of saving our country when in danger, are of a higher obligation" than a "strict observance of the written laws."[78]

These incidents yield Levinson a queer distillation: "The role of the great political leader is *often* to assume the almost Nietzschean task of going beyond the law in an effort *to transform* the society which he purports to lead."[79] We condone Lincoln's "dubious" behavior, he continues, because "his memorable vision of what this country was truly about, which involved transcending the existing constitutional structure and its support for slavery, has prevailed. . . ."[80] But this reads subsequent events back into 1861. The suspension of habeas corpus was altogether unrelated to slavery; it was designed to protect the capital from a potential enemy. Lincoln himself wrote in August, 1862, "My paramount object in this struggle is to save the Union, and is not either to save or to destroy slavery."[81] There was no commitment to freeing the slaves in the early years of trial; that emerged as the fearful losses mounted and as the North came to believe that once and for all the cancer which had eaten away at the vitals of the nation must be eradicated.

Stranger yet is Levinson's question, "Was Nixon's offense his disobedience of the law or, rather, his failure [unlike Lincoln] to present a plausible case for his violations of law as necessary to 'national security?' "[82] Since the publication of Levinson's article, Nixon himself has explained that his "national security" measures were meant to stifle dissenters in order to prevent "those that we were negotiating with in Paris" from "gain[ing] the impression that they represent a majority." He too assimilated this to Lincoln's action for "the purpose of preserving the Constitution and the Nation," though he conceded that "in Lincoln's case it was the survival of the Union in war time" that was at stake. But he concluded that "This nation was torn apart in an ideological way by the war in Vietnam, as much as the Civil War tore apart the nation when Lincoln was President."[83] Vietnam, however, was 6,000 miles away, not next door as was Maryland; and habeas corpus was suspended in Maryland to insure defense of the capital, not to gag dissent in the North. No President has been subjected to more incessant, vitriolic calumny during the progress of a war than Lincoln, yet he never resorted to wide-scale illegality to counter it. Levinson compares the incommensurable. Nixon did not merely *fail* "to present a plausible case"; under the circumstances, it was impossible to do so. It would open a frightening chapter in our history were dissent stifled to facilitate peace negotiations!

The great "Nietzschean task of going beyond the law in order to transform the society"[84] has led to a Hitler. Germany did not have to wait for the verdict of posterity for "the final assessment . . . whether the bet as to shape the shape of the future is won or lost;"[85] in the process of realizing Hitler's apocalyptic vision Germany was razed to the ground. Nothing in the Jefferson and Lincoln incidents warrants Levinson's extravagant extrapolation; neither conceived of himself as a "super-

---

[77]S. Levinson, *supra* note 1, at 42.

[78]A. SCHLESINGER, *supra* note 70, at 24–25.

[79]S. Levinson, *supra* note 1, at 42 (emphasis added).

[80]*Id.*

[81]S. E. MORISON, *supra* note 48, at 616.

[82]S. Levinson, *supra* note 1, at 42.

[83]N.Y. Times, May 20, 1977, § A, at 16, col. 1.

[84]*See* note 79 *supra* and accompanying text.

[85]S. Levinson, *supra* note 1, at 42.

man." A democracy which depends for its salvation on the vision of a "superman" has confessed its impotence and is on the road to dictatorship.

Finally, Levinson remarks, "if law is *only* that which the courts are prepared to enforce . . . then it becomes impossible, by definition, to accuse those institutions of disobeying the law."[86] The "enforce" definition was uttered by Holmes in the role of jural philosopher, but he did not find it incompatible with his recognition of "the right of the majority to embody their opinions in law,"[87] to which he felt bound to give effect despite his disagreement. As judge, Justice Holmes stated that when a legislature "has intimated its will . . . that will should be recognized and obeyed."[88] He condemned uncurbed judicial discretion to alter the law and identify personal predilections with constitutional mandates, and he recognized the perversion of due process that made such practices possible.[89] He accepted the "will" of the people when he could ascertain it and refused to change it to correspond to his predilections. Not every phrase of the Constitution lends itself to such analysis; some provisions are amorphous and afford judicial leeway. But "due process" and "equal protection," which today furnish the bulk of the Court's business, are, as I have elsewhere documented,[90] not among them.

VI

In a brilliant study, THE LIMITATIONS OF SCIENCE, J. W. N. Sullivan pointed out that Heisenberg's "principle of indeterminacy" had shaken the doctrine of strict causality in the atomic realm, but concluded that for practical purposes men can continue to rely on "cause and effect."[91] So too, whatever the philosophical doubts about the nature of the rule of law, I consider that society may safely continue to rely on it. With Charles McIlwain, I would urge that "[t]he two fundamental correlative elements of constitutionalism for which all lovers of liberty must yet fight are the legal limits to arbitrary power and a complete political responsibility of government to the governed."[92] Without the rule of law there is no accountability; recognition that Nixon had violated constitutional limits led to his banishment. It is not merely that respect for law binds our disparate elements together. Men cannot live without civil order. Law furnishes protection against the disruptive forces that would return us to the blood feud, against arbitrary power; it assures an accused that he will be impartially tried under existing law; and it furnishes a medium for the reconciliation of conflicting interests. In a recent monograph, the English Marxist historian, E. P. Thompson concluded:

> [T]he rule of law itself, the imposing of effective inhibitions upon power and the defense of the citizen from power's all-intrusive claims, seems to me to be an unqualified human good. To deny or belittle this good is, in this dangerous century when the resources and pretensions of power continue to enlarge, a desperate error of intellectual abstraction.[93]

---

[86]*Id.* at 99 (emphasis in original).
[87]*Id.* at 38.
[88]Johnson v. United States, 163 F. 30, 32 (1st Cir. 1908).
[89]Baldwin v. Missouri, 281 U.S. 586, 595 (1930) (dissenting opinion).
[90]R. BERGER, *supra* note 24, at 166–220.
[91]J. SULLIVAN, THE LIMITATIONS OF SCIENCE 69, 72 (1949).
[92]C. MCILWAIN, CONSTITUTIONALISM: ANCIENT AND MODERN 146 (rev. ed. 1947).
[93]E. P. THOMPSON, WHIGS AND HUNTERS: THE ORIGIN OF THE BLACK ACT 266 (1975).

INDEX